I0822004

1 & 2 THESSALONIANS

Zondervan Exegetical Commentary Series: New Testament

1 & 2 THESSALONIANS

ZONDERVAN
Exegetical Commentary
ON THE
New Testament

GARY S. SHOGREN

CLINTON E. ARNOLD
General Editor

For Karen

οὐκ ἐγκακεῖ καλοποιοῦσα
She does not grow weary in doing good
2 Thessalonians 3:13

ZONDERVAN ACADEMIC

1 and 2 Thessalonians

Published in Grand Rapids, Michigan, by Zondervan. Zondervan is a registered trademark of The Zondervan Corporation, L.L.C., a wholly owned subsidiary of HarperCollins Christian Publishing, Inc.

Requests for information should be addressed to customercare@harpercollins.com.

Zondervan titles may be purchased in bulk for educational, business, fundraising, or sales promotional use. For information, please email SpecialMarkets@Zondervan.com.

ISBN 978-0-310-49287-0 (ebook)

Library of Congress Cataloging-in-Publication Data

Shogren, Gary Steven.
1 and 2 Thessalonians / Gary S. Shogren.
p. cm.—(Zondervan exegetical commentary series on the New Testament)
Includes bibliographical references (pp. 41–47) and indexes.
ISBN: 978-0-310-24396-0 (hardcover)
1. Bible N.T. 1 and 2 Thessalonians—Commentaries. I. Title.
BS2725.53.A76 2012
227'.81077—dc23 2011044547

Cover design: Tammy Johnson
Interior design: Beth Shagene

Printed in the United States of America

---

25 26 27 28 29 30 31 32 33 34 35 /TRM/ 20 19 18 17 16 15 14 13 12 11 10 9 8 7 6

Contents

Series Introduction

This generation has been blessed with an abundance of excellent commentaries. Some are technical and do a good job of addressing issues that the critics have raised; other commentaries are long and provide extensive information about word usage and catalogue nearly every opinion expressed on the various interpretive issues; still other commentaries focus on providing cultural and historical background information; and then there are those commentaries that endeavor to draw out many applicational insights.

The key question to ask is: What are you looking for in a commentary? This commentary series might be for you if

- you have taken Greek and would like a commentary that helps you apply what you have learned without assuming you are a well-trained scholar.
- you would find it useful to see a concise, one- or two-sentence statement of what the commentator thinks the main point of each passage is.
- you would like help interpreting the words of Scripture without getting bogged down in scholarly issues that seem irrelevant to the life of the church.
- you would like to see a visual representation (a graphical display) of the flow of thought in each passage.
- you would like expert guidance from solid evangelical scholars who set out to explain the meaning of the original text in the clearest way possible and to help you navigate through the main interpretive issues.
- you want to benefit from the results of the latest and best scholarly studies and historical information that help to illuminate the meaning of the text.
- you would find it useful to see a brief summary of the key theological insights that can be gleaned from each passage and some discussion of the relevance of these for Christians today.

These are just some of the features that characterize the new Zondervan Exegetical Commentary on the New Testament series. The idea for this series was refined over time by an editorial board who listened to pastors and teachers express what they wanted to see in a commentary series based on the Greek text. That board consisted of myself, George H. Guthrie, William D. Mounce, Thomas R. Schreiner, and Mark L. Strauss, along with Zondervan senior editor at large Verlyn Verbrugge, and former Zondervan senior acquisitions editor Jack Kuhatschek. We also enlisted a board of consulting editors who are active pastors, ministry leaders, and seminary professors to help in the process of designing a commentary series that will be useful to the church. Zondervan senior acquisitions editor Katya Covrett has now been shepherding the process to completion.

We arrived at a design that includes seven components for the treatment of each biblical passage. What follows is a brief orientation to these primary components of the commentary.

Literary Context

In this section, you will find a concise discussion of how the passage functions in the broader literary context of the book. The commentator highlights connections with the preceding and following material in the book and makes observations on the key literary features of this text.

Main Idea

Many readers will find this to be an enormously helpful feature of this series. For each passage, the commentator carefully crafts a one- or two-sentence statement of the big idea or central thrust of the passage.

Translation and Graphical Layout

Another unique feature of this series is the presentation of each commentator's translation of the Greek text in a graphical layout. The purpose of this diagram is to help the reader visualize, and thus better understand, the flow of thought within the text. The translation itself reflects the interpretive decisions made by each commentator in the "Explanation" section of the commentary. Here are a few insights that will help you to understand the way these are put together:

1. On the far left side next to the verse numbers is a series of interpretive labels that indicate the function of each clause or phrase of the biblical text. The corresponding portion of the text is on the same line to the right of the label. We have not used technical linguistic jargon for these, so they should be easily understood.
2. In general, we place every clause (a group of words containing a subject and a predicate) on a separate line and identify how it is supporting the principal assertion of the text (namely, is it saying when the action occurred, how it took place, or why it took place?). We sometimes place longer phrases or a series of items on separate lines as well.

3. Subordinate (or dependent) clauses and phrases are indented and placed directly under the words that they modify. This helps the reader to more easily see the nature of the relationship of clauses and phrases in the flow of the text.
4. Every main clause has been placed in bold print and pushed to the left margin for clear identification.
5. Sometimes when the level of subordination moves too far to the right — as often happens with some of Paul's long, involved sentences! — we reposition the flow to the left of the diagram, but use an arrow to indicate that this has happened.
6. The overall process we have followed has been deeply informed by principles of discourse analysis and narrative criticism (for the Gospels and Acts).

Structure

Immediately following the translation, the commentator describes the flow of thought in the passage and explains how certain interpretive decisions regarding the relationship of the clauses were made in the passage.

Exegetical Outline

The overall structure of the passage is described in a detailed exegetical outline. This will be particularly helpful for those who are looking for a way to concisely explain the flow of thought in the passage in a teaching or preaching setting.

Explanation of the Text

As an exegetical commentary, this work makes use of the Greek language to interpret the meaning of the text. If your Greek is rather rusty (or even somewhat limited), don't be too concerned. All of the Greek words are cited in parentheses following an English translation. We have made every effort to make this commentary as readable and useful as possible even for the nonspecialist.

Those who will benefit the most from this commentary will have had the equivalent of two years of Greek in college or seminary. This would include a semester or two of working through an intermediate grammar (such as Wallace, Porter, Brooks and Winbery, or Dana and Mantey). The authors use the grammatical language that is found in these kinds of grammars. The details of the grammar of the passage, however, are discussed only when it has a bearing on the interpretation of the text.

The emphasis on this section of the text is to convey the meaning. Commentators examine words and images, grammatical details, relevant OT and Jewish background to a particular concept, historical and cultural context, important text-critical issues, and various interpretational issues that surface.

Theology in Application

This, too, is a unique feature for an exegetical commentary series. We felt it was important for each author not only to describe what the text means in its various details, but also to take a moment and reflect on the theological contribution that it makes. In this section, the theological message of the passage is summarized. The authors discuss the theology of the text in terms of its place within the book and in a broader biblical-theological context. Finally, each commentator provides some suggestions on what the message of the passage is for the church today. At the conclusion of each volume in this series is a summary of the whole range of theological themes touched on by this book of the Bible.

Our sincere hope and prayer is that you find this series helpful not only for your own understanding of the text of the New Testament, but as you are actively engaged in teaching and preaching God's Word to people who are hungry to be fed on its truth.

Clinton E. Arnold, general editor

Author's Preface

The Thessalonian letters have lately begun to receive the attention due them, with several important works appearing in just the last few years. The reader who wishes for further information should consult the bibliography. I particularly recommend the commentaries by Abraham Malherbe, Gene Green, and Gordon Fee; the collection of essays edited by Raymond F. Collins, *The Thessalonian Correspondence*, is likewise a precious resource.

I am especially delighted to see the amount of interest being given to Christian mission and pastoral ministry in these two letters. If the time I have spent in study has taught me anything, it is that I should put my books aside for a while and imitate the apostle:

- to make myself more available to speak to groups, no matter their size
- to find a handful of brothers and serve as their mentor
- to take a more active role in personal evangelism
- to participate in work projects that tangibly show Christ's love
- above all, to pray for the advance of the gospel

Among the contributors to this series, there are a number of alumni from my *alma mater*. I feel privileged to be included among them. Like the apostle, you exert a constant pressure on me to serve our Lord with excellence.

For those who have given me their valuable suggestions, many thanks: Jimmy Snowden, Fred Zaspel, Bill Isley, Pastor Steve Dyson, Brent McNamara, David Macario, and Fred Putnam. And, of course, many thanks to the general editor, Clinton Arnold, to acquisitions editor Katya Covrett, and to production editor Verlyn D. Verbrugge.

Thanks to our fellow missionaries at WorldVenture, our supporters, and to my friends and colleagues at Seminario ESEPA of Costa Rica, for their encouragement and for being so understanding about my writing ministry: *gracias, compañeros y compañeras.*

This is for you, Karen, remembering everything you are and everything you do.

Glory to God!

Gary Steven Shogren
Summer, 2011

Abbreviations

Abbreviations for books of the Bible, pseudepigrapha, rabbinic works, papyri, classical works, and the like are readily available in sources such as the *SBL Handbook of Style* and are not included here.

AB	Anchor Bible
ABD	*Anchor Bible Dictionary*. Ed. D. N. Freedman. 6 vols. New York, 1992.
ACCS	Ancient Christian Commentary on Scripture
AnBib	Analecta biblica
ANF	*Ante-Nicene Fathers*
ASV	American Standard Version
BA1CS	The Book of Acts in Its First Century Setting. Ed. Bruce W. Winter. 5 vols. Grand Rapids, 1993 – .
BBR	*Bulletin for Biblical Research*
BDAG	Bauer, W., F. W. Danker, W. F. Arndt, and F. W. Gingrich. *Greek-English Lexicon of the New Testament and Other Early Christian Literature.* 3rd ed. Chicago, 2000.
BDF	Blass, F., A. Debrunner, and R. W. Funk. *A Greek Grammar of the New Testament and Other Early Christian Literature.* Chicago, 1961.
BETL	Bibliotheca ephemeridum theologicarum lovaniensium
Bib	*Biblica*
CBET	Contributions to Biblical Exegesis and Theology
CBQ	*Catholic Biblical Quarterly*
CEV	Contemporary English Version
DLNT	*Dictionary of the Later New Testament and Its Developments.* Ed. R. P. Martin and P. H. Davids. Downers Grove, IL, 1997.
DPL	*Dictionary of Paul and His Letters.* Ed. G. F. Hawthorne, R. P. Martin, and D. G. Reid. Downers Grove, IL, 1993.
EBib	Études bibliques
EDNT	*Exegetical Dictionary of the New Testament.* Ed. H. Balz and G. Schneider. 3 vols. Grand Rapids, 1990 – 93.
EKKNT	Evangelisch-Katholischer Kommentar zum Neuen Testament
ESV	English Standard Version
EvQ	*Evangelical Quarterly*

ExpTim	*Expository Times*
FF	Foundations and Facets
GNB	Good News Bible
HCSB	Holman Christian Standard Bible
HTR	*Harvard Theological Review*
ICC	International Critical Commentary
IVPNTC	InterVarsity Press New Testament Commentary
JB	Jerusalem Bible
JBL	*Journal of Biblical Literature*
JETS	*Journal of the Evangelical Theological Society*
JSJSup	Journal for the Study of Judaism Supplements
JSNT	*Journal for the Study of the New Testament*
JSNTSup	Journal for the Study of the New Testament Supplement Series
JSPSup	Journal for the Study of Pseudepigrapha Supplement Series
KJV	King James Version
L&N	*Greek-English Lexicon of the New Testament: Based on Semantic Domains*. Ed. J. P. Louw and E. A. Nida. 2nd ed. New York, 1989.
LCL	Loeb Classical Library
LEH	Lust, Johan, Erik Eynikel, and Katrin Hauspie, eds. *Greek-English Lexicon of the Septuagint*. Stuttgart, 2003.
LNTS	Library of New Testament Studies
LSJ	Liddell, H. G., R. Scott, H. S. Jones, eds. *A Greek-English Lexicon*. 9th ed. with revised supplement. Oxford, 1996.
LXX	Septuagint
MM	Moulton, J. H., and G. Milligan, eds. *The Vocabulary of the Greek Testament*. London, 1930.
MNTC	Moffatt New Testament Commentary
MSJ	*The Master's Seminary Journal*
NA	Nestle-Aland, *Novum Testamentum Graece*
NAB	New American Bible
NASB	New American Standard Bible
NCB	New Century Bible
NDBT	*New Dictionary of Biblical Theology*. Ed. Brian S. Rosner et al. Downers Grove, IL, 2000.
NEB	New English Bible
NET	New English Translation (online Bible translation)
NETS	NET Bible translation of the LXX
NICNT	New International Commentary on the New Testament
NIDNTT	*New International Dictionary of New Testament Theology*. Ed. C. Brown. 4 vols. Grand Rapids, 1975 – 1985.
NIGTC	New International Greek Testament Commentary

NIV	New International Version
NIVAC	NIV Application Commentary
NJB	New Jerusalem Bible
NKJV	New King James Version
NLT	New Living Translation
NovT	*Novum Testamentum*
NPNF[1]	*Nicene and Post-Nicene Fathers*, Series 1
NPNF[2]	*Nicene and Post-Nicene Fathers*, Series 2
NRSV	New Revised Standard Version
NTS	*New Testament Studies*
OED	*Oxford English Dictionary*
PG	Patrologia Graeca, ed. J.-P. Migne.
PNTC	Pillar New Testament Commentary
REB	Revised English Bible
RevExp	*Review and Expositor*
RSV	Revised Standard Version
SBLDS	SBL Dissertation Series
SBT	Studies in Biblical Theology
SC	Sources chretiennes, Paris, 1943-
SNTSMS	Society for New Testament Studies Monograph Series
SP	Sacra pagina
TDNT	*Theological Dictionary of the New Testament.* Edited by G. Kittel and G. Friedrich. Translated by G. W. Bromiley. 10 vols. Grand Rapids, 1964–1976.
TEV	Today's English Version
TJ	*Trinity Journal*
TLG	*Thesaurus Linguae Graecae*
TLNT	*Theological Lexicon of the New Testament*. Ed. Ceslas Spicq. Trans. and ed. James D. Ernest. 3 vols. Peabody, MA, 1994.
TNIV	Today's New International Version
TNTC	Tyndale New Testament Commentary
TR	Textus Receptus
TS	*Theological Studies*
TynBul	*Tyndale Bulletin*
UBS	United Bible Societies' *Greek New Testament*
WBC	Word Biblical Commentary
WTJ	*Westminster Theological Journal*
WUNT	Wissenschaftliche Untersuchungen zum Neuen Testament
WW	*Word and World*
ZNW	*Zeitschrift für die neutestamentliche Wissenschaft und die Kunde der älteren Kirche*

Introduction to 1 and 2 Thessalonians

The letters to the Thessalonians were elements of an innovative solution to a grave predicament. The apostles had been thrown out of town and were banned from returning. They had removed themselves to a distance of 190 miles (300 km) as the crow flies. Now, how could they keep in touch with their newly planted church? In the case of these letters, there were exceptional circumstances: the church was only a few months old; it was undergoing fierce harassment; persecution had cut off their lines of communication to the apostles; Satan himself was conspiring to keep the apostles and the church apart. The Thessalonian church urgently needed a word of encouragement from its founders.

In the middle of this crisis, Paul and Silas fixed on a fresh stratagem: they commissioned the junior member of the missionary team to serve as their traveling representative. While in hindsight this method seems characteristically Pauline (see Acts 19:22), it may not have been an obvious choice when he first tried it. After all, Timothy himself was new to the ministry. Nevertheless, he put himself at risk, traveling north and slipping into Thessalonica, not once, but three times (a subsequent visit after the church was planted and then to deliver the two letters). While there, he would have acted by the light of "What would Paul and Silas do?" His commission also involved listening and observing. He needed to return safely to Paul and Silas to tell them the questions that the church was asking. The crucial first round trip resulted in the writing and sending of 1 Thessalonians.

Paul and Silas were hugely relieved when Timothy returned from that first deputation to tell them that *there was still a Thessalonian church.* The church had not only survived hell's onslaught but was positively thriving: "just now Timothy has come to us from you and has announced the good news" (1 Thess 3:6). First Thessalonians is an outpouring of their relief and gratitude to God for his protection of their Thessalonian "children."

On his second and third trips to Thessalonica, Timothy arrived with a small scroll in his baggage.[1] The two Thessalonian letters are short notes and can be read

1. We should not award 1 Thessalonians the honor of being the first Christian letter. At the least, the short letter of James as president of the Jerusalem Council preceded it by many months (Acts 15:23 – 29). His letter followed a pattern that would characterize later letters: a written document that was carried by envoys who could also propound and apply its message (see

one after the other in less than an hour. The first letter especially sparkles with life: reading it aloud in the Greek lets the hearer capture the alliteration and other devices that Paul included — for example, the repetitive use of π in 1 Thess 1:2. Paul also favored triads, groups of three words to express a theme in a striking manner (so 1:5 — "not simply as words ... but also with *miracles* and in the operation of *the Holy Spirit*, and in the great sense of *certainty*"). They were read to all the local brothers and sisters (5:27). Within a few years, the letters were copied and collected for the edification of all Christians, people far separated in space and time from the original recipients. Thus, these early examples of long-distance apostolic communication came to form part of the canon.

Letters, carried and interpreted by Paul's associates, were the medium by which any Pauline church could hear from its apostle within weeks of having posed questions to him, even if he were in another region. Only in the last century and a half has the speed of interchurch communication surpassed what Paul attained when he sent 1 Thessalonians.

The Church

The City of Thessalonica

Thessalonica, a city at the crossroads. From AD 44 on, Thessalonica served as the provincial capital of Macedonia. Like many of Paul's urban centers, it was a well-populated city that was built on a crossroads. It was a stopping point along the Via Egnatia, the Roman road that ran from Byzantium (Istanbul) westward, eventually terminating at the embarking point for travel by sea to Italy and Rome. Thessalonica lay ninety miles (144 km) west along the Via from Philippi. It also straddled north-south trade routes. Thessalonica was, and still is, a natural port. The southwest view from the city across the bay is stunning; there is Mount Olympus, home of the pantheon headed by Zeus.

As a "free city," Thessalonica had a fair amount of local autonomy that the city's leaders were anxious to retain; this may explain why the local officials seemed particularly nervous about political disturbances. The city was a prominent center for the worship of the Roman emperors.

Thessalonian Jews. Jews had imperial permission to acquire land and erect synagogues, conduct regular worship, and raise funds to send to Jerusalem. Despite their

Acts 15:25 – 27, 30 – 35; 16:4 – 5). Beyond that, Paul already had perhaps fifteen years of experience behind him when he arrived in Macedonia, and may have written other letters; see too Abraham J. Malherbe, *The Letters to the Thessalonians: A New Translation with Introduction and Commentary* (AB 32B; New York: Doubleday, 2000), 13. Malherbe even speculates that Paul wrote a letter, now lost, to the Thessalonians and says that it is probable that they had written back, all before Paul penned 1 Thessalonians. See Abraham J. Malherbe, "Did the Thessalonians Write to Paul?" in *The Conversation Continues: Studies in Paul and John in Honor of J. Louis Martyn* (ed. Robert T. Fortna and Beverly R. Gaventa; Nashville: Abingdon, 1990), 255.

legal status, many of their neighbors disliked Jews as a people (see comments on 1 Thess 2:14 – 16). For example, Roman historian Tacitus "criticizes Jewish proselytism, misanthropy, separatism, and their refusal to worship the emperor."[2]

Acts 17:1 – 2 indicates that the Thessalonian Jews, unlike their counterparts in Philippi, possessed their own synagogue building.[3] Jews met on the Sabbath to recite creedal statements, pray, hear the Scriptures read, hear some sort of exposition and exhortation, and perhaps sing. If Gentiles wished to hear the Bible taught, they might have had to stand apart from the Jewish worshipers. Perhaps they would hear a message similar to this:

> Let us, therefore, fix deeply in ourselves this first commandment as the most sacred of all commandments, to think that there is but one God, the most highest, and to honour him alone; and let not the polytheistical doctrine ever even touch the ears of any man who is accustomed to seek for the truth, with purity and sincerity of heart.[4]

Thessalonian pagans. Most Westerners are familiar with the labors of Hercules or other classical myths and legends. Nevertheless, one cannot understand a religion simply by reading its formative stories. Greek religion was a system of rituals directed to heaven. Ritual was vital in popular thinking. Worshipers had to perform visible actions, since the gods could not read minds and could only understand people's motives through what they did.

Religion existed on two levels, the civic and the domestic. To be a good citizen meant to pay respect to the patron deities. This included participation in feasts, sacrifices, celebrations, games, and other public events. Every occasion had its religious turn, from banquets to games to business transactions.

Domestic religion involved women more than did the public; it was their temple, although the male head of the family was the titular priest. There were household shrines to Hestia, goddess of the hearth. Banquets were dedicated to the gods. Births, marriages, rites of passage, and funerals all included their religious element. Fortune-telling and astrology were important facets of life; so were pilgrimages to oracle shrines (such as the famous one at Delphi): people sought answers to questions of love, success at business, and health.

Jews in Thessalonica were taught to live in accordance with the Mosaic law; meanwhile, the Gentiles lived according to an entirely different set of mores. The gods of

2. S. T. Carroll, "Tacitus," *ABD*, 6:306.

3. There exists no direct proof for a first-century synagogue in the excavations or inscriptions of Thessalonica. The earliest reference to any synagogue there dates from the fourth century AD at the earliest, and it is not Jewish but Samaritan. So Helmut Koester, "Archäologie und Paulus im Thessalonike," in *Frühchristliches Thessaloniki* (ed. Cilliers Breytenbach and Ingrid Behrmann; Studien und Texte zu Antike und Christentum 44; Tübingen: Mohr Siebeck, 2007), 1 – 9; also H. L. Hendrix, "Thessalonica," *ABD*, 6:527. Despite this lack of evidence, the best conclusion is that there was a synagogue of indeterminate size in Thessalonica and that it had been there since the late second or early first century BC. See Christoph vom Brocke, *Thessaloniki — Stadt des Kassander und Gemeinde des Paulus* (WUNT 2: 125; Tubingen: Mohr Siebeck, 2001), 217 – 33.

4. Taken from Paul's contemporary, Philo, *Decalogue* 65 (trans. Jonge).

Mount Olympus were said to live as lusty mortals would, if mortals had magical powers. More sophisticated Macedonians would have regarded the sexual adventures of the gods as metaphors, designed to teach some philosophical truth or another.

Thessalonica had all the vices of any bustling trade city. Theatrical works slid more and more toward the violent and sexually crude. Arrivals by sea or land would demand drink, gambling, and sex, and part of the economy of the city was keeping its visitors satisfied. Young men in particular were expected to have an active sex life, with slaves, prostitutes, or lovers. Engaging in too much sex was thought to be a sign of self-indulgence and economic wantonness, but not an offense against God or the gods. Bisexuality was more common in Macedonia and Achaia than in other parts of the empire, especially because of the shortage of marriageable women.[5] Friendships between men even might be cemented by a sexual relationship. Forcible homosexual intercourse was shameful only for the "female" in the relationship. Women for their part were expected to keep themselves faithful to their husbands, in great part so that they were guaranteed to bear only legitimate children. Not all women kept themselves faithful. Men were expected to keep their wives from any embarrassing fallout from their activities; fathering illegitimate children was one sure way to shame the wife.[6]

Some have suggested that the Thessalonians in particular had depraved sex lives, based on infiltration of the so-called Cabiri cult into local culture.[7] This was a mystery cult based on the myth of how two brothers kill a third brother. The nature of their practices is obscure, in part because of the difficulty in excavating the ancient city. Some have suggested that there was a gross sex cult in Thessalonica that emphasized the male organ; this suggests a possible background for Paul's use of σκεῦος (lit.,"vessel") with the meaning of male genitals in 1 Thess 4:4. Nevertheless, Koester gives a wise summing up when he says that while the Cabiri cult was present, we have little idea what it was like and no clue as to whether Paul was writing against it in 1 Thess 4.[8] At this time it seems best not to appeal to the Cabiri cult in favor of any particular exegesis.

5. See comments on 1 Thess 4:1 – 12. We do not know if it is coincidental that Paul's writings about homosexuality occur in two passages: in a letter sent from Corinth (Rom 1:18 – 32) and a letter sent to Corinth (1 Cor 6:9 – 10).

6. See the fine article by G. W. Peterman, "Marriage and Sexual Fidelity in the Papyri, Plutarch and Paul," *TynBul* 50.2 (1999): 163 – 72.

7. Karl Paul Donfried, "The Cults of Thessalonica and the Thessalonian Correspondence," *NTS* 31 (1985): 336 – 56. Also Robert Jewett, *The Thessalonian Correspondence: Pauline Rhetoric and Millenarian Piety* (FF; Philadelphia: Fortress, 1986), 127 – 32. Jewett draws out some rather fantastic conclusions based on a small amount of evidence, for example, that the Cabiri cult has strong parallels with Paul's gospel and therefore paved the way for its positive reception. Vom Brocke, *Thessaloniki*, 117 – 21, replies that the more this cult is studied, the more tenuous our understanding of it appears. Another recent work, which shows the influence of Rome in Thessalonica, is by Christopher Steimle, *Religion im römishen Thessaloniki: Sakraltopographie, Kult und Gesellschaft 168 v. Chr. – 324 n. Chr.* (Studien und Texte zu Antike und Christentum 47; Tübingen: Mohr Siebeck, 2008); an older article by Charles Edson is still of some value, "Cults of Thessalonica (Macedonia III)," *HTR* 41.3 (1948): 153 – 204.

8. Helmut Koester, "Archäologie und Paulus im Thessalonike," 2.

The Second Missionary Journey

What we call Paul's second missionary journey began around the year AD 49, some time after the Jerusalem Council had affirmed that Gentiles were full Christians and not obligated to follow the Mosaic covenant (Acts 15:1 – 29). The team launched out from Antioch (15:40) and, at the beginning, consisted only of Paul and Silas; along the way they added young Timothy (16:1 – 3). The journey began as an inspection tour of the churches that Paul and Barnabas had planted in Galatia. Although the team apparently had designs to go on to evangelize western Asia Minor (16:6 – 8), they were summoned by God to preach in Macedonia (16:9 – 10). They began with the city of Philippi, where they planted a church but also receive a vicious whipping from the Roman authorities (16:11 – 40).[9] From there they followed the Via Egnatia westward to Thessalonica.

The walk to Thessalonica would have taken about four days if Paul and Silas were able to maintain a normal pace after their beating in Philippi. Paul, Silas, and Timothy are the only three ever mentioned in connection with the work in that city; the three also seem to have labored together in the subsequent ministry in Corinth (2 Cor 1:19).

For those fortunate enough to have seen Paul on his first Sabbath there, they heard a word of exhortation from a man who, with his companion, had obviously been physically abused in a brutal fashion. The gossip was that they had been shamed: accused of being instigators, publicly stripped of their clothes, beaten with rods, and then thrown into prison (see 1 Thess 2:2). Paul availed himself of his right to speak in the Thessalonian synagogue, always focusing on a scriptural exposition of how a man named Jesus was the Messiah (Acts 17:2 – 3).

The author of Acts states that Paul spent "three Sabbath days" in Thessalonica (Acts 17:2). It is virtually certain that he is referring only to the initial stage of their work there and not to their entire stay. (1) Luke tends to telescope events together in order to focus on his larger theological interests, not on the small details. (2) From what may be gleaned from the Thessalonian letters, the depth of their doctrinal understanding seems well out of proportion to a visit of only a few weeks. (3) Time would have been needed for the team to show themselves a model of manual labor (1 Thess 2:9; 2 Thess 3:6 – 9). (4) Time would also have been needed for the conversion of Gentiles straight out of paganism (1 Thess 1:9), people who would have taken more time to disciple than the others. (5) The Philippians more than once sent him financial help while he was in Thessalonica (Phil 4:16). (6) There needs to have been sufficient time to designate what seem to be leaders of the church (1 Thess 5:12).[10]

9. The author of Acts may imply that he was with them in Troas and crossed with them to Philippi, but then did not meet up with the team until some years later. This is the most logical reading of the so-called "we-passages," which begin in Acts 16:10 – 17. Then the use of "we" ceases, to begin anew in 20:5.

10. See on this Malherbe, *Letters to the Thessalonians*, 60 – 61; Gordon Fee, *The First and Second Letters to the Thessalonians* (NICNT; Grand Rapids: Eerdmans, 2009), 6.

It is probable that Jason was the host for the band of new disciples (Acts 17:7); it was a generous act that would shortly land him in trouble. Within a short time, the Christian preachers became city-wide news. A riot was instigated by some Jews and carried out by local ruffians (17:5). Jason was physically dragged before the city leaders with some other Christians (17:6).[11] Paul's Jewish opponents twisted his message, just as the Sanhedrin had done before Pilate, making out that Jesus was a rival to Caesar's throne (17:7). Jason was forced to post bond as guarantee against a breach of the peace.[12]

Paul and Silas were compelled to leave the city. Rather than continue along the Via Egnatia, they got off the main highway, traveling south for fifty miles (80 km) to preach in a relatively small town called Berea. It is possible that this was not their original itinerary. Had they kept heading west along the Via they would have eventually arrived at Dyrrachium, where a ship could have taken them over the Adriatic Sea to Italy. Romans 1:13 suggests that Rome had been Paul's goal for some years. Was the stopover at Berea an expedient, from which location the team could keep a close eye on Thessalonica and Philippi without jeopardizing Jason or the others?[13]

Whatever the plan, Jews from Thessalonica derailed it by following them to Berea and again stirring up a mob (Acts 17:10 – 15). What followed next has to be inferred from 1 Thess 2 – 3 and Acts 17. Paul traveled by sea to Athens (Acts 17:14), leaving instructions "for Silas and Timothy to join him as soon as possible" (17:15). It seems that Silas and Timothy did in fact join him in Athens. Still "Satan blocked us" (1 Thess 2:18c) — that is, Paul and Silas — from returning to Thessalonica, and so "we" instead sent Timothy (3:1 – 2). Silas too went to Macedonia but apparently not to Thessalonica (there is no mention of it either in Acts or in the letter).[14]

Finally, Timothy and Silas rejoined Paul in Corinth, Timothy bearing good news of the believers in Thessalonica (Acts 18:1, 5; 1 Thess 3:6). Timothy had little time to rest, since the most likely interpretation is that it was he who immediately returned with the letter of 1 Thessalonians. That letter bears the names of all three and indicates their presence together in Corinth when it was composed. A round trip from Athens to Macedonia would have taken 3 – 4 weeks, not to mention the time that the travelers spent with the churches.

The first letter is at heart a record of the apostles' gratitude to God. Their thanksgiving must not be glossed over as a formality, as if they were bowing their heads to

11. For information about the "politarchs" or city authorities in Thessalonica and elsewhere in Macedonia, consult the full article by G. H. R. Horsley, "Politarchs," *ABD*, 5:384 – 89. They formed a group of around five members in larger cities.

12. Concerning Jason's role in all this, see F. M. Gillman, "Jason,"*ABD*, 3:649. Many Jews in the Diaspora used "Jason" as a Greek version of the Hebrew name Joshua, implying that Jason may have been one of the Jewish converts mentioned in Acts 17:4.

13. F. F. Bruce, *1 & 2 Thessalonians* (WBC 45; Waco, TX: Word, 1982), xxvi.

14. The whereabouts of Silas during this period are vague. Allan Wainwright proposes that he had to return to Galatia in order to clarify certain points about the Jerusalem decree. His hypothesis must remain just that. See "Where Did Silas Go? (And What Was His Connection with *Galatians*?)," *JSNT* 8 (1980): 66 – 70.

give thanks before getting to the "meat" of the letter (in 1 Thess 4:1). The giving of thanks and the reports of their prayer are in fact a large part of the letter's substance. Next, they provide a model for how the church should live; the Thessalonians must imitate the apostles (1:6; 2:1 – 12) and also the Judean churches (2:14 – 16).[15] The closest New Testament parallel is found in Acts 20:17 – 35, where Paul reminds the Ephesian elders that he had lived among them as an example, and he instructed them to "keep watch over yourselves and all the flock" (Acts 20:28, 35); Paul implies they should follow the pattern he has given. In the same way, the Thessalonians must have blameless character, labor hard, take diligent care of their charges, and endure persecution. Next, he teaches them about the resurrection of the saints, a doctrine they seem to have forgotten or failed to apply (see below under "Eschatology in Thessalonica").

Upon his next return to Corinth, Timothy brought back further questions from the church, prompting the second letter hard on the heels of the first. The church had perhaps been shaken by news that the day of the Lord was at hand. Paul has a cure: that Day must be preceded by the final Apostasy and the coming of the "Man of Lawlessness." Beyond that, the general theme of the letter is the justice of God as revealed in the gospel. Christ will come and save his people and destroy those who have rejected him. In a time of great persecution, the Thessalonians are assured that God is watching over them and that in the future he will make all things right.

Jewish apocalypses often dealt with the issue of theodicy, the problem of evil in the world. Most particularly they wondered, *Why do the wicked persecute the saints, and what will a just God do to rectify the matter?* First Enoch 62:11 is but one example: the Lord will deliver the rulers of the earth "to the angels for punishments in order that vengeance shall be executed on them — oppressors of his children and his elect ones." In other letters, Paul does not go into details about the parousia as the moment of God's vengeance on those who mistreat the church. Nevertheless, it is a theme that he would have found throughout Daniel and in the Olivet Discourse (Matt 24:41 – 46) and would later be developed in the book of Revelation.

Life in the Thessalonian Church

The composition of the church. Acts 17:4 states that "some" Thessalonian Jews came to the faith, along with "a large number of God-fearing Greeks and quite a few prominent women." First Thessalonians paints a different picture: when Paul addresses the group as a whole, he states that they had "turned away from idols to God" (1 Thess 1:9); that is, they seem to have been converted from full paganism with no stopover in the synagogue system.

This tension may be explained by how the gospel would spread in a new city. Paul

15. So Malherbe, *Letters to the Thessalonians*, 130 – 31.

would plant his churches with Jews and God-fearers and some pagans. Then, rapid growth took place among Gentiles, with less growth among the smaller population of Jews. By the time Paul wrote his first letter to Thessalonica, the church in the majority was already Gentile Christian.

Who was the typical Christian in Thessalonica at the time of 1 Thessalonians? He or she was from a pagan background, spoke *koinē* Greek as a first language, could not read or write, kept house or was a manual laborer or a slave,[16] had never set foot inside a synagogue, had newly pledged to an ethic that was sharply different from that of the local environment, shared his or her faith with unbelievers, experienced serious harassment from family and society, and knew someone who had been physically punished, imprisoned, or maybe killed for the faith.

Meetings. By the time of 1 Thessalonians, that church may have consisted of several assemblies, each with a few dozen members, in various parts of the urban area. Aristarchus and Secundus of Thessalonica were able to serve as trustees of the Jerusalem offering (see Acts 20:4), probably because they were men of means. Perhaps they, along with Jason, were patrons of house churches. The assemblies did not meet in temples, shrines, or theaters, but in homes.[17] "All in all, in the context of the cult expression of religion in the Roman era, earliest Christian worship would have seemed a fairly modest, even unimpressive affair."[18] Still, Christians from the lower strata must have been impressed: they found themselves received into rich surroundings, not as servants but as members of a family.

A "family church." Jews and Greeks defined themselves through their kinship relationships. The Thessalonian church was famous for a new species of family love (φιλαδελφία, 1 Thess 4:9) of one member for another regardless of blood ties or class structure. What a comfort that must have been, since the Thessalonian believers had been torn away from family, friends, and city and, for the Jews, synagogue and nation. This trauma was deeper than would be a similar experience in our contemporary Western world, where tribal and civic connections are not so strong. There exists a social science category of "fictive family" or "fictive kinship" that is defined as treating others "as if" they were members of a new family. The Christian gospel stretches those categories past the breaking point: because God truly was their Father, the believers regarded other Christians as brothers and sisters on a deeper, even literal, sense.[19] An outsider to the faith would have found remarkable the leveling

16. So Paul assumes in 1 Thess 4:11; it is implicit in 1 Thess 2:9; 2 Thess 3:6–13 as well.

17. Richard Ascough tries to reconstruct a situation in Thessalonica, in which Paul evangelized and met together with other leatherworkers. That is, the church arose out of an association of artisans. This might explain why Paul speaks so frequently about manual labor. Ascough must make many leaps of logic in order to arrive at his conclusions. See Richard S. Ascough, *Paul's Macedonian Associations* (WUNT, Series 2, 161; Tübingen: Mohr Siebeck, 2003), 165–76.

18. Larry W. Hurtado, *At the Origins of Christian Worship: The Context and Character of Earliest Christian Devotion* (Grand Rapids: Eerdmans, 2000), 40.

19. See the full study by Trevor J. Burke, *Family Matters: A Socio-Historical Study of Kinship Metaphors in 1 Thessalonians* (JSNTSup 247; London: T&T Clark, 2003). He quotes a third-century AD complaint by Minucius Felix (174) that Christians "indiscriminately call each other brothers and sisters."

effect that the gospel had on human relationships. At least in theory, no Christian was less important than the most rich, powerful, or well-connected. No one was considered too dull to learn God's truth.[20] For the women, religion was no longer confined to the home, since the "sisters" stood side by side with men as cobelievers and worshipers.[21]

Scripture. The new Christians, particularly those from a Greek background, moved within a culture that venerated the spoken word. They might have gone to public readings of poetry or literature, witnessed Greek plays, or listened to orators. Some few may have listened to philosophers. The church honored group readings, too, since the Word read there was from God himself (1 Tim 4:14). The believers learned to correlate their experience of God with the Jewish Scriptures, celebrating their faith that they were the beneficiaries of a new covenant (see comments on 1 Thess 3:13; 2 Thess 2:6–7). Meanwhile, in another location in the city the synagogue met and studied the same Scriptures. Yet the Christians understood that the Jews had rejected the Messiah promised in the prophetic writings (1 Thess 2:15).

Letters. As the apostolic envoy, Timothy would have been the first to read the Thessalonian letters to the believers there, most of whom were illiterate. If he read it aloud, it would take less than a half hour to go straight through 1 Thessalonians. The letters we now know in the NT were not originally documents for exegesis, to be stored in a library. It is better to think of 1 Thessalonians as a script, which Timothy read aloud, recreating as it were the presence of Paul and Silas and himself. Since he had heard Paul dictate it, he could provide the nuances of expression that he had heard from Paul. In the earliest church, such readings from apostolic literature began to supplement readings from the OT.[22]

Teaching. The apostles were known principally as teachers, and Timothy did his share of instructing the church (1 Thess 3:2). First Corinthians 14:26 implies that there might be plural teachers within any given meeting. Whether there were regular, appointed leaders in Thessalonica cannot be proven conclusively, although they are probably mentioned in the first letter: "those who labor among you and who lead you in the Lord and admonish you" (1 Thess 5:12).

Charismata. The Thessalonian church was a charismatic church. If Paul found any fault with their experience of the Spirit, it was that they were a trifle timid about

20. People of the lower classes, from artisans downward, were thought incapable of appreciating philosophy. "Plying a trade was denigrated as it left no time for building friendships or developing one's virtue. Thus, artisans were considered incapable of attaining virtue or they were viewed as uneducated" (Ascough, *Paul's Macedonian Associations*, 172).

21. Hence a Christian woman would have discarded the principle that was later written down in Plutarch: "A wife ought not to make friends of her own, but to enjoy her husband's friends in common with him. The gods are the first and most important friends. Wherefore it is becoming for a wife to worship and to know only the gods that her husband believes in" (Plutarch, *Mor* 140D; trans. Babbitt [LCL]).

22. About a century after 1 Thessalonians, Justin Martyr would write: "And on the day called Sunday, all who live in cities or in the country gather together to one place, and *the memoirs of the apostles* or the writings of the prophets are read, as long as time permits; then, when the reader has ceased, the president verbally instructs, and exhorts to the imitation of these good things" (*1 Apol.* 67, *ANF* 1:186, emphasis added).

the gift of prophecy. Paul exhorts them to pay due attention to supernatural utterances and to be discerning (1 Thess 5:19 – 21).

Evangelism. Paul implies that the Thessalonians actively shared their faith. This may have taken the form of one-on-one evangelism and even extensive mission work. The question of Thessalonian evangelism is one of the larger interpretative issues of 1 Thessalonians. See "Were the Thessalonian Believers Evangelistic?" at 1 Thess 1:8.

Persecution. The Thessalonian churches knew from the beginning that following Christ would lead to trouble, some of it violent (1 Thess 1:6; 3:3 – 5; 2 Thess 1:6 – 7; see also 1 Thess 2:14). Persecutions may have been economic, familial, social, or physical. The persecution seems to have begun with the arrest of Jason (Acts 17:6) and been ongoing. It is not certain that persecution led to the death of any Christian in Thessalonica (1 Thess 4:13), although 2:15 may be a hint that it had. But given the relatively high death rate among them, it is also possible that the Thessalonians had died of age, illness, accident, or in childbirth.

The Thessalonian Church and the Rest of the Story

Paul finally was able to revisit Thessalonica during his third missionary journey, around the year AD 55 – 56. He left his main base of ministry, Ephesus, to pass through Macedonia (Acts 20:1); he then went south to Achaia for three months (Acts 20:2 – 3). Paul mentions in 2 Cor 7:5 only that "when we came into Macedonia, we had no rest, but we were harassed at every turn — conflicts on the outside, fears within." He returned north and traveled to Jerusalem, perhaps in the year AD 58 (Acts 20:3), setting out from Philippi (Acts 20:6).

In 2 Cor 8:1 – 5, Paul speaks of the warm generosity of the Macedonian Christians for the Jerusalem fund — and that despite their "extreme poverty." This description could characterize both Thessalonica and Philippi. Paul's plan, it seems, was that each church would appoint one or two men to represent them and to verify that the money arrived in Jerusalem. Thessalonica selected Aristarchus and Secundus. We know little about Secundus.[23] Aristarchus was a Jewish believer (Col 4:10 – 11). He was present when Paul was swept up in the Ephesian riot (Acts 19:29). He accompanied Paul by ship to Rome (Acts 27:2) and seems to have accepted imprisonment with him (Col 4:10; Phlm 24).

When Demas deserted Paul, he went to Thessalonica (2 Tim 4:10) — a large city where maybe he could spend his life without seeing any Christians. Thessalonica, like most Pauline churches, then disappears from the New Testament narrative. Yet, two additional footnotes are appropriate. First, after nearly two millennia, including five centuries under Turkish rule, there is still a church in the city of Thessalonica. A more horrific note concerns the Jewish people of the city. From about AD

23. See J. F. Watson, "Secundus," *ABD*, 5:1065. Watson says he was a Gentile, but offers no proof.

1500 – 1700, Thessalonica was host to the single largest Jewish colony in the world. In 1943, under the Nazi occupation, nearly the entire Jewish population was deported and executed.[24]

Critical Issues

Integrity of 1 Thessalonians

A few have suggested that one or both of the letters is a "composite"; that is, some later scribe stitched together several shorter Pauline letters into larger ones. Walter Schmithals, for example, dissected 1 – 2 Thessalonians into four original letters. He then rearranged these components in chronological order so as to reveal the evolution of Paul's dealings with Thessalonica. Supposedly they show the picture of a church that was infected with Gnosticism.[25] The reconstruction is extraordinarily speculative and based on his overarching and unproven premise that Gnosticism existed in the middle of the first century, and that Paul was fighting it on every front.

A regular presupposition in these reconstructions is that Paul could not have written a letter that jumped from theme to theme as 1 Thessalonians might appear to do. Why, for example, would a single letter need two thanksgiving sections?[26] Some help is afforded us by remembering that Paul was not writing as a professor of rhetoric, but as a pastor, one whose exuberant style was due to his relief that his church had avoided disaster. In seminary, homiletics professors insist that every sermon must have one main idea; after all, there is always the next Sunday to develop a new topic. But a letter is not a sermon. It is a communiqué that would take weeks to deliver by hand, weeks to digest, and weeks to receive a reply if and when one was sent. Therefore, an apostle writing from Corinth to Thessalonica did not have the luxury of writing on one theme only; he had to touch on all the topics that lay at hand.

According to one theory, 1 Thess 2:13(14) – 16 is an "interpolation," an anti-Jewish message that found its way into the letter some time after Paul's death. B. A. Pearson's 1971 article has been the touchstone for discussion in recent decades.[27] He argues that the text was interpolated early enough into the manuscript transmission so that the original text did not survive. He takes the statement to be some scribe's thoughts about the destruction of Jerusalem in AD 70.[28]

24. Vom Brocke, *Thessaloniki*, 232 – 33.

25. Walter Schmithals, *Paul and the Gnostics* (trans. John E. Steely; Nashville: Abingdon, 1972), 123 – 218.

26. Earl J. Richard, *First and Second Thessalonians* (SP; Collegeville, MN: Liturgical, 1995), 11. He divides 1 Thessalonians into an "Earlier Missive" (2:13 – 4:2, excluding 2:14 – 16), a "Later Missive" (1:1 – 2:12 + 4:3 – 5:28), and a non-Pauline interpolation (2:14 – 16).

27. Birger A. Pearson, "1 Thessalonians 2:13 – 16: A Deutero-Pauline Interpolation," *HTR* 64 (1971): 79 – 94.

28. Ibid., 82 – 83. The main recent commentator to reject the authenticity of 2:14 – 16 is Richard, *First and Second Thessalonians*, 17 – 19. He points to supposedly non-Pauline vocabulary and ideas, stating for example (17) that "imitation" in 2:14 "is not used properly." His comments have the unintended result of revealing how difficult it is to excise this passage from the letter.

Against Pearson one should consider several things. First, the syntax of the paragraph fits within its context.[29] Second, Pearson must assume that the divine "wrath" refers to AD 70, not to some event in Paul's lifetime or to the eschatological judgment. Third, he disregards the way in which the passage fits within the letter as a whole, with its themes of persecution and imitation.[30] Fourth, he cannot account for the fact that all ancient manuscripts and versions contain this paragraph.[31] There is little solid proof that 1 Thess 2:13 – 16 did not come from Paul's pen. We are left to wrestle with its meaning as we do with any other difficult passage.

Authorship of 2 Thessalonians

There is no serious debate over whether Paul wrote the first letter. The same cannot be said of 2 Thessalonians, and in some circles it is now taken as a given that it is post-Pauline or even anti-Pauline.[32] This is a wholly modern concern and has been most extensively argued by Wolfgang Trilling.[33] The earliest lists of the New Testament books, including Marcion's, contained two letters to Thessalonica. For example, the Muratorian Canon states that Paul wrote to Corinth and Thessalonica once, and that "he wrote to the Corinthians and to the Thessalonians once more for their reproof." Irenaeus refers to the letter as "Second Thessalonians" (Irenaeus, *Haer.* 3.7.2).

The objections to 2 Thessalonians fall into two categories. (1) Literary: the style of the letter looks close enough to 1 Thessalonians that it makes some think it is a poor imitation of the real letter; or, the second letter lacks the warmth of the first. (2) Theological: 2 Thessalonians shows that the day of the Lord cannot be at hand, since the eschatological Apostasy and the Man of Lawlessness are not on the scene, whereas 1 Thessalonians 5:2 makes the parousia a "thief in the night" that will take all by surprise.

The fact that the author placed his own signature at 2 Thess 3:17 has not convinced everyone that Paul signed it. Perhaps it was a sort of "stealth" letter, sent in to discredit and replace 1 Thessalonians. By the same token, the warning against false letters (2 Thess 2:2) has been taken to mean that the author is denouncing 1 Thessalonians as the fake — a letter as "supposedly, from us" — and offering his own version of apocalyptic eschatology as genuine. With regard to this issue, we will argue under "Eschatology in Thessalonica" later in this introduction that both letters are

29. Jon A. Weatherly, "The Authenticity of 1 Thessalonians 2.13 – 16: Additional Evidence," *JSNT* 42 (1991): 79 – 98.

30. As also Ben Witherington III, *1 and 2 Thessalonians: A Socio-Rhetorical Commentary* (Grand Rapids: Eerdmans, 2006), 82 – 83; Karl P. Donfried, *Paul, Thessalonica, and Early Christianity* (Grand Rapids: Eerdmans, 2002), 200.

31. The interpolation theory can point to no external evidence. All manuscripts of 1 Thessalonians include these verses. The only textual variant worth noting is that some manuscripts of the Vulgate omit the very end of 2:16, that God's "wrath has come upon them unto the end."

32. We will not enter into all the many details of the debate, but direct the reader to Malherbe, *Letters to the Thessalonians*, 364 – 70; D. A. Carson and Douglas J. Moo, *An Introduction to the New Testament* (2nd ed.; Grand Rapids: Zondervan, 2005), 536 – 42.

33. Wolfgang Trilling, *Untersuchungen zum zweite Thessalonicherbrief* (Leipzig: St. Benno, 1972).

firmly rooted in the Olivet Discourse; the gospel tradition itself teaches both the suddenness of the parousia and the coming of apocalyptic signs before the end.

With regard to the similar language, these alone of Paul's letters purport to have flowed from his pen within months or more likely weeks and indicate that his posture toward the church had not changed. The tone is calmer in the second letter, because Paul was not writing as a man who has recently been relieved from a huge burden of anxiety.

Dates

There are two viewpoints with regard to the second missionary journey of Paul. The view that is held by the great majority of scholars states that Paul and team arrived in Macedonia during the reign of Emperor Claudius (AD 41 – 54; see Acts 11:28). His arrival at Corinth is rather easily dated because of the so-called "Gallio inscription" discovered in Delphi. The inscription implies that Gallio's proconsulship began in 51 or 52. The book of Acts states that he was proconsul when Paul had already been in Corinth for a year and a half (see Acts 18:11 – 12). This puts Paul's arrival in Corinth around AD 50, and his work in Thessalonica earlier that same year. A second datum is the arrival of Aquila and Priscilla and Corinth, which is said to have taken place after they had been expelled from Rome (see Acts 18:2), an event that is hard to pin down precisely, but probably took place in AD 49.

Most scholars date 1 Thessalonians and (if genuine) 2 Thessalonians during Paul's earlier months in Corinth, perhaps before the arrival of Gallio. We could thus reconstruct the events:[34]

48 or 49	Jerusalem Council
49 or 50	Paul and team arrive in Macedonia, evangelize Thessalonica
50	Paul arrives in Corinth; Aquila and Priscilla arrive from Rome
50 or 51	Paul writes 1 Thessalonians; then 2 Thessalonians

The other major viewpoint is most famously associated with Gerd Lüdemann, building on the research by John Knox. He argues that Aquila and Priscilla were expelled from Rome in AD 41 and not, as is commonly calculated, in 49. Paul must have already evangelized Macedonia before he met them in Corinth. This would place the Macedonia campaign in the very late 30s and 1 Thessalonians in the year 41.[35] Therefore, he concludes, the book of Acts gets it wrong when it places the Galatian ministry before the Greek one, and Paul wrote 1 Thessalonians long before

34. The reader should consult the standard introductions; also Robert Jewett, *A Chronology of Paul's Life* (Philadelphia: Fortress, 1979), 38 – 40; Malherbe, *Letters to the Thessalonians*, 71 – 74; and especially Rainer Riesner, *Paul's Early Period: Chronology, Mission Strategy, Theology* (trans. Doug Stott; Grand Rapids: Eerdmans, 1998), 157 – 211.

35. Gerd Lüdemann, *Paul Apostle to the Gentiles: Studies in Chronology* (trans. F. Stanley Jones; Philadelphia: Fortress, 1984), 238.

the time of Gallio. The great majority of scholars have rejected the Knox-Lüdemann thesis as untenable, depending as it turns on a redating of the Jewish expulsion and a highly skeptical reading of the book of Acts.

Chronological Order of the Letters

For some centuries, a minority of scholars has argued that while both letters are genuine, their order in the canon is reversed. If the early church canons got the order wrong, it was because they tended to list the longer letter first (e.g., 1 and 2 Corinthians). The most recent major commentary that holds to the priority of 2 Thessalonians is that by Charles Wanamaker. His argument is complex and depends on internal evidence, for example, that Paul is more likely to have autographed his original letter than his second (2 Thess 3:17). He argues that reversing the order of the letters can help resolve some issues of interpretation.[36] This theory has failed to convince most scholars, and its supposed evidence is usually capable of being interpreted to support the priority of 1 Thessalonians.[37]

Eschatology in Thessalonica

Some expect that the eschatology of 1 – 2 Thessalonians should bear a strong resemblance to Mark 13, since all were composed in the first Christian generation. In particular, Beasley-Murray in his influential monograph compared the Thessalonian letters principally with Mark.[38]

A better method is to compare the two letters with *all three Synoptic apocalypses.* That sort of study reveals that neither Mark nor Luke contains parallels to all the material found in these two letters. Only Matthew's gospel (1) provides parallels for all of Paul's eschatological teaching in the two letters, and (2) uses technical vocabulary in the same way that Paul does. From textual considerations, it could even be supposed that Paul knew and taught something resembling the Matthean tradition.[39]

There are four elements in Matthew's special material and in the Thessalonian epistles that are *not* found in Mark: (1) Matt 24:12: "the love of most will grow cold" (not in Mark or Luke; see Paul's concern about love in light of the coming of Christ in

36. Charles A. Wanamaker, *The Epistles to the Thessalonians: A Commentary on the Greek Text* (NIGTC; Grand Rapids: Eerdmans, 1990), 37 – 45.

37. See especially Malherbe, *Letters to the Thessalonians*, 361 – 64.

38. George R. Beasley-Murray, *Jesus and the Future: An Examination of the Criticism of the Eschatological Discourse, Mark 13, with Special Reference to the Little Apocalypse Theory* (London: Macmillan, 1954), 232 – 34. His observations should be compared with the detailed chart by Béda Rigaux, *Saint Paul: Les épîtres aux Thessaloniciens* (EBib; Paris: Gabalda, 1956), 98 – 101. There is an inherent flaw in Beasley-Murray's approach, namely, that he favored Markan parallels over the parallels that are found in Matthew or Luke, even when the other gospels seem to be closer to Paul. He has to conclude that the Pauline eschatological material comes from Mark "helped out by Q" (234).

39. Our viewpoint is not dependent on any date for the final publication of Matthew's gospel. One supporter for the Matthean view is J. B. Orchard, "Thessalonians and the Synoptic Gospels," *Bib* 19 (1938): 19 – 42, esp. 37 – 38.

1 Thess 3:12; 5:13; 2 Thess 1:3, and other passages). (2) Matt 24:10: many "will turn away." (3) Matt 24:43: "If the owner of the house had known at what time of night the thief was coming" (in Luke, not in Mark). (4) Matt 24:49: people in the world are drunk (in Luke, not in Mark). If Paul's eschatological terms come close to the teachings of any gospel, it is Matthew.[40]

There are other synoptic traditions that inform Paul's teaching, all found in Matthew and many found in Mark or Luke as well.

In 1 Thessalonians:

- Matt 10:17 – 18 (the abuse experienced by the Judean Christians in 1 Thess 2:15 – 16)
- Matt 24:8 ("birth pains"; see 1 Thess 5:3)
- Matt 24:13 ("the one who stands firm to the end will be saved"; see 1 Thess 3:5)
- Matt 24:31 (the gathering of the elect by the angels; see 1 Thess 3:13; 4:16 – 17)
- Matt 24:33 ("right at the door"; see below; also see our comments on 1 Thess 4:17 with regard to "welcome," ἀπάντησις)
- Matt 24:36 ("about that day or hour no one knows"; see 1 Thess 5:2)
- Matt 24:42 ("keep watch"; cf. 1 Thess 5:6 – 7)
- Matt 24:49 (drunkenness is a symbol of being unprepared; see 1 Thess 5:6 – 8)

In 2 Thessalonians:

- Matt 24:6 (the disciples should not be "alarmed"; see 2 Thess 2:2, the Thessalonians should not be "disturbed"; both texts use θροέω)
- Matt 24:4 – 5, 11 (eschatological deception and false prophets; see 2 Thess 2:2, 9 – 12)
- Matt 24:15 ("abomination that causes desolation"; see 2 Thess 2:3 – 12)
- Matt 24:30 (the Son of man comes "with power and great glory"; see 2 Thess 1:7 – 10)
- Matt 24:31 (gathering of the saints; cf. 2 Thess 2:1)

And in both letters:

- Matt 24:9 – 12 (Christians will suffer tribulations; see 1 Thess 2:14; 3:3, 7; 2 Thess 1:4 – 8).

Paul and Matthew coincide in the use of a semitechnical word group. Paul uses ἀπάντησις, which may be paraphrased as going out to "welcome" the Lord (see comments on 1 Thess 4:17). Matthew too knows of a "meeting" (ἀπάντησις) in Matt

40. Other Matthean passages that may have influenced Paul's theology in these letters are Matt 10:23; 13:20 – 21.

25:6 and a cognate (ὑπάντησις) in Matt 25:1. That is, only Matthew's version of the Olivet Discourse and Paul use this word group to refer to the church going forth to meet Christ at his coming, and neither Mark nor Luke nor the other NT writers use it eschatologically.

There is one point that is absent from the Olivet traditions of all three Synoptic Gospels: the resurrection of the saints. In fact, Jesus' pronouncement that "the one who stands firm to the end will be saved" (Matt 24:13; see also 10:22) might sound unnervingly close to "salvation will come to those who manage not to die before Christ returns."

In 1 Thessalonians, Paul provides the missing datum. The key to understanding the Olivet discourse from a *post-Easter* perspective is: "If we believe that Jesus died and rose again, well ... God will gather together with [Jesus] those who have died in him" (1 Thess 4:14). Here is a comparison of the Matthean Olivet Discourse (using ESV) and Paul's teaching in the two Thessalonian letters:

Matt 24:30–31	1 Thess 4:16–17	2 Thess 1:6–7
The sign of the Son of Man	The Lord himself	At the revealing of the Lord Jesus
will appear ... in heaven	will come down from heaven	from heaven
and then all the peoples of the earth will mourn when they see the Son of Man coming on the clouds of heaven, with power and great glory.		with his powerful angels, with blazing fire
And he will send out his angels	with the commanding shout of the archangel's voice [also "with all his holy angels" 3:13]	
with a loud trumpet call	with the sound of the trumpet of God	
	New information: THE DEAD IN CHRIST WILL FIRST BE RESURRECTED	
and [the angels] will gather his elect from the four winds, from one end of heaven to the other. [Note too 25:1, 6: the "virgins" go out to meet the bridegroom]	Next, we who are still alive and remain will be taken up together with [those who were dead] in the clouds to welcome the Lord in the air. And so we will always be with the Lord.	

Even apart from the fact that the resurrection is not mentioned in this Matthean material (as it is, for example, in Matt 22:30), it is still not certain how the Thessalonians missed out on that doctrine. In other instances, when Paul addresses any issue in these two letters, there is usually no lack of explanation of why he might have brought up a certain point. But in 1 Thess 4:13–18 there seems no self-evident answer to the singular mystery: Due to what circumstances did Paul now have to inform them about the resurrection of the saints? What could possibly have gone wrong so that the Thessalonians missed out on this doctrine, which, as a casual reading of his letters shows, was central to Paul's theology? Some of the viewpoints are as follows:

(1) The least probable explanation is that of Walter Schmithals, who finds Gnosticism behind most of the problems that plagued Paul's churches. In this case, some outsider had taught the Thessalonians that the resurrection was a spiritual experience, not a bodily one.[41] This theory has multiple difficulties, not least of which is why Paul did not contradict the Gnostic teaching head-on, but was content to declare flatly that the dead would rise physically.

(2) Equally unlikely is the idea that the Thessalonians had not been taught the resurrection of the saints simply because the doctrine had not yet become a part of Christian doctrine. C. L. Mearns has argued that the earliest church believed that the resurrection was not future but "realized." Then, within two decades, believers started to die, forcing Paul to invent the comforting idea of a future resurrection.[42] Mearns fails to explain the fact that many Christians must have died before AD 50 as, we are told, Paul well knew (Acts 8:1; 9:1). One must also discard the testimony from Acts 23:6; 24:15 and Paul's letters that he had been a Pharisee and thus, by definition, had believed in the resurrection of the saints long before he believed in Jesus. The Jesus tradition too reveals that the final resurrection was a staple of Christian doctrine. Moreover, if Paul were just now putting the doctrine together for the first time, how may one account for its appearance in books by other authors in the NT canon?

(3) W. D. Davies attributes the church's confusion to Paul himself. Paul had taught them about the spiritual resurrection, as in Rom 6. He had also told them that physical death was a signal of spiritual failure, as in 1 Cor 11:27–32.[43] Therefore, the Thessalonians put two and two together and reckoned that their dead companions had been judged by God, perhaps for some secret sin. As to Davies's view, it is of course possible that Paul had taught them about a spiritual resurrection—even though he did not write it down in detail until he penned Romans. Yet, the grief in Thessalonica does not seem to be rooted in any supposed moral failure on the part of the dead, nor does Paul point out that those who had died were obviously less righteous than the survivors, which would surely have been the more direct counterargument.

41. Schmithals, *Paul & the Gnostics*, 163–64.

42. See C. L. Mearns, "Early Eschatological Development in Paul: The Evidence of 1 Corinthians," *JSNT* 22 (1984): 20. See the brief discussion by Wanamaker, *Thessalonians*, 164–65. Mearns's revisionist interpretation runs counter to another theory, that Paul's viewpoint evolved from an eschatological resurrection toward a mystical one. For further information see Ben F. Meyer, "Did Paul's View of the Resurrection Undergo Development?" *TS* 47 (1986): 363–87.

43. W. D. Davies, *Paul and Rabbinic Judaism: Some Rabbinic Elements in Pauline Theology* (4th ed.; Philadelphia: Fortress, 1980), 291.

(4) Perhaps the explanation for their being "uninformed" was circumstantial: that the apostles were quickly expelled from the city and did not have the chance to teach the doctrine of the resurrection. Against this, I think it highly implausible that Paul took the time to teach them details such as the Apostasy, the "Man of Lawlessness," and the restrainer and yet omitted to mention that Christians would be resurrected. This is especially the case when one considers that the resurrection of Jesus, the church's union with him, and the final judgment of humanity are building blocks of the basic gospel, not to be left for later catechetical instruction under the category of "last things."

(5) A more credible possibility, developed by Joseph Plevnik and others, is to view 1 Thess 4 against a backdrop of OT and apocalyptic thinking.[44] According to this theory, Paul taught them that the living Christians would be "assumed" into heaven. After the apostles left town and believers began to die, the Thessalonians supposed that the dead would forever be disadvantaged. While this viewpoint has the advantage of a set of traditions that actually existed, it has weaknesses as well. It still does not answer why Paul did not teach them about the final resurrection, which, as we have seen, was a basic tenet. If one wished to argue that Paul followed only the gospel traditions that foretold the assumption of believers, the question is still left begging, why did he do so? Of importance too is that when Paul describes the Christian hope, he does not contrast it with the "assumption" model but with paganism, which lacks a resurrection.

(6) It may be that the resurrection doctrine, while known, had not changed the deep assumptions of the believers.[45] This older view is still a promising direction. In a commentary series such as this one, the insights of pastoral theology will shed light on how the Thessalonians' eschatology was derailed. In the academy, knowledge, once brought into being, is supposed to continue to exist, able to be recovered; a commentator, for example, should be counted on to know and apply Walter Schmithals's view of Gnosticism. An axiom of pastoral ministry, by contrast, is that the flock, once taught a thing, cannot be assumed from that point on to *remain taught*. A church is a dynamic, growing, and changing group. Members are added to and subtracted. In the best of circumstances part or all of a church might forget what it has at one time known — by losing knowledge, by forgetting to apply it, or by misapplying it. There is no way I know of to teach a flock so that it retains a doctrine "once and for all."

44. Joseph Plevnik, "The Taking Up of the Faithful and the Resurrection of the Dead in 1 Thessalonians 4:13 – 18," *CBQ* 60 (1984): 274 – 83; later, "The Destination of the Apostle and the Faithful: Second Corinthians 4:13b – 14 and First Thessalonians 4:14," *CBQ* 62 (2000): 83 – 95; Wanamaker, *Thessalonians*, 166.

45. See I. Howard Marshall, *1 and 2 Thessalonians* (NCB; Grand Rapids: Eerdmans, 1983), 120 – 22; Gene L. Green, *The Letters to the Thessalonians* (PNTC; Grand Rapids: Eerdmans, 2002), 213 – 15; Seyoon Kim, "The Jesus Tradition in 1 Thess 4.13 – 5.11," *NTS* 48 (2002): 225 – 42.

In that light, let us pursue this sixth option, given what Paul stresses in the text itself.

- The Thessalonians were "*uninformed*" (1 Thess 4:13), which in context might not mean a complete lack of information. Since Paul contrasts this paragraph with 4:1 – 12, he may only be saying that "you do not truly grasp the resurrection doctrine as you did this other material" or "you do not know it in a way that you put it into practice." If one were to view the statement through the modern taxonomy of learning, Paul could perhaps be taken to mean that Thessalonians could "recall" the resurrection doctrine without being able to "comprehend" or "apply" that knowledge to a new situation.
- The main problem in Thessalonica was *grief*, which Paul compares to the sort of grief that a pagan traditionally felt after losing a loved one. The Thessalonians were grieving because of a pagan assumption, that they would never again see their companions; for that reason, Paul promised them that they would meet deceased Christians (4:17). Grief after the manner of the pagans does not seem an appropriate response at the death of someone who would be resurrected (against viewpoint 5 above) but live in a second-class state.
- Paul's solution is that *there is a resurrection of the dead* (4:14 – 15) as the necessary consequence of the death and resurrection of Jesus. He does not try to prove an afterlife, or the gathering of the saints at Jesus' coming, or the bare fact of Jesus' coming. It is the resurrection and that alone that is the missing point, and it is that doctrine that would have been the stumbling block for a Christian who had come out of paganism.
- It is of help to recall what Paul *implied elsewhere in the letter*: ever since the team arrived in Thessalonica, the church was able to view their story through the lens of the Matthean tradition. The Jewish believers were being beaten and expelled from synagogues; there was persecution from the local government; there was family disintegration as a result of the gospel; there may have been a famine; their sister churches in Judea had also long been under fire. As becomes clear in 2 Thess 2:1 – 2, it was a context where all it took was for someone to say: "The day of the Lord is at hand" or "has come."

Under extreme stress, living as all people did, with death at their elbow and with the additional possibility that members of their group might be killed, their thoughts would have flown in a dozen different directions. We know today better than ever that people who are grieving not uncommonly suffer from lack of concentration and forgetfulness. The Thessalonians' thought processes, not yet deeply formed by the resurrection doctrine, could have included the inability to apply it properly. Paul's "we do not want you to be uninformed" (1 Thess 4:13) would be an appropriate introduction or reintroduction to the resurrection doctrine.

It is my opinion that we do not have enough evidence to confirm any of the above viewpoints. Nevertheless, it requires the fewest assumptions and does justice to the known data to conclude that the Thessalonians were earlier taught the resurrection as we know it from 1 Thess 4 and other passages, and that under duress some failed to apply it properly; some "forgot" it altogether.

In 1 Thess 5:2, the day is like a thief in the night; yet according to 2 Thess 2 the believers can know that the day is not at hand. Some scholars have wondered how Paul could have taught two programs that were apparently at variance with each other: in the first, the day of the Lord comes suddenly and surprises everyone; in the second, the day of the Lord cannot come now, because there are signs that must first take place.[46]

It helps to define our terms, first with regard to the church's knowledge — the church cannot positively know the time of the day of the Lord (1 Thess 5:2). But negatively, the church can rule out that the day of the Lord is immediately at hand, based on unfulfilled eschatological events (2 Thess 2:3). The church's ignorance is real but not absolute.

Second, what is meant by "suddenness" (5:3)? Believers should not be taken unaware, if they are walking in the light; unbelievers will be, because they are walking in darkness and because they do not expect Christ to come. The suddenness of the Day is qualitatively different for the world than it is for the "children of light."

Third is the question of intervening signs. According to Matthew 24, this entire age is marked by evidences that Satan is at work. All sorts of signs must take place before Christ's return, including the particularly vital work of God, that is, the worldwide spread of the gospel (Matt 24:14). There is no indication that Paul, who was so strongly influenced by this tradition, had jettisoned Jesus' predictions of the many signs that would precede the (surprising) coming of the end.

Fourth is the meaning of imminence. Evangelicals bandy back and forth the question of whether Christ's coming is imminent. For example, one exegete deduces from the Scriptures that Christ's coming is imminent; he then defines the word "imminent," but not on a firm basis of the relevant texts; he then reads that definition back into the New Testament and concludes that there is an imminent return of Christ (the pre-tribulational rapture) and years later the second coming of Christ.[47]

46. Some say that with the destruction of Jerusalem and with the failure of the parousia to materialize, the church reached for Jewish apocalyptic symbols in order to make sense of the intervening period, and that the (pseudepigraphical?) epistle of 2 Thessalonians dates from that period. L. J. Lietaert Peerbolte, "The KATÉXON/KATÉXΩN of 2 Thess 2:6–7," *NovT* 39/2 (1997): 138–50, states that a pseudepigraphic author of this letter gestures toward some unknown "restrainer" without identifying him, because — according to Peerbolte — the author himself does not know who the restrainer could be.

47. See Robert L. Thomas, "Imminence in the NT, Especially Paul's Thessalonian Epistles," *MSJ* 13/2 (2002): 191–214. Like Thomas, some use the term "imminent" to mean "it could happen at any moment, without intervening signs, but that could mean immediately or in a thousand years." Nevertheless, this definition of "imminent" is *not* the accepted meaning of the English word, which is "impending threateningly, hanging over one's head, ready to befall or overtake one; close at hand in its incidence; coming on shortly" (*OED*). One cannot legitimately use the English word to mean "it will not necessarily come soon, but could happen any moment and must be without intervening events."

This is not a sound methodology. The NT vocabulary must be defined on its own terms, not ours. Neither the Olivet Discourse nor Paul's letters speak of any imminence that denies that signs will take place before the coming of Christ.[48]

One must give due attention to the strong *intertextuality* between Matt 24 – 25 and these two letters.[49] Taken together, the letters jointly exhaust almost all of the material found in the Matthean tradition. Yes, Paul addresses the Thessalonians' immediate needs based on two interpretative cruxes (the resurrection of the dead; the signs of the end). But the broader paradigm that he teaches in 1 and 2 Thessalonians is what the tradition has given him, and his source material allows the expectation of the "thief in the night" to live side-by-side with warnings about the signs of the end.

Since the middle of the nineteenth century, many Bible students have looked to 1 Thess 4:13 – 17 and 2 Thess 2:1 and asked whether the gathering of the church is to take place *before* or *after* the final tribulation and the coming of the Man of Lawlessness. As shown by the parallels provided above, it apparently did not occur to Paul to describe any gathering other than that which occurs at the coming of the Son of Man at the end of the age. The eschatological outline of Matt 24:30 – 31 is extraordinarily similar to that of 1 – 2 Thessalonians, save for the additional datum of the resurrection of the saints in 1 Thess 4. Thus, when Paul described the resurrection/rapture, a Thessalonian who was already familiar with the Olivet tradition would have understood it as the same event as the coming of the Son of Man and the gathering of the saints as taught in Matt 24:31. When readers of today ask the Thessalonian texts whether the rapture might not take place before the tribulation, they are seeking something that the letters simply are not designed to provide.[50]

48. Paul nowhere links the "work stoppage" in 2 Thess 3:6 – 15 with eschatology. When we study this relevant passage, we will attempt to demonstrate that the problem of work had nothing to do with any eschatological misperception.

49. There is a superb comparison between the eschatology of Jesus and of Paul by Ben Witherington III, *Jesus, Paul and the End of the World: A Comparative Study in New Testament Eschatology* (Downers Grove, IL: InterVarsity Press, 1992).

50. The reader should consult the useful volume: Richard R. Reiter, ed., *Three Views on the Rapture: Pre-, Mid-, or Post-tribulation* (Grand Rapids: Zondervan, 1984). D. Edmond Hiebert, *The Thessalonian Epistles: A Call to Readiness* (Chicago: Moody Press, 1971), 200 – 203, promotes the pretribulational viewpoint. We leave to one side the question of whether anyone prior to the nineteenth century ever taught a pretribulational rapture. As far as I can see, if anyone taught the doctrine, they left no impact in the historical record. I am taking into account the reference that is falsely attributed to Ephraem of Syria and is thought by some to teach a pretribulational rapture.

Outline of 1 and 2 Thessalonians

1 Thessalonians

I. Introduction (1:1)

II. Thanksgiving for God's Saving Intervention (1:2 – 10)

- A. The apostolic team regularly gives thanks for them (1:2)
- B. The apostles gratefully affirm their salvation before God (1:3 – 5)
- C. The apostles recognize growth in the believers (1:6 – 10)

III. The Apostolic Team as a Pattern for the Thessalonians (2:1 – 12)

- A. The apostolic team met with success, even though it was under fierce attack (2:1 – 2)
- B. The apostolic team served God in an exemplary manner (2:3 – 12)

IV. Recapitulation: Why They Regularly Give Thanks for the Thessalonians (2:13 – 16) [Inclusio with 1:2]

- A. The Thessalonians received the gospel as the divine message (2:13a)
- B. That message was active among them (2:13b)
- C. They became imitators of the established Judean churches (2:14 – 16)

V. Paul and Silas' Frustrated Travel Plans and a Solution (2:17 – 3:13)

- A. Paul and Silas had a deep desire to revisit the Thessalonians, but Satan hindered them (2:17 – 20)
- B. Timothy carried out a reconnaissance of the Thessalonian church (3:1 – 5)
- C. Timothy returned (3:6a)
- D. Timothy conveyed joyful information about the state of the church (3:6b – 10)
- E. The new information makes Paul and Silas pray all the more (3:11 – 13)

VI. *Paraenesis:* The Gospel Ethic in a Gentile Environment (4:1 – 12)

- A. The Thessalonians should continue to thrive in the gospel ethic (4:1 – 2)
- B. God's will for them includes sexual holiness (4:3 – 8)
- C. God's will also includes that each believer live in love (4:9 – 12)
  1. The Thessalonians already excel in love for the Christian family (4:9 – 10)
  2. One expression of love is a particularly Christian social ethos (4:11 – 12)

VII. Instruction about the Return of Christ (4:13 – 5:11)

- A. Dead Christians will be raised to be with Jesus ahead of the living (4:13 – 18)
- B. Christians should live in holiness, even without knowing the timing of the end (5:1 – 11)

VIII. Final Exhortations (5:12 – 22)

- A. The apostles speak to all church members (5:12 – 13)
- B. The apostles give specific instructions to the leadership (5:14 – 15)
- C. The apostles return to speak to members generally (5:16 – 22)

IX. Conclusion (5:23 – 28)

- A. The apostles pray for the Thessalonians' full sanctification at the return of Christ (5:23 – 24)
- B. The apostles ask the Thessalonians to pray for the apostles' work (5:25)
- C. The apostles direct the congregations to other actions (5:26 – 27)
- D. The apostles give a benediction to the Thessalonians (5:28)

2 Thessalonians

I. Introduction (1:1 – 2)

II. Thanksgiving and Prayer for the Believers in Tribulation (1:3 – 12)
   - A. The apostolic team gives thanks, since the Thessalonians' faith and love for one another are thriving (1:3)
   - B. The apostles have a positive opinion of how they have managed to live under persecution (1:4 – 10)
   - C. The apostles pray for the Thessalonians in accordance with their hard circumstances (1:11 – 12)

III. Instruction concerning the End Times (2:1 – 12)
   - A. The Thessalonians must not become confused about the end of the age (2:1 – 3a)
   - B. The apostles remind them that they already possess the information they need to stay on course (2:3b – 12)

IV. A Second Thanksgiving, an Exhortation, and a Prayer for the Thessalonians (2:13 – 17)
   - A. The apostles give thanks because of God's election and call (2:13 – 14)
   - B. They remind the Thessalonians that they are responsible to hold fast to apostolic doctrine (2:15)
   - C. They pray that the God of salvation will encourage and strengthen the Thessalonians (2:16 – 17)

V. A Request for the Thessalonians' Prayer (3:1 – 5)
   - A. The apostles ask the Thessalonians to pray that Paul's team will have success in their current evangelistic work (3:1)
   - B. They ask for prayer that the team be delivered from evil people (3:2)
   - C. They affirm that the Lord is faithful and will protect the Thessalonians (3:3)
   - D. They are convinced that through the Lord's faithfulness, the Thessalonians will carry out the apostolic commands (3:4)
   - E. They pray that the Thessalonians will grow, particularly with regard to love and endurance (3:5)

VI. *Paraenesis:* The Problem of Disorderly Thessalonian Disciples (3:6 – 15)
   - A. The church should stay away from members who are living disruptively (3:6)
   - B. The church knows full well that Christians should work to support themselves (3:7 – 10)
   - C. Some Thessalonians are living disruptively, not working but "meddling" (3:11)
   - D. The apostles command these disorderly persons to work for their living and to cease their troublesome behavior (3:12)
   - E. The church must not allow these new distractions to discourage them from doing the right thing (3:13)
   - F. The church must stay aloof from disorderly members but not cut them out from the fellowship of the church (3:14 – 15)

VII. Conclusion (3:16 – 18)
   - A. The apostles give the Thessalonians a blessing of peace (3:16)
   - B. Paul signs the letter with his own handwritten greeting, in order to authenticate it (3:17)
   - C. The apostles give a benediction to the Thessalonians (3:18)

Select Bibliography

Commentaries on Thessalonians

Ambrosiaster. *Commentaries on Galatians-Philemon*. Translated and edited by Gerald L. Bray. Ancient Christian Texts. Downers Grove, IL: InterVarsity Press, 2009.

Beale, G. K. *1–2 Thessalonians*. IVPNTC. Downers Grove, IL: InterVarsity Press, 2003.

Best, Ernest. *A Commentary on the First and Second Epistles to the Thessalonians*. Reprint, Peabody, MA: Hendrickson, 2003.

Bruce, F. F. *1 & 2 Thessalonians*. WBC 45. Waco, TX: Word, 1982.

Calvin, John. *Commentaries on the Epistles of Paul the Apostle to the Philippians, Colossians, and Thessalonians*. Translated and edited by John Pringle. Reprint, Grand Rapids: Eerdmans, 1948.

Chrysostom, John. *Homilies on First Thessalonians*. In vol. 13 of *NPNF*[1]. Edited by Philip Schaff. Reprint, Grand Rapids: Eerdmans, 1979.

———. *Homilies on Second Thessalonians*. In vol. 13 of *NPNF*[1]. Edited by Philip Schaff. Reprint, Grand Rapids: Eerdmans, 1979.

Elias, Jacob. *1 and 2 Thessalonians*. Believers Church Bible Commentary Series. Scottdale, PA: Herald, 1995.

Fee, Gordon D. *The First and Second Letters to the Thessalonians*. NICNT. Grand Rapids: Eerdmans, 2009.

Frame, James E. *A Critical and Exegetical Commentary on the Epistles of St. Paul to the Thessalonians*. ICC. Edinburgh: T&T Clark, 1912.

Gaventa, Beverly Roberts. *First and Second Thessalonians*. Interpretation. Louisville: John Knox, 1998.

Gorday, Peter, ed. *Colossians, 1–2 Thessalonians, 1–2 Timothy, Titus, Philemon*. ACCS. Downers Grove, IL: InterVarsity Press, 2000.

Green, Gene L. *The Letters to the Thessalonians*. PNTC. Grand Rapids: Eerdmans, 2002.

Hendriksen, William. *Exposition of I–II Thessalonians*. Grand Rapids: Baker, 1955.

Hiebert, D. Edmond. *The Thessalonian Epistles: A Call to Readiness*. Chicago: Moody Press, 1971.

Holmes, Michael W. *1 & 2 Thessalonians*. NIVAC. Grand Rapids: Zondervan, 1998.

Holtz, Traugott. *Der Erste Brief an die Thessalonicher*. EKKNT 13. Zürich: Benziger/Neukirchen-Vluyn: Neukirchener, 1986.

Malherbe, Abraham J. *The Letters to the Thessalonians: A New Translation with Introduction and Commentary*. AB 32B. New York: Doubleday, 2000.

Marshall, I. Howard. *1 and 2 Thessalonians*. NCB. Grand Rapids: Eerdmans, 1983.

Milligan, George. *St. Paul's Epistles to the Thessalonians*. London: MacMillan, 1908.

Morris, Leon. *The Epistles of Paul to the Thessalonians: An Introduction and Commentary.* TNTC. Revised ed. Grand Rapids: Eerdmans, 1984.

———. *The First and Second Epistles to the Thessalonians.* NICNT. Revised ed.; Grand Rapids: Eerdmans, 1991.

Plummer, Alfred. *A Commentary on St. Paul's First Epistle to the Thessalonians.* London: Robert Scott, 1918.

Richard, Earl J. *First and Second Thessalonians.* SP 11. Collegeville, MN: Liturgical, 1995.

Rigaux, Béda. *Saint Paul: Les épîtres aux Thessaloniciens.* EBib. Paris: Gabalda, 1956.

Theodoret of Cyrus. *Interpretatio in xiv epistulas sancti Pauli.* In vol. 82 of PG. Paris: Migne, 1857–66.

Trilling, Wolfgang. *Der Zweite Brief an die Thessalonicher.* EKKNT 14. Zürich: Benziger/ Neukirchen-Vluyn: Neukirchener, 1980.

Wanamaker, Charles A. *The Epistles to the Thessalonians: A Commentary on the Greek Text.* NIGTC. Grand Rapids: Eerdmans, 1990.

Weima, Jeffrey A. D. "1 and 2 Thessalonians." Pages 404–43 in *Zondervan Illustrated Bible Backgrounds Commentary: New Testament,* vol. 3 (ed. Clinton E. Arnold; Grand Rapids: Zondervan, 2002).

Witherington, Ben, III. *1 and 2 Thessalonians: A Socio-Rhetorical Commentary.* Grand Rapids: Eerdmans, 2006.

Books and Articles on Thessalonians

Aune, David E. *Prophecy in Early Christianity and the Ancient Mediterranean World.* Grand Rapids: Eerdmans, 1983.

Barclay, John M. G. "Conflict in Thessalonica." *CBQ* 55 (1993): 512–30.

Beale, G. K., and D. A. Carson, eds. *Commentary on the New Testament Use of the Old Testament.* Grand Rapids: Baker, 2007.

Beasley-Murray, George R. *Jesus and the Future: An Examination of the Criticism of the Eschatological Discourse, Mark 13, with Special Reference to the Little Apocalypse Theory.* London: Macmillan, 1954.

———. *Jesus and the Last Days: the Interpretation of the Olivet Discourse.* Peabody, MA: Hendrickson, 1993.

Bockmuehl, Markus. "1 Thessalonians 2:14–16 and the Church in Jerusalem." *TynBul* 52 (2001): 1–31.

Boring, M. Eugene, Klaus Berger, and Carsten Colpe, eds. *Hellenistic Commentary to the New Testament.* Nashville: Abingdon, 1995.

Bousset, Wilhelm. *The Antichrist Legend: A Chapter in Christian and Jewish Folklore.* Translated by A. H. Keane. Reprint, Atlanta: Scholars, 1999.

Brant, Jo-Ann. "The Place of *Mimēsis* in Paul's Thought." *Studies in Religion* 22 (1993): 285–300.

Brundage, James A. *Law, Sex, and Christian Society in Medieval Europe.* Reprint, Chicago: University of Chicago Press, 1990.

Burke, Trevor J. *Family Matters: A Socio-Historical Study of Kinship Metaphors in 1 Thessalonians.* JSNTSup 247. London: T&T Clark, 2003.

Byskorg, Samuel. "Co-Senders, Co-Authors and Paul's Use of the First Person Plural." *ZNW* 87 (1996): 230–50.

Cahill, Lisa Sowle. "Sexual Ethics, Marriage, and Divorce." *TS* 47 (1986): 102 – 17.

Carson, D. A. *A Call to Spiritual Reformation: Priorities from Paul and His Prayers*. Reprint, Grand Rapids: Baker, 1992.

Cerfaux, Lucien. *Christ in the Theology of St. Paul*. Translated by Geoffrey Webb and Adrian Walker. New York: Herder and Herder, 1959.

Clarke, Andrew D. *Called to Serve: A Pauline Theology of Church Leadership*. LNTS. Edinburgh: T&T Clark, 2008.

———. *Serve the Community of the Church: Christians as Leaders and Ministers*. First-Century Christians in the Graeco-Roman World. Grand Rapids: Eerdmans, 2000.

Collins, Raymond F., ed. *Studies on the First Letter to the Thessalonians*. BETL 66. Leuven: Leuven University Press, 1984.

———. *The Thessalonian Correspondence*. BETL 87. Leuven: Leuven University Press, 1990.

Copan, Victor A. *Saint Paul as Spiritual Director: An Analysis of the Concept of the Imitation of Paul with Implications and Applications to the Practice of Spiritual Direction*. Paternoster Biblical Monographs. Eugene, OR: Wipf & Stock, 2008.

Cosby, Michael B. "Hellenistic Formal Receptions and Paul's Use of APANTĒSIS in 1 Thessalonians 4:17." *BBR* 4 (1994): 15 – 34.

Cullmann, Oscar. *Christ and Time: The Primitive Christian Conception of Time and History*. Philadelphia: Westminster, 1950.

Davies, W. D. *Paul and Rabbinic Judaism: Some Rabbinic Elements in Pauline Theology*. 4th ed. Philadelphia: Fortress, 1980.

Deidun, T. J. *New Covenant Morality in Paul*. AnBib 89. Rome: Pontifical, 1981.

De Jonge, Marinus. "Light on Paul from the Testaments of the XII Patriarchs." Pages 100 – 115 in *The Social World of the First Christians: Essays in Honor of Wayne A. Meeks*. Edited by L. Michael White and O. Larry Yarbrough. Minneapolis: Fortress, 1995.

Dickson, John P. *Mission-Commitment in Ancient Judaism and in the Pauline Communities*. WUNT 2/159. Tübingen: Mohr Siebeck, 2003.

Dixon, Paul S. "The Evil Restraint in 2 Thess 2:6." *JETS* 33/4 (1990): 445 – 49.

Donfried, Karl P. "The Cults of Thessalonica and the Thessalonian Correspondence." *NTS* 31 (1985): 336 – 56.

———. "Paul and Judaism: 1 Thessalonians 2:13 – 16 as a Test Case." *Interpretation* 38 (1984): 242 – 53.

———. *Paul, Thessalonica, and Early Christianity*. Grand Rapids: Eerdmans, 2002.

Donfried, Karl P., and I. Howard Marshall. *The Theology of the Shorter Pauline Epistles*. New Testament Theology. Cambridge: Cambridge University Press, 1993.

Dunn, James D. G. *The Theology of Paul the Apostle*. Grand Rapids: Eerdmans, 1998.

Edson, Charles. "Cults of Thessalonica (Macedonia III)." *HTR* 41/3 (1948): 153 – 204.

Elgvin, Torleif. "'To Master His Own Vessel.' 1 Thess 4.4 in Light of New Qumran Evidence." *NTS* 43 (1997): 604 – 19.

Ellis, J. Edward. *Paul and Ancient Views of Sexual Desire: Paul's Sexual Ethic in 1 Thessalonians 4, 1 Corinthians 7 and Romans 1*. LNTS. Edinburgh: T&T Clark, 2007.

Fee, Gordon D. *God's Empowering Presence: The Holy Spirit in the Letters of Paul*. Peabody, MA: Hendrickson, 1994.

———. *Pauline Christology: An Exegetical-Theological Study*. Peabody, MA: Hendrickson, 2007.

Fowl, Stephen E. "A Metaphor in Distress: A Reading of NHΠΙΟΙ in 1 Thessalonians 2.7." *NTS* 36 (1990): 469 – 73.

Furnish, Victor Paul. *Theology and Ethics in Paul*. Nashville: Abingdon, 1968.

Gaventa, Beverly Roberts. "Apostles as Babes and Nurses in 1 Thessalonians 2:7." Pages 193 – 207 in *Faith and History: Essays in Honor of Paul W. Meyer*. Edited by J. T. Carroll et al. Atlanta: Scholars, 1991.

Gilliard, Frank D. "Paul and the Killing of the Prophets in 1 Thess. 2:15." *NovT* 36 (1994): 259 – 70.

———. "The Problem of the Antisemitic Comma between 1 Thessalonians 2.14 and 15." *NTS* 35 (1989): 481 – 502.

Gilliland, Dean S. *Pauline Theology & Mission Practice*. Grand Rapids: Baker, 1983.

Gundry, Stanley N., ed. *Five Views on Sanctification*. Grand Rapids: Zondervan, 1987.

Harrison, J. R. "Paul and the Imperial Gospel at Thessaloniki." *JSNT* 25/1 (2002): 71 – 96.

Haufe, Günter. "Reich Gottes bei Paulus und in der Jesustradition." *NTS* 31 (1985): 467 – 72.

Hock, Ronald F. *The Social Context of Paul's Ministry: Tentmaking and Apostleship*. Philadelphia: Fortress, 1980.

Jewett, Robert. *A Chronology of Paul's Life*. Philadelphia: Fortress, 1979.

———. *The Thessalonian Correspondence: Pauline Rhetoric and Millenarian Piety*. FF. Philadelphia: Fortress, 1986.

Johnson, Stephen C. "The 'Future' of Preaching Apocalyptic Eschatology and Christian Proclamation." *Restoration Quarterly* 49 (2007): 129 – 41.

Johnston, George. " 'Kingdom of God' Sayings in Paul's Letters." Pages 143 – 56 in *From Jesus to Paul: Studies in Honor of Francis Wright Beare*. Ed. P. Richardson and J. C. Hurd. Waterloo, Ont.: Wilfrid Laurier, 1984.

Kim, Seyoon. *Christ and Caesar: The Gospel and the Roman Empire in the Writings of Paul and Luke*. Grand Rapids: Eerdmans, 2008.

———. "The Jesus Tradition in 1 Thess 4.13 – 5.11." *NTS* 48 (2002): 225 – 42.

———. "Paul's Entry (εἴσοδος) and the Thessalonians' Faith (1 Thessalonians 1 – 3)." *NTS* 51 (2005): 519 – 42.

Klijn, A. F. J. "1 Thessalonians 4:13 – 18 and its Background in Apocalyptic Literature." Pages 67 – 73 in *Paul and Paulinism: Essays in Honour of C. K. Barrett*. Edited by M. D. Hooker and S. G. Wilson. London: SPCK, 1982.

Ladd, George Eldon. *A Theology of the New Testament*. Revised ed. Grand Rapids: Eerdmans, 1993.

Lambrecht, Jan. *Pauline Studies: Collected Essays*. Leuven: Leuven University Press, 1994.

Longenecker, Richard N., ed. *Life in the Face of Death: The Resurrection Message of the New Testament*. Grand Rapids: Eerdmans, 1998.

Lövestam, Evald. *Spiritual Wakefulness in the New Testament*. Translated by W. F. Salisbury. Lund: Gleerup, 1963.

Lührmann, Dieter. "The Beginnings of the Church at Thessalonica." In *Greeks, Romans, and Christians*. Edited by David L. Balch, Everett Ferguson, and Wayne A. Meeks. Minneapolis: Fortress, 1990.

Lyons, George. *Pauline Autobiography: Toward a New Understanding*. SBLDS 73. Atlanta: Scholars, 1985.

Malherbe, Abraham J. " 'Gentle as a Nurse': The Cynic Background of 1 Thessalonians ii." *NovT* 12 (1970): 203 – 17.

———. "God's New Family in Thessalonica." Pages 115 – 25 in *The Social World of the First Christians: Essays in Honor of Wayne A. Meeks*. Edited by L. Michael White and O. Larry Yarbrough. Minneapolis: Fortress, 1995.

———. *Paul and the Popular Philosophers*. Minneapolis: Fortress, 1989.

———. *Paul and the Thessalonians: The Philosophic Tradition of Pastoral Care*. Philadelphia: Fortress, 1987.

Marshall, I. Howard. *Kept By the Power of God: A Study of Perseverance and Falling Away.* Reprint, Minneapolis: Bethany, 1974.

———. *New Testament Theology: Many Witnesses, One Gospel.* Downers Grove, IL: InterVarsity Press, 2004.

Martin, Dale B. *The Corinthian Body.* New Haven, CT: Yale University Press, 1995.

Mearns, C. L. "Early Eschatological Development in Paul: The Evidence of I and II Thessalonians." *NTS* 27 (1981): 137–57.

———. "Early Eschatological Development in Paul: The Evidence of 1 Corinthians." *JSNT* 22 (1984): 19–35.

Meeks, Wayne A. *The First Urban Christians: The Social World of the Apostle Paul.* 2nd ed. New Haven, CT: Yale University Press, 2003.

Morris, Leon. *Word Biblical Themes.* Dallas, TX: Word, 1989.

Munck, Johannes. "1 Thess. I. 9–10 and the Missionary Preaching of Paul: Textual Exegesis and Hermeutic Reflections." *NTS* 9 (1962–63): 95–110.

Nicholl, Colin R. *From Hope to Despair in Thessalonica: Situating 1 and 2 Thessalonians.* SNTMS 126. Cambridge: Cambridge University Press, 2004.

O'Brien, P. T. *Gospel and Mission in the Writings of Paul: An Exegetical and Theological Analysis.* Grand Rapids: Baker, 1995.

Orchard, J. Bernard. "Thessalonians and the Synoptic Gospels." *Bib* 19 (1938): 19–42.

Oropeza, B. J. *Paul and Apostasy: Eschatology, Perseverance, Falling Away in the Corinthian Congregation.* WUNT 2/115. Tübingen: Mohr Siebeck, 2000.

Paddison, Angus. *Theological Hermeneutics and 1 Thessalonians.* SNTSMS 133. Cambridge: Cambridge University Press, 2005.

Pate, C. Marvin, and Douglas W. Kennard. *Deliverance Now and Not Yet: The New Testament and the Great Tribulation.* Studies in Biblical Literature 54. New York: Peter Lang, 2003.

Pearson, Birger A. "1 Thessalonians 2:13–16: A Deutero-Pauline Interpolation." *HTR* 64 (1971): 79–94.

Peerbolte, L. J. Lietaert. "The KATÉXON/KATÉXΩN of 2 Thess 2:6–7," *NovT* 39/2 (1997): 138–50.

Peterman, G. W. "Marriage and Sexual Fidelity in the Papyri, Plutarch and Paul." *TynBul* 50/2 (1999): 163–72.

Pitre, Brant. *Jesus, the Tribulation and the End of the Exile: Restoration Eschatology and the Origin of the Atonement.* WUNT 2/204. Tübingen: Mohr Siebeck, 2005.

Plevnik, Joseph. "The Destination of the Apostle and of the Faithful: Second Corinthians 4:13b–14 and First Thessalonians 4:14." *CBQ* 60 (2000): 83–95.

———. "The Taking Up of the Faithful and the Resurrection of the Dead in 1 Thessalonians 4:13–18." *CBQ* 60 (1984): 274–83.

Plummer, Robert L. *Paul's Understanding of the Church's Mission: Did the Apostle Paul Expect the Early Christian Communities to Evangelize?* Paternoster Biblical Monographs. Eugene, OR: Wipf & Stock, 2006.

Ridderbos, Herman. *Paul: An Outline of His Theology.* Translated by J. R. DeWitt. Grand Rapids: Eerdmans, 1975.

Riesner, Rainer. *Paul's Early Period: Chronology, Mission Strategy, Theology.* Translated by Doug Stott. Grand Rapids: Eerdmans, 1998.

Russell, R. "The Idle in 2 Thess 3.6–12: An Eschatological or a Social Problem?" *NTS* 34 (1988): 105–19.

Sailors, Timothy. "Wedding Textual and Rhetorical Criticism to Understand the Text of 1 Thessalonians 2.7." *JSNT* 80 (2000): 81–98.

Schippers, R. "The Pre-Synoptic Tradition in 1 Thessalonians II:13–16." *NovT* 8 (1966): 223–34.

Schlueter, Carol J. *Filling Up the Measure: Polemical Hyperbole in 1 Thessalonians 2:14–16*. JSNTSup 98. Sheffield: JSOT, 1994.

Schmithals, Walter. *Paul & the Gnostics*. Translated by John E. Steely. Nashville: Abingdon, 1972.

Schnabel, Eckhard J. *Paul the Missionary: Realities, Strategies and Methods*. Downers Grove, IL: InterVarsity Press, 2008.

Schreiner, Thomas R. *New Testament Theology: Magnifying God in Christ*. Grand Rapids: Baker, 2008.

Schreiner, Thomas R., and Ardel B. Caneday. *The Race Set Before Us: A Biblical Theology of Perseverance & Assurance*. Downers Grove, IL: InterVarsity Press, 2001.

Shelton, Jo-Ann. *As the Romans Did: A Sourcebook in Roman Social History*. 2nd ed. Oxford: Oxford University Press, 1998.

Spicq, C. "Les Thessaloniciens 'inquiets' étaient-ils des paresseux?" *Studia Teologica* 10 (1956): 1–13.

Stanley, Christopher D. "Who's Afraid of a Thief in the Night?" *NTS* 48 (2002): 468–86.

Stanley, David. *Christ's Resurrection in Pauline Theology*. AnBib 13. Rome: Pontifical Biblical Institute, 1961.

———. "Imitation in Paul's Letters: Its Significance for his Relationship to Jesus and to His Own Christian Foundations." Pages 127–41 in *From Jesus to Paul: Studies in Honor of Francis Wright Beare*. Edited by P. Richardson and J. C. Hurd. Waterloo, Ont.: Wilfrid Laurier, 1984.

Stauffer, Ethelbert. *New Testament Theology*. Translated by John Marsh. New York: Macmillan, 1955.

Steimle, Christopher. *Religion im römishen Thessaloniki: Sakraltopographie, Kult und Gesellschaft 168 v. Chr.—324 n. Chr*. Studien und Texte zu Antike und Christentum 47. Tübingen: Mohr Siebeck, 2008.

Still, Todd D. *Conflict at Thessalonica: A Pauline Church and Its Neighbors*. JSNTSup 183. Sheffield: JSOT, 1999.

———. "Eschatology in the Thessalonian Letters." *RevExp* 96 (1999): 195–210.

Strecker, Georg. *Theology of the New Testament*. Translated by M. E. Boring. Louisville: Westminster John Knox, 2000.

Trilling, Wolfgang. *Untersuchungen zum zweite Thessalonicherbrief*. Leipzig: St. Benno, 1972.

Turner, Seth. "The Interim, Earthly Messianic Kingdom in Paul." *JSNT* 25/3 (2003): 323–42.

Vom Brocke, Christoph. *Thessaloniki—Stadt des Kassander und Gemeinde des* Paulus. WUNT 2/125. Tübingen: Mohr Siebeck, 2001.

Wallace, Daniel B. *Greek Grammar beyond the Basics: An Exegetical Syntax of the New Testament*. Grand Rapids: Zondervan, 1996.

Walton, Steve. *Leadership and Lifestyle: The Portrait of Paul in the Miletus Speech and 1 Thessalonians*. SNTSMS 108. New York: Cambridge University Press, 2000.

———. "What Has Aristotle to Do with Paul? Rhetorical Criticism and 1 Thessalonians." *TynBul* 46 (1995): 229–50.

Ware, James. "The Thessalonians as a Missionary Congregation: 1 Thessalonians 1,5–8." *ZNW* 83 (1992): 126–31.

Weatherly, Jon A. "The Authenticity of 1 Thessalonians 2.13–16: Additional Evidence." *JSNT* 42 (1991): 79–98.

Weima, Jeffrey A. D. "An Apology for the Apologetic Function of 1 Thessalonians 2.1–12." *JSNT* 68 (1997): 73–99.

———. "'But We Became Infants Among You': The Case for ΝΗΠΙΟΙ in 1 Thess 2.7." *NTS* 46 (2000): 547–64.

Wengst, Klaus. *Pax Romana and the Peace of Jesus Christ*. Philadelphia: Fortress, 1987.

Wenham, David. *Paul: Follower of Jesus or Founder of Christianity?* Grand Rapids: Eerdmans, 1995.

Wiles, Gordon P. *Paul's Intercessory Prayers: The Significance of the Intercessory Prayer Passages in the Letters of St. Paul.* SNTSMS 24. Cambridge: Cambridge University Press, 1974.

Winter, Bruce W. "The Entries and Ethics of Orators and Paul (1 Thessalonians 2:1–12)." *TynBul* 44 (1993): 55–74.

———. "'If a Man Does not Wish to Work ...': A Cultural and Historical Setting for 2 Thessalonians 3:6–16." *TynBul* 40 (1989): 303–15.

———. *Seek the Welfare of the City: Christians as Benefactors and Citizens.* First-Century Christians in the Graeco-Roman World. Grand Rapids: Eerdmans, 1994.

Witherington, Ben, III. *The Acts of the Apostles: A Socio-Rhetorical Commentary.* Grand Rapids: Eerdmans, 1998.

———. *Jesus, Paul and the End of the World: A Comparative Study in New Testament Eschatology.* Downers Grove, IL: InterVarsity Press, 1992.

Witmer, Stephen E. *Divine Instruction in Early Christianity.* WUNT 2/246. Tübingen: Mohr Siebeck, 2008.

Wright, N. T. *Paul in Fresh Perspective.* Minneapolis: Fortress, 2005.

———. *The Resurrection of the Son of God.* Minneapolis: Fortress, 2003.

Yarbrough, O. Larry. *Not Like the Gentiles: Marriage Rules in the Letters of Paul.* SBLDS 80. Atlanta: Scholars, 1985.

1 Thessalonians 1:1 – 10

CHAPTER 1

Literary Context

Letters have always followed conventional forms; such predictability allows the reader to grasp the message with less need for conscious interpretation. In this letter, Paul's opening address to the readers (1:1) resembles the standard Greco-Roman form. Nevertheless, one can also speak of a Pauline style — he amplifies the standard form with theological meaning, thus "Christianizing" it. The church exists "in God the Father and the Lord Jesus Christ" (1:1c). As in many letters of the day, the apostle gives them a greeting, but again, he expresses himself in familiar gospel terms, "grace" and "peace" (1:1d).

In the trove of ancient letters we now possess, the author might then give brief thanks to the gods before moving on. Here in 1:2 – 10, Paul shows gratitude to heaven precisely because of the Thessalonians' relationship to God and because of God's working in them through Christ. The thanksgiving ceases to be a formality and reveals itself at the very heart of the message.

This extended giving of thanks also functions as an *exordium*.[1] In ancient rhetoric, the *exordium* was a section of short to moderate length in which an author called to mind the positive aspects of their mutual relationship. In an age when time and distance might have a chilling effect on a friendship, an author did well to reestablish the reality and the value of their attachment before going on to deal with new issues. In Paul's hands, this *exordium* not only sets the tone of the letter (in the case of 1 Thessalonians, gratitude and appreciativeness), it also foreshadows how the new disciples have abandoned their previous Gentile conduct and how they now hope in the Lord's return. Some debate exists over the extent of the *exordium* in this letter, whether it is 1:2 – 5 or 1:2 – 10.[2] Nevertheless, what matters for today's reader is the content of this *exordium*, not its precise boundaries.

More so than in the typical Pauline letter, 1 Thessalonians should be read "from the inside out." That is, the modern reader may begin with 2:17 – 3:13 in order to discover the ground of the apostles' overwhelming gratitude: "But just now Timothy

1. See R. P. Martin, "Worship," *DPL*, 985.

2. Consult Wanamaker, *Thessalonians*, 72 – 73. Witherington, *1 and 2 Thessalonians*, 52, chooses 1:2 – 3.

has come to us from you and has announced the good news of your faith and your love" (3:6). The original readers, of course, knew of Timothy's mission before they first broke the seal of this letter. First Thessalonians is all the more effective because Paul omits a detailed retelling of the events that had led to this deep joy until several paragraphs into the body of the letter.[3] That is, in the written version, *result* (our joy) precedes *cause* (you have survived).

Paul's thanksgiving here is effusive: "all the time," "when," "without fail." He is repetitive, with the artlessness of true emotion, as he describes their eagerness to hurry into God's presence in order to give thanks. Why this passion? And why does their gratitude seem less breathless in the second letter (2 Thess 1:3 – 4)? It is because at the precise point of writing the first letter, communication with Thessalonica had just been reopened after weeks or months of silence. Their thankfulness is sharpened by the fear that things might have turned out "in vain" (1 Thess 3:5) — but thank God, they did not!

In other letters (e.g., 2 Thessalonians, Romans, Ephesians) Paul moves directly from thanksgiving to the main theme. And so in 1 Thessalonians, the *exordium* is a bridge to teaching about the apostolic team (2:1 – 12). But thanksgiving does not end after 1 Thess 1 — a distinctive trait of this letter is that three times more Paul has recourse to grateful words (2:13; 2:19 – 20; 3:9 – 10; see also 5:16, 18).

➡ **I. Introduction (1:1)**

II. Thanksgiving for God's Saving Intervention (1:2 – 10)

A. The apostolic team regularly gives thanks for them (1:2)

B. The apostles gratefully affirm the Thessalonians' salvation before God (1:3 – 5)

C. The apostles recognize growth in the believers (1:6 – 10)

III. The Apostolic Team as a Pattern for the Thessalonians (2:1 – 12)

Main Idea

Paul, Silas, and Timothy greet the Thessalonians and then declare that they regularly and fervently give thanks to God for them. The team's gratitude is based on their confidence that the new disciples are among the elect, a judgment that is based first on their own eyewitness testimony and second on the talk about their changed behavior that has spread to Macedonia, Achaia, and "everywhere."[4]

3. In a Greco-Roman letter, an author might have chosen to use the rhetorical device known as *narratio*: the recounting of the events that led the author to write the letter. Paul uses that form in Gal 1:11 – 2:14.

4. Similar to Rom 1:8; Eph 1:15; Col 1:4; Phlm 4 – 7.

Translation

(See next two pages.)

Structure

The letter begins with a normal Greco-Roman introduction: name of the sender; name of the recipient; greeting (see also 2 Thess 1:1 – 2). Paul's style is at its most sparse in this letter; in other letters his introductions give more detail.

"We give thanks to God" (1:2) sets the emotional tone for the rest of chapter 1. Paul develops in 1:2 – 3a *how they give thanks and pray*. First is the adverb "all the time" (πάντοτε); then "for every one of you"; then in 1:2d an adverbial participle "with gratitude we speak concerning you." Following the punctuation of NA[27], we attach the adverb (ἀδιαλείπτως) at the end of 1:2 to the participle in 1:3: "without fail remembering before God." The syntax is not tightly structured, with the result that the thoughts seem to come all in a rush. It is this very flood of words that reflects the high emotion of Paul, Silvanus, and Timothy.

Paul then moves on to the content of their prayers (1:3 – 5), doing so with participles that unpack the initial "we give thanks," as in Eph 1:16; Phlm 4. The first, "remembering" (1:3), leads to a description of the Thessalonians' three *Christian activities in the now*: work, hard labor, and endurance, which are inspired by the three divine graces of faith, love, and hope.

With the other participle Paul turns his attention to *God and his work in the Thessalonian Christians*: "we acknowledge" God's choice of them (1:4). They are able to perceive God's election for a reason, "because" (causal use of ὅτι) of what they have seen in Thessalonica. Paul uses, as he does in 1 Cor 4:20 and elsewhere, the rhetorical device known as antithesis: the gospel came not (οὐκ) in word only but (ἀλλά) with miracles and (καί) in the Holy Spirit and (καί) in a great sense of certainty. The final clause of this set uses reminder language ("and you know") to point to the behavior of the missionaries in Thessalonica. He thus foreshadows the truth that God will not work through people of whom he does not approve (1 Thess 2:4).

In 1:6 we highlight Paul's change of focus to the Thessalonians, "in your turn, you" (καὶ ὑμεῖς). Verse 6 outlines *the initial effects of the gospel in Thessalonica*: they became "imitators" of Paul and of the Lord Jesus and received the message in tribulation and with the Spirit's joy. Then in 1:7 – 10 Paul shows how, having received the message, they have quickly *become the caliber of Christian that others could imitate*; they "became the pattern" for other believers in the region. It was natural for the Thessalonians to be examples of gospel life, once they had truly received it, and the clause is marked with "as a result" (ὥστε).

But Paul is not finished there, for the Thessalonians have also sent forth the gospel as evangelists. With the marker of clarification "for" (γάρ) he expands on what

1 Thessalonians 1:1 – 10

1a	Sender	Paul, Silvanus, and Timothy,
1b	Recipient	to the church of the Thessalonians,
1c	Identification	which is in God the Father and the Lord Jesus Christ:
1d	Greeting	grace to you and peace.
2a	Prayer	**We give thanks to God**
2b	Time	all the time
2c	Reference	for every one of you;
2d	Restatement	[with gratitude] we speak concerning [you]
2e	Simultaneous	when we pray,
3a	Content #1 (of 2a, c)	[1] without fail remembering [before God]
3b	List	[1] your work that arises from your believing, and
3c	List	[2] your hard labor that comes from your love [for others], and
3d	List	[3] your endurance that comes from the hope you have,
3e	Source	[1] [faith, love, and hope] in our Lord Jesus Christ,
3f		[2] [as you live] in the presence of our God and Father.
4a	Content #2 (of 2a, c)	[2] We acknowledge [before God], brothers and sisters whom God loves,
4b	Content	that you were chosen,
5a	Cause (of 4c)	because the gospel that we brought came to you not simply
5b	Manner/ List	[1] as words [that we spoke], but also
5c	List	[2] with miracles and
5d	List	[3] in [the operation of] the Holy Spirit, and
5e	List	[4] in the great sense of certainty [we had in the gospel].
5f	Reminder language	[5] *And you know* how we were among you for your sake.

6a	Comparison (with 5g)	In your turn,
6b	Assertion	**you became imitators of the pattern**
6c	List Source	[1] given by us and
6d	List	[2] by the Lord [Jesus].
6e	Manner (of 6b)	You received the message
6f	Circumstance/ List	[1] in highly distressing circumstances,
6g	Circumstance	[2] [yet] with the joy that comes from the Holy Spirit.
7a	Result (of 6e-g)	As a result you [in your turn] became the pattern
7b	Advantage	for all the believers in Macedonia and in Achaia.
8a	Explanation	For you see, from you **the word of the Lord has sounded forth,**
8b	Place/ List	[1] not only in Macedonia and in Achaia,
8c	Place/ List	[2] but everywhere,
8d	Explanation	**news of your faith in God has gone out**,
8e	Result	so that we have no need to say anything [about you].
9a	Explanation	That's because **they themselves are talking about us**,
9b	Content/ List	[1] about what kind of welcome we had from you, and
9c	Content	[2] how you turned away from idols to God
9d	Result/ List	[1] to serve the God who is living and true and
10a	Result	[2] to await his Son from heaven,
10b	Description	he whom [God] raised from the dead,
10c	Apposition	Jesus our Savior
10d		from [God's] coming wrath.

he said in 1:7. I will argue that the apostles expected their disciples to be evangelistic, and that that is precisely what the Thessalonians were doing. Paul begins to conclude the section with a result clause, "so that [ὥστε] we have no need to say anything."

Paul goes on to develop further why the apostles don't have to say anything, reinforced by a marker "for, because" (γάρ): they are saying what kind of an entrance the apostles had and how the Thessalonians reacted. They turned to God — their conversion represented by two infinitives, "serve" God and "await" his Son from heaven. The apostle goes beyond the mere description of their conversion: he recounts the apostolic kerygma, emphasizing its christological and eschatological elements in a way that anticipates the teaching of the rest of the letters.

Exegetical Outline

➡ **I. Introduction (1:1)**

II. Thanksgiving for God's Saving Intervention (1:2 – 10)

- A. The apostolic team regularly gives thanks for them (1:2).
- B. The apostles gratefully affirm their salvation before God (1:3 – 5).
  1. Their faith, love and hope are manifested in their behavior (1:3).
  2. The gospel was not simply words but the medium for God's power (1:4a).
  3. God's love and election are witnessed by the Spirit's miracles and the apostles' confidence in the gospel (1:5c-e).
  4. The believers have the apostolic team as an example (1:5f).
- C. The apostles recognize growth in the believers (1:6 – 10).
  1. They have become imitators of the apostolic team (1:6).
  2. They have become a model for the gospel (1:7 – 10).
     - a. In every place people are talking about them (1:7 – 9a).
     - b. Their conversion is exemplary (1:9b – 10).
       - i. They welcomed the apostolic team (1:9b).
       - ii. They turned away from paganism (1:9c).
       - iii. They turned to the true God and now await the eschatological salvation (1:10).

Explanation of the Text

1:1 Paul, Silvanus, and Timothy, to the church of the Thessalonians, which is in God the Father and the Lord Jesus Christ: grace to you and peace (Παῦλος καὶ Σιλουανὸς καὶ Τιμόθεος τῇ ἐκκλησίᾳ Θεσσαλονικέων ἐν θεῷ πατρὶ καὶ κυρίῳ Ἰησοῦ Χριστῷ· χάρις ὑμῖν καὶ εἰρήνη). Paul follows the common formula of naming the sender (in the nominative case), naming the recipient (dative case), and then offering a blessing or greeting. Paul and Silvanus were Roman citizens (Acts 16:37 – 38) and bore Latin names that served as the equivalents of their Hebrew names, Saul and Silas. Silvanus was a prophet and a leading member of the Jerusalem church (Acts 15:27, 30, 32, 40). Timothy was a member of the church at Lystra and probably came to faith in Christ during Paul's first missionary journey. From the moment he joined Paul and Silas (Acts 16:1 – 3), Timothy became a regular fixture in Acts and the Pauline letters (though not in Galatians or Ephesians), not to mention in Heb 13:23: "I want you to know that our brother Timothy has been released."

It is not unusual for Paul to mention others as senders of a letter, without meaning to imply that they were coauthors. Nevertheless, the first person plural "we," "us," and "our" will be found in an unusually high frequency throughout this first letter (though note 2:18; 3:5; 5:27; in the first two, Paul is referring to his individual reaction to events). Paul oscillates between "we" and "I" in 2:17 – 3:6, "we" being he and Silas (not Timothy; see comments).

According to Malherbe, Paul is using an "editorial we," and Paul alone must be considered the author.[5] But this theory does not satisfactorily explain how "I" can also mean Paul. He uses the "we" as he does in Colossians (1:3, 4, 9; 4:8), to speak concretely of himself and other associates. Silvanus and Timothy are present with him in Corinth and are true cosenders of the message. We cannot now determine to what extent Silas (or Timothy) has a hand in the letter's composition.[6] The facts that Paul speaks of "I" and gives his signature in the second letter show that his voice is the dominant one in their composition.

Usually Paul refers to "the church/saints in such-and-such a city." Only here and in 2 Thess 1:1 does he speak of the people ("the church of the Thessalonians") rather than the city (those in Rome, those in Colossae). Paul remarks that they are "in [ἐν] God the Father and the Lord Jesus Christ," which denotes the relationship in which the church dwells.

"Grace to you and peace" is the stereotypical Pauline greeting, the pair found in all his epistles except 1 – 2 Timothy (which have "grace, mercy and peace," as does 2 John 3). Divine "grace" (χάρις) is a Hellenistic concept, and Paul may have adopted the term from his pagan environment. For that reason many have suggested that he has combined a Greek term with the Hebrew *šālôm*. But this explanation does not do justice to the evidence. The closer parallel to Paul's greeting is the Greek rendering of the Hebrew *ḥesed* ("kindness, loving-kindness"; see Exod 34:6, Yahweh abounds in "love and faithfulness"). That is, "grace" too has its roots in the OT. For Paul and the other Christian authors, a prayer for God's grace is typically found at the end of letters as well (all Pauline letters; Heb 13:25; *1 Clem.* 65.2; also Rev 22:21).

The greeting "peace" comes from the Hebrew

5. Malherbe, *Letters to the Thessalonians*, 86 – 89. On the other hand, Bruce, *1 & 2 Thessalonians*, 11, believes that the "we" refers to the three senders.

6. See Fee, *Thessalonians*, 4.

greeting (1 Sam 1:17; found in Greek Jewish literature, e.g., in Jdt 8:35, "go in peace"). The prophets had also announced the coming "good news ... [of] peace" (Isa 52:7; Nah 1:15). "Grace and peace" came to greater prominence as part of the stock vocabulary of the earliest Christian church (see, e.g., 1 Pet 1:2; 2 Pet 1:2; Rev 1:4; *1 Clement inscr.* — "May grace and peace from almighty God through Jesus Christ be yours in abundance").

The Textus Receptus and hence the KJV add "from God our Father, and the Lord Jesus Christ" after "peace." The clause has some manuscript support, but it is best explained as an addition by some early scribe who was thinking of 2 Thess 1:2.

1:2 We give thanks to God all the time for every one of you; [with gratitude] we speak concerning [you] when we pray (Εὐχαριστοῦμεν τῷ θεῷ πάντοτε περὶ πάντων ὑμῶν, μνείαν ποιούμενοι ἐπὶ τῶν προσευχῶν ἡμῶν). Paul, Silas, and Timothy pray regularly for the Thessalonians and give God thanks for them. This prayer report is not polite religious jargon, such as Christians tend to fall into ("I'll be praying for you!"). Rather, it is a realistic and powerful description of how they speak when they enter the presence of God.[7] The Christian's prayer is efficacious because there is a living God who hears prayers and responds. It is frequent because it is proper to offer him regular thanks for what he has done and to pray for his further intervention.

The language of 1:2 is similar to 2 Thess 1:3 (the latter does not have "every one," πάντων). This is the first of several thanksgivings in 1 Thessalonians that are based on "to give thanks" (εὐχαριστέω), a verb common in Paul's letters.[8] While the verb could mean "to pray," Paul's orientation here is thankfulness for God's past and present work in the Thessalonians. "All the time" (πάντοτε) is the first of many references to time in the two letters. It expresses positively the same truth that is communicated by the litotes "without fail" at the end of 1:2.[9]

The prepositional phrase "for every one of you" (περὶ πάντων ὑμῶν) goes with "we give thanks." Alternately it could be attached to what follows, yielding a meaning like "concerning every one of you we speak, whenever we pray." There are two reasons why the first option — "we give thanks for every one of you" — is the better. First, many manuscripts insert "you" after "remembering" (μνείαν); while it may not have been part of the original text, nevertheless "for every one of you" was thought by *koinē* speakers to go more naturally with "we give thanks." Second, the parallel in 2 Thess 1:3 suggests that the former option is correct.[10]

The plural "you" does not indicate "you as a group" but "all of you individually." The thanksgiving in Rom 1:8 closely parallels our section: "First, I thank my God through Jesus Christ for all of you, because your faith is being reported all over the world." That letter was addressed to a city where many of his Christians friends were known individually (Rom 16:3 – 15) and could be prayed for by name.

"We speak concerning you" (μνείαν ποιούμενοι)

7. For a technical analysis of Pauline thanksgivings, see Peter Arzt-Grabner, "Paul's Letter Thanksgivings," in *Paul and the Ancient Letter Form* (ed. Stanley E. Porter and Sean A. Adams; Pauline Studies 6; Leiden: Brill, 2010), 129 – 58.

8. The verb was well-known in Hellenism and in the deuterocanonical books of the LXX; nevertheless, in the LXX of the canonical books, synonyms such as "give thanks" (ἐξομολεγέομαι) predominate. See the parallel in 2 Macc 1:11: "Having been saved by God out of grave dangers we thank him greatly. . ."

9. Litotes is a figure of speech whereby a positive truth is expressed by the negation of its opposite, sometimes for the sake of irony. In English: "Not bad!"; "It was no picnic!" It is a favorite device of Acts, e.g., in 20:12 (NKJV): "they brought the young man in alive, and they were *not a little* comforted."

10. So Wanamaker, *Thessalonians*, 73 – 74, citing another parallel, 1 Cor 1:4. Likewise, Rigaux, *Thessaloniciens*, 359.

in our expanded translation is a well-attested use of the middle voice of the verb "to do, make" (ποιέω). The reader might be tempted to translate this hyperliterally, rendering it something like "to make remembrance for oneself." Nevertheless, in this case usage determines meaning, and the phrase should be smoothed out as "to remember someone" to a third party; even better is "to mention someone" or "to speak to someone concerning another." The NT has several examples where this construction is used as prayer language (see Rom 1:9; Eph 1:16; Phlm 4).[11]

We supply "with gratitude" in the second clause, since the verbal participles (e.g., "we speak," ποιούμενοι) are connected with the "give thanks" (εὐχαριστοῦμεν) and further develop it. The Greek calls for stronger language than the "make mention" that is found in most translations, a rendering that might leave the reader with the idea that the apostles speak casually about them. As an example of how this phrase is appropriate for describing passionate prayer, *1 Clem.* 56.1 says that the Corinthians are to pray fervently for the repentance of the rebellious Christian. "When" (ἐπί) in this context refers to the time(s) of their prayers.[12]

1:[2e] – 3a Without fail remembering [before God] (ἀδιαλείπτως μνημονεύοντες). Paul describes how he and his company pray concerning the Thessalonians; gratitude is an overarching theme of their ministry to the church. Some interpreters attach "without fail" (the adverb ἀδιαλείπτως) to "we speak" (μνείαν ποιούμενοι) in 1:2 ("we speak concerning [you] without fail when we pray").[13] It is better to follow the NA[27] text, which links it with "remembering" (μνημονεύοντες) in 1:3. First, the parallel in Rom 1:9 suggests that Paul favored placing the adverb before the verb. Second, the rhythm of the Greek is smoother if the adverb is attached to 1:3.[14] This is the view we adopt in our translation.

In English, 1:3 and 5:17 are traditionally rendered "pray without ceasing." But can this really mean *perpetual* intercession, given the demands of daily life? Should prayer claim the sum total of one's waking hours? Fortunately there are some ancient Jewish and Christian parallels that help to unlock its specific meaning. In 3 Macc 6:33 there is a banquet during which there is *uninterrupted* thanksgiving to heaven.[15] In this case, the author could be referring to long hours of prayer. This would lead to an understanding of 1:2e-3a as "we pray often and heedless of the time."

Paul's letters themselves hint at this meaning here. Especially noteworthy is 2 Cor 11:28, which many commentators take to be a reference to prayer: "I face daily the pressure of my concern for all the churches." Even more clear are Col 2:1 and 4:12, where Paul's prayer for the believers is a fight or struggle. How wonderfully this mirrors the prayers of our Lord, who was known to arise before dawn to pray (Mark 1:35) or to pray long into the night (Matt 14:23). He taught his followers to

11. See BDAG, μνεία 2. Also BDAG, ποιέω 7.

12. BDAG, ἐπί 18. a., marker of temporal associations. It is possible, but unlikely, that Paul is referring to regular occasions of prayer; e.g., the apostles Peter and John kept the traditional Jewish daily cycle in Acts 3:1; 10:9. That alternate rendering would be "at our prayer times."

13. So Wanamaker, *Thessalonians*, 74; Fee, *Thessalonians*, 21; Green, *Thessalonians*, 87.

14. So Bruce, *1 & 2 Thessalonians*, 11 – 12. It is perhaps a relief to see that even the *koinē* preacher Chrysostom was puzzled by the sentence's syntax; see *Homilies on First Thessalonians* 1 (*NPNF*[1] 13:324).

15. It is the sense we might have gotten from a parallel usage of the adjective in a first-century BC inscription that refers to an *incessant* cough (MM, 9). An interesting usage is found in the pseudepigraphal *T. Levi* 13.2 (ed. Charlesworth): "Teach your children letters also, so that they might have understanding throughout all their lives as they *ceaselessly* read the law of God." That is, the literate son will be able to read the law throughout his lifetime, regularly and often, but of course not uninterruptedly. If *T. Levi* provides a true parallel, then the Christian's prayer should be regular, but not necessarily perpetual.

pray and never give up (Luke 18:1). Be sure also to study the example of Moses, who told Israel how "I lay prostrate before the Lord those forty days and forty nights because the Lord had said he would destroy you" (Deut 9:25).

Praying "night and day" also has a pedigree in the Psalms, where the phrase does not mean "evening and morning prayers" but desperate, unending intercession for God's help: "Lord, you are the God who saves me; day and night I cry out to you. May my prayer come before you; turn your ear to my cry" (Ps 88:1 – 2). During the Maccabean revolt the people were summoned to call on the Lord day and night (2 Macc 13:10 – 12), which added up to three straight days of prayer, weeping and fasting "without ceasing."

Here is where the immediate postapostolic literature can also shed some light, since it purports to be faithful to the apostolic practice of the first century. In those books, "prayer without ceasing" bears a close resemblance to the uninterrupted prayer of thanksgiving in 3 Macc 6:33. Ign. *Eph.* 10.1 seems to quote 1 Thess 5:17 and applies it to a regular ministry of prayer. Ignatius and also Polycarp in Pol. *Phil.* 4.3 use the adverb "ceaselessly" (ἀδιαλείπτως); yet they do not give specifics as to prayer's duration. Further along in the second century, however, Herm. *Sim.* 9.11.7, "without ceasing" (ἀδιαλείπτως) refers to an all-night prayer vigil. Ign. *Pol.* 1.3 likewise refers to losing sleep. Polycarp for his part did "nothing else night and day except praying for everyone and for the churches throughout the world, for this was his constant habit" (*Mart. Pol.* 5.1). Even on the verge of arrest Polycarp prayed two full hours for "everyone who had ever come into contact with him, both small and great, known and unknown, and all the universal church throughout the world" (*Mart. Pol.* 7.3 – 8.1). In other words, the apostolic fathers believed that Christians should pray daily and for extended periods of time, and that this practice had been learned from the apostles.

It seems best to conclude that Paul and team engaged in *regular, extended, and strenuous* prayer. "It would not be adequate to make an equation [of praying without ceasing] with what we call today 'the spirit of prayer,' a readiness to place oneself in the presence of God."[16] In no fashion does unceasing prayer transgress the Lord's command, "when you pray, do not keep on babbling like pagans" (Matt 6:7). The Gentiles in Jesus' day viewed prayer as efficacious to the extent that it repeated large quantities of "power" words, which would somehow effect change in the cosmos. Christian prayer, by contrast, is powerful in that it is directed to a powerful God. Today there are Christians who reason that repeated prayer somehow reflects a person's lack of faith. I have heard too many times, from the pulpit or in conversation, that the Christian should learn to speak to God once and for all about some necessity, and then simply "leave it with him." Yes, surely in some extraordinary case the Spirit might lead in that direction. Nevertheless, this practice has no basis in the doctrine of prayer as taught by the OT, Jesus, the apostles, or the earliest church fathers.

For all this, we translate "without fail" in an attempt to capture the regimen of their intercession and thanksgiving. The NLT also does well with "we ... pray for you constantly" (see also 1 Thess 2:13; Rom 1:9; 2 Tim 1:3). Since Paul directs that his readers follow the same discipline in 5:17, he must have regarded it as practicable for a nonapostle to obey. In other texts, Paul, Ignatius, and Polycarp thought it a reasonable standard for bishops and widows as well as for the laity.[17]

16. Spicq, "ἀδιαλείπτως," *TLNT*, 1:34. Were it not an uncommon word, I would have suggested that Paul prayed *assiduously.*

17. 1 Tim 5:5; Ign. *Eph.* 10.1; Pol. *Phil.* 4.3.

The verb "remembering" (μνημονεύοντες) refers to prayer in Ign. *Magn.* 14.1, "Remember me in your prayers." As with "we speak" (μνείαν ποιούμενοι) in 1:2, a participle unpacks the previous verb "we give thanks." This verbal participle could be causal ("because we remember") or temporal ("when[ever] we remember"). Yet, since there is nothing that demands either of these interpretations, it is best to follow the rule of leaving it an attendant circumstance, thus: "we give thanks and we remember."[18]

1:3b-d Your work that arises from your believing, and your hard labor that comes from your love [for others], and your endurance that comes from the hope you have (ὑμῶν τοῦ ἔργου τῆς πίστεως καὶ τοῦ κόπου τῆς ἀγάπης καὶ τῆς ὑπομονῆς τῆς ἐλπίδος). The Thessalonian disciples are carrying out activities that confirm the inner changes they have experienced. Here is one of the "triads" (patterns of three; sometimes Paul uses dyads, patterns of two) that are sprinkled throughout the two letters. The dyads and triads have the effect of communicating Paul's effusiveness as he reflects on Thessalonians' response to an appalling situation. The three virtues of faith, love, and hope are given as fundamentals in 1 Thess 3:5 – 6; 5:8; and then in 1 Cor 13:13.[19]

Each virtue — faith, love, hope — is in the genitive case. Translators have tried to capture Paul's meaning, given the various options for translating these genitive words. Among the solutions, the two most viable are attributive genitives: "your faithful work, your loving deeds, and the enduring hope you have" (NLT).[20] Meanwhile, the NIV offers a genitive of production/producer:[21] "your work produced by faith, your labor prompted by love, and your endurance inspired by hope."

Is one option more credible than the others? Yes, especially if one begins by looking at all three genitives ("faith," "love," and "hope") together rather than one at a time. While there is no rule of grammar that demands that all genitives in a triad must be of the same type, it is the logical place to start. "Endurance of hope" (τῆς ὑπομονῆς τῆς ἐλπίδος) makes best sense if "hope" (ἐλπίδος) is a genitive of production/producer: "your endurance that is produced by your hope." It then yields a smooth reading to make the other two this same type of genitive, as does the NIV. This is also the interpretation given by John Chrysostom in his homily to a *koinē*-speaking congregation.[22] It is the view reflected in our translation.

"Faith," "love," and "hope" are not some invisible qualities that bear no relationship to the real world. They are vibrant realities that express themselves visibly. "Faith" (πίστεως) in this context is not a creed but the action of believing that produces

18. See Daniel B. Wallace, *Greek Grammar Beyond the Basics: An Exegetical Syntax of the New Testament* (Grand Rapids: Zondervan, 1996), 640 – 45; Green, *Thessalonians*, 87.

19. There is a fine analysis of the "gospel of faith, hope and love" in Karl P. Donfried and I. Howard Marshall, *The Theology of the Shorter Pauline Epistles* (New Testament Theology; Cambridge: Cambridge Univ. Press, 1993), 53 – 58.

20. See Wallace, *Grammar*, 86 – 88.

21. Wallace, *Grammar*, 104 – 6. Exegetes who label the three as subjective genitives are pointing in the same direction as Wallace; nevertheless, Wallace distinguishes between the genitive of production/producer and the subjective genitive: Wallace, *Grammar*, 105, n. 89 — "With a subjective gen., the head noun is transformed into a verb; with a gen. of producer, the head noun is transformed into the direct object of the verb 'who produces.' " Attributive genitives and genitives of production/producer (or, as some would prefer, subjective genitives) are not the only two options. Rigaux, *Thessaloniciens*, 362 – 63, for example, would like to render the first phrase as an epexegetical genitive, something like "the act of having faith in Christ." His interpretation does not yield a natural understanding; for example, "labor that is love" would not suggest itself to the reader as the obvious sense of "labor of love."

22. See Chrysostom, *Homilies on First Thessalonians* 1 (*NPNF*[1] 13:324). Likewise: Leon Morris, *The First and Second Epistles to the Thessalonians* (NICNT; rev. ed.; Grand Rapids: Eerdmans, 1991), 39 – 43.

hard work (see comments on 1:8; see also 3:5). Likewise, love manifests itself in "your hard labor," or as Green puts it, "hard, strenuous, and exhausting labor."[23] But, to whom is their love directed? Although "faith" and "hope" are Godward, "love" in this verse seems to be the love between people. For example, Paul regularly speaks of love one for another (3:12; 4:9 – 10; 5:13), and it seems to be this mutual love in which they are flourishing (3:6; also 2 Thess 1:3).

The Thessalonians passed through extraordinary testing, even while Paul was still present in the city (Acts 17:5 – 9). Jason and others had to post bail as guarantee against further disturbances. If they forfeited the bond or lost their income because of their commitment to Christ, some of the believers would be laboring simply to survive.

Love is a theme repeated throughout this letter, and for good reason: Paul bases his teaching on the Olivet Discourse (see Introduction). Although we hear little preaching today about a particular sign of the end, one is that "the love of many will grow cold" (Matt 24:12; see also the prophecy in 2 Tim 3:2 – 3, that people will become "without love"). I have translated it as "love for others," since it may have extended beyond the Christian family and included the love that leads to evangelism.

"The endurance of hope" is a common NT motif; likewise, "the one who stands firm to the end will be saved," as Jesus said (Mark 13:13). In 2 Thess 1:4 the traits of faith and endurance are thrown into sharper relief during tribulation (see also 2 Thess 3:5; 2 Cor 1:6). The same holds true in Revelation, where Ephesus is noted for its endurance (Rev 2:2 – 3; see also 3:10; 13:10). In 2 Thess 3:5 Paul prays that the Thessalonians might endure, since they know what the future holds. By contrast, the pagans are known as those who have no hope in the resurrection (see comments on 1 Thess 4:13) and thus grieve piteously at the death of their friends.

1:3e-f [Faith, love, and hope] in our Lord Jesus Christ, [as you live] in the presence of our God and Father (τοῦ κυρίου ἡμῶν Ἰησοῦ Χριστοῦ ἔμπροσθεν τοῦ θεοῦ καὶ πατρὸς ἡμῶν). The Thessalonians are to define themselves with reference to the Father and the Son and (in 1:5) with reference to the Spirit. There are two ways to connect this clause with the preceding context: (1) it refers only to the third part of the triad, hope;[24] (2) it refers to each of the three parts. Some versions purposely leave it vague. The second option is preferable; since Paul is speaking in triads, it is natural that he follows a triad with language that qualifies all three parts (there are two further examples of triads doing so in 2:10 and 12). For this reason we include the triad in brackets. All three have their source in "our Lord Jesus Christ."

The phrase "in the presence of our God and Father" is not immediately clear. First Thessalonians offers some parallels: (1) perhaps the phrase is *prayer language*, as in 3:9. This might suggest that "the presence of God" is where the apostles are praying and giving thanks, and Paul is looking ahead to 1:4. (2) Perhaps it is *eschatological* language, referring to being in Christ's or God's presence after the parousia in 2:19 and 3:13. (3) The best interpretation is that it is *relational* language, as shown by what immediately precedes it, "our Lord Jesus Christ." Paul describes the sphere in which the Thessalonians experience faith, love, and hope in Christ, that is, in the presence of the gracious God.[25]

23. Green, *Thessalonians*, 90.

24. So CEV, GNB, NIV, NJB; Witherington, *1 and 2 Thessalonians*, 59; Bruce, *1 & 2 Thessalonians*, 12.

25. See the analysis in Wanamaker, *Thessalonians*, 76, who relates "God's presence" to prayer.

1:4 We acknowledge [before God], brothers and sisters whom God loves, that you were chosen (εἰδότες, ἀδελφοὶ ἠγαπημένοι ὑπὸ [τοῦ] θεοῦ, τὴν ἐκλογὴν ὑμῶν). The prayer of Paul, Silas, and Timothy consists in thanksgiving, and their thanksgiving rests on assumptions regarding the Thessalonians' standing before God. "We acknowledge" (εἰδότες, based on οἶδα) means "recalling" or "recognizing";[26] their confident thanksgiving is *because* they possess the information that follows. In the LXX "know" (γινώσκω) is the verb typically used for "acknowledging" or "confessing"; for example, "because I *knew* that the Lord is great, and our Lord in comparison with all the gods" (Ps 134:5 LXX [NETS] [135:5 MT]). Therefore, either form of "to know" (οἶδα or its synonym γινώσκω) could have worked equally well in 1 Thess 1:4. With regard to Greek synonyms, misunderstanding may arise, especially by using outdated word study tools. To give a recent example: "*Oida* (perfect of *horaō*) is to see with the mind's eye (that is, 'to know by reflection'), while *ginōskō* is to know by observation."[27] This sort of distinction yields no light on verses such as 1:4. Preachers should exercise care on this point, anticipating that their listeners may previously have heard these outdated myths.

Paul then affirms their membership in God's family: they are "brothers and sisters" (ἀδελφοί). The Christian use of "brothers and sisters" is predicated upon their adoption by God the Father (Gal 3:26 – 29) and their status as heirs of Abraham. It is correct in 1:4 to translate the term as "brothers and sisters," as do GNB, NRSV, NLT, and the NIV. It is the faithful contemporary rendering of the noun, more accurate than "brothers" or "brethren" (NASB, HCSB, ESV, NKJV).[28] "Brothers and sisters" is also much better than the colorless "dear friends" (so the CEV). Paul uses the term about 130 times. He and the other NT authors invest it with a meaning that goes well beyond the Jewish idea of co-membership in the chosen race.[29] The NT concept also supersedes the Greco-Roman ideal of friendship.[30] Paul's constant use of kinship language is a characteristic trait of 1 Thessalonians.

"Whom God loves" (ἠγαπημένοι) is a perfect participle, indicating that God's love was initiated in the past. In this verse Paul is not speaking generally of God's love for humanity, but more

26. See L&N 29.6.

27. This is the mistaken assumption found in the commentary by Linda L. Belleville, *2 Corinthians* (IVPNTC; Downers Grove, IL: InterVarsity Press, 1996), 153.

28. The NRSV has a footnote at 1 Thess 1:4 and 2 Thess 1:3 et al., saying "Gk *brothers*." The editors thereby imply that while they have given "brothers and sisters" as an acceptable *paraphrase*, the Greek *literally* has "brothers." This is misleading, since ἀδελφοί, depending on the context, may equally refer to all males, "brothers," or to "brothers and sisters" or "siblings." Odder still is the rendering of the ESV. In the body of the text it renders ἀδελφοί as "brothers" (never "brothers and sisters"). Then at the first use of the term in each letter, one encounters a footnote, as for 1 Thess 1:4: "Or *brothers and sisters*. The plural Greek word *adelphoi* (translated 'brothers') refers to siblings in a family. In New Testament usage, depending on the context, *adelphoi* may refer either to men or to both men and women who are siblings (brothers and sisters) in God's family, the church." In other words, the ESV editors have conceded that rendering ἀδελφοί as "brothers *and sisters*" in this context would be the more accurate and literal rendering. In fact, even the traditionalist Colorado Springs Guidelines would not take issue with our "brothers and sisters," since it states that "the plural *adelphoi* can be translated 'brothers and sisters' where the context makes clear that the author is referring to both men and women." See "Colorado Springs Guidelines": www.bible-researcher.com/csguidelines.html.

29. See Jer 22:18; Jdt 7:30; *2 Bar.* 78:4 (ed. Charlesworth) — "Are we not all, the twelve tribes, bound by one captivity as we also descent from one father?"; Acts 2:37; 23:1, 6. "Sister" might also serve as a term of endearment (Song 4:10, etc.; Tob 8:4).

30. See the useful discussion by W. Günther, "Brother, Neighbor, Friend," *NIDNTT*, 1:254 – 60. Ernest Best, *A Commentary on the First and Second Epistles to the Thessalonians* (repr.; Peabody, MA: Hendrickson, 2003), 71, claims that Jews and Greeks used "brother" of their fellows; there is some evidence for this Jewish use of the plural, but none for its use in Hellenism.

particularly of love for his redeemed people (see also 2 Thess 2:13, 16; Col 3:12). Divine love is a natural counterpart to divine "election" (ἐκλογήν), which refers to a past event (Eph 1:4, Col 3:12). "Your" (ὑμῶν) technically could denote either the subject or the object of that action. As a subjective genitive, it would mean "your choice of something." But clearly in this context it is an objective genitive, implying that "someone chose you."[31] There is an implied "divine passive" here, the name of the deity being omitted, as was often the case in Jewish and Christian God-language.

The same sort of syntax is found in 2 Pet 1:10: "Therefore, my brothers and sisters, make every effort to confirm your calling and election," that is: *eagerly make sure that God really has called and elected you.* "Election" is also used of God's choice of his people in Rom 9:11; 11:5. A parallel in 2 Thess 2:13 employs the synonymous "choose" (αἱρέω). Paul combines the vocabulary of love and election in Rom 11:28–29: despite Israel's hardening toward the gospel, "as far as election [of the Israelites] is concerned, they are loved on account of the patriarchs, for God's gifts and his call are irrevocable." Thus, in this one short statement, the apostle applies two fundamental biblical attributes to the Thessalonian church: like Israel of old, they are beloved and they are chosen. (See "Theology in Application" under 2 Thess 2:13–17 for Paul's doctrine of election). Later in 1 Thess 2:16, it is the synagogue, not the church, that hinders the gospel's spread to the nations and thus faces God's wrath.

1:5a-e Because the gospel that we brought came to you not simply as words [that we spoke], but also with miracles and in [the operation of] the Holy Spirit, and in the great sense of certainty [we had in the gospel] (ὅτι τὸ εὐαγγέλιον ἡμῶν οὐκ ἐγενήθη εἰς ὑμᾶς ἐν λόγῳ μόνον ἀλλὰ καὶ ἐν δυνάμει καὶ ἐν πνεύματι ἁγίῳ καὶ [ἐν] πληροφορίᾳ πολλῇ). Paul now points to the visible evidences of their conversion. He begins by describing the apostles' ministry. The word we have translated "because" (ὅτι) may be taken in a variety of ways (the reader should consult BDAG). (1) Indirect discourse that would be based on the participle "knowing" (εἰδότες) in 1:4. In that case it would be translated: "we acknowledge that you were chosen ... that the gospel came to you." (2) An explanatory clause: "we acknowledge that you were chosen ... in that the gospel came to you." (3) A causal clause: "we acknowledge ... because, or on the basis that, the gospel came to you." In response to these options, it can be observed that (2) would be awkward theologically, since it would equate election with the manner in which the gospel went forth. The first option works better syntactically and theologically, but it would indicate that Paul and the others are using the language of v. 5 in prayer, as if they were informing God how the gospel entered Thessalonica. The most pleasing option is (3); the apostolic team has good cause for acknowledging God's election of the Thessalonians, in that God worked through them in an effective way. In choosing (3) we side with the majority of English versions.[32] "Paul here shows none of the contemporary Western church's anxiety about appealing to experience as part of the overall reality of coming to Christian faith."[33]

"Come to you" is the best rendering of the Greek expression (γίνομαι εἰς) that is capable of other interpretations. Despite the lack of a definite article before "in the Holy Spirit" (ἐν πνεύματι ἁγίῳ), it is

31. Wallace, *Grammar*, 116–19. See George Eldon Ladd, *A Theology of the New Testament* (rev. ed; Grand Rapids: Eerdmans, 1993), 589. For a detailed discussion of election, refer to Witherington, *1 and 2 Thessalonians*, 65–70.

32. See ESV, NASB, NIV, NJB, NKJV, NRSV. So too Wanamaker, *Thessalonians*, 78.

33. Fee, *Thessalonians*, 29.

clear from the context that the Holy Spirit is the referent.[34]

It is typical of Paul to contrast a positive declaration with its negative (see also 1 Thess 2:4, 13).[35] Here he prefaces the triad "miracles ... Holy Spirit ... certainty" with "*not* simply as words that we spoke" (οὐκ ... ἐν λόγῳ μόνον); in 1:6 and 7 as in 2:12 Paul shows that the ministry of course was "of the word." A parallel may be found in Rom 10:17, that faith comes by hearing (ἀκοή, as in 1 Thess 2:13), and hearing comes by a word (ῥῆμα) about Christ. For someone whose ministry was fundamentally verbal — speaking, writing, and even, as here, praying — Paul was dismissive of any undertaking fueled by grandiloquence or mere talk. His aversion is most clear in 1 Cor 4:20, where the apostle cuts the support from under the pseudo-intellectuals of the Corinthian church. No, the kingdom of God is not a matter of mere "word" but of "power." This contrast is foreshadowed in 1 Thess 1:5, which is made less harsh by the addition of "not simply" (or "not only") and "but also." Verbal communication is fine, says Paul, but only insofar as it is empowered by the Spirit.

"Power" or, as we have it, "miracles" (δύναμις), could point in two directions: Paul may be speaking of an *efficacious message* — that is, the gospel message that powerfully changed lives. Or he may be speaking of *powerful miraculous deeds* that confirmed the message.[36] Both are semantically and theologically workable. In the first case, the changed lives of the Thessalonians are a most effective proof that the Spirit has worked in them — no one saw the Spirit, but the effects of his presence are obvious (see John 3:8; Rom 1:16). Nevertheless, the evidence for the second interpretation is stronger. The early church often linked the authentic proclamation of the gospel with impressive miracles. According to Mark 16:20, "Then the disciples went out and preached everywhere, and the Lord worked with them and confirmed his word by the signs that accompanied it." Hebrews 2:4 is similar: "God also testified to it by signs, wonders and various miracles, and by gifts of the Holy Spirit distributed according to his will."[37]

Paul uses the same language elsewhere in less ambiguous ways. His northeastern Mediterranean work was characterized "by the power of signs and wonders, through the power of the Spirit of God" (Rom 15:19; also Gal 3:5). Our verse differs from Rom 15:19 mainly in that here Paul adds "and" before Spirit, thus creating a characteristic triad — in miracles and in the Spirit and in certainty.[38] The new disciples in Thessalonica have cast their lot with the living and true God (1:9), a God who does miracles (1:9), unlike their old dead, impotent idols.

The Christian today takes as assured that the Holy Spirit is at work within the church. But how revolutionary that paradigm was in AD 50, when Paul declared that his ministry was done through the power of the Spirit. With few exceptions, the Jews did not regard themselves as people of the Spirit. Two decades earlier, the young rabbi Saul

34. See the discussion in James Moulton, *A Grammar of New Testament Greek*, Vol. III: *Syntax*, by Nigel Turner (Edinburgh: T&T Clark, 1963), 175 – 76.

35. Rigaux, *Thessaloniciens*, 374.

36. Ambrosiaster, *Commentaries on Galatians-Philemon* (trans. and ed. by Gerald L. Bray; Ancient Christian Texts; Downers Grove, IL: InterVarsity Press, 2009), 101 – 2, suggests miracles of healing.

37. One interpretation of Heb 2:3 – 4 is that *only* "those who heard" (the apostles) performed miracles. This is a textbook example of fallacious logic: that if the Bible attributes X to a particular Group A, then the attribute X is true *only* of Group A. In Heb 2:4, the miraculous signs would be limited to the apostles only if the author so indicated, for example, if the verse included the word "only." Neither the continuation or cessation of miracles may be inferred from Heb 2:3 – 4.

38. See Green, *Thessalonians*, 96. A good overview may be found in G. H. Twelftree, "Signs, Wonders, Miracles,"*DPL*, 875 – 77.

engaged in religious work that was in the main verbal: teaching, dialogue, argument and counterargument, citation of tradition. It is only as an apostle of the new covenant that he finds himself empowered by the Spirit of whom the ancients prophesied (see, e.g., Ezek 36:22 – 32; Joel 2:28 – 29). There is some indication that the first-century Essenes thought that some of their members were prophets, yet their perspective cannot compare with Christian theology (see comments on 1 Thess 5:19 – 20). "The sect of the Nazarenes was evidently marked out within first-century Judaism by its claim to have been given the Spirit of God in a new and exceptional way."[39]And to stretch the point further, we now hear of the Spirit working in this mainly Gentile congregation in Macedonia. Its members are numbered with God's chosen ones, and they experience the work of the Spirit, the signs and the prophetic gifting foreseen by Joel and Ezekiel.

Besides the Spirit and power, Paul perceives a third expression of God's working, in what we have translated a "great sense of certainty" (πληροφορίᾳ πολλῇ).[40] Most lexical reference works understand the phrase as we have, as one's *deep confidence* that the gospel message is true. A minority opinion suggests that it is not a subjective feeling but rather "every kind of richness."[41] Spicq argues that "if St. Paul had meant [complete assurance], he would have written *en pasē parrēsia* (Phil 1:20; cf. 2 Cor 3:12; 7:4; 1 Tim 3:13; *meta pasēs parrēsias*, Acts 28:31); and at any rate it would be odd for the apostle to emphasize his personal conviction."

Spicq's argument is unsustainable: (1) it rests on his supposition of how an author *should* have expressed himself, always a tricky business; (2) he insists that "confidence" (παρρησία) was *the* Pauline expression for confidence (it is not, see πείθω and πεποίθησις); (3) πληροφορία as "fullness" supposedly is the meaning that best fits in the other NT usages (it does not, as we will see); (4) how rare could it really have been for Paul to mention his personal conviction, if seven verses later he marvels at the fact that "we found courage in our God" to speak to the Thessalonians (2:2)?

The more common interpretation of the phrase is that it refers to one's inner confidence (so in Col 2:2; Heb 6:11; 10:22). This is not some mere human disposition; Paul regards it as proof of God's involvement in the Thessalonian campaign, ranking it along with miracles and the Spirit as a manifestation of the supernatural.

Paul does not specify who experienced this inner certainty. Is it the Thessalonian readers,[42] or is it the team of confident preachers?[43] In favor of the former, Paul is clearly impressed by the change that has taken place in their lives. His message has turned out to not be mere words, but the channel of the Spirit's work in them — hence the NLT's interpretation, "the Holy Spirit gave you full assurance that what we said was true." This is the sense

39. James D. G. Dunn, *The Theology of Paul the Apostle* (Grand Rapids: Eerdmans, 1998), 417; see 416 – 19.

40. According to MM, 519 – 20 the word "full confidence" (πληροφορία) "does not occur in classical writers or the LXX"; the major reference tools and commentaries are in agreement. Nevertheless, a fresh TLG search confirms that it *did* exist in classical Greek. There is a single extant pre-Christian reference, in the sixth century BC. See in Aesop, *Fab.* 69.3 the phrase "a confident work" (πληροφορίας ἔργον).

41. See Ceslas Spicq, "πληροφορέω, πληροφορία," *TLNT*, 3:120; Green, *Thessalonians*, 96; especially Rigaux, *Thessaloniciens*, 377 – 79.

42. So NLT. See Bruce, *1 & 2 Thessalonians*, 14.

43. See Best, *Thessalonians*, 76; Malherbe, *Letters to the Thessalonians*, 112; Morris, *Thessalonians* (NICNT), 47; Wanamaker, *Thessalonians*, 79. Fee thinks it refers to both groups (Fee, *Thessalonians*, 35); idem, *God's Empowering Presence: The Holy Spirit in the Letters of Paul* (Peabody, MA: Hendrickson, 1994), 45. This sort of "both … and" interpretation is often unsatisfying, especially — as in this case — when it is possible to narrow it down to a single option. The majority of versions leaves it vague: KJV, NIV, NASB, CEV, HCSB.

we find in Col 2:2, where Paul struggles for the Colossians and is present in the Spirit (in prayer?) so that all Christians might have "complete confidence" (NLT; see also Heb 6:11; 10:22).

Nevertheless, there is strong evidence in other passages that it was the apostles who acted with "complete assurance" in God and in his gospel message. In Acts, one of the supernatural signs of the Spirit's work is that the apostles have confidence to speak out in the face of tribulation (see the use of "courage" [παρρησία] in Acts 4:13, 29, 31; also the use of "speak fearlessly" [παρρησιάζομαι]). Since the first two parts of the triad refer to manner in which the message was brought, it is more likely that the third part of the triad would follow suit, thus favoring the thought that "great sense of certaintiy" would refer to the heralds of the gospel. It is later, in 1:6, that Paul moves on to show how the Thessalonians responded, with "in your turn" apparently indicating a change of focus. Thus the context guides us to follow the lead of the GNB, which renders 1:5 as "we brought the Good News to you ... with complete conviction of its truth."

There are other texts that back up this interpretation and amplify it. First, Paul seems to be glancing at Matthean tradition (see Introduction): "When they arrest you, do not worry about what to say or how to say it. At that time you will be given what to say, for it will not be you speaking, but the Spirit of your Father speaking through you" (Matt 10:19–20).

Second, some decades later, it appears that Clement of Rome has this passage in mind: "Having therefore received their orders and being fully assured [from the cognate verb πληροφορέω] by the resurrection of our Lord Jesus Christ and full of faith in the Word of God, they went forth with the firm assurance [πληροφορία] that the Holy Spirit gives, preaching the good news that the kingdom of God was about to come" (*1 Clem.* 42.3). Here is evidence that the earliest of Paul's readers attributed this "confidence" not to the Thessalonians but to the apostles.

Finally, there is a parallel in 1 Corinthians, which also describes the arrival of Paul in a new city. First Corinthians 2:3 could be read to mean that Paul's courage in Macedonia had turned into "weakness with great fear and trembling." Nevertheless, I do not find the contrast between 1 Cor 2 and 1 Thess 1–2 to be stark. First Corinthians goes on to parallel Paul's point in our letter, that the Holy Spirit was the invisible actor in that drama: "What I spoke and proclaimed was not meant to convince by philosophical argument, but to demonstrate the convincing power of the Spirit, so that your faith should depend not on [the mere verbiage of] human wisdom but on the power of God" (1 Cor 2:4–5 NJB).

1:5f And you know how we were among you for your sake (καθὼς οἴδατε οἷοι ἐγενήθημεν [ἐν] ὑμῖν δι' ὑμᾶς). Paul concludes for now his description of the apostles' work; he will pick up and develop the theme in detail in 2:1–12. This verse contains the first use of "reminder language," by which Paul states a truth and then tells the Thessalonians that they already know that truth. First Thessalonians is saturated with "reminder language"; 2 Thessalonians features it to a lesser extent.[44] He typically uses "know" (οἶδα), "remember" (μνημονεύω), or "witness" (μαρτύρομαι).

Paul does not introduce reminder language a propos of nothing, as if to casually remark that the Thessalonians have heard or seen certain things before now. Nor in 1–2 Thessalonians is it a way to offer rebuke ("you should know better!"), as it is in

44. Reminder language is found in 1 Thess 1:5, 2:1, 2:2, 2:5, 2:9, 2:10, 2:11, 3:3, 3:4, 5:1, 5:2; 2 Thess 2:5, 2:6, 3:7.

another context (1 Cor 6:2 – 3). Rather, he is evoking the shared experience of his audience. The fact that he uses reminder language six times in 1 Thess 2:1 – 12 indicates that he is striving to link what he now says with what they already know, thus cementing in their minds that these declarations have a sturdy base in their previous experience.

The verb he now uses is one of the most common in the New Testament, "to be, become, etc." (γίνομαι). It sometimes is used to denote behavior (see "how we lived" in the NIV). But in 1:5 his theme is the supernatural characteristics of their ministry in that city — not ministerial ethics, but ministerial modus operandi.

1:6a-d In your turn, you became imitators of the pattern given by us and by the Lord [Jesus] (καὶ ὑμεῖς μιμηταὶ ἡμῶν ἐγενήθητε καὶ τοῦ κυρίου). The Thessalonians were converted to the evangel and also to being evangelists (see below, "In Depth: Were the Thessalonian Believers Evangelistic?"). The apostles "were" a certain way among them, whereas the Thessalonians "came to be" imitators. It is useful to add "in your turn" to account for the emphatic "and you too" (καὶ ὑμεῖς) and to play up the repetition of the verb "to be, become" (γίνομαι). "By ([lit.] 'of') us and by the Lord" (ἡμῶν ... καὶ τοῦ κυρίου) are objective genitives attached to "imitators."[45] Later in the verse Paul shows how the Thessalonians imitated the behavior of the apostolic team. They also followed the pattern of the Judean church (2:14). In the second letter Paul tells them to pattern themselves after the apostles' work ethic (2 Thess 3:6 – 13). See "Theology in Application" for more discussion concerning "imitation."

S. E. Fowl examines this imitation language and claims that "as the letter unfolds, it seems [to the reader] that the Thessalonians are less steadfast than they once were.... Paul hopes to confirm the Thessalonians' faith."[46] His analysis shares the weakness of a certain erroneous hermeneutic, that *any positive exhortation in a letter exists in order to correct an existing negative situation in the church.* That is, if an apostle says "Love one another," it must follow that the recipients were not doing so. In the case of this letter, that sort of approach is particularly unconvincing; it does not do justice to Paul's consistently positive tone.

1:6e-f You received the message in highly distressing circumstances (δεξάμενοι τὸν λόγον ἐν θλίψει πολλῇ). Paul, like all followers of Jesus' teaching, knows that the Christian gospel is inherently coupled with persecution; in Paul's letters this link is nowhere more apparent than in 1 – 2 Thessalonians. "Receive the message [word]" (δεξάμενοι τὸν λόγον) is a common term for receiving the gospel[47] (see also 2:13). "Received" (δεξάμενοι) is adverbial to the principal verb "you became" (ἐγενήθητε). The syntax of this participle is hard to pin down. Some options are: You became imitators of us and of Jesus

- *by* receiving the message in highly distressing circumstances (participle of means or cause)
- *with the result that* you received the message (participle of result)
- *when* or *after* you received the message (temporal participle)
- *and* you received the message (attendant circumstance participle)

45. John Calvin, *Commentaries on the Epistles of Paul the Apostle to the Philippians, Colossians, and Thessalonians* (trans. and ed. by John Pringle; repr. Grand Rapids: Eerdmans, 1948), 243, makes two minor errors in his comments on the verse: he reads "Lord" as "God," not Jesus, by citing a parallel with Exod 14:13 (*sic*, should be 14:31).

46. S. E. Fowl, "Imitation of Paul/Christ," *DPL*, 429.

47. See "receive the word" in Luke 8:13; also Acts 8:14; 11:1; 17:11. See G. P. Benson, "Note on 1 Thessalonians 1:6," *ExpTim* 107/5 (1996): 143 – 44.

Some NT students assume that the use of an aorist participle implies that "receiving" came first and "became imitators" second. Although this can happen, the tendency is toward contemporaneous action, as Wallace notes: "When the aorist participle is related to an *aorist* main verb, the participle will often be contemporaneous (or simultaneous) to the action of the main verb."[48]

Each of the four options is to some degree suitable; the difficulty lies in how the "in highly distressing circumstances" fits with the previous action. Did the Thessalonians receive the word in tribulation, thus imitating the pattern of Jesus and the Pauline team? It is unlikely, since Jesus did not "receive" the gospel. Option 2 avoids that problem, as does 3. Perhaps the key lies in making the participle "receiving" less strongly connected with the main verb than it would be in Option 1. Option 4 ("and you received the message") is best; it maintains the two actions in a loose relationship. Thus, we might paraphrase: "At the moment when you received the gospel, and in much affliction, you started out on a path of discipleship that entails imitating Jesus and his apostles."[49]

The expression "highly distressing circumstances" could refer to eschatological tribulation (Matt 24:21, which is itself based on Dan 12:1 LXX); or, as in 1:6, to trials and tribulations in general (all other Pauline references to θλίψις and θλίβω, including 1 Thess 3:3–4 and 2 Thess 1:4). The second option is correct, since Paul knows that the day of the Lord is *not* at hand, and Christians should not fear that they are in the eschatological period (2 Thess 2:3). His teaching on the trials of this age is neatly summed up in Acts 14:22: "we must go through many hardships to enter the kingdom of God." What makes the Thessalonian case notable is that they were in the middle of extreme tribulation (see Introduction) when they had hardly taken their first breaths as Christian disciples.[50]

1:6g [Yet] with the joy that comes from the Holy Spirit (μετὰ χαρᾶς πνεύματος ἁγίου). The Thessalonians' joy, like the apostles' confidence in the gospel (1:5), is a manifestation of the supernatural. Its astounding presence proves that God is at work in them. "From the Spirit" (πνεύματος) is best taken as a genitive of source.[51] There is a parallel in Rom 14:17, with its joy "in the Holy Spirit" (ἐν πνεύματι ἁγίῳ), and of course in the list of the Spirit's fruit in Gal 5:22. Paul's theology in our letter is similar to that found in Gal 5. *How do we know that the Thessalonians are the elect and the beloved of God? Because they have received the Spirit. But, how do we know that they have the Spirit? Through behavioral evidence* — in this case, the disciples are filled with joy despite their circumstances.

There is an important pastoral principle here. How does Paul (or any pastor) know that they aren't just experiencing the initial high spirits that are present in fresh converts to any movement? For even the Lord warned that "the seed falling on rocky ground refers to someone who hears the word and at once *receives it with joy* [μετὰ χαρᾶς]. But since they have no root, they last only a short time. When *trouble* [θλίψις] *or persecution* comes because of the word, they quickly fall away" (Matt 13:20–21; is this another case of Paul interacting with the Matthean tradition?). Apart from their "fruit" (behavior), there exists no method for divining that

48. Wallace, *Grammar*, 624. Also BDF §339.

49. So the NIV, which avoids the problem by moving one clause around: "You became imitators of us and of the Lord, for you welcomed the message in midst of severe suffering with the joy given by the Holy Spirit."

50. For a study of the vocabulary of "tribulation," see R. Schippers, "θλίψις," *NIDNTT*, 2:807–9.

51. Vaticanus and some manuscripts of the Vulgate add "and" (καί) before "Spirit" (πνεύματος), making it "with joy *and from* the Holy Spirit." With NA[27] we reject this highly unlikely reading, given its weak support in the manuscripts and the awkward genitive of "and from the Holy Spirit."

they are true believers; perhaps sufficient time has passed, and they are still rejoicing after an initial stretch of tribulation. In any case, time would bear out Paul's assurance. The Macedonian churches still enjoyed a reputation for joy in tribulation some seven years later, providing Paul with a fulcrum for his appeal in 2 Cor 8:2: "In the midst of a very severe trial, their overflowing joy and their extreme poverty welled up in rich generosity."

1:7 As a result you [in your turn] became the pattern for all the believers in Macedonia and in Achaia (ὥστε γενέσθαι ὑμᾶς τύπον πᾶσιν τοῖς πιστεύουσιν ἐν τῇ Μακεδονίᾳ καὶ ἐν τῇ Ἀχαΐᾳ). The Thessalonians have not only imitated the apostles and Jesus; they have themselves become a pattern for others Christians.[52] We add "in your turn" again to play up the repetition of "became." Paul and his team served as patterns (1:6; 2 Thess 3:7) and expected that Christian leaders would do the same (Phil 3:17; 1 Tim 4:12; Titus 2:7). Peter likewise employed this technical use of "example" (τύπος; see 1 Pet 5:3). Yet in this letter, Paul observes that not only the leaders of the Thessalonian church function as models; the believers in general have become patterns for others.

In the phrase "for all the believers" (πᾶσιν τοῖς πιστεύουσιν), the dative shows how the Thessalonians gave some advantage to others.[53] There are two directions we could assign the participle: (1) for *all who were already believers* when they heard of the Thessalonians, these believers benefitting from sound direction on how to live; (2) all who *were coming to believe* as a result of hearing about the lifestyle that these Christians exhibited. The Greek is not specific, and so we leave it vague as well.

A geographical note is in order. The Thessalonians, in the far north, had already affected people as far south as Achaia, some weeks journey away whether by land or sea. Yet, Paul had probably not been apart from the Thessalonians for more than several months. Had their reputation reached Athens and Corinth before Paul dictated 1 Thessalonians? This is almost certainly what has happened, given that Paul speaks of third parties in 1 Thess 1:9; unnamed people appear on stage to say what they know about the events in Thessalonica. This is amazingly rapid, but not implausible; Thessalonica and Corinth were ports, and other cities with churches were strung along major land routes.

1:8a-d For you see, from you the word of the Lord has sounded forth, not only in Macedonia and in Achaia, but everywhere, news of your faith in God has gone out (ἀφ' ὑμῶν γὰρ ἐξήχηται ὁ λόγος τοῦ κυρίου οὐ μόνον ἐν τῇ Μακεδονίᾳ καὶ [ἐν τῇ] Ἀχαΐᾳ, ἀλλ' ἐν παντὶ τόπῳ ἡ πίστις ὑμῶν ἡ πρὸς τὸν θεὸν ἐξελήλυθεν). We now detect that the Thessalonians are engaged in evangelism. We supply "you see," since Paul is giving proof for his claim he has made in 1:7, and since "for" (γάρ) is a marker of clarification.[54] "The word of the Lord" in this context is as a traditional label for the gospel message (see also 2 Thess 3:1). "Lord" (κύριος) is a reference to the Lord Jesus Christ, as it usually is in 1 – 2 Thessalonians. The genitive "of the Lord" may refer to the message *about* Jesus or the message that comes *from* him; the context indicates that it is a message about Jesus to which Paul refers.

"Sounded forth" (ἐξήχηται) is the perfect tense of a verb (ἐξηχέω) that is found in the NT only here. The verb conveys a sense of a loud, clear sound.

52. A number of weighty manuscripts supports a plural reading, "you became *examples*"; we follow manuscripts B, D and others and the NA[27] in following the singular. Whether Paul wrote "example" or "examples" makes little difference in the context, since the singular would be collective. Ignatius in the same way uses the singular to speak of all the disciples in Magnesia in Ign. *Magn*. 6.2.

53. Wallace, *Grammar*, 142 – 44.

54. See BDAG, γάρ 2.

Now, it is common to hear in sermons that the verb "literally" means the sound of a thunderclap (its reference in Sir 40:13) or that it "literally" means that the Thessalonians "gossiped" the gospel (it refers to the spread of a rumor in 3 Macc 3:2). This is the fallacy of importing into one context all the significance that a word can take elsewhere. Here it simply means to "sound forth."

The phrase "faith toward God" (ἡ πίστις ὑμῶν ἡ πρὸς τὸν θεὸν) is a figure of speech in which the part is used for the whole (a synecdoche): Paul uses the part ("your faith") to represent the whole (the preaching of the gospel by the Pauline team and its reception by the Thessalonians). This verse contains a chiastic structure:

A The word of the Lord has sounded forth
  B not only in Macedonia and in Achaia
  B′ but everywhere
A′ news of your faith in God has gone out.

The apostle expands on the specific geographical reference of 1:7: not only in the two provinces of Macedonia and Achaia, but "everywhere." Hyperbole is typical of 1 and 2 Thessalonians, including geographical exaggeration (2 Thess 3:1; see Rom 16:19: "everyone has heard about your obedience"). Still, it is not outlandish to imagine that there were reports from beyond Macedonia and Achaia; perhaps they were already coming in from Asia Minor or Rome (as reported by Priscilla and Aquila? Acts 18:2) by the time of 1 Thessalonians.

There is some indication that Paul wrote 1 Thess 1:7 – 8 under the literary influence of Isa 66 LXX. The Septuagint differs significantly from the Hebrew (as shown here in the NETS translation of Isa 66:18b – 19f):

I am coming to gather all the nations and tongues,
And they shall come and shall see my glory.
And I will leave signs upon them ["upon *the nations*," apparently],
and from them I will send forth those who are saved to the nations,
to Tharsis and Phoud and Loud and Mosoch and Thobel[55]
and to Greece[56] (Ἑλλάς); and to the islands far away —
those who have not heard my name or seen my glory,
and they shall declare my glory among the [Gentile] nations.

First, the saved remnant — which in Isa 66 is the remnant of Israel — will "go forth"[57] to Gentile nations. Paul alludes to the same chapter of Isaiah (Isa 66:15 – 16) in 2 Thess 1:7 – 8, leaving the impression that the passage was one to which he had frequent recourse.[58] Thus, by coming to Christ, the Thessalonian Greeks have fulfilled prophecy: Javan (Greece) was turning to God. What is more, depending on one's reading of the last phrase, they go on to declare God's glory among the nations. See "In Depth: Were the Thessalonian Believers Evangelistic?"

55. To use their better-known names: Tarshish (Gibraltar? Spain?); Put (N. Africa?); Loud (Lud; N. Africa? W. Asia Minor?); Mosoch (Meshech; E. Asia Minor?; Meshech is not found in the Hebrew text); Tubal (E. Asia Minor?). Little evidence exists for the notion that the latter two have something to do with Moscow and Tobolsk.

56. The Hebrew text's "Javan" becomes Ἑλλάς. The latter could mean Macedonia, both Macedonia and Achaia, or just the Roman province of Achaia; see LSJ.

57. The Hebrew text uses *šlḥ*; the LXX uses ἐξαποστέλλω; both of these are appropriate terms for the "sending forth" of apostles.

58. See Bruce, *1 & 2 Thessalonians*, 151.

IN DEPTH: Were the Thessalonian Believers Evangelistic?

As the Macedonian Christians knew, "the first task of the Church is to preach the Word."[59] Nevertheless, Christians have interpreted the Thessalonians' "mission" in two broad ways: Does Paul mean that "the gospel is going forth from you" through conscious evangelism on their part?[60] Or does he refer to a spreading awareness of their "personal testimony" that may in turn attract others to Christ?[61] Some use the terms "centrifugal" mission (believers go out to win others) and "centripetal" (people are drawn inward to the faith through the church's good testimony). There is evidence that the first interpretation is Paul's intent, that he expected the Thessalonians to take part in evangelism and that they were succeeding in that task.

The language that "from you the word of the Lord has sounded forth" implies conscious effort.[62] James Ware looks at other NT uses of "word of the Lord," "word," or "word of God" and argues that these phrases must refer to the active transmission of the gospel: the word of the Lord sounding out "cannot refer to mere reports of the Thessalonians' conversion."[63]

In other words, people in Macedonia and Achaia are hearing about the Thessalonians' conversion to the gospel (1:8–9a). Yet this is no confused rumor; they possess details; that is, they could coordinate what they know of the Thessalonians' testimony with a basic outline of the apostolic kerygma (1:9–10). This implies that somebody is purposefully communicating the theological meaning of the Thessalonian experience.

The Thessalonians are to have love for non-Christians (3:12), in imitation of

59. Ethelbert Stauffer, *New Testament Theology* (trans. John Marsh; New York: Macmillan, 1955), 157.

60. So Green, *Thessalonians*, 101–2; Bruce, *1 & 2 Thessalonians*, 16; Malherbe, *Letters to the Thessalonians*, 117–18, 124, 130–31; G. K. Beale, *1–2 Thessalonians* (IVPNTC; Downers Grove, IL: InterVarsity Press, 2003), 59–60; Michael W. Holmes, *1 & 2 Thessalonians* (NIVAC; Grand Rapids: Zondervan, 1998), 54; Marshall, *1 and 2 Thessalonians*, 56; Robert L. Plummer, *Paul's Understanding of the Church's Mission: Did the Apostle Paul Expect the Early Christian Communities to Evangelize?* (Paternoster Biblical Monographs; Eugene, OR: Wipf & Stock, 2006), 135–38.

61. Fee, *Thessalonians*, 43–45; Wanamaker, *Thessalonians*, 83; John P. Dickson, *Mission-Commitment in Ancient Judaism and in the Pauline Communities* (WUNT 2/159; Tübingen: Mohr Siebeck, 2003), 94–103. Victor Copan argues that Paul taught his disciples to live a life that reflected the gospel, but not to be evangelists themselves. See Victor A. Copan, *Saint Paul as Spiritual Director: An Analysis of the Concept of the Imitation of Paul with Implications and Applications to the Practice of Spiritual Direction* (Paternoster Biblical Monographs; Eugene, OR: Wipf & Stock, 2008), 223–26. See the fine overview of interpretations in Plummer, *Paul's Understanding of the Church's Mission*, 1–42.

62. Fee, *Thessalonians*, 43, argues that this forces the grammar of the sentence to say something it does not, but he does not take into account parallels such as the missionary text Luke 24:47.

63. James Ware, "The Thessalonians as a Missionary Congregation," *ZNW* 83 (1992): 127 n. 8. The data do not support all of Ware's conclusions (see esp. 1 Thess 4:15). Yet he is correct that in Acts and the NT letters, "word of the Lord" is *generally* a reference to someone actively proclaiming the gospel (Acts 8:25; 13:44, 48, 49; 15:35, 36; 16:32; 19:10, 20; 2 Thess 3:1).

the apostles' love for their converts. In that case, they should have the same concern for their Gentile neighbors that Paul and his team showed for them. It is possible that "love for others" is love for outsiders that results in evangelism.

Because of the Thessalonians' love, they are (for the most part) willing to support themselves by hard labor (1:3). Paul uses language that parallels how the apostles themselves operated in the same manner (2:9).[64] We will see in 2 Thess 3:6 – 16 that Paul may have been speaking about Thessalonian evangelists in 1 Thess 1:3. Moreover, there are other Pauline texts that indicate he planted *evangelistic* churches.[65]

It is the heart of Christian discipleship that the beginner imitate the teacher. In the case of Thessalonica, they imitate Jesus and the Pauline team and thus provide a model for other Christians. Nevertheless, it is not simply the Christian ethic that the Thessalonians determined to follow. They also imitated *that which evangelistic Christians like Paul, Silas, and Timothy were doing.*[66]

Conclusion: The Thessalonians have come full circle and have become "evangelized evangelists." This was likely the team's desire in all their churches. For the most part the apostle did not need to push his churches to do evangelism: "Paul was confident that his congregations would continue his missionary activity, as the power of God at work in his preaching of the gospel continued to be active in those who had believed the message."[67] So, why does Paul bring up the point in 1 Thessalonians? First, he seems pleased that a church that labored under heavy persecution was active in the faith. They couldn't even get a message out to Paul, who was desperate to get some news; yet they somehow managed to circulate the gospel around Greece. Second, he mentions evangelism because their level of success had made it absolutely clear that the Spirit was at work. They imitated Paul in such a way that they too showed themselves approved by God (1 Thess 2:4) and carried his gospel with heavenly power.

1:8e So that we have no need to say anything [about you] (ὥστε μὴ χρείαν ἔχειν ἡμᾶς λαλεῖν τι). Paul uses more hyperbole, but justifiably. The evidence of the Thessalonians' conversion is so arresting that it stands on its own without fear of contradiction.

1:9a-b That's because they themselves are talking about us, about what kind of welcome we had from you (αὐτοὶ γὰρ περὶ ἡμῶν ἀπαγγέλλουσιν ὁποίαν εἴσοδον ἔσχομεν πρὸς ὑμᾶς). It was their "welcome," their initial contact with the Thessalonians that has struck people as noteworthy. They

64. Malherbe, *Letters to the Thessalonians*, 108 – 9.

65. In particular see Plummer, *Paul's Understanding of the Church's Mission*; P. T. O'Brien, *Gospel and Mission in the Writings of Paul: An Exegetical and Theological Analysis* (Grand Rapids: Baker, 1995).

66. Ware, "The Thessalonians as a Missionary Congregation," 127, traces the role of imitation in 1:6 – 8 and shows that they imitated the apostles by becoming evangelists.

67. Ibid., 131.

are talking "about us" (περὶ ἡμῶν), that is, the apostolic team.[68] Who is talking? First, the Macedonians (1:8): their neighbors in Philippi and Berea and others are recounting the marvelous thing that had happened in Thessalonica. The unusual severity of the tribulations in Thessalonica itself seems to have disrupted interchurch communication so badly that Paul could not rely on the regular network that he favored, personal reports (1 Cor 1:11) and official communiqués (1 Cor 7:1). Yes, talk trickled in from everywhere, though not from the church itself. When, Paul wondered, would Timothy come back to him with a first-hand report (3:1 – 2)?

The "welcome we had" (εἴσοδον ἔσχομεν) may be paraphrased as "we received a welcome."[69] Paul interprets the team's "welcome" in Thessalonica in the light of gospel tradition. He echoes the Markan tradition of Jesus' charge to the disciples, which is expanded in Matt 10:11 – 14:

> Whatever town or village you enter, search there for some worthy person and stay at their house until you leave. As you enter the home, give it your greeting. If the home is deserving, let your peace rest on it; if it is not, let your peace return to you. If anyone will not welcome you or listen to your words, leave that home or town and shake the dust off your feet.

Later on we will argue that Paul interprets his Macedonian experience in terms of Matt 10:17 – 18, where Jesus predicts that the synagogues will flog the disciples. But Paul and team had also encountered at least a few willing ears in the Macedonian towns. They received an open door from the new convert Lydia, a hostess who refused to take "no" for an answer (Acts 16:14 – 15); hospitality from Jason (17:7); and a receptive Jewish audience in Berea (17:11).

1:9c And how you turned away from idols to God (καὶ πῶς ἐπεστρέψατε πρὸς τὸν θεὸν ἀπὸ τῶν εἰδώλων). Paul gives an outline of the gospel message in 1:9b – 10. It has a rhythmic style, implying that it might be a formula. In other passages Paul will capture the readers' attention with "reminder language." Here he accomplishes the same end by repeating a teaching that they recognized and probably knew by heart. Acts 26:20 is similar to 1 Thess 1:9: "I preached that they should repent and turn to God."[70] Perhaps he has written 1:9 – 10 by turning imperative verb forms ("you, turn away from idols!") into infinitives, so that it fits syntactically with his point in this chapter.

Language such as "turn," "serve," and the "living and true God" is straight from the OT.[71] This religious use of "turned away" (ἐπιστρέφω) is well attested in the LXX to denote conversion to God or, negatively, apostasy from God. It appears only three times in the Pauline letters (here; 2 Cor 3:16; Gal 4:9), but is attributed to Paul twice more in Acts (14:15; 26:18); Jesus sends Paul to the Gentiles "to open their eyes and turn from darkness to light, and from the power of Satan to God, so that they

68. One would have expected that people were talking about "you," the Thessalonians. It is probably for that reason that a scribe — whose correction is represented by Vaticanus and some other manuscripts — smoothed this by changing ἡμῶν to ὑμῶν (talking about "you," plural). Another possible cause for the emendation is "itacism," one of the changes in the pronunciation of vowels through the centuries; the two pronouns "you" and "us" sounded like "hee-MOAN" and rhymed at the time that some early manuscripts were copies, leaving the door open for a scribe to misunderstand what he heard.

69. See the full study in John Gillman, "Paul's εἴσοδος: The Proclaimed and the Proclaimer (1Thes 2,8)," in *The Thessalonian Correspondence* (ed. Raymond F. Collins; BETL 87; Leuven: Leuven Univ. Press, 1990), 62 – 70.

70. See G. Bertram, "ἐπιστρέφω, ἐπιστροφή," *TDNT*, 7:727 – 28.

71. Jeffrey A. D. Weima, "1 and 2 Thessalonians," in *Commentary on the New Testament Use of the Old Testament* (ed. G. K. Beale and D. A. Carson; Grand Rapids: Baker, 2007), 872.

may receive forgiveness of sins and a place among those who are sanctified by faith in me" (26:18; see also James in Acts 15:19).

So striking is the resemblance of this language with the LXX that some have theorized that 1:9b – 10 was originally composed by Hellenistic Jewish proselytizers, not by Christians or by Paul. Supposedly they designed these lines in order to convince Gentiles of the folly of idolatry.[72] Bruce, for example, wonders how this statement could have been composed by a Christian when it doesn't even mention the death of Jesus; he points to the weight given Jesus' death in the kerygma in 1 Cor 15:3 – 8. He concludes that it began as a Jewish statement, and that the church later tacked on the reference to Jesus' resurrection and future coming in 1:10 in order to Christianize it.[73]

The better explanation is that this is a Christian evangelistic formula that happened to be an apt description of Gentile converts. Of its five lines, three (C, B′, A′) could make sense only as specifically Christian teaching:

A Turn away [or "you turned"] from idols to God,
  B to serve the God who is living and true
    C and to await his Son from heaven,
  B′ he whom God raised from the dead,
A′ Jesus our Savior from God's coming wrath.

The word here rendered as "idol" (εἴδωλον) appears as early as Homer, where it means "shadow, form."[74] No pagans would call their cult images "idols," since it would imply that the god was a fake. Here it has its pejorative meaning as used by the Jews and later the Christians: "Many even from Israel gladly adopted [Antiochus's] religion; they sacrificed to *idols* and profaned the sabbath" (1 Macc 1:43, emphasis added).[75] Paul saw idols everywhere he turned; it had not been long since he had passed through Athens, and "he was greatly distressed to see that the city was full of idols" (Acts 17:16).

It is not now possible to determine which Thessalonian idols Paul means — there were so many gods and goddesses in Thessalonica that to list them would have taken up the bulk of the letter![76] The important thing is that the Thessalonians had turned away from their cult images in order to serve Christ; in so doing, the Gentile converts were tacitly accepting that the statues were not tangible representations of a deity.

Paul was in Corinth as he wrote this letter. In a twist of irony, some of the believers in that city would later fail to grasp that an idol is "nothing." Those disciples were "weak" in the Christian faith (see 1 Cor 8:4 – 13).

1:9d To serve the God who is living and true (δουλεύειν θεῷ ζῶντι καὶ ἀληθινῷ). Turning away from idols does no good unless idolaters turn to serve the Creator. Paul uses a term that in this context speaks of religious service: "serve" (δουλεύω) underlies Paul's understanding of his own vocation, as seen in his frequent use of "servant" (δοῦλος). This verb is used of "serving" or "worshiping" a deity in pagan, Jewish, and Christian literature.

"Living God" was language typical of the synagogue.[77] By contrast, idols are dead and false, as Isaiah pointed out (Isa 40:18 – 24; 41:21 – 24; 44:9 – 20; 46:5 – 7), and Hellenistic Jews spoke in

72. For example, Wis 14:12, which begins: "For the idea of making idols was the beginning of fornication, and the invention of them was the corruption of life"; or Sir 30:19: "Of what use to an idol is a sacrifice? For it can neither eat nor smell."

73. Bruce, *1 & 2 Thessalonians*, 18.

74. In *Iliad* 5.541 it refers to the "shadows" that are the souls in the underworld.

75. εἴδωλον occurs 88 times in the LXX (see, e.g., 4 Kgdms 17:12); also in Philo and Josephus.

76. Vom Brocke, *Thessaloniki*, 116 – 17.

77. See Rigaux, *Thessaloniciens*, 391.

the same terms: "The Apostle, in ascribing to God the epithets *true and living*, indirectly censures idols as being dead and worthless inventions, and as being falsely called gods."[78] The later Christian apologists directed to their pagan audiences the same message:

> The majesty of the one God, which keeps together and rules all things, has come to be so forgotten, that the only befitting object of worship is, above all others, the one which is especially neglected; and that men have sunk to such blindness, that they prefer the dead to the true and living God, and those who are of the earth, and buried in the earth, to Him who was the Creator of the earth itself.[79]

1:10a And to await his Son from heaven (καὶ ἀναμένειν τὸν υἱὸν αὐτοῦ ἐκ τῶν οὐρανῶν). The gospel message is inherently eschatological: believers await the future intervention of God through his Son. The Christian hope is sometimes pictured in heavenly or spatial terms ("our citizenship is in heaven," Phil 3:20), sometimes in future-temporal terms ("we eagerly await a Savior," same verse).[80] First Thessalonians 1:10 is the earliest extant formulation of the Christian expectation of the parousia. It is not simply a future hope, but it also has a "heavenly" aspect, since the Son is now in heaven until his coming.[81] This dual temporal and vertical orientation in the earliest NT literature lends credence to the authenticity of the speech attributed to Peter in Acts 3:20 – 21a: "that [the Lord] may send the Messiah, who has been appointed for you — even Jesus. Heaven must receive him until the time comes for God to restore everything."

The rare verb "await" (ἀναμένω) is a *hapax* in the NT. In the LXX it refers to waiting for God's intervention (Jdt 8:17; cf. also Ign. *Phld.* 5.2). The Thessalonians have been converted not merely to monotheism, but to a christological-eschatological faith: they await God's Son. The creed in 1:10 is intrinsically Christian. Throughout this letter, Paul portrays the Thessalonians as people who live in expectation of Christ and orient their lives to that event.

1:10b He whom [God] raised from the dead (ὃν ἤγειρεν ἐκ [τῶν] νεκρῶν). The resurrection of Jesus lies at the heart of the gospel. The reference here foreshadows the eschatological hope in 4:13 – 18, where the believers' destiny is determined by Jesus' resurrection. "He whom" (ὃν) has as its antecedent "Son" (τὸν υἱόν). The stereotyped phrase "he raised Jesus from the dead" (ἤγειρεν τὸν Ἰησοῦν ἐκ νεκρῶν) is common in Paul's letters, especially Romans and 1 Corinthians. Christians by definition confess their faith in the resurrection of Jesus (Rom 10:9; 1 Cor 15:4).[82] Our verse also has other

78. Calvin, *Thessalonians*, 245.

79. Lactantius, *Inst.* 2.1 (*ANF* 7:40), early fourth century.

80. A. T. Lincoln has demonstrated that both perspectives are thoroughly Jewish and early Christian, and that the "vertical" language is not a later innovation of the Hellenistic church. See A. T. Lincoln, *Paradise Now and Not Yet: Studies in the Role of the Heavenly Dimension in Paul's Thought with Special Reference to his Eschatology* (SNTSMS 43; Cambridge: Cambridge Univ. Press, 1981).

81. Contra Christopher L. Mearns, "Early Eschatological Development in Paul: The Evidence of 1 and 2 Thessalonians," *NTS* 27 (1980 – 81): 137 – 57. Mearns proposes that prior to 1 Thessalonians, Paul had assumed that Jesus' parousia took place at his resurrection. He then argues that Paul's eschatological statements in these letters were freshly minted, in part in order to respond to the unexpected deaths of believers at Thessalonica. This is extraordinarily unsteady logic: our earliest evidence (1 – 2 Thessalonians) reveals a church with a strong eschatological orientation, and Paul is not springing it on believers here for the first time.

82. There is a theory that these verses outline an "eschatological gospel," a message more primitive and apocalyptic than the one later described in 1 Cor 15:3 – 5. The better explanation is that Paul is adapting the one gospel to the Thessalonians' special needs: suffering, rejection by the synagogue, the death of their companions. It is worth underscoring that Paul was teaching 1 Cor 15:3 – 5 to the Corinthians at the time he was writing 1 Thess 1:9 – 10; that is, at the same general time (AD

language that is typical of Paul: the Son rose not "from the state of death" but "from among (ἐκ) dead people" (see, e.g., the pivotal use of the phrase in 1 Cor 15 and Rom 6).

In 1:9d and 10a Paul lays emphasis on the power of the true God: "to serve the God who is living and true" (1:9d) has as its companion "he whom [God] raised from the dead." That is, the living God alone is able to give life. It is this very combination of ideas that the Athenians found so incredible (Acts 17:22 – 32): that God is the Creator, that he cannot be represented by idols, that he is the life-giver, that he raised Jesus from the dead, and that he has fixed a day of judgment. Paul preached in Athens the basic message that he had recently preached in Thessalonica. And because God truly exists and gives life, the Thessalonians have experienced his ability to changes their lives.

1:10c-d Jesus our Savior from [God's] coming wrath (Ἰησοῦν τὸν ῥυόμενον ἡμᾶς ἐκ τῆς ὀργῆς τῆς ἐρχομένης). Salvation is eschatological; that is, it may be framed in terms of Jesus' future coming to damn the unbeliever or to rescue the believer (see esp. 2 Thess 1:5 – 10). Paul speaks of "Jesus"; the Savior is the same Jesus who walked on the earth in Judea (1 Thess 2:14 – 15), died, and was raised. Paul refuses to distinguish Jesus from the Son of God or the Christ, as later errorists did (see 1 John 2:22). Jesus is entitled God's "Son" in 1:10; "our Lord Jesus" in 2:19 and 3:13; "Jesus," "Lord," and "Christ" in 4:13 – 17; "Lord" in 5:2; "our Lord Jesus Christ" in 5:9.

Because "rescues" or "saves" (ῥυόμενον) is an attributive participle, it might be rendered "Jesus who saves us," "who will save us," or even "who has saved us." "Jesus our Savior" is the best choice; as in the Greek, it leaves vague whether it denotes past, present, or future deliverance.[83] The verb may imply "to rescue from danger, with the implication that the danger in question is severe and acute."[84] Isaiah emphasized that no idol could "save" (Isa 44:17, 20); but the living God can, declares Isaiah (Isa 45:17), and Paul reaffirms that teaching.

The Thessalonian letters emphasize a pattern of earthly tribulation for the believers, future rescue for them, and divine destruction for their tormenters and for all the wicked. By entering into the faith, the Thessalonians have opened the door to persecution: "And in fact, you yourselves know that we were destined for this very thing, because even when we were with you, we told you that we would be put through such afflictions" (1 Thess 3:3b – 4b).

The disciples also know that they are part of God's saving work on the planet: Jesus is coming to spare them from the coming wrath. Verse 10 is closely parallel to 5:9: "Because God has not assigned us to feel his coming wrath [ὀργή], but rather to obtain salvation [σωτηρία] through our Lord Jesus Christ" (see also Heb 9:28). Paul will continue to develop the teaching on divine retribution (as seems the likely interpretation of 1 Thess

50), the creeds were proclaimed in two contexts (Thessalonica and Corinth). See the argument by I. H. Marshall, *New Testament Theology: Many Witnesses, One Gospel* (Downers Grove, IL: InterVarsity Press, 2004), 240; also D. M. Stanley, *Christ's Resurrection in Pauline Theology* (AnBib 13; Rome: Pontifical Biblical Institute, 1961), 82.

83. Contra Morris, *Thessalonians* (NICNT), 54, who says that "saves" (ῥυόμενον) is a "timeless present." The difficulty with his interpretation lies in the fact that a participle does not generally have temporal reference; that is to say, this present participle does not speak of present time per se. In the last few decades, grammarians have shown that only in the indicative mood does a verb refer to time. For this same reason, the "coming [ἐρχομένης] wrath" in 1:10 is known to be future in time only because of the future nature of "coming."

84. L&N, 21.23. "Save" (ῥύομαι) is used of the rescue of Lot from Sodom in 2 Pet 2:7, and in the Lord's Prayer, "deliver us from the evil one" (Matt 6:13). In a number of passages (e.g., Rom 15:31; 2 Thess 3:2; 2 Tim 3:11; 4:18) it refers to the deliverance of Paul from human persecution. Jesus is eschatologically ὁ ῥυόμενος in Rom 11:26, paraphrasing Isa 59:20.

2:16d; also 5:1 – 10; 2 Thess 1:5 – 9; 2:8; 2:12), reflecting on God's wrath in the two letters almost as much as his salvation.

Like his salvation, God's wrath too is future, it is "coming" (ἐρχομένης). Paul's language reflects the Hebrew *habbāʾ* ("to come," from *bôʾ*), which was a popular attribution of the eschatological time, as in the key Jewish phrase *hāʿôlām habbāʾ* ("the age to come"; Paul uses a Greek version of that phrase in Eph 1:21).

This commentary takes the view that the coming of Christ to "rapture" the church in 4:15 – 17 is synchronous with the coming of the Son of Man to gather the elect in Matt 24:30 – 31. There are others who argue that *if* the church will not face God's wrath (1 Thess 1:10, 5:9), and *if* by definition the tribulation is God's wrath, *then* it is necessary for the church to already be "off-planet" when the tribulation begins.[85] The logic is weak: in Matthew 24 and throughout Revelation, God's people are said to be on earth during the end-time tribulation but not as the recipients of God's wrath. When Paul corrects the Thessalonians' fear that they were in the final tribulation (2 Thess 2:1 – 12), he does not state, "Oh, but as you know, by definition, no Christian will face God's wrath, and therefore will not enter the tribulation." Rather, he argues that the great Apostasy and the Man of Lawlessness are not present.

Apart from "wrath" (ὀργή), there is a second biblical term for wrath or anger (θυμός). Why does Paul use one term and not the other, given that both were available to him? Older commentaries tended to concentrate on the various synonyms for wrath, love, life, and so forth. Some of the data they used are now outdated. It can now be shown, for example, whether a NT author invented a particular Greek term or whether two terms that had distinct meanings in the classical Greek came to be interchangeable in the *koinē* period.[86] In the case of "wrath" there is no fine shade of contrast between the two synonyms. Either may refer to human or divine anger in the LXX and NT, and their meanings broadly overlap.

Both Testaments show that the wrath of God should not be whittled down to mere "anthropomorphism." Most famously, C. H. Dodd took this reductionist approach in his commentary on Rom 1:18, calling God's wrath "a thoroughly archaic idea." Wrath denotes "some process or effect in the realm of objective facts," not "a certain feeling or attitude of God towards us."[87] That is, the divine working could only have been grasped by the primitive human mind by analogy to human anger: "God will deal with your sin as an angry man would." But in reality, said Dodd, God does not feel anger; rather, he is showing us that sin leads inevitably to one's doom.

Dodd's interpretation seems to have been shaped more by his philosophical assumptions than by a close reading of Scripture. For the exegete who wishes to know what God's wrath means in 1:10, there is no better instructor than the rest of the Thessalonians letters: it is something from which people must be "saved" (1 Thess 1:10; 5:9), it is "unexpected destruction" (5:3), "tribulation," "blazing fire," "retaliation," "eternal destruction," "separated from the presence of the Lord" (2 Thess 1:6 – 9), and "perishing" (2:10). The Bible describes God's wrath as a personal attitude, with all the se-

85. Note esp. that Paul D. Feinberg in Reiter, ed., *Three Views on the Rapture*, 50 – 71, places great stress on this idea.

86. See the article by H.-C. Hahn, "ὀργή," *NIDNTT*, 1:105 – 13.

87. C. H. Dodd, *The Epistle of Paul to the Romans* (MNTC; New York: Harper and Brothers, 1932), 21 – 24. Surprisingly, Fee, *Thessalonians*, 196 – 97, seems to agree with that hermeneutic. For an exposition of the theme and a refutation of Dodd, see G. L. Borchert, "Wrath, Destruction," *DPL*, 991 – 93; also Best, *Thessalonians*, 84 – 85; Ladd, *Theology of the New Testament*, 447.

riousness that it uses to describe his love or his mercy (cf. Exod 32:11 – 12).

Paul had to chart a careful course when he spoke to pagans about God's anger. On the one hand was the popular notion of the gods as beings of quick and fiery tempers. Virgil based the plot of his hugely influential *Aeneid* (late first century BC) on the anger of Juno:

> I tell about a war and the hero ... a man [Aeneas] much travailed on sea and land by the powers above, because of the brooding wrath of Juno.... Can a divine being be so persevering in anger? (*Aeneid* 1.1 – 10)

In popular religion, the gods were capricious, irritable, and easily offended. What human knew when they might commit some action or neglect some duty that a divinity might find irksome?

On the other hand, the philosophers rejected what they regarded as the foolish myths of these people. A deity could not have passion, since that implied change. God was changeless, immutable, forever existing in a state of perfect detachment. On that basis, the second-century Celsus made fun of the Christian God, who had "passions" such as wrath. Origen's rebuttal is found in the majestic *Contra Celsum*; unfortunately his answer to Celsus consisted in a capitulation to the philosopher's position, anticipating Dodd's view:

> We speak, indeed, of the "wrath" of God. We do not, however, assert that it indicates any "passion" on His part, but that it is something which is assumed in order to discipline by stern means those sinners who have committed many and grievous sins.[88]

That is, both Origen and Celsus favored the Greek doctrine of the "impassibility of God." In that form, it is an unbiblical idea that has found favor among many theologians throughout the centuries, but one which does not capture the biblical revelation of a God of holy passion.

These Thessalonians knew they would escape God's wrath, even though as Gentiles they used to do precisely those deeds that would bring his judgment on the human race. Their conversion was a striking demonstration of the power of God to bring about his will on the earth already during this age. According to Judaism, the world would have to wait until the eschatological kingdom before God would eliminate the cluster of sins associated with the apostate Gentiles, particularly idolatry and sexual sin.

That kind of universal change is predicted in Zech 14:9: "The LORD will be king over the whole earth. On that day there will be one LORD, and his name the only name." Zechariah shows how the Shema confession of God's name (Deut 6:4) will finally be actualized on earth. But what is the situation already in Macedonia? Before the coming of the end, Macedonian Gentiles have turned their backs on idolatry and the fornication associated with it (1 Thess 4:1 – 8) and, as we will see, are being called into the future kingdom and made worthy of it during this age (2:12; 2 Thess 1:5). This is a living God indeed, who can effect powerful conversion through his Spirit.

Thus Paul has come full circle. The Thessalonians are thriving within tribulation; God has preserved them; and the God in whom they believe is the God who through Jesus will deliver them from the ultimate end-time horror.

88. Origen, *Cels.* 4.72 (*ANF* 4:529). According to Origen, *Cels.* 4.71 (*ANF* 4:529), God speaks to people as a father speaks to young children. He calls this "anthropopathic" language, that is, God speaking as if he had human emotions.

Theology in Application

The Gentile converts to Christian faith had experienced a fundamental paradigm shift when they came to accept the existence of only one God. They would have been impressed that this new God had somehow "beaten" Fate by resurrecting one who was destined to die. How then should the apostles teach these people to pray to this sovereign and powerful God? First Thessalonians is a source for a number of doctrines; two special contributions happen to be intertwined in ch. 1: a theology of prayer, and teaching and learning by imitation. To this we will add learning to pray by imitation.

Theology of Prayer

The two Thessalonian letters not only serve as archives of Paul's prayers; they are "holographs," recordings of prayer even as they are being offered.[89] They provide a challenge for pastors, who might find great benefit in imitating the apostles. In his *A Call to Spiritual Reformation*, D. A. Carson goes directly to the Pauline prayer passages and uses them as a guide for Christians today. Unfortunately, notes Carson, "by and large, our thanksgiving seems to be tied rather tightly to our material well-being and comfort."[90] Is our gratitude stronger for the rescue of a lost sheep or for the retrieval of lost car keys? If, as Carson proposes, we look to the apostle and judge our prayers by the priorities shown in his prayers, we are unlikely to be found wanting with regard to our hierarchy of values. In other terms, our "thank-you" list is like the dipstick of a car; it is a gauge of what lies hidden in the heart.

One point is clear: Paul prayed a great deal. Perhaps we don't regard prayer with apostolic seriousness, giving it the sort of gravity the apostles gave it in Acts 6:4, who maintain they "will give ... attention to prayer and the ministry of the word." Here are a few suggestions:

1. *Pray and give thanks for all your believers, all the time.* As a pastor of a church of 125 members some years ago, I wrote up a list of cards on which I wrote people's names. No matter what the size, there must be some plan for praying for the sheep by name, and "at all times."
2. *Pray and give thanks in the "gaps."* Instead of complaining about the red light or when the computerized answering service puts you on hold, fill these spaces with prayer. And by the way, this does not excuse you from carving out larger uninterrupted spaces so that you may pray with full attention.
3. *Above all, pray and give thanks with an eye to biblical content.* Pray with a

89. 1 Thess 1:2 – 5; 2:13 – 16; 3:11 – 13; 5:23 – 25, 28; 2 Thess 1:2 – 5, 11 – 12; 2:13 – 17; 3:16, 18.

90. D. A. Carson, *A Call to Spiritual Reformation: Priorities from Paul and His Prayers* (repr.; Grand Rapids: Baker, 1992), 41.

gratitude that reflects what God is doing. How easy it is to have a constant, low-grade level of resentment toward the flock. How easy to dissipate that cloud by thanking God for each individual, and for specific gospel reasons.

4. *Finally, let "leak out" the things you've told God.* Paul allowed his churches to listen in on his prayers. There is joy in visiting a family or seeing children in Sunday school and being able to say, "I pray for you, you know."

Teaching and Learning by "Imitation"

One cannot appreciate the distinctive contribution of the Thessalonian letters without a basic understanding of the apostles' method of teaching/learning. Mimesis is literally the "imitation" of the teacher, who for his or her part provides a "model" or "pattern" (τύπος, see 1:7). For example, 3 John 9 – 12 is at heart a call to imitation, where the elder holds up Demetrius as a proper model and Diotrophes as a negative one: "Dear friend, do not imitate what is evil but what is good" (3 John 11).[91] Of course the ultimate pattern is provided by Jesus, to whom all the faithful should look (Heb 12:2).

Mimesis was especially suitable to a culture where few were literate. Pastors could not ask their people to read a guide to discipleship and then fill in the accompanying workbook. Rather, the teachers lived out the qualities of the well-rounded disciple, giving a pattern of character, behavior, and skill sets.

Mimesis was a favorite of the rabbis, Jesus ("Follow me!"), and the apostles.[92] Paul provided a living pattern when he was present; he also went on to develop a sort of "distance teaching" — holding himself up as a model to his disciples *in writing*, usually connecting their present need with something his readers had earlier seen him do with their own eyes. Examples of mimesis abound in the Pauline letters. In 1 Cor 9, Paul urges the Corinthians to suspend their rights for the sake of love, imitating his own pattern even as he imitated Christ (1 Cor 11:1; see more broadly, 1 Cor 4:16). Paul not only offered himself as a model, but he trained his protégées to do the same for their own disciples (1 Tim 4:12; Titus 2:7).

Christian leaders must assume that they are always being watched and imitated. At no time may they "let down their hair." Mimesis is not the same as an instructional video, which asks the viewer to imitate a skill set without concerning themselves with the moral character of instructor. Mimetic discipleship is the imitation of the pattern

91. Other examples: in the second century, Polycarp would urge his readers in Philippi to imitate the endurance of Paul, citing Phil 2:16 as an example; also of outstanding Christians of the day, such as Ignatius; and beyond that, "others from your congregation" (Pol. *Phil.* 9.1). Philo urged his readers to imitate Moses, since "he established himself as a most beautiful and Godlike work, to be a model for all those who were inclined to imitate him" (Philo, *Moses* 158). Heb 11:1 – 12:3 is a detailed list of good examples from the Scriptures.

92. Imitation of one's master is the very heart of Christian discipleship: if the exegete compares the language of the gospels with that of the Pauline letters, it turns out that the "*mathētēs* [disciple] ... and the *mimētēs* [imitator] are one and the same" (W. Michaelis, "μιμέομαι, μιμητής, συμμιμητής," *TDNT*, 4:673.

holistically, and the pattern is in theory always on duty. A flawed model will result in a flawed disciple, who will beget flawed followers in turn.[93]

Today mimesis has largely fallen out of favor in Western education, which tends to encourage students to discover their own personal style. Nevertheless, imitation of a "master" is widely used to teach such divergent skills as cooking, art, gardening, home renovation, tennis, the martial arts, golf, aerobics, and even surgery. The church often overlooks this potent method, which can be employed to teach the basic skills of prayer, Bible study, teaching methods, and others. Evangelism Explosion employs mimesis to good effect.

Learning to Pray by "Imitation"

Let us combine the first two applications. In general the North American church fails to teach its people to pray. For some the training begins and ends with, "Forget about formal prayers you may have learned. Prayer is just talking to God, so just speak to him as you would to another person." Given the importance of good praying and its difficulty, this sort of negligence is appalling.

Solid biblical praying is best created through a living model for people to imitate. Paul taught the new converts the relevant truths; he also said, in effect, "Listen to me and pray as I do." Rather than teaching a class on prayer, why not select a smaller number of people and say to them, "Let's pray together for three months, and we'll also talk about what the Bible says about prayer"?

Your church's prayer list is in itself didactic, since it provides Christians with a pattern to imitate, coaching them: "Here we show what the church regards as the hierarchy of God's values, so pray according to these priorities." I've done a nonscientific study of the prayer lists of a handful of churches. They implicitly transmitted that the highest duty in prayer was for the sick or bereaved. Next in importance: people in the armed services. Those are good things, but out of proportion to their importance. The missionaries seemed a bit squeezed. Rarely were the people asked to pray as Paul did in this letter, that the church would be steadfast, grow in love, and be generally blameless.

93. There's an excellent cautionary tale in James Baldwin's *Go Tell It on the Mountain* (1952; repr., New York: Facts on File, 2010). There had been a series of church meetings. Gabriel was the youngest preacher of the group; the others were black ministers of great renown who had come from all over to participate. But when the doors were shut, the preachers took it that they had permission to be themselves since there were no laypeople present. One of the preachers made a vicious slur against a woman who had just served them. "I don't think it's right," said Gabriel, "to talk evil about nobody. The Word tell me it ain't right to hold nobody up to scorn." "Now you just remember," Elder Peters said, as kindly as before, "you's talking to your elders." "Then it seem to me," he said, astonished at his boldness, "that if I got to look to you for a example, you ought to be a example."

CHAPTER 2

1 Thessalonians 2:1 – 16

Literary Context

The study of this section is complicated more than is usual by doubts about Paul's purpose here. He describes the work he and his team did in Thessalonica in some detail in 2:1 – 12. Until recent years most scholars felt he was defending the team against pagan or Jewish attack. Alfred Plummer expressed the idea nearly a century ago: "In what follows we may regard it as certain that the writers are replying to charges and insinuations which their Jewish opponents had made against them."[1] Alternatively, Paul is calming the Thessalonians' own real or potential doubts about them.[2] Thus, scholars have read the "antitheses" (e.g., "not with sneaking craftiness," 2:3) as responses to charges ("Paul and his team are crafty!").[3] Some link 2:1 – 12 ("We are not the type to abandon their children!") with 2:17 – 3:10, taking that passage as a defense for Paul and Silas's absence: "We made every possible effort to see you in person with great desire ... and Satan blocked us" (2:17 – 18).[4]

This general approach has several weaknesses. For one, Paul nowhere implies that the team is under attack for its integrity or for its absence. Paul knew how to speak up when he was attacked; in another context, he sallied forth to undermine the claim of his detractors (2 Cor 11:12). Second, he affirms in clear terms to the Thessalonians that "you maintain a good memory of us at all times" (3:6). Where is the tottering reputation he is trying to protect?[5]

1. Alfred Plummer, *A Commentary on St. Paul's First Epistle to the Thessalonians* (London: Robert Scott, 1918), 20, who speaks of "Jewish opponents"; also Morris, *Thessalonians* (NICNT), 52. Marshall, *1 and 2 Thessalonians*, 61, states that "he must have felt that he was being accused." See Seyoon Kim, "Paul's Entry (εἴσοδος) and the Thessalonians' Faith (1 Thessalonians 1 – 3)," *NTS* 51 (2005): 519 – 42. Kim jumps from the mere possibility of such opponents to the supposition (526): "Are we to fail to perceive the real presence of the opponents of the Christian faith in Thessalonica?" to (527) "the opponents are clearly denigrating Paul." All very well, but where is the proof? Fee, *Thessalonians*, 53, draws a similar conclusion: Timothy returned to Paul and brought news of "a considerable smear campaign against Paul."

2. See esp. on this theme, J. A. D. Weima, "An Apology for the Apologetic Function of 1 Thessalonians 2.1 – 12," *JSNT* 68 (1997): 73 – 99; also Bruce W. Winter, "The Entries and Ethics of Orators and Paul (1 Thessalonians 2:1 – 12)," *TynBul* 44 (1993): 55 – 74.

3. So Mearns, "The Evidence of I and II Thessalonians," 145; Fee, *Thessalonians*, 53.

4. Green, *Thessalonians*, 111 – 14.

5. Kim, "Paul's Entry," 539, argues that 1 Thess 3:6 has the same function as 2 Cor 7:6 – 7, where Titus returns to Paul from Corinth with encouraging news. The parallel is not, as Kim claims, a particularly strong one, despite the similarity of language: Titus's report had to do principally with how the Corinthians received the "sorrowful letter."

A better direction is to show how the apostles' ministry corresponds neatly with the life of the Thessalonian church (as in 1:6). Paul then goes into another statement about imitation: you imitate the Lord Jesus; you imitate Judean churches and the prophets (2:14 – 16a). The Lord Jesus, the churches, and the prophets are not under attack *in this document* because of doubts about their character; rather, along with the Pauline team, they were models of how to proclaim God's message in spite of trouble from their fellow-countrymen.[6]

Therefore, we underscore the continuity of 2:1 – 16 with the previous chapter, where the apostles were said to provide a *model for their disciples to imitate*. A benefit of this viewpoint is that within the text of the letter itself, Paul equates discipleship with imitation of the teacher:

1:6 "you became imitators [of us]"
2:1 – 12 here is how we live and work

In addition to following their ethical behavior, the believers were emulating the team by projecting themselves beyond the limits of their local church: "the word of the Lord has sounded forth [from Thessalonica]" (1:8). They had in a remarkably short time become effective evangelists. Since imitation of the persecuted evangelist is the motif that runs through these two chapters, it is likely that Paul is focusing on imitation in 2:1 – 12.[7] This view is well articulated by Malherbe: "A writer might also describe his own life in detail, in antithetic form, in order to provide a basis for the practical advice he would give."[8]

Yes, 1 Thess 2 has some parallels with 2 Cor 7, where Paul defends himself. Yet the student of Scripture must allow for the fact that the same *form* may in a different context serve a different *function*. Two parallels will suffice. In 1 Sam 12:3 Samuel offers a challenge to the nation:

> Here I stand. Testify against me in the presence of the LORD and his anointed. Whose ox have I taken? Whose donkey have I taken? Whom have I cheated? Whom have I oppressed? From whose hand have I accepted a bribe to make me shut my eyes? If I have done any of these things, I will make it right.

What was Samuel's intent? Ostensibly, it was to establish his reputation beyond reproach. Yet his purpose extended to the future. Israel was passing through a transi-

6. For that reason, some argue that Paul is not defending himself but distinguishing himself from false teachers generally. See Ambrosiaster, *Commentaries on Galatians-Philemon*, 103.

7. See Carol J. Schlueter, *Filling Up the Measure: Polemical Hyperbole in 1 Thessalonians 2:14 – 16* (JSNTSup 98; Sheffield: JSOT: 1994), 32 – 33, for a list of parallels between 1 Thess 1 and 2.

8. Malherbe, *Letters to the Thessalonians*, 155; Wanamaker, *Thessalonians*, 93. Marshall, *1 and 2 Thessalonians*, 61, reads too much into Malherbe when he expresses doubt as to "why Paul, a Christian preacher, should have gone to such pains to describe himself in terms of the ideal philosopher." It should be kept in mind that Paul's purpose may not be identical to Dio's but was using similar language to show that Paul and Silas were approved by God and should be emulated.

tion, from the judges to a "king to lead us, such as all the other nations have" (1 Sam 8:3). Moses had warned that the sin of kings is rapaciousness (Deut 17:14 – 17), and Samuel repeated that warning (1 Sam 8:11 – 18). Samuel's vindication of himself has a broader function as a caveat — *let Saul and all future kings beware of violating the law; may they hold on to my example; may Israel reject a greedy king!*

Acts 20:17 – 35 sheds further light on what is going on. On one level Paul gives an "apology" for his work. Yet for what purpose does he rehearse all the details of his honesty and labor before the Ephesian elders? The apostle, like Samuel of old, is looking ahead, warning the elders themselves to follow his example:

> I know that after I leave, savage wolves will come in among you and will not spare the flock. Even from your own number men will arise and distort the truth in order to draw away disciples after them. So be on your guard! Remember that for three years I never stopped warning each of you night and day with tears. (Acts 20:29 – 31)

In 1 Thess 2:1, Paul turns from thanksgiving to a description of their missionary venture for a church that, in turn, has become a beacon of evangelism. Do you Thessalonians experience severe persecution? So have we when we spoke boldly (2:2), so have the churches of Judea, the Christian prophets (2:14 – 15), and come to think of it, so did our definitive model, the Lord Jesus (1:6; 2:15). In great detail, here, brothers and sisters, is "how we proclaimed to you the gospel of God" (2:9). And that is precisely how you should live generally, and this is how you should share the gospel with others.[9]

The latter part of the section is thought by some to be an interpolation — that is, words that were added into the letter after the destruction of Jerusalem, perhaps by a person with an anti-Semitic agenda. There is little historical foundation for the idea (see Introduction). But what is the purpose of the section? It is to contrast the gospel-preaching Gentile believers of Thessalonica with the gospel-blocking unbelievers of Judea. The church will be saved from God's wrath (1:10), whereas the unbelieving Jews are compounding God's anger toward them (2:16). In a city where the synagogue has enticed both the mob and the government to persecute Christians, it is important to define one's terms: *Who is pleasing to God, and who is rebelling against him?*

9. See the excellent development of the "imitation" view by George Lyons, *Pauline Autobiography: Toward a New Understanding* (SBLDS 73; Atlanta: Scholars, 1985), 182 – 201.

Main Idea

Paul describes his team's mission in Thessalonica principally in order to shape the behavior of his readers, using the teaching method known as "mimesis." They communicated the gospel with success because God, who tests their hearts, approved them and worked through them despite opposition. The Judean churches provided a similar positive model. If the Thessalonians follow these models, they too will have God's approval.

Translation

(See next three pages.)

Structure

The bulk of this section concerns the manner in which the apostles evangelized Thessalonica. Paul is repeating and developing the information that already appeared in ch. 1: the success of the missionary venture and Paul's gratitude for their imitation of the apostolic team (2:1 – 13) and now, additionally, their imitation of the Judean churches (2:14 – 16). The central theme is how a true evangelist acts, given that there is a God who "tests our inner motives" (2:4e). While this is crucial information for any Christian, it is especially imperative for the Thessalonian church, from which the gospel "sounds forth" (1:8).

Paul begins by reminding the readers ("you yourselves know") that the team encountered good results in Thessalonica and felt braver than they normally should have. They faced furious opposition (2:1 – 2, ἀλλά being used in 2:2 to denote unfavorable conditions for success).

1 Thessalonian 2:1 – 16

1a	Reminder language	**You yourselves know**, brothers and sisters,
1b	Content	that the welcome we had from you was not without good results.
2a	Concession	Even though we had just suffered and had been badly treated in Philippi,
2b	Reminder language	as you know,
2c	Contra-expectation	still
		we found courage in our God to communicate to you the gospel of God,
2d	Circumstance	in the face of [even more] opposition.
3a	Assertion	**Our entreaty to you was**
3b	List -Manner	not with lies,
3c	Manner	not with corruption,
3d	Manner	not with sneaking craftiness.
4a	Basis (for 3)	No, in the same way that we have been tested and
		found worthy by God
4b	Purpose	to be entrusted with his gospel,
4c	Comparison	**that's how we communicate [it]**:
4d	Contrast	not striving to please people, but rather
4e	Contrast	the God who tests our inner motives.
5a	Expansion (of 3-4)	That is to say, **we did not come**
5b	Time	at any time
5c	Manner/List	with flattering words,
5d	Reminder language	as you know,
5e	Manner/List	not with some pretext for greed—
5f	Appeal to God	God himself is our witness!—
6a	Manner/List	not looking for prestige,
6b	Source	not from you or
6c	Source	from anyone else,

Continued on next page.

Continued from previous page.

7a	Concession/List	even though we could have insisted on acting all important and
7b	Concession/List	on being a burden to you,
7c	Basis (for 7a-b)	since we are apostles of Christ.
7d	Contrast/List	No, **we took the position of little children among you.**
7e	Manner	[Or if you please] how a wet-nurse might cherish her very own little ones;
8a	Result	so then, because we had this longing for you,
8b	Assertion	**we determined to share with you** not only
8c	Content/List	the gospel of God, but also
8d	Content/List	our very selves,
8e	Cause (of 8)	because you had become beloved to us.
9a	Reminder Language	For **you remember**, brothers and sisters,
9b	Content/ List	our labor and our hardship,
9c	Content/ List	how night and day we worked,
9d	Purpose	so as not to be a burden to anyone of you;
9e	Content List	that's how
		we proclaimed to you the gospel of God.
10a	Reminder Language	**You are witnesses—**
10b	Appeal to God	**and so is God!—**
10c	Manner/ List	that we were pleasing [to God],
10d	Manner/ List	right and blameless
10e	Content	with you who came to believe,
11a	Reminder Language	just as you know,
11b	Manner	how we were with each one of you,
11c	Comparisons	as a father with his own sons and daughters;
12a	Manner /List	that's how we entreated you,
12b	Manner /List	that's how we comforted you,
12c	Manner /List	that's how we implored you

12d	Manner	to walk worthy of the God
12e	Description	who called you into his own glorious kingdom.
13a	Thanksgiving	So, for this reason,
		we give thanks to God
		without fail:
13b	Cause	Because . . .
		when you received the proclaimed word from us, [that is, the word] of God,
		. . . you received it,
13c	Contrast	not as a human message, but
		as what it really is,
13d	Contrast	the word of God,
13e	Description	the same [word] that is active in you believers.
14a	Restatement	**You became imitators**, brothers and sisters,
		of God's churches in Judea
14b	Sphere	[which are] in Christ Jesus
14c	Cause	because you also endured the same things from your fellow countrymen
14d	Source List	that they suffered from the Judeans,
15a	Description List	those who killed the Lord Jesus and
		the prophets, and
15b	Description List	persecuted us, and
15c	Description List	do not live pleasing to God, and
15d	Description List	are hostile to all
16a	Means	by hindering us from speaking
		to the Gentiles
16b	Purpose	so that they might
		be saved;
16c	Cause	for so their sins were at all times such as to warrant [God's wrath];
16d	Result	[God's] wrath has come upon them unto the end.

There are three major metaphors in 2:3 – 12: being like a child (2:3 – 7d, see comments for proof of this exegesis), like a wet-nurse (2:7e – 8), and like a father (2:9 – 12). As in 1:5, Paul uses antithesis throughout 2:3 – 7c ("not this ... but that"). With "our entreaty to you was not" (2:3) he offers several negative statements, marked with "not ... not ... not ... not" (οὐκ ... οὔδε ... οὔδε ... οὔτε, etc.). In 2:4 there is a side comment, marked by "but" or, in our translation, "No" (ἀλλά). Paul offers a comparison "in the same way [καθώς] that we have been tested and found worthy by God," with the point of comparison marked by "so thus" or, as we have expanded it, "that's how" (οὕτως).

Paul then expands this comparison with an additional antithesis: "not" (οὐχ) striving to please people "but rather" (ἀλλά) God. Here then, says Paul, is what an authentic presentation of the gospel must *not* be: it is not the pleasing package of the street preachers who are on the make for a stipend. Rather, a preacher of the gospel has pure inner motives, which are tested by God. Paul calls on the Thessalonians and God himself to bear witness that he is telling the truth.

With "but" or "instead" (ἀλλά) in 2:7d Paul turns from "what we did not do" to the positive "what we did do": we were as free from guile as "little children"; we did not engage in grown-up deception and manipulation.

The controlling metaphor from 2:7e – 9 is the "wet-nurse." She "cherishes" her little ones; Paul reminds the Thessalonians in another antithesis that the apostles did not simply share a verbal message (2:8c) "but also" their "very selves." This sharing was expressed by the fact that they worked night and day, taking upon themselves the burden and not putting it on their charges, just as a mother might do (2:9).

The third main metaphor (2:10 – 12) is that they acted "as a father" to their disciples, and he repeatedly calls on the Thessalonians or God himself to bear him witness (2:10), as elsewhere in the chapter. The point of comparison is that a father instructs his children (2:11 – 12).

Verse 13 provides an *inclusio* (the closing bracket) to the theme begun in 1:2 — the apostles give thanks to God "for this reason" (διὰ τοῦτο), that is, that the gospel was successful. Paul slips in one more antithesis: the Thessalonians received the message not (οὐ) as a human one, but (ἀλλά) as the word of God. He explores that further with "because" (γάρ, which is better left untranslated). Paul does not introduce an entirely new theme but continues the "imitation" motif of 1:6 – 7, which, as I seek to prove, Paul has in mind throughout 2:1 – 12.

Verses 14 – 16 are not a later interpolation (see the Introduction) but an integral part of Paul's original letter. The Thessalonians, like their Judean fellows, must keep faithful to the gospel despite opposition. The Jewish religious establishment was going to any length to impede the spread of the gospel to the nations. With the cadence of an ancient prophet, Paul uses a string of participles and an adjective ("killed," "persecuted," "do not live pleasing to God," "are hostile to all," and "hindering us") to describe the unbelieving Jews, and shows in 2:16 that the end result (εἰς τό) of their actions is God's wrath. No wonder, then, that the Thessalonians encounter opposition from their own "fellow countrymen" (2:14) as they carry out their desire to evangelize Greece and other regions.

Exegetical Outline

→ **I. The Apostolic Team as a Pattern for the Thessalonians (2:1 – 12)**

- A. The apostolic team met with success, even though it was under fierce attack (2:1 – 2).
- B. The apostolic team served God in an exemplary manner (2:3 – 12).
  1. They did not come to perpetrate a fraud (2:3).
  2. Rather God himself had tested them and found them worthy to proclaim the gospel (2:4).
  3. They did not exhibit the normal character traits of the popular teachers of the day (2:5 – 12).
     - a. They didn't flatter the powerful in order to receive money or recognition (2:5 – 6).
     - b. They declined the treatment befitting Christ's apostles (2:7a-c).
     - c. They assumed humbler roles (2:7d – 11).
       - i. They were as guileless as small children (2:7d).
       - ii. They were as gentle and nurturing as nursemaids (2:7e).
       - iii. They took on the low social status of manual workers (2:8 – 9).
       - iv. They showed themselves of blameless character (2:10).
       - v. They took on the role of loving fathers (2:11).
     - d. They taught their hearers to act as they themselves did, in a manner worthy of God (2:12).

II. Recapitulation: Why They Regularly Give Thanks for the Thessalonians (2:13 – 16) [*inclusio* with 1:2]

- A. The Thessalonians received the gospel as the divine message (2:13a-d).
- B. That message was active among them (2:13e).
- C. They became imitators of the established Judean churches (2:14 – 16).
  1. They suffered at the hands of their own fellow countrymen (2:14).
  2. Judeans killed Jesus and the Christian prophets (2:15a).
  3. Judeans persecuted Paul and Silas and other Christians (2:15b).
  4. Judeans displeased God and offended other people (2:15c-d).
  5. Judeans hindered the Gentile mission (2:16a-b).
  6. The Judeans had gone the way of the ancient nations of Canaan (2:16c-d).

Explanation of the Text

2:1 You yourselves know, brothers and sisters, that the welcome we had from you was not without good results (Αὐτοὶ γὰρ οἴδατε, ἀδελφοί, τὴν εἴσοδον ἡμῶν τὴν πρὸς ὑμᾶς ὅτι οὐ κενὴ γέγονεν). "For" (γάρ) here is a "narrative marker to express continuation or connection"; it does not indicate causation (see BDAG) and is best left untranslated. Paul has previously noted that people everywhere were talking about God's work in Thessalonica (1:8b – 9a); he now reminds the readers that they themselves know all about it. This is the second use of "reminder language" in this letter (see 1:5); there are a total of six instances in ch. 2. What did they "know"? "The welcome we had from you" (τὴν εἴσοδον ... τὴν πρὸς ὑμᾶς) echoes language of 1:9. Paul uses "yourselves" (αὐτοὶ) to intensify "you know" (οἴδατε). "You yourselves know" is a parallel to "they themselves are talking about us" in 1:9.

"Not in vain" or "not without good results" (οὐ κενή) is the figure of speech known as litotes, the stating of a positive fact by means of negating its opposite (see comments on 1:2). Paul uses the same figure in a later letter to show that God's grace is potent, even when there are inhospitable circumstances: "his grace toward me [Saul the persecutor!] did not prove vain" (1 Cor 15:10 NASB). Paul's reminder to the church here is poignant, since later on he admits he had truly been vexed over whether the Thessalonian work "*had* been in vain" (εἰς κενὸν γένηται, 3:5).

2:2a-b Even though we had just suffered and had been badly treated in Philippi, as you know (ἀλλὰ προπαθόντες καὶ ὑβρισθέντες καθὼς οἴδατε ἐν Φιλίπποις). Paul shows with "even though" (ἀλλά) why their success in Thessalonica was contrary to what might have been expected: the apostles had arrived in less than optimal condition. The compound verb "suffer before" (προπάσχω) is a *hapax legomenon*, that is, a word used only here in the New Testament. The verb may take two meanings: it may refer to hardship that others imposed on them, or it may have a "psychological" meaning, that they were inwardly dispirited.[10] In that case, it would be similar to the use of "could stand it no longer" in 3:1. The first meaning is preferred: the verb is paired with being "badly treated"; that is, Paul seems focused on what others were doing to them. The parallel in Phil 1:30 shows that when Paul thought of Philippi, he thought of physical suffering, not mental anguish. The fact that "suffer" (πάσχω) and the like are so prominent in the early Christian vocabulary (see, e.g., 1 Thess 2:14; 2 Thess 1:5) reveals much about the nature of Christian experience in apostolic times. "Badly treated" (ὑβρισθέντες) speaks of gross insult, whether verbal or physical.[11] According to Acts 14:5, Paul and Barnabas were "badly treated" at Iconium; in that case, there was an attempt to stone them.[12]

The words "suffered" and "been badly treated" truly capture their earlier experience in Philippi. They had tried to help a girl of low social status by exorcising a demon from her (Acts 16:18). This led to their being hauled by brute force before the magistrates (16:19), where they were derided for being Jews (16:20 – 21), stripped of their clothing, flogged, and jailed (16:22 – 23).

Indeed, the fact that Paul and Silvanus were Roman citizens worsened the shame of their experience; in theory they were exempt from such

10. See MM, 543.

11. See MM, 647, where "abuse the body" (εἰς τὸ σῶμα ὑβρίζω) means to subject to corporal punishment.

12. See the use of "insult" (ὑβρίζω) of the bad treatment of the servants in the parable of the vineyard in Matt 22:6; of the Son of Man in Luke 18:32.

gross insult (Acts 16:37 – 39).[13] Public shaming does not have the impact in the West today that it did in Paul's day. Fortunately, NT scholars have of late drawn attention to the significance of shame in Jewish and in Greco-Roman circles. Note, for example:

> Thus witnessed and endorsed by a sizable proportion of the Philippian populace — including a substantial number of fellow Romans — their degradation could not have been more complete.... Uncontested, the shame of their beating and bonds would henceforth obtrude upon all social relations in Philippi. There would be no honour for them or for their message.[14]

Contrary to cultural norms, the apostolic team did not attempt to hide the fact of their beating. Nor could they have hoped to gain sympathy, as if their experience was proof of the sincerity of their beliefs. They were marked upon their arrival in Thessalonica as troublemakers. Yet, as Calvin comments:

> We know that the minds of men are weakened, nay, are altogether broken down by means of ignominy and persecutions. It was therefore an evidence of a Divine work that Paul, after having been subjected to evils of various kinds and to ignominy, did, as if in a perfectly sound state, shew no hesitation in making an attempt upon a large and opulent city, with the view of subjecting the inhabitants of it to Christ.[15]

There are parallels in Heb 10:32 – 33 and in Rom 8:36, where Paul applies Ps 44:22 to his own experience: "For your sake we face death all day long; we are considered as sheep to be slaughtered." If the Thessalonians wished to be Christians, they might expect the same outrageous treatment that Paul and Silas had received.

"As" (καθώς) is the language of comparison and leads into further reminder language: "you know" (οἴδατε).[16]

2:2c-d Still we found courage in our God to communicate to you the gospel of God, in the face of [even more] opposition (ἐπαρρησιασάμεθα ἐν τῷ θεῷ ἡμῶν λαλῆσαι πρὸς ὑμᾶς τὸ εὐαγγέλιον τοῦ θεοῦ ἐν πολλῷ ἀγῶνι). According to ch. 1, the Thessalonians had experienced the powerful operation of the Spirit; Paul now shows that they could also find supernatural courage, as had their apostles. When the verb "speak boldly" (παρρησιάζομαι) is complemented by an infinitive,[17] it takes the meaning of "have the courage, venture." The infinitive "communicate" or "speak" (λαλῆσαι) denotes the oral ministry of Paul and his team. Here we must guard against seeking fine distinctions between synonyms, for example, for "speak" (λαλέω and λέγω). In older Greek, λαλέω might give a sense of relatively informal speech, whether conversation or chatter, but in the first century that distinction no longer held.[18] Paul could be referring here to anything from a quiet conversation to a preaching session.

God had empowered Paul and the team to articulate whatever was needed to communicate the gospel. This does not mean that they were at liberty

13. See MM, 647, where a papyrus links citizenship with exemption from beatings: "your citizenship, however, will in no way be injured thereby, nor will you be subjected to corporal punishment."

14. Brian Rapske, *The Book of Acts and Paul in Roman Custody* (BA1CS 3; Grand Rapids: Eerdmans, 1994), 303 – 4.

15. Calvin, *Thessalonians*, 248.

16. See καθώς with reminder language in 1 Thess 1:5; 2:2; 2:5; 3:4; 4:1; 4:6; 4:11.

17. See BDF §392 for the complementary use of the infinitive.

18. See LSJ, λαλέω. It is used of Jesus' preaching in Matt 13:3 and of the apostolic preaching generally in 1 Thess 2:16. In Acts 18:9, in a vision that occurred shortly after the writing of 1 Thessalonians, Jesus appeared to Paul and charged him, "Do not be afraid; keep on speaking [from λαλέω], do not be silent."

to ramble on, as did the Cynic philosophers of that era. The Cynics used volubility and insult as teaching tools: "Having himself attained moral freedom, the philosopher felt compelled to turn others to it by harshly pointing out their shortcomings and holding up the fulfillment of human potential that the rational life would bring."[19] The apostles' boldness is no public nuisance, but the "great sense of certainty we had in the gospel" (1:5). Yes, he was frank to point out what the hearers needed, but in a fashion he was as gentle as a nurse (2:7).

"Gospel" followed by a noun in the genitive is never easily translated. Here it could be a subjective genitive ("God announces good news to us") or objective ("we announce good news about God"). Either may be made to fit; this is why Wallace[20] suggests that both may be in the author's mind here and in 2:8 – 9, under a category known as a "plenary genitive": God produces the good news, a message that in turn others preach concerning God. Other important examples are found in Mark 1:1 and Rev 1:1.

We have added "even more" because the hostility they faced in Thessalonica was the perpetuation of their experience in Philippi. The noun "opposition" (ἀγών) in its literal sense is a gathering of people or by extension the venue in which they assemble, perhaps to see games. Another meaning is the competitive games themselves. Socrates recounts, "I have undertaken in my time many *contests* of speech" (Plato, *Prot.* 335a); the author of Hebrews says, "Let us run ... the *race*" (Heb 12:1; see also 1 Tim 6:12). The word can be rendered "struggle," that is, an inner, psychological turmoil due to the circumstances. While this is possible, the more common use of ἀγών is a reference to "hardships," as in the many "labors" of Hercules (Sophocles, *Trach.* 159). What reinforces this latter sense of the word is Paul's reference to his trials in Philippi: "For it has been granted to you on behalf of Christ not only to believe in him, but also to suffer for him, since you are going through the same struggle [ἀγών] you saw I had, and now hear that I still have" (Phil 1:29 – 30; also Col 2:1).

2:3 Our entreaty to you was not with lies, not with corruption, not with sneaking craftiness (ἡ γὰρ παράκλησις ἡμῶν οὐκ ἐκ πλάνης οὐδὲ ἐξ ἀκαθαρσίας οὐδὲ ἐν δόλῳ). This is not just a reminder of how the team behaved or a defense against those who might charge them with charlatanism. Rather, Paul is telling his disciples how one must live in order to see the power of God at work.[21]

As in 2:1, it is best to leave "for" (γάρ) untranslated. "Entreaty" (παράκλησις) is capable of various meanings, even within 1 Thessalonians. It may mean encouragement[22] or, as here, "exhortation" or "entreaty."[23] Paul exhorts/encourages the Thessalonians here in writing (4:1, 10; 5:11; see 2 Thess 3:12). Later we learn that when he had sent Timothy on his return mission north, he too was expected to "exhort" (1 Thess 3:2).

Verse 3 sounds as if Paul is leaving verses 1 – 2

19. Abraham J. Malherbe, *Paul and the Popular Philosophers* (Minneapolis: Fortress, 1989), 59. So too T. Paige, "Philosophy,"*DPL*, 715: the Cynics' "ideal of 'boldness' (*parrēsia*) in speech was displayed by public preaching which was often caustic, abusive and arrogant in exposing the 'sins' of the audience. They compared their manner to surgery on a patient with gangrene."

20. Wallace, *Grammar*, 119 – 21.

21. Walton carries out a comparison of 1 Thess 2 with the Miletus speech in Acts 20. He argues that in both texts, Paul is not defending himself against specific detractors, but is setting himself up as an example to believers and to leaders of the church (e.g., in 5:12 – 13). See Steve Walton, *Leadership and Lifestyle: The Portrait of Paul in the Miletus Speech and 1 Thessalonians* (SNTSMS 108; New York: Cambridge Univ. Press, 2000), ch. 5.

22. See παρακαλέω in Deut 3:28; 1 Thess 4:18; 2 Thess 2:17; παράκλησις in Acts 13:15; 2 Thess 2:16; esp. 2 Cor 1:3 – 7.

23. See παρακαλέω in 1 Thess 4:1; the verb and παράκλησις both in Rom 12:8. Exhortation is an apostolic ministry according to Acts 15:32; 16:40.

and moving to a new topic, that is, the behavior of the apostles. But he would not perceive that he was changing themes. Paul does here what he has already done—juxtapose the theme of the powerful entrance of the gospel with a reminder of the team's integrity (1:4–5). One manifestation of God's working was that the apostles spoke in a trustworthy fashion. Here in 2:3 Paul is not distancing his team from a hypothetical sincerely mistaken preacher, but from the wily—through whose devices God will not reveal himself in power. "Deceit" or "lies" (πλάνη) is sometimes used of the deceit of religious apostates. "Corruption" (ἀκαθαρσία) in this context means moral corruption. It is the opposite of holiness (4:7) and a work of the flesh—that is, a characteristic of the person not fashioned by the Spirit (Gal 5:19).

A few years earlier, Paul and Barnabas had run across a master of "craftiness" (see also 1 Pet 2:1) in Cyprus, the court magician Bar Jesus (Acts 13:10). Not only did he oppose God's truth, but he did so with deceptive tactics.

These new believers lived in a town where traveling philosophers might appear and deliver a pastiche of myth and popular philosophy, seasoned by sex and financial rip-off. They might collect money and make a profit, or endeavor to win the patronage of some wealthy person.[24] Despite Paul's extraordinary efforts to avoid this label, people still charged him with being disingenuous—"regarded [us] as imposters" (2 Cor 6:8).[25]

2:4a-b No, in the same way that we have been tested and found worthy by God to be entrusted with his gospel (ἀλλὰ καθὼς δεδοκιμάσμεθα ὑπὸ τοῦ θεοῦ πιστευθῆναι τὸ εὐαγγέλιον). It is not as if God has intervened through Christ and then abandoned his apostles to develop human strategies to spread the message. All that pertains to salvation, including its proclamation, begins and ends with divine intervention. God tests and approves those true envoys who aid its spread around the world.

This verse contains one of the many contrasts and comparisons found in this chapter. Translating the connective simply as "no" (ἀλλά) well underscores the contrast that Paul intends. Within this contrast lies a comparison that begins with "in the same way" (καθώς): in the same way that God tested us and found us worthy heralds, so we performed our duty in that same trustworthy manner.

Paul will speak of "testing" (from δοκιμάζω) again in 5:20–21: "Do not disdain prophetic messages. But rather put all of these to the test." He too will offer a reliable prophecy or "oracle from the Lord" concerning the resurrection of the saints (see comments on 4:15; cf. also 1 John 4:1). Paul and his team were tested "by God," a concept known from Jer 17:10—"I the Lord search the heart and examine the heart, to reward each person according to their conduct, according to what their deeds deserve." In classical Greek the verb was used of testing people to see if they were fit for public office.[26]

Paul will later tell Timothy to appoint deacons in Ephesus, but only after they have been tested by others in the church (1 Tim 3:8–10). Their examination too consists of ensuring that they are free of the vices that cast doubt on their integrity: they are to be "worthy of respect, sincere, not indulging in

24. Dio Chrysostom, *Oratory* 32, said that some Cynic preachers "posting themselves at street-corners, in alleyways, and at temple-gates, pass round the hat and play upon the credulity of lads and sailors and crowds of that sort." Other types "come before you as men of culture either declaim speeches intended for display, and stupid ones to boot, or else chant verses of their own composition, as if they had detected in you a weakness for poetry."

25. Although see his sarcastic comment in 2 Cor 12:16—"crafty fellow that I am, I caught you by trickery!"

26. See LSJ, δοκιμάζω; of a calvaryman, Lysias, *Against Alcibiades* 1.22. According to Lysias, *Against Alcibiades* 15.6 (Lamb), certain men "passed their scrutiny in compliance with the laws."

much wine, and not pursuing dishonest gain," and with "a clear conscience." More broadly, Christians in general should examine themselves (Gal 6:3 – 4), but always with the awareness that people tend to deceive themselves and rationalize their motives and actions (see 1 Cor 4:3 – 4).

Paul uses an aorist infinitive "to be entrusted" (πιστευθῆναι). The aorist has suffered from a long history of misunderstanding, and even now many believe that it denotes *a point of time*. This is not so. The aorist does not as such indicate a punctilear action, nor, as the most baffling version of the myth has it, does it mean an action performed once and for all, never to be repeated. The kind of action to which an aorist verb refers can only be determined by the context and in some cases by the nature of the verb itself. In this instance, the aorist does not necessarily indicate some "moment" in which God committed the gospel to the apostolic team, nor does it specify a past action, although from the context we may infer that it did take place in the past. This verse coincides with Gal 2:7 ("I had been entrusted with ... the gospel," πεπίστευμαι τὸ εὐαγγέλιον; cf. also Rom 3:2; 1 Tim 1:11; Titus 1:3). The information in this verse provides the readers with a normative pattern for preaching the gospel: not just anyone can communicate it; gospel heralds need to live according to its truth and live under God's scrutiny and approval.

2:4c-e That's how we communicate [it]: not striving to please people, but rather the God who tests our inner motives (οὕτως λαλοῦμεν, οὐχ ὡς ἀνθρώποις ἀρέσκοντες ἀλλὰ θεῷ τῷ δοκιμάζοντι τὰς καρδίας ἡμῶν). Paul's standard goes far beyond being true to oneself; he must remain true to God, or else he could cast away the hope for God's power in his work.

The issue that Paul and his companions faced was not simply to get along well with people. Obscured from modern eyes are the social and economic implications of their approach to ministry. Principally, they might have tailored their message so as not to affront the rich and powerful. An apostle with the prudence not to cause offense might have attracted patronage, prestige for his message, a pleasant hall in which to teach it, and a well-earned respite from manual labor. But they decided not to alter the content or the method of their preaching. The "people" (ἀνθρώποις) mentioned here are not only "men," but "men and women." In Paul's day self-promoting philosophers tried to take in both prominent men and women as patrons.

Paul employs the verb "please" (ἀρέσκω) a total of fourteen times in his letters.[27] The reader senses a certain tension in his usage, since he states in various locations that:

- All humans must seek to please God (2:4; this is impossible outside of life in the Spirit, Rom 8:8).
- It is a vice to please oneself; Christ sets the pattern (Rom 15:1 – 3).
- It is a vice to be a "people pleaser" (2:4; see Gal 1:10).

Nevertheless, it can be a virtue to seek to please humans. Paul sets himself up as the pattern in 1 Cor 10:33 – 11:1: "I try to please [ἀρέσκω] everyone in every way ... so that they may be saved. Follow my example, as I follow the example of Christ"; also Rom 15:2: "Each of us should please our neighbors for their good" (see also Eph 6:5 – 6). Overseers must have a pleasing reputation among non-Christians (1 Tim 3:7), as should all believers (1 Thess 4:11 – 12)

The solution to this disparity is not far from hand. "Pleasing God" is a fundamental rule for the Christian life. It lies opposite flattering oneself or pleasing a human who can do one good, which is

27. See the study by H. Bietenhard, "ἀρέσκω," *NIDNTT*, 2:814 – 17.

corruption and deceit. The other side of the coin is that those who seek to please God will also seek to please other humans in love. As Christ taught, the second commandment is to love one's neighbor (Matt 22:39). This means that the minister actively chooses to sacrifice his or her own preferences in order to serve the other. Later in the chapter, Paul will show how Judeans have displeased God and also become an irritant to other humans.

In the phrase "but the God who" (ἀλλὰ θεῷ), Paul does not repeat "to please" God (ἀρέσκοντες); it is implied from the previous clause and here it takes its positive meaning, as under #1 above. Paul repeats the reference to "tests" (δοκιμάζοντι). He knows that there is no way to escape the piercing eye of God. The Thessalonians too, after living their whole lives as pagans, are now following a God who can read their minds and analyze their motives.

Too many church leaders throughout history have used the defense, "I am accountable to God, not to man!" as camouflage. To demand an accounting is supposedly an insult to "God's man," whom God will correct if he needs it. Paul leaves no room for this nonsense. In fact, on another occasion, he insisted that trustees from every church travel to oversee the large Jerusalem offering (1 Cor 16:1 – 3).

"Inner motives" (καρδία) is a better rendering than "heart." In English, as in other European languages, "heart" indicates the seat of the emotions (e.g., "a person's feeling of or capacity for love or compassion").[28] Preachers should remind the flocks that "heart" is something different in 2:4, and indeed in most biblical passages. BDAG offers the useful rendering, "center and source of the whole inner life, with its thinking, feeling, and volition." It is a standard Jewish and Christian affirmation that human motives are inscrutable, even to the individual him- or herself, and that only God knows what lies in the heart (see, e.g., 1 Chr 28:9: "[The Lord] understands every desire and every thought"; Luke 16:15: "You are the ones who justify yourselves in the eyes of others, but God knows your hearts"; also Ps 139:1; Rom 8:27; Rev 2:23).

The apostles' preaching had such positive results because God approves of their motives. Nevertheless, "his message, the gospel, stands or falls with his integrity as its preacher.... *Therefore* it is absolutely necessary for him to defend his integrity."[29] Paul does not say that the gospel's success rests principally on his good reputation before others; it is rather God's evaluation of his ministry that is paramount ("God ... tests our inner motives!"; "God himself is our witness!"). At the point that God does not approve them, he will, one infers, cease to work through them by his Spirit, with miracles, conviction, courage, and the conversion of Gentiles (see 1:5 – 6; 2:2).

Paul gives thanks to God because the Thessalonians received the gospel as God's word, not the word of humans, no matter how admirable those preachers might be (1:5; 2:13). The team's integrity is of such importance, first of all because God is ever watching. Paul closely mirrors the spirituality of the psalmists; he declares before God that he has "integrity," inviting God to "prove him" and distancing himself from evil people, who use deception as their tool. Note the echoes of Ps 26:1 – 7:

> Vindicate me, O Lord,
> for I have walked in my *integrity*,
> and I have trusted in the Lord without wavering.
> *Prove* me, O Lord, and try me;
> *test* my heart and my mind.
> For your steadfast love is before my eyes,
> and I walk in your faithfulness.
> I do not sit with men of *falsehood*,
> nor do I consort with *hypocrites*.

28. *Concise Oxford English Dictionary.*

29. Kim, "Paul's Entry," 540.

I hate the assembly of evildoers,
and I will not sit with the *wicked*.
I wash my hands in innocence
and go around your altar, O LORD,
proclaiming thanksgiving aloud,
and telling all your wondrous deeds. (ESV; emphasis added)

Paul is mostly concerned to show a tight connection between living in righteousness and the intervention of God.

2:5a-d That is to say, we did not come at any time with flattering words, as you know (οὔτε γάρ ποτε ἐν λόγῳ κολακείας ἐγενήθημεν, καθὼς οἴδατε). Paul continues to expand on the antithesis ("what we did not do") in order to show these disciples what a sound pattern for ministry looks like. As with the prayer language in 1:2–3, this is a sweeping statement: "(not) at any time" (ποτε).

The power of "flattering words" might escape today's Western reader, who tends to regard sweet talk with immediate suspicion. Yet in the ancient world flattery could prove to be an effective trick. The fact that God's Word often condemns smooth talk is telling, since its rebukes make sense only in a situation where offenses are likely ("a flattering mouth works ruin," Prov 26:28b; "those who flatter their neighbors are spreading nets for their feet," Prov 29:5).[30] In a society that operates on a system of honor and dishonor, flattering words have a higher probability of luring the recipients into gullibility. In the New Testament, the Pharisees and Herodians try to flatter Jesus into lowering his defenses (Mark 12:14). There is a notable demonstration of flattery and its horrific results in Acts 12:20–23: Herod Agrippa I sits enthroned before the crowds of Tyre and Sidon and gives a speech. The people keep shouting "This is the voice of a god, not of a man" (Acts 12:22). Herod dies because he is enticed by their words, blasphemous though they be.[31]

The false prophets in the time of Jeremiah tell the multitude only what it wanted to hear — that the nation is deserving of the good times that are surely coming (Jer 23:17). Paul for his part denounces flattery (Rom 16:18) and promotes integrity in speech (2 Cor 4:2; 1 Tim 4:12; Titus 2:7–8). The apostolic team did not tell the Thessalonians what they wanted to hear; their poor reception in Philippi and in Thessalonica was ample proof that his message was no crowd-pleaser.

"As you know" (καθὼς οἴδατε) is the fourth use of reminder language in the letter; Paul now begins to border on a distracting amount of repetition.

2:5e Not with some pretext for greed (οὔτε ἐν προφάσει πλεονεξίας). The popular pagan philosopher would try to make a living from his words. It was far easier than manual labor; as we might say, "It's indoor work and no heavy lifting." Paul cannot regard that practice as an acceptable career decision; no, if someone preached about the gospel *for the purpose of gain*, it must be labeled greed or "hunger for money" (πλεονεξία). As with the comment about "flattery," the fact that Paul and others keep mentioning this possibility means that it was a credible threat within the primitive church.[32]

This passage does not prohibit Christian work-

30. See also Philo: "And with [unwholesome pleasure] there walk as her most intimate friends, bold cunning, and rashness, and *flattery* (κολακεία), and trick, and deceit, and false speaking" (*Sacrifices* 22, Jonge). Thoughtful philosophers too found fault in obsequious behavior; note Plutarch's essay, where the title says it all: "How to Tell a Flatterer from a Friend," *Mor.* 48E–74E (trans. Babbitt).

31. In his version of this incident, Josephus, employs both κόλαξ ("flatterer") and κολακεία ("flattery"). See *Ant.* 19.8.2 (§345–46).

32. Most of the principal biblical texts that deal with pastoral ministry offer some comment about greed: Acts 20:33–35; 2 Cor 7:2; 1 Tim 3:3; 3:8; Titus 1:7; 1 Pet 5:2. See also the detailed instructions about itinerant teachers in *Did.* 11–13, which warns about these "Christ-traders" (*Did.* 12.5).

ers from receiving financial support, as Paul himself sometimes permitted himself to do, notably from Philippi (2 Cor 11:9; Phil 4:10 – 20). While the line between seeking support and indulging in greed can be a thin one, still the line exists and is biblical. The pastor or missionary must not be driven by gain, must not focus on money, must not seek unreasonable compensation, and must be faithful even when there is a threat of losing support.[33]

2:5f God himself is our witness! (θεὸς μάρτυς). Paul holds back from using reminder language yet a fifth time and calls out to a higher authority, invoking God as "witness." Paul uses the same language in Rom 1:9 and Phil 1:8.

God is the one who has tested and approved of the apostles, and he alone has absolute knowledge of whether someone has greed as a motive. The invoking of God or a god as a witness to human behavior was a longstanding practice. In the Bible, Laban does so with Jacob (Gen 31:49 – 50) and Moses before Israel (Num 16:1 – 40). Levi on his deathbed was said to declare, "The Lord is my witness and his angels are witnesses, and you are witnesses, and I am witness, concerning the word from your mouth" (*T. Lev.* 19.3, ed. Charlesworth). A near parallel to 1 Thess 2:5 is Samuel's invoking of the Lord before the Israelite nation: " 'The Lord is witness against you, and also his anointed [Saul] is witness this day, that you have not found anything in my hand.' 'He is witness,' they said." (1 Sam 12:5). Paul would never have used this language lightly, given his knowledge that God is the living God who will uncover and condemn every lie. In 2:10, Paul will again use reminder language and also invoke God as a witness.[34]

2:6 Not looking for prestige, not from you or from anyone else (οὔτε ζητοῦντες ἐξ ἀνθρώπων δόξαν, οὔτε ἀφ' ὑμῶν οὔτε ἀπ' ἄλλων). Paul has said that his team does not use flattering speech in order to "honor" their hearers, nor are they interested in gaining human "glory" or "honor" or "prestige" (δόξαν).[35] This is consistent with the teaching of Jesus, who disdained human honors (John 5:41, 44; 7:18; 12:43). In a society where personal reputation was of great moment, many philosophers focused on winning the respect of their hearers. The known exceptions, some of the Cynic preachers, were antiestablishment and acted clownishly in order to mock contemporary values. But even they did so to boost their own self-image.

"Not ... not ... or" (οὔτε) shows that Paul and his team are not eager to receive honor from anyone: not from Thessalonian pagans, not from the Jewish synagogue, not from rich leading citizens ... not even from their own converts. This stands in marked contrast with Christian workers throughout the centuries who reject honors from those "outside" the church, but who would be loathe to lose the adulation of those "inside."

Paul's words in 1 Thess 1 – 2 find a striking parallel in Dio Chrysostom, from a speech he gave in Alexandria a half century later. His hearers have no interest in sound teaching because they had previously been turned off by huckstering philosophers:

> But to find a man who in plain terms and without guile speaks his mind with frankness, and neither for the sake of reputation nor for gain makes false pretensions, but out of good will and concern for his fellow-men stands ready, if need be, to submit to ridicule and to the disorder and the uproar of the mob ... I feel that I have chosen that role, not

33. Janet M. Everts offers a superb analysis of Paul's teaching on "Financial Support," *DPL*, 295 – 300.

34. In other contexts, Paul invokes God as witness to his fervent longing for absent friends (Rom 1:9; Phil 1:8; see also Rom 9:1; 2 Cor 1:23; 11:31; Gal 1:20).

35. See BDAG, 257: "honor as enhancement or recognition of status or performance."

of my own volition, but by the will of some deity. (*Oratory* 32, trans. Crosby)

2:7a-b Even though we could have insisted on acting all important and on being a burden to you (δυνάμενοι ἐν βάρει εἶναι). Paul now turns to the hypothetical, that is, how the team *might* have acted differently: "we could have insisted" (δυνάμενοι) is a participle of concession, "even though."[36] "A burden" (ἐν βάρει) with "to be" (εἶναι) is an idiomatic phrase: literally, "throw one's weight around... *wield authority, insist on one's importance.*"[37] This might include financial dependence on the Thessalonians, as it perhaps does in 2 Cor 12:16, where he uses the cognate verb "to be a burden" (καταβαρέω, see 2:3) and declares that he did not (financially?) take advantage of the Corinthians (see also 1 Thess 4:6). According to 1 Thess 2:9 (also 2 Thess 3:8; cf. 2 Cor 11:9), the apostles worked with their hands so as not to financially burden (ἐπιβαρέω) the Thessalonians.

Paul foreshadows the theme that will come up in 1 Cor 9:1 – 27, that while he has certain rights as an apostle, he reserves the right of not availing himself of them (see also Phlm 8 – 9). Acts and the Pauline letters give a picture of Paul who can be bold and unbending on the one hand, but who maintains a light touch when it comes to asserting his own privileges.

2:7c Since we are apostles of Christ (ὡς Χριστοῦ ἀπόστολοι). Paul and Silas are apostles; ὡς is not "as if we were" here but rather "since we are." Given how Paul uses "we," he probably means to include Silas, but not Timothy. The noun "apostle" (ἀπόστολος) appears eighty times in the New Testament; 1 Thess 2:7 may have been its first use in Christian writing.[38] Its core meaning is "delegate" or "envoy," although it also had also gained a new, technical use of "apostle." In the two Thessalonian letters the noun appears only here.

The plural "apostles" is surprising, since one might not expect anyone other than Paul to be so named. Yet the New Testament shows surprising variety with its use of the term. First, there are the Twelve, including Matthias, who followed Christ from the days of John the Baptist and then served as witnesses to his resurrection (Acts 1:20 – 26). The number twelve seems to be fixed, even into eternity (Rev 21:14). But second, there are other Christian envoys who do not fulfill the qualifications of Acts 1, who are not numbered with the Twelve, yet who are designated as apostles because they do the work of a pioneering missionary. These include Silas (1 Thess 2:7), Barnabas (Acts 14:14; perhaps also the implication of 1 Cor 9:5 – 6), Andronicus and Junia (Rom 16:7);[39] and James the brother of the Lord (Gal 1:19). Meanwhile, Epaphroditus (Phil 2:25) and certain "brothers" (2 Cor 8:23) appear to be "representatives" of specific churches but are not necessarily "apostles" in this second category.

Paul is an anomaly. He was neither a follower of Jesus on earth nor an original witness of his resurrection; thus we might be tempted to put him with the second, more generic type of apostle. Yet he makes it clear that he is a witness of the resurrection through a special vision (1 Cor 9:1) and that he does apostolic miracles. In 1 Thess 4:15 he assumes the apostolic prerogative of passing along new doctrine "by an oracle from the Lord"; this is a right he ascribes to apostles in Eph 3:5. He does not claim to be of the Twelve, nor does the New Testa-

36. Wallace, *Grammar*, 634 – 35.

37. BDAG, 167.

38. The cognate "apostolate" (ἀποστολή) occurs only four times; the cognate verb "to send" (ἀποστέλλω) appears 132 times, although its meaning is often general, with no implication of sending out an apostle.

39. That Junia was a woman, and that Paul means to label her and Andronicus as "apostles" is virtually certain; see the standard commentaries on Romans.

ment ever hint that the appointment of Matthias as the twelfth was invalid. We do best to follow Paul's lead and understand him as an exceptional case (1 Cor 15:8), not of the Twelve but equal to them in divine calling.

2:7d No, we took the position of little children among you (ἀλλὰ ἐγενήθημεν ἤπιοι ἐν μέσῳ ὑμῶν). Paul and his team follow the paradigm offered by Jesus, that the least on earth are the greatest in the kingdom. Thus, rather than acting like imposing apostles, they take on the role of small children.

This verse contains the most difficult textual problem in these two letters.[40] Either (1) the apostolic team took the position of "infants" (νήπιοι) or (2) they were "kind/gentle" (ἤπιοι). The reason for the variant is simple: in this sentence, the words sound nearly identical if read aloud and could look deceptively alike to the eye of a copyist. Most versions use "gentle" (ἤπιοι); a few versions have "infant" or "young children" (νήπιοι; NIV, CEV, NLT).

"Kind, gentle" (ἤπιοι) is favored by the great majority of manuscripts, including the Byzantine family. Most of the earliest manuscripts have νήπιοι ("infants"), but many of these were corrected by later scribes to ἤπιοι by the elimination of the letter *nu* (ν). ἤπιοι is accepted by most commentators and most English versions. Chrysostom expounded it the same way: "'But we were gentle,' he says; we exhibited nothing that was offensive or troublesome, nothing displeasing, or boastful."[41]

"Infants" (νήπιοι) is noteworthy for being one of the few changes in the UBS Greek NT between its second and third/fourth editions. "Infants" (νήπιοι) should be accepted as the original reading, following the stronger early manuscript evidence, but also because of the rule of preferring the more difficult reading (*lectio difficilior*) (for detailed proof, see "In Depth: 'Gentle' (ἤπιοι) or 'Infants' (νήπιοι) in 1 Thess 2:7?").[42]

IN DEPTH: "Gentle" (ἤπιοι) or "Infants" (νήπιοι) in 1 Thess 2:7?

A pastor may use the NRSV in the pulpit and read 1 Thess 2:7 as "we were gentle." Members who brought their NIV see "we were like children among you" and might assume that these are just two ways of translating the original. Without an explanatory footnote they won't realize that "gentle" and "children" (or "infants") are translations of two sound-alike but distinct Greek words that appear in the manuscript evidence.

There is one correct answer, since Paul must have dictated one or the other; but was it "gentle" or "infants"? The evidence for these readings is as follows:

40. See Bruce Metzger, ed., *A Textual Commentary on the Greek New Testament* (2nd rev. ed.; New York: United Bible Society, 2005), 561 – 62.

41. See John Chrysostom, *Homilies on First Thessalonians* 2 (*NPNF*[1] 13:330). Abraham J. Malherbe, "'Gentle as a Nurse': the Cynic Background of 1 Thessalonians ii," *NovT* 12 (1970): 203 – 17, argues that Paul uses terms common to Cynic preachers, who valued frank speech but also knew the value of gentleness and of acting as a nurse. Best, *Thessalonians*, 101, also prefers "gentle."

42. Fee, *Thessalonians*, 65 – 71, provides an extensive argument in favor of "infant"; see too Green, *Thessalonians*, 127; Burke, *Family Matters*, 154 – 57. The reader should also refer to the excellent analysis of the textual problem by Jeffrey A. D. Weima, "'But We Became Infants Among You': The Case for ΝΗΠΙΟΙ in 1 Thess 2.7," *NTS* 46 (2000): 547 – 64.

External Evidence (i.e., evidence from the manuscript history)

"Gentle" (ἤπιοι) is attested by most manuscripts, some versions, and possibly Clement of Alexandria. The weighty witnesses are א[2] (Codex Sinaiticus) A C[2] D[2] Ψ, but in all of these except A, the original text "infants" was later changed to "gentle" by a corrector, who crossed out a *nu* (ν) because he believed that an earlier scribe had accidentally miswritten the word. This is denoted by the superscript [2] above the *sigla*. "Gentle" (ἤπιοι) was selected by UBS[2] and NA[25] as the original reading.

"Infants" (νήπιοι) is the reading preferred by UBS[3/4] and NA[26/27] and clearly has the better attestation. It is supported by some 70 manuscripts, including 𝔓[65] א* B C* D*; some versions; a few Byzantine manuscripts. "Infants" (νήπιοι) is supported by the earliest manuscript of 1 Thessalonians: 𝔓[65] is a papyrus scrap from the middle of the third century that contains 1 Thess 1:3–2:1, 6–13. While the testimony of Clement of Alexandria from the second century might be taken as a weighty early witness *against* "infants" (νήπιοι), as it turns out, his testimony is ambiguous.[43]

Internal Evidence (that is, the evidence from the biblical text)

Neither "child" or "gentle" would be out of place in a Pauline letter. The Pauline literature uses "child" (νήπιοι) eleven times (e.g., of his converts as his spiritual children). He does not use it consistently, as some commentators claim, in a demeaning sense of childishness.[44] Paul uses "gentle" (ἤπιοι) only once (2 Tim 2:24), but in an appropriate parallel, to describe a virtue that a Christian teacher should have: "And the Lord's servant... must be *kind* to everyone." Overall, such "considerations of what the author was more likely to have written are... inconclusive"; that is, the internal evidence does not solve the problem.[45]

The discipline of textual criticism asks that we explain how a hypothetical original reading could have given rise to the other(s). Two principles come into play in 2:7. First, *is there a known mechanism to explain how a second reading would have arisen in some manuscripts?* Yes, and a very simple one: if the copyist were reading the exemplar, he might accidentally skip the *nu* (ν) that begins the word "child" (νήπιοι): ΕΓΕΝΗΘΗΜΕ*ΝΝ*ΗΠΙΟΙ would thus be turned into ΕΓΕΝΗΘΗΜΕ*Ν*ΗΠΙΟΙ and the word would be altered to "gentle" (ἤπιοι). Since "gentle" (ἤπιοι) is also a known Greek word, it would look and sound plausible.

43. See Clement of Alexandria, *Paed.* 1.5.19 (*ANF* 2:214). Although he cites 1 Thess 2:7 with the reading "gentle" (ἤπιοι), Clement does not provide a clear testimony: in context, he is speaking about how children need instruction. He then makes a play on words between ἤπιος, νήπιος and νεήπιος (gentle—child—silly): "So then, the child is gentle" (ἤπιος οὖν ὁ νήπιος). Is this simple coincidence, or could Clement's awareness of the variant reading ἤπιος have suggested the play on words?

44. 1 Cor 3:1; Eph 4:14. In 1 Cor 13:11 it describes Christians during this age of partial knowledge; "be as a child" (νηπιάζω) is used of innocence toward evil in 1 Cor 14:20.

45. Metzger, *Textual Commentary*, 561.

It is, however, equally possible that a scribe might double the nu (ν) and turned "gentle" (ἤπιοι) into "little children" (νήπιοι).

The second principle of textual criticism that applies to 2:7 is "the more difficult reading is to be preferred" (*lectio difficilior*): *Is one reading harder to make sense of, without being absurd?* In the case of 2:7, the answer is a clear affirmative: "little children" (νήπιοι, "we became infants among you, like nurse-maids") is significantly more difficult than "gentle" (ἤπιοι, "we were gentle among you, like nurse-maids"). It runs contrary to intuition, but according to *lectio difficilior*, it is not the easier reading that is more likely to be true, but the more difficult. A scribe would be more likely to "correct" an original text "little children" (νήπιοι) to "gentle" (ἤπιοι) with a simple elimination of a *nu* (ν). The question then remains: Is "little children" (νήπιοι) so difficult as to be ridiculous? According to the translators of most English versions, it is, and so they go with "gentle" (ἤπιοι).

Nevertheless, there is mitigating internal evidence that downgrades the reading "infants" (νήπιοι) from "impossible" to "difficult" and thereby presses us to accept the strong manuscript testimony of "infants."

First, it is to be conceded that if the apostle wrote "infants," he would have been jumping from metaphor to metaphor. But Paul was not averse to doing so, and quickly, as even a cursory reading of his letters reveals. *I was a child, now I am an adult; we see in a mirror, then we will see face to face; I know in part, then I will know fully* (1 Cor 13:11 – 12). Not only are these metaphors rapidly shifting, they cannot really be understood as metaphors of the same thing; they do not neatly line up one with each other. Again: *the law is a guardian of you minor children;* no, *you are a slave to the "elements";* no, *the law is Hagar the slave woman and you are her slave children* (Gal 4). In 1 Thess 2 he uses at least two metaphors, wet-nurse and father (1 Thess 2:7 – 8, 11 – 12). Nurses "cherish" their babies, fathers "instruct" children who are past their infancy. Could his argument carry the weight of a third metaphor?

According to our understanding of 2:17 (see commentary), Paul was just about to apply a metaphor of childhood to the apostles. They "were made orphans"; that is, Paul describes their circumstances and the resulting psychological state as being orphaned. Some have interpreted this exactly backwards, as if Paul were saying that the *Thessalonians* had been orphaned from their parents, the apostles; but that is not what Paul wrote. The implied metaphor in 2:17 is that the apostles are children. The point of comparison has now changed from children's lack of guile to the anxiety of small children who cannot see their parents' "faces." Therefore, the question over whether the apostles can be portrayed as wet-nurses, fathers, *and* small children, within a few verses, is a moot one; without doubt they are so described, once one reads through 2:17. What is of greater concern is whether Paul can move from "infants" to "wet-nurses" virtually in the same breath.

Weima points out in other contexts that Paul can begin with one metaphor; that metaphor then reminds Paul of another point of contact, and he pivots rather awkwardly into a second metaphor.[46] For example, in 2 Cor 2:14, Paul and Titus are *chained captives* who are being displayed in a triumphal parade. Paul then turns around and makes them the *incense* that is burned at such processions. It is as if Paul, literally thinking on his feet, offers a metaphor, then says, "Wait, this other works too, and what does it matter if the two images don't fit together with precision?" As a second example, Paul writes: "I am again in the pains of childbirth until Christ is formed in you" (Gal 4:19)—but who is pregnant, the apostle with labor pains or the Galatians in whom Christ is taking form? In comparison with 2 Cor 2 or Gal 4, the leap from "infants" to "nurse" hardly jars the reader: "We were innocent of grown-up machinations and motives, like infants. I say infants, but come to think of it, it's also true that we were like a wet-nurse who takes care of infants." Far from being an absurd movement from one metaphor to another, this sort of rhetoric should truly be labeled as distinctively Pauline and thus a possible reading of 2:7.

On another level, the grammar and the rhetoric of the section indicate that Paul is not developing the previous material when he makes the "wet-nurse" statement, but has moved to another theme. Jeffrey Weima and Gordon Fee have produced detailed work on this section, particularly the rhetoric of 2:3–8 and the use of "as if" (ὡς ἐάν) in 2:7.[47] As noted in the Structure section above, the rhetorical device "antithesis" (*not this, but that*) is one of the outstanding features of the passage; by Weima's count, Paul uses eight such antitheses. The "but that" (ἀλλά) part of the antithesis always concludes the comparison. To properly appreciate Paul's rhythm throughout the section "the ἀλλά in 2.7b, therefore, cannot introduce a new sentence but rather concludes the preceding negative phrases in 2.5–7a."[48] This would lead to a structure of "we took the position of little children among you" as the conclusion to what had gone before, not the introduction to what follows about the wet-nurse. One would put a period after "among you."

Yet another aspect of Paul's style shows that 2:7e does not naturally follow upon the preceding material but marks the start of a new sentence. As Fee points out, the wet-nurse clause is "a (typical) Pauline sentence that begins with

46. Weima, "'But We Became Infants Among You,'" 557.

47. Weima, "'But We Became Infants Among You,'" esp. 554–59; Fee, *Thessalonians*, 65–71.

48. Weima, "'But We Became Infants Among You,'" 556. He refers to his own verse divisions, not mine.

a 'as/thus(so)' contrast." This yields for Fee a translation of: "As a nursing mother cares for her children, so with deep longing we shared with you."[49]

How does this all affect our modern versions of the Greek Testament? While the text of NA[27] (and the UBS[4]) is correct in reading "infants," its punctuation of the verse weakens rather than reinforces that editorial decision. The punctuation of a Greek New Testament has been added by its editors; it is supposed to help the reader by indicating the natural flow of the passage. As rendered in English, NA[27] would read: " ... as apostles of Christ. But we became infants among you, as a nurse cherishes her own little ones." The editors thus unwittingly move the reader from "infants" toward what follows, the wet-nurse metaphor. But in fact, there is no need to put a period after "apostles of Christ." The better choice for NA[27] would have been to use a comma after the "apostles" statement and then put the full stop at the end of the "infants" material: "as apostles of Christ we could have asserted our authority. Instead, we were like young children among you." It would have issued into a new paragraph: "Just as a nursing mother cares for her children, etc." (see the NIV). This is supported by the structure and grammar of the section. A full stop would make the switch from "infants" to "wet-nurse" less abrupt than the quickly changing metaphors of 2 Cor 2:14. What might appear a dubious interpretation to a student who reads the Greek text of 1 Thess 2 clause by clause, following the punctuation of the modern edition, seems more likely when the text is read aloud and the punctuation put to one side.

Therefore, we agree with the critical text, that Paul wrote "little children" (νήπιοι); nevertheless, the punctuation of NA[27] should be amended in order to bracket the "little children" material with what goes before.

What then does Paul mean by becoming like "little children" (νήπιοι)? In Jesus' teaching in Matt 11:25, the "little children" (νήπιοι) are those of humble status who are chosen to receive God's mysteries.[50] Is 1 Thess 2:7 its parallel? In part, although careful attention must be paid to Paul's exact point in 2:4b – 7b: the apostles did not use adult tricks of guile, flattery, and pretext in order to gain human approval. *In this way* they became like little children.[51]

We may picture his point thus: a three-year-old is fighting with another child for possession of a

49. Fee, *Thessalonians*, 66 – 67.

50. Matt 11:25 par.; cf. Matt 21:16; παιδίον (and in Luke, βρέφος) is used to refer to small children in Mark 10:13 – 16.

51. Stephen Fowl analyzes the passage and concludes that Paul wanted to say that the apostles are like infants, that is, are *gentle* and not, like adults, *demanding*. But then Paul, says Fowl, has to backtrack, since infants are very demanding indeed — his metaphor is "in distress" and Paul saves it by turning to a second metaphor, that of a nurse. See his "A Metaphor in Distress: A Reading of ΝΗΠΙΟΙ in 1 Thessalonians 2.7," *NTS* 36 (1990): 472.

toy. He knows what he wants and he does not care that the others have rights as well. That child is not innocent, at least not in the eyes of those who believe in depravity. However, on another level the child *is* free from adult trickery: he does not compliment Mother on her new hairstyle in order to gain favor from those in power; he does not bribe other children to form an alliance; he does not leak accusations about how the other boy is hoarding toys to the detriment of the common good. On this level the child is innocent because he is incapable of executing such gamesmanship. Like the small child, the apostles have nothing to do with the low cunning of the pop philosopher.

Again, we translate the conjunction (ἀλλά) as "no," see above in 2:4. "We were ... in the midst of you" (ἐγενήθημεν ... ἐν μέσῳ ὑμῶν) speaks of behavior, and we paraphrase it as "took the position of ... among you." Paul's point is that they had not gone to the Thessalonians with the garb of apostolic rank, but rather as the socially unprepossessing. The apostolic team evangelized according to God's pattern (2:6 – 7b); so should any would-be Thessalonian evangelists.

2:7e [Or if you please] how a wet-nurse might cherish her very own little ones (ὡς ἐὰν τροφὸς θάλπῃ τὰ ἑαυτῆς τέκνα). As was his style at times (see "In Depth" section, above), Paul abruptly turns the metaphor on its head and explores another aspect of their relationship to the disciples: they became their wet-nurses. It is best to begin a new sentence. Thus the added phrase "or if you please" underscores how Paul is whipping from one metaphor to another. The introductory expression (ὡς ἐάν) means "how" or "as if we were," not as it may sometimes be, the temporal meaning "when, as soon as."

A "nurse" (τροφός) is a woman who breastfeeds children; she is either the mother herself or someone to whom the child was given — to use the older term, a wet-nurse. Since Paul inserts "her very own" (ἑαυτῆς), the second direction fits the flow of thought: it is as if a nurse were nursing, not the children of her employer, but her own babies.[52] The verb "cherish" (θάλπω) is used twice in the NT: here and in Eph 5:29 (where it describes how the husband cherishes the wife). While "little ones" (τέκνα) could refer to offspring of all ages, in this context it refers to the very young. Paul's point is that a nurse would not only love her own children, she would know best how to care for them. The apostle is not averse to using maternal language of his behavior toward his disciples (see 1 Cor 3:1; see the scriptural background in Num 11:12; Isa 66:13).

This attitude nicely parallels what Plutarch would say some decades later, that the sincere friend will speak the truth but will do so kindly: "For a friend is not a dull tasteless thing, nor does the decorum of friendship consist in sourness and austerity of temper, but its very port and gravity is soft and amiable."[53]

2:8a So then, because we had this longing for you (οὕτως ὁμειρόμενοι). Because Paul and his team had maternal longings, they acted in a generous manner. "So then" (οὕτως) may refer to what comes before or to what follows. In this case, it points forward to the main finite verb "we determined." They "had this longing for you" (ὁμειρόμενοι), which in this type of context signifies "a warm inward attachment."[54] Moulton and Milligan state that this rare word may mean a yearning for another person; for example, an inscription on a sepulcher reads that the grieving parents were "greatly desir-

52. See NASB, "as a nursing mother tenderly cares for her own children." Also Fee, *Thessalonians*, 74 – 75; Green, *Thessalonians*, 128.

53. Plutarch, "How to Tell a Flatterer from a Friend" (trans. Goodwin).

54. H. W. Heidland, "ὁμείρομαι," *TDNT*, 5:176.

ing their son."[55] It conveys well the deep maternal feeling of the "nurse."[56] The verb shows the cause for the approach that they took, "because" (διότι) you had become beloved to us" (v. 8e).

2:8b-e We determined to share with you not only the gospel of God, but also our very selves, because you had become beloved to us (ὑμῶν εὐδοκοῦμεν μεταδοῦναι ὑμῖν οὐ μόνον τὸ εὐαγγέλιον τοῦ θεοῦ ἀλλὰ καὶ τὰς ἑαυτῶν ψυχάς, διότι ἀγαπητοὶ ἡμῖν ἐγενήθητε). The team did not march into Thessalonica, drop off a message, and withdraw; they made their very persons available to the new disciples up to the point when they were forced to leave. Verse 8 forms a chiasmus that puts special emphasis on their care for them:

A Because we had this longing for you
  B We determined to share with you
  B′ Not only the gospel of God but also our very selves
A′ Because you had become beloved to us

With regard to "we determined" (εὐδοκέω) BDAG offers: "to consider something as good and therefore worthy of choice, *consent, determine, resolve.*" The team did not merely feel a preference but went on to make a decision. "To share" (μεταδοῦναι) in other contexts may speak of helping the needy, e.g., an orphan sharing in Job's bread (Job 31:17 LXX; cf. Rom 12:8; Eph 4:28). Paul uses it here of the imparting of a spiritual blessing (cf. Rom 1:11).

Again Paul speaks in the negative and then in the positive: "not only ... but also" (οὐ μόνον ... ἀλλὰ [καί]; see also 1:5, 8). "Even" or "also" (καί) heightens Paul's meaning. It is better to render what follows not with "our very souls" (τὰς ἑαυτῶν ψυχάς) but with "our very selves." In Western vocabulary, "soul" might convey some vague intangible part of the person. This is precisely the opposite of what Paul means. "Here the reference is not so much to the giving of physical life in death as to the giving of that which constitutes life, e.g., time, energy, and health."[57] By imparting their "very selves," they worked longer hours and got less sleep as a concrete token of love. "Because" (διότι) shows the cause that lay behind this outpouring of commitment. Not only are the Thessalonians "beloved" by God (1:4), but also by God's emissaries.

2:9a-c For you remember, brothers and sisters, our labor and our hardship, how night and day we worked (μνημονεύετε γάρ, ἀδελφοί, τὸν κόπον ἡμῶν καὶ τὸν μόχθον, νυκτὸς καὶ ἡμέρας ἐργαζόμενοι). Again, this is reminder language. It is one thing for Paul to state in 2:8 that the team loved the disciples; he goes further and triggers a strong visual memory. Educational theorists are fond of saying that we remember 20 percent of what we hear, 50 percent of what we see, and a greater percentage of what we hear *and* see.[58] The mental image of an apostle doing menial labor should have been unusually striking and memorable to a Thessalonian, because it would have created cognitive dissonance. This is the disquieting feeling that comes when one is confronted with contradictory data: *an apostle as a person of authority and dignity clashes with his doing menial labor*. Because of this sense memory, the team's manual labor lingered on as a living parable of their love and commitment.

55. MM, 447.

56. Nevertheless, the verb does not necessarily refer to feelings *toward a person*, as shown in Herodotus, *Hist.* 7.44.1 (Godley) — "[Xerxes] desired to see the ships contend in a race."

57. E. Schweizer, "ψυχή (New Testament)," *TDNT*, 9:648. See too G. Harder, "Soul," *NIDNTT*, 3:683.

58. The actual percentages that are given vary from person to person, since these data seem to be passed along by word of mouth. Nevertheless, there is broad consensus that visual memories are more lasting than audible, and that a combination of sensory input (hearing, seeing, smelling, touching) plus actual participation by the learner provides the most lasting memories.

"For" (γάρ) again (see 2:1; 3:3) points to what follows. Paul has already used the word "labor" (κόπον) to describe what the Thessalonians did (1:3). "Hardship" (μόχθον) appears three times in his letters (2 Cor 11:27; 1 Thess 2:9; 2 Thess 3:8) as half of a dyad; "labor and hardship" can be paraphrased as "hard labor." On Paul's missionary tours, hard labor was always present, whether in his teaching work or in his manual labor. In 2 Thess 3:6 – 15, Paul will deal with those in the church who have not imitated his dedication to hard work.

The genitive "night and day" (νυκτὸς καὶ ἡμέρας) denotes the kind of time, not its duration: "Paul is not suggesting here that he and his colleagues were working 24-hour shifts among the Thessalonians, but that they labored both in daytime and nighttime."[59] He reminds them again of their work "night and day" as an example to the believers in 2 Thess 3:8. Paul speaks elsewhere of erratic sleep (2 Cor 11:27, "[I] have often gone without sleep"; see also 1 Cor 4:12). His prayer ministry ate into his sleep (2 Tim 1:3, again with genitives of time). He also taught "night and day" (Acts 20:31).

We do not know at what Paul and his team "worked" in Thessalonica. The brevity of their stay probably means that he did not have time to set up a leatherworking shop. Perhaps he, Silas, and Timothy took whatever work was available. Later Paul joined with Priscilla and Aquila in the leatherworking trade in Corinth (Acts 18:3), which arrangement was perhaps in place as he wrote 1 Thessalonians. The second-century AD Rabban Gamaliel was attributed with the saying, "Fitting is learning in Torah along with a craft, for the labor put into the two of them makes one forget sin. And all learning of Torah which is not joined with labor is destined to be null and cause sin."[60] Although Jewish rabbis respected manual labor, it was considered menial among the Greeks, especially among people with dreams of being accepted as philosophers. Thus Paul's decision to follow the rabbinic ethos had both economic (2:9b) and social implications in this Hellenistic environment. He was deliberately throwing status points to the winds; "he was stepping down the social ladder for the sake of Christ."[61]

2:9d So as not to be a burden to any of you (πρὸς τὸ μὴ ἐπιβαρῆσαί τινα ὑμῶν). That is, Paul's work also had a pastoral as well as pragmatic purpose. The infinitive with this preposition and article (πρὸς τό) is not common in the New Testament; in this case, it shows the purpose of their continual labor.[62] "Not to be a burden" (μὴ ἐπιβαρῆσαι, from ἐπιβαρέω) in this statement and its echo in 2 Thess 3:8 and 2 Cor 11:9 refer to burdening a church financially. The simple verb "burden" (βαρέω) has a similar meaning in 1 Tim 5:16, where the church is burdened by a widow who should rely on other resources. While the church in Thessalonica seems to have included members from across the social spectrum, Paul does not propose to burden "any of you," whether rich or poor.

2:9e That's how we proclaimed to you the gospel of God (ἐκηρύξαμεν εἰς ὑμᾶς τὸ εὐαγγέλιον τοῦ θεοῦ). Here Paul moves to a positive declaration of how he preached. "Preach" or "proclaim" (κηρύσσω) means to announce a message, as in the synagogue (Acts 15:21; Rom 2:21), but we must not restrict this to a formal address delivered from a pulpit. The verb may refer to any sort of public proclamation.

59. Wallace, *Grammar*, 124.

60. *m.* ʾ*Abot* 2:2 A-B (trans. Neusner).

61. See Ben Witherington III, *The Acts of the Apostles: A Socio-Rhetorical Commentary* (Grand Rapids: Eerdmans, 1998), 547. See also Ronald F. Hock, *The Social Context of Paul's Ministry: Tentmaking and Apostleship* (Philadelphia: Fortress, 1980).

62. See BDF §402 (5).

2:10a-b You are witnesses — and so is God! (ὑμεῖς μάρτυρες καὶ ὁ θεός). As in 2:5, he invokes both the Thessalonians and heaven as witnesses. For one who believes that God's wrath will fall on the deceitful (2 Thess 2:10), this is risky business, if he is not sure that he is telling the truth.

2:10c-e That we were pleasing [to God], right and blameless with you who came to believe (ὡς ὁσίως καὶ δικαίως καὶ ἀμέμπτως ὑμῖν τοῖς πιστεύουσιν ἐγενήθημεν). No matter how odd their technique appeared to the citizens of Thessalonica, God held it with high regard. Again, Paul uses "we were" (from γίνομαι) to describe their behavior, as in 1:5; 2:7.

Paul uses a triad of adverbs here. In order to avoid awkward English, the Greek adverbs are best translated as adjectives. "That" (ὡς) is not "how," but rather a marker of discourse content (see BDAG) showing to what it is that they and God witnessed. We have added "to God," which is implicit from the context and from the use of "pious = pleasing to God" (ὁσίως appears only here in the NT; 1 Tim 2:8 and Titus 1:8 use the adjectival form). "Right" (δικαίως) reflects a key word group of the Greek Bible, referring to being right/righteous before God. "Blameless" (ἀμέμπτως) is not common in the LXX, but its adjective cognate does make an appearance to describe Abram (Gen 17:1) and Job (Job 1:1). The triad implies that Paul and his team are (vertically) in the right, and that this rightness expresses itself (horizontally) toward the disciples. The apostolic team is in all ways "above reproach."[63] Once again, we have seen how the apostles are models to these evangelistic disciples, for they too were a pattern toward all those who believe.

2:11 Just as you know, how we were with each one of you, as a father with his own sons and daughters (καθάπερ οἴδατε ὡς ἕνα ἕκαστον ὑμῶν ὡς πατὴρ τέκνα ἑαυτοῦ). Paul now turns to his third family metaphor, how they were like fathers to the new disciples. "Just as" (καθάπερ) is relatively frequent in Paul (twelve occurrences; apart from him, only in Heb 4:2). As a comparison conjuction it is aptly used in this new instance of reminder language. "Each one" (ἕνα ἕκαστον) is followed by "of you" (ὑμῶν, a partitive genitive). The fatherhood metaphor is more typical of Paul than the metaphors in 2:7 (note, e.g., 1 Cor 4:15: "Even if you have ten thousand guardians in Christ, you do not have many fathers, for in Christ Jesus I became your father through the gospel").[64] It is comparable to the work of God himself: "As a father has compassion on his children, so the Lord has compassion on those who fear him" (Ps 103:13). In Judaism and in the Greco-Roman world, it was expected that a father would give moral instruction to his sons. "Sons and daughters" (τέκνα) may refer to male and female offspring, from babies through adulthood (cf. also John 1:12).

2:12a-c That's how we entreated you, that's how we comforted you, that's how we implored you (παρακαλοῦντες ὑμᾶς καὶ παραμυθούμενοι καὶ μαρτυρόμενοι). The readers are not left to imagine what an ideal father is like in Paul's mind. We have translated this triad of participles in a staccato manner, to match Paul's tone. The first, "entreated" (παρακαλοῦντες), is a cognate to their guileless "entreaty" (παράκλησις) in 2:3. Its direct object "you" is the assumed object of all three verbs. "Comforted" (παραμυθούμενοι) is used again in 5:14 to

63. Leon Morris, *Thessalonians* (TNTC; Grand Rapids: Eerdmans, 1984), 22.

64. See also 2 Cor 12:14; Gal 4:19; cf. John in 3 John 4. Pierre Chantraine, ed., *Dictionnaire étymologique langue grecque: histoire des mots* (4 vols.; Paris: Klincksieck, 1968–80), 415, dismisses the viewpoint that πατήρ in 2:11 was meant to contrast with νήπιοι in 2:7, that is, fatherly *versus* childish. Along those lines, Bruce, *1 & 2 Thessalonians*, 36, provides a few Homeric examples of "gentle (ἤπιος) as a father." See also P. Beasley-Murray, "Pastor, Paul as,"*DPL*, 654–58.

speak of encouragement for those whose stamina is flagging; the gift of prophecy can also bring "comfort" (1 Cor 14:3).[65] "Implored" (μαρτυρόμενοι, from μαρτύρομαι, not to be confused "to testify," μαρτυρέω) is found in Paul's letters (here; Gal 5:3; Eph 4:17) and also in his mouth in Acts (Acts 20:26; 26:22). It may take the meaning of "to testify"; here "implore" is better, for it captures the strong emotion of the verse.

2:12d-e To walk worthy of the God who called you into his own glorious kingdom (εἰς τὸ περιπατεῖν ὑμᾶς ἀξίως τοῦ θεοῦ τοῦ καλοῦντος ὑμᾶς εἰς τὴν ἑαυτοῦ βασιλείαν καὶ δόξαν). God's call to the Thessalonians and the coming of the kingdom define the Christian's existence. In order to do justice to the divine call and to the kingdom, the Thessalonians must learn from the apostles to "walk worthy." The grammatical construction (εἰς τό + the infinitive) is in this context not an infinitive of purpose; rather, the verb "implore" with this construction means "implore someone to do something." "Walk" (περιπατεῖν) is language typical in Hebrew (*hālak*) and in biblical and nonbiblical Greek (see LSJ) to denote a way of life.

How does a Thessalonian "walk worthy"? Among other points, by imitating Paul and his team, in the areas that he mentions in 1 Thess 2. "The God who called you" uses the present participle (καλοῦντος). Contrary to one fallacious idea, the present participle does not specify that the time of this call is present (thus, "God who is now calling you").[66] I have rendered it as the past tense, to make it match its parallel in 2 Thess 2:14 ("God *called* you ... through the gospel we preached"; see also 1 Thess 4:7).

Paul then defines the goal of the disciples: not only their rescue from God's wrath, but positively their deliverance into his kingdom.[67] The phrase (lit.) "the kingdom and the glory" (τὴν ... βασιλείαν καὶ δόξαν) is a hendiadys, the use of "and" (καί) for the "co-ordination of two ideas, one of which is dependent on the other" — thus yielding a meaning like "his glorious kingdom."[68] Most take the kingdom reference to be eschatological; Plummer opts for a present meaning, "the existing spiritual kingdom which the Thessalonians had already entered," which interpretation would make 2:12 a parallel to Col 1:13.[69] But the evidence points firmly toward the eschatological: "glory" is code for the future manifestation of God's reign (see Matt 25:31; Rom 5:2; 8:17 – 18; Col 3:4; 2 Thess 2:14).

Verse 12 is markedly similar to 2 Thess 1:5, and together they are Paul's only two positive references to entering the kingdom. "God's kingdom" in 2 Thess 1:5 is "his own ... kingdom" in 1 Thess 2:12. Both times Paul refers to the eschatological age into which the church will enter having escaped God's judgment. Paul used the phrase "will [not] inherit the kingdom of God" in his evangelism and instruction (in 1 Cor 6:9 – 10; cf. 15:50; Gal 5:19 – 21; Eph 5:5).[70] While that catchphrase might impress a modern reader as some generic Jewish formula, the parallels indicate that it was probably of the apostle's own composition. "Will

65. See G. Braumann, "παραμυθέομαι," *NIDNTT*, 1:328 – 29.

66. As thinks Fee, *Thessalonians*, 83, following Best, *Thessalonians*, 108. Although Best's commentary has some fine insights, his handling of the Greek verb is disappointing.

67. See the overview in L. J. Kreitzer, "Kingdom of God/ Christ," *DPL*, 524 – 26.

68. On hendiadys, see BDF §442 (16). If "kingdom and glory" sounds reminiscent of the Matthean Lord's Prayer — "yours is the kingdom and the power and the glory" — it does not imply a Pauline dependence on this prayer, since the closing benediction seems only to have been added to the text as late as the late fourth century.

69. Plummer, *First Thessalonians*, 28.

70. There are a number of references to the future kingdom in the other New Testament books and in the Apostolic Fathers, for example, Acts 14:22; Heb 12:28; Jas 2:5; 2 Pet 1:11; Rev 11:15; 12:10; *1 Clem.* 50.3; *2 Clem.* 5.5; 9.6; *Did.* 10.5; *Mart. Pol.* 20.2; *Barn.* 21.1; Herm. *Sim.* 9.12.3; *Diogn.* 10.2.

not inherit the kingdom" is equal to facing God's "coming wrath" (1 Thess 1:10); 1 Thess 2:12 and 2 Thess 1:5 provide the positive side, being declared "worthy" to enter in.

The New Testament does not distinguish between the "gospel of the kingdom" and the Christian gospel of grace, as some (especially dispensationalists) have imagined. That which Jesus began to teach from the beginning (Matt 4:17, 23) was what he charged his disciples to preach during his days on earth (10:7): that God as King had drawn near in Jesus and was beginning to impose his will on the natural order, human beings, and the spiritual realm (12:28). It is that same gospel, newly seen through the prism of the death and resurrection of Christ that is preached through this age (24:14; Acts 1:3).

Acts regularly labels the Christian message with kingdom language (Acts 8:12; 14:22; 19:8; 20:25; 28:23, 31; see Col 4:11; Rev 1:9; see also *1 Clem.* 42.3, a text discussed under 1 Thess 1:5). Paul uses specific kingdom terms about a dozen times in his letters, demonstrating that it formed part of his basic instruction of new disciples. It is even arguable that Paul based his language on that of the Olivet Discourse:[71]

- Matt 24:14: "And this gospel of the kingdom will be preached ... and then the end will come"
- 1 Thess 2:12: "[We preached that you] walk worthy of the God who called you into his own glorious kingdom"
- 1 Thess 2:16 "[God's] wrath has come upon them unto the end"

2:13a So, for this reason, we give thanks to God without fail (Καὶ διὰ τοῦτο καὶ ἡμεῖς εὐχαριστοῦμεν τῷ θεῷ ἀδιαλείπτως). Paul turns once again to thanksgiving, with echoes of 1:2, and gives out more details of the Thessalonians' "imitation." "So, for this reason" resembles 3:5, which likewise directs the readers' attention to what follows in the context.[72] Paul and his team give thanks that the Thessalonians received the word of God, the very thing for which they were grateful in 1:4 – 5. The use of the personal pronoun "we" as the subject of "we give thanks," along with the reappearance of "without fail" (ἀδιαλείπτως), is especially appropriate: 2:13 marks the end of an *inclusio* (the use of similar words to "bookend" the discussion of a theme) that began in 1:2 with "we give thanks."

2:13b Because when you received the proclaimed word from us, [that is, the word] of God (ὅτι παραλαβόντες λόγον ἀκοῆς παρ' ἡμῶν τοῦ θεοῦ). Paul develops why they give thanks, using the causal "because" (ὅτι). He reaches back to the introductory thanksgiving and once again underscores that when they received the word, God was working in a supernatural way. "When you received" (παραλαβόντες) is here and other contexts the language of oral tradition, used also by Paul of his teaching of new believers.[73] "Proclaimed" (ἀκοῆς) is a common Greek word, but not easy to render in English: BDAG rightly offers "the word of proclamation" for λόγον ἀκοῆς (see also Heb 4:2). The phrase "of God" (τοῦ θεοῦ) describes that message: Paul has delayed it to the end of the clause, hence giving it greater emphasis.

2:13c-d You received it, not as a human message, but as what it really is, the word of God (ἐδέξασθε οὐ λόγον ἀνθρώπων ἀλλὰ καθώς ἐστιν ἀληθῶς λόγον θεοῦ). Paul comes back to the theme of 1:8 – 10, how the Thessalonians received the

71. So agrees David Wenham, *The Rediscovery of Jesus' Eschatological Discourse* (Gospel Perspectives 4; Sheffield: JSOT, 1984), 283.

72. BDF §442(12). So most versions, especially the NJB: "Another reason why we continually thank God for you is...."

73. 1 Thess 4:1; 2 Thess 3:6; cf. 1 Cor 11:23; 15:1, 3; Gal 1:9, 12; Phil 4:9.

gospel. The verse begins to become redundant,[74] with its repetition of "God," but that is not unusual for this emotionally charged letter and Paul's insistence on God's intervention. The gospel has a divine origin (Gal 1:11). There is again the Pauline stylistic contrast ("not this, but that") with "but" (ἀλλά). He again hearkens back to the beginning of the letter (1:5, "not simply as words that we spoke, but also with miracles"). "Word of God" in this section does not refer to the Bible as a book, but rather to God's message as contained in the gospel. As the apostle would say in Rom 10:17, "Consequently, faith comes from hearing the message, and the message is heard through the word about Christ."

2:13e The same [word] that is active in you believers (ὃς καὶ ἐνεργεῖται ἐν ὑμῖν τοῖς πιστεύουσιν). "The same [word]" (ὅς καί) has as its antecedent "the word of God" (λόγον θεοῦ), the relative pronoun changing to the nominative so as to form the subject of the clause. The Thessalonians had faith in God (1:3, 8; see 2 Thess 1:10), and the gospel message did a mighty work in them (1:5; see Rom 1:16; Phil 2:13). This is rooted in a prophetic theme, epitomized in Isa 55:11: "so is my word that goes out from my mouth: It will not return to me empty, but will accomplish what I desire and achieve the purpose for which I sent it." In their turn, the Thessalonians are now responsible to pray that Paul has the same kind of success as he goes on to preach in Achaia (2 Thess 3:1; also Eph 6:19 – 20). The gospel is not a series of philosophical chats, but a message through which the King himself changes lives.

2:14a-b You became imitators, brothers and sisters, of God's churches in Judea, [which are] in Christ Jesus (ὑμεῖς γὰρ μιμηταὶ ἐγενήθητε, ἀδελφοί, τῶν ἐκκλησιῶν τοῦ θεοῦ τῶν οὐσῶν ἐν τῇ Ἰουδαίᾳ ἐν Χριστῷ Ἰησοῦ). Paul expands on the imitation motif, but in a direction that the first-time reader may find puzzling: they follow the pattern of Judean churches. This section is not a later insertion or a digression on Paul's part (see the Introduction). It clearly parallels the material in chapter 1: the Thessalonian idol worshipers received the gospel; the Jews in Judea did not; rather, the unbelieving Jews brutally treated all Christians, going so far as to try to prevent the spread of the gospel.

We translate the verb as "you became" (ἐγενήθητε, as in 1:6, 7); that is, when God acted in them, they became followers of the pattern of persecution that had been in place in Jerusalem and Judea. "Of the churches" (τῶν ἐκκλησιῶν) is an objective genitive, linked with the action noun "imitators"; that is, *you imitated the churches*. Paul does not mean to imply that the Thessalonians set out to imitate these other believers; the imitation is of the order that "your experience resembles theirs." These are "God's churches,"[75] part of a network of congregations that now comprise his true people (see 2 Thess 1:4). Paul uses the phrase "church *of God*" several times in connection with persecution, perhaps to emphasize that to persecute the church is to withstand God himself; so might a former student of Gamaliel have reasoned (Acts 5:39; 9:4 – 5).[76]

The phrase "in Christ Jesus" or "in Christ" is common in Paul (approx. eighty-eight times) and may be regarded as a key to a concept of equality in Christ: "There is neither Jew nor Gentile ... for you are all one in Christ Jesus"; "in Christ Jesus neither circumcision nor uncircumcision has any value" (Gal 3:28; 5:6). Paul does not speak in terms of a Gentile church in Macedonia and a Jewish one in

74. Literally, "when you received the proclaimed word from us of God, you received it not as the word of humans but just as it truly is the word of God."

75. Compare with the language of Acts 20:28; 2 Cor 1:1; 1 Tim 3:5.

76. For the same idea, see also 1 Cor 15:9; Gal 1:13; 2 Thess 1:4.

Judea; their race and geography are less important than their shared identity. It just happens that the Judean church is the archetype of other suffering congregations.

2:14c-d Because you also endured the same things from your fellow countrymen that they suffered from the Judeans (ὅτι τὰ αὐτὰ ἐπάθετε καὶ ὑμεῖς ὑπὸ τῶν ἰδίων συμφυλετῶν καθὼς καὶ αὐτοὶ ὑπὸ τῶν Ἰουδαίων). Their imitation of the Judean churches consists in suffering at the hands of their own people. The compound noun "fellow-countrymen" is a *hapax legomenon* in the New Testament. We take this as a reference to Thessalonians who reject the gospel; naturally they are primarily Gentiles.

Paul does not simply give a report of the historical data but also an interpretation of those events through the lens of Jesus' teaching. Matthew 10:16–25 gives a detailed prediction; the disciples will be handled over to councils (lit., "sanhedrins") and synagogues, flogged by Jews, and turned over to Roman governors. There is hatred, even by family members. The parallel in Luke 21:12 mentions being put in prisons. Paul's experiences matched these predictions precisely.

Paul uniformly uses "the Judean" (ὁ Ἰουδαῖος) to mean "Jew." Yet a more fitting translation in this special case is "the Judeans" (τῶν Ἰουδαίων). Paul is not concerned primarily with their religion but with their region: Thessalonians suffer at the hands of Thessalonians, while the churches in "Judea" (2:14a) are persecuted by Judeans.[77] When Jews or Gentiles receive Christ, they find themselves cut off from their former people and persecuted by them. This is the main theme of 1 Peter, summed up in 4:4: "[The heathen] are surprised that you do not join them in their reckless, wild living, and they heap abuse on you." Yet beyond this, underlying Paul's statement is the logic of from the lesser to the greater (*a minore ad maius*): if the people of the covenant act this way when their fellow Jews receive Christ, then imagine the reaction of the Gentiles among whom you live.

2:15a Those who killed the Lord Jesus and the prophets (τῶν καὶ τὸν κύριον ἀποκτεινάντων Ἰησοῦν καὶ τοὺς προφήτας). After looking at 2:16, we will ask whether Paul is being anti-Semitic. From the outset the reader must recognize that Paul is not speculating about race but is responding to a concrete historical situation. The synagogue wielded great power in Judea and enough in Macedonia to cause serious persecution to the Christians there.[78]

Like a prophet of old, Paul is building a case against his own nation, naming their iniquities, each one of which is worthy of divine wrath.[79]

77. The NKJV, unusually for a traditionalist version, renders it "the Judeans." The CEV translates "by their people," which captures Paul's intent but not his language.

78. See the thought-provoking analysis by Frank D. Gilliard, "The Problem of the Antisemitic Comma between 1 Thessalonians 2.14 and 15," *NTS* 35 (1989): 481–502. Gillard notes that Paul uses the second attributive order of the participles. He compares its use here with the other instance of the second attributive in 1 Thessalonians. He then proposes, based on the analogy of the other passages, that no comma should be placed between "Jews" in 2:14 and "who killed" in 2:15; thus, Paul's condemnation is not directed at "the Jews" but "the-Jews-who-killed-Jesus, etc." This is similar to the NLT, "*some of* the Jews even killed the Lord Jesus." On this point, Gilliard is affirmed by Markus Bockmuehl, "1 Thessalonians 2:14–16 and the Church in Jerusalem," *TynBul* 52 (2001): 11. For our part, we agree with Gilliard that there is no call for adding this comma; for example, in 2:14 he has just referred to "the churches in Judea" (τῶν ἐκκλησιῶν ... τῶν οὐσῶν) and the comma is not appropriate after "churches" in that case either. Yet the other examples of the second attributive position (1 Thess 1:10; 2:4; 2:12; 4:5; 4:17; 5:9–10) do not seem to follow the same rule, and so they weaken rather than support his case. See also Gilliard, "Paul and the Killing of the Prophets in 1 Thess. 2:15," *NovT* 36 (1994): 259–70.

79. See Schlueter, *Filling Up the Measure*, 111–85, who analyzes the use of prophetic hyperbole in 1 Thessalonians.

First, they "killed the Lord Jesus." Whether or not the Jews physically executed Jesus was moot, since the church saw in their complicity with the Romans a participation in that crime.[80]

The Judeans also killed "prophets." The question is wide open: Are these Christian prophets, or prophets of the old covenant?[81] One should begin with a parallel in the Synoptic tradition: given Paul's affinity with the Matthean tradition, in particular Matt 23 – 24, he almost certainly is echoing Jesus' lament in Matt 23:29 – 36 = Luke 11:47 – 51. Jesus called the residents of Jerusalem the "descendants of those who murdered the prophets" (Matt 23:31; cf. 5:12). So, is not Paul referring to OT prophets? It is not so easy, since to this Jesus added, "I am sending you prophets" (Matt 23:34). These are surely Christian prophets, since Jerusalem "will" (future tense) kill and crucify them. Therefore, Paul could have had Matt 23 in mind and still meant *either* Israel's prophets *or* prophets after Pentecost.

The evidence for their being OT prophets is this: (1) there is no reference to the murder of any particular Christian prophet in Acts or the Pauline letters, although perhaps Stephen, a man full of the Spirit, should count as one (Acts 6:5); (2) the tradition that Israel killed its prophets was a commonplace (Neh 9:26; see also 2 Chr 36:15 – 16; Jer 2:30); (3) Acts 7:52 implies that Paul/Saul had heard Stephen saying that Israel killed its prophets.[82]

In favor of Christian prophets, the two times Paul mentions prophecy in these letters he is thinking of Christian charismatics (1 Thess 5:19 – 22; likely 2 Thess 2:2). Even more important, the order in the Greek of 2:14 – 15 seems to place the prophets firmly in the *now*:

> God's churches in Judea
> The Lord Jesus
> *Prophets*
> Us

While either answer is suitable, the weight of the evidence tilts toward these being Christian prophets.[83] It is worth noting that at least one Judean Christian prophet was well-known to the Thessalonians: Silas himself (see Acts 15:32). In another setting, the whole world is guilty of shedding "the blood of your holy people and your prophets" (Rev 16:6).

2:15b-d And persecuted us, and do not live pleasing to God, and are hostile to all (καὶ ἡμᾶς ἐκδιωξάντων, καὶ θεῷ μὴ ἀρεσκόντων, καὶ πᾶσιν ἀνθρώποις ἐναντίων). Paul pushes the argument to its logical outcome: the Jews had persecuted their own Lord, Christian prophets, and now "us." Who is included in this group, and how did they persecute "us"? Many commentators gloss over the historical fact of persecution in the early church, but according to Acts 4:3, their trouble began from the earliest days. In the grandest of ironies, Paul was the Jew who was most notable for persecuting the church within its first decade.[84] His was no mere bureaucratic mission, but a crusade of hate: "I was so obsessed with persecuting them that I even hunted them down in foreign cities" (Acts 26:11). The church ended up being scattered from Jerusalem to other locations in the northeast Mediterranean. In another supreme irony, the persecution in

80. "You [Israelites], with the help of wicked men, put him to death" (Acts 2:23; see also 3:15; 4:10; 5:28; 7:52). Paul blames the Romans also for Jesus' death in 1 Tim 6:13.

81. A textual variant in D and in Marcion adds "their own" to "prophets" (ἰδίους, so also TR, KJV, NKJV), which makes them the OT prophets. But the manuscript evidence speaks decisively toward its omission.

82. Favoring the view that these are the OT prophets: Best, *Thessalonians*, 115; Wanamaker, *Thessalonians*, 114; Green, *Thessalonians*, 144.

83. See esp. Fee, *Thessalonians*, 97 – 98.

84. In his testimony, Paul regularly made reference to his role as persecutor; see Acts 22:4 – 5; 26:9 – 11; 1 Cor 15:9; Gal 1:13 – 14; Phil 3:6; 1 Tim 1:13.

which Saul participated served to spread the gospel to Jews of other regions and then to Gentiles (Acts 11:19).[85]

Paul's reference to "us" is not simply a token of his solidarity with persecuted Judean Christians; he himself had faced risk from Judeans. There is the briefest reference in Acts 9:29 that Hellenistic Jews plotted to murder him after his conversion; Acts 22:17–21 is an account of the same event, where Jesus in a vision warns him to flee Jerusalem. Nor should Silas's experiences in Judea be overlooked; he was known as one of the "men who have risked their lives" for the gospel (15:26–27) and was, of course, in favor of the Gentile mission that Jews tried to hinder. As for the third member of the team, Timothy apparently had not visited Judea or been persecuted there.

"Do not live pleasing to God" (θεῷ μὴ ἀρεσκόντων) is the foil to 2:4 ("striving to please ... God"): Paul, Silas, and Timothy, all Jews themselves, are pleasing to God, while the nation of Israel as a whole is not. Some have wondered whether "hostile to all" (πᾶσιν ἀνθρώποις ἐναντίων) is boilerplate anti-Jewish slander. Diaspora Jews were widely regarded as misanthropic, in part due to their ritual separation from the Gentiles. Said Tacitus in the early second century: "Among themselves they are inflexibly honest and ever ready to shew compassion, though they regard the rest of mankind with all the hatred of enemies."[86] The Alexandrian Apion was a contemporary of Paul. According to Josephus, he wrote an anti-Jewish book in the 40s and repeated a libel, "when he mentions an oath of ours, as if we 'swore by God, the maker of the heaven, and earth, and sea, to bear no good will to any foreigner, and particularly to none of the Greeks.'"[87] Whether or not anti-Semitism yet existed as an abstract idea, the fact remains that the Jews tended to stand out in the Hellenistic world, and because of their "otherness" many people could not abide them.

Was Paul then trading on popular prejudice, baiting the Jews so as to build up the self-esteem of Gentile Christians? Not at all; again, he is referring to concrete historical experiences. Given that the next participle is not preceded by a conjunction "and" (καί), it is probable that the "hindering" (κωλυόντων) in v. 16 is meant to define and expand on "hostile to all" (see exposition of 2:16). Paul is thinking of the Jews' demonstrable antipathy to Gentile evangelism rather than making a sociological slur: "they are hostile to all people, in that they hinder us from evangelizing them."[88]

2:16a-b By hindering us from speaking to the Gentiles so that they might be saved (κωλυόντων ἡμᾶς τοῖς ἔθνεσιν λαλῆσαι ἵνα σωθῶσιν). As noted above, this phrase unpacks "hostile to all." "Hindering" (κωλυόντων) is not necessarily an official decree; it is the same word used of the disciples' blocking of the children who wanted to be with Jesus in Matt 19:14, but the similar application of the verb is probably coincidental. "To the Gentiles" (τοῖς ἔθνεσιν) could be rendered "to the nations," but "Gentiles" better conveys the prejudicial use of the term and is found in most English versions.

Who is being "hindered" in this clause? Is the "us" (ἡμᾶς) a reference to his missionary team,

85. Bockmuehl ("1 Thessalonians 2:14–16," 18–28) goes so far as to say that there had just been a persecution in Judea during the years AD 48–49. His argument, however, is largely inferential from these verses. Similar to Bockmuehl, see Wanamaker, *Thessalonians*, 113; also Robert Jewett, "The Agitators and the Galatian Congregation," *NTS* 17 (1970–71): 204–6; Jewett thinks that there was an especially strong circumcizing movement in the late 40s, but again the evidence is unconvincing.

86. Tacitus, *Hist.* 5.5 (trans. Church and Brodribb).

87. Josephus, *Ag. Ap.* 2.1.11 (§122).

88. So too Green, *Thessalonians*, 146, giving approval to the NIV (1984): "hostile to all men *in their effort to* keep us from speaking to the Gentiles" (emphasis added).

Jewish Christians, or Christians in general? When and how did they try to hinder "us" from speaking to the Gentiles about the gospel? What was their motive; is it implied by the "so that" (ἵνα) clause, that "in order that Gentiles not be saved, they hindered us from speaking"?[89]

From the earliest, there was official sanction against the disciples by the Jewish leaders (Acts 4:17–21), who ordered them to stop preaching Jesus. The Sadducean leadership of the temple persecuted the apostles because of an implied accusation (*you have rejected God's Messiah*), because of an anti-Sadducean doctrine (*God raised him from the dead*), and because they were evangelizing other Jews (Acts 4:2). Saul attacked the church (8:1–3) before the first Gentile (ch. 10) and even the first Samaritan (ch. 8) had been evangelized. That is, the early persecutions were a strictly intramural affair in Israel. It is likely that Saul's zeal was aroused because he saw that the gospel might lead to a deprecation of the Torah among Jewish — not Gentile — believers.

The evangelism of Cornelius (see Acts 11:2–3) and Paul and Barnabas's first journey attracted the attention of some reactionary Christians who insisted that Gentiles must enter the Mosaic covenant in order to be saved (15:1, 5). These "Judaizers" would dog Paul for the rest of his ministry. Yet Paul's language in 1 Thessalonians is not targeted against Judaizers, who did not so much block Gentile evangelism as preach that the converts then take on themselves the yoke of the Torah.

The best explanation of this "hindering" is that the non-Christian leaders of synagogues, first in Judea and later in the Diaspora, threw obstacles in the way of Christians when they wished to speak to God-fearers or to pagans about the gospel. This is precisely what happened in Thessalonica (Acts 17:5; see also 13:45–51), and it particularly affected Paul, whose method was to do his initial evangelism in the synagogue to try to win Jews and God-fearing Gentiles.

2:16c For so their sins were at all times such as to warrant [God's wrath] (εἰς τὸ ἀναπληρῶσαι αὐτῶν τὰς ἁμαρτίας πάντοτε). Paul declares with prophetic authority that the Jews' rejection of the gospel both for themselves and for others would lead them to God's eschatological wrath. Verse 16 b-c does not yield to quick and easy interpretation. One should start with "for so" (εἰς τό), which introduces an infinitive of result; we have paraphrased "such as to warrant" (ἀναπληρῶσαι) a form that may more literally mean "to fill up" or "make complete." The accusative "sins" is the subject of the infinitive (contra BDAG).

This statement seems cryptic because Paul depends on his hearers being able to recall the language of the OT; we mark the clause as a definite scriptural allusion. Genesis 15:16 speaks of how the children of Abraham will live in Egypt until the fourth generation, "for the sins of the Amorites are not complete yet [or *up until now*]" (LXX, my translation), that is, have not yet reached the point at which God will judge them. The verse is hard to read literally and is therefore usually rendered in a dynamic fashion:

> for the iniquity of the Amorites is not yet complete (NKJV)
>
> for the sins of the Amorites do not yet warrant their destruction (NLT)

Paul has adapted the Genesis tradition by sub-

89. Todd Still states that "forbid us" refers specifically to the synagogue in Thessalonica and its opposition directed against Paul, Silvanus, and Timothy. But this is an unlikely referent: in this verse Paul's main interest is *Judean* Jews as the counterpart to Thessalonian pagans. See Todd D. Still, *Conflict at Thessalonica: A Pauline Church and Its Neighbors* (JSNTSup 183; Sheffield: JSOT, 1999), 136.

stituting "always, at all times" (πάντοτε) for "not yet": "with the result that they *always* fill up the measure of their sins" (NASB). The Amorites could count on more time before God's judgment fell on them, but not the Judeans of Paul's day. The measure of their sins is already — has always been! — sufficient to warrant divine judgment. The irony is palpable: in Palestine, righteous Abraham had lived among wicked Amorites, but their sins had not yet reached their limit. Now the Christian saints are living among Abraham's descendants, and it is that Jewish nation that deserves God's immediate wrath.

Paul's language may also recall the Matthean tradition. Jesus says: "Complete what your ancestors started!" (Matt 23:32; see also Dan 8:23, 2 Macc 6:14) in his condemnation of the Jewish religious hierarchy, given immediately before his announcement of the destruction of the temple and other eschatological signs.

2:16d [God's] wrath has come upon them unto the end (ἔφθασεν δὲ ἐπ' αὐτοὺς ἡ ὀργὴ εἰς τέλος). The Judeans will face the destiny that the Thessalonians have escaped through Christ, that is, the divine wrath (ὀργή).[90] While the seriousness of this pronouncement is clear, the reader might be left confused as to its time. The two variables are: (1) What does the verb "has come" (ἔφθασεν) tell us about the time of God's wrath? (2) What does the phrase we have translated "unto the end" (εἰς τέλος) mean?

The verb "came" or "has come" is aorist. A textual variant in B D and the Majority Text has the perfect form; nevertheless, the meanings of the tenses would overlap in this sort of context, and the translation "has come" is suitable either way. Few commentators are confident about the verb's meaning and thus express a variety of possible interpretations. First, Paul (or, as some say, a later author using Paul's name) may be thinking of some recent event, which he took to be a manifestation of divine wrath; it would mean something like "God's wrath *has just* come on them *as we know*." In that case, there is a nice parallel in *T. Levi* 6.11 (see below).[91]

Second, Paul might be looking forward to an imminent parousia or the imminent destruction of Jerusalem; in that case it is "God's wrath has *as good as* come."[92]

Third, this aorist may be the so-called proleptic or futuristic usage, whereby a future event is presented as so certain that one might express it as already accomplished.[93] This usage occurs elsewhere in statements about God's eschatological plan (Heb 4:10; Jude 14; also Rom 8:30, in my opinion). It would yield a meaning of "God's wrath *will come* upon them, *be sure that he will see to it*." Yet the proleptic aorist is rare in the NT, and one wonders whether the readers would have caught Paul's meaning.

A fourth possibility is based on the striking verbal coincidence with Matt 12:28 and Luke 11:20: "But if it is by the Spirit [Luke, 'finger'] of God that I drive out demons, then the kingdom of God has come to you" (the same phrase, ἔφθασεν ἐπ'). The key verbs in Matthew and Luke are not proleptic aorists but represent a past action: the kingdom of God really has drawn near, already, but it is not

90. We supply "God's," which in fact is added in by D and a few other Western manuscripts, but in any event it is implicit from the context.

91. Green, *Thessalonians*, 148 – 49, states that some recent harsh events are glimpses of the final wrath. Others, arguing that the letter was written after AD 70, usually point to the destruction of Jerusalem; see Pearson, "1 Thessalonians 2:13 – 16," 82 – 83.

92. Orchard, "Thessalonians and the Synoptic Gospels," 22; for a variation of this view, Best, *Thessalonians*, 120.

93. Wallace, *Grammar*, 563 – 64.

fully manifest.[94] With his fondness for Matthean tradition, Paul has perhaps picked up this use of the verb and applied it to the dark side of eschatology: God is already angry at you who reject Christ and even impede the gospel; given your rebellion, God always (πάντοτε) has just cause to be full of wrath.

This fourth option makes as good sense of the verb as other interpretations; it even has a parallel with the difficult verb of Rom 1:18: "The wrath of God is being revealed from [ἀποκαλύπτεται] heaven against all [Gentile] godlessness."[95] Paul also uses the same verb and tense in Rom 1:17 to describe the revelation of divine righteousness. In this age of the gospel, both saving righteousness and damning wrath are "out in the open," as it were, known facts that are components of the gospel.

"Unto the end" (εἰς τέλος) presents two difficulties. First, the textual: it is not absolutely certain that Paul wrote it. The Greek manuscripts and other versions are unanimous in including the phrase; some manuscripts of the Latin Vulgate omit it. This leaves open the remote possibility that some early scribe added the final clause as a comment on 2:15 – 16, remarking in the margin that God's wrath had "finally" fallen upon them after Paul's demise. Later Greek scribes would have assumed that it was a marginal *correction*, not a *comment*, and moved it into the body of the text. Nevertheless, the external evidence (*some* manuscripts of *one* version) is exceedingly scanty and probably indicates that the variant arose within the transmission of the Latin, not Greek, text. Like the rest of this section, 2:16d remains stubbornly a part of 1 Thessalonians.

One possible understanding is that "the wrath of God has come upon them *at last*" (so the NIV, emphasis added) or "ultimately" or "recently." There is a helpful literary parallel that might back this translation: the text is so close to *T. Levi* 6.11 that it could be regarded as an allusion to that Jewish work.[96] In it Levi tells how he and Simeon slew the Shechemites to punish them for the rape of Dinah and other sins. He states that their action, although it caused Jacob grief, was the manifestation of God's judgment and concludes that "the wrath of God ultimately [εἰς τέλος] came upon [the Shechemites]" (ed. Charlesworth). As in the case of the Shechemites, Paul may be thinking of some recent, tangible, and noneschatological manifestation of God's judgment. Jewett believes that the panic in Jerusalem in AD 49, which killed ten (or twenty) thousand Jews, was the referent. Others have mentioned a difficult famine. For those who believe this passage to be post-Pauline, then the destruction of Jerusalem and the temple in AD 70 would be the natural choice.[97]

The other possible translation is "unto the end" (εἰς τέλος).[98] This is the more natural interpretation. Paul indeed uses "end" eschatologically in

94. So Marshall, *1 and 2 Thessalonians*, 80 – 81; Wanamaker, *Thessalonians*, 117.

95. See Malherbe, *Letters to the Thessalonians*, 177, who also mentions 1 Cor 1:18 and *1 En* 84.4.

96. Best, *Thessalonians*, 122, replies that, given that *T. Levi* 6.11 is lacking in some manuscripts, it may be an interpolation added after the composition of 1 Thessalonians. Similarly Marinus De Jonge, "Light on Paul from the Testaments of the XII Patriarchs," *The Social World of the First Christians: Essays in Honor of Wayne A. Meeks* (ed. L. Michael White and O. Larry Yarbrough; Minneapolis: Fortress, 1995), 112 – 13, who argues that the literary influence goes in the opposite direction, that 1 Thessalonians had an influence on the developing text of the Testaments. The fact that the manuscripts do reveal an evolution of the text, partly under Christian influence, may mean that this is so, but it is difficult to prove.

97. Nevertheless, Orchard, "Thessalonians and the Synoptic Gospels," 22, states that Paul himself was speaking of the destruction of Jerusalem, based on Jesus' known prediction.

98. The Vulgate is no more specific than the Greek with its "usque in finem" ("to the limit? until the end?").

1 Cor 15:24 ("then the end will come") and also in Phil 3:19. What is more, if 1 Thessalonians was shaped with reference to the Matthean tradition, then it is natural to think that the "end" is the last day, as in Matt 24:6, 13, 14. The full expression of God's wrath will be eschatological. Paul anticipates that wrath here as he does in 2 Thess 1, but has no current events in mind.[99]

Our verse echoes another Matthean tradition, John the Baptist's words against the Pharisees and Sadducees, "You brood of vipers! Who warned you to flee from the coming wrath?" (Matt 3:7). They will experience the "unquenchable fire" (3:12) and their membership in the Abrahamic covenant will be of no help in the divine judgment. Paul has, perhaps consciously, joined with John and pitted himself against conventional Jewish soteriology. For the author of 2 Maccabees, for example, Israel's misfortunes in this age are disciplinary, but cannot in the end be punitive:

> In the case of the other nations the Lord waits patiently to punish them until they have reached the full measure of their sins; but he does not deal in this way with us, in order that he should not take vengeance on us afterwards when our sins have reached their height. Therefore he never withdraws his mercy from us. Although he disciplines us with calamities, he does not forsake his own people. (2 Macc 6:14 – 16)

This is a soteriology of (near-) universal salvation for the covenant people, Israel; but Paul for his part saw no hope in it for those who rejected the prophets and the Messiah.

The textual emendation of 1 Thess 2:14 – 16 (see the Introduction) is not necessary if it is seen in the context of Paul's experience. For one, Paul himself had been the most infamous persecutor of the church until this time; and later, as a Jewish Christian, he was just as renowned for his concern about his fellow Israelites (Rom 9:1 – 5). Yet as a proclaimer of the gospel of Christ, he was fully aware that Israelites were not only rejecting the gospel, but also that some were actively opposing it and trying to stop its spread. Like the Israelites of old, they stood in the way of God's spokespeople; like their ancestors, they were under God's wrath. As a student of the prophets Paul would later string together OT verses (Rom 3:10 – 18) to prove that even those "under the law" (3:19) would face God's wrath. By the same token, all who received Christ will be rescued from that wrath (1 Thess 1:10; 2 Thess 1:6 – 9).

The synagogue's opposition to Gentile evangelism was hardly an abstract question; it directly affected people like the Thessalonians. If such Jews had had their way, the new disciples would even now be pagans, awaiting the divine judgment. The Thessalonians can rest assured that God has not forgotten the synagogue's attempt to abandon them to their heathen darkness (see "In Depth: Was Paul Anti-Semitic?"). Nor would God ignore the sin of the pagans in harming his people (2 Thess 1:8).

99. See Morris, *Thessalonians* (NICNT), 85; especially C. Marvin Pate and Douglas W. Kennard, *Deliverance Now and Not Yet: The New Testament and the Great Tribulation* (Studies in Biblical Literature 54; New York: Peter Lang, 2003), 123 – 29, who find the roots of Paul's teaching in Jesus' own. Still, *Conflict at Thessalonica*, 36; R. Schippers, "The Pre-Synoptic Tradition in 1 Thessalonians II:13 – 16," *NovT* 8 (1966): 223 – 34.

IN DEPTH: Was Paul Anti-Semitic?

It is a tragic fact that the church has used passages like this one to stereotype and denounce the Jews as a group: John Chrysostom preached eight harsh sermons against the Jews;[100] Luther wrote, *On the Jews and Their Lies* (1543).[101] They both offered biblical texts and personal experience to prove their cases. The strong content of this section was thrown into high relief after the Holocaust. Some Christians skip over the text, as does the Revised Common Lectionary of the Anglican liturgy. Others go so far as to deny that Paul could not have written it and that it was a later scribal addition.

Anti-Semitism appears in various forms; two have come to the fore within the last century. First is the belief that the Jewish race is inferior; the presence of Jews leads to a degradation of society; Jews must not be allowed to mingle with or intermarry with the supposed superior majority race. This sort of "racist" anti-Semitism is akin to the anti-African prejudice. It is broad enough to include a hatred of Jews on a cultural, religious, or ethnic basis. Some first-century Greeks and Romans singled out the Jews as objects of group hatred, for their religious and cultural otherness or clannishness. We keep in mind that Paul's own Jewishness does not necessarily save him from suspicion of anti-Semitism: the "self-hating Jew" is a known persona (or stereotype) throughout history.

A second type is subtle but still as harmful and is sometimes associated with the pseudo-historical "Protocols of the Elders of Zion," according to which there exists a cabal of Jewish leaders who are secretly gaining control over governments, the economic system, the press, and other key sources of power. Rank-and-file Jews might be decent people; indeed, they are probably unaware of what their leaders are up to. This form of anti-Semitism is the "conspiracy" type and may be compared with theories concerning how the Masons, the Illuminati, or the Trilateralists are the driving force behind contemporary history.

Both types of anti-Semitism may be packaged together, as they were in Nazism.

100. John Chrysostom, "Eight Homilies Against the Jews"; see www.fordham.edu/halsall/source/chrysostom-jews6.html.

101. Luther's violent language is apparently due to his frustration that they refused to believe the gospel, even when it was presented clearly. His essay should be read in context with his other writings, especially those of his later years, which testify to the same hair-raising vehemence when he addresses a variety of themes. In Part XII, Luther may have our passage in mind when he prays, "O God, heavenly Father, relent and let your wrath over them be sufficient and come to an end, for the sake of your dear Son! Amen." Yet he goes on to ask Christians rulers: "Burn down their synagogues, forbid all that I enumerated earlier, force them to work, and deal harshly with them, as Moses did in the wilderness, slaying three thousand lest the whole people perish. They surely do not know what they are doing; moreover, as people possessed, they do not wish to know it, hear it, or learn it. Therefore it would be wrong to be merciful and confirm them in their conduct. If this does not help, we must drive them out like mad dogs, so that we do not become partakers of their abominable blasphemy and all their other vices and thus merit God's wrath and be damned with them." See Martin Luther, "On the Jews and Their Lies," 1543, trans. by Martin H. Bertram: www.humanitas-international.org/showcase/chronography/documents/luther-jews.htm.

How do we understand Paul's strong language in 1 Thessalonians in his own context? First, we must understand the population demographic in which he lived. The Jews in the Diaspora, as best as can be estimated, outnumbered Christians, probably for centuries. Therefore, until the conversion of Constantine, the synagogue was a greater potential threat to the church than the church could be in return.

Second, Paul's condemnation of "the Jews" here, like the language of John's gospel,[102] has principally to do with the Jewish leadership elite in Judea. By extension it applied to the Jewish synagogue establishment in Macedonia and elsewhere in the Diaspora. Especially pernicious is that some Jews actively tried to block the Gentiles from hearing the gospel. Paul does not hypothesize about some underground Zionist conspiracy, but instead points to public actions that the synagogue had taken to impede his work.

Third and foremost, the greatest issue for Paul was how Israelites in general, his own race, were even then reacting toward the gospel. His experience told him that the majority of Jews found the gospel a "stumbling block" (1 Cor 1:23). In Rom 11:31 Paul states that Israel — apart from those few who have already had faith in the gospel — is "disobedient" to God (cf. also Rom 10:21).

Paul followed closely the approach taken by the Hebrew prophets and the Lord Jesus, in showing that God's ancient people were in fact furthest from the truth, and that Gentiles would come to salvation despite the conventional assumptions of the synagogue. He developed this theme further in Gal 4:21 – 5:1 and Rom 9 – 11. Although Justin Martyr is harsher than Paul is his critique of Israel, his theology takes the same line:

> Those who have persecuted and do persecute Christ, if they do not repent, shall not inherit anything on the holy mountain. But the Gentiles, who have believed on Him, and have repented of the sins which they have committed, they shall receive the inheritance along with the patriarchs and the prophets.[103]

Like Chrysostom and Luther, Paul wrote having had abrasive encounters with the Jewish establishment. Like them, he prayed for Jews to come to Christ and had seen a small measure of good results. Yet more than the other two, Paul's theology was also guided by a hopeful element in his eschatology: "Israel has experienced a hardening in part until the full number of the Gentiles has come in, and in this way all Israel will be saved" (Rom 11:25 – 26; see commentaries for the variety of interpretations of this passage). If in the end God has a

102. Among others, John 1:19; 2:18; 5:10; 7:1; 9:22; 11:8; 13:33; 18:12; 19:7; 19:38; 20:19.

103. Justin Martyr, *Dial.* 26 (*ANF* 1:207); Justin is also evangelistic toward Jews and states that he prays for them.

place for "all" or even many Jews, then racist anti-Semitism by definition must be unrighteous.

Christians today must show with great care that Paul is not racist or anti-Semitic in this passage and explain why it should not and must not lead to anti-Semitism.

Theology in Application

Theology in Thessalonica

The Thessalonians have not only clung to Christ; they have also sent the gospel out to Macedonia, Achaia, and, well, everywhere (1:8)! The apostle now turns his attention to an uncommon theme for his letters: *how to be people worthy of sharing God's Word.* I use the word "sharing," knowing full well that some prefer proclaim, announce, or preach. These latter terms usually imply a monologue given to a group of people, perhaps in a formal meeting. "Sharing the gospel" is not only good apostolic language (see 1 Thess 2:8), it more accurately describes the evangelism that the whole people of God carry out.

The apostles did not simply teach the Thessalonians a new way of life. They demonstrated to them that God works only through believers who are willing to do things God's way, rejecting the world's wisdom in their methods. Christian integrity does not consist in being true to oneself, as Paul's contemporary Seneca taught.[104] It consists of being true to God.

The Jews of Paul's day should have taken the message of the God of Israel to the world. Yet Jesus gave Jewish missionaries a failing grade because of their condescension to others (Matt 23:13 – 15). Paul followed suit in Rom 2:17 – 24 (alluding to Isa 52:5) that "God's name is blasphemed among the Gentiles because of you" (Rom 2:24).

It was the Pauline team that did what Israel should have done, glorifying God by transmitting the gospel in alignment with the divine character: in humility, without guile, without interest in money, with care for each person, and with an eye to

104. Seneca, *Ep.* 20, "On Practicing What You Preach" (trans. Gummere): "Far different is the purpose of those who are speech-making and trying to win the approbation of a throng of hearers, far different that of those who allure the ears of young men and idlers by many-sided or fluent argumentation; philosophy teaches us to act, not to speak; it exacts of every man that he should live according to his own standards that his life should not be out of harmony with his words, and that, further, his inner life should be of one hue and not out of harmony with all his activities. This, I say, is the highest duty and the highest proof of wisdom — that deed and word should be in accord, that a man should be equal to himself under all conditions, and always the same."

God's coming judgment. So too the gospel "sounds forth" from Thessalonica (1:8). If Thessalonians want to see the mighty power of God at work, they must forget about money, fame, or even protection from danger.

Biblical Theology

How a Christian shares the gospel directly reflects the nature of God. By contrast with the biblical God, the Olympian gods cared more about visible offerings and tangible honors than they did about the inner motives.

Paul knew that the eternal gospel would have no effect in Thessalonica if God did not open a successful entrance for the Word (1:9; 2:1), working through his team in the power of the Holy Spirit. This is why they paid such close attention to their attitudes and actions.

The church of Ephesus was later to experience a failure along these lines. Paul predicted that people would be greedy for their own gain (Acts 20:25 – 35). Perhaps six years after his talk to the elders at Miletus, he wrote to Timothy in Ephesus that church officers must not be lovers of money or proud (see 1 Tim 3:3, 8; 6:3 – 10; also Titus 1:7). Later the *Didache* would have to devote three chapters to detailed instructions on how to spot a false teacher; one bad sign was if a prophet asked for money (*Did.* 11.12).

Paul thanks God because the Thessalonians received their message as the Word of God. In so doing, he communicates one of his major assumptions about evangelism. If it has success, then this must have been the work of God; why else would he be thanking God? That is, behind the apostles' success was that they prayed. In fact, later on he tells the Thessalonians: "Pray for us, brothers and sisters, that the word of the Lord might run well and be glorified by its hearers" (2 Thess 3:1). The successful sharing of the Word is prayerful sharing.

Paul did not go around giving seminars in which he promoted "Proven Methods for Successful Evangelism" or "The Seven Irrefutable Principles of Preaching." The heart of the matter is that neither strategy nor methodology will have success in bringing down the power of God from heaven.

Message of this Passage for the Church Today

It is not enough to communicate the Bible. Its message will remain mere words if the Spirit does not act to change people's lives. The further a Christian strays from the apostolic model, the less likely it will be that the Word will have an impact.

The need for prayer. I was shocked by the outcome of a little experiment I did. I selected from my shelf four informative homiletics texts, which I had to read in college and seminary. One was a classic from the late nineteenth century; the others were more recent. I scanned through them to see what the writers had to say about prayer and its role in preaching and evangelism. First, the older book emphasized the importance of how to organize one's thoughts and of how to develop sound biblical exegesis. It offered no instruction about prayer.[105] I laid it aside, assuming that it was an aberration. But the second book told the same story. Likewise the third and the fourth. All of these authors waxed eloquent about how only God's Word will change people's lives. Not one connected that truth with the need for prayer, neither in the exegesis nor in the delivery of a message or its follow-up. I imagine that all of these writers would rail against the creeping secularization of Western civilization. Yet in effect they have offered secularized guides to preaching and evangelism by not urging preachers to their knees. Missionary texts too regularly fall into the same mistake.

The place of methodology. "Strategic planning" is not a new invention. Paul employed methods and strategies. He spoke little about them in his letters, because there was no need at the moment. Above all, his main theological assumption was that no strategy or method could bring about a "good entrance" of the Word.

Paul's heirs travel thousands of miles and pay a great deal of money to learn the methods that other growing churches have used. Perhaps the key to success is a certain style of music, expanding the parking lot, providing better childcare, developing a vision statement, or a dozen other tools for success, most of which are probably useful ideas. The danger comes when a man-made method takes the Christian's interest away from the Holy Spirit's activity. "Where your treasure is, there your heart will be also" (Matt 6:21). A method becomes your treasure when it becomes your focus.

But let us turn this phenomenon on its head. In the circles I travel in, I have also seen people distance themselves from these so-called "secular methods" and declare their intention to "reject these new idols." Yet, what happens next? Perhaps they minister with an uninterrupted connection with the Holy Spirit. But it is also possible that they simply continue along with outdated methods, while at the same time downplaying the Spirit's work as much as any secularist might.

Methods are like presuppositions: we all have them, and there is no use denying it. The trick is to identify what we are bringing to the table and then to evaluate it by Scripture. But whether a person uses the latest thing or traditional techniques, all of these must be laid to one side in favor of devoting much time and effort in asking God to do miracles in the lives of one's hearers, be they Christians or not.

Holy motives. Communicators of God's Word cannot "earn" God's favor by behaving themselves. Nevertheless, they can block the power of God through sinful motives, attitudes, and actions.

Paul was aware of the power of money. In the country where I work, "*el televangelista*" is nearly synonymous with "con-artist." "Invest in my ministry and God will

105. It will be obvious to his fans that I am not thinking of Charles Spurgeon's *Lectures to My Students*. Spurgeon was adamant about the need of "The Preacher's Private Prayer," in Chapter III.

bless you a hundredfold, just as he has me," he shouts as he shows off his tailored suit and Rolex watch. Less extreme is the pastor who finds it easier to rebuke a poor person than to rebuke a member of an influential family or a rich donor.

With regard to pastors, I do not know anyone personally who seems to want to become rich. However, Jesus did not simply warn about riches, but about their "deceitfulness" (Matt 13:22). Paul too condemned those who imagined that "godliness is a means to financial gain" (1 Tim 6:5). Some pastors enter into heated salary negotiations, perhaps justifying themselves that they are not after a pot of gold, but they would like to have economic security, especially for the sake of their children. Yes, the church should provide for its leaders, but economic considerations by definition are perilous.

The issues that Paul mentions in this chapter — money, authority, and recognition — can become like a virus, to ruin the communication of God's Word.

CHAPTER 3

1 Thessalonians 2:17 – 3:13

Literary Context

At the heart of this section is the occasion that prompted Paul to write the letter: the return of Timothy with good news about the Thessalonian church (3:6). The apostle also gives details about why Timothy went to them in the first place.

Many ancient letters contained an "itinerary," that is, a description of the author's travel plans. Romans 15:22 – 29 is an example of a Pauline itinerary. Nevertheless, in 1 Thessalonians, he does not write about his future travel; rather, he describes what he wished he could have done but did not.

Some have thought that this section and perhaps 2:1 – 13 is apologetic, that is, to excuse Paul and Silas for having sent Timothy instead of going to Thessalonica themselves. There may be some truth in that, although the exegete should remember Timothy had earlier explained in detail why Paul and Silas had not been able to return; why would Paul need to offer another excuse? It is better to see 2:17 – 3:13 fundamentally as an affirmation of their love and concern for the Thessalonians. Paul also underscores what they value in that church: their love (3:12; see 1:3 and 4:9 – 10) and the prospect of being holy at the end of the age (3:13; see 5:23). Paul ends with a prayer that God and Jesus Christ will bless the believers in Thessalonica and that Paul and Silas will be able to see them soon (3:11 – 13). This eschatological reference ties the section into the other references to the parousia in the letter and the pressing need to be found holy at Christ's coming.

IV. Recapitulation: Why They Regularly Give Thanks for the Thessalonians (2:13 – 16) [*inclusio* with 1:2]

➡ **V. Paul and Silas' Frustrated Travel Plans and a Solution (2:17 – 3:13)**

- **A. Paul and Silas had a deep desire to revisit the Thessalonians, but Satan hindered them (2:17 – 20)**
- **B. Timothy carried out a reconnaissance of the Thessalonian church (3:1 – 5)**
- **C. Timothy returned (3:6a)**
- **D. Timothy conveyed joyful information about the state of the church (3:6b – 10)**
- **E. The new information makes Paul and Silas pray all the more (3:11 – 13)**

VI. *Paraenesis:* The Gospel Ethic in a Gentile environment (4:1 – 12)

Main Idea

Paul assures the Thessalonians that he and Silas had yearned for a return visit to their city, but they had been blocked by Satan. Timothy's trip to Thessalonica accomplished what the apostles would have liked to have done. The news upon his return gives Paul and Silas much relief and leads them to pray even more for these disciples in tribulation.

Translation

(See next three pages.)

Structure

The section describes what has taken place between the departure of the team from Macedonia to the return of Timothy. Paul turns away from the oppression given by unbelieving Jews in 2:16 to another set of troubles, marking the transition with "meanwhile we" (ἡμεῖς δέ, a better translation of the conjunction δέ than merely "and"). He delineates five actions/events in 2:17–3:10 that are predicated on the forced separation of Paul and Silas from the Thessalonians, and the happenstance that young Timothy was able to go to and from the church unchecked.

First: "we made every possible effort to see you" (2:17e); the parallel "we resolved to go to you" (2:18) is marked by "and so" (διότι). The language is highly emotive here: orphaned, face-to-face, heart, abundantly, every possible effort, great desire, all alone, and so forth. Paul develops that resolution in 2:19–20, saying that their desire was because (marked by γάρ twice) the Thessalonians were so valuable to them.

Second: following hard on the first statement is that "Satan blocked" Paul and Silas (2:18c). Paul introduces this event with a bare "and" (καί), which seems to be a deliberate understatement on his part. It is an abrupt, harsh description, without elaboration: *Satan just shut us down.*

Third: the apostles came up with a "Plan B" (3:1–5), marked with "and so" (διό in 3:1a, διὰ τοῦτο in 3:5a) and a further note about how unbearable it was to be separated from their friends. Thus, they sent Timothy alone to Thessalonica (3:2). He was charged with (εἰς τό denoting purpose) "strengthening" (3:2d) and "encouraging" them (3:2e). The apostles were concerned "lest" (μηδένα + infinitive in 3:3a; similarly, "whether," μή πως in 3:5c) they had been shaken (3:3a). Of course, Paul states, using reminder language and "for" (γάρ), they already well knew that they would be experiencing this sort of persecution (3:3b–4).

Fourth: Timothy returns to Paul and Silas in, we infer, Corinth and gives them a good report about the church (3:6–8). It is syntactically striking that his return is

1 Thessalonians 2:17 – 3:13

2:17a	Simultaneous	Meanwhile we, brothers and sisters,
17b	Cause	because we were made orphans from you
17c	Time	for a time
17d	Manner	[orphaned from you] in person, not in our hearts
17e	Action #1	**made every possible effort to see you in person,**
17f	Manner	with great desire.
18a	Restatement of 17e	And **so we resolved to go to you,**
18b	Expansion	to be sure, I, Paul, more than once,
18c	Action #2	and **Satan blocked us.**
19a	Cause/Rhetorical question	[We wanted to see you], because **who gives us**
19b	List	hope and
19c	List	joy, or
19d	List	who is a prize to boast of—
19e	Rhetorical question	if not you all in the presence of our Lord Jesus at his coming?
20	Restatement of 19	**Yes, it is you all who bring us pride and joy.**
3:1a	Time	And so,
		when we could stand it no longer,
1b	Action	**we determined to be left all alone in Athens,**
2a	Action #3	and **we sent Timothy,**
2b	Expansion	our brother and
2c	Expansion	God's coworker in the gospel of Christ,
2d	List/Purpose	to strengthen you and
2e	List/Purpose	encourage you
2f	Advantage	for the sake of your faith
3a	Circumstance	lest in some way you had been shaken by these afflictions.

3b	Reminder language	And in fact, **you yourselves know**
3c	Content	that we were destined for this very thing,
4a	Cause	because even when we were with you, we told you
4b	Content	that we would be put through [such] afflictions,
4c	Event	just as it took place,
4d	Reminder language	as you know.
5a	Time	And so, when I could stand it no longer,
5b	Restatement of 2a	**I sent to find out about your faith,**
5c	List/ Expansion	wondering whether the tempter had perhaps tempted you and
5d	List/ Expansion	our labor had been in vain.
6a	Action #4	But **just now Timothy has come** to us from you and
6b	Action	**has announced** the good news
6c	List/Content	of your faith and
6d	List/Content	your love and
6e	List/Content	that you maintain a good memory of us at all times and
6f	List/Content	that you long to see us just as
6g	Comparison	we also long to see you.
7a	Manner	And in that way we are encouraged about you, brothers and sisters,
7b	Sphere	in the middle of our affliction and distress,
7c	Cause	because of your faith.
8a	Assertion	That's because, now we are alive
8b	Condition	if you stand firm in the Lord!
9a	Rhetorical question	**What kind of thanksgiving can we repay God concerning you**
9b	Cause	because of all the joy with which we rejoice
9c	Cause	on account of you
9d	Sphere	before our God?

Continued on next page.

Continued from previous page.

10a	Manner	Unreservedly,
10b	Time	night and day
10c	Action #5	**we are asking [God]**
10d	Content	to be able to see you in person and
10e	Purpose	to put in order
10f	Content	any things that are lacking in your faith.
11a	Entreat/Expansion of Action #6	Now **may our God and Father himself and**
11b	Entreaty	**our Lord Jesus direct our steps to you.**
12a	Entreaty	And **may the Lord make you to increase and abound**
12b	Sphere	in love for one another and
12c	Sphere	for all people,
12d	Comparison	just as our love does for you,
13a	Result	so that your entire person may be made strong
		in blamelessness,
13b	Result	[that is] with regard to holiness,
13c	Sphere	before our God and Father,
13d	Time	at the coming of our Lord Jesus
13e	Manner	with all his holy [angels]. Amen.

expressed in a genitive absolute, possibly for dramatic effect: "Timothy has come ... and has announced the good news" (ἐλθόντος Τιμοθέου ... εὐαγγελισαμένου). Timothy's report is described as a brief list (3:6c-g).

Fifth: Paul and Silas react to the good news to the Thessalonians (3:7 – 10) and offer up prayer (3:11 – 13). They are encouraged "in that way" or "for that reason" (διὰ τοῦτου, 3:7a), followed up by "because of" (διά, 3:7c), "because" (ὅτι, 3:8a) and "for" (γάρ, left untranslated in 9a). Paul once again reverts to highly emotional language as he reports how they pray and give thanks to God for the Thessalonians. Suddenly, the reader is reminded that this was exactly how the letter began, with their unceasing prayer in 1:2 – 3. That text and 3:9 – 10 form an *inclusio* — two similar passages that stand at the beginning and end of a section of text. Now that we learn of the results of Timothy's journey and report, we understand why the apostles were so exuberant in the opening verses. Paul began the first chapter writing about the *effect*; only now do we learn about the *cause*.

In 3:11 – 13 Paul not only reports how they pray; he goes ahead and prays for them, then and there as he dictates the letter. He introduces the benediction with "and" (δέ), but it is better translated as "now," to match the flow of thought in the original and also to remind English readers of benedictions that they have heard in church, as in, "And now may the Lord, etc." (see also 5:23). It is theologically significant that the apostles pray to both "our God and Father" and "our Lord Jesus," a pattern that one finds throughout these early Pauline letters. There are two main petitions. First, he prays that the Father and the Lord Jesus "direct our steps to you." This is meant to be taken literally, asking that the apostles will be able to return to Thessalonica. The second petition is much longer and has to do with the spiritual growth of the disciples, that they will abound in love, resulting in complete holiness.

Exegetical Outline

➡ **I. Paul's and Silas's Deep Desire to Revisit the Thessalonians, but Satan's Hindrance (2:17 – 20)**

II. Timothy and the Thessalonian Church (3:1 – 10)

- A. Timothy's reconnaissance with the Thessalonian church (3:1 – 5)
- B. Timothy's return (3:6a)
- C. Timothy's joyfully conveying information about the Thessalonian church (3:6b – 10)

III. The New Information Makes Paul and Silas Pray All the More (3:11 – 13)

- A. To be able to visit them (3:11)
- B. That the Thessalonians' love may continue to grow (3:12)
- C. That they may be ready for Christ's coming (3:13)

Explanation of the Text

2:17a-c Meanwhile we, brothers and sisters, because we were made orphans from you for a time (Ἡμεῖς δέ, ἀδελφοί, ἀπορφανισθέντες ἀφ᾽ ὑμῶν πρὸς καιρὸν ὥρας). Now Paul returns to the first person plural with "meanwhile we" (ἡμεῖς δέ). "Brothers and sisters" draws the readers' attention as Paul turns to a new theme: where they had been since last seen in Thessalonica. It is difficult to harmonize precisely this section of the letter with Acts 17 (see the Introduction, "The Second Missionary Journey," for details).

In order to impress on the disciples their commitment to Thessalonica, Paul describes the psychological state of the team during the period of separation. In 2:1–12, he and Silas were like children, mothers, and fathers. Now they are like "orphans," lost and worried. The verb "to be made an orphan" (ἀπορφανίζω) was at times used in a generic sense of "being deprived of";[1] nevertheless, the more specific sense of "to be made an orphan" makes good sense in a letter where family relationships are so key. Perhaps readers would have expected Paul to say "*you* were orphaned from *us*," since Paul and team were "fathers/mothers" to the Thessalonians.[2] But the natural sense of the verb shows that he is building on 2:7: now the little children have walked off and lost their parents.[3]

The phrase "for a time" (πρὸς καιρὸν ὥρας) usually indicates a relatively short period, not to be thought of as more than a period of weeks. Paul is probably not indicating the whole elapsed time since his departure from Thessalonica, but rather between their departure and the decision to send Timothy. Paul will later write something similar to the Romans, but instead will say that he had been hindered for a long time (τὰ πολλά, Rom 15:22; see 1:10, 13). That time period probably spanned eight or so years, commencing at the point he first started on the Via Egnatia but was then diverted to Berea (Acts 17:10).

2:17d [Orphaned from you] in person, not in our hearts (προσώπῳ οὐ καρδίᾳ). The apostolic team is physically but not emotionally separated from their Thessalonian friends. They are apart, literally, "with respect to the face" (προσώπῳ), "face" having reference to presence "in person." Paul later speaks of believers who have never met him personally (Col 2:1). But despite their geographical separation from Thessalonica, the team was not orphaned with respect to the "heart." In this case—unlike 2:4—"heart" (καρδία) *does* refer to the seat of the emotions.[4] The "orphans" feel a strong bond with the church that distance cannot dilute. Here as always in his letters, Paul is no dispassionate functionary.

2:17e-f Made every possible effort to see you in person, with great desire (περισσοτέρως ἐσπουδάσαμεν τὸ πρόσωπον ὑμῶν ἰδεῖν ἐν πολλῇ ἐπιθυμίᾳ). This strong statement is fortified with Paul's use of an adverb, a strong verb, and a prepositional phrase. "Every possible" (περισσοτέρως) means "even much more." Paul uses it elsewhere to speak of Titus's deep commitment to the Corinthians (see 2 Cor 7:15). They also "make every effort" (σπουδάζω); he uses this verb elsewhere in the context of "do your best to come to me quickly" (2 Tim 4:9; 4:21; Titus 3:12). Paul augments this further

1. Chantraine, *Dictionnaire*, "ὀρφανός," 829.

2. Bruce, *1 & 2 Thessalonians*, 54; Green, *Thessalonians*, 150; and Calvin, *Thessalonians*, 261, take it that the *Thessalonians* were the orphans.

3. John Chrysostom, *Homilies on First Thessalonians* 3 (*NPNF*[1] 13:334) interprets it correctly, that the *apostles* felt like orphans. See also Wanamaker, *Thessalonians*, 120.

4. See BDAG, καρδία 1. b.

by saying "with great desire" (ἐν πολλῇ ἐπιθυμίᾳ). The language is unequivocal: it was not for lack of serious, heartfelt effort that Paul and Silas did not return to Thessalonica.

2:18a And so we resolved to go to you (διότι ἠθελήσαμεν ἐλθεῖν πρὸς ὑμᾶς). Added as it is to the phrases at the end of 2:17, this verse lends an air of drama to their dilemma. "And so" or "that is why" (διότι) we resolved this action. "Resolved" (ἠθελήσαμεν) is a better rendering than merely "to wish," seeing that the clause is meant to draw a conclusion from their feelings in 2:17.

2:18b To be sure, I, Paul, more than once (ἐγὼ μὲν Παῦλος καὶ ἅπαξ καὶ δίς). And still Paul pushes on, telling of his own multiple attempts to revisit them. Because this is such a personal heart desire of his, he lapses from first person plural to the singular "I, Paul" (ἐγὼ ... Παῦλος). Paul as an individual breaks in and interrupts the more consistent "we"—the senders of the letter.

The language now alternates back and forth from "I" to "we":

2:17 *we* were made orphans from you
2:17 *we* made every possible effort
2:18 *we* resolved to go to you, to be sure, *I, Paul,* more than once –
2:18 and Satan blocked *us*
3:1 when *we* could stand it no longer, *we* determined to be left alone in Athens
3:2 *we* sent Timothy, *our* brother
3:4 when *we* were
3:4 *we* told you
3:5 when *I* could stand it no longer
3:5 *I* sent to find out about your faith
3:5 *our* labor
3:6 Timothy has come to *us* from you [and back consistently to the plural "we"]

One possible interpretation is that Paul has been using "we" as an "epistolary" or editorial plural; that is, that Paul is writing as the sole author, and "we" is a device, not a literal reference to himself and Silas (but not Timothy—he is referred to in the third person). Yet Samuel Byskorg offers a thorough analysis of the first person plural in the epistolary genre and demonstrates that a literary plural is unlikely. In Greco-Roman letters it was extraordinarily rare, with perhaps nine known examples. It is more common but still unusual in Jewish letters: "The samples of [Jewish] letters with several senders referred to above exhibit no instance of the literary plural.... The 'we' of these letters mostly includes all the senders." He offers the rule, that "if other criteria of analysis allow an interpretation of either a real or a literary plural, the former is to be preferred."[5]

There are other telling arguments in favor of "we" being literally the plural, "we, Silas and I." (1) There is no clear evidence that Paul elsewhere uses an epistolary plural: "we" and "I" have their normal reference to plural or singular.[6] (2) Paul writes with Silas and Timothy in 1 – 2 Thessalonians to a degree that he does not, for example, represent Sosthenes in 1 Corinthians. (3) There are "we" statements that would hardly function as having a singular reference, such as 2:6 (where "we" = "apostles," plural, not Paul as "an" apostle) and 2:18 (where the plural "we resolved" alternates with "I, Paul"—otherwise, Paul would be repeating himself and probably mystifying his audience by the switch). (4) First Thessalonians 2:17 – 3:6 would be confusing if Paul were going back and forth between Paul-as-we and Paul-as-I.

Thus, "we" in this section means Paul and Silas (see comments on 1:1). As elsewhere in the Thessalonian letters, Paul makes reference to the prayers,

5. Samuel Byskorg, "Co-Senders, Co-Authors and Paul's Use of the First Person Plural," *ZNW* 87 (1996): 230 – 50.

6. So Green, *Thessalonians*, 156 – 57. Contra Malherbe, *Letters to the Thessalonians*, 184; Morris, *Thessalonians* (NICNT), 93.

ministry, and travel plans of three men who have deep ties with the church and whose representation in the letters would have come as a great comfort to them during their trials.

"To be sure" (μέν) captures Paul's emphatic tone. "More than once" (ἅπαξ καὶ δίς, lit., "once and twice") is an idiomatic phrase that does not literally mean "twice" but "more than once, and perhaps multiple times" (see also Phil 4:16, where Paul refers to the multiple gifts that the Philippians had sent Paul).

2:18c And Satan blocked us (καὶ ἐνέκοψεν ἡμᾶς ὁ Σατανᾶς). With "and" (καί) Paul reveals why their plan did not succeed: something "blocked" or "hindered" them. Because the Greek language is highly inflected (i.e., syntax is demonstrated by word endings), sentence structure is more elastic than it is in English. As in this verse, it was possible to delay the subject until the end of a clause. Here Paul delays the subject of the verb for the sake of emphasis, making it something like: "and he blocked us ... Satan!"

"Satan" (ὁ Σατανᾶς, an alternate spelling is Σατάν) is a loanword; that is, it was transliterated from the Hebrew *śāṭān*. The word was at times used to mean any sort of adversary (cf. 1 Kgs 11:14; also Sir 21:27 — "When an ungodly person curses an adversary, he curses himself"). It could also be used to refer to the chief angelic adversary of God's people (see Job 1:6). It was translated into Greek as "devil/adversary" (διάβολος). In intertestamental Jewish literature, Satan played a larger role than he did in the Old Testament; at Qumran Belial or the angel of darkness is the being who stands behind the evil inclination and prompts people to sin.[7]

In the Gospels and Revelation, "Satan" is a common name for the principal adversary of God. It is used ten times in Paul's letters and in a Pauline speech in Acts 26:18. A messenger of Satan causes Paul's thorn in the flesh (2 Cor 12:7). Satan is the cause of false teaching (2 Cor 11:14; 1 Tim 5:15) and temptation (1 Cor 7:5). He is the one who stands behind the Man of Sin (2 Thess 2:9). Paul uses "devil" (διάβολος) eight times in his letters, more or less interchangeably with "Satan"; he uses the term "child of the devil" for Elymas in Acts 13:10.

From the very beginning Satan hoped to pull human beings away from God (Gen 3:5), and his longing is that they follow idols. Now, under the power of the gospel, some are turning back from idols (1 Thess 1:10). No wonder, then, that Satan wished to block the evangelists, who have turned a small but growing number of Gentiles away from false gods to follow the true and living Creator.[8] The reader might be saddened at this point, thinking back a few sentences and drawing the inevitable conclusion that the Judeans who oppose the Gentile mission (2:15 – 16) are actively participating in a satanic work.

In this verse and in 2 Thess 2:9, Paul demonstrates no interest in the more arcane mysteries of the apocalypses of the Second Temple period. Nevertheless, he dwells within the conceptual framework of Daniel and Revelation. His universe has ample space for battles between spiritual powers. We find more details by comparing 1 Thess 2:18 with Acts 16:6 – 10:

> Paul and his companions traveled throughout the region of Phrygia and Galatia, having been *kept* [κωλυθέντες] by the Holy Spirit from preaching the word in the province of Asia. When they came to the border of Mysia, they tried to enter Bithynia, but the Spirit of Jesus *would not allow*

7. See W. F. Foerster, "διάβολος — The Later Jewish View of Satan," *TDNT*, 2:75 – 79; also W. F. Foerster and K. Schäferdiek, "σατανᾶς," *TDNT*, 7:151 – 65.

8. See the development of this theme in Stauffer, *New Testament Theology*, 66.

> [οὐκ εἴασεν] them to. So they passed by Mysia and went down to Troas. During the night Paul had a vision of a man of Macedonia standing and begging him, "Come over to Macedonia and help us." After Paul had seen the vision, we got ready at once to leave for Macedonia, concluding that God had called us to preach the gospel to them.

This extraordinary chain of events led Paul and his team to cross over to Macedonia, and within a short time, to plant the faith in Thessalonica. Apart from the "night vision," Acts does not give details of how the Spirit communicated his wishes to the team. Some have suggested that they were not allowed by local governments to cross over into Asia (as Paul would later find himself able to do on his third missionary journey) and Bithynia. While this is a possible interpretation, the pattern of Acts suggests an explanation that comes from the supernatural realm. In Acts 13:2, "the Holy Spirit said" refers to a word given by one of the prophets who was present, during a period of worship and fasting. This resulted in Saul, Barnabas, and Mark's campaign in Cyprus. After the Jerusalem Council, Silas and Judas Barsabbas went to Antioch as witnesses of the Council's decision: they were both known as prophets (Acts 15:32).

Later in Acts, God sent a word of prophecy to warn Paul about the trouble he would face in Jerusalem (Acts 20:22–23; 21:10–14; see the standard commentaries for the difficulties surrounding prophecy in that section). Given the general trend within Acts, the most natural interpretation of 16:6–7 is that someone, perhaps Silas, uttered a prophecy that warded them off from Asia and Bithynia, but did not go on to give positive direction as to where to go. Then in Acts 16:9–10 Paul had a vision that they interpreted as guiding them to cross over to Macedonia. The Spirit thus gave them three signals concerning where they were to go.

So, God at times gives the apostle a direct word about where to go or not go. Yet now, Paul states that it is Satan, not the Spirit, who has hindered him and Silas (but apparently not Timothy) from going to Thessalonica. But how did they apprehend that this hindering was from Satan and not from the Spirit (as in Acts 16:7)? Bruce believes it was possible to discern the impediment's *source* from its *result*: "It was probably evident—in retrospect, if not immediately—that the one check worked out for the advance of the gospel and the other for its hindrance."[9]

While plausible, this is impossible to prove. After all, Acts 16:6–7 implies that the gospel was "hindered" from going into Asia and Bithynia; that is, the advance of the gospel was checked by Jesus. What did Satan's block look like, to make it distinguishable from what Jesus did? Again, the facts of the case are elusive. In the case of the blocked path from Athens to Thessalonica, it is possible that Satan was hindering them by means of the onerous bail that Jason had posted, a legal prohibition that obstructed the two senior members but not Timothy. Paul might have employed a hermeneutic that interpreted any problem caused by the government to be satanic. Many other speculations are possible, ranging from bad weather to illness to spiritual warfare. Nevertheless, by some method—perhaps more supernatural knowledge given through Silas?—Paul knows it is Satan who has blocked their path, not just random circumstance and not the Holy Spirit.

The reader must press still further and understand Paul in the broader context of the Scripture.

9. Bruce, *1 & 2 Thessalonians*, 58; Best, *Thessalonians*, 84–85. See the section in Ladd, *Theology of the New Testament*, 440–42.

Paul would have believed that, while Satan could do harm to the saints, he could never do so apart from God's permission. This is demonstrated clearly by Job 1:12; 2:6. The doctrine is even clearer in Dan 10:10 – 15, where Daniel prayed fervently for enlightenment, the angel who came in answer was blocked, and Michael came to relieve him and send him on his way to Daniel. Behind these accounts is the faith that Satan cannot act apart from divine leave.

It is probable that on his first reconnaissance Timothy had communicated to the church the specific details of why Paul and Silas had not returned; this reference to Satan was therefore comprehended in light of the information that they already possessed. Immediately helpful for the Thessalonians was the knowledge that it took the archenemy of God, Satan himself, to keep Paul and Silas from personally visiting them.

Paul communicates several important theological points in one statement. First, Satan is a foe whose presence is immediately palpable, not simply an abstract principle of evil. Second, he is able to impede such key apostles as Paul and Silas. Third, Satan's hindrance continues, despite the many prayers to God for relief. Fourth, Paul and his team continue to pray for the satanic barrier to be eliminated, even though it has not been lifted thus far — their battle with Satan required vigilance. Fifth, Paul is not reticent about admitting that he, an apostle, has been successfully held up by Satan. Something similar appears in 2 Cor 12:7, where the "thorn in my flesh" is "an messenger of Satan, to torment me." His spiritual modesty is a rebuke to those leaders who through the centuries have dared to imply that Satan is their trained poodle.[10]

2:19a-d [We wanted to see you], because who gives us hope or joy, or who is a prize to boast of — if not you all (τίς γὰρ ἡμῶν ἐλπὶς ἢ χαρὰ ἢ στέφανος καυχήσεως — ἢ οὐχὶ καὶ ὑμεῖς). Here is why they want to visit the Thessalonians; it is an affectionate cry from the heart.

"Crown" (στέφανος) might refer to the headwear of a king; this is how it is consistently used in Revelation. It may also refer to a prize won for athletic or civic achievement, a chaplet woven of some flowers or branches and is a symbolic honor given to a victor.[11] It is used metaphorically by Paul to speak of the success he hopes to gain (here and in 1 Cor 9:24 – 25).

In Paul's usage, "boasting" (καύχησις) is double-edged. It may refer to prideful attitudes by sinful people (Rom 3:27). But positively, it may refer to legitimate glorying in God (Rom 15:17) or in what a person can do in God's power (1 Cor 15:31): "Let the one who boasts boast in the Lord" (1 Cor 1:31, which uses the cognate verb; also 2 Cor 10:17). This positive use is Paul's intent here. The prize here is not some crown that he anticipates receiving: rather, the Thessalonians themselves are those concerning whom Paul will glory at the coming of Christ. Philippians 4:1 is similar, where Paul speaks of the Philippians' steadfastness in the faith: "Therefore, my brothers and sisters, you whom I love and long for, my joy and crown, stand firm in the Lord in this way, dear friends!"

"If not you all" (ἢ οὐχὶ καὶ ὑμεῖς) is awkward; Paul probably adds the particle (ἤ, lit., "or") to make it parallel with the preceding phrases.

2:19e In the presence of our Lord Jesus at his coming? (ἔμπροσθεν τοῦ κυρίου ἡμῶν Ἰησοῦ ἐν τῇ αὐτοῦ παρουσίᾳ;). Paul returns to the eschatologi-

10. In 2 Thess 3:1 – 5 we will examine how Christians may turn to prayer to counterattack Satan and possibly find success.

11. Contra Richard Chenevix Trench, *Synonyms of the New Testament* (9th ed. rev.; reprint; Grand Rapids: Eerdmans, 1980), 78 – 81, who mistakenly states that στέφανος always signifies a prize, and that διάδημα is always a royal crown.

cal, "at" (ἐν) Jesus' second coming.[12] The parousia is not simply a deliverance from God's wrath (1:10), but positively a time of glory and rejoicing. "In the presence of" (ἔμπροσθεν) is used of appearing before God or Christ, for example, at the judgment (Matt 25:32; 2 Cor 5:10). In other contexts the preposition may refer to prayer or more generally to existence in God's presence (1 Thess 1:3; 3:9). "Coming" (παρουσία) is a semitechnical expression in the New Testament. The return of Jesus came to be called his parousia[13] or epiphany (ἐπιφάνεια, e.g., 2 Thess 2:8) or revelation (ἀποκάλυψις, 1 Cor 1:7; 2 Thess 1:7). At Jesus' coming the Thessalonian converts will redound to the team's credit.

2:20 Yes, it is you all who bring us pride and joy (ὑμεῖς γάρ ἐστε ἡ δόξα ἡμῶν καὶ ἡ χαρά). Again, Paul affirms how they deeply value the disciples. We render "for" (γάρ) as "yes" in order to give it its proper emphatic meaning. Paul answers his own rhetorical question in 2:19 by echoing—although not word for word—his reference to "hope and joy or who is a prize to boast of." Here he uses "glory" (ἡ δόξα) rather than the synonymous "prize to boast of." We translate it with the present tense, although from the context, Paul is thinking ahead to the second coming.

3:1 And so, when we could stand it no longer, we determined to be left all alone in Athens (διὸ μηκέτι στέγοντες εὐδοκήσαμεν καταλειφθῆναι ἐν Ἀθήναις μόνοι). Paul changes direction and returns to the details of his and Silas's enforced absence. The chapter division here is not ideal, since the apostle simply reverts to the original point in 2:17–18 after the parenthetical 2:19–20. With "and so" (διό) Paul continues to recount their abortive trip to Thessalonica. He uses in 3:1–2 the first person plural (Paul and Silas), whereas he will go to the first person singular in 3:5 (see comment on 2:18). "When we could stand it no longer" (μηκέτι στέγοντες) is a verbal participle, connected with the indicative "we determined." It could be construed as causal ("because we could stand it no longer"), but the whole tenor of the section is the *chronology* of their actions, yielding a temporal participle "when."

"We determined" (εὐδοκήσαμεν) is the same verb used in 2:8 with regard to giving their very selves to the Thessalonians. In the face of a satanic impediment, the apostles did not complain, nor were they paralyzed. They made hard and pragmatic choices, "to be left all alone in Athens," while Timothy went to do what was possible. Paul has already spoken of their being orphaned from the Thessalonians, and so "all alone" brings out the poignancy of their situation. We note here again that Acts does not hint at Silas's being with Paul in Athens, nor of the two of them together making plans to send Timothy to Thessalonica.

3:2a-c And we sent Timothy, our brother and God's coworker in the gospel of Christ (καὶ ἐπέμψαμεν Τιμόθεον, τὸν ἀδελφὸν ἡμῶν καὶ συνεργὸν τοῦ θεοῦ ἐν τῷ εὐαγγελίῳ τοῦ Χριστοῦ). "And we sent" is the follow-up to "we determined" in 3:1. If the Thessalonians were hoping for the triumphal return of the apostles, they had a letdown: only Timothy showed up.

Timothy is not only their "brother" but also "God's coworker" (συνεργὸν τοῦ θεοῦ) in the gospel. Other NT passages refer to coworkers in the horizontal sense of one's fellows in the work (e.g., Timothy himself in Rom 16:21; cf. also the plural in 1 Cor 3:9). Many manuscripts smoothed what they saw as a theological difficulty by emending to

12. BDAG, ἐν 10. b.

13. "At his coming" (ἐν τῇ αὐτοῦ παρουσίᾳ) found here, also 3:13; 1 Cor 15:23. παρουσία refers to the Lord's coming in 1 Thess 2:19; 3:13; 4:15, 5:23; 2 Thess 2:1; 2:8. For the παρουσία of the Man of Sin, see 2 Thess 2:9.

"*servant* of God and *our* coworker" (διάκονον τοῦ θεοῦ καὶ συνεργὸν ἡμῶν). This is almost certainly an intentional emendation, since the copyists tended to balk about statements about "synergy" with God.

The solution lies not in altering the text but in a correct understanding of working with God. One must imagine that God's power is possible only through the working of the apostolic team. It is that the team is working along with God, who ensures that the "word" of preaching is not mere talk but the conduit of the divine power (1:5). Paul's underlying point is: *Let no Thessalonian voice disappointment that the apostles themselves had not visited them!* They must acknowledge that Paul and Silas have not simply dispatched a messenger boy; Timothy is a true part of the apostolic team, and he too can minister to their needs in God's power.

A round trip from Athens to Macedonia would have taken three or four weeks, not to mention the time that Timothy spent with the church. This event was a momentous step in Timothy's experience. He was probably in his early twenties and had only a few months earlier joined the team as the junior member (Acts 16:1 – 5). Yet here he is carrying out a solo mission to dangerous Thessalonica, one that would end in triumph. He would repeat that success on other occasions (Acts 19:22).

3:2d-f To strengthen you and encourage you for the sake of your faith (εἰς τὸ στηρίξαι ὑμᾶς καὶ παρακαλέσαι ὑπὲρ τῆς πίστεως ὑμῶν). Timothy went north not simply to gather information, but to carry out apostolic ministry. "To" (εἰς τό + infinitive) can denote a result; in this context what follow are infinitives of purpose.[14] With "to strengthen you" (εἰς τὸ στηρίξαι ὑμᾶς), Paul employs a verb that he uses four times in these two letters (here; 1 Thess 3:13; 2 Thess 2:17; 3:3). This is a typically Pauline approach in 1 Thessalonians: the disciples are doing well, and the apostles want them to grow even more. Timothy will "encourage" them (παρακαλέσαι) "for the sake of your faith." "Faith" (πίστις) in this paragraph, as in 1:3, is their active trust in God as tested by hard circumstances. Through Timothy's work, the Thessalonians will have a stronger confidence in the Lord.

3:3a Lest in some way you had been shaken by these afflictions (τὸ μηδένα σαίνεσθαι ἐν ταῖς θλίψεσιν ταύταις). Now we know why Paul and Silas were unable to stand it any longer (3:1) — they thought that the church might have suffered real damage during the time of the satanic blockade. Paul begins with a phrase that is not easily translated; "lest in some way" (τὸ μηδένα) is acceptable and points to a shaking up that might have occurred before Timothy's arrival. The implied subject of "been shaken" (σαίνεσθαι) is the Thessalonians, "lest [you] being shaken." "Shaken" (σαίνω) is a *hapax legomenon* in the NT, a word more at home in poetic Greek. Its literal sense was of a dog wagging its tail. By extension, it was used of humans fawning on others in order to gain favor.[15] Some therefore read the verse to mean that the Thessalonians had been confused by some smooth talker.[16]

Nevertheless, the other meaning offered fits more neatly here: "to cause to be emotionally upset, *move, disturb, agitate*."[17] Satan was pressing upon them with "by these afflictions" (ἐν ταῖς θλίψεσιν ταύταις); and there is no evidence that he was using *flattery* as such as one of his weapons. "Afflictions" here and the cognate verb "afflict" (θλίβω)

14. Wallace, *Grammar*, 590 – 92.

15. Aeschylus, *Cho.* 194 (trans. Smyth): "hope is merely *flattering* me"; 419 – 20: "To what could we more fittingly appeal than to those very miseries we have endured from the woman herself who bore us? She may *fawn upon* us, but they are past all soothing."

16. Especially, MM, 567; Morris, *Thessalonians* (NICNT), 96.

17. See BDAG, σαίνω 2.

in 3:4 were commonly used to denote Christian tribulation in general (in 1 – 2 Thess; Rom 5:3; 8:35; Phil 1:17), or semitechnically, of the eschatological tribulation (Matt 24:21; 24:29; Rev 7:14; but never in Paul).[18]

Seyoon Kim offers a detailed analysis of Paul's "entrance" into Thessalonica. When he comes to this shaking up of the Thessalonians, he concludes that the devil must have created doubts specifically about the apostles' integrity. That is, since Paul speaks about integrity in 2:1 – 12, he must be touching on the very point that at issue.[19] Kim's argument fails to convince, since in this verse, it seems to be persecution in general that is "shaking" the believers' faith.

3:3b – 4b And in fact, you yourselves know that we were destined for this very thing, because even when we were with you, we told you that we would be put through [such] afflictions (αὐτοὶ γὰρ οἴδατε ὅτι εἰς τοῦτο κείμεθα· καὶ γὰρ ὅτε πρὸς ὑμᾶς ἦμεν, προελέγομεν ὑμῖν ὅτι μέλλομεν θλίβεσθαι). Again Paul uses elaborate "reminder language." He had taught the Thessalonians not only that tribulation was a possibility, but that it was the Christian's destiny. The implied subject of "you know" (οἴδατε) is strengthened to "you yourselves" with the intensive use of the pronoun "yourselves" (αὐτοί). They know that "we" (in the sense of "we Christians") are "destined for this very thing" (εἰς τοῦτο κείμεθα). This passive verb implies "God" as the doer of the action. Paul did not simply observe the harsh realities of pagan Macedonia and calculate that the Christians would be at risk. According to the worldview throughout the NT, God has destined the Christians for trials in this world.

Paul hearkens back to their previous knowledge, drawing on the team's teaching in Thessalonica. The temporal clause "when we were with you" (ὅτε πρὸς ὑμᾶς ἦμεν) shows the context of when they taught. He reiterates his teaching, using the infinitive of the verb "afflicted." It would be unjust to the context to load more meaning on the statement than Paul intended, to make it say that "we the church are going to pass through the eschatological tribulation." Rather, the Christian per se is a person who can expect trials from the world.

3:4c-d Just as it took place, as you know (καθὼς καὶ ἐγένετο καὶ οἴδατε). Paul has circumscribed a large circle: you saw us experience tribulation, you became imitators of us, we foretold tribulations for you, they came about, you know this full well, I'm telling you that you know this, and now we're all aware of what is going on. With this comparative clause Paul uses "as" (καθώς) to give the Thessalonians a firm reminder of their experience: it has taken place and they know it. "Took place" (ἐγένετο) refers to events of which the Thessalonians are daily all too aware; thus Paul again uses standard reminder language.

3:5a-b And so, when I could stand it no longer, I sent to find out about your faith (διὰ τοῦτο κἀγὼ μηκέτι στέγων ἔπεμψα εἰς τὸ γνῶναι τὴν πίστιν ὑμῶν). Paul seems to hop from topic to topic. He now leaves off speaking about his anxiety and his previous teaching; now he gets back to the main theme: *what of Timothy's mission* (3:2)? "And so" (διὰ τοῦτο) returns us to the decision that Paul and Silas took. Yet here, Paul replaces the "and so, when we could stand it no longer ... we sent Timothy" (3:1 – 2) with the first person singular: "when I [myself; κἀγώ] could stand it no longer." Paul "sent" Timothy (πέμπω, repeating a key verb from 3:2).

18. See also in Jewish eschatology: Dan 12:1; Zeph 1:15; *As. Mos.* 8.1. For an overview of the word group, see esp. H. Schlier, "θλίβω, θλίψις," *TDNT*, 3:139 – 48.

19. Kim, "Paul's Entry," 523 – 24.

Years later, Timothy would go on a similar mission to Macedonia to communicate details about Paul and gather information about the church in Philippi (Phil 2:19, 23).

3:5c-d Wondering whether the tempter had perhaps tempted you and our labor had been in vain (μή πως ἐπείρασεν ὑμᾶς ὁ πειράζων καὶ εἰς κενὸν γένηται ὁ κόπος ἡμῶν). Here is the source for Paul's angst: If Satan was blocking the apostles from entering Thessalonica, what dark deeds might he be doing behind those drawn curtains? After all, their tribulation was not just from angry synagogue leaders or impulsive Gentiles, but was orchestrated by Satan. Their doubt is expressed in "lest perhaps" (μή πως), which we paraphrase as "wondering whether."[20] Paul has a deep sense of apprehension. The following verb is subjunctive to denote the consideration of a possibility.[21] "Test, try" (πειράζω) in the context of satanic work means to "entice to improper behavior, tempt" (see BDAG). The verb appears twice here, first as an indicative and then as "the tempter," a substantival participle (see parallel in the temptations of Jesus, Matt 4:3).

The reader must push through the whole sentence in order to capture Paul's meaning. It is not as if the apostles were uncertain whether Satan had tempted them — of course he had. Rather, they wondered whether, as a result of that temptation, their apostolic labor might have come to nothing. "Had been in vain" (εἰς κενὸν γένηται) is rhetorically parallel to 3:3, "shaken by these afflictions"; nevertheless it goes further than "shaken," since Paul seems to imply that the whole Thessalonian project could have failed (for more, see below).

There is a biblical basis for his language. Paul elsewhere applies Isa 49 to his work among Gentiles (Isa 49:6 in Acts 13:47), and it is probable that he is now thinking of Isa 49:4 (KJV) — "Then I said, I have laboured in vain, I have spent my strength for nought, and in vain: yet surely my judgment is with the Lord, and my work with my God." Paul and the team wondered if in the end their work in Thessalonica had been a waste of time. They knew from the prophet Isaiah that failure was an option.

There are broader questions that must be addressed if we are to understand the team's apprehensions. First is the *psychological*. How can they have reconciled their deep unease with other biblical truths, in particular Matt 6:25 ("do not be worry about your life") or Phil 4:6 ("do not be anxious about anything, but in every situation, by prayer and petition, with thanksgiving, present your requests to God")?[22] The answer lies in what motivates the anxiety. On the one hand, Jesus told his followers not to be anxious about their own daily needs, since this demonstrated a failure of confidence in God. The remedy is prayer and trust. On the other hand, love for one's fellow Christians could produce a righteous anxiety, especially when they are in distress. A proper course of action would, of course, include prayer — and no one could fault Paul and his team with neglecting that — but also deep concern and the desire to rush to the aid of the needy. This is what we see in 1 Thessalonians. Paul emulates Moses, the prophets, and the Lord Jesus himself. The opposite of this positive, loving type of anxiety would be lukewarm indifference.

The second point of interest is the *soteriological*. Had Paul genuinely feared that the Thessalonians might have defected because of Satan's onslaught? We say "defected," that language being preferable to "lost their salvation." In this letter, salvation is

20. See BDAG πως 2.b.; the enclitic particle must not to be confused with the interrogative πῶς, "How?"

21. See Wallace, *Grammar*, 467 – 68 (a deliberative rhetorical subjunctive).

22. See esp. Matt 6:25 – 34, where Jesus says not to "worry" six times.

eschatological, and one cannot lose what one does not yet have. Those who turn from God under Satan's onslaught are said to "be shaken" (2 Thess 2:2 – 3), or they might fall away (2:3), or in terms of 1 Thess 1:9, they might turn away once more from the living God.[23]

Here are some points to consider. Paul gives no hint that his fear is purely hypothetical. In that case he could have said: "We feared lest our work was in vain (which we all know cannot really happen)." Sometimes exegetes point to the conditional or hypothetical nature of a sentence (notably Heb 6:4 – 6) or the subjunctive mood of the verb in this sort of context and argue that the idea of defection is purely speculative and not a real possibility. But this is simply not how the Greek language works.

Paul and the team were deeply fearful. Fear results from what might really happen, not from what cannot happen and is only hypothetically possible. Their anxiety is not due to some mere abstract conjecture.

Paul does not say that their work would end in vain because Satan would have killed the Thessalonian believers or dispersed the church. It is "temptation" that is said to result in disaster — that is, the believers caving in under Satan's onslaught and becoming shipwrecked in their faith.

Nevertheless, Paul also indicates that God's chosen cannot be led away by the Man of Lawlessness, in that ultimate and most insidious deception of Satan in the end times (2 Thess 2:10 – 12; cf. 1 Thess 5:4, 9). This teaching seems to be drawn from the Olivet Discourse (Matt 24:24: "For false messiahs and false prophets will appear and perform great signs and wonders to deceive, if possible, even the elect").

Finally, the apostles' concern for the Thessalonians was eventually eliminated through eyewitness observation. They were able to conclude that "the welcome we had from you was not without good results" (2:1) because Timothy had just reported that the church was still alive and thriving (3:6). In addition, they had heard about their faith indirectly from others (1:7 – 8). That is, their relief is grounded on hard evidence.

To conclude, Paul and Silas trusted that God would protect the chosen ones; they suspected, rightly, that Satan was trying to pulverize the Thessalonians; they did not know the outcome of that battle until they had evidence as reported by Timothy and others.[24] Any doctrine of perseverance must take all of these truths into account. Yet Paul's concern here is not one of systematic theology ("what could happen?") but a pastoral one ("what has happened/is happening?"). He is a model of Jesus' teaching, that one may discern a person's inner life only by outward manifestations ("fruit," Matt 7:16), not by guessing about what lies hidden beneath the surface.

3:6a But just now Timothy has come to us from you (Ἄρτι δὲ ἐλθόντος Τιμοθέου πρὸς ἡμᾶς ἀφ' ὑμῶν). Upon this verse turns the epistle; everything hinged on Timothy's arrival in Corinth and the news he brought. The conjunction (δέ) is "but," since this verse stands in contrast to the anxiety that went before. For this reason too "now" (ἄρτι) is better rendered with the more vivid "just now."[25] "Timothy has come" (ἐλθόντος Τιμοθέου) is a genitive absolute, as is "has announced" (εὐαγγελισαμένου).[26] By switching from finite verbs and adverbial participles to this new form,

23. See the excellent overview by B. J. Oropeza, *Paul and Apostasy: Eschatology, Perseverance, Falling Away in the Corinthian Congregation* (WUNT 2/115; Tübingen: Mohr Siebeck, 2000), 22 – 34.

24. See particularly Green, *Thessalonians*, 165.

25. "Now" (ἄρτι) with a genitive absolute is found only here in the NT. In the LXX, it is found only in 2 Macc 9:5 and 10:28 and denotes immediacy, "as soon as."

26. A genitive absolute typically provides a context of time ("when, now"); see Wallace, *Grammar*, 654 – 55.

Paul introduces a change of rhythm in order to arrest the audience's attention. "To *us* from *you*" indicates that Silas and Paul were together when Timothy arrived; only Acts indicates that Paul and Silas had ever been separated during this portion of the journey.

3:6b-d And has announced the good news of your faith and your love (καὶ εὐαγγελισαμένου ἡμῖν τὴν πίστιν καὶ τὴν ἀγάπην ὑμῶν). Paul has now taken us full circle: Timothy is reporting the information that Paul assumes at the beginning of the letter, that the Thessalonians are still there and that they have faith and love (1:3). "And has announced the good news" (καὶ εὐαγγελισαμένου ἡμῖν) is the second genitive absolute. The word broadly means "announce good news" and not necessarily "evangelize."[27] The good news is that the Thessalonian place of assembly is not some Ground Zero that Timothy gazed on in horror, but a thriving body of believers.

3:6e And that you maintain a good memory of us at all times (καὶ ὅτι ἔχετε μνείαν ἡμῶν ἀγαθὴν πάντοτε). Not only are the Thessalonians still followers of Christ; they are also continuing to be loyal to the missionary team. "At all times" (πάντοτε) and "memory" (μνείαν) sound similar to the prayer language Paul used in 1:2 – 3 (also Rom 1:9; Eph 1:16; Phil 1:3 – 4; Phlm 4); nevertheless, it is not prayer language here. But neither does it speak of mere warm feelings, that they had "pleasant memories" of Paul and his team (so the NIV).[28] A good translation would be "maintain a recollection." It refers to maintaining and practicing a teacher's model or pattern by the disciple, a dynamic that is strongly present in this letter as well as in Hellenism and Judaism. "A disciple continued to be guided by the exemplary life of his teacher in his absence by remembering him."[29] The implication is: "you maintain a good memory of us always and use that mental picture as a guide for your own actions."

3:6f-g And that you long to see us just as we also long to see you (ἐπιποθοῦντες ἡμᾶς ἰδεῖν καθάπερ καὶ ἡμεῖς ὑμᾶς). The Thessalonians deeply miss the people who, from one perspective, were the proximate cause of their trials. They continue to reciprocate the feelings and motives of the apostolic team. The team was thwarted from seeing the Thessalonians by Satan (2:17 – 18), and the Thessalonians too wish to see "us." Paul does not let the parallel go unnoticed. In the NT, the verb "long to" (ἐπιποθοῦντες) is found only in Paul (see 2 Tim 1:4) and James 4:5 and 1 Pet 2:2. Timothy has disclosed that the friendship between apostles and Thessalonians is a mutual one (cf. also Rom 1:11 – 12).

3:7 And in that way we are encouraged about you, brothers and sisters, in the middle of our affliction and distress, because of your faith (διὰ τοῦτο παρεκλήθημεν, ἀδελφοί, ἐφ᾽ ὑμῖν ἐπὶ πάσῃ τῇ ἀνάγκῃ καὶ θλίψει ἡμῶν διὰ τῆς ὑμῶν πίστεως). Paul and Silas are experiencing further trials of their own, but if the Thessalonians are well, then "in that way" their spirits are lifted. Once more Paul uses the verb "encouraged" (παρεκλήθημεν). Among Christian friends there is mutual support: Timothy encourages the Thessalonians (3:2), and Paul and Silas are encouraged to hear of them (see also Phil 2:19). "Brothers and sisters" (ἀδελφοί) captures the listeners' attention and also underlines the fact that they have a shared experienced: Paul and Silas too need encouragement in their times of trial.

27. See Wanamaker, *Thessalonians*, 133.

28. So Green, *Thessalonians*, 167; Fee, *Thessalonians*, 123, and the majority of English versions.

29. Malherbe, *Letters to the Thessalonians*, 207; also his "God's New Family in Thessalonica," in *The Social World of the First Christians: Essays in Honor of Wayne A. Meeks* (ed. L. Michael White and O. Larry Yarbrough; Minneapolis: Fortress, 1995), 121.

The fact of apostolic suffering was a pattern for all Christian tribulation: you saw us suffer, now you suffer, and we too are continuing to suffer. "Affliction" (ἀνάγκη) and "distress" (θλίψις) are often seen together in the LXX.[30] In the NT, "affliction" (ἀνάγκη) may refer to an eschatological tribulation (Luke 21:23) or, as here, to the ongoing distresses of Christians during this age (cf. 1 Cor 7:26; 2 Cor 6:4; 12:10).

It is not clear to which trials the apostle is now referring. Is it the persecutions in Macedonia, some unnamed distress in Achaia, or simply the apostolic trials in general? Regardless, it is "because of your faith" (διὰ τῆς ὑμῶν πίστεως) that Paul and Silas have received encouragement. The phrase has specific reference to the positive news that Timothy has brought (1:3).

3:8 That's because, now we are alive if you stand firm in the Lord! (ὅτι νῦν ζῶμεν ἐὰν ὑμεῖς στήκετε ἐν κυρίῳ). Paul tends to repeat himself when he is emotionally moved, and so he states the obvious once more. We take the conjunction (ὅτι) as the marker of a causal clause, explaining why Paul can say they are encouraged in 3:7. For them to "live" is not physical life, but a life of joy. Some translations offer some version of "now we really live." "Stand in the Lord" uses a typically Pauline verb, "to stand" (στήκω); it has the sense "to be firmly committed in conviction or belief" (so BDAG).[31] Paul will exhort them later to "stand" in 2 Thess 2:15, using the imperative mood: "be firmly committed [στήκω] and hold tight to the traditions that you were taught."

3:9 What kind of thanksgiving can we repay God concerning you because of all the joy with which we rejoice on account of you before our God? (τίνα γὰρ εὐχαριστίαν δυνάμεθα τῷ θεῷ ἀνταποδοῦναι περὶ ὑμῶν ἐπὶ πάσῃ τῇ χαρᾷ ᾗ χαίρομεν δι' ὑμᾶς ἔμπροσθεν τοῦ θεοῦ ἡμῶν). Paul's rhetorical question comes across as more powerful than his declarations of gratitude. Certainly, he and Silas give thanks to God, but what kind of thanksgiving could possibly be sufficient?

The emotion continues to build. They rejoice before God because of the joy the Thessalonians have given them! The use of the cognate words "joy" (χαρά) and "rejoice" (χαίρω) are like the language of Hebrew poetry, which tends to use pairs of cognate words in order to emphasize a deep truth. Since this sort of repetition does not function well in English, "rejoice with joy" is not the best rendering. The NIV does better with, "for all the joy we have." "Before" (ἔμπροσθεν) is again prayer language as in 1:3, standing before the God who is always present for Christians.

3:10a-d Unreservedly, night and day we are asking [God] to be able to see you in person (νυκτὸς καὶ ἡμέρας ὑπερεκπερισσοῦ δεόμενοι εἰς τὸ ἰδεῖν ὑμῶν τὸ πρόσωπον). Paul's language swells. Now he gives a prayer report to show what is an appropriate response to this spiritual feeling. This is still technically a part of the rhetorical question that began in 3:9, but we have broken it up in order to make it smooth English. As in 2:9, he uses the genitive "night and day" (νυκτὸς καὶ ἡμέρας) to denote "by night, by day." "Asking" (δεόμενοι) is a participle connected with "we rejoice" (χαίρομεν) in 3:9; their rejoicing is ever yoked with the "unceasing" prayer of which this letter is so redolent.

Up to this point the prayer language is familiar from other letters; but it is the term "unreservedly" (ὑπερεκπερισσοῦ) that gives the translator pause, since the compounded adverb is hard to render into proper English. BDAG offers "*quite beyond all measure* (highest form of comparison imaginable)"; L&N 78.34 suggests "extreme earnestness." These are fine as far as they go, but they sound

30. Weima, "1 and 2 Thessalonians," 874.

31. See also Rom 14:4; 1 Cor 16:13; Gal 5:1; Phil 1:27; 4:1.

tamer than the original. The expression "flat out" would capture Paul's mood, but is too idiomatic. Hence we have chosen "unreservedly."

Paul and Silas are petitioning God with εἰς τό, which shows the goal of their prayer.[32] At last we see what this team is praying for: that they might see the Thessalonians. As in 2:17, he uses an expression for a face-to-face meeting (τὸ πρόσωπον ὑμῶν) to refer to a personal visit. But beyond that, implicit in their prayer is that the satanic obstacle might prove to be no hindrance at all, that Paul and Silas will be able to once again head north and not simply send their agent to spy out the land. This prayer report should be studied in tandem with 2:18. Satan can seek to block the apostles, but lying behind that action, God has given him permission to do so. Thus the solution is not to rebuke Satan or to calculate boundaries of a territorial spirit, but to go directly to God and ask him to alter circumstances.

3:10e-f And to put in order any things that are lacking in your faith (καὶ καταρτίσαι τὰ ὑστερήματα τῆς πίστεως ὑμῶν). To be sure, this letter was already designed to fill the gaps in their lives, particularly in 4:13 – 18. Beyond that, Timothy was acting as the apostolic envoy who knows how to strengthen them. But Paul and Silas wish to do the same, and in person. "To put in order" (καὶ καταρτίσαι; BDAG suggests "to fix up any deficiencies") is the second concern. With "lacking in your faith" (τὰ ὑστερήματα τῆς πίστεως ὑμῶν) Paul does not distinguish between faith as "doctrine" and faith as "practice"; likely in this statement, the one blends into the other.

Timothy would go north with 1 Thessalonians, then return to Corinth; Paul would then write the second letter and send it with Timothy. From that point until Paul's return to Macedonia on his third missionary journey, we know little of these believers. The data we have suggest that Silas would go to Macedonia, but apparently not to Thessalonica (Acts 18:5). Thus, neither Paul nor Silas would be able to revisit Thessalonica for six or seven years more, perhaps at the time of the writing of 2 Corinthians. We do not know if Satan kept blocking them or if, as in Ephesus, "a great door for effective work" (1 Cor 16:9) had opened to them in Corinth and other locales, and they were loathe to leave. Green states that God answered the apostles' prayer, pointing to Acts 19:21 – 22, where Paul again passed through Macedonia.[33] This is stretching a point, since many years would pass before that next visit. The better interpretation is that God did not immediately answer their prayer.

3:11a-b Now may our God and Father himself and our Lord Jesus (Αὐτὸς δὲ ὁ θεὸς καὶ πατὴρ ἡμῶν καὶ ὁ κύριος ἡμῶν Ἰησοῦς). With "now" Paul concludes this section. The words Paul dictates are at once a real prayer and also an exemplar of the apostles' prayers for the Thessalonians.

Grammatically the verbs (see below) catch the eye. The optative mood (as in "*may* God do something") was rarely used in the first century. The spread of *koinē* Greek since the third century BC meant that many of the finer classical usages were left behind as Greek became an international second language. As part of this evolution, the optative was in "strong retreat."[34] It was being subsumed into the subjunctive and is virtually extinct in modern Greek. In the LXX it occurs in nearly four hundred verses, but in the New Testament only sixty-eight times. Paul uses it twenty-eight times; his stereotyped "Never!" (μὴ γένοιτο; lit., "may it not be") accounts for fourteen (ten times in Romans alone, three times in Galatians, once in 1 Cor 6:15).

32. BDF §402(2).

33. Green, *Thessalonians*, 152, 174.

34. BDF §357.

Apart from that, many are "voluntary optatives," used "to express an obtainable wish or a prayer."[35] This appears three times in this prayer: "direct" (κατευθύναι), "increase" (πλεονάσαι) and "abound" (περισσεύσαι) in 3:11–12. What is remarkable for our purposes is the high frequency of nine optatives in the Thessalonian letters.[36] The fact that the LXX Psalms used the optative in prayer may have prompted Paul to use this antiquated form, because it sounded like "biblical" prayer language.

"Our God and Father himself" (αὐτὸς δὲ ὁ θεὸς καὶ πατὴρ ἡμῶν) is not a common phrase, but "God himself" is found again with an optative in 1 Thess 5:23 (cf. also Rev 21:3).[37] Isaiah 54:5 LXX provides a parallel with this letter: "he who rescues you is the God of Israel himself" (pers. trans.; 54:4 MT).

Integral to the apostle's theology is that Paul prays to the Lord Jesus just as he prays to the Father. He does not defend or justify the practice. We can only assume that the new disciples had heard him praying to God the Father and to the Lord Jesus from the very first. There is syntactical tension here that reveals something of his theology; technically there is disagreement between the plural subjects "our God and Father *and* our Lord Jesus" and the singular verbs of which they are the subject. In English we would have to imagine a sentence such as "God and Jesus directs us" in order to hear the same grammatical discord. It is common in the Pauline literature to see Jesus assume many of the roles of God.

3:11b Direct our steps to you (κατευθύναι τὴν ὁδὸν ἡμῶν πρὸς ὑμᾶς). The Lord of the angelic hosts can break the satanic blockade whenever it pleases him so to do. And so the team prays about a concrete aspect of their ministry, the possible return north of the full apostolic team. The verb "direct" (κατευθύναι) is a common one in the Jewish literature.[38] This is a prayer that God will give them "clear passage."

3:12a And may the Lord make you to increase and abound (ὑμᾶς δὲ ὁ κύριος πλεονάσαι καὶ περισσεύσαι). Paul goes on to pray for the Thessalonians themselves, using two optatives from the verbs "increase" and "abound." The subject of the verb is "the Lord," the referent of which is consistently the Lord *Jesus* in these two letters. Jesus is not simply some powerful angel who, like Michael in Dan 10:13, 21, can make a show of power; here he does what only God does, working deep within the hearts of his people to incline them toward righteousness. "Increase" (πλεονάζω) is used of the abounding of Christian virtue in 2 Thess 1:3 and 2 Pet 1:8. Paul uses the language of "abounding" or "thriving" here and in 1 Thess 4:1, 10 to affirm that the disciples are on the right path and to pray for or encourage further growth. As prayer was pivotal in bringing about their conversion, so it is in their growth.

3:12b-c In love for one another and for all people (τῇ ἀγάπῃ εἰς ἀλλήλους καὶ εἰς πάντας). Just as they are already renowned for their love (1:3), so now Paul prays that they grow still more. "One another" is the language used in a broad set of reciprocal actions within the Christian community.[39] "And for

35. Wallace, *Grammar*, 481.

36. Three times in this prayer; twice in 5:23; twice in the prayer of 2 Thess 2:17; in 3:5 (repeating the "direct," κατευθύναι, of 1 Thess 3:11), then again in 3:16. They are all aorist optatives.

37. In 2 Thess 2:16 it is reversed: "the Lord Jesus Christ himself and God our Father."

38. A good parallel to 3:11 using the same verb is found in the Apocrypha, where Judith prays that God will give her direction (Jdt 12:8).

39. E.g., in Paul's letters: Rom 12:10; 13:8; but most particularly in this letter: 1 Thess 3:12; 4:9; 4:11; 5:11; 5:15; also 2 Thess 1:3. It is also typical of Johannine language: examples include John 13:14; 1 John 3:11; 2 John 5.

all people" could refer to Christians of other communities (see 1:7), but a better rendering is a reference to love they have for "the whole human race" (JB).[40] Their love for outsiders and their desire to take the gospel to them contrasts with the forbidding stance of the synagogue toward the Gentile nations (2:15 – 16).

Here may be a veiled reference to the Olivet Discourse: apostates will "hate each other" and "the love of most will grow cold" (Matt 24:10, 12). By maintaining their love — no, by abounding in love — the Macedonians are standing firm against apostasy, whether it is the end time or not. The author of *2 Clement* may have had either Matthew or 1 Thessalonians in mind when he urged his audience, "let us love one another, that we all may enter into the kingdom of God" (*2 Clem.* 9.6); he understood that those who are worthy of the kingdom are loving. Paul will next speak of love in 1 Thess 5:8, of the breastplate that is love. It is right to pray that others may be more loving and to expect that the glorified Lord Jesus — preacher of the Olivet Discourse — might answer that prayer.

3:12d Just as our love does for you (καθάπερ καὶ ἡμεῖς εἰς ὑμᾶς). All of 1 Thess 2 – 3 has shown the apostles' love in the feelings they express, but more importantly, in the actions they have taken. He reminds the disciples that they have an excellent model of mutual love in the apostolic team; once again, Paul and his team are the "pattern" the disciples should imitate.

3:13a-b So that your entire person be made strong in blamelessness, [that is] with regard to holiness (εἰς τὸ στηρίξαι ὑμῶν τὰς καρδίας ἀμέμπτους ἐν ἁγιωσύνῃ). Paul now orients his readers toward the parousia; their present behavior will affect how they stand before God in his judgment. "So that" (εἰς τό) leads to an infinitive of result. The NIV, NRSV, and NJB start a new sentence and make the infinitive "strengthen" (στηρίξαι) sound as if it too were an optative ("May he strengthen your hearts so that . . . ," NIV), but this is to neglect the causal relationship between growing in love and being strengthened in holiness. The NLT is better: "May he, as a result, make your hearts strong. . . ." "Strengthen" (from στηρίζω) described Timothy's work among them in 3:2; his ministry has its counterpart in the spiritual realm when the apostles pray toward the same end. "Hearts" (τὰς καρδίας) is not a reference to the emotional life, but to the whole inner person (cf. 2:4).[41]

Their "blamelessness" (ἀμέμπτους) may be summed up as perfect "holiness" (ἁγιωσύνη; cf. the other references in Rom 1:4; 2 Cor 7:1). God's will in 1 Thess 4:3 is represented by the cognate "holiness" or "sanctification" (ἁγιασμός). Paul prays at the end of the letter for this very point, that they will be holy and ready at Christ's return (5:23).

3:13c-d Before our God and Father, at the coming of our Lord Jesus (ἔμπροσθεν τοῦ θεοῦ καὶ πατρὸς ἡμῶν ἐν τῇ παρουσίᾳ τοῦ κυρίου ἡμῶν Ἰησοῦ). Again we return to eschatology: here, as in 2:19, "before" (ἔμπροσθεν + genitive) refers to the parousia or the judgment. The saints will stand before "our God and Father" in the coming of Jesus. This statement has implications regarding the person of Christ, especially when Paul's Christology is contrasted with the theology of Second Temple Judaism. Within the Jewish hope, the messianic figure may range from being a central eschatological person to being eliminated entirely; or there may be two or even three messiahs.

40. Cf. Gal 6:10. See also Wanamaker, *Thessalonians*, 143.

41. Paul uses the "double accusative." Wallace, *Grammar*, 186, categorizes this particular use as the double accusative of object-complement, with a verb of "making, appointing."

But Christian theology is christocentric in a way that Judaism has never been Messiah-centric.[42] In Judaism, the Messiah does not mediate the presence of Yahweh as Christ does for God; he certainly does not fulfill the scriptural predictions of the epiphany of Yahweh.[43] In 3:13, Paul goes even beyond Matt 16:27: "For the Son of Man is going to come in his Father's glory with his angels." Jesus does not simply gather the saints to the Father; he embodies God's presence by his own person.

3:13e With all his holy [angels]. Amen (μετὰ πάντων τῶν ἁγίων αὐτοῦ. [Ἀμήν]). The Lord Jesus is accompanied by other holy beings in his parousia, but by whom? "All his holy ones" (πάντων τῶν ἁγίων αὐτοῦ) is simple enough syntax: it is the substantive use of the adjective "holy." There are two major interpretations of these "holy ones." The first is that they are holy *human beings* — either saints of the old covenant or Christian saints.[44] The second is that they are holy *angels*.[45] A compromise solution is that *both human and angelic beings* are intended.[46]

In favor of the interpretation that these are human saints are the many New Testament references to Christians, so much so that "the holy ones" or "saints" (οἱ ἅγιοι) is a semitechnical term for believers.[47] It appears that this is the sense of 2 Thess 1:10, which uses a Hebrew-type parallelism:

> when he comes to be glorified among his saints
> and
> to be worshiped among all who have believed

This verse does not necessarily contain a reference to Jesus coming *with* holy ones; rather, the saints glorify and worship him at the point of his revelation.

There is one possible NT picture of Christ coming to earth *with* human saints, in Rev 19:14: "The armies of heaven were following him, riding on white horses and dressed in fine linen, white and clean." This interpretation of 19:14 rests on the identification of the armies with saints in 19:7 – 8: "His bride has made herself ready. Fine linen, bright and clean, was given her to wear. (Fine linen stands for the righteous acts of God's holy people.)." Yes, they wear fine linen ... but then so do angels in Rev 15:6, who are "dressed in clean, shining linen ... [with] golden sashes around their chests." The referent of "the armies" in Rev 19:14 is in the end difficult to pin down.

In favor of the second view, that these are "holy angels," there exist many references to the coming of Yahweh or the appearing of the Son of Man or the parousia of Christ with angels.[48] Deuteronomy

42. Well-spoken is the observation of Marinus de Jonge: "Because a central tenet of Christianity has always been the conviction that Jesus was the Christ (the Messiah expected by Israel), much attention has been paid to the study of Jewish expectations of the Messiah. The Christian focus upon the person of Jesus has led to an undue concentration on the *person* of the Messiah in Jewish thought, even in the works of recent scholars." See "Messiah," *ABD*, 4:777.

43. The indispensable analysis of the Christology of these letters is by Gordon D. Fee, *Pauline Christology: An Exegetical-Theological Study* (Peabody, MA: Hendrickson, 2007), 31 – 83; also in Fee's *Thessalonians*, in loc. Some exceptions give hints of the divinity of the messianic figure: Ps 2:7; Isa 9:6 (the everlasting king is called "mighty God"); Mic 5:2. The literature of the Second Temple does not follow that lead: even the strongly messianic *Ps. Sol.* 17 speaks of a merely human son of David.

44. So Calvin, *Thessalonians*, 272. *Did.* 16.6 – 7 regards the saints as those who have just been resurrected and caught up with Christ.

45. So the majority of commentators: Green, *Thessalonians*, 181; Best, *Thessalonians*, 152 – 53; Wanamaker, *Thessalonians*, 145.

46. Morris, *Thessalonians* (NICNT), 111 – 12; Weima, "1 and 2 Thessalonians," 875, allows that this is possible.

47. Commonly in epistolary introductions, such as 1 Cor 1:2. Also notably Rom 8:27; 1 Cor 6:1 – 2; Eph 4:12; Col 1:26; there are also occurrences in Acts, Hebrews, Jude, Revelation.

48. See the useful article, C. A. Newsom and D. F. Watson, "Angels," *ABD*, 1:248 – 55.

33:2 speaks of Yahweh descending from Sinai: "The LORD came from Sinai and dawned over them from Seir; he shone forth from Mount Paran. He came with myriads of holy ones from the south, from his mountain slopes."[49] In Jude 14, "Enoch, the seventh from Adam, prophesied about these men: 'See, the Lord is coming with thousands upon thousands of his holy ones.'" This is a direct reference to the pseudepigraphal *1 En.* 1.9 (ed. Charlesworth): "Behold, he will arrive with ten million of the holy ones in order to execute judgment upon all." These "holy ones" are angelic, as in *1 En.* 60.4; 61.10.

The "clouds" of heaven in Dan 7:13; Mark 14:62; and Rev 1:7 might also denote the heavenly armies. In the Matthean version of the Olivet Discourse, the angels come with the Son of Man in order to collect the elect from the four corners of the earth (Matt 24:31); according to 24:36, these same angels do not know the day or hour of the parousia. Angels are also assigned to gather the wicked together for the fiery judgment (Matt 13:39, 41, 49). Besides all this evidence lies the parallel in 2 Thess 1:7: "the revealing of the Lord Jesus from heaven with his powerful angels" (μετ' ἀγγέλων δυνάμεως αὐτοῦ). The breadth of the evidence shows that 1 Thess 3:13 refers to angels, as does 2 Thess 1:7 (but they are not mentioned in 2 Thess 1:10).

The referent of "*his* angels" is not precise: its antecedent may be the Lord Jesus or God the Father. The parallel "his" in Matt 16:27 give no definitive help either; in Mark and Luke, Jesus simply refers to "the" angels. In 3:13, there is an allusion to Zech 14:5 (NETS) — "And the Lord my God will come and all his holy ones with him." By contrast, in Matt 24:31 the Son of Man comes with "his angels," and here the pronoun "his" clearly refers to the Son of Man. The parallel in 2 Thess 1:7 also makes the angels belong to the Lord Jesus. The parallels in Zechariah, Matthew, and 2 Thessalonians point to "all the holy angels" *of the Lord Jesus*. We conclude that Paul is speaking in 1 Thess 3:13 of how the Thessalonian believers will measure up in the presence of God, at the return of Jesus when he comes with his holy angels.

There is a minor textual problem at the end of this prayer, a phenomenon that is encountered at the close of prayers in other letters. Many strong witnesses include an "Amen" (ἀμήν), while other strong ones omit it. It may have been added in the margin by a pious scribe, assuming that it was appropriate conclusion to a prayer.[50]

49. This is a difficult verse to translate, as reflected as early as the LXX, which differs somewhat from the Hebrew: "The Lord has come from Sina, and appeared to us from Seir, and hasted from Mount Pharan with myriads of Kades; at his right, angels with him" (Deut 33:2 NETS translation of the LXX). See other versions for the variety of translations.

50. "Since it is very difficult to reach a confident decision, and since the external attestation is rather evenly balanced, a majority of the Committee decided to include ἀμήν, but enclose it with square brackets" (Metzger, *Textual Commentary*, 563). The NLT is the only major English version to include it. For parallels where Paul undoubtedly inserts the Amen, see Rom 9:5; 11:36; Eph 3:21; Phil 4:20; 1 Tim 1:17. Where doubt exists in the manuscripts, typically in the last verse of a letter, see, e.g., 1 Cor 16:24; 2 Cor 13:13; esp. 1 Thess 5:28; 2 Thess 3:18.

Theology in Application

Theology in Thessalonica

Many of the Thessalonians had come to Christ from paganism. Their gods were of superhuman power, but they were bound to the Fates just as were human beings. This meant that no Gentile, no matter how pious, could use prayer to substantially redirect future events; what would be would be. The most that could be hoped for was that the regular sacrifices and visible religious duties would ameliorate some of the excesses of divine caprice, even while one's Fate rolled on.

When the gospel arrived in Thessalonica, those Gentiles heard, perhaps for the first time, that there might exist a "living and true" God (1:9), one who freely "chose" (1:4) and who was in no way bound by Fate. This made stunning changes in the way in which the new believers saw the universe. Instead of fear and fatalism, believers could turn to the true God for help, even during hard circumstances, and ask for circumstances to change with regard to something as mundane as travel plans or something as profound as spiritual growth. "The God to whom we pray is no pitiless deity ... but is the Father who can do all things, has control of every situation and is near me in every time of need."[51] The fact that Paul thanks this God for the blessings that have happened also indicates that God is their source and that he is not simply a bystander to Fate.

Biblical Theology

For the Christian, prayer is entering into a personal relationship with the almighty God through his Son Jesus Christ.

Satan, too, is a reality in the Christian life. While many Western Christians reject the idea of a personal evil being,[52] it is a part of the apostolic gospel that he exists and that he makes himself known by trying to harm the gospel work — at times successfully — by blocking plans or by harming believers. Paul understands that to rightly exegete one's circumstances, we cannot relegate what happens to mere happenstance. By contrast, the believer who does not have direct access to a prophetic word from God must show great care in ascribing this thing to Satan or that thing God, lest he or she make a disastrous mistaken identification.

Paul asks God that their faith be strengthened (3:10), but the apostle does not let up on his own efforts toward achieving that end. Neither did he know anything of "follow-up" as a brief period of instruction after a person makes a profession.

51. Stauffer, *New Testament Theology*, 177.

52. See "Most American Christians Do Not Believe That Satan or the Holy Spirit Exist," in the Barna Report of April 13, 2009, which states that only about 35 percent of professing Christians in America believe that the devil is a personal being. Online: www.barna.org/barna-update/article/12-faithspirituality/260-most-american-christians-do-not-believe-that-satan-or-the-holy-spirit-exist.

Another modern notion is that once a person makes a profession of faith in Christ, it is up to the Holy Spirit to preserve them, and the evangelist's work is done. That is, if they are true Christians, they will survive; if they do not persevere, it must not have been the real thing. The Bible reader seeks in vain for this sort of laissez-faire discipleship. Rather, urgency is the key characteristic of Paul's work in taking his disciples from conversion through maturity. At every stage, prayer is a nonnegotiable.

By putting an imaginative spin on the apostolic prayers in this and other letters, we might be able to picture Paul and his companions at prayer:

Setting: One evening in Corinth before the sending of 1 Thessalonians

Paul: Our God and our Father, our Lord Jesus, our hearts are full of thanks. You have given us spiritual children, Father. It was you who sent the Spirit to convert them from their false idols. We did not do that, Lord, but you intervened and chose out for yourself a people for your name.

Silas: God and Father, you have made us love them. And they love each other so much. Miriam was even shunned by her parents because she refused to give up her new Christian friends. Be a Father to her, Savior; let the church embrace her as their own sister.

Paul: Be with those who can't find work because of their faith; we don't even know who they might be in this very hour. Let no one be discouraged, Lord, but let them seek work and find it so that they can support themselves in a godly way.

Timothy: Samuel was beaten in the synagogue, Lord Jesus, and did not deny your name. May all Christians of Thessalonica follow you even as they learn that this is normal for those who follow you.

Silas: Let no one panic, Lord, or lose hope. May everyone endure. *[He prays at length and mentions many by name].*

Paul: Thank you so much, Father, for these young disciples. *[He too prays for dozens of individuals and mentions details about a number of them].* You've planted deep within us the desire to nurture them. But now you have placed us so far away, and we can only reach them in writing. For so many weeks Satan has blocked us. May it please you, Father … *[he tears up and cannot speak].*

Silas: Lift Satan's blockade, we petition you, O Lord. No power in heaven or on earth can defy you. We confess that the Thessalonians are in your care; Timothy has brought us a good report; but in your mercy we pray that you would let us see the church with our own eyes.

And so on and so on…

Message of This Passage for the Church Today

One is impressed with the holy activism of the Pauline team through this section. If we were to follow the apostolic pattern laid down here, we would warn our people of all the possibilities that lie ahead, just as the apostles were frank about the possibility of persecution. In Greek mythology, Cassandra was a prophetess who foresaw horrible events, only to suffer the curse of being disbelieved. The apostolic message is more positive, given that we depend not on the Fates but on the almighty God.

Nevertheless, do we as preachers prepare our flocks for hard times? It's more of a crowd-pleaser to preach prosperity, conventional morality, how to succeed in business with God on our side, family values, politics, or theology that doesn't connect with real-life events — such as death, divorce, disease, addiction, unemployment, or rejection. In particular, a faithful Christian will warn people that tribulation is typical of Christianity, not an aberration. With regard to suffering, any pastor today who is not warning the flock about a great false teaching of our day, the Prosperity Gospel, is leaving the door open for trouble.

When speaking about signs of the end, focus not just on earthquakes and rumors of war, but also the grave danger that "the love of most will grow cold."

A certain proportion of Christians imagine that prayer is not about changing things, but rather changing our attitude about circumstances. Other Christians exaggerate Jesus' warning against vain "babbling" in prayer (Matt 6:7) and pray once and for all, "leaving it all in God's hands." But Jesus was not speaking against continual, fervent prayer, such as we find summarized in 1 Thess 3:10. In Christian prayer, one prays with passion and in communication with a divine Person, aided by the Holy Spirit.

Pray for matters that perhaps, according to your theology, are already sure things. Do you pray for your people? That they will continue to grow and be steadfast? Or even, as Paul implies here, that they will stay Christian? "But I believe in eternal security!" you might answer. Very well, and so do I. But the Holy Spirit carries out his work in part through the prayer of fellow believers.

CHAPTER 4

1 Thessalonians 4:1 – 12

Literary Context

First Thessalonians 4:1 marks a major turning point in the letter. The apostle had already described what kind of pattern the Thessalonians should follow (2:1 – 12). Now he turns to direct exhortation: *do this, don't do that.* This type of writing is technically known as *paraenesis.* When the Thessalonians later read the letter aloud, they will hear the echo of Paul's oral instruction: "That's how we entreated you face-to-face, that's how we comforted you, that's how we implored you to walk worthy of God" (cf. 2:12).

Paul is writing *paraenesis* to a congregation that has, according to a close reading of the text, not fallen into sin.[1] Nor does he suggest that Timothy has brought back troubling news about the Thessalonians. But Paul is sending the letter from Corinth, where his senses are daily bombarded by evidence of Gentile practices (as in 1 Cor 6:9 – 11). If the Thessalonians are going to backslide, these are the sins that might entrap them. Therefore, Paul tells them what every Gentile congregation needed to hear, while heartily affirming that they are doing well and should simply keep on in the same direction.

In the next section (4:13 – 18) Paul will turn to a particular aspect of theology that seems to elude them: the resurrection of the saints at Christ's parousia.

V. Paul and Silas' Frustrated Travel Plans and a Solution (2:17 – 3:13)

➡ **VI. *Paraenesis:* The Gospel Ethic in a Gentile Environment (4:1 – 12)**

- **A. The Thessalonians should continue to thrive in the gospel ethic (4:1 – 2)**
- **B. God's will for them includes sexual holiness (4:3 – 8)**
- **C. God's will also includes that each believer live in love (4:9 – 12)**
  - **1. The Thessalonians already excel in love for the Christian family (4:9 – 10)**
  - **2. One expression of love is a particularly Christian social ethos (4:11 – 12)**

VII. Instruction about the Return of Christ (4:13 – 5:11)

1. Some commentators argue that the Thessalonians had indeed fallen into the sort of sin that Paul here rejects: "Paul now turns to the first of the two matters where their 'faith' is 'deficient' (3:10)," see Fee, *Thessalonians*, 143. Also Green, *Thessalonians*, 181 – 84, 187 ("certain members" were living in sexual sin); also Robert Jewett, *The Thessalonian Correspondence*, 105 – 6.

Main Idea

When Paul wrote 1 Corinthians, he rebuked them for one sin after another: their involvement with incest and prostitutes, their lawsuits, and their lack of love. By stark contrast, the apostle did not correct the Thessalonians for any such behavior. He only has to urge them to continue in living right with regard to sex (4:3 – 5), relationships (4:6), Christian love (4:9 – 10), and work (4:11 – 12).

Translation

(See next two pages.)

Structure

With "beyond that" (λοιπὸν οὖν) Paul for the first time gives his readers a word of exhortation, which is the theme throughout this section. The content of his teaching is already well-known in Thessalonica: "just as" (καθώς) they received from the apostles (4:1c), "just as" (καθώς) they are doing (4:1d), and "because" (γάρ) they already know the apostolic commands. One might summarize the section by the highly optimistic note that they are doing well, and they should only "thrive even more" (4:1e).

The apostle's task is to verify those truths and to reaffirm that they should continue on that path. The first area of Christian behavior is that of a sexual ethic and its social implications. Paul explores the theme in 4:3 – 8 by using infinitives: to "abstain" (4:3) from fornication, to "know" (4:4) how to control one's own body, to not "transgress by taking advantage of" (4:6) other Christians through sexual misbehavior. As he often does in this letter, Paul uses the rhetorical device of antithesis in order to distinguish between Christian behavior and pagan: yes, abstain from fornication; yes, control your own body; no (μή) to harming other Christians. Within 4:4 – 5 he includes another antithesis: yes, in holiness and honor, no (μή) to Gentile lust.

In 4:7 there is yet another *inclusio*, bracketing 4:3 and 4:7 – 8 with references to God's will. Holiness in the realm of sexuality is not just some admirable virtue; rather, it proceeds from the person of God himself. There is further antithesis in these verses: not impure but holy; not human authority but God's.

The second area that Paul addresses is introduced by a transitional marker, "now concerning" (περὶ δέ, 4:9). With respect to love within the Christian family (4:9 – 12), the same truth applies that *you are doing well, so* (δέ, 4:10b) *keep on and keep growing.* Paul twice signals his knowledge of their love by "for" (γάρ): you are taught by God (4:9) and you love others (4:10). Once again Paul does not need to introduce some new doctrine or convince them that family love is a virtue to be desired. Positively,

1 Thessalonians 4:1 – 12

1a	Exhortation	Beyond that, brothers and sisters, **we urge and entreat you**
1b	Sphere	in the Lord Jesus
		that—
1c	Comparison	just as you received
		from us [teaching on]
		how you must conduct your lives in a manner pleasing to God, [in fact]
1d	Comparison	just as you are indeed conducting yourselves—
1e	Exhortation	that you thrive even more.
2a	Reminder language	**You know what commands we gave you**
2b	Agency	by the Lord Jesus,
3a	Reminder	[that] **this is what God desires:**
3b	Content	your holiness;
3c	Expansion #1	that you would abstain from immoral sexual practices,
4a	Expansion #2	that each one of you would know how to control his or her body
4b	Manner	in holiness and honor,
5a	Manner	not in lustful passions,
5b	Comparison	just as do the Gentiles,
5c	Description	who do not know God,
6a	Expansion #3	not transgressing by taking advantage of one's brother or sister
6b	Sphere	in such a matter,
6c	Cause	since the Lord is the one who avenges
		all situations
		of this nature,
6d	Reminder	just as we likewise told you and warned you.

7a	Cause	For [it is] **God who called us,**
7b	Purpose	not to be impure, but
7c	Contrast	[to live] in holiness.
8a	Assertion	So for that reason,
8b	Inference	**the one who rejects [this command] does not reject human authority**, but
8c	Inference	God, who has given his Holy Spirit to you.
9a	Assertion	Now, concerning family love, **you do not need us to write [anything] to you.**
9b	Cause	[I say this] because **you yourselves are [apparently] taught by God**.
9c	Content	to love one another.
10a	Example	And **you even practice this toward all the brothers and sisters in all of Macedonia**.
10b	Exhortation	So, **we [simply] entreat you,** brothers and sisters,
	Expansion	to thrive even more, and
11a	Expansion	to make it your ambition to live peaceably, and
11b	Expansion	to keep to your own business, and
11c	Expansion	to work with your own hands,
11d	Reminder language	just as we commanded you,
12a	Purpose	in order that you might conduct yourselves properly
12b	Reference	with respect to those outside [the people of God] and
12c	Purpose	to have no need of anything.

in 4:11 he does underscore with infinitives some of the ways that Christians should express their love: to live peaceably, to keep to their own business, and to work with their own hands. These loving social behaviors have as their purpose "that" (ἵνα as marker of purpose, 4:12) they will have a good reputation and have no need of anything.

Exegetical Outline

➦ **I. The Thessalonians Should Continue to Thrive in the Gospel Ethic (4:1 – 2).**

II. God's Will for Them Includes Sexual Holiness (4:3 – 8).

- A. They must refrain from illicit sexual behaviors (4:3).
- B. They must maintain self-control (4:4).
- C. They must avoid stereotypical Gentile passions (4:5).
- D. They must not mistreat their "brothers and sisters" through sexual adventurism (4:6).
- E. They must remember that the Christian sexual ethic is based in God's calling (4:7 – 8).
  1. All holiness is rooted in God's person (4:7).
  2. Holiness was taught by the apostolic team, but the teaching comes from God, not from human authority (4:8).

III. God's Will Also Includes That Each Believer Live in Love (4:9 – 12).

- A. The Thessalonians already excel in love for the Christian family (4:9 – 10).
  1. The apostles see no need to teach them what they are already practicing (4:9a).
  2. It is evident that God has taught them directly (4:9b).
  3. They show family love to all Macedonian believers (4:10a).
  4. They must continue to grow in love (4:10b).
- B. One expression of love is a particularly Christian social ethos (4:11 – 12).
  1. They should seek a quiet and harmonious lifestyle (4:11a).
  2. They should do manual labor (4:11b).
  3. They should then enjoy the fruit of a good work ethic (4:12).
     - a. Those outside of Christ's family will approve of what they see believers doing (4:12a-b).
     - b. Believers will not be in economic need themselves (4:12c).

Explanation of the Text

4:1a-b Beyond that, brothers and sisters, we urge and entreat you in the Lord Jesus (Λοιπὸν οὖν, ἀδελφοί, ἐρωτῶμεν ὑμᾶς καὶ παρακαλοῦμεν ἐν κυρίῳ Ἰησοῦ). Earlier Paul had said, "Now we are alive if you stand firm in the Lord" (3:8). He then related how the team prayed that the Thessalonians might stay strong in love and in holiness (3:11 – 13). Now in 4:1 – 11 he shows in concrete detail what it means for the Thessalonians to be holy and loving in their behavior. The section should have caused the disciples to remember the oral teaching of the apostles (2:12).

Most English versions translate the opening as "finally" (λοιπὸν οὖν), giving the impression that the letter is drawing to a close. This is not a good translation, since in this context it means "beyond that" or "beyond what I have already written."[2] When read aloud in the congregation, it would gather afresh the attention of hearers for a new section of teaching, as would "brothers and sisters."[3]

Paul uses two verbs for his appeal: "urge" (ἐρωτῶμεν), which could simply mean "to ask," but in contexts where a teacher is pressing people how to live, it has this stronger meaning. He also "entreats" them (παρακαλοῦμεν). With reference to teaching them "in the Lord Jesus" (ἐν κυρίῳ Ἰησοῦ), see comments on 4:2.

4:1c-e That — just as you received from us [teaching on] how you must conduct your lives in a manner pleasing to God, [in fact] just as you are indeed conducting yourselves — that you thrive even more (ἵνα καθὼς παρελάβετε παρ' ἡμῶν τὸ πῶς δεῖ ὑμᾶς περιπατεῖν καὶ ἀρέσκειν θεῷ, καθὼς καὶ περιπατεῖτε, ἵνα περισσεύητε μᾶλλον). The new disciples received the Christian code of behavior by the apostles' teaching. Paul twice refers to oral teaching about how to walk "in a manner pleasing to God" (cf. 2:12; see also Col 1:10). This verb was conventionally used to denote the "receiving" (παρελάβετε) of oral tradition (cf. its use in 1 Cor 11:23 and 15:1 – 3). "Passed on" (παρέδωκα; 1 Cor 15:3) is another semitechnical term of oral tradition. In a culture with a low rate of literacy, Christian instruction usually depended on oral repetition: the learner heard the teacher's words, repeated them back, and passed them along to others.

"How" (πῶς) introduces a so-called indirect question, a transformation of *how should you walk, etc.*? Paul rules out the notion that the Christian ethic is merely optional: rather, it is obligatory; it "must" be done. "Must" (δεῖ) is an impersonal verb, which usually takes an infinitive as its subject (e.g., Acts 5:29: lit., "to obey God is necessary"). Here δεῖ has two subjects. The first infinitive is "walk/conduct oneself" (περιπατεῖν), a verb found everywhere in Paul's letters (see already 2:12; also 4:12). Like all Jews, Paul was well acquainted with the equivalent Hebrew verb, *hālak*. For example: "Was it not the Lord, against whom we have sinned, in whose ways *they were not willing to walk*, and whose law they did not obey?" (Isa 42:24b NASB).[4] From this verb is derived *halakah*, the label the rabbis gave to ethical instruction. The second infinitive is "please God" (ἀρέσκειν θεῷ; see comments on 2:4).

2. MM, 380 states that λοιπόν is used "sometimes simply to mark transition to a new subject like an emphatic οὖν." Cf. also 2 Thess 3:1. In Phil 3:1 λοιπόν signals a transition, but is not even close to the end of the letter. In the case of Philippians, a proper understanding of λοιπόν weakens the theory that the letter as it now stands is a clumsy redaction of two or more shorter letters.

3. See similarly Rom 12:1, "Therefore, I urge you, brothers and sisters."

4. See also Prov 15:21.

These two words do not point to distinct actions, as if "conducting yourselves" and "pleasing God" were two different tasks. Rather, they form a "hendiadys," the expression of a single idea by means of two similar words, joined by a conjunction (in this case, "and," καί; again see 2:12).[5] The translator should blend them together, yielding a meaning like "conduct your lives in a manner pleasing to God" or "live in order to please God." In 4:1 Paul introduces an implicit contrast between the old and new covenants: while the Judeans do not please God (2:15), the Gentiles can do so if they are in Christ. Because of God's intervention in the world, Christian instruction is on a different plane than the rabbinic *halakah*: they can walk in holiness because they enjoy a supernatural empowerment not available under the old covenant.

The Majority Text (and thus the KJV/NKJV) omits "just as you are indeed conducting yourselves" (καθὼς καὶ περιπατεῖτε), but it is supported by all the older manuscripts and we follow the NA[27] in including it. The clause reinforces our observation that Paul is not offering the Thessalonians any word of rebuke. The CEV translation is excellent: "You are already living that way, but try even harder."

4:2 You know what commands we gave you by the Lord Jesus (οἴδατε γὰρ τίνας παραγγελίας ἐδώκαμεν ὑμῖν διὰ τοῦ κυρίου Ἰησοῦ). Paul again turns to reminder language; the Thessalonians already "know" what he is about to say (οἴδατε; see comments on 1:5). This letter is a reinforcement of known oral commands (παραγγελίας). But what does Paul mean that the teaching is "by" or "through" (διά) the Lord Jesus? Here is part of the answer:

> His instructions ... have the character of authoritative apostolic ordinances, behind which stands the full authorisation of Christ Himself. Thus when he beseeches and admonishes the Thessalonians Paul can refer to the directions which were given "by the Lord Jesus" at the founding of the church, 1 Th. 4:2; cf. 2 Th. 3:10.... In the apostle's saying, then, the readers have to do with the Lord Himself.[6]

This is as useful as far as it goes, but one must press further. It is likely that the teaching authorized "by" (διά) the Lord Jesus should be similar to "we urge and entreat you *in* (ἐν) the Lord Jesus" (4:1). Perhaps Paul refers to:

1. teaching that has its source in some specific sayings of Jesus, that is, oral tradition that would later become a part of the written gospels[7]
2. teaching that has its roots in the preaching of the *apostles* of Jesus, but not necessarily referring to a specific saying of Jesus[8]
3. teaching that was revealed through charismatic prophecy (see "word of the Lord" in 4:15)[9]

It would seem logical to choose option 1 if there were some specific saying of Jesus that fit the situation; yet there is no true parallel in the preserved gospel tradition. Option 3 would be unusual, since it would hardly require a fresh word of prophecy to reveal that God wants the Thessalonians to be holy. Option 2 has the benefit of a parallel in 2 Thess 3:6, where "command ... in the name of our Lord Jesus Christ" turns out to be the apostles' teaching about work. This is the best option: when the apostles arrived, they contextualized the gospel to a Gentile audience, having determined that sexual and social holiness needed to be allotted a greater proportion. Their preaching possibly included the Jerusalem decree that ordered Gentile Christians to abstain from sexual immorality (Acts 15:29).[10]

5. See BDF §442(16).

6. O. Schmitz, "παραγγέλλω, παραγγελία," *TDNT*, 5:764.

7. Mentioned but not accepted by Best, *Thessalonians*, 158; in the same way Marshall, *1 and 2 Thessalonians*, 105.

8. Wanamaker, *Thessalonians*, 149; Bruce, *1 & 2 Thessalonians*, 79.

9. Best, *Thessalonians*, 158.

10. See, e.g., Green, *Thessalonians*, 190.

Perhaps it is no coincidence, then, that Paul sounds like James's appeal to heaven's authority: "It seemed good to the Holy Spirit and to us ..." (Acts 15:28). What Paul does in 1 Thess 4:2 is underscore that in questions of holiness, the Christian cannot rely on conscience or customs, but on God's standards as given through the Lord Jesus and the Holy Spirit and applied by the apostles. He will deal further with that theme in 4:8.

4:3a-b [That] this is what God desires: your holiness (τοῦτο γάρ ἐστιν θέλημα τοῦ θεοῦ, ὁ ἁγιασμὸς ὑμῶν). Here then is the heart of the matter: the rule for Christian behavior comes from God. Paul will add in 2 Thess 2:13 that it is the Spirit who carries out this work of holiness, and he holds that all believers have the Spirit (1 Cor 12:13). Later in Rom 12:2, Paul will declare that as Christians surrender themselves to God, their minds enjoy an ever-growing ability to grasp what is his will. Paul does not teach that there are esoteric heavenly mysteries into which only a select few might be initiated (as possibly claimed the errorists of 1 Tim 1:3 – 4). Rather, the ability to know God's will is for all who follow Christ and heed the apostolic doctrine.

The phrase "will of God" (θέλημα τοῦ θεοῦ) contains a "subjective genitive" — hence, "the will of God" means "that which God wants." In the Christian faith, the divine will is not some information set to which people should align themselves. Rather, it refers to what a personal God desires. Jesus, too, defined discipleship as doing the Father's will (Matt 12:50).

What does God desire, or what "pleases the Lord"? "Your holiness" (ὁ ἁγιασμὸς ὑμῶν). This is a better translation than "your sanctification," a word that on the one hand is uncommonly used and on the other is used with distinctive meanings within the various theological systems.[11]

Holiness is a theological term that tends to elude definition. We might start with what it is *not* in 4:3 (and 4:4, 7):

- Holiness is not adherence to a temple ritual nor submission to the Torah. Gentiles were excluded from the full temple system, and they also had been told by the apostles that they must not submit to the yoke of the law.
- Holiness cannot be defined simply as "separation" or being "called apart" without further definition and ethical application.
- Holiness is not an abstraction or simply "positional" truth; it has wide-ranging practical implications concerning everyday actions.
- Holiness is not merely a corporate characteristic, as in the phrase "one holy, catholic church." The call to holiness in this verse is for individual believers in Thessalonica and everywhere.

As to a positive definition of holiness, in Judaism and Christianity it is God who defines the holy: "Your ways, O God, are holy" (Ps 77:13). The Old Testament is replete with verses about how holiness is rooted in and measured by the holiness of Yahweh himself: for example, "You are to be holy to me because I, the Lord, am holy, and I have set you apart from the nations to be my own" (Lev 20:26). For this reason it is impossible to construct a biblical ethic of holiness that is not only theocentric, but Yahweh-centric.

A major implication is that the gospel does not offer a way of life that the whole world can follow; the Christian ethic presupposes a knowledge of God in Christ and the desire and ability to model

11. O. Procksch, "ἁγιασμός," *TDNT*, 1:113, appears to be saying that in the New Testament letters, this term is used "preponderantly in the field of Gentile Christianity," that is, in letters addressed to Gentiles. This proposal is moot, since most NT letters are written to predominantly Gentile churches. He further disproves his case by noting that the letter to the Hebrews uses the term.

oneself on him: "Follow God's example, therefore, as dearly loved children" (Eph 5:1). This puts the lie to those who do not follow Christianity but profess to admire Christ's teaching, and that usually in a bowdlerized form. Holiness means conforming to the character of God and at the same time rebuffing what is not in accordance with his character.

The Thessalonian context provides excellent help with regard to God/the gods and one's own ethic. A Thessalonian could look across the bay and have a wonderful vista of Mount Olympus. Yet the gods who dwelt there were the opposite of a role model (see the Introduction). They each had their own agenda, as can be proven from the Trojan War, where deities supported one side or the other. The philosophers, by contrast, found the myths repugnant:

> Shall our youth be encouraged to beat their fathers by the example of Zeus [as is recounted in Hesiod], or our citizens be incited to quarrel by hearing or seeing representations of strife among the gods [as in Homer]? ... [Rather] this is our first and great principle — God is the author of good only. And the second principle is like unto it: — With God is no variableness or change of form.[12]

For Plato, there was one god, and he was worthy of imitation. If someone were to choose to follow after Ares, then "when under the influence of love, if they fancy that they have been at all wronged, are ready to kill and put an end to themselves and their beloved" (*Phaedrus* 252d). Conversely, the one who imitated the true Supreme Being would pursue the philosophical life: "The philosopher believed that contemplation brings knowledge of God and results in likeness to him (cf. *Phaedrus*). Each person is fashioned by what he/she contemplates."[13] The "imitation of God" is found in philosophy (e.g., Socrates, Plato, Seneca, Epictetus) and in Judaism (Philo, the rabbis). Yet the God of the philosophers differs from Yahweh, as much as a lofty philosophical "unmoved mover" does from a God of love and wrath.

4:3c That you would abstain from immoral sexual practices (ἀπέχεσθαι ὑμᾶς ἀπὸ τῆς πορνείας). A primarily Gentile congregation at Thessalonica needed to receive continual reminders concerning what God expected in the way of sexual morality. There are several theories as to why Thessalonica in particular was in danger. The viewpoint of Walter Schmithals falters from the outset: they were falling into sin because of some Gnostic aberration that allowed its adherents to divorce the actions of the body from the inner spirit and thus render moot the question of sin for the enlightened.[14] His viewpoint founders for lack of evidence: (1) Why doesn't Paul here refute anything resembling Gnosticism as it is known from historical evidence? (2) Where in this letter does Paul indicate that they might be sexually immoral?

Some scholars have suggested that a specific Thessalonian religion was an enemy to sexual holiness. The cult of the Cabiri was supposed to have been bloody and also orgiastic. For example, K. P. Donfried argues that the cult of the "Cabiri" brothers was prominent in Thessalonica in Paul's day and that it had rituals that might have been known for sexual promiscuity.[15] His viewpoint falters because of the growing awareness that we know very little about the Cabiri cult, despite the claims of Donfried and others.

There is some evidence to suggest that the god Cabirus was called "the Most Holy" by its adherents. Vom Brocke argues that it is no coincidence that Paul uses the language of holiness so much in

12. Plato, *Republic* (trans. Jowett), 378 – 80.

13. Charles H. Talbert, *Reading the Sermon on the Mount: Character Formation and Ethical Decision Making in Matthew 5 – 7* (Grand Rapids: Baker, 2006), 96.

14. Schmithals, *Paul & the Gnostics*, 156 – 57.

15. See Donfried, "The Cults of Thessalonica," 336 – 56.

this letter—he calls them to follow the true God, whose holiness excludes fornication; by implication this God is the true counterpart of the false Most Holy Cabirus.[16] While this conclusion appears to possess some logic, it has two weaknesses. (1) The small amount of evidence for the cult in first-century Thessalonica should give the reader pause before making a connection between Paul's words and the background of Thessalonian paganism. (2) From the side of the biblical text, while it is true that "holiness" is used several times in 1 and 2 Thessalonians, this is not a particularly high frequency. Most of the references in this letter appear in this one section (in 4:3, 4, 7; also 2 Thess 2:13; and a synonym ἁγιωσύνη in 3:13). Moreover, Paul uses the term in three other letters (Rom 6:19, 22; 1 Cor 1:30; 1 Tim 2:15; see also Heb 12:14; 1 Pet 1:2), all apparently with the same meaning. The cognates "sanctify" (ἁγιάζω) and "holy" (ἅγιος) are scattered through his letters. That is, "holy" is not a term especially associated with Thessalonica, and by extension, a local Cabiri cult.

A better explanation is that Paul was aware that the Thessalonian context offered particular dangers (see the Introduction). The fact that he wrote from Corinth was a sharp reminder of what was possible; for that reason, his teaching here about fornication might have more to do with Corinth than with any problem in Thessalonica.

"Abstain" (ἀπέχεσθαι) when used in the middle voice means "keep away, abstain, refrain from," in this case from sexual immorality (see also 1 Pet 2:11). James, the leader of the Jerusalem church, had earlier written to the Gentile churches, using the same two key words "abstain" and "immorality": "It seemed good to the Holy Spirit and to us not to burden you with anything beyond the following requirements: You are to *abstain* [ἀπέχεσθαι] from ... *sexual immorality* (πορνεία; Acts 15:28–29; see also 15:20; 21:25).[17]

This was sent as a letter to Antioch, and Paul and Silas bore the message to those who had already come to faith in Galatia (Acts 16:4). Given our acceptance of the Acts account as accurate, a reasonable supposition is that they took that message to the new converts in Macedonia and Achaia.

Paul's converts were Gentiles from a variety of backgrounds. Some had been "God-fearers" and had attended to the reading of the OT in the synagogue. They would have heard the LXX's usage of the "immorality" (πορνεία) word group to speak of sexual sin generally and prostitution specifically. That is, they had a ready definition of sexual morality that the gospel then reinforced. But when Gentiles who had never been connected with the synagogue first heard preaching against "immorality," they might have been puzzled by the sense that the apostles now gave the word. The noun form "immorality" (πορνεία), although known, was rarely used in first-century Thessalonica.[18] It could mean consorting with a "prostitute" (its cognate πόρνη), but it might also refer to other irregular sexual practices. All this is to say that a Thessalonian Gentile might have understood "immorality"

16. Vom Brocke, *Thessaloniki*, 117–21.

17. The rendering of πορνεία in Acts 15:29 NJB as "illicit marriages" is unacceptable. That translation agrees with the view espoused by Ernst Haenchen (*The Acts of the Apostles: A Commentary* [trans. R. McL. Wilson; Philadelphia: Westminster, 1971], 449), who takes πορνεία as the prohibited degrees of marriage (incest) found in Lev 18:6–18; the case for this depends on the hypothesis that the Apostolic Decree was based on that passage of Leviticus.

18. There are a mere eight extant classical references to πορνεία: five from Aeschines and Demosthenes (fifth century BC, both of which deal with an exchange about the same situation of possible homosexual prostitution), a possible use in a fragment from Aristophanes (fifth to fourth century), and two fragments from Theopompus (fourth century). MM, 529, also states that πορνεία "originally meant 'prostitution.'" Nevertheless, because of Theopompus's references to orgies and because of the paucity of evidence, it is not possible to link it strictly to prostitution with its implied economic transaction, despite the word's etymological relationship with πορνή.

as exaggerated sexual activities. They would be offensive, not because they affronted the gods, but because they implied disrespect to family or the *polis* or because they showed a lack of self-control or led to financial embarrassment.

It was in Jewish and Christian contexts that the noun form "immorality" (πορνεία) came into more general usage, to describe *any sexual activity outside of heterosexual marriage*. The LXX uses it fifty times, if one includes the Apocrypha. It refers, for example, to Tamar's prostitution (Gen 38:24), to the unfaithful "wife" Israel (Hos 1:2), or even to mere sexual desire (Tob 8:7). Whether using this specific term (πορνεία) or not, the OT condemns all sorts of sexual sin: seduction of a virgin (Exod 22:16), incest (Lev 18:6 – 18), bestiality, homosexual intercourse, and cross-dressing (Lev 18:22 – 23; 20:13; Deut 22:5). Adultery is that subcategory of fornication that transgresses a marital relationship (see Sir 23:23; Matt 19:9) and is a capital crime. Adultery is intercourse with a married woman (Lev 20:10), but apparently the converse is not true; that is, it is not adultery when a woman commits fornication with a married man. Consorting with prostitutes, which Paul strictly forbids in 1 Cor 6:15 – 16, is treated more ambivalently; women can be stoned for prostitution (Deut 22:20 – 21); marrying a prostitute is expressly banned only for priests (Lev 21:7); and fathers are prohibited from prostituting their daughters (Lev 19:29). But there is no general ban on prostitution.

During the Second Temple period, *The Testaments of the Twelve Patriarchs* uses πορνεία twenty-five times. As *T. Reu.* 4.6 explains, immorality opens the path to idolatry: "the sin of *promiscuity* is the pitfall of life, separating man from God and leading on toward idolatry" (ed. Charlesworth; see also 1 Cor 10:6 – 13). Wisdom of Solomon 14:12, 26 states that it works the other way too; that is, idolatry can lead to all sorts of sexual sins. The NT uses the noun πορνεία twenty-five times. As Paul says in Rom 1, apostasy consists in not giving thanks to the Creator (cf. Rom 1:21 with 1 Thess 1:2); its results are felt in Gentile religion (idolatry, 1 Thess 1:9) and Gentile sexuality (fornication, 4:3 – 5).

What kinds of sexual sins might the term "sexual immorality" (πορνεία) include? *T. Benj.* 9.1 warns against the homosexual "immorality" of Sodom, whereas *T. Reu.* 1.6 applies the term to incest (see also 1 Cor 5:1). Josephus even tells of sexual immorality (πορνεία) committed against statues of Herod Agrippa's daughters after the death of that king in AD 44.[19] The rabbis looked down on the institution of slavery because it led to the sexual use of slaves, a crime that made a reappearance during the era of American slavery. Hillel said, "Lots of slave girls, lots of lust."[20] For Gentiles, sex with slaves was the norm.

Paul's definition of sexual sin generally follows Jewish standards, except that he categorically forbids consorting with prostitutes. In short, the biblical data confirm that "Paul's condemnation of extramarital sex was sweeping and unqualified. When he used the term *porneia*, Paul's meaning was unequivocal — it embraced any and all sexual relationships outside of marriage."[21]

In Thessalonica, Paul and the synagogue would have been perceived as unhealthily inhibited about sexual expression. To be sure, a handful of Greco-Roman philosophers took a view that was closer

19. Josephus, *Ant.* 19.9.1 (§357).

20. See *m. ʾAbot* 2:7.

21. James A. Brundage, *Law, Sex, and Christian Society in Medieval Europe* (Chicago: Univ. of Chicago Press, 1990), 61. See the brief but useful development of the theme by G. P. Carras, "Jewish Ethics and Gentile Converts: Remarks on 1 Thess 4,3 – 8," in *The Thessalonian Correspondence* (ed. Raymond F. Collins; BETL 87; Leuven: Leuven Univ. Press, 1990), 312, who argues that Paul means by *porneia* what the Hellenistic Jews meant, a rejection of all hetero- and homosexual sexual activity that is not between a husband and wife, including "incest, homosexuality, prostitution, and adultery."

to the Judeo-Christian ethic. Among the Stoics, the first-century Musonius Rufus stands out. According to him, both husbands and wives are responsible to be sexually faithful. He advocates the cultivation of deep marital love and respect. Procreation is one aspect of marriage, but marriage is raised to a higher level by the devotion of the spouses to each other. Musonius harshly condemns all sex, whether hetero- or homosexual, committed with anyone but the marriage partner.[22] Yet a high-minded ethic like that of Musonius was hardly popular in Thessalonica; in fact, it's probable that the first converts in Thessalonica had never even heard that any Greeks took such a strict view of sex.

The members of the Thessalonian church included Jews, Gentiles who had spent time in the synagogue, and a growing portion of people saved directly from paganism. Thus the apostles needed to expound on the Decree's prohibition of fornication so as not to leave the disciples there without direction. When the team preached there, they probably taught some version of the formula that "no immoral, impure or greedy person ... has any inheritance in the kingdom of Christ and of God" (Eph 5:5; also 5:3; see the other "vice lists" in 1 Cor 6:9–10; Gal 5:19–21; Col 3:5). They learned that one's sexual ethic, like all aspects of holiness, was rooted in God himself: "The body, however, is not meant for sexual immorality but for the Lord, and the Lord for the body" (1 Cor 6:13–14). It was God who banned fornication, that is, every sort of sexual activity outside of marriage (1 Cor 7:2), and not just those activities that brought shame on the individual, the family, or the city.[23] In 1 Thess 4:3, Paul simply reinforces this teaching, with no indication that they have let him down.[24]

4:4 That each one of you would know how to control his or her body in holiness and honor (εἰδέναι ἕκαστον ὑμῶν τὸ ἑαυτοῦ σκεῦος κτᾶσθαι ἐν ἁγιασμῷ καὶ τιμῇ). This is the most complex verse in the Thessalonian correspondence because of the difficulty of the language of the clause "control/possess one's own body/vessel [σκεῦος]." The NASB simply leaves it as "possess his own vessel." Most likely, the Thessalonians knew what Paul meant by σκεῦος; they had heard it from him before. Or, they could ask Timothy for further enlightenment. Today we have no Timothy to clarify matters. The best interpretation, which we will demonstrate below, is that *all Christians, men and women, should know how to maintain control of their bodies in a way that pleases God in sexual holiness.*

"Know" (εἰδέναι) is not simply cognizance of the right behavior, but also the doing of it.[25] Like "abstain" in 4:3, it is an infinitive used to give further expression to "your holiness" and takes an accusative subject "each one [of you]" (ἕκαστον [ὑμῶν]). "Control" (κτᾶσθαι) shows what they are to know; in other contexts the verb may mean "possess" or "acquire or gain possession." Moulton and Milligan offer evidence that in later *koinē* Greek another meaning grew in popularity, to "gradually obtain the complete mastery of."[26]

22. See J. Edward Ellis, *Paul and Ancient Views of Sexual Desire: Paul's Sexual Ethic in 1 Thessalonians 4, 1 Corinthians 7 and Romans 1* (LNTS; Edinburgh: T&T Clark, 2007), 108–11; also "The Sex Ethics of Stoicism" under the article "πόρνη," *TDNT*, 6:583–84; Musonius Rufus, frag. 12 (found in Beverly Roberts Gaventa, *First and Second Thessalonians* [Interpretation; Louisville: John Knox, 1998], 52–53).

23. See D. F. Wright, "Sexuality, Sexual Ethics," *DPL*, 871–75.

24. A century later, the Roman Christian Hermas was described as one who "abstains from every evil desire" (Herm. *Vis.* 1.2.4), a statement that seems to allude to this letter.

25. BDAG, οἶδα 3; George Milligan, *St. Paul's Epistles to the Thessalonians* (London: MacMillan, 1908), 49.

26. MM, 362. Commentators have tended to focus on literary Greek, not on the papyri, and deduced that "possess" is the meaning only in the perfect tense and that "acquire" is to be preferred here. Thus Milligan adds as a corrective, "to judge from the papyri it would seem as if at least in the popular language this meaning [possess] was no longer confined to the perf[ect tense]. See Milligan, *Thessalonians*, 49.

The noun "vessel" (σκεῦος) presents the interpreter with unusual difficulties. In other contexts, it was used literally of a container (Mark 11:16); here it is a metaphor, but of what? Two millennia of interpretation have produced the following options:

1. "Vessel" means "a wife," making Paul's command that each man figure out how "possess" or "acquire a wife."[27]
2. "Vessel" is a circumlocution for the penis.[28] Some take the genitalia as a metonymy for the whole human body.[29] While the natural interpretation would be that the command applied only to the men of the community,[30] some commentators suggest that the metaphor should be extended to the sexual lives of all members, male or female.[31]
3. The view here favored, "vessel" is a metaphor of the human body.[32] According to this reading, Paul uses the generic sense of the masculine pronouns (ἕκαστον and ἑαυτοῦ) as "his or her" and refers to all readers, men or women.

The interpretation of the clause in option 1 as "acquire a wife" is complicated at the outset by demographical considerations. The task of finding a wife in first-century Macedonia was not as simple as making up one's mind to get married. Many Greeks "exposed" their female babies; that is, they abandoned them to die because of the financial

27. This is the view of Augustine, *Marriage and Concupiscence* 1.8.9; see Peter Gorday, ed., *Colossians, 1–2 Thessalonians, 1–2 Timothy, Titus, Philemon* (ACCS, New Testament 9; Downers Grove, IL: InterVarsity Press, 2000), 80. See esp. Witherington, *1 and 2 Thessalonians*, 114–16; Burke, *Family Matters*, 185–93; Malherbe, *Letters to the Thessalonians*, 226–28. C. Maurer ("σκεῦος," *TDNT*, 7:365) states that "either the unmarried in Thessalonica are being urged to marry as a remedy against fornication (ingressive sense) or those who are married are being told to hold their own wives in esteem (durative sense)." O. Larry Yarbrough, *Not Like the Gentiles: Marriage Rules in the Letters of Paul* (SBLDS 80; Atlanta: Scholars, 1985), 65–87, points to the language of Tob 4:12 and *T. Levi* 9:9–10, which both speak of "obtaining a wife" and keeping oneself from fornication. Because those passages also warn against intermarrying with Gentiles, Yarbrough suggests that Paul wrote to urge the community to keep itself apart from the Gentile world. Yarbrough does not explain why Paul would use such a remote metaphor as "obtain a *vessel*" when he could just as easily have said "obtain a wife" or "know how to respect and honor your wife" (CEV; see GNB). There are two further variations of the interpretation that "vessel" means "wife." Jouette Bassler proposes that Paul is suggesting that they acquire a "spiritual wife," that is, that a couple agree to live together without "passion," that is, any sex at all. See "Σκεῦος: A Modest Proposal for Illuminating Paul's Use of Metaphor in 1 Thessalonians 4:4," in *The Social World of the First Christians: Essays in Honor of Wayne A. Meeks* (ed. L. Michael White and O. Larry Yarbrough; Minneapolis: Fortress, 1995), 53–66. This viewpoint runs counter to Paul's teaching in 1 Cor 7:3–6. D. Fredrickson, "Passionless Sex in 1 Thessalonians 4:4–5," *WW* 23 (2003): 23–30, says that "vessel" (σκεῦος) means the receptacle for semen, that is, the woman, and that Paul is in favor of sex within marriage, but only if the sex carried out without desire. There is an excellent rebuttal of this viewpoint in the full study by J. E. Ellis, *Paul and Ancient Views of Sexual Desire*; also by Robert W. Yarbrough in his very useful "Sexual Gratification in 1 Thess 4:1–8," *TJ* 20 NS (1999): 215–32.

28. For this viewpoint, see BDAG, σκεῦος 3; Donfried, "The Cults of Thessalonica," 342. Some commentaries tactfully use the Latin equivalent, *membrum virilis*, "male member."

29. So Wanamaker, *Thessalonians*, 152–53.

30. Fee, *Thessalonians*, 146–50. See also Torleif Elgvin, "'To Master His Own Vessel.' 1 Thess 4.4 in Light of New Qumran Evidence," *NTS* 43 (1997): 604–19; Jay E. Smith, "Another Look at 4Q416 2 ii.21, a Critical Parallel to First Thessalonians 4:4," *CBQ* 63 (2001): 499–504. Both argue based on the Qumran text that "vessel" means male member, as also in 1 Sam 21. Both succeed in demonstrating only that the Qumran text is open to a great many interpretations and that the key proof text 4Q416 is murkier in meaning than 1 Sam 21 and 1 Thess 4.

31. This is the view of Robert W. Yarbrough, "Sexual Gratification in 1 Thess 4:1–8," 220–21. Yarbrough gives a careful analysis of the data. Nevertheless, he seems to make a leap of logic from: (a) "vessel" was a common metaphor of the male member; to (b) by extension, Paul means to include the female genitalia as well. It is difficult to prove (a), and (b) would be even more of a strained application even if (a) were really the case.

32. So ESV, NIV, NJB, NLT, NRSV, REB. See the excellent analysis by Rigaux, *Thessaloniciens*, 503–7, who regards these verses as parallels with statements within 1 Cor 4–6. The "body" interpretation is the view of Tertullian, *Res.* 16 (*ANF* 3:556); see Gorday, *Colossians, 1–2 Thessalonians, 1–2 Timothy, Titus, Philemon* (ACCS), 80; also John Chrysostom, *Homilies on First Thessalonians* 5 (*NPNF*[1] 13:344); Bruce, *1 & 2 Thessalonians*, 83; Calvin, *Thessalonians*, 274.

burden that they caused. This led to a population tipped disproportionately toward the males, such as in China today due to its "one-child policy." Particularly in Greece, a man might have to wait until his thirties in order to marry a girl who was scarcely in puberty. This lack of brides explains in part the prevalence of homosexual partnering as a measure against the long interim before a marriage could be consummated. Added to this was the higher mortality of women because of the risks of childbirth (see comments on 5:3). For the Christian man in Macedonia, the lack of available Christian women might have been an impediment to marriage. Of course, this situation would also have been the case in Corinth, and Paul seemed undeterred from telling Corinthian men to get married (1 Cor 7:2a).

In favor of option 1 is the argument that "vessel" (σκεῦος) means a wife in 1 Pet 3:7, where she is called "the weaker vessel" (KJV). Besides the difficulties attached to using a Petrine metaphor to interpret Paul, this argument is easily turned on its head. If the wife is a weaker vessel, then by implication there is a corresponding stronger vessel, that is, the husband. In 1 Pet 3:7, both spouses are vessels, which, if anything, adds evidence for option 3.

A strong proponent of option 1, C. Maurer implies that "possess a vessel" was a Hebrew euphemism for having sex with one's wife. In fact that phrase nowhere appears in Hebrew, and Maurer is only speculating that a Hellenistic Jew *could have* combined two expressions ("acquire a wife" and the metaphorical use of "vessel") to form that phrase.[33]

With regard to option 2, isn't it true that "vessel" (Heb. *k^e lî*) was a popular euphemism for the "male member"? For example, in 1 Sam 21:5 (ESV): "And David answered the priest, 'Truly women have been kept from us as always when I go on an expedition. The vessels of the young men are holy even when it is an ordinary journey. How much more today will their vessels be holy?' " But in fact, this is to interpret one unclear verse (1 Thess 4:4) with a second unclear verse (1 Sam 21:5). David could have been using *k^e lî* to signify either the body in general or possibly the male sexual member in particular, but his meaning is not at all certain, whether in the Hebrew or in the LXX.[34]

Against options 1 and 2, we should not take for granted that only the men needed a warning against sexual immorality. While it was assumed that men would be sexually adventurous, Greeks and Romans also reproached women for being insatiable. Some argued that a man might be able to better control himself by the dictates of reason.[35] Any show of interest in sex on the part of the woman was a sign of promiscuity.[36] Besides this cultural background, it would have been uncharacteristic for Paul to define holiness as *that the males know how to control their sexual organs*, or *that a man know how to acquire/respect a wife*, leaving no word for underage males or females or celibates (he speaks about women and sexual sin in 1 Tim 5:11; Titus 2:5; perhaps 2 Tim 3:6). This is an argument against both options 1 and 2; note how in 1 Cor 7, the one text where Paul does deal with sexuality in great detail, he speaks equally to both sexes and covers a variety of life situations.[37]

33. C. Maurer, "σκεῦος," *TDNT*, 7:361, 365 – 67.

34. In the first part of David's statement, *k^e lî* in the Hebrew has no corresponding word in the LXX; he merely says that "we have kept ourselves from woman." Therefore, in the LXX, reading *k^e lî* as "body" or "person" is at least as likely as "male member." David goes on to use the word "vessel" at the end of the verse, but again it hardly seems to refer to sexual organs in the Hebrew; in the Greek, David says that his journey "shall be consecrated today through my implements [from σκεῦος]" (NETS). In this phrase, "implements" seems to refer to weapons, another meaning of that noun.

35. See Dale B. Martin, *The Corinthian Body* (New Haven, CT: Yale Univ. Press, 1995), 219 – 28.

36. See Peterman, "Marriage and Sexual Fidelity," 168 n. 21.

37. See 1 Cor 7:2 – 40; we take 1 Cor 7:1 ("It is well for a man not to touch a woman," NRSV) to be a slogan of super-spiritual Corinthians that Paul takes up and modifies to his own purposes.

None of these three options is an obvious victor. In this case it should be remembered that both options 1 and 2 rely on rather obscure assumptions ("vessel" means a "wife"; "vessel" is Hebrew for the male member) that have yet to be demonstrated. The simplest reading is option 3, that this is a commandment for all men and women, since all have — or better *are* — their own "vessel" (as in 1 Pet 3:7). Here we are on safer ground, since Paul regularly speaks of the Christian's body in terms of a "container" when he speaks of personal holiness.

For example, the body is a temple that contains the Holy Spirit (1 Cor 6:19; cf. 1 Thess 4:8). He uses "vessel" (σκεῦος) itself in 2 Tim 2:21: "who cleanse themselves from the latter will be *instruments* for special purposes, made holy, useful to the Master and prepared to do any good work." It must ever be kept in mind that for Paul it would be a foreign concept to use "vessel" in some Platonic sense, as if the body were the container for the true person, which is the soul or spirit. Paul is clear on this matter: God is the Creator and Redeemer of the body, which is part of the "real person."

Christians, male or female, are to exercise control over themselves "in holiness and honor" (ἐν ἁγιασμῷ καὶ τιμῇ). That is to say, self-control is of singular interest to a holy God. We have seen in 4:1 that our ethic is defined by the nature of God, that his very person reveals what is to be considered holy or honorable. Some have suggested that "honor" (τιμῇ) is the attitude a man shows his wife (i.e., following option 1 above), but it is better seen as the "honor" or even "decency" to be practiced by all Christians.

4:5 Not in lustful passions, just as do the Gentiles, who do not know God (μὴ ἐν πάθει ἐπιθυμίας καθάπερ καὶ τὰ ἔθνη τὰ μὴ εἰδότα τὸν θεόν). Paul contrasts the Christian path of "holiness and honor" with the Gentile quest to satiate their sexual desires. He first rules out "lustful passions" (ἐν πάθει from πάθος, while singular in the Greek, is better rendered by the plural). πάθος is used elsewhere of "suffering" (*Barn.* 6.7, often in Ignatius), but in the NT it always denotes sinful human desires (so Rom 1:26; Col 3:5). One could take "of lust" (ἐπιθυμίας) as a subjective genitive ("passions engendered by lust"); the better option is that it is a descriptive genitive ("desires that are lustful").

We have rejected option 1 of 4:4, that Paul is speaking of a man and his wife. It is doubtful that Paul is now describing the marital sexual relationship, as if to say that passionate sex is inadmissible even within a Christian marriage. Hebrews 13:4 does not, as some might suggest, provide an exact parallel: "Marriage should be honored by all, and the marriage bed kept pure." For there the author goes on to tell us whom he considers are the defilers of marriage: "the adulterer and all the sexually immoral." That is, it is not a warm physical relationship as such that is the concern of Heb 13:4, but its violation by extramarital sin. First Thessalonians 4:5 has the same lesson, that the Thessalonians should not let the way of Gentile fornication be their practice, since by definition it is lustful.

"Just as" leads us to a comparison. "The Gentiles, who do not know God" has a nice parallel in 4:13: "just like other people, who have no hope." The verb "know" speaks of a personal knowledge; in 2 Thess 1:8, "those who do not know God" will face his fiery vengeance. This affirms our point about the Christian ethic (see comments on 4:3).

4:6a-b Not transgressing by taking advantage of one's brother or sister in such a matter (τὸ μὴ ὑπερβαίνειν καὶ πλεονεκτεῖν ἐν τῷ πράγματι τὸν ἀδελφὸν αὐτοῦ). This clause, which has also been much debated, should be taken to mean *that impure sexual practice is a path that leads to defrauding one's fellow-believers*. Paul begins with two infinitives that lie parallel to "abstain" in 4:3 and "know" in 4:4 — God also wills that they not *transgress* and *take advantage*. "Transgress" and "take advantage" possess only one article (τό); thus they should be taken as a hendiadys, the expressing of one idea by joining two words together with "and" (see 2:12; 4:1). Their meaning is along the lines of "transgressing by taking advantage."

What is not so clear is the phrase "in such a matter" (ἐν τῷ πράγματι). There are two major interpretations: (1) Paul *is not* still speaking about sexual sin, but of defrauding one's fellow Christians generally;[38] (2) Paul *is* still speaking about sexual sin and developing its ramifications for the Christianity community.[39]

An examination of the language will help to better identify his point. "Transgressing" (ὑπερβαίνειν) has the sense of a moral overstepping. Some argue that the verb takes "his or her brother or sister" (τὸν ἀδελφὸν αὐτοῦ) as a direct object and that it means "disregarding" someone or, more fully, "act against with force or cunning" against someone.[40] The view we take is that the verb is intransitive (not using a direct object) in the sense of simply "transgressing." Nor should the Christian "take advantage" (πλεονεκτέω), the verb that does take "brother or sister" as its direct object. In Paul's letters, the verb typically refers to theft. If that is the case here, then "defraud in business" (πλεονεκτεῖν ἐν τῷ πράγματι) might fit, with the dative "business" meaning commercial business or work. On the other hand, "business" (πράγμα) is capable of other meanings; in fact, "an affair" was a euphemism for a sexual liaison.[41] As such it anticipates the "all situations of this nature" in 4:6.

The context too shows that Paul is still speaking of illicit sex. First, he is clearly speaking of sexual sin in 4:3 – 5: God's will is that they refrain from fornication and that they know how to control themselves honorably, not as the pagans do. Later in 4:7 onward, he again speaks against "impurity" (ἀκαθαρσία) and in favor of "holiness" (ἁγιασμός), two words already used in the context of sexual activity in 4:3 – 4. That is, Paul is likely not talking about sex, then changing to some other theme, and then switching back to sex again. It is better to take all of 4:3 – 8 to concern the holiness that excludes fornication, so that 4:6 warns against the damage that may be caused by sexual sin: they are taking advantage of others.[42] Paul thus opens up the social side of this transgression, and in a way that surpassed the philosophical moralists of his day. These illicit sexual actions harm all who are connected with either transgressor, be they spouses, fiancé(e)s, family members, or any fellow Christians.

In a later passage, Paul would show how adultery is ruled out by the love commandment (Rom 13:9 – 10, quoting Lev 19:18):

> The commandments, "You shall not commit adultery," [et al.] are summed up in this one command: "Love your neighbor as yourself." Love does no harm to its neighbor. Therefore love is the fulfillment of the law.

Here in 4:6, Paul shows that if any Christian, man or woman, commits fornication with any other Christian, it is by definition the defrauding of a "brother or sister." Already in Israel, it was a grave offense to have intercourse with the wife of one's "brother" (Lev 18:16), but in that case it was a biological brother. Adultery between Christian and Christian was of that level of lewdness: they

38. For example, G. Delling, "πλεονεκτέω," *TDNT*, 6:271.

39. Best, *Thessalonians*, 166; Fee, *Thessalonians*, 150 – 51; Wanamaker, *Thessalonians*, 154 – 56.

40. J. Schneider, "ὑπερβαίνω," *TDNT*, 5:744.

41. See BDAG, πράγμα 3. The noun is used to refer to the homosexual relationship of Aristogeiton and his boy lover Marmodius. Their pederastic arrangement was consensual and was held up by some to be an ideal.

42. Of course, Paul would emphasize that fornication is first of all an offense against God, a theme that is even more strikingly put in 1 Cor 6:18 – 20, along with the truth that it is sin against one's own body.

are taking the wife of a "brother" and also invite the condemnation found in Deut 27:22: "Cursed is anyone who sleeps with his sister" (see also 2 Sam 13:1 – 22). This makes Paul's attention-getting "brothers and sisters" in 4:1 even more impressive: when Christians engage in sexual adventurism with another believer, they have ceased to behave as they should act toward a sibling. Paul will make the same assumption in 1 Tim 5:2b when he tells Timothy, treat "younger women as sisters, with absolute purity."[43]

4:6c-d Since the Lord is the one who avenges all situations of this nature, just as we likewise told you and warned you (διότι ἔκδικος κύριος περὶ πάντων τούτων, καθὼς καὶ προείπαμεν ὑμῖν καὶ διεμαρτυράμεθα). If the Thessalonians needed further motivation to be sexually pure and self-controlled, Paul gives them a lesson in eschatology: no matter how cleverly the sin is concealed, the Lord will avenge the defrauded person. God is called the avenger in the Old Testament, notably in Ps 79:10: "make known among the nations that you *avenge* the outpoured blood of your servants" ("you" refers to Yahweh God).

"The Lord" throughout this section of 1 Thessalonians is the Lord Jesus, giving him yet another role of Yahweh God. In 2 Thess 1:8 the Lord Jesus inflicts "retaliation" (the cognate noun, ἐκδίκησις, is a cognate noun of "avenger," ἔκδικος) on the wicked. While it is stock teaching that the Lord will avenge his people on outsiders, it is also true that the Lord will avenge one Christian against another. This eschatological act falls in the category of 2 Cor 5:10, that "we must all appear before the judgment seat of Christ, so that each of us may receive what is due us for the things done while in the body, whether good or bad." "All situations of this nature" (περὶ πάντων τούτων), like the "matter" (πράγμα) earlier in the verse, seems to be an example where Paul uses a circumlocution for sexual transgression.

Paul then goes on to use more reminder language as in 4:2. The apostles have "told" them previously and "warned" (διεμαρτυράμεθα) them, which means "to exhort with authority in matters of extraordinary importance, frequently with reference to higher powers and/or suggestion of peril."[44] According to Acts, the latter verb is a favorite of Paul's.

4:7 For [it is] God who called us, not to be impure, but [to live] in holiness (οὐ γὰρ ἐκάλεσεν ἡμᾶς ὁ θεὸς ἐπὶ ἀκαθαρσίᾳ ἀλλ' ἐν ἁγιασμῷ). Paul underscores the seriousness of his instruction at this point: yes, the Lord Jesus will avenge those who have defrauded their brothers and sisters. He provides a cause for their behavior with "for" (γάρ). But the eschatological judgment is not the only frame of reference; their very call to the gospel by God meant that they were summoned to leave behind their Gentile ways (4:5). "*It is God* who called us" shows the appropriate emphasis in this clause, with Paul emphasizing "God" by leaving this word until the end of the clause. Paul uses two key words here: "impure/impurity" (ἀκαθαρσίᾳ, see 2:3) and "holiness" (ἁγιασμῷ, see 4:3, 4).

4:8 So for that reason, the one who rejects [this command] does not reject human authority, but God, who has given his Holy Spirit to you (τοιγαροῦν ὁ ἀθετῶν οὐκ ἄνθρωπον ἀθετεῖ ἀλλὰ τὸν θεὸν τὸν [καὶ] διδόντα τὸ πνεῦμα αὐτοῦ τὸ ἅγιον εἰς ὑμᾶς). The apostolic ethic is rooted in the person and nature of God: God summons human beings to be like him. Paul begins with "so for that

43. Did the Corinthians exaggerate this doctrine (1 Cor 7:1), insisting that couples live together as brother and sister, a practice that would gain popularity in the second century? This was never Paul's intention, as can be shown from 1 Thessalonians and 1 Cor 7:3 – 6.

44. BDAG, διαμαρτύρομαι 2.

reason" (τοιγαροῦν),[45] perhaps employing a multisyllabic word in order to make the Thessalonians slow down in order to consider this truth. "Reject" (ἀθετέω) is used of divine commandments in other passages (Mark 7:9; Luke 7:30; Heb 10:28; Herm. *Mand.* 3.2). Paul strikes a familiar note, that his message is not (merely) a human one but derives from God: to reject it is to reject God himself (see 1 Thess 2:13).

This is a truth in the gospels as well: those who reject the apostles reject Jesus; and those who reject Jesus, reject him who sent Jesus (see Luke 10:16, where "reject" [ἀθετέω] appears four times). Green argues on the basis of this verse that some men of the community were still living a lifestyle of pagan sexuality, and that someone was denigrating the apostolic teaching as being merely "from a man."[46] However, there is little evidence in the text that Paul is doing anything more than reminding the Thessalonians of a teaching that in the Gentile world was particularly out of the ordinary.

God is the one who "gives," or more likely "has given" (διδόντα),[47] the "Holy Spirit," a title for the Spirit that Paul frequently uses. Christians should be holy because God commands it and because his Spirit, who is holy, is within them. By invoking the Holy Spirit here, Paul also alludes to the prophetic new covenant, which said that God would place the Spirit in the hearts of his people and teach them directly (see "Theology in Application" as well as the phrase "taught by God" in 4:9): "And I will put my Spirit in you and move you to follow my decrees and be careful to keep my laws" (Ezek 36:27). Yet Paul has changed the LXX's future tense "I will give" (δώσω) the Spirit, and with the participle implies that already God has given his Spirit to the Thessalonians. These disciples of Jesus find themselves in the age of fulfillment: Jesus has come, and God is pouring out his Spirit on his people, exchanging their natural pagan ways for supernatural.

4:9a Now, concerning family love (Περὶ δὲ τῆς φιλαδελφίας). Paul uses "now, concerning" (περὶ δέ plus the genitive) to turn to a new theme. We have converted the traditional "brotherly love" to "family love," to make it clear that this is love between siblings, regardless of gender. The term deserves close attention, since "in profane Greek and the LXX [family love] φιλαδελφία is confined to the love of those who are brothers by common [i.e., biological] descent."[48] Fourth Maccabees is typical of the Jewish usage, in its account of the famous Seven Brothers who were martyred one after another:

> But although nature and companionship and virtuous habits had augmented the affection of family ties, those who were left endured for the sake of religion, while watching their brothers being maltreated and tortured to death. Furthermore, they encouraged them to face the torture, so that they not only despised their agonies, but also mastered the emotions of *brotherly love* [φιλαδελφία]. (4 Macc 13:27 – 14:1; see also 13:23)

That is, family love (φιλαδελφία) was limited to family commitment between blood relatives; the Seven Brothers' love for their faith had to transcend all, since their family love would naturally forbid them from allowing brother after brother to

45. An emphatic marker of result, "often associated with exhortation" (L&N, 89.47), in the NT only here and in Heb 12:1.

46. See Green, *Thessalonians*, 200 – 201. Schmithals, *Paul & the Gnostics,* 140 – 41, predictably, pinpoints this opponent of Paul as a Gnostic, who was supposedly accusing Paul of not possessing the Spirit.

47. Since this is a participle, the time of the action is not indicated; in fact, many manuscripts read an aorist participle instead of the present διδόντα. T. F. Deidun, *New Covenant Morality in Paul* (AnBib 89; Rome: Pontifical Biblical Institute, 1981), 56, argues that it speaks to a *continuous* work of the Spirit in the heart, but this is an overinterpretation of the present participle.

48. So MM, 668.

be executed in cruelly inventive ways.[49] In Hellenistic Greek, Philadelphus was a common epithet for people who were devoted to their blood relatives: Attalus II Philadelphus, for example, apparently founded and gave his name to Philadelphia (see Rev 1:11; 3:7).

A single exception to the rule that "brotherly love" equals "love for siblings" in the Jewish literature is found in 2 Macc 15:14, where the prophet Jeremiah is described with the adjective form as "a man who loves the family [φιλάδελφος] of Israel." That is, a Jewish writer could think in terms of one's love for the whole Jewish people and enlarge the sphere wherein that term "family love" could properly be used, but always maintaining the biological tie.[50] But the NT extends such love far beyond the biological family or even, as with Jeremiah, the Jewish nation.[51] Now the concept has become spiritualized so that all Christians are family members, and love for other believers may in the truest sense be termed family love. In Pauline usage, Jesus was the first of many brothers and sisters (Rom 8:29), and the church is called the "family of believers" in Gal 6:10 (cf. 1 Pet 2:17).[52]

There were other tangible symbols of the new family membership in the church. First, "the place of meeting, the house, served to reinforce the reality of Christians becoming members of the same brotherhood and sisterhood."[53] Second was the sharing of the "holy kiss" among members of the Christian family (see comments on 5:26). It is impressive that the concept of family membership and the family kiss were features of the church as early as the 40s. Within so short of time, Jews and Gentiles were living with a consciousness of being one family.

Paul follows up on the reality of family love in 4:10 by referring to the "brothers and sisters" who lived outside the scope of Thessalonica, referring to believers in all of Macedonia.

4:9a-c You do not need us to write [anything] to you. [I say this] because you yourselves are [apparently] taught by God to love one another (οὐ χρείαν ἔχετε γράφειν ὑμῖν, αὐτοὶ γὰρ ὑμεῖς θεοδίδακτοί ἐστε εἰς τὸ ἀγαπᾶν ἀλλήλους). Not only have the Thessalonians remembered and put into practice what the apostles taught them — a marvel in itself, given the weaknesses of human nature — but according to Timothy's report, God himself has been teaching them. He writes this only in order to tell them that "you do not need us to write anything to you," a comment Paul will make again in 5:1. Verse 9 stands in contrast with Heb 5:12, where the recipients *did* need written instruction: "you need someone to teach you ... again."[54] Paul goes on with "because" (γάρ) to explain why he states what he does in v. 9a: they are taught by God. He uses the pronoun to make "you" (ὑμεῖς) emphatic. This is further underscored by "yourselves" (αὐτοί); we might represent it by, "you yourselves, yes, I'm talking to you!"

They are "taught by God" (θεοδίδακτοι). In this

49. See similar references in Philo, *Joseph* 215; *Embassy* 87; Josephus, *Ant.* 4.2.4 (§26), speaking of the brothers Moses and Aaron; *J.W.* 1.14.1 (§275); 1.24.6 (§485) of Herod the Great.

50. Contra Burke, *Family Matters*, 169, who regards 2 Macc 15:14 as a metaphorical, not extended-biological, usage of the term. Wayne A. Meeks points to a scattered few groups that used "brother" language, particularly the Qumran sect. Nevertheless, it must be remembered that the Qumran Jews regarded themselves as kin precisely because they were the remnant of the Jewish family and thus biologically related. See Meeks, *The First Urban Christians: The Social World of the Apostle Paul* (2nd ed.; New Haven, CT: Yale Univ. Press, 2003). Some Roman clubs used fraternal language, but only rarely.

51. Paul uses the noun here and in Rom 12:10; in other NT authors, see Heb 13:1; 1 Pet 1:22; 2 Pet 1:7; see also φιλάδελφος in 1 Pet 3:8.

52. See P. H. Towner, "Households and Household Codes," *DPL*, 417 – 21; also "4.3 The Household," in P. T. O'Brien, "The Church," *DPL*, 128.

53. Green, *Thessalonians*, 203.

54. Contra Green, *Thessalonians*, 202 – 3, who thinks that the Thessalonians were not as loving as they could have been.

verse the compound adjective "taught by God" makes its first appearance in literary Greek. It is used only here in the NT, and its next use is in the second-century *Epistle of Barnabas*.[55] The word may have been coined by Paul himself. While it may have referred to the Thessalonians' growth through attending to the message of the gospel or to the Scriptures, the most natural reference of "taught by God" is to a supernatural working of God in their hearts. The OT speaks of this divine work: "I will praise the LORD, who counsels me; even at night my heart instructs me" (Ps 16:7).

Yet the apostle is going far beyond Ps 16. While King David may have enjoyed such special guidance, in the new age the dam has broken, and even former pagans experience God's immediate direction. Witmer is most likely correct in saying that Paul is giving a shorthand reference to Isa 54:13 (NETS), that "I will make all your sons taught by God" (διδακτοὺς θεοῦ; in the Hebrew, they are taught by "Yahweh," not God); after all, the apostle favors this same section of Isaiah when he speaks about the church in Gal 4:27.[56]

There is also a Johannine saying of Jesus, "It is written in the Prophets, 'They will all be taught by God'" (John 6:45), which in fact quotes directly from the Isa 54 passage. Jesus' teaching was that all should listen to him since in this new age God is speaking to them through him. Witmer interprets Paul to mean that God's teaching of the Thessalonians is mediated through the apostolic teaching and is not to be considered apart from it: that is, Paul has no doctrine of "direct unmediated instruction" by God.[57] This is unnecessary, unless we reduce the phrase "you do not need" to mere rhetoric. The better interpretation is that Paul is pleasantly surprised that God is working among them even when the apostles cannot.[58]

What has God been teaching them? A fundamental Christian virtue is to "love one another" (εἰς τὸ ἀγαπᾶν ἀλλήλους). God has not simply taught them that they *ought* to love one another or filled them in on a theology of love; he has taught them with the result that they *practice* love. Paul uses the reciprocal pronoun "one another" (ἀλλήλους); "one frequently finds this pronoun in 'paraenetic' sections [i.e., passages of exhortation concerning behavior], basing the exhortation on the organic connection that believers have with the risen Christ."[59] "Love for one another" in the Christian context is synonymous with "family love" (φιλαδελφία).

4:10a And you even practice this toward all the brothers and sisters in all of Macedonia (καὶ γὰρ ποιεῖτε αὐτὸ εἰς πάντας τοὺς ἀδελφοὺς [τοὺς] ἐν ὅλῃ τῇ Μακεδονίᾳ). Again, Paul remarks on the astounding fact that the Thessalonians have affected people in the greater region of Macedonia. They serve not just as "patterns" (1:7), a reputation that one might admire at a distance. Instead, they tangibly demonstrate family love to Christians who live in other parts of Greece. Paul does not mention Achaia as he does in 1:7, which is probably not surprising, for their connection with the

55. *Barn.* 21.6: "Be *instructed by God*, seeking out what the Lord seeks from you, and then do it, in order that you may be found in the day of judgment."

56. See Stephen E. Witmer, "θεοδίδακτοί in 1 Thessalonians 4.9: A Pauline Neologism," *NTS* 52/2 (2006): 239–50.

57. Stephen E. Witmer, *Divine Instruction in Early Christianity* (WUNT 2/246; Tübingen: Mohr Siebeck, 2008), 162–64.

58. This is the view of Clement of Alexandria, who alludes to 1 Thess 4 when he writes that mere human instruction cannot bring about radical inner change. He goes through a list of Greek and Persian leaders and shows how their tutors gave them military training. Nevertheless, their human nature remained fundamentally unaltered; the leaders have innumerable sexual partners, they are "practised in intercourse like the wild boars." On the other hand, "our Instructor is the holy God Jesus, the Word, who is the guide of all humanity. The loving God Himself is our Instructor." *Paed.* 1.7 (*ANF* 2.223). Clement thus makes a strong statement of the deity of Christ.

59. Wallace, *Grammar*, 351.

Achaean church is still nascent. "Even" (καί) refers to the pleasant surprise that their love extends beyond local borders. With "you ... practice this," the antecedent of "this" (αὐτό) might conceivably have been the feminine noun "family love" (τῆς φιλαδελφίας), but the neuter infinitive "to love" (τὸ ἀγαπᾶν) is more proximate and of the correct grammatical gender. How the Thessalonians showed love to "all the brothers and sisters in all of Macedonia" is not specified, but it must have been an observable behavior. Gaventa suggests "intercessory prayer, financial support, and hospitality."[60]

4:10b So, we [simply] entreat you, brothers and sisters, to thrive even more (παρακαλοῦμεν δὲ ὑμᾶς, ἀδελφοί, περισσεύειν μᾶλλον). How pleasing for the apostles that they only need to charge them to "thrive" (περισσεύειν) in their love.[61] The adverb in this context (μᾶλλον) has the idea of "to a greater or higher degree, more" (BDAG).

Compare this statement with 1 Cor 13, where an entire weighty chapter exists to correct the Corinthians' imperfect love that leads them to sin clumsily against others (1 Cor 8:12) and to use their spiritual gifts to serve themselves (14:4, 13 – 19). In the case of the Thessalonians, Paul simply entreats them to continue on (as he does with regard to their general conduct of life [4:1] and mutual encouragement [5:11]). There is a parallel in Phil 1:9, "And this is my prayer: that your love may abound more and more." Nevertheless, in that text he did have to correct divisive behavior in Philippi (Phil 4:2).

Paul's words suggest that the Thessalonians themselves can decide to love one another in greater measure. The counterpart is his prayer in 3:12, where he prays that the Lord make them "increase and abound in love for one another and for all people." Thus does prayer function side-by-side with exhortation and with the Christian's commitment to grow. This dynamic eliminates on the one hand a view of sanctification as self-reliance, and and on the other a passive acquiescence so as to "let God" do his work.

4:11 And to make it your ambition to live peaceably, and to keep to your own business, and to work with your own hands, just as we commanded you (καὶ φιλοτιμεῖσθαι ἡσυχάζειν καὶ πράσσειν τὰ ἴδια καὶ ἐργάζεσθαι ταῖς [ἰδίαις] χερσὶν ὑμῶν, καθὼς ὑμῖν παρηγγείλαμεν). Paul now asks the Thessalonians to live as Paul had previously commanded with regard to a favorite topic of his, the work ethic. More than with any other theme, the apostles are held up as the pattern. Paul uses an unusual verb, here rendered "to make it your ambition" (φιλοτιμεῖσθαι); some versions have "aspire." The verb at times denoted a practice of the Greco-Roman elite. In lieu of being taxed, the wealthy were expected to make generous donations to their cities, in public works, entertainments, food distributions, and so forth. In many cases this became a contest of who could outstrip one's peers, since the greater gift bespoke the power and wealth of the donor as well as his magnanimity.[62]

Paul, however, uses the verb to speak of a striving to render service, not in order to receive admiration from others but in order to serve God.[63] The verb normally takes an infinitive; this verse has three: "to live peaceably" (ἡσυχάζειν),[64] to "keep

60. Gaventa, *First and Second Thessalonians*, 58; also Wanamaker, *Thessalonians*, 161.

61. See Wallace, *Grammar*, 603 – 5, for material on "indirect discourse."

62. Herod the Great was a master of ostentation, "indeed was very ambitious to leave great monuments of his government to posterity; whence it was that he was so zealous in building such fine cities, and spent such vast sums of money upon them" (Josephus, *Ant*. 15.9.5 [§330]).

63. See also Rom 15:20; 2 Cor 5:9; Josephus, *Ant*. 3.8.6 (§207) uses it of zeal for God's service, likewise *Ant*. 10.2.1 (§25) with φιλοτιμία.

64. See the useful analysis by Spicq, "ἡσυχάζω, ἡσυχία, ἡσύχιος," *TLNT*, 2:179 – 82.

to your own business" (πράσσειν), and to "work" (ἐργάζεσθαι). These are not verbs that would suit the ostentatious philanthropist, who worked for recognition and whose wealth was inherited or derived from the labor of others.

First, Paul says to "live peaceably" (ἡσυχάζειν). This is not the way the verb is used in classical and *koinē* Greek or in the LXX, where it typically means "to be at rest." In the NT Paul uses it to denote a quiet lifestyle linked with diligent work.[65] Some take this in the sense of 1 Tim 2:2, where he asks that believers pray for the government, so that their quietness is not disturbed. Nevertheless, Paul's concern is not principally related to government interference, but rather promotes a lifestyle that best reflects the Christian message, which he himself has modeled.

Second, he asks them to "keep to your own business" (πράσσειν τὰ ἴδια), a known idiom that means to mind one's own affairs. On the surface, this might seem to contradict Phil 2:4, "looking not to your own interests but each of you to the interests of the others," let alone the various commands to intervene in the lives of other believers (above all, 1 Thess 5:14–15). The difference is easily resolved. In 4:11 he rules out not a wholesome care for others but meddling in others' affairs (cf. 1 Tim 5:13; 1 Pet 4:15). Some suggest that the Pastoral Letters promote mere respectability, that rather than turn the world upside-down with the gospel, Christians are to stay at home, be quiet and dignified, and obey the government (e.g., 1 Tim 2:2). Nevertheless, "quiet" does not necessarily mean passivity; 1 Thessalonians combines a radical commitment to the gospel and the return of Christ with a conventional manner of living.

Third, he tells them "work with your own hands" (ἐργάζεσθαι ταῖς [ἰδίαις] χερσὶν ὑμῶν). As in the case of Paul and Silas's work (2:9), the focus is on manual labor, a grade of work that some would despise. He is not telling those with higher qualifications to quit and to take up manual labor; rather, he knows the typical Thessalonian believer is not suited for anything other than manual labor. Yet their work takes on sacred meaning if it expresses their family love; it is transformed into "your hard labor that comes from your love" that Paul commended in 1:3. Paul is anticipating an issue that would need to be addressed in his second letter, namely, that some were neglecting their work (2 Thess 3:11). But already in 1 Thessalonians he introduces the theme of the work ethic before he receives a report about the possible eschatological confusion of 2 Thess 2:2. This pushes the interpreter to conclude that the problem of work was not caused by eschatological confusion over the day of the Lord (2:1–2).

4:12 In order that you might conduct yourselves properly with respect to those outside [the people of God] and to have no need of anything (ἵνα περιπατῆτε εὐσχημόνως πρὸς τοὺς ἔξω καὶ μηδενὸς χρείαν ἔχητε). Paul marks out two positive consequences of a quiet, self-sustaining lifestyle: a *good reputation with non-Christians* and *economic stability*. The clause shows the purpose of 4:11, "in order that" (ἵνα). He uses περιπατέω ("conduct yourselves") to denote a manner of life, as in 4:1. It is modified by the adverb "properly"

65. See also 2 Thess 3:12, where he uses the cognate ἡσυχία. Paul may have resonated with Philo in *Abraham* 27, apart from the latter's speculation over the etymology of "Noah," which he supposes means "rest": "the appellation 'rest' is likewise appropriate, since the opposite quality to rest is unnatural agitation, the cause of confusion, and tumults, and seditions, and wars, which the wicked pursue; while those who pay due honour to excellence cultivate a tranquil, and quiet, and stable, and peaceful life." In *1 Clem.* 63.1, the verb is used when Corinthians are told to submit to their leaders, cease from dissension, and live in godly peace.

(εὐσχημόνως, see also Rom 13:13; 1 Cor 14:40). In classical Greek, this adverb denoted the dignity of a gentleman;[66] here it is the quiet decorum that befits Christians of every class. "With respect to" (πρός) we take as similar to the dative of reference. "Those outside" (τοὺς ἔξω) refers to those who do not belong to a particular group; in this case, "outside the people of God." Paul uses the language of the "outsider" the same way in 1 Cor 5:12 – 13 and Col 4:5. It was always Paul's desire that Christians make a sincere and positive impression on non-Christians.[67] It was also a typically Pauline idea that people should work in order to not be in want (Eph 4:28).[68]

Theology in Application

We will focus here on *sexual ethics* and leave until 2 Thess 3:6 the question of a Christian work ethic.

Theology in Thessalonica

Jesus warned his followers about sexual sin: "anyone who looks at a woman lustfully has already committed adultery with her in his heart" (Matt 5:28; this is also the teaching of the OT, see Job 31:1). Yet it would not have done for the apostles simply to reiterate this small quantity of Jesus' teaching on the topic. As the gospel spread to the Gentiles, its preachers had to adapt the gospel to a new audience, and that involved expanding and clarifying the Christian teaching on sexuality.

The Jerusalem church was early on conscious of this need. Although all accepted the fact that Gentiles were receiving the gospel (Acts 11:18), few could picture them becoming disciples unless they were circumcised. In so doing, the Gentiles would be taking on themselves Torah, whose laws would have covered all sexual contingencies. While the Apostolic Council rejected this reactionary opinion, it did make a point of prohibiting the Gentiles from idolatrous practices and from their regular companion, sexual immorality (Acts 15:20, 29).

The church set the limits of fornication from the Scriptures. "It may be said that the Old Testament moral teaching is taken over as *content* when it rings true to the Christian's understanding of his calling, but that its claim upon the Christian *as law* is rejected."[69] It is clear from the sum of Paul's teaching on the topic that "fornication"

66. See Aristotle, *Eth. nic.* 1.10.13 (trans. Rackham): "the truly good and wise man will bear all kinds of fortune in a *seemly* way, and will always act in the noblest manner that the circumstances allow."

67. Rom 13:8 – 10; 1 Cor 9:19 – 23; 2 Cor 8:21; Gal 6:10; see also Matt 5:16; 1 Pet 4:15.

68. See Bruce W. Winter, *Seek the Welfare of the City: Christians as Benefactors and Citizens* (First-Century Christians in the Graeco-Roman World; Grand Rapids: Eerdmans, 1994), 51. Winter theorizes that 4:11 does not mean "lacking for nothing" but rather "dependent on *nobody*"; in this viewpoint, Paul was already rejecting the dependence on patronage that would arise in the second letter. Winter develops the idea further (53 – 57) with regard to 2 Thess 3:6 – 18. Winter's explanation, though popular among some commentators, fails to explain why people sought patronage *after* Paul's departure from the city or why Paul does not specifically mention patronage in either letter.

69. Joseph Jensen, "Does *Porneia* Mean Fornication? A Critique of Bruce Malina," *NovT* 20 (1978): 161 – 62.

included the content of the Torah; he even went beyond it, for example, by mandating an absolute restriction against visiting prostitutes.

Paul himself, in 1 Cor 7, shows a healthy respect for the power of sexual temptation. It must have been a burden on Paul to address the Gentiles' sexual practices. Should we guess that Jewish Christian women were the ones to address the new female Gentile disciples, giving them detailed instruction? Whether or not this is true, we do infer from 1 Thessalonians that Paul left nothing to chance and did not restrict himself to abstract exhortations about sex.

Biblical Theology

The Christian sexual ethic is not simply one more code of behavior. Rather, it presupposes that people who had been far from God would radically change direction. Centuries earlier, God had promised a remapping of the inner person so that Israelites would be enabled to obey the Torah. According to Isa 30:20b – 21, God would steer each person directly:

> Your teachers will be hidden no more; with your own eyes you will see them. Whether you turn to the right or to the left, your ears will hear a voice behind you, saying, "This is the way; walk in it."[70]

In Ezekiel and Jeremiah this theme of the new covenant came to its fullest expression:[71]

> And I will put my Spirit in you and move you to follow my decrees and be careful to keep my laws. (Ezek 36:27)

> "No longer will they teach their neighbor, or say to one another, 'Know the LORD,' because they will all know me, from the least of them to the greatest," declares the LORD. (Jer 31:34a)

These passages predict that Israel would be returned to the Promised Land and that their predilection to idolatry would be wiped out. Their obedience to Yahweh would spring from within, as God himself taught them in an integral and soul-transforming fashion. It is not the exegete's imagination that makes us connect Paul with this prophetic hope. From the oral tradition Paul knows that Christ died to establish the new covenant (1 Cor 11:25); Paul is a "minister of a new covenant" (2 Cor 3:6), which covenant is based in the Holy Spirit's presence; there are two covenants, the old and, by implication, the new (Gal 4:24).[72]

70. See also 2 Chr 6:27; Isa 54:13: "All your children will be taught by the LORD."

71. Deidun looks over the (later) rabbinic literature and notes that "the *combination* of these two prophetic texts [from the Ezekiel and Jeremiah] is widely attested in Jewish tradition in contexts concerning messianic times, with particular reference to the immediacy of God's teaching." See Deidun, *New Covenant Morality in Paul*, 20.

72. Again, see Deidun, *New Covenant Morality in Paul*, 33 – 41. Although a few recent works take his volume into

Now the Gentiles were directly "God-taught," while the synagogue, despite its rigorous study of the Torah, had closed themselves off from God. Paul as evangelist and as theologian affirms that the Thessalonians' ability to live free from fornication or idolatry is an endowment of God through the Spirit (Ezek 36:27) and not simply the enforcement of a "boundary marker" by the apostles.[73] Although the Christian ethic has some parallels in first-century Stoicism and Judaism,[74] its nature as the life in the Spirit distinguishes it from all other "isms."

In the specific case of the Christian sexual ethic, this whole section shows that it is God-given. Sexual sin is first and foremost an affront to God (cf. Ps 51:4), who made the body (see also 1 Cor 6:18 – 20) and who gave commandments concerning sexuality. To reject that ethic is to reject God himself (1 Thess 4:8) and to invite his vengeance (4:6). Our sexual ethic is not, as many seem to assume today, a minor or even a dispensable component of the Christian's moral life.

Message of This Passage for the Church Today

This section is one of the key passages concerning Christian sexuality, and Paul's candor sets us an example that we should speak in concrete terms about the topic.

When the Pauline team set foot in Thessalonica, two paradigms of sexual mores came into collision. When we say that the gospel demanded a "paradigm shift," we do not mean that the apostles had new answers to people's questions; rather, they provided answers for questions that the apostles themselves had framed. Some people today disparage preachers who "answer questions that no one is asking." Yet in this area, Paul might have faced similar charges; after all, the Thessalonian pagans were not waiting around for answers on how to stop living in fornication. Those Gentiles who wanted to put a stop to sexual philandering were usually people who had themselves been cheated on! Paul had to create thirst for a new way even as he offered the gospel as that way.

Today's preachers of the gospel must follow the apostle's lead. Some Christians today sincerely want help to abstain from sex apart from marriage. But let us not limit ourselves to people of goodwill. The data suggest that the large majority of U.S. residents who marry do not come to the altar as virgins. It takes no calculator to infer that many — probably the majority — of Christian people have had sexual experience before they marry. No preacher can simply assume that the flock is behaving as it should or even that they would like to do the right thing. Nor can they simply answer the questions that people are asking; they must allow the gospel to raise new questions, to create a new paradigm.

account (e.g., Malherbe, *Letters to the Thessalonians*; Dunn, *The Theology of Paul the Apostle*), Deidun's contributions are generally underappreciated.

73. F. Thielman, "Law," *DPL*, 534 – 35.

74. See G. Strecker, *Theology of the New Testament* (trans. M. E. Boring; Louisville: Westminster John Knox, 2000), 46; Weima, "1 and 2 Thessalonians," 878 – 79.

We must grapple with the same tension with regard to the sexual education of our children. One school of thought has it that we wait for the children to take the initiative: "I'll answer their questions as they raise them." This is a dangerously passive stance, when an active approach is called for. Who would advocate such a wait-and-see posture about any other theme except the awkward one of sexuality? Who would say, "I'll talk my children about what to do if the house is on fire ... once they begin to ask questions"? Most children who have not previously been exposed to questions of sexuality through the media or friends or school simply do not have the tools to formulate the right questions and may keep silent out of shame. No, it depends on the parent, not simply to provide answers but also to point out what the important questions are.

As I grow older, I try hard to avoid saying that "things aren't like they used to be." Nevertheless, in this case I plead a compelling reason. In 1995 I published a book on addiction[75] and mentioned that beyond drugs and alcohol, some people might get addicted to pornography. I was visualizing magazines bought by a furtive customer at the convenience store. Roughly ten years later, I began to write this commentary, and the new landscape was unrecognizable. People have exploited electronic media to expand the frontiers of Gentile sin far beyond what Paul could have imagined. Men and women can view sexual material or engage in sexual interaction of every variety without leaving their desk. It is likely that pornography is now the single greatest besetting sin among Christians and their leaders. In addition, a friend who is writing a book on this topic informs me that American women have nearly caught up with the men in their use of pornographic material;[76] but the apostles have already anticipated that, teaching that men and women both need to control their bodies.

Here is another area where the pastor must understand the realities of the present day: no preacher should ever declare from the pulpit that "whatever a husband and wife do behind closed doors is fine." God bless these pastors for their innocence of the world's harsh realities, but they are culpably naive about the degrading things that people do. Jesus is present in the bedroom, and Christian sex should be characterized by Christian virtues: love, patience, generosity, and joy; never pain, selfishness, shame, or exploitation.

In this age of sexual apostasy, Christians can demonstrate the power of the gospel simply by living the normal Christian (i.e., miraculous) sexual ethic. At the same time, we must have apostolic courage to spell out precisely what is immorality in its various forms and to teach against them all.

75. Gary Steven Shogren, *Running in Circles: How to Find Freedom from Addictive Behavior* (Strategic Christian Living Series; Grand Rapids: Baker, 1995).

76. See Brent Edward McNamara, *No More Hiding, No More Shame: Finding Freedom from Pornography Addiction* (Mustang, OK: Tate, 2011). It is available as a digital download, see www.tatepublishing.com/bookstore/book.php?w=978-1-61739-268-9.

CHAPTER 5

1 Thessalonians 4:13 – 18

Literary Context

In 4:1 – 12, Paul took up various points of Christian ethics, and he affirms that the Thessalonians already know and practice them. To put it another way, there is nothing that a Thessalonian would have found new or confusing. By contrast, in 4:13 – 18 Paul helps the believers navigate a topic they have perhaps never heard or, as is more likely, have forgotten to apply in their situation. Thus, 4:13 – 18 is the only paragraph that contains material new to them: that at his parousia, Jesus will resurrect the dead saints so that they will enjoy his coming with those who are still alive. Then in 5:1, the apostle returns to material that, again, he is sure they well know.

These verses serve to draw together and unite the various threads of eschatological hope: believers in Jesus will escape from God's wrath (1:10; 5:9; by implication 2:16); they must be holy at Jesus' coming (3:13; 5:1 – 11, 23); and they joyfully anticipate the parousia in part because their fallen friends will be there too (4:17 – 18).

The fact that Paul does not have to explore the topic further in 2 Thessalonians indicates that the matter was settled.

VI. *Paraenesis:* The Gospel Ethic in a Gentile Environment (4:1 – 12)

➡ **VII. Instruction about the Return of Christ (4:13 – 5:11)**

A. Dead Christians will be raised to be with Jesus ahead of the living (4:13 – 18)

B. Christians should live in holiness, even without knowing the timing of the end (5:1 – 11)

VIII. Final Exhortations (5:12 – 22)

Main Idea

For all their strong grip on Christian doctrine (e.g., Jesus doing the work of Yahweh, the person of the Spirit, the work of Satan, Jesus' death and resurrection), the Thessalonians are missing something essential: that Christ's resurrection guarantees the resurrection of believers who have died before his return. Most likely Paul had taught that doctrine to them, but in a time of persecution they were forgetting to apply it; we invite the reader to look over the material in the Introduction, under "Eschatology in Thessalonica."

Translation

(See next page.)

Structure

Paul has already said plenty about the Lord's return, but now he turns his full attention to eschatology. He uses a litotes, "we do not wish you to be uninformed" to mean "let us fill you in on information you are lacking." Once the Thessalonians have a proper grasp on the fate of their dead companions, they will not be emotionally distraught. Paul uses comparative language "just like [καθώς] other people" (4:13), in order to draw a firm distinction between the people of hope (see 1:3) and the hopeless pagans. His aim is pastoral, and he knows that good hope is rooted in good doctrine. Thus Paul begins with a word of hope in 4:13, starting an *inclusio* that will end with his charge to his hearers to comfort one another by means of the same information (4:18).

The Thessalonians' main problem concerned those Christians who had died (using the common euphemism "fallen asleep") in contrast with those "who still live and remain here" (4:15). Paul offers two proofs for the eschatological resurrection, a doctrine that will surely boost their spirits.

The first proof is that the resurrection of Jesus provides a full solution to their doubts (4:14). The adverb "thus" or "in the same way" (οὕτως) signals that Paul will be drawing an inference from the protasis: if we believe that God raised Jesus from the dead, then it is safe to assume that God will resurrect believers as well. This act is called a "gathering together with Jesus." Paul reflects the language of the Olivet Discourse, where the angels gather the elect (Matt 24:31). He also anticipates 4:17e, "so we will always be with the Lord"; and 2 Thess 2:1, God "gathers us together to Christ."

Paul offers a second proof in 4:15. I will argue in the commentary that this is not a summary of Jesus' teaching or an *agraphon*, a hitherto unwritten teaching of Jesus. Rather, it is "an oracle from the Lord Jesus" given through a living communication as prophecy, perhaps recently to Paul or Silas. The content of the message is introduced by "that" (ὅτι, to introduce indirect discourse); it is brief but direct: "We who still live and remain here until the Lord's coming will in no way go ahead of those who have died" (v. 15).

Paul then begins at the beginning and describes the second coming. It is best to take 4:16 – 17, not as part of the prophetic oracle of 4:15, but as a summary description of the parousia that uses traditional language of angels and trumpet, but in

1 Thessalonians 4:13 – 18

13a	Disclosure formula	Now—**we do not want you to be uninformed**, brothers and sisters, concerning those who have died,
13b	Result	that you might not be in distress,
13c	Comparison	just like other people, who have no hope.
14a	Basis	If we believe that Jesus died and rose again… well,
14b	Inference	in the same way,
		God will gather together with [Jesus] those who have died in him.
15a	Basis	For **we say this to you by an oracle from the Lord**,
15b	Content	that we who still live and
		remain here until the Lord's coming
15c	Content	will in no way go ahead of those who have died.
16a	Basis…	Because the Lord himself,
16b	Association	with the commanding shout of the archangel's voice and
16c	Association	with the [sound of the] trumpet of God,
16d	…Event	will come down from heaven, and
16e	Event	the dead in Christ will first be resurrected.
		Next,
17a	Sequence	we who still live and remain will be taken up together
17b	Association	with [those who were dead]
17c	Place	in the clouds
17d	Purpose	to welcome the Lord in the air.
17e	Result	And so we will always be with the Lord.
18	Inference (from 14-17)	So then, **encourage one another with these words.**

which the resurrection of the dead is strongly featured. Instead of the angels simply going to gather the saints from the four corners of the earth, which one would expect having heard Matt 24:31, the dead in Christ make a sudden appearance in 4:16e: "and the dead in Christ will first be resurrected."

Paul then introduces the believers who are still living (4:17). There is a nice contrast between "and" (καί) the dead will rise, "next" (ἔπειτα) the living. One might almost paraphrase it as "*only then* will the living be taken up." They will rise to be with the resurrected dead; the resurrected believers once again serve as a point of reference, if at some moment we had forgotten that they had already been made alive. It will all happen "so" (καὶ οὕτως, 4:17e), that is, "in this manner." There is no need for the sort of grief that their pagan neighbors exhibit (4:13), since every believer will enjoy Christ's presence forever.

To round out his *inclusio* in this section, Paul is not simply concerned with informing them about eschatology, but about comforting them and giving them the tools so that they can "encourage one another" (4:18).

Exegetical Outline

➡ **I. The Apostles Perceive That the Thessalonians Are Missing an Important Piece of Teaching and Move to Fill It (4:13).**

II. The Basis for This Doctrine Is Found in the Gospel and Also in New Revelation (4:14 – 15a).

- A. According to the gospel, Jesus died and rose again; Christians will do the same (4:14).
- B. By a prophetic oracle the apostles have more details that they now transmit to the Thessalonians (4:15a).

III. The Apostolic Eschatology Reveals Truths Relevant to the Thessalonians' Confusion (4:15b – 17).

- A. At the Lord's coming, the risen dead will be the first to go to meet Jesus (4:15b – 16).
- B. Then the living believers will ascend to join with the resurrected dead in welcoming Jesus (4:17a).
- C. All Christians will be with the Lord Jesus forever (4:17b-e).

IV. The Benefit of This Doctrine Is to Encourage Living Christians (4:18).

Explanation of the Text

4:13a Now — we do not want you to be uninformed, brothers and sisters, concerning those who have died (Οὐ θέλομεν δὲ ὑμᾶς ἀγνοεῖν, ἀδελφοί, περὶ τῶν κοιμωμένων). Paul appreciates how people learn. He began in 4:1 – 12 by going over what the Thessalonians already clearly grasped, that is, the familiar themes of sexual purity and brotherly love. He now takes them to an area where they are not clear. To be sure, they have been awaiting Jesus' coming from heaven (1:10) with his holy angels (3:13); yet they are wondering whether they will see their fallen comrades again at that parousia. Paul uses "now" (δέ) to turn their attention to this new theme and brings them to full attention with "brothers and sisters" (ἀδελφοί). "We do not want you to be uninformed," he says; as throughout this chapter, "we" means Paul and Silas. The infinitive "to be uninformed" (ἀγνοεῖν) might be rendered "to be or stay ignorant," but as this has an insulting tone in English, we render it in a way that does not imply criticism. The clause is a typical formula for disclosing new information (see 1 Cor 10:1; 12:1; 2 Cor 1:8).

There are two ways to translate "those who have died" (τῶν κοιμωμένων). The verb in some contexts had first of all the sense of literal sleep. Second, it served as a metaphor, denoting death; its cognate, "sleeping-place" (κοιμητήριον), is the root of the English word "cemetery." The same double meaning of "sleep/death" occurs in the synonym for "sleep" (καθεύδω). This latter verb is used in Dan 12:2 to speak of the dead who will be resurrected, and Paul will use it in 1 Thess 5:10; probably it denotes "death" there as well.

Sleep came to be a metaphor for death at least as early as Homer: "So there the poor fellow lay, sleeping a sleep [from κοιμάω] as it were of bronze, killed in the defense of his fellow-citizens" (*Iliad* 11.241, trans. Butler). Homer believed neither in soul sleep nor in the resurrection; therefore, the metaphor does not imply a doctrine of soul sleep or that the person would "awake" at the resurrection. The comparison with sleep has to do with the appearance of the body to the survivors. Some Jewish literature pairs the verb "sleep" (κοιμάω) and resurrection (2 Macc 12:45); thus, Paul is using language that would have been a metaphor about death for Greeks or Jews.[1]

It is therefore a mistake to render the verb with a supposed literal equivalent, that is, "to fall asleep" (many versions, including KJV, NASB, ESV, NJB; the NIV and REB have "sleep in death"); to his readers it simply meant "to die." It is parallel to "the dead" (i.e., οἱ νεκροί) in 4:16. Nevertheless, the wordplay between sleep and death does form a part of the plot of John 11:11, where Lazarus is thought by the disciples to be peacefully sleeping off his illness, whereas Jesus meant that Lazarus had died. But only in the postapostolic period did Christians begin to make a regular play on the double meaning of the verbs.

4:13b-c That you might not be in distress, just like other people, who have no hope (ἵνα μὴ λυπῆσθε καθὼς καὶ οἱ λοιποὶ οἱ μὴ ἔχοντες ἐλπίδα). Greco-Roman piety demanded that each family member properly grieve over the loss of a loved one. For their part, Thessalonian Christians have broken with their biological kin and pledged their

1. Contra Colin R. Nicholl, *From Hope to Despair in Thessalonica: Situating 1 and 2 Thessalonians* (SNTSMS 126; Cambridge: Cambridge Univ. Press, 2004), 23, who believes that Paul is giving the verb κοιμάω a new, specifically Christian sense: "we suggest that the portrayal of the Christian dead as 'asleep' ... is a significant, if subtle, affirmation ... that deceased Christians will rise from the dead to be with Christ at his parousia." See also Fee, *Thessalonians*, 167 – 68.

deepest fidelity to the new family of faith. This leads to the reassigning of the role of "survivors" from blood relatives to members of the church. Are the Thessalonians therefore expected to rend their garments, as they would have done out of respect for their deceased biological parents?

Not precisely, answers Paul, but it is not for any lack of family feeling. Nor are they to follow the lead of the philosophers, who urged that people moderate their grief to a reasonable level. The Christian survivors' reaction is based on their hope in God. But what is the specific point of contrast in "that you might not be in distress, just like other people." Is Paul saying (1) that they should not grieve at all, because only those devoid of hope feel grief?[2] Or is he saying (2) that they must not grieve in the same manner that the hopeless Gentiles do?[3] Almost certainly the second is his intended meaning; "he meant simply to restrain excessive grief, which [grief] would never have had such an influence among them, if they had seriously considered the resurrection, and kept it in remembrance."[4]

This interpretation is fitting in light of how grief is handled in other NT passages. One of the most poignant images of sorrow is that of Martha and Mary sitting in mourning for Lazarus; hardly less moving or less significant is that "Jesus wept" on the way to Lazarus's grave (John 11:35). Yet in 11:24 – 27, Jesus and Martha both declare their faith in the resurrection. This resurrection hope transforms anguish into sorrow that is moderated by hope. Other examples of godly sorrow include when the Christians "mourned deeply" over the martyred Stephen (Acts 8:2). Sorrow is positively represented in the Pauline letters (e.g., Rom 9:2; 2 Cor 6:10; Phil 2:27). In fact, "the Bible everywhere assumes that those who are bereaved will grieve, and their grief is never belittled."[5] Therefore Thessalonians should not grieve in the unmitigated manner of the hopeless.

Paul compares other people with those "who have no hope." The church is surrounded on all sides by Greeks. Their funeral rites reflect their belief in the irremediable loss of the loved one. For them, death was, as N. T. Wright puts it, a "one-way street."[6] The author of Hebrews seems to have Gentiles in mind when he refers in Heb 2:15 to "those who all their lives were held in slavery by their fear of death," an anxiety not readily grasped today when medical science always holds out the hope of yet one more miracle treatment.

4:14a If we believe that Jesus died and rose again (εἰ γὰρ πιστεύομεν ὅτι Ἰησοῦς ἀπέθανεν καὶ ἀνέστη). The hope that Christians have, that which lifts them from utter distress, is made possible only by the death and resurrection of Jesus. The Christian hope is not merely wishful thinking, but a confident expectation. Paul uses "for" (γάρ), which need not be translated into English so long as the causal sense is implied. The function of this protasis (the "if" clause) is not to question whether Jesus' death and resurrection are true, but to draw a conclusion — *if* the resurrection is believed to be true (and by definition a Christian does so believe, 1:10), *then* what follows is also true.[7] Paul uses the same sort of logic in 1 Cor 15:12: "If it is preached that Christ has been raised from the dead, how can some of you say that there is no resurrection of the dead?"

"We believe that Jesus died and rose again" is

2. So the GNB, NJB. The CEV captures this interpretation: "Then you won't grieve over them and be like people who don't have any hope."

3. So Nicholl, *From Hope to Despair*, 23 – 26. Apparently too the NKJV, NLT.

4. Calvin, *Thessalonians*, 279.

5. D. A. Carson, *How Long O Lord? Reflections on Suffering and Evil* (2nd ed.; Grand Rapids: Baker, 2006), 112.

6. N. T. Wright, *The Resurrection of the Son of God* (Minneapolis: Fortress, 2003), 81.

7. See Best, *Thessalonians*, 187; Fee, *Thessalonians*, 169 n. 21.

fundamental to the Pauline kerygma. It may seem strange to modern ears that the point that "Jesus died" would be a part of someone's creed, as if that could ever be debated. Yet that doctrine was precisely in doubt in the Hellenistic world and would later come under fire in Gnosticism. The Greeks had plenty of stories of gods and goddesses who passed among humans in disguise, but who, being immortal, did not die. The Gnostic *Gospel of Philip* 22 makes Jesus' death to be spiritual, not literal. Other Gnostics imagined that God miraculously made Simon of Cyrene look like Jesus, so that he was crucified in his place while Jesus watched from the crowd.

Paul for his part makes the point that without Jesus' death, there is no resurrection of Jesus and hence no hope for the resurrection of the Christian. The Apostles' Creed affirms this truth with Paul and turns aside the Gnostics with its declaration that Jesus "suffered under Pontius Pilate, was crucified, dead, and buried." His death was "for us" (5:10). "Rose again" (ἀνέστη) is the typical verb for the resurrection both of Jesus and the saints and is repeated in 4:16. The passage in 1 Cor 15:52 uses another verb to say that "the dead will be raised" (οἱ νεκροὶ ἐγερθήσονται).

4:14b Well, in the same way, God will gather together with [Jesus] those who have died in him (οὕτως καὶ ὁ θεὸς τοὺς κοιμηθέντας διὰ τοῦ Ἰησοῦ ἄξει σὺν αὐτῷ). Paul argues that belief in Jesus' resurrection leads to a corollary, namely, the resurrection of the saints. This is translated "well, in the same way" (οὕτως καί), so that it doesn't seem as if "we believe" in 4:14a is the *cause* of final resurrection. Rather, this is an example of evidence–inference, where "the speaker infers something (the apodosis) from some evidence."[8] *Jesus rose (so we believe) from the dead; in the same way God will resurrect the saints.*

Paul delays the explicit promise that God will resurrect the dead believers. In this verse, "[God will] gather together" (ἄξει, from ἄγω) the dead. In the gospel tradition, the parousia involves the gathering of people from around the world: "And he will send his angels with a loud trumpet call, and they will gather [from a compound of ἄγω, ἐπισυνάγω] his elect from the four winds, from one end of the heavens to the other" (Matt 24:31).[9] Similar language appears in 2 Thess 2:1, where the saints are "gathered together" unto Christ (the cognate form ἐπισυναγωγή). Likewise, the ancient text *Did.* 10.5 instructs the church to pray that God will "gather [συνάγω] [the church] ... from the four winds into your kingdom." Paul will show in 4:16 that this gathering is accomplished through resurrection, not through a summoning together of the spirits of the disembodied dead.

For the expression "those who have died" (from κοιμάω), see 4:13. "In" (διά) is not the language Paul typically uses to speak of being in Christ; nevertheless, that seems to be his sense here, giving a parallel to "the dead in Christ" (οἱ νεκροὶ ἐν Χριστῷ) at the end of 4:16. An alternative might be that these saints died because of their association with Jesus, that is, that they were martyrs; or perhaps the phrase "with Jesus" (διὰ τοῦ Ἰησοῦ) is connected not with the participle but with the verb "will gather": "through Jesus, God will bring with him those who have fallen asleep" (ESV). But this latter seems to be an awkward rendering of διά, which seems to connect better with the words that immediately precede it, "have died."

Paul is at odds with some Christian thinking of our day; our eschatology has been affected over the centuries by foreign influences. In particular, we have become accustomed to the phrase "immortal soul," that the soul lives in a mortal body but does

8. Wallace, *Grammar*, 683.

9. A cognate verb occurs in Matt 13:30. In 13:39–42, 49–50, the angels gather up the wicked.

not really require it. The roots of that idea lie in Greek philosophy: for example, Plato has Socrates say that for the philosopher, one's final purification

> consists in separating the soul as much as possible from the body, and accustoming it to withdraw from all contact with the body and concentrate itself by itself; and to have its dwelling, so far as it can, both now and in the future, alone by itself, freed from the shackles of the body.... Will [the philosopher] be grieved at dying? Will he not be glad to make that journey?[10]

Thus the philosopher realizes that death is not a frightening loss, since the soul is better off without the body. Paul for his part sees that death is indeed a cause for sorrow, but grief that is transformed by the Christian's hope for the resurrection.

In the Bible, immortality is an attribute of God, meaning that he is not susceptible to death (1 Tim 1:17). This is nowhere said to be a characteristic of the human soul, even when it teaches that the soul or spirit remains conscious after death.[11] Immortality (Rom 2:7; 1 Cor 15:53–54) or "eternal life" (Rom 6:23) in Pauline terms is always associated with the eschatological resurrection: God in the future will give eternal life, transforming the human body into an undying form. This meant that Paul had his work cut out for him as he taught about life and death "to an audience that denied an afterlife or held that immortality was theirs by natural endowment" or held to a hereafter of shadows.[12]

4:15a For we say this to you by an oracle from the Lord (Τοῦτο γὰρ ὑμῖν λέγομεν ἐν λόγῳ κυρίου). Paul now gives the cause for his assertion in 4:14 by revealing the source of his doctrine: a direct revelation from the Lord Jesus. He uses language that is reminiscent of the LXX. "Lord" (κυρίου) is a subjective genitive, indicating that "the Lord spoke." The LXX typically uses "word [ῥῆμα] of the Lord" to refer to a word of prophecy.[13] Its synonym (i.e., λόγος) also occurs in the LXX and functions interchangeably with ῥῆμα.[14] The phrase in Thessalonians, "by an oracle from the Lord," is based on an instrumental usage of "by" (ἐν). A parallel may be found in 1 Kgs (3 Kgdms LXX) 13:18, where a prophet falsely claims that an angel had spoken to him "by a word of the Lord" (ἐν ῥήματι κυρίου).

The question now arises whether Paul might be referring to a saying of Jesus from his earthly ministry (as he does about marriage in 1 Cor 7:10; cf. also 11:23).[15] In a variation of that position, Seyoon Kim has argued forcefully that Paul has inferred 4:15–16 from the Jesus tradition in general, but not from a specific saying.[16] The difficulty is that there is no known Jesus tradition that resembles the material in 1 Thessalonians. In that case, it would have to be an *agraphon*, that is, an

10. Plato, *Phaedo* (trans. Tredennick) 67d-e, 68b.

11. Luke 16:19–31, which, though parabolic, is still a portrayal that depends on accepted truths; 2 Cor 5:6–9; Phil 1:21–23; Rev 6:9–11.

12. Gary S. Shogren, "Mortality and Immortality," *DLNT*, 776.

13. For example, to Abram in Gen 15:1; from God on Sinai to Moses in Exod 24:4; to Balaam in Num 24:13; to Nathan in 2 Sam 7:4; to Elijah in 1 Kgs 17:24; to Isaiah in Isa 66:5.

14. This is explicit in 1 Kgs 13—"λόγος" of the Lord is used in 1 Kgs 13:1, 9, 17; while ῥῆμα appears as its parallel in 1 Kgs 13:18, 21. This is parallel with the stereotyped "this is what the Lord says" (1 Kgs 13:2, 21).

15. So David Wenham, *Paul: Follower of Jesus or Founder of Christianity?* (Grand Rapids: Eerdmans, 1995), 310–11, who suggests that Paul may have borrowed Matt 25:1–13 and applied it to Christians who have died and then "arisen" to meet the bridegroom. See also S. Kim, "Jesus, Sayings of," *DPL*, 475–77. Among other exegetes, David Hill, *New Testament Prophecy* (New Foundations Theological Library; Atlanta: John Knox, 1979), 130–31, 166, proposes that 1 Thess 4:15 is a summary of the Lord's teaching, not an *agraphon* or an oracle.

16. See Kim, "Jesus Tradition," 234–37; similarly Wanamaker, *Thessalonians*, 170–71; Green, *Thessalonians*, 222. See the analysis on Paul and the Jesus tradition by Michael Thompson, *Clothed with Christ: The Example and Teaching of Jesus in Romans 12.1–15.13* (JSNTSup 59; London: T&T Clark, 1992), 70–76.

oral tradition not included in the gospels.[17] This hypothesis must remain a speculation. The better interpretation is that it is a word given to a Christian prophet such as Silas (he was a prophet, see Acts 15:32) or even to Paul himself.[18] It would fall into the category of revelation that Jesus promised in John 14:26, that the Spirit would "teach [them] all things." Paul is known to pass along new truth given directly by God: coincidentally he would disclose a similar "mystery" in 1 Cor 15:51, the parallel passage parallel to 1 Thess 4:13 – 18.[19] He will soon teach the Thessalonians to hold prophecy in its proper honor (5:20) but also to beware of false messages (the deceiving "spirit" in 2 Thess 2:2).

4:15b That we who still live and remain here until the Lord's coming (ὅτι ἡμεῖς οἱ ζῶντες οἱ περιλειπόμενοι εἰς τὴν παρουσίαν τοῦ κυρίου). The new datum is not the fact that Jesus will return, but that at the parousia dead believers will ascend first, to be followed by living Christians. Paul relates the content of this revelation in an "indirect discourse," that is, "the ὅτι clause contains *reported speech or thought*."[20]

"We who still live and remain" (ἡμεῖς οἱ ζῶντες οἱ περιλειπόμενοι, see also 4:17) has two present tense participles. But the present tense does not necessarily imply that the actions take place in present time, as if Paul were speaking of those *now* alive and *now* remaining; substantival present participles do not necessarily indicate an action that takes place at the time of the statement.[21] Our translation restates what the Greek says, no more and no less.

Scholars have tended to overinterpret Paul's use of the first person plural, that is, "*we* who live and remain." There is sufficient evidence elsewhere that Paul did not expect necessarily to live until the parousia or that, by implication, the parousia was near at hand.[22] First, the apostle faced death daily; even if a man of his age might expect to enjoy another twenty years of life, his lifestyle was by no means normal. With his constant encounters with near-fatal beatings, exposure, imprisonments in unhealthy conditions, malnutrition, bandits, shipwreck, and other threats to life (cf. 2 Cor 11:23 – 27), one should wonder how such a man could expect to see any future event, let alone Christ's return.

Second, Paul's intention here is to speak about believers who are living at the time of the parousia. He uses "we" for the simple reason that he was then alive and speaks of what living Christians should expect were the parousia immediate. He goes further and includes the Thessalonians in the "we," even though some of them at that moment are facing death. Only the living write and read letters, and so the words are geared to those "who still live."[23]

17. For example, Acts 20:35, "It is more blessed to give than to receive." See the overview by W. D. Stroker, "Agrapha," *ABD*, 1:92 – 95. Strecker, *Theology of the New Testament*, 212, regards 4:16 – 17 as an apocalyptic tradition from Jewish Christianity. Joachim Jeremias, *Unknown Sayings of Jesus* (trans. R. H. Fuller; 2nd ed.; London: SPCK, 1964), 80 – 83, takes it as a saying of Jesus that had been slightly modified in transmission.

18. See esp. Best, *Thessalonians*, 189 – 94; also Malherbe, *Letters to the Thessalonians*, 267 – 70; John Chrysostom, *Homilies on First Thessalonians* 8 (*NPNF*[1] 13:355).

19. John Chrysostom in his *In principium actorum* (PG 51.93.16 – 19, four sermons on Acts, a work not included in the *NPNF* series) asserts that Paul possessed the full range of charismatic gifts; he quotes this verse and others to show that Paul had the gift of prophecy. D. E. Aune, *Prophecy in Early Christianity and the Ancient Mediterranean World* (Grand Rapids: Eerdmans, 1983), 253 – 56, carefully examines 1 Thess 4:15 and concludes it was a prophetic oracle given by someone other than Paul, perhaps Silas.

20. Wallace, *Grammar*, 456.

21. Stanley E. Porter, *Idioms of the Greek New Testament* (Biblical Languages: Greek 2; Sheffield: JSOT, 1992), 181.

22. Best, *Thessalonians*, 194 – 96.

23. See too Origen, *Cels.* 5.17 (*ANF* 4:550): "Paul, as one who is alive and awake, and different from those who are asleep [κοιμάω], speaks as follows ..."; Origen then quotes 1 Thess 4:15 – 17.

Third, in other contexts, where appropriate, Paul could speak as if he were identifying with believers who were already dead: "We know that the one who raised the Lord Jesus from the dead will also raise us [the dead] with Jesus and present us [the dead] with you [the living Corinthians] to himself" (2 Cor 4:14; see also 1 Cor 6:14). Paul is offering no prediction in 1 Thessalonians as to whether or not the parousia would take place during his lifetime (see also comments on 5:1 – 2; 2 Thess 2:1 – 2).

4:15c Will in no way go ahead of those who have died (οὐ μὴ φθάσωμεν τοὺς κοιμηθέντας). Paul now delivers the content of the word from the Lord: believers who manage to survive until the parousia will certainly not be the first to be summoned to go out and meet Christ. He uses "in no way" (οὐ μή), the Greek double negative making it especially emphatic: living Christians "will in no way go ahead" (φθάσωμεν). This verb often has the more general sense of "come, arrive" (as in 2:16; Matt 12:28); here alone in the NT it means "go ahead of" or "precede."[24] The parousia is not just the coming of Christ from heaven. There is also movement on the part of Christians, the dead first and then the living. The rendezvous will take place "in the air" (1 Thess 4:17). For "died" (κοιμάω as metaphor for death) see 4:13.

4:16a-c Because the Lord himself, with the commanding shout of the archangel's voice and with the [sound of the] trumpet of God (ὅτι αὐτὸς ὁ κύριος ἐν κελεύσματι, ἐν φωνῇ ἀρχαγγέλου καὶ ἐν σάλπιγγι θεοῦ). The apostle has just shown that God will "gather together" the dead Christians; now he demonstrates what the parousia will be like and how the dead will be resurrected and go ahead of the living believers.

The word "because" (ὅτι) here is causal; that is, Paul shows *on what grounds* he has made the claim in v. 15. The phrase "the Lord himself" has its roots in the Scriptures (e.g., Isa 7:14 LXX; cf. also *T. Sim.* 6.5 [ed. Charlesworth] — "the Lord God shall appear on earth, and Himself save men"). For Paul, an integral part of the end of the age is that God's people will be gathered to the Lord they love; see also 4:17, "so we will always be with the Lord." The parousia will mark a new phase in the Christians' relationship with their Savior. It is this personal relationship that contrasts with the pantheistic eschatology of Sallustius in the fourth century AD: "Souls that have lived in accordance with virtue have as the crown of their happiness that freed from the unreasonable element and purified from all body they are in union with the gods and share with them the government of the whole universe"; that is, there is no resurrection and no personal loving communion with God.[25]

The Lord comes with blasts of sound, introduced by "with" (ἐν). Are there three (i.e., shout, voice of the archangel, trumpet of God) or two (i.e., shout made with the voice of the archangel, trumpet)? Most versions leave the question unanswered. The NJB, however, makes an explicit identification between the shout and the archangel: "at the signal given by the voice of the Archangel." This gives the best sense, since otherwise there would be a shout and then some other noise, voiced by the angel. "With the commanding shout" (ἐν κελεύσματι) is an authoritative command, not simply a loud noise.

There is a parallel in Joel 3:16 that likewise refers to the eschatological epiphany: "The Lord will roar from Zion and thunder from Jerusalem; the earth and the heavens will tremble." Another parallel is found in Philo, whose death occurred around the time Paul wrote 1 Thessalonians. Philo is speaking of God's power to bring people to repentance, no

24. MM, 666 – 67.

25. Sallustius, *Concerning the Gods and the Universe* 21 (trans. Nock).

matter where they have strayed: "God, by *one single word of command* [ἑνὶ κελεύσματι], could easily collect together men living on the very confines of the earth, bringing them from the extremities of the world to any place which he may choose, so also the merciful Saviour can bring back the soul after its long wandering."[26]

Morris comments that Paul has no particular archangel in view. Yet he reads too much into the absence of the definite article, thinking it must therefore mean "*an* archangel."[27] The Greek article does not function as does the English, and Paul could easily be speaking of "the" or "an." Only in this passage and Jude 9 do we find this compound noun "archangel" (i.e., lead angel). Michael is the one named in the Jude passage. His name is also found in the OT, in Dan 10:13, where he is an angelic "prince" (ἄρχων). Michael and his angels fight the dragon and his forces in Rev 12:7.

Within the elaborate models of postbiblical Judaism, Michael emerges as the special defender of Israel.[28] According to *3 (Greek) Baruch* 11.2, it is Michael who holds the keys to the kingdom of heaven. While Paul does not name the angel here, it seems likely that he has Michael in mind. He is in some way associated with the resurrection of the saints in Dan 12:1, and it is even possible that Michael is the "restrainer" of 2 Thess 2:6–7 (see comments on that passage). Nevertheless, Paul's focus is not on the layer upon layer of angelical hierarchy that one finds in the apocalyptic tradition. As this verse stresses at the beginning, the central figure is "the Lord himself," and all other beings are subordinated to him.

The "trumpet of God" at the resurrection is clearly a parallel to 1 Cor 15:52: "... at the last trumpet. For the trumpet will sound, the dead will be raised imperishable." The trumpet too finds its background in the OT[29] and in the Jesus tradition: "And he will send his angels with a loud trumpet call" (Matt 24:31). What Paul does not include here in 1 Thess 4:16 is the plurality of "holy angels" from 3:13, nor does he explain the role of the angels in gathering the elect, as stated in the Olivet Discourse.[30]

Oddly, some imagine that Paul's words here are derived from Jewish apocalyptic language. This cannot be so, for one searches in vain in known Jewish apocalypses to find any statement of a descending Messiah that resembles 4:16. Rather, Paul has woven together elements from the OT descriptions of "theophany" (the glorious appearing of the Lord) and the Jesus tradition, along with a fresh revelation.

4:16d Will come down from heaven (καταβήσεται ἀπ' οὐρανοῦ). Paul now moves to the central event of the parousia: Jesus will descend from heaven; that is, he will come down to the earth, and the saints will meet him in the air. The same vocabulary is found in John 6:38, but there Jesus speaks of his mission on earth: "I have come down from heaven [καταβέβηκα ἀπὸ τοῦ οὐρανοῦ] not to do

26. Philo, *Rewards* 117 (trans. Jonge). Philo uses "gathering" (συνάγωγος). See the use of the cognate verb "gather" (συνάγω) in *Did.* 10.5, discussed under 4:14 above.

27. Morris, *Thessalonians* (TNTC), 93.

28. See the useful article by D. F. Watson, "Michael," *ABD*, 4:811. See esp. *1 En.* 20.5 (ed. Charlesworth): "Michael, one of the holy angels, for (he is) obedient in his benevolence over the people and the nations." Also *War Scroll* 16.6–7. In the Gospel of Judas, Michael is he who distributes spirits to human beings.

29. The loud trumpet signaled the epiphany of Yahweh in Exod 19:16: "On the morning of the third day there was thunder and lightning, with a thick cloud over the mountain, and a very loud trumpet blast. Everyone in the camp trembled." See also Zech 9:14; Heb 12:18–21. Michael blows the trumpet, and so do other angels, in late Judaism: see *Apoc. Mos.* 22.1.

30. Schippers, "Pre-Synoptic Traditions," 233: "Paul has completely incorporated the pre-synoptic tradition into his letter to the Thessalonians." Contra the minimalist position of C. M. Tuckett, "Synoptic Tradition in 1 Thessalonians?" pages 160–82 in *The Thessalonian Correspondence* (ed. Collins), who argues there is hardly any dependence on the Synoptic tradition in this letter.

my will but to do the will of him who sent me." More closely related conceptually to 1 Thess 4:16 is the descent of angels from heaven (Rev 10:1; 18:1; 20:1); the ascent of Jesus to heaven with the promise that he will "return" (Acts 1:11); and Paul's later statement that "we eagerly wait a Savior from [heaven], the Lord Jesus Christ" (Phil 3:20). The topography of 1 Thess 4:16 runs from the surface of the earth, to the air, and then to heaven. While theologians across two millennia have proposed that heaven is not really vertically "up from" the surface of the planet, the New Testament writers were comfortable with that language as one way to describe the relative positions of heaven and earth.

4:16e And the dead in Christ will first be resurrected (καὶ οἱ νεκροὶ ἐν Χριστῷ ἀναστήσονται πρῶτον). Here is the solution to the Thessalonians' grief: as Christ was resurrected, so now will those who died in him be resurrected at his parousia. This resurrection is the first part of the gathering of the saints. Paul does not develop, as he will in 1 Cor 15:35–49, the nature of the resurrection body.

We render the verb "will be resurrected" (the future passive, ἀναστήσονται) rather than the traditional "will rise," which might be confused with the rising "in the air" (4:17). Many have noted the odd fact that nowhere does Paul write that the wicked will be resurrected. One has to draw that from Acts 24:15, where he states before Felix, "there will be a resurrection of both the righteous and the wicked." This omission of the resurrection of the damned in 1 Thess 4 seems to be due to his interest in "the dead in Christ," including the fatalities that some believers in Thessalonica have already suffered. The same seems true of 1 Cor 15:52: the dead believers will be raised incorruptible, and we [living Christians] will also be changed. In Acts 24, by contrast, Paul is speaking to non-Christians and gives out the truth that would be applicable to them as well. Paul uses "first" in 4:16 (πρῶτον) to denote a chronological order, following it up with "next" (ἔπειτα) in 4:17.

The author of Hebrews later reminded his readers that the eschatological "resurrection of the dead" was among the "first lessons of the Christian message" (Heb 6:1–2 GNB). How then had the Thessalonians missed out on this basic tenet? It is possible that there were countercurrents that pushed against the resurrection doctrine. In Macedonia, it would have been all but impossible to encounter the resurrection teaching in any venue apart from the synagogue and the newly planted church. Everything about the Greek worldview, be it in popular religion or erudite philosophy, resisted what would have seemed like the reviving of rotting cadavers. This, rather than some hypothetical Gnostic tendency, is the best explanation of why some in Corinth rejected the resurrection. Like the Sadducees and the Hellenists, they jibed, "How are the dead raised? With what kind of body will they come?" (1 Cor 15:35). Paul reminds the Corinthians of certain points of Christology and the doctrine of creation to show that it is not outlandish.

We have little idea of why some in Ephesus would say that the resurrection had already taken place (2 Tim 2:18), although in that case, they may have been anticipating what would blossom in the second century: Gnostics would reject the doctrine wholesale, along with the incarnation, death, and resurrection of Jesus.[31] Hence the Fathers as early as the second century fought hard against a hyperspiritualized Christianity that rejected God's

31. Modern Gnostics understand the resurrection of the saints as the receiving of the higher knowledge (gnosis) during this life. See the contemporary Gnostic teaching by Stephan A. Hoeller, "The Gnostic Catechism": www.webcom.com/gnosis/ecclesia/catechism.htm. "Question 89. How and when is our resurrection to take place? It takes place by Gnosis while we are still in earthly life."

continued interest in the material world.[32] The best explanation for the Thessalonians is that they heard that truth, but then had trouble grasping it when it was no longer a hypothetical question but a crisis over what would happen to the fallen ones in their small congregations. Nevertheless, it is unlikely that the question of "why" can be answered definitively unless further information be forthcoming. See the Introduction, "Eschatology in Thessalonica."

4:17a-d Next, we who still live and remain will be taken up together with [those who were dead] in the clouds to welcome the Lord in the air (ἔπειτα ἡμεῖς οἱ ζῶντες οἱ περιλειπόμενοι ἅμα σὺν αὐτοῖς ἁρπαγησόμεθα ἐν νεφέλαις εἰς ἀπάντησιν τοῦ κυρίου εἰς ἀέρα). The people of Christ will go forth to meet him at his parousia in two stages: first, the resurrected dead; "next," the living believers. Paul now speaks of this second group. He repeats the phrase from 4:15, "we who still live and remain" as a rubric for living Christians. They will be "taken up together with those who were dead . . . in the air." Paul is still speaking in terms of vertical movement: Christ descends from heaven, the dead arise, and living Christians are snatched upward with them into the "clouds" and into the "air."

Paul uses the future passive of the verb "taken" (from ἁρπάζω). The Latin Vulgate translates the verb as *rapiemur*, a form of *rapio*; from this is derived the English word "rapture." God "takes" Paul from earth to the third heaven in 2 Cor 12:2, 4. But in itself the Greek verb does not convey vertical movement, that is, of being "caught *up*"; it could refer to "being taken from one place to another." For example, in Acts 8:39 the Spirit snatches (form of ἁρπάζω) Philip from the Gaza Road to Azotus. Some have concluded that the rapture must mean the transportation of the saints from earth to another location, heaven, to wait out the tribulation. This is not indicated: rather, when the believers are caught up from one place to another, it is from earth to "the air." The verb "taken up" is a "divine passive," since God is the one who gathers the saints (see also 4:14).[33]

First Thessalonians 4:17 is the only explicit New Testament reference to the saints being raptured "upward" at the parousia;[34] other terms, such as "gather," while easily accommodating the idea of an ascent, do not demand a vertical movement. The reference to Enoch's translation in Gen 5:24 likewise does not say that Enoch went "up," but simply that God "took" or (in the LXX) "transferred" him.[35]

"Cloud" has a variety of uses in eschatological passages. It may allude to the innumerable heavenly armies (cf. Jude 14; 1 Thess 3:13); to literal clouds, betokening the ascension into the upper air; to the cloud of glory on which sits the Son of Man; or to a heavenly cloud that transports Christ or his saints (Matt 24:30). The closest parallel to 1 Thess 4:17 is Rev 11:11 – 12, where the slain witnesses are resurrected and ascend into heaven in a cloud. So, "cloud" as heavenly vehicle is the pre-

32. The tension that occurred between church and the Hellenistic world is evidenced by the clause "I believe . . . in the resurrection of the body" in the Apostles' Creed. As early as the first and second century we hear denials of the resurrection in *1 Clem.* 24 – 27; *Barn.* 21.1; *2 Clem.* 9.1, 5 ("And let none of you say that this flesh is not judged and does not rise again. . . . If Christ, the Lord who saved us, became flesh (even though he was originally spirit) and in that state called us, so also we will receive our reward in this flesh." Justin Martyr tells Trypho in *Dial.* 80.4 – 5 (*ANF* 1:239) that "some who are called Christians . . . say there is no resurrection of the dead, and that their souls, when they die, are taken to heaven. . . . But I and others, who are right-minded Christians on all points, are assured that there will be a resurrection of the dead." Justin Martyr and Tertullian wrote whole treatises on the topic of the resurrection.

33. Wallace, *Grammar*, 437 – 38.

34. So Leon Morris, *Word Biblical Themes* (Dallas: Word, 1989), 49.

35. The LXX does not use the verb "catch up" (ἁρπάζω) of Enoch in Gen. 5:24, but rather "transferred" (μετατίθημι); Wis 4:10 – 11, however, uses both verbs to describe Enoch's experience.

ferred understanding, as is shown by Acts 1:9, 11: "After [Jesus] said this, he was taken up before their very eyes, and a cloud hid him from their sight.... 'This same Jesus, who has been taken up from you into heaven, will come in the same way as you have seen him go into heaven.'" "In the air" is simply the atmosphere.

"Together" (ἅμα) is used in the parable of the tares in Matt 13:29, where the master forbids the servants from uprooting the weeds and hence damaging the grain. Here in 1 Thess 4:17 it signifies the reuniting of the people of Christ in the eschatological moment; we all join together, and it is the ascension of the living believers that is the second step that will complete the assembling of God's people.

Paul does not divulge here the truth of 1 Cor 15:51, the "mystery" that "we will not all sleep [die], but we will all be changed"; that is, the living believers too must undergo a transformation. Paul calls it a "mystery," perhaps another new revelation. Since he doesn't mention it here, and since it seems to be new information in 1 Cor 15, it is unlikely that the doctrine of the "transformed living" was a part of the apostolic preaching at the time of 1 Thessalonians.

In our translation, "to welcome" follows the lead of most English versions by making a verb of the prepositional phrase "for a meeting" (εἰς ἀπάντησιν). The basic translation "to meet" or "to welcome" is technically correct, but what happens after the Christians meet the Lord in the air? Where do they go? Paul does not say, neither here or in 1 Cor 15:52. In some systems of eschatology, Christ comes close to the earth, to the atmosphere, to receive the saints and then takes them back with him to heaven.[36] Another interpretation is that Christ comes back, the saints go forth to meet him, and then they accompany him as he continues on his way to earth.

In the absence of explicit details, is there some implicit indication of what is to follow? Apparently so: the Greek "meeting" (ἀπάντησις as here, and its cognate ὑπάντησις)[37] is not simply going to encounter someone, but rather "the action of going out to meet an arrival, especially as a mark of honour."[38] When a dignitary came to visit a city in those days, the inhabitants would pay him tribute by going out of the city to meet him at the proper time. They would then *accompany him back* to the city he was planning to enter. This is what happened in John 12:13, where the crowd on Palm Sunday came out of Jerusalem to meet Jesus (ὑπάντησις) and accompany him back in to the city. Moreover, the Olivet Discourse contains the metaphor of a ruler coming to the city, which he then enters; "when you see all these things: know that he is near, right at the gates" (Matt 24:33 NJB).[39]

What makes Paul's language unusual is the

36. See Plevnik, "The Taking Up of the Faithful," 274 – 83. He states that this verse is parallel to 2 Cor 4:13 – 14, and since the latter passage speaks of being led into God's presence in heaven, 1 Thess 4:17 must also speak of going on to heaven. Therefore, the Thessalonians did not know about the resurrection because Paul had only taught them about the translation of the saints to heaven at Christ's coming. Plevnik's point falters in assuming that passages that sound similar are making the same point. See also his "The Destination of the Apostle and the Faithful," 83 – 95

37. See the Matthean parable of the ten maidens (Matt 25:1 – 13); five of them apparently go forth in order to meet the groom and then walk back with him to the wedding feast, from which the girls had originally set out; however, we do not possess enough detailed information about wedding customs to make absolute claims. The language in the better manuscripts of Matt 25:6, "to meet" (εἰς ἀπάντησιν) is identical to what Paul uses here — another tantalizing clue that Paul is working with the Matthean tradition. Notice that in Matt 25:1, ὑπάντησις is interchangeable with the ἀπάντησις of 25:6. In both verses, some manuscripts have the words switched.

38. LSJ, "ἀπάντησις." See also MM; the Hellenistic references show that this is not a Semiticism.

39. The NRSV and ESV also have "gates," which preserves the metaphor — the Son of Man comes as a king to the gates of his city. See the synoptic parallel in Mark 13:29. The alternative translation, which is not so strong a possibility, is that this refers to the door of a habitation (see NIV), as indeed several

spatial reorientation of the "meeting." He turns the horizontal action of the dignitary's approach, reception, and entrance into a gated city into a vertical action: when Christ comes, he "will come down" to his domain, and his subjects ascend "in the clouds ... in the air," as befits his deserved honor.[40] Based on this conventional usage of "meeting" (ἀπάντησις), it may be concluded with a relatively high degree of certainty that Paul envisions Jesus coming in the air; resurrected believers and then living ones will ascend to honor him, and *they will then accompany him back to the earth.*[41] This lies close to the thought of 2 Thess 1:10: "when he comes to be glorified among his saints and to be worshiped among all who have believed." Paul's language, while taken from earlier tradition, would have sounded political to residents of the empire: Christ, not Caesar, is the true king, the one whom Christians should receive as their sovereign; Christ's peace, not Caesar's "peace and security" (1 Thess 5:3), is the true reality.[42]

4:17e And so we will always be with the Lord (καὶ οὕτως πάντοτε σὺν κυρίῳ ἐσόμεθα). In John's gospel, Jesus promises, "I will come back and take you to be with me that you also may be where I am" (John 14:3). For his part, Paul shows that Jesus will come, not just to take individuals to him, but to gather together and be with his people as a body. The apostle uses "and so" (καὶ οὕτως) to demonstrate that the resurrection and rapture of the saints is the manner in which they are united forever with him. Paul leaves open what is the exact meaning of being "always ... with the Lord." This state is beyond human description, even for an apostle who is disclosing a prophetic word (4:15). But he has made the point the Thessalonians needed to hear: we, that is, the living and the dead, will be together with Jesus, and living Christians may be confident that they will see their deceased friends in his presence.

4:18 So then, encourage one another with these words (Ὥστε παρακαλεῖτε ἀλλήλους ἐν τοῖς λόγοις τούτοις). Paul concludes with "so then" (ὥστε) in order to show the Thessalonians what to do with this information. In Gnosticism, information about the true nature of resurrection would have

metaphors of the Synoptic apocalypse speak of the lord of the household and his servants.

40. So E. Peterson, "ἀπάντησις," *TDNT*, 1:380 – 81. Among other authors, this is one of those cases where one side errs by reading too much meaning into a word, and the other side refutes what is in effect a straw man. For example, John Chrysostom, *Homilies on First Thessalonians* 10 (*NPNF*[1] 13:356) states that such a coming by a king by definition includes the giving of rewards for the faithful subjects and the immediate judgment of the city's rebels; the type of expanded meaning of the concept is approved by Lucien Cerfaux, *Christ in the Theology of St. Paul* (trans. Geoffrey Webb and Adrian Walker; New York: Herder and Herder, 1959), 39 – 42. A better way forward is shown by M. R. Cosby, "Hellenistic Formal Receptions and Paul's Use of ΑΠΑΝΤΗΣΙΣ in 1 Thessalonians 4:17," *BBR* 4 (1994): 15 – 34. He demonstrates that the word does not necessarily carry all the baggage that is sometimes attributed to its meaning (citizens prepare the reception; the offering sacrifices; judgment of rebels who are jailed within the city). Nevertheless the word can be shown generally to describe "a loose pattern to play against when describing the coming of a heavenly king" (15). Similarly Malherbe, *Letters to the Thessalonians*, 277; Bruce, *1 & 2 Thessalonians*, 102 – 3. Doubtful is the theory of N. T. Wright, that it was Paul who originally combined "meeting" with parousia in order to pit Christ against the earthly usurper, the emperor. See N. T. Wright, *Paul in Fresh Perspective* (Minneapolis: Fortress, 2005), 74. The easiest refutation of Wright's point is that it was not Paul who first applied these terms to the second coming; he found them in the gospel tradition (παρουσία: Matt 24:27, 37; see also Jas 5:8; "meeting" [ἀπάντησις], see our analysis above).

41. So S. Turner, "The Interim, Earthly Messianic Kingdom in Paul," *JSNT* 25 (2003): 331. See also the essay by Douglas J. Moo, defending the posttribulationist view timing of the rapture, in Reiter, *Three Views on the Rapture*, 169 – 211. Wanamaker, *Thessalonians*, 169 – 70, states that the reference to the clouds means that they accompany Christ back to heaven.

42. Seyoon Kim, *Christ and Caesar: The Gospel and the Roman Empire in the Writings of Paul and Luke* (Grand Rapids: Eerdmans, 2008), 6; N. T. Wright, *Paul in Fresh Perspective*, 54 – 56, 142 – 43.

been part of a higher plane knowledge, not able to be absorbed by rank-and-file Christians. But Paul does not make this information private and individualistic but corporate; if properly grasped, it will lead them to "encourage one another" (παρακαλεῖτε ἀλλήλους); see also 5:11: "so then, encourage and build up one another." "With these words" are not simply words of emotional support, but words of revelation that are by nature encouraging, on which they should base their speech to other believers and help them to throw away their un-Christian grief.

Theology in Application

With the doctrine of the resurrection, Gentile converts were to accept and put into daily practice a radically new paradigm.

Theology in Thessalonica

The Jewish colony in Thessalonica differed from its religious context in many respects. Most Jews believed that history was moving toward a final conclusion (a telic view of history), an end that was in God's hands. In addition, most Jews believed in the resurrection of the body as the redemption of God's physical creation (cf. Dan 12:2 – 3). In the story of Lazarus, Martha is quoted as giving a simple but definite confession: "I know he will rise again in the resurrection at the last day" (John 11:24). An inscription from Rome (second or third century AD) over the grave of a twenty-year-old Jewish wife reflects that view of the resurrection:

> Here lies Regina.... She will live again, return to the light again, for she can hope that she will rise to the life promised, as is our true faith, to the worthy and to the pious, in that she has deserved to possess an abode in the hallowed land.... Your hope of the future is assured. In this your sorrowing husband seeks his comfort.[43]

A few of the new Christians in Thessalonica came from that synagogue background, but most did not.

The Greek view of death varied widely.[44] The followers of Plato, for example, believed in the reincarnation, or transmigration, of the soul: the soul goes into a new body (perhaps human, perhaps animal) and recalls something of the experience and wisdom of past lives. Others Greeks believed that death was the end of existence. For example, the Epicureans thought that human consciousness dissolved with the body:

> Accustom yourself to believe that death is nothing to us, for good and evil imply awareness, and death is the privation of all awareness; therefore a right understanding

43. Harry J. Leon, *The Jews of Ancient Rome* (Philadelphia: Jewish Publication Society, 1966), 335. See the detailed analysis of the Jewish doctrine of the resurrection by C. Brown, "ἀνάστασις," *NIDNTT*, 3:259 – 75.

44. See the indispensable study by Wright, *The Resurrection of the Son of God*, 32 – 84.

> that death is nothing to us makes the mortality of life enjoyable, not by adding to life an unlimited time, but by taking away the yearning after immortality.[45]

The Stoics believed in the survival of death, but not as personal beings. According to Marcus Aurelius:

> The souls which are removed into the air after subsisting for some time are transmuted and diffused, and assume a fiery nature by being received into the seminal intelligence of the universe, and in this way make room for the fresh souls which come to dwell there. And this is the answer which a man might give on the hypothesis of souls continuing to exist.[46]

These ideas, along with the lore of the mystery religions, were always minority views, held by people with some taste for philosophy or for arcane religion. For his part, Paul was writing to Greeks who had "no hope" apart from Christ, that is, people who held to the majority opinion that the soul would travel to a gloomy underworld. Even if they might encounter their dead friends in the life beyond, it would be in a realm of shadows, known for its drab hopelessness.[47] Tombstones have been recovered from all over the empire, and they reveal something of the popular mindset. An inscription from Thessalonica itself shows the misery of death; the widower built a tomb "that later he would have a place to rest together with his dear wife, when he looks upon the end of life that has been spun out for him by the indissoluble threads of the Fates."[48]

How does one carry on when the future looks so baleful? Some Greeks would simply cry and wail against the destiny that awaits all people.[49] Others urged acquiescence to one's inevitable fate. Paul's contemporary Seneca — whose brother, Gallio, crossed paths with Paul as proconsul of Corinth — took a typical philosophical approach. Grief, like all passions, should be moderated, and the wise man should control himself. If someone should tell Seneca that " 'One should be allowed a certain amount of grieving, and a certain amount of fear,' I reply that the 'certain amount' can be too long-drawn-out, and that it will refuse to stop short when [eventually] you so desire."[50]

Paul went directly against the grain, preaching the resurrection of Jesus and also

45. Epicurus, "Letter to Menoeceus" (trans. Hicks).

46. Marcus Aurelius, *Meditations* 4.21 (trans. Long).

47. Wright, *The Resurrection of the Son of God*, 82.

48. M. Eugene Boring, Klaus Berger, and Carsten Colpe, eds., *Hellenistic Commentary to the New Testament* (Nashville: Abingdon, 1995), 494. Another funerary inscription from the third century AD reveals that some Hellenized Jews seem scarcely distinguishable from the Greeks with regard to their despair over the afterlife: "I, the son of Leontius, lie dead, Justus, the son of Sappho ... (and left) my poor parents in endless mourning.... And having gone to Hades, I, Justus, lie here with many of my own kindred, since mighty Fate so willed. Be of good courage, Justus, no one is immortal" (see P. W. van den Horst, "Jewish Tomb Inscriptions in Verse," in *Hellenism, Judaism, Christianity: Essays on their Interaction* [CBET; Kampen: Kok Pharos, 1994], 35).

49. Gaventa, *First and Second Thessalonians*, 67: "people in desperate pain will seek and grasp for comfort wherever they can find it, in an effort to manage the pain of loss. Paul takes a strikingly different strategy."

50. Seneca, *Ep.* 116, "On Self-Control" (trans. Gummere).

the future resurrection of all humanity: "I have the same hope in God these [Pharisees] themselves have, that there will be a resurrection of both the righteous and the wicked" (Acts 24:15).[51]

Since the Thessalonians seem to have missed out on the implications of the resurrection doctrine, Paul writes to fill in this gap in their understanding. They should not grieve as others do. Yet Christianity is not Stoicism. When Christians lose friends from church, who are, at the deepest level of truth, family members, their grief should be shaped and moderated by the resurrection hope that lies at the foundation of the gospel.

Biblical Theology

Paul is the most prominent spokesman in the Scriptures for the doctrine that death is the result of human sin. While this is implicit in Gen 2:17; 3:19, and in other places, neither the authors of the OT, the literature of Second Temple Judaism, nor the NT authors give it the strong development found in Rom 5:12 and its context. In addition, Paul makes the corollary doctrine of the resurrection an integral component of divine salvation: "just as Christ was raised from the dead through the glory of the Father, we too may live a new life" (Rom 6:4b; see also 8:11).

The resurrection is not some isolated doctrine. It is part and parcel of the truth that God is the "living God, who made the heavens and the earth and the sea and everything in them" (Acts 14:15). Within this worldview, God has the authority to redeem life out of death.[52] If God can create life from nonlife, he is ready to create life even from the bodies of the dead.

To the surprise of many, in no Scripture does one find the Greek phrase "the immortality of the soul." To be mortal simply means to be capable of death. Human beings since the sin of Adam have been inherently mortal, that is, subject to bodily death and decay. No mortal may inherit the eschatological kingdom (1 Cor 15:50), and therefore the dead must be resurrected and the living transformed into immortality (1 Cor 15:51 – 53). As a second-century preacher would come to express it: "So great is the life and immortality which this flesh is able to receive, if the Holy Spirit is closely joined with it, that no one is able to proclaim or to tell 'what things the Lord has prepared' for his chosen ones" (*2 Clem.* 14.5).[53]

Some contemporary views of the afterlife suffer from reductionism. According to Rudolf Bultmann, no God will break into history to save us. There is no coming kingdom, parousia, Satan, demons, or three-storied universe consisting of heaven, earth, and hell:

51. For the Pharisees' view see Josephus, *Ant.* 18.1.3 (§14); *J.W.* 2.8.14 (§163).

52. See P. S. Johnston, "Death and Resurrection," *NDBT*, 444 – 47.

53. Beginning in the second century, a number of heresies (Marcionism, various strands of Gnosticism) rejected these implications of the OT, being informed by Greek assumptions. See, e.g., Tertullian, *Res.* 24; 41; 57 (*ANF* 3).

> This conception of the world we call mythological because it is different from the conception of the world which has been formed and developed by science.... In this modern conception of the world the cause-and-effect nexus is fundamental ... modern science does not believe that the course of nature can be interrupted or, so to speak, perforated, by supernatural powers.[54]

Bultmann concluded that the apocalyptic message calls modern hearers outside themselves to an existentialist understanding of their reality. But in fact Bultmann approximated the approach of many philosophers of Paul's day, who understood the old pagan myths as mere metaphors. Paul for his part could not accept that sort of ahistorical hermeneutic, since for him the literal history of Jesus was the foundation of the gospel. In the case of the believer's resurrection, no mere feeling of hopefulness provided the foundation for Paul's confidence that God would raise people from the dead just as he had Jesus.

Message of This Passage for the Church Today

Paul wrote this letter as a Christian pastor. He knew the value of theology for altering human psychology and insisted on the Thessalonians encouraging one another with good eschatology (4:18). They could now appreciate yet another facet of Christ's gift of salvation, the physical and the eschatological level.

It is regrettable that so many of today's Christians read volume after volume of "pop eschatology" and yet seem at a loss to better understand their future hope. For example, I just browsed through a painfully detailed study that "proved" that Prince Charles of England is the antichrist, and that no other possible candidate is possible. We should include here the growing set of people who supposedly have died and then returned to write up what they saw in heaven. But where is the flood of popular interest in the truly fundamental themes of the end times: judgment, vindication, resurrection, kingdom, and others — not to mention their traveling companions, joy, hope, faith, and mutual encouragement? Where are the teachers who will work through the details of eschatology so as to draw the larger conclusions about the divine nature? Eschatology, like any other part of our belief system, must be *doxological*; that is, it must lead to glorifying God.

Then too, many Christians neglect the resurrection doctrine and place too much weight on the doctrine of dying and going to heaven. Two books that we commend as a corrective are by Rebecca Price Janney, *Who Goes There? A Cultural History of Heaven and Hell* (Chicago: Moody Press, 2009); and N. T. Wright, *Surprised by Hope: Rethinking Heaven, the Resurrection, and the Mission of the Church* (New York: Harp-

54. R. Bultmann, *Jesus Christ and Mythology* (New York: Scribner, 1958), 15. Without giving away any support to postmodernism, still I must say it is jarring to read Bultmann a mere fifty years after he gave this speech and to see how badly out of fashion his "modern" approach to truth has become.

erOne, 2008). There is also a fine section by Beverly Gaventa in her Thessalonians commentary on "Preaching and Teaching Eschatology."[55]

Let us explore how a proper emphasis on the resurrection might affect our proclamation.

The Christian funeral. "He is no longer suffering; he is in heaven, where we will join him; God will comfort the bereaved with his loving presence." Such is the form into which the funeral oration has evolved. The difficulty with it is not that it is mistaken, but that it is ill-proportioned. Paul would probably have preached a funeral sermon along the lines of: "He testified to Christ in his life, despite opposition, right to the end; he is in the presence of Christ; he will be resurrected when Christ returns, where we will see him in the presence of our Lord; God comforts us by reminding us that he has destroyed death in Jesus."

Evangelism. When Paul proclaimed the resurrection of Jesus at Athens, he was mocked (Acts 17:31 – 32). His modern counterparts might be tempted to skip over the eschatological resurrection of the saints as a necessary corollary to the Easter faith. But what is demanded of us today is not avoidance but an insightful biblical and cultural interpretation of the resurrection message to each generation. One route is to take advantage of our contemporaries' obsession with their health. The media are saturated with medical reports, health advice, and new diets. Western culture is also obsessed with staying young, to the point of having multiple elective surgeries. People feel youth — and thus, life — slipping away, and there is no brake against it. With extended life spans, people are living long enough to experience more diseases, such as arthritis, Alzheimer's, cancer.

The gospel does not promise some final release from the physical body but its perfect transformation. Take the woman with arthritic fingers: in Christ, she can look forward to, not reincarnation (as an animal, or if she is lucky, another human being who in turn is doomed to growing old again), nor the laying aside of the body, to live as a disembodied spirit, nor being extinguished. Rather, she can experience the transformation of that very hand so that the joints work precisely as her Maker intended, and in ways beyond our current reckonings.

By the same logic, those who do not know God cannot flee him through extinction or reincarnation or a flight into the cosmos as a phantom. No, such people will stand resurrected to give account of what they have done in the body (2 Cor 5:10), and will then exist forever in bodies that can experience torment and the pain of absence from God (Rev 20:13). If the resurrection is the bedrock the Christian's expectation, it is also the terror of those without hope.

55. Gaventa, *First and Second Thessalonians*, 76 – 79.

CHAPTER 6

1 Thessalonians 5:1 – 11

Literary Context

Paul moves from fresh teaching about Christ's return (4:13 – 18) to teaching that he is confident the Thessalonians have already absorbed: how to be ready for Christ's coming. Negatively, one does not prepare by calculating the date of his return; positively, true readiness is spiritual and involves walking in God's ways. It is not clear why the apostle rehearses doctrine that is not at immediate risk. One explanation is that the Thessalonians were starting to show signs that they misunderstood the question of end-time chronology (2 Thess 2:1 – 2). A better explanation is that the early church commonly combined the truth of the Lord's return with exhortation to vigilence and holiness; since Paul has spoken about the parousia, he goes on naturally to talk about readiness.

In 5:4 – 11, the apostle speaks in general terms about walking in the light. In the following section (5:12 – 22) he delves into specific behaviors that should characterize the Christian. Finally, Paul will end the letter praying that God will make the Thessalonians fully holy, ready to meet Christ at the parousia (5:23).

VI. *Paraenesis:* The Gospel Ethic in a Gentile Environment (4:1 – 12)
VII. Instruction about the Return of Christ (4:13 – 5:11)
  A. Dead Christians will be raised to be with Jesus ahead of the living (4:13 – 18)
➡ **B. Christians should live in holiness, even without knowing the timing of the end (5:1 – 11)**
VIII. Final Exhortations (5:12 – 22)

Main Idea

Paul now examines the coming of Christ from the angle of daily living. First, no one knows the time of his return; it cannot be anticipated by mathematical calculation. Second, to prepare for this surprise means living in anticipation of the eschatological kingdom, in holy alertness.

Translation

(See next two pages.)

Structure

Although Paul has been speaking of eschatology in the previous section, he now signals a change of direction with "now about" (περὶ δέ, 5:1; see the same construction in 4:9). In contrast to what has gone before, the Thessalonians are not confused or ill-informed about the ethical implications of their eschatology: they "have no need" of more information (5:1b), "because" (causal use of γάρ) they know perfectly well that the day of the Lord comes as a thief in the night (5:2). Here Paul associates that Day with the parousia of Jesus in 4:15 — when Jesus comes, he initiates the day of Yahweh.

The apostle now describes two contrasting groups of people, the world (5:3) and the people of God (5:4 – 5). The destructive power of that Day is expressed with three traditional metaphors: it will be "like a thief in the night" (5:2c), like a military invasion from out of nowhere, and "as birth pains." Paul uses emphatic negation: "in no way" (οὐ μὴ) will they escape (cf. Amos 2:14 – 15).

Paul draws a clear line between "them" and "you/we" (5:3 – 5): "they" will be taken unaware by the parousia, "but you" (ὑμεῖς δέ) Thessalonians will not (5:4). Yet how will the believers not be surprised, given that for them too the Day is like a thief? This tension is resolved by focusing on the nature of the surprise: Christians do not know *when* Christ will return (5:1), but they will be prepared because (γάρ; 5:5a) they are walking according to their new nature, as children of the day and of the light.

In 5:6 Paul now marks a change in direction from "indicative" to "hortatory subunctive" with "so then" (ἄρα οὖν). He begins this section, as he does so often in this letter, with an antithesis: "let us not let ourselves fall asleep ... but let us keep alert." Another antithesis follows as he provides the reason (marked by γάρ) for his preceding exhortation: people of the night are wicked (5:7), but because "we belong to the day," we should behave as such (5:8a). The believers should be vigilant and put on the divine armor that protects those who are in Christ (5:8b-d). Here Paul alludes to the "armor of God" language from Isa 59:17; it is a favorite motif that he will use in other letters.

In 5:9 – 10 the apostle summarizes this section but also reaches back to earlier sections of the letter. He is leaving the Thessalonians on a high note about putting on God's armor "because" they are people who will receive not wrath but salvation (5:9a-b); this alludes back to his gospel outline in 1:9 – 10. In 5:10, this future salvation is through the death of Christ (cf. 5:9c with 4:14a) "so that" (ἵνα) it will be enjoyed by all believers, living or dead.

1 Thessalonians 5:1 – 11

1a	Assertion	Now, concerning times and dates, brothers and sisters,
1b	Assertion	**you have no need [for us] to write you**,
2a	Cause	because you yourselves know perfectly well
2b	Content	that the day of the Lord will come
2c	Comparison	like a thief in the night.
3a	Simultaneous	When they will be saying, "Peace and security,"
3b	Assertion / Simultaneous	then **unexpected destruction will befall them,**
3c	Comparison	[sudden] as birth pains on a pregnant woman,
3d	Result	and **they will in no way escape.**
4a	Contrast	But **you, brothers and sisters, are not in darkness,**
4b	Result	so that the day would surprise you
4c	Comparison	like a thief.
5a	Cause – List	For **you are all children of light and**
5b	Cause – List	**the children of the day.**
5c	Cause – List	**We are not of the night nor**
5d	Cause – List	**of the darkness.**
6a	Inference	So then, **let us not let ourselves fall asleep,**
6b	Comparison	as do other people,
6c	Contrast (to 6a)	but **let us keep alert and exercise self-control.**

7a	Basis	[I say this because] **those who fall asleep do so at night**
7b	Basis	and **those who get drunk do so at night.**
8a	Basis	But because we belong to the day,
8b	Exhortation	**let us exercise self-control**
8c	Means	by putting on faith and love
		as a breastplate and
8d	Exhortation	as a helmet
		the sure expectation of our [coming] salvation.
9a	Cause	[This is the confidence we have] because God has not assigned us to feel [his coming] wrath, but rather
9b	Contrast	to obtain salvation
9c		through our Lord Jesus Christ,
10a	Description	who died for us,
10b	Result	so that,
		whether we are [still] keeping alert or
10c	Alternative	whether we have [already] died,
10d	Result	we shall live together with him.
11a	Inference (from 1-10)	So then, **encourage and build up one another,**
11b	Comparison	just as you are already doing.

As in 4:18, Paul ends the section stating that on the basis of these gospel truths, the Thessalonians must therefore (διό) continue to encourage and build up one another (5:11).

Exegetical Outline

→ **I. The Apostles Begin with Known Eschatological Teaching (5:1 – 5).**
- A. They remind the Thessalonians that they already possess this teaching (5:1).
- B. The day of the Lord will come as sudden destruction (5:2 – 3).
- C. The Thessalonian Christians, being who they are, will not be taken by surprise (5:4 – 5).

II. The Apostles Turn to Ethical Exhortation Based on This Teaching (5:6 – 11).
- A. They should be alert and self-controlled (5:6 – 8a).
- B. They should put on the eschatological "armor of God" (5:8b).
- C. They should have the confidence that they will live with Christ at the resurrection (5:9 – 10).
- D. They should encourage each other with these eschatological truths (5:11).

Explanation of the Text

5:1 Now, concerning times and dates, brothers and sisters, you have no need [for us] to write you (Περὶ δὲ τῶν χρόνων καὶ τῶν καιρῶν, ἀδελφοί, οὐ χρείαν ἔχετε ὑμῖν γράφεσθαι). The destiny of the Christian dead has now been settled. Thus, Paul turns to the related issue of when Christ will return. Once again, his teaching has firm roots in the oral teaching of Jesus. The Olivet Discourse itself was a response to the disciples' inquiry, "Tell us, when will these things happen? And what will be the sign that they are all about to be fulfilled?" (Mark 13:4). Acts 1:6 – 7 also begins with the question of eschatological timing when the disciples asked, "Lord, are you at this time going to restore the kingdom to Israel?" There Jesus corrected them: "It is not for you to know the times or dates the Father has set by his own authority." Thomas Aquinas commented on Acts 1:7, "Whereby, as Augustine says '*He scatters the figures of all calculators and bids them be still.*' For what He refused to tell the apostles, He will not reveal to others."[1]

The pattern, then, is that whenever the disciples seek knowledge about when the parousia will occur, Jesus responds with his own agenda. He tells them to defend themselves against deceivers (Matt 24:4 – 5), to beware of interpreting wars, famines, and earthquakes as irrefutable signs that the end is near (24:6 – 8), to remain watchful (24:42), to not be violent or drunk (24:49 – 50), and to be witnesses to all nations (Acts 1:8).

Paul pairs together "times and dates" (τῶν χρόνων καὶ τῶν καιρῶν), the same words used in Acts 1:7. It is not fruitful to look for subtle distinctions between these synonyms. In the LXX and the NT, "over a large area of the usage … the two words mean the same thing.… In particular, in those theologically important cases which speak of the 'time' or 'times' which God has appointed or

1. Thomas Aquinas, *Summa*, Question 77, Art. 2 (Cosimo, Vol. V, Part III); Aquinas is citing Augustine, *Civ.* 18.53.

promised, the two words are most probably of like meaning."[2] They speak of general chronological information; the translation of "times and dates" is fitting. Paul is in line with the gospel tradition that the time of the parousia is unknowable until after "all signs have been fulfilled" (Matt 24:32 – 34).

Paul tells the Thessalonians (lit.) that "you have no need to be written to you." Some versions render it that way, while others more helpfully offer a free translation such as "we/I have no need to write." The Thessalonians had already received this teaching from the apostolic team, probably in a package resembling the Matthean tradition: "about that day and hour no one knows" (Matt 24:36). While it is true that Paul may be using the rhetorical device "I don't need to tell you" only as a set-up to tell them anyway, there is no evidence here that the Thessalonians have begun to be preoccupied with dates as they would be in 2 Thess 2:1 – 2.[3]

5:2 Because you yourselves know perfectly well that the day of the Lord will come like a thief in the night (αὐτοὶ γὰρ ἀκριβῶς οἴδατε ὅτι ἡμέρα κυρίου ὡς κλέπτης ἐν νυκτὶ οὕτως ἔρχεται). The Thessalonians are already aware of the terrible suddenness with which the day of the Lord will come. Paul underscores that they have previous knowledge by adding the pronoun "you yourselves [αὐτοί] know" this. In so doing he also distinguishes "you" from "they," establishing their group identity and the knowledge that their group possesses. In fact, the Thessalonians know this information "perfectly well" (ἀκριβῶς), that is, with precision and accuracy; it is the same term Luke used to describe his own careful research into the gospel tradition (Luke 1:3).

Paul taps into a long tradition concerning the day of the Lord. The OT prophets portrayed it as the coming of Yahweh in judgment and destruction: "See, the day of the Lord is coming — a cruel day, with wrath and fierce anger — to make the land desolate and destroy the sinners within it" (Isa 13:9). The term might apply to any divine intervention against sin, no matter at what point in history it might occur (Lam 2:22; Joel 1:15). But beyond that usage, especially as the term is developed in Joel, divine judgment in this age is a foreshadowing of the horrific final day of Yahweh: "The sun will be turned to darkness and the moon to blood before the coming of the great and dreadful day of the Lord" (Joel 2:31; see Mal 4:5).

Jesus spoke in terms of that Day in his Olivet Discourse (see his use of Joel in Matt 24:29), as did Peter on Pentecost (Acts 2:17 – 21). Paul too spoke of a future Day (1 Cor 3:13), as also Peter in 2 Pet 3:10. Revelation 6:12 – 17 foresaw cosmic and terrestrial disasters: "For the great day of their wrath has come, and who can withstand it?" (6:17). In 1 Thessalonians, the Day is portrayed as a day of judgment, from which the believers will be spared (1 Thess 5:9; cf. 5:4).

With regard to this eschatological Day, some students split words beyond what is warranted by the biblical texts. They assume that a literal exegesis must lead to the conclusion that, for example, the day of Christ is to be distinguished from the day of the Lord. In fact, Paul uses such terms as day of the Lord, day of Christ, day of the Lord Jesus

2. So H. Hübner, "χρόνος," *EDNT*, 3:488. Also consult James Barr, *Biblical Words for Time* (SBT First Series; rev. ed.; Naperville, IL: Allenson, 1969), 44; see throughout the volume for an exhaustive study. Malherbe, *Letters to the Thessalonians*, 288, regards it as "hendiadys," that is, a pair of synonyms that should not be distinguished in meaning; so too Bruce, *1 & 2 Thessalonians*, 108 – 9. In contrast, William Hendriksen, *An Exposition of 1-II Thessalonians* (New Testament Commentary; Grand Rapids: Baker, 1955), 121, goes beyond the known use of the words and instead offers the ungainly "concerning the duration-periods and the appropriate seasons.... A trifle less exact but, perhaps, more understandable would be the rendering, 'Now concerning the *How Long?* and the *When?*'"

3. For which, see Kim, "Jesus Tradition," 239.

Christ, or simply Day more or less interchangeably, without intending to lend fine shades of meaning to each one.[4] His readers did not need a decoder, since all these "day" references are variations of the Hebrew "day of Yahweh."

What is remarkable from the standpoint of Paul's Christology is that the day of Yahweh predictions find their fulfillment in the coming of the Lord *Jesus*; all of the "day" references are therefore indirect but unmistakable affirmations of Christ's deity. Compare, for example, "That day belongs to the Lord, the LORD Almighty — a day of vengeance, for vengeance on his foes" (Jer 46:10) with 2 Thess 1:7c – 8b, "at the revealing of the Lord Jesus from heaven with his powerful angels, with blazing fire ... [to] dispense retaliation" on that Day. To be sure, some scholars have suggested that when early Gentile Christians used the LXX, they mistakenly applied Yahweh passages to the Lord Jesus, since the LXX used "Lord" (κύριος) to translate Yahweh and Adonai. But the apostle Paul cannot have been confused on that score. He had a firm grasp both on the Hebrew text and the LXX; when he refers to Yahweh passages as predictions of the Lord Jesus, he was assuming that Jesus is Yahweh.

As this apostolic use of the Old Testament implies, one cannot gain a proper definition of the day of the Lord without thinking of the coming of Jesus in his parousia. Above all, the day of Yahweh was a day of revelation of God in his righteousness; the coming of Jesus too is his "coming" (4:15) or "revealing" (2 Thess 1:7) or "appearance" (2:8). Jesus already laid the foundation for this identification when he connected the end of the age with the "day" of the Son of Man (Luke 17:24, 30); as noted above, this day should not be distinguished from, for example, Paul's "day of the Lord Jesus Christ."

With regard to Pauline terminology, parousia and "day of the Lord" are identical or nearly so. In 4:15, Paul speaks of the "coming" (παρουσία) and immediately follows it up with "the day of the Lord" (5:2, 4), which will come as a thief. This matches the rest of the NT: Jesus said that the Son of Man would come as a thief (Matt 24:43 – 44; see also Rev 3:3, 16:15); in 2 Peter it is the day of the Lord that is the thief (2 Pet 3:10); in Rev 16:14 – 15 "the great day of God the Almighty" is linked with Jesus' coming "like a thief." The connection between day of the Lord and parousia is just as close in 2 Thessalonians. In 2:1 – 2, Paul states that he will speak about the parousia, but then goes on to discuss the day of the Lord. In 1:10, Jesus will come "on that Day" to judge the wicked; at his parousia in 2:8 he comes and destroys the Man of Lawlessness. At most, one might state that in some passages the day of the Lord looks like it takes place over a period of eschatological time, and that the parousia is instantaneous. Paul himself does not make that fine distinction; in practical terms, to speak about the day of the Lord is to speak of Christ's parousia.

Paul reaches into the biblical tradition for three metaphors of what the wicked will experience: (1) a thief who comes by night to steal; (2) a land that clings to the illusion of peace that is then brutally invaded; (3) a pregnant woman who feels her first contraction.

First, the day "will come like a thief in the night" (ὡς κλέπτης ἐν νυκτὶ οὕτως ἔρχεται), the present tense of the verb pointing to the future event that "will come." The Synoptic apocalypse in Matt 24 has the fullest version of this metaphor: "Therefore keep watch, because you do not know on what day your Lord will come. But understand this: If the owner of the house had known at what time

4. See "the day of the Lord" (outside of 1 – 2 Thess in 1 Cor 5:5), "day of [the] Lord Jesus Christ" (1 Cor 1:8); "the day of Christ Jesus" (Phil 1:6); "the day of Christ" (Phil 1:10; 2:16); "the day of the Lord Jesus" (1 Cor 5:5 some mss; 2 Cor 1:14); or simply the "Day" (1 Cor 3:13; 2 Thess 1:10; 2:3; 2 Tim 1:12, 18; 4:8).

of night the thief was coming, he would have kept watch and would not have let his house be broken into" (24:42 – 43; see Luke 12:39; also 2 Pet 3:10; Rev 3:3; 16:15). Today the "thief in the night" has become for many readers a dead metaphor. Moreover, in suburban North America, "thief" does not strike the same emotional chord or immediacy as does, for example, *ladrón* in the Spanish versions.

In Latin America the thief who forces his way into the house is a daily anxiety. There are men in our seminary's neighborhood who spend night after night in a chair with a club or machete, awaiting a possible break-in. How they would appreciate knowing what night and what hour the thief would come![5] Perhaps "burglar" (Matt 24:43 NLT) or to use the current favorite "home invader" captures the feel of that term in English.

5:3a-b When they will be saying, "Peace and security," then unexpected destruction will befall them (ὅταν λέγωσιν, εἰρήνη καὶ ἀσφάλεια, τότε αἰφνίδιος αὐτοῖς ἐφίσταται ὄλεθρος). Paul now moves to his second metaphor, comparing the parousia with a devastating military invasion. It is better to translate them as saying "security" rather than "safety" (ἀσφάλεια), since the former is the more commonly used term today to denote protection against military invasion. The language has its roots in Jeremiah's complaint against Judah: "They dress the wound of my people as though it were not serious. 'Peace, peace,' they say, when there is no peace" (Jer 6:14); and in Jesus' teaching about the end, with its comparison with a sudden flood (Matt 24:37 – 39).[6]

It seems more than coincidence that Paul echoes a well-known slogan of the Roman Empire, *Pax et securitas* ("Peace and security"), which comes from living under the *Pax romana*. Seyoon Kim states that Paul "apparently was critical of the imperial propaganda of *pax et securitas* for its hubris and inadequacy."[7] Not even the Roman Empire, with its Caesar who proclaimed himself the divine savior, would protect them from God's judgment. Paul foresees the sudden destruction of the wicked, employing terms that are as terse as they are catastrophic. As Zephaniah said, "the great day of the Lord is near — near and coming quickly" (Zeph 1:14). Again, as with "will come" (ἔρχεται) in 5:2, Paul uses a present tense "befalls them" (ἐφίσταται) to describe an assured future event. The fact that the word order is disjointed (adjective - indirect object - verb - noun) underscores the unexpectedness of the event ("then suddenly will fall on them ... *destruction*"). The eschatological destruction is "eternal" according to 2 Thess 1:9 (see comments). "Unexpected" or "sudden" (αἰφνίδιος) is familiar military term from late Judaism.[8]

5:3c-d [Sudden] as birth pains on a pregnant woman, and they will in no way escape (ὥσπερ

5. See too the study Christopher D. Stanley, "Who's Afraid of a Thief in the Night?" *NTS* 48 (2002): 468 – 86; he applies some principles from sociology and argues that the thief imagery would be particularly frightening to women and the poor, and that male writers were using androcentric language in order to control women.

6. But see Malherbe, *Letters to the Thessalonians*, 292, 301 – 2, 304. Malherbe argues that Paul is reacting to a specific set of circumstances in Thessalonica, namely, false prophets who were arguing that the end was *not* near and were telling their followers to enjoy a life of peace and security. This led to lax morality but also resulted in grief when some Christians died. But there is no indication in this passage that the Thessalonians are morally lax, nor is there a rebuke to some false teacher in that city.

7. Kim, *Christ and Caesar*, 43. He goes on to say that "yet [Paul] may well have taken the *pax Romana* as a precondition for his successful mission, the like of which he did not quite see present outside the Roman world." See too Peter Oakes, "Remapping the Universe: Paul and the Emperor in 1 Thessalonians and Philippians," *JSNT* 27/3 (2005): 301 – 22.

8. See Josephus, *Life* 253 — "[I] placed the most faithful of my armed men upon the avenues, to be a guard to us; lest John should unexpectedly fall upon us." Luke 21:34 uses the word to speak of the sudden coming the eschatological day.

ἡ ὠδὶν τῇ ἐν γαστρὶ ἐχούσῃ, καὶ οὐ μὴ ἐκφύγωσιν). The final metaphor has to do with the suddenness of labor pains. In today's terms, we are conditioned to think not of birth pains but of "contractions"; yet it is the traditional rendering that captures the original, since labor is presented as a painful and grievous experience. Childbirth in the age of Paul was risky in the extreme, and the large number of women who died while giving birth lowered the life expectancy of women to somewhere in their twenties or thirties.[9]

The woman's first contraction might therefore be the harbinger of death. The onset of labor is thought to "catch" her, leaving her helpless and immobile; this is the basis for the woe concerning pregnant women in Matt 24:19, who will be unable to run away. Isaiah 13:6 – 9 contains several of the points found in Paul: "Wail, for the day of the Lord is near; it will come like destruction from the Almighty ... [all] will writhe like a woman in labor. ... See, the day of the Lord is coming."

The pain of childbirth is a common trope in Judaism, as in this description of the final judgment carried out by the Son of Man (*1 En.* 62.4, ed. Charlesworth):

> Then pain shall come upon them
> as on a woman in travail with birth pangs —
> when she is giving birth (the child) enters the
> mouth of the womb,
> and she suffers from childbearing.

Jesus said that some signs are the "*beginning* of birth pains" (Matt 24:8; Mark 13:8); that is, they foreshadow the end but do not prove that the end is immediate. Yet these early pains will come more rapidly and strongly. Some Jews taught that the messianic "birth pangs" were the struggle to bring forth a new world — that is, the pains were a means to a good end (see also Rom 8:19, 22 – 23; cf. Isa 66:7). There is nothing of this nature in 1 Thess 5; "it is unlikely that there is any thought of the 'they' having these birth pangs because they are bearing some child, figuratively speaking. The anguish of the pangs is all they have."[10]

While today's readers might think of that first contraction as something relatively predictable — since due dates can now be rather accurately predicted — even in our times it seems to come as a surprise. Paul is speaking about people who are not only taken by surprise by their first birth pain, but also — if we extend the metaphor further, as Isaiah certainly did — did not know they were pregnant nor even perceive that pregnancy was an option. For birth pains are also for the strong men who are caught in (perceived) womanly weakness. As in Isa 13, those who war against God are emasculated and thus humiliated, writhing like a woman in labor.

Paul uses again an emphatic negative "in no way" (οὐ μή), followed by "escape" (ἐκφύγωσιν). The inability of the wicked to flee from their doom is a common Jewish theme. Paul seems to be making a definite allusion to Amos 2:14 – 15 LXX:

> ... flight shall perish from the runner, the strong shall *by no means* (οὐ μή) retain his strength and the fighter shall *by no means* save his soul; and the archer shall *by no means* stand, and he who is swift on his feet shall *by no means* escape, and *by no means* shall the horseman save his soul. (NETS, slightly paraphrased by author)

Paul may also have been thinking of the judgment pronounced by Jesus in Matt 23:33, a tradition already echoed in 1 Thess 2:14 – 16: "You snakes! You brood of vipers! How will you escape [or 'flee'] being condemned to hell?"

9. Jo-Ann Shelton, *As the Romans Did: A Sourcebook in Roman Social History* (2nd ed.; Oxford: Oxford Univ. Press, 1998), 91.

10. See the useful overview by C. Gempf, "The Imagery of Birth Pangs in the New Testament," *TynBul* 45/1 (1994): 123.

5:4 But you, brothers and sisters, are not in darkness, so that the day would surprise you like a thief (ὑμεῖς δέ, ἀδελφοί, οὐκ ἐστὲ ἐν σκότει, ἵνα ἡ ἡμέρα ὑμᾶς ὡς κλέπτης καταλάβῃ). The world will be surprised by sudden destruction. But not these Christians brothers and sisters! Paul uses "but" (δέ) to begin this contrast and describes the believers in 5:4–6. They are not "in darkness"; later he will say that they are "of the day" and "not of the night nor of the darkness." The believers live on a different plane of existence than people of the world. Light has its biblical sense of entry into the realm of salvation: "The people walking in darkness have seen a great light; on those living in the land of deep darkness a light has dawned" (Isa 9:2). People of the light are those who have a relationship with the saving God, who has broken into the world's darkness. Beyond that basic meaning, Paul brings forth some related metaphors: people who walk in the light of day can see, those in darkness are ignorant and surprised by a thief; people of the day are awake, while people of the night are drunk or have dozed off. (See "In Depth: Light and Darkness, Day and Night")

IN DEPTH: Light and Darkness, Day and Night

When Paul uses these terms, he reaches back to the Hebrew Scriptures and to the teaching of Jesus.[11] This means that light and darkness are words of salvation, not of philosophical speculation on the cosmos nor intellectual enlightenment. "The LORD is my light and my salvation" declares the psalmist in Ps 27:1. There is also an eschatological aspect in the prophets: "Arise, shine," declares Isa 60:1. But for the wicked, the day of the Lord will bring darkness, not light. "Darkness" throughout both Testaments is a common metaphor for lostness (see Isa 9:2; also Matt 5:14–16; John 1:4–9; 8:12). Believers are called "people of the light" in Luke 16:8.

The Qumran community in particular used this sort of biblical language, but worked from a different cosmology. Human beings belong to opposing camps that correspond to the angelic world.[12] The sect understood itself as the people of the light: "sons of light" and "sons of darkness" are a constant motif in the Dead Sea Scrolls, the latter corresponding to those who follow Belial (i.e., Satan).[13] They went beyond Scripture in that their light/darkness language reflected a larger dualism in the cosmos: God and Belial rule over two spheres.

11. See the treatment of all four gospels by H.-C. Hahn, "φῶς," *NIDNTT*, 2:493–95; H. Conzelmann, "φῶς," *TDNT*, 9:310–58.

12. "And in the hand of the Prince of Lights is dominion over all the sons of justice; they walk on paths of light. And in the hand of the Angel of Darkness is total dominion over the sons of deceit; they walk on paths of darkness" (1QS 3.20–21a, trans. Martínez and Tigchelaar, 1.76). Paul in 2 Cor 6:14 uses similar language. Although some have used this passage and Col 1:12–13 to argue that Paul was borrowing from Qumran tradition, the facts prove no more than that Paul and Qumran shared common roots in Judaism, esp. Isaiah.

13. God's covenant, according to 1QS 1.9–11, allows the righteous "to be united in the counsel of God and walk in perfection in his sight, complying with all revealed things concerning the regulated times of their stipulations; in order to love all the sons of light, each one according to his lot in God's plan, and to detest all the sons of darkness, each one in accordance with his guilt in God's vindication" (trans. Martínez and Tigchelaar, 1.71).

The "spirit" that helped the members live righteously was a variant on the conventional Jewish teaching of the "inclination to good," whose opposite, the "evil inclination," was fostered by Belial.[14]

God rescued the Christians from the power of darkness and brought them into the light, says Paul in Col 1:12 – 13, using Exodus language to describe salvation in Christ. The apostle's gospel work is a "light for the nations" in Acts 26:17 – 18: "I am sending you to them to open their eyes and turn them from darkness to light, and from the power of Satan to God." The Thessalonians had joined God's people who would receive the final salvation (1 Thess 1:10) and who even then were already in the light. Paul speaks of the "deeds of darkness" (Rom 13:12) and of putting on the armor of light. Darkness is the realm of damnation (Acts 26:18; Col 1:13; Eph 5:8; see 1 Pet 2:9). In Rom 2:19, Paul satirizes the synagogue for claiming to be "a light for those who are in the dark"; he is almost certainly using Judaism's own language as it tried to proselytize Gentiles.

The reader must not confuse Paul's teaching with that of the Gnostics: they used Platonic categories to say that the initiates were in reality scattered sparks of light that had become imprisoned in bodies. Thus Gnostic salvation is enlightenment, or rather, a new recognition of one's real nature of light.[15]

One point of difficulty in this section is whether Paul means to say that the parousia will come as a surprise to Christians. On the one hand, the "thief in the night" metaphor seems strictly to apply to the world of darkness. Yet throughout the tradition on which he bases his teaching, all people will be taken by surprise: "Therefore keep watch, because *you* do not know on what day your Lord will come" (Matt 24:42, italics added). It is the church that Jesus warns about his return: "Look, I come like a thief! Blessed is the one who stays awake and remains clothed, so as not to go naked and be shamefully exposed" (Rev 16:15).

The solution to this tension lies in recognizing the various levels of preparedness. The Christians will not be taken by surprise, but not because they possess an esoteric method of calculating the date of the parousia. The most that can be said is that the Christian has *negative* information, that the day of the Lord is *not yet* at hand (2 Thess 2:3). Positively, the believer is said to be "ready" if he or she is always walking in God's light, even though the event itself will come as a surprise.

5:5 For you are all children of light and the children of the day. We are not of the night nor of the darkness (πάντες γὰρ ὑμεῖς υἱοὶ φωτός ἐστε καὶ υἱοὶ ἡμέρας. οὐκ ἐσμὲν νυκτὸς οὐδὲ σκότους). Paul now speaks positively of the nature of the believers. Strikingly, he again turns to the language of "all" (πάντες). Unlike the more generic "child" (τέκνον), Paul chooses to designate every believer

14. On Paul's rejection of the Jewish teaching of the good and evil inclinations, see G. S. Shogren, "The 'Wretched Man' of Romans 7:14 – 25 as *Reductio ad absurdum*," *EvQ* 72/2 (April 2000): 119 – 34.

15. With regard to the Gnostics, see H. Conzelmann, "σκότος," *TDNT* 7:437: "Transcendent salvation is consistently depicted by light (the world of light). But darkness does not have to be mentioned as its opposite."

as a "son" (υἱός). The term normally refers to male offspring or descendants. The NT uses both terms to refer to people of either sex who share a spiritual commonality.[16] While it is possible to identify a brief chiastic structure in 5:5 (light-day, night-dark), one should not make too much of it; in fact, in Greek the rhythm is less striking than in English. Paul does not develop those four terms but rather emphasizes day versus night as his main motif in 5:6 – 8. Night is for sleep and drunkenness; day implies self-control and preparedness.

5:6 So then, let us not let ourselves fall asleep, as do other people, but let us keep alert and exercise self-control (ἄρα οὖν μὴ καθεύδωμεν ὡς οἱ λοιποί, ἀλλὰ γρηγορῶμεν καὶ νήφωμεν). Paul has spoken the truth about believers in 5:4 – 5; he now issues an exhortation based on that truth. "So then" (ἄρα οὖν) shows that the "indicative" of the previous two verses provides the foundation for the "hortatory subjunctives" of 5:6 – 10. Paul gives a contrast: "Let us not do that, but do this." Apart from Eph 5:14, which may have been a pre-Pauline tradition, Paul uses "to sleep" (καθεύδω) only in 1 Thess 5 (verses 6, 7 [2x], 10). In 5:6 – 7 it clearly refers to a way of life. By contrast, he uses "to sleep/die" (κοιμάω) exclusively to refer to the death of believers.[17] This does not mean that the reverse is true, that he never used "to sleep" (καθεύδω) as a metaphor of death, only that his preferred term is κοιμάω. This will make a difference in the exegesis of 5:10, where there is controversy over whether "sleep" refers to death or to the lack of alertness.

"Sleep" imagery is used in several ways. Sleep in some of Jesus' parables does not seem to be a moral fault but a natural fact of real life (Matt 13:25; 25:5). Nevertheless, it may be sinful: sleep in Prov 6:10 refers to the napping of people who should be more industrious. "Falling asleep" may be a sign of spiritual carelessness, particularly in the face of God's impending judgment (Isa 56:10; Rom 13:11 – 14). In 1 Thess 5:6, sleep is what "other people" do; the comparative clause (ὡς οἱ λοιποί) refers to "outsiders" (as in 4:13).

The positive side is "let us keep alert and exercise self-control" (γρηγορῶμεν καὶ νήφωμεν), where Paul uses two more hortatory subjunctives. Again, this language is traditional. "To keep alert" (γρηγορέω) is used in a number of eschatological passages to warn Christians to stay vigilant, particularly because they do not know when Jesus will return.[18] "To exercise self-control" (νήφω) is less frequent.[19] Daniel 5:1 – 31 provides good background for Paul's warning: Belshazzar feasted, drunk and unwary, until a hand spelled out his imminent judgment.

5:7 [I say this because] those who fall asleep do so at night and those who get drunk do so at night (οἱ γὰρ καθεύδοντες νυκτὸς καθεύδουσιν, καὶ οἱ μεθυσκόμενοι νυκτὸς μεθύουσιν). Again Paul uses the conduct of outsiders as a contrast to Christian behavior. If believers are not of the night/darkness, they should not act as such. He offers this maxim by way of explanation of what he has just said. Both statements begin with a substantival participle; this is followed by "at night" (νυκτός), a genitive of time — "the *kind* of time, or time *within which* the word to which it stands related takes place."[20]

Sleep and drunkenness are stereotypical of nighttime. "Sleep can also become stupefaction,

16. So, e.g., Eph 2:2 and 5:6, υἱοί of disobedience; 2:3, τέκνα of wrath; 5:8, τέκνα of light.

17. See 1 Cor 7:39; 11:30; 15:6, 18, 20, 51; 1 Thess 4:13, 14, 15. See also Matt 27:52; Acts 7:60; 13:36; 2 Pet 3:4.

18. E.g., Matt 24:42 – 43; 25:13 and parallels; see Rev 3:2 – 3; 16:15.

19. See 1 Thess 5:8; 2 Tim 4:5; 1 Pet 1:13; 4:7; in 1 Pet 5:8 too it stands side-by-side with "keep alert" (γρηγορέω).

20. Wallace, *Grammar*, 122 – 24; see also 1 Thess 2:9; 3:10.

and here it is a judgment of Yahweh on those who sleep and a help to those who remain awake (Is. 51:20; 1 S. 26:12, cf. v. 7)."[21] Drunkenness may refer to literal intoxication (Eph 5:18, and consistently in the LXX),[22] but also by extension the overall numbing of one's sensibilities towards God. *T. Jud.* 14.1 (ed. Charlesworth) shows that application: "And now, my children, I tell you, do not be drunk with wine, because wine perverts the mind from the truth, arouses the impulses of desire, and leads the eyes into the path of error."

In his major work on Thessalonica, Vom Brocke proposes that the Thessalonian cult of Dionysus serves as the possible background for this verse. One of their rites was a drunken "midnight feast." Therefore, Paul would be reminding the readers of a specific aspect of their pagan past and contrasts it with the Christian life of alertness and sobriety.[23] But there is no indication that Paul has Dionysian rites in mind, especially given that people "get drunk ... at night" sounds more like a truism than a cultic reference. Paul also condemns "sleep" in this passage, which has nothing to do with late-night Dionysian feasts. He elsewhere combines "night" and "drunkenness" as traits of the old life for other readers, with no obvious reference to any Dionysus cult (Rom 13:13; 1 Cor 5:11; 6:10; 11:21; Gal 5:21; Eph 5:8 – 18).

Paul can use the same imagery with a closer correlation of "night" with this age and "day" with the age to come: "The night is nearly over; the day is almost here.... Let us behave decently, as in the daytime, not in carousing and drunkenness" (Rom 13:12a, 13a).

5:8 But because we belong to the day, let us exercise self-control by putting on faith and love as a breastplate and as a helmet the sure expectation of our [coming] salvation (ἡμεῖς δὲ ἡμέρας ὄντες νήφωμεν, ἐνδυσάμενοι θώρακα πίστεως καὶ ἀγάπης καὶ περικεφαλαίαν ἐλπίδα σωτηρίας). Paul again turns to a positive exhortation, based on the "indicative" of the foregoing verse. He contrasts believers with the world and adds further emphasis (the pronoun "we," ἡμεῖς), to contrast them with those who sleep and get drunk. He repeats in simpler terms what he has just said:

> You are all children ... of the day. We are not of the night (5:5).
> So then, let us ... exercise self-control (νήφωμεν) (5:6).
> We belong to the day (5:8).
> Let us exercise self-control (νήφωμεν) (5:8).

The broad meaning of the present participle "belong" (ὄντες; lit., "be") is not disputed, but its syntax is less than clear. It could be adjectival to the pronoun "we." This is a relatively common construction, as in 1:4, "brothers and sisters whom God loves." In that case one should opt for a translation such as "we who are of the day should exercise self-control" (so KJV, GNB, NJB, NKJV, NLT).

Alternatively, ὄντες could be adverbial, modifying the imperative, "let us exercise self-control" (νήφωμεν). The only adverbial participle that works here is the causal: "*because/since* we belong to the day" (so ESV, HCSB, NASB, NIV, NRSV).[24]

Which is the best interpretation is almost a toss-up. The causal use of the participle is slightly preferable if only because the syntax is less awkward.

21. A. Oepke, "καθεύδω," *TDNT*, 3:434.

22. H. Preisker, "μέθω, μεθύω, μέθυσος, μεθύσκομαι," *TDNT*, 4:546.

23. Vom Brocke, *Thessaloniki*, 128 – 29.

24. Wallace, *Grammar*, 631, observes that in the category of causal participles "aorist and perfect participles are amply represented, but the present participle is also frequently found here." The participle could be taken as an "attendant circumstance" and thus have an imperative sense: "Be children of day and be sober." But in such cases both the participle and the imperative verb are usually both in the aorist; in our verse they are both in present (see Wallace, *Grammar*, 640 – 45). Beyond that, it would be strange for Paul to command the Thessalonians to be children of the day when they are already such (5:5).

Both interpretations yield nearly the same meaning; thus, the differences between one English version and another are barely noteworthy. A number of commentators do not even make a case for one view or another.[25]

The armor of God is a trope borrowed from Isaiah, who anticipated the coming wrath of God against injustice: "[Yahweh] put on righteousness as his breastplate, and the helmet of salvation on his head; he put on the garments of vengeance and wrapped himself in zeal as in a cloak" (Isa 59:17). Yet in Paul's usage, it is always the believer who puts on the armor:

Rom 13:12: armor of light
1 Thess 5:8: breastplate of faith and love; helmet of the hope of salvation
Eph 6:11 – 17: God's whole armor: belt of truth, breastplate of righteousness, shoes of the gospel, shield of faith, helmet of salvation, sword of Spirit, which is the Word of God
2 Cor 6:7: weapons of righteousness for the right and left hands

It is to be noted that (1) some terms are constant; for example, salvation is always the helmet. (2) Yet Paul seems free to alter the metaphor; that is, one piece of armor does not consistently denote one and the same spiritual concept. (3) The weapons are for offense and defense in Isaiah and 2 Corinthians, and primarily for defense in 1 Thessalonians, Romans, and Ephesians. (4) The Isaiah passage and all of Paul's references occur in close proximity to light/darkness language, marking Paul's dependence on Isaiah.

The key to interpreting the genitives "breastplate *of* faith and love" and "helmet, the hope *of* salvation" is likewise found in Isaiah LXX. The Lord puts on "righteousness as his breastplate." This indicates that Paul uses the genitive of apposition: the Christian's breastplate *consists of* faith and love, while the hope for salvation *is like* a helmet.[26]

The metaphors are not intrinsic to the nature of the piece of armor. It cannot be inferred, for example, that the hope for salvation in some way protects the head, while faith and love protect the heart. It is enough to say that both articles protect vital areas.

Behind the benefits of the *Pax romana* lay naked militaristic force. Yes, Roman peace provided a good environment for the spread of the gospel, but it came at a horrific cost of human life and dignity.[27] According to Paul, the Christian cannot take up literal arms, be they the weapons of the imperialist or the revolutionary zealot. They ready themselves with supernatural virtues such as faith and love. Despite the tribulation in which they find themselves, they are supernaturally enabled to bear the Spirit's fruit for which they are already well-known (1:3).

"Hope" (ἐλπίδα) is followed by another genitive, "salvation" (σωτηρίας), which is best taken as an objective genitive, "the salvation for which we hope." A legitimate expansion is "sure expectation of our coming salvation," since in this context it is not wishful thinking but rather confidence in God's future action. This piece of armor well suits the soteriology of the letter, in which salvation is eschatological and attached to the return of Jesus (1:10; 5:9). The Thessalonians are vitally protected by the fact that their Savior is on his way. Because of this future orientation, we have added "coming" to our translation.

25. Fee, *Thessalonians*, 195 has the "causal" view; Bruce, *1 & 2 Thessalonians*, 112, takes the adjectival interpretation. Neither defends their perspectives.

26. Also called the "epexegetical" genitive; Wallace, *Grammar*, 95 – 100.

27. See, e.g., Julius Caesar, *On the Gallic War*. Caesar prided himself on his clemency toward his enemies and his desire to avoid bloodshed. Nevertheless his chronicle outlines how he crushed barbarian Gaul through one bloody campaign after another, from 58 – 51 BC.

5:9a-b [This is the confidence we have] because God has not assigned us to feel [his coming] wrath, but rather to obtain salvation (ὅτι οὐκ ἔθετο ἡμᾶς ὁ θεὸς εἰς ὀργὴν ἀλλὰ εἰς περιποίησιν σωτηρίας). Paul shows once more why the believers are to live in confident expectation of salvation. He repeats the truth of 1:10, that the return of Christ will save us from the eschatological wrath of God. This verse is a causal statement, "because [ὅτι] God has not assigned [ἔθετο] us." God has determined that his people will not face his eschatological wrath. The day of the Lord (5:2) is at its core a "day of wrath" (Zeph 1:15).

By contrast, "but" (ἀλλά), believers are destined to "obtain salvation." The thought is similar to the "hope of salvation" in 5:8. "Obtain" (περιποίησις) is the noun form of περιποιέω and speaks of the "experience of an event of acquisition."[28] It also appears in 2 Thess 2:14 to speak of obtaining Christ's glory. The action noun is followed by an objective genitive; that is "the obtaining of salvation" is equal to "[we] will obtain salvation."

5:9c – 10a Through our Lord Jesus Christ, who died for us (διὰ τοῦ κυρίου ἡμῶν Ἰησοῦ Χριστοῦ, τοῦ ἀποθανόντος ὑπὲρ ἡμῶν). Whereas in 1:10 Paul has pointed to Christ's resurrection as the basis for escaping God's wrath, here it is his death. In 4:14 he speaks of both his death and resurrection. Although Paul does not develop the details of soteriology, the phrase "for us" (ὑπὲρ ἡμῶν) implies that Jesus' death was for the believers' benefit. He taught this from his first message in the synagogue in Thessalonica, "that the Messiah had to suffer and rise from the dead" (Acts 17:3). At the same time when Paul was writing this letter, he was also passing along to the Corinthians the tradition that "Christ died for [ὑπέρ] our sins" (1 Cor 15:3). This formulation was typical of Paul, and he used it eight times in his letters (here; Rom 5:6, 8; 14:15; 1 Cor 15:3, 2 Cor 5:14, 15 [2x]). His language bears a resemblance to Jewish martyrs who died for their nation,[29] but in Christian theology "Christ's death for us" came to have a central position in the theology of atonement.

5:10b-d So that, whether we are [still] keeping alert or whether we have [already] died, we shall live together with him (ἵνα εἴτε γρηγορῶμεν εἴτε καθεύδωμεν ἅμα σὺν αὐτῷ ζήσωμεν). With 5:10 – 11, Paul recapitulates his eschatological instruction, just as he did in 4:17 – 18, moving on to exhort them to encourage one another on the basis of that teaching. Verse 10 is open to two interpretations of the phrase "whether we sleep" (καθεύδωμεν). Paul has used two synonyms in this letter, both of which could mean "sleep" or "die" (καθεύδω and κοιμάω). An attentive exegete knows that an author might switch from one synonym to another and not necessarily signify a change of meaning or even of emphasis; it is the context that must make clear the author's intent. Most versions translate 5:10 with some form of "fall asleep" and leave to the reader to decide whether Paul is speaking of (1) the sleep of careless living or (2) the sleep of death.[30]

Interpretation 1 traces the use of "keep alert" (γρηγορέω) through 5:6 – 7, noting that it is a virtue that stands opposite of "fall asleep" (καθεύδω). By this route, the interpretation of 5:10 is "whether we are alert or whether we are dozing, we will live together with him." Alertness, while important, is not an absolute necessity for participating in the resurrection; Christ will still take the negligent Christian with him.

28. BDAG, περιποίησις 2.

29. See Henk J. De Jonge, "The Original Setting of the Χριστὸς ἀπέθανεν ὑπέρ Formula," pp. 229 – 35 in Collins, *The Thessalonian Correspondence*.

30. Those with some version of "whether we are awake or asleep" include KJV, NKJV, NIV, ESV, HCSB, NJB, NRSV, NASB, REB.

Interpretation 2 looks to 4:15 for the interpretive key: "that those who live and remain until the coming of the Lord will not precede those who have 'fallen asleep' [κοιμάω]." In this view, Paul employs the same contrast here, to conclude the entire section on the destiny of living and dead believers: "whether we are alive and alert or whether we are deceased when he comes."[31]

The first interpretation has the advantage of identifying one and the same meaning for the verb in 5:6 – 7 and 10. Nevertheless, the second interpretation is the better choice. Paul switches to the less likely term for "to die" (καθεύδω) because it has stuck in his mind from 5:6 – 7. The rendering "died" is perfectly correct, given that "sleep" was a fixed metaphor for death.

Paul is not simply speaking of being biologically alive in 5:10, but of being "watchful." It is skating on thin ice to deduce that the verse "expresses the 'blessed hope' that *all believers, spiritual or not*, will be caught up to meet the Lord when he comes for his Church."[32] Throughout this section, Paul has lent no support to the notion that watchfulness is merely the desired ideal; rather, it is the very nature of the children of light that they will not be caught by the eschatological "thief." According to 5:3 – 5, it is the world that will be found napping when Christ returns. Hence we translate 5:10 as "still keeping alert" versus "have already died."

One should take Paul's language on its own terms, as one should do for the teaching about the ten virgins in Matt 25:1 – 13. In Jesus' parable, sleep is not a vice — even the five wise virgins drift off, but still they are prepared for the bridegroom when he finally comes. Nor is sleep a symbol of physical death from which the maidens are "awakened." No, sleep is simply a part of the parable's plot, providing for the possibility of delay in the bridegroom's appearance. Yet just as Paul would teach in 1 Thess 5:10, there are the prepared and the unprepared; there is no third category, no unprepared ones who will be allowed to enter the wedding banquet.

Whether the Christian is alive and alert or has died in the interim, "we shall live together with him." Paul uses the future indicative to highlight the eschatological nature of the resurrection. "Him" is "our Lord Jesus Christ" from 5:9. Paul uses the phrase "together with" (ἅμα σύν) for the second time; in 4:17 it was with the resurrected saints, and here it is with the Lord Jesus. He highlights the unity of Christ with his people.

5:11 So then, encourage and build up one another, just as you are already doing (Διὸ παρακαλεῖτε ἀλλήλους καὶ οἰκοδομεῖτε εἷς τὸν ἕνα, καθὼς καὶ ποιεῖτε). Paul ends this eschatological teaching as he did in 4:18, with a call to action; here he uses "so then" (διό). A proper use of eschatological truth is to benefit and enhance the spiritual life of other Christians. As is implicit from 5:1 – 2, the believers can carry out this task with nothing more than a generalized knowledge of end-time chronology. Their encouragement and edification is to be mutual; he uses the synonymous phrases "one another" (ἀλλήλους) and "one to another" (lit., "one to one," εἷς τὸν ἕνα).

The word that is here translated "encourage" (παρακαλεῖτε) could also be rendered as "entreat, exhort" (its sense in 2:12; 4:1, 10; 5:14). Nevertheless, Paul has also used it to refer to comforting people who might otherwise remain in profound emotional distress (3:2, 7; 4:18). "Encourage" in fact suits 5:11 better (1) because that meaning makes it parallel with the similar 4:18, and (2) because 4:18 and 5:11 both speak of the resurrection hope at the

31. CEV; identical to GNB, similarly NLT. So Ambrosiaster, *Commentaries on Galatians-Philemon*, 110; Marshall, *1 and 2 Thessalonians*, 141; Best, *Thessalonians*, 218 – 19.

32. So T. R. Edgar, "The Meaning of 'Sleep' in 1 Thessalonians 5:10," *JETS* 22/4 (1979): 349, emphasis added. Contra, see Bruce, *1 & 2 Thessalonians*, 114.

coming of Christ. Paul also directs them to build up or edify (οἰκοδομεῖτε) one another. This refers to actively promoting the growth and strength of one's fellow Christians. As the apostle stressed in 1 Cor 8:1, to contribute to the edification of other believers, even those who seem different, weak, or uninformed, is a primary duty of love.

Encouragement and edification are excellent ways to express the "familial love" that Paul enjoins in 4:9. When we picture a lack of love, we must think more broadly than outright hatred. For example, both the person who turns to eschatological speculation and the person who panics are likely to love others less than they should. In fact, soon the Thessalonians will be tempted away from love precisely because they have supposedly received inside information about the time of the end (2 Thess 2:1 – 2); the result is panic and deceptive speech. If they will return to the apostolic truth that the time of the end is incalculable, they could enjoy afresh the "eternal encouragement and good hope" of the gospel (2 Thess 2:16). But in this first letter, Paul finds no fault in their current behavior; with "just as" (καθώς) he signals that they are "already" (the best rendering of καί here) doing what is needful.

Theology in Application

In this chapter, Paul deals with two of the principal motivations for holy Christian behavior. The first is that the Thessalonians must be watchful as they await Jesus' coming. The second basis for holy living can exist side-by-side with the eschatological: they must live out what is already true ("you are all children of light and the children of the day").

Be Watchful in the Expectation of Jesus' Coming

Biblical theology. According to Sicilian legend, Damocles was invited to sit on the king's throne for a day. On making himself comfortable, he looked up and noticed that a huge and terrifying sword suspended over his head, hanging by a horse's hair. Damocles fled, unable to keep himself fixed on the spot, no matter what the benefits of being "king."

In their evangelistic work, the apostles announced the impending threat of the judgment of God on the whole world. Paul and his team has earlier proclaimed the final judgment in Thessalonica (1:10; 5:3; 2 Thess 1:6 – 9; 2:12). Although traditional Jews were already fully aware of that expectation, Paul had to start from scratch among the Gentiles. The Greeks were undoubtedly more apprehensive about the dangers they could see around them, such as earthquakes, disease, and poverty. This is why Paul needed to introduce the teaching that "in the past God overlooked such ignorance, but now he commands all people everywhere to repent. For he has set a day when he will judge the world with justice by the man he has appointed. He has given proof of this to everyone by raising him from the dead" (Acts 17:30 – 31). That is, they had to begin to wrap their minds around the fact that history would end and they would then face their Creator.

Human beings are able to make rational decisions based on what they reason to be true. This is one of those abilities that separate them from animals, which are not able to anticipate the future based on conscious calculation. A rational response to the truth of Christ's coming should be fear that works repentance. Yet according to Paul, repentance is not the fruit of rationality; if people turned to Christ in the face of the approaching end, it was because God had enlightened them.

The Thessalonian believers did not fit in the world around them. The synagogue told them that they were alienated from the God of Israel. The Greeks told them that they were insulting the ancient gods. Everyone told the Christians that they were a source of offense. But the gospel informed them of something better. Not only were they destined to escape God's wrath (5:9); they had also been altered from within and turned into a new kind of creation, one suited to a better (future) world.

Message of this passage for the church today. There is a slogan that originated with a certain atheist comedian but was picked up by Christians and placed on T-shirts: "Jesus is coming . . . everyone look busy!" This is an uncouth version of what many Christians have pondered: *If you knew Christ was coming this week, what would you change?* Holy apprehension about the end has been around ever since the Lord unnerved his followers with a parable about ten virgins.

There are Christians who have sought to remain vigilant by constructing arcane systems that spit out data about when Christ might come (see Theology in Application under 2 Thess 2:1 – 12). This is not simply misdirected fervor; rather, it is thoroughly antibiblical. In the Scriptures, preparedness is not based on knowing a date but on *not* knowing a date. It is defined as living as children of the day even when the day of the Lord is unpredictable.

Life in the light of Christ's return is not some mystical experience. Rather, it reveals itself in concrete, everyday actions as empowered by the Spirit. In this letter alone, "readiness" includes the following: deeds of love, patience, peace, gentleness, mutual encouragement, hard work, behaving righteously with regard to alcohol use and sexual behavior, treating other believers properly, evangelism, thanksgiving, and prayer.

If preparedness and vigilance can take many forms, so can its opposite, sleepiness — that is, distraction from the divine things. From 1 Thessalonians alone we might mention these: drunkenness, which is not merely the overconsumption of alcohol or drugs but insensitivity toward God; idolatrous reliance on the government for peace and security; blocking the spread of the gospel or even not actively participating in its spread; sins of speech such as lying, trickery, or hypocrisy; greed and egotism; a poor work ethic; apostasy or even stunted spiritual growth; lack of sexual self-control; taking advantage of others in any way; taking God's truth lightly; being a troublemaker; being impatient or vengeful; making light of God's word as given through charismatic utterance; or any other failure of full holiness (5:23).

God summons every believer to watchfulness, since every human being has a deficit of attention when it comes to holiness. Yet in Christ, as we have seen, God's people have the ability to remain watchful. If they drift off, this is not because they lack the means; rather they lack the willingness to focus on the future deeds of God and to act appropriately.

Live Out What Is Already True

Biblical theology. The Bible everywhere assumes that good works are at heart the reaction to the coming of God to save. After the exodus, the Ten Commandments demand obedience in this way: "And God spoke all these words: 'I am the Lord your God, who brought you out of Egypt, out of the land of slavery. You shall have no other gods before me'" (Exod 20:1 – 3).

There is implicit causation in the first commandment: God has acted on your behalf, and *therefore* you must worship him alone. Whether in the face of that archetypical redemption from Egypt or military deliverance by the judges or the return from exile, Israel was commanded to obey because God had already intervened in their history. There is much of this motif in the NT as well; for example, Christ has died for people (5:10), and therefore they should serve God through him (5:4 – 8).

Yet Paul's gospel goes far beyond the paradigm of the old covenant (see comments on ch. 4). Not only has God acted in historical deeds; he has also intervened in the very person of each Christian. Converts are already "children of the light" and "children of the day" (5:5). This designation cannot be reduced to "people enlightened by the gospel" or "people who live in an ethical manner." Rather, God has made them a "new creation" (2 Cor 5:17).

This arrangement is, of course, not the power of positive thinking, that is, *to think better of yourself and you will become better*. There is an authentic spiritual — and what we today might call psychological — reordering of the believer in Christ that goes beyond the humanly possible. This is why we cannot sift through Christian texts and find any coherent ethic that does not begin and end with Christ and with God's work in human beings.[33] It may not be secularized and keep its integrity.

Message of this passage for the church today. Prior to their first act of Christian behavior, God had already transformed the Thessalonians. He had rewritten and continues to alter their internal code, so that their thoughts, motivations, internal

33. Did Paul have a system of ethics? Because of the limited extent of Pauline literature and its occasional purpose, one must exercise great caution in taking the observation "Paul does not address this issue" and drawing from it the conclusion that "Paul has no interest in it." Thus Victor Furnish (*Theology and Ethics in Paul* [Nashville: Abingdon, 1968], 209 – 10) goes too far when he says that "Paul has as little concern for ethics in a *systematic* sense as he has for a 'systematic theology.' Nowhere in his letters does he deal in a deliberative, reflective, critical way with the questions which an *ethicist* per se must always examine." Furnish's work is still essential after four decades. He is to be especially commended in that he tries to tackle all of the difficult questions: what is God's will; how to find God's will; how to carry out God's will; etc. Nevertheless he is not at his best when he deals with the role of the new covenant in Pauline theology. For this reason he compares Paul's ethic with that of the OT and intertestamental Judaism, but does not stress that Paul is dealing with an entirely different set of assumptions.

conversation, feelings, and inclinations had all been touched by God Spirit. Christian behavior is not simply God's command; it is actually a possibility that was not available to them before they met Christ.

Since we have dealt with the positive side of the Christian walk, we might further define the new life in Christ by ruling out *what it does not mean.*

Legalism. The legalist has little appreciation that Christians are endowed with a new ability to know the right path and obey it. Therefore, the more that people attempt to achieve legalistic holiness, the more they will fail. When people come to your church from out of a legalistic background, they need to hear over a long time a great deal about God's love and acceptance of them in Christ. But beware of a slingshot effect, since people freed from legalism might be tempted to whip over to license. Others will attempt to define holiness as some sort of middle-of-the-road approach to the Christian life. But God's holiness is not some spiritual Goldilocks's bed; it is not "moderation in all things."

A merely intellectual appreciation of the doctrine of the new life. There are people who seem to grasp all the facts about the new life. Yet they seem to falter when it comes to launching out into the new behavior that this truth demands. This is the sort of tension found in James 2: a person *claims to have faith* in the miracle of new creation but has no extraordinary *works* that reflect those new abilities.

All-at-once sanctification. Like many Christians of a certain age, I have memories of youth rallies where we were called upon to surrender fully, to "present your bodies a living sacrifice, holy, acceptable unto God" (Rom 12:1 KJV). But what happened next? People who went forward on Sunday night typically found themselves on Monday or Tuesday right back where they had begun. They wanted to step into the light, but they didn't appreciate that walking is by definition a series of many steps (as Paul makes clear in Rom 12 – 13).

Isolation. This is the conclusion that some seem to draw from the Bible, that if we are new creatures in Christ, we are self-sufficient and do not need regular communion with other believers. They need to know that God never intended his people to be lone wolves, but a "holy nation." For example, the Thessalonians were experiencing the new life in and through the love they had for the Christian family (1:3; 4:9 – 10). First John also provides help: "Anyone who claims to be in the light but hates a brother or sister is still in the darkness" (1 John 2:9). But we can hear the objection: "What do you mean? I don't hate anybody!" Hatred cannot be defined merely as harsh feelings about another person. Rather, it is the absence of love. To refuse the embrace of fellow Christians is to despise them, and the person who lives alone for God has wandered off the path of light.

CHAPTER 7

1 Thessalonians 5:12–22

Literary Context

When a Greco-Roman letter with pretensions to moral instruction was drawing to a close, the author generally offered a list of terse imperatives. Paul too gives a set of short commands, in which he focuses on life in the Christian community. One cannot read through this list and draw a hasty conclusion that whatever Paul commands addresses a known problem within Thessalonica; that is, one cannot assume that they were *not* rejoicing, *not* praying without ceasing, *not* respecting their leaders. Any "mirror-reading" of a letter must take into account that there are all sorts of motives for which a writer might command a thing.

Verse 12 shows that many of these activities are social ones — that is, dealing with human interaction between the "brothers and sisters" of the church family (as in 1:4; 2:1, etc.). Paul has shown great interest in Christian love in this letter (1:3; 3:6, 12; 4:9–10; 5:8). He could claim they had modeled all these virtues mentioned in this section, to the point of not seeking to take revenge on the synagogue, whom they have left in God's hands (2:16).

Other directions have to do with the relationship of the community to God: joy, prayer, and charismatic discernment (5:16–22). The instruction about discerning prophecy (5:19–22) foreshadows the church's subsequent confusion about the day of the Lord (the "spirit/Spirit" of 2 Thess 2:1–2). Perhaps the church failed to identify and reject a word that purported to say that the end was at hand.

VII. Instruction about the Return of Christ (4:13–5:11)

➡ **VIII. Final Exhortations (5:12–22)**

- **A. The apostles speak to all church members (5:12–13)**
- **B. The apostles give specific instructions to the leadership (5:14–15)**
- **C. The apostles return to speak to members generally (5:16–22)**

IX. Conclusion (5:23–28)

Main Idea

As members of God's true family, the Thessalonians must practice behaviors that reflect their identity as children of the Father. These must include a holy interrelationship among members and between members and their leaders, a life of fervent prayer together, and the careful discernment of prophetic messages.

Translation

1 Thessalonians 5:12–22

12a	Exhortation	And now	**we appeal to you**, brothers and sisters,
12b	Exhortation		[A] to respect those
12c	Object		[1] who labor among you and
12d			[2] who lead you in the Lord and
12e			[3] admonish you and
13a	Restatement		to esteem them profoundly in love
13b	Cause		because of their work.
13c	Exhortation		[B] **Be at peace** among yourselves.
14a	Exhortation		[For your part], **we encourage you**, brothers and sisters:
14b	List		**[1] admonish the disruptive.**
14c	List		**[2] Comfort the discouraged.**
14d	List		**[3] Stand by the weak.**
14e	List		**[4] Be patient toward everyone.**
15a	List		**[5] See to it that no one returns evil for evil,**
15b			but at all times [you are to] **pursue good**,
15c			both to one another and to all people.
16	Exhortation		[C] **Rejoice always.**
17	Exhortation		**Pray without fail.**
18a	Exhortation		**In everything give thanks,**
18b	Reason		for this is the will of God in Christ for you.
19	Exhortation		[D] **Do not stifle the Spirit.**
20	Exhortation		**Do not disdain prophetic messages.**
21a	Contrast	But rather	**put all [of these] to the test.**
21b	Exhortation		**Hold on to what is proven good.**
22a	Exhortation		**Keep away from every sort of evil.**

Structure

In v. 12 Paul directs the reader's attention to a new theme with the discourse marker "and now" (δέ). He had been speaking in 5:1 – 11 about how Christians should live as they anticipate the day of the Lord. Now he gives more general direction or *paraenesis*, with no direct reference to eschatology. The passage is simple in that it is composed mainly of brief commands. The principal difficulty lies in determining how these short phrases relate to one another. They should be separated into three groups:

First, commands for members of the church: 5:12 – 13 consists of directions for how they should treat their leaders. There are two infinitives that sum up that relationship: "respect" and "esteem." He describes the leaders in 5:12c-e with three tasks, indicated by substantival participles: they labor, lead, and admonish. These works make them worthy of respect and esteem. Furthermore, the Thessalonian believers should live in peace among themselves; this time Paul uses an imperative, the first in this section, but by no means the last.

Second, the leaders are to perform certain duties in 5:14 – 15, introduced by "and" (δέ, which we have marked as "for your part") and denominated by six imperative verbs: admonish, comfort, stand by, be patient, see to it (that no one returns evil for evil), and pursue good. The first four verbs have various groups as their direct objects; they are people who might actually be found in Thessalonica, such as disruptive people or those who have grown discouraged during their various trials.

Third, Paul again turns to instruct the whole church. The fact that he uses *asyndeton* — that is, he gives clauses that do not use any conjunction or other discourse marker — lends the passage a staccato rhythm. The prayer life of the church is described with three imperatives in 5:16 – 18: "rejoice ... pray ... give thanks." It is best to group 5:19 – 22 together. All five imperatives here have to do with the prophetic gift, which should not be quenched or despised. "But rather" (and Paul now does link 5:21 to 5:19 – 20 with δέ) the church should discern what supposed prophecy is from God and what is not. "Keep away from every sort of evil" applies in the first instance to false prophecy, but it also has broader ethical applications.

Exegetical Outline

➡ **I. The Apostles Speak to Members Generally (5:12 – 13).**

A. They should respect their leaders (5:12 – 13b).

B. They should live in peace (5:13c).

II. The Apostles Give Specific Instructions to the Leadership (5:14 – 15).

A. They should treat people according to their various situations (5:14).

B. They should not allow Christians to take vengeance and should promote well-doing (5:15).

III. The Apostles Return to Speak to Members Generally (5:16–22).

A. They should live and pray according to the apostolic pattern (5:16–18).

B. They should respond properly to charismatic manifestations (5:19–22).

Explanation of the Text

5:12 And now we appeal to you, brothers and sisters, to respect those who labor among you and who lead you in the Lord and admonish you (Ἐρωτῶμεν δὲ ὑμᾶς, ἀδελφοί, εἰδέναι τοὺς κοπιῶντας ἐν ὑμῖν καὶ προϊσταμένους ὑμῶν ἐν κυρίῳ καὶ νουθετοῦντας ὑμᾶς). We render the start as "and now" (δέ) to mark the change of rhythm as Paul begins to draw the letter to a close. Paul issues a series of brief instructions, beginning with a rarely seen command concerning how the congregation should behave toward its leaders. He asks them to "respect" or "recognize" (εἰδέναι) their leaders,[1] labeling them with three substantival present participles "those who labor ... [those] who lead ... [those who] admonish."[2] Paul is not speaking of three groups but one. "Labor" shows that they have followed the apostolic example of labor and hardship in 2:9 (see also Heb 13:7). The leaders of the church follow Paul in validating their ministries through their own work, so as not to burden their hearers.

With the verb "lead" (substantival participle) Paul explores their particular task. He identifies "leadership" as a charismatic gift in Rom 12:8. The overseer must "manage his own family well" (the verb used twice in 1 Tim 3:4–5), and special attention is due to the "elders who direct the affairs of the church well" (1 Tim 5:17).[3] Another activity of these people is to "admonish" (another participle, νουθετοῦντας), a speaking ministry of warning people away from bad actions.[4] The Thessalonians are to respect these leaders, not simply with verbal honors but by paying careful attention to their spiritual direction, even when it consists in warning them away from pet habits. Admonishment must be offered in kindly, paternal, but not paternalistic, terms (1 Cor 4:14).

Much ink has been spilled over whether these people were church officials or perhaps simply outstanding members of the church.[5] A large part of this debate lies in the use of the loaded term "office," since each student of the text brings to the table a paradigm, perhaps one informed by denominational background. Rather than ask whether these are officers, the exegete should focus on what they do. In the Pastoral Letters, the persons in authority seem to be operating within a more developed structure, and so those letters should be read in

1. See H. Seesemann, "οἶδα," *TDNT*, 5:117. The verb in the sense of recognizing an authority is found in Ign. *Smyrn.* 9.1 — "It is good to acknowledge God and the bishop." Οἶδα is parallel in that passage to τιμάω, "honor."

2. Were these participles singular, the order article-substantival-καί-substantival would fall under the Granville Sharp Rule, so that the "the laborers" would automatically be identical to "[those] who lead" and "[those who] admonish." While the rule does not technically apply here — it does not apply when the substantivals are plural — the intended sense is of one group. See the clear discussion of the Granville Sharp Rule in Wallace, *Grammar*, 270–90.

3. See particularly B. Reicke, "προΐστημι," *TDNT*, 6:700–703.

4. BDAG, νουθετέω has "to counsel about avoidance or cessation of an improper course of conduct."

5. See the good balance by Milligan, *Thessalonians*, 71–72. Wanamaker, *Thessalonians*, 191–95, following the lead of Wayne Meeks, proposes that these leaders are patrons of the church, who take the leadership based on their social rank. While the hosts of churches did have a level of preeminence, other aspects of Paul's theology, such as equality in Christ of all believers, run counter to the bestowal of authority on the socially powerful.

that way. In 1 Thess 5, they are "recognizable," they "lead," and they offer admonishment that they have reason to expect will be acted upon. This opens the possibility that early congregations possessed a college of leaders charged with specific functions. This is clearly the case in Acts 14:23, where Paul and Barnabas appointed elders in each of the Galatian churches, which occurred a short time after their founding.[6] It is also the case in nearby Philippi, although this is attested perhaps a decade later than 1 Thessalonians (Phil 1:1).

5:13a-b And to esteem them profoundly in love because of their work (καὶ ἡγεῖσθαι αὐτοὺς ὑπερεκπερισσοῦ ἐν ἀγάπῃ διὰ τὸ ἔργον αὐτῶν). Paul now intensifies his directive: not only should they respect their leaders, but they should also hold them in highest esteem. The infinitive "esteem" (ἡγεῖσθαι) stands parallel to "respect" in 5:12. The language of this statement should electrify the reader; Paul uses the adverb that we rendered "unreservedly" in 3:10 (ὑπερεκπερισσοῦ; see also Eph 3:20). The fact that Paul links the respect due them to the quality of their work does not weigh against the possibility that these people hold an official position in the church (as shown by 1 Tim 5:17). Rigaux may be correct concerning the need for the teaching in this letter: since the Thessalonian church has had these leaders for such a short time, they have no settled tradition concerning how the church should treat them.[7]

5:13 Be at peace among yourselves (εἰρηνεύετε ἐν ἑαυτοῖς). Paul wants Christians to live at peace, but with whom? A textual variant in this verse has "live at peace among *them*" (αὐτοῖς), which might mean, "with the leaders." The import would be that those who respect their leaders and eschew unruliness (5:14) will foster a peaceful atmosphere in the church. The critical text "among one another/yourselves" (ἐν ἑαυτοῖς) is mutual and horizontal, that all believers should seek to live in peace with all others. Both readings make good sense in the context.

However, the reading accepted by the NA[27], "among yourselves," is to be preferred. First, Paul typically points us toward "among one another/yourselves." Second, in 5:13 and 5:15, Paul links peace with a rejection of revenge as he does later in Rom 12:17 – 21. Thus the text refers to general congregational life — all Christians should take it upon themselves to be at peace with all other disciples, a teaching based in Mark 9:50 ("be at peace with each another" [ἐν ἀλλήλοις]) and developed further in Rom 12:18 ("live in peace with [μετά + genitive] everyone") and in most of Paul's letters. The Thessalonians now possess a supernatural ability to live in harmony, fostered by the Holy Spirit. This new power stands in contrast to the transitory "peace and security" of the deluded people of the end times (1 Thess 5:3).

It is necessary to add a note concerning the commands in 5:13 – 22, all of which are present imperatives. At one time it was thought that an imperative mood reflected the time of the tense.[8] It is now clear that, first, the present and aorist tenses mark time only within the indicative mood. That is, a present imperative does not necessarily indicate a deed which must be done in the pres-

6. "It is not really possible to define the duties of 'leaders' over against the bearers of other charismatic gifts. It is possible that congregational leadership lay in the hands of men who were also prophets and teachers" (Strecker, *Theology of the New Testament*, 186 – 94, who has a useful section on charismatic gifts). On p. 191, he deals with the "leaders" in Rom 12:8 and 1 Thess 5:12. He identifies the "bishops and deacons" in Phil 1:1 as a committee of charismatically gifted people.

7. Rigaux, *Thessaloniciens*, 581. Rigaux goes too far when he hypothesizes that the church had a natural resentment of authority figures.

8. H. E. Dana, and Julius R. Mantey, *A Manual Grammar of the Greek New Testament* (New York: Macmillan, 1927), 206 – 8.

ent. Further, one still hears the approach that the present imperative means "keep on doing" and the aorist "start doing." Many studies have disproved this "rule," even when they limit themselves to the small amount of test data provided by the New Testament. Wallace's definition fits this context nicely: the present imperative often conveys a *general rule for life*.[9]

5:14a-b [For your part], we entreat you, brothers and sisters: admonish the disruptive (παρακαλοῦμεν δὲ ὑμᾶς, ἀδελφοί, νουθετεῖτε τοὺς ἀτάκτους). Now Paul addresses those who have the responsibility to "admonish." Verses 14 – 15 yield two interpretations. First, Paul may be speaking to Christians in general, and the "brothers and sisters" may be the same addressees from 5:12 all the way through 22. This yields a consistent and pleasing sense, that all Christians are responsible to help all their companions (4:18; 5:11), and should thus admonish those who get out of line.[10]

But the other interpretation is preferable, that Paul is turning to address the leaders of the church. After all, the verb "admonish" (νουθετέω) in this section is a prerogative of leadership.[11] Thus we paraphrase, "for your part" rather than simply "and" (δέ). Since we have used "brothers and sisters" as the best rendering of the plural of "brother" (ἀδελφοί), we will not at this late point change course concerning the gender of the people in 5:14. If the referent was "leaders, who are brothers/males," that would have been known to the Thessalonians; it is a point that may not now be proved or disproved by the masculine plural form, which could, after all, be generic and refer to both men and women.

The leaders of the church might need to admonish "disruptive people" (τοὺς ἀτάκτους), which is a substantival use of the adjective. In the case of this word, the etymology offers some help: the initial vowel (α-) indicates the negation of the quality, while the root speaks of being in order. "Disorderly" (as in the ASV) is an accurate rendering, being literal and also not giving more definition to the word than it has in the original.

Disorderliness often refers to actively mischievous disruption, as in Philo: "seditious, faithless, *disorderly*, impious, unholy, unsettled, unstable" (*Sacrifices* 32).[12] This is the basis for the translation "unruly" (so KJV, NKJV, NASB). Paul several times condemns dissensions/divisions (1 Cor 1:10; Gal 5:20). Or the disorder could be passive or accidental, that is, caused by one who disrupts the peace without meaning to do so. Paul does not offer any further explanation of whether these people mean to do harm.

Several translations go well beyond what Paul actually says. "Undisciplined" (NJB) assumes too much. Later on in 2 Thess 3, the disorderly may have been highly disciplined and motivated. "Lazy" (NLT, HCSB) is incorrect, as is "idle(r)" (ESV, GNB, NIV, NRSV, REB). While laziness may be a cause for disorderliness, the inverse is not true: "disorderly" does not mean "lazy." Neither is there evidence to connect the disorderly of 1 Thess 5:14 with the work issues in 4:11 – 12 and 2 Thess 3:6 – 15. Indeed, neither 1 Thess 4:11 – 12 nor 5:13

9. See the detailed account of tenses of the imperative in Wallace, *Grammar*, 714 – 25. The present imperative "is used for the most part for general precepts — i.e., for habits that should characterize one's attitudes and behavior — rather than in specific situations" (721).

10. Neither Bruce, *1 & 2 Thessalonians*, 122, nor Malherbe, *Letters to the Thessalonians*, 316, see in this verse a group of special leaders such as elders.

11. So John Chrysostom, *Homilies on First Thessalonians* 10 (*NPNF*[1] 13:367) — "Here he addresses those who have rule."

12. See also the full study by Milligan, *Thessalonians*, 152 – 54, "Note G: On ἀτακτέω and its cognates." The word group may overlap with "unruliness" (ἀκαταστασία), as found in 1 Cor 14:33, 2 Cor 12:20, Jas 3:16. See too G. Delling, "ἄτακτος (ἀτάκτως), ἀτακτέω," *TDNT*, 8:48.

prove that any Thessalonians were yet refusing to work. Second Thessalonians is another case: much of Paul's ethical instruction in the second letter has to do with actual outbreaks of disruption in the community that are connected with failing to work (see comments on 2 Thess 3:6–15).

It is conceivable that Paul is not dealing in 1 Thess 5 with real cases but merely various types of people with whom the leaders might need to deal. Nevertheless, it is more likely that there is continuity over the two letters, and that disruptive people as early as 1 Thessalonians were not working to support themselves for some reason or another.[13]

5:14c Comfort the discouraged (παραμυθεῖσθε τοὺς ὀλιγοψύχους). The leaders of the church should imitate the apostles in another ministry, that is, by offering comfort (see Paul in 1 Thess 2:12). In the KJV, an attempt was made to make sense of a little-known adjective through its etymology, hence producing the translation "feebleminded," which implies a mental limitation; that translation is now invalidated. Rather Paul, like Isaiah (Isa 35:4; 57:15 LXX), refers people who are discouraged, not necessarily one who is by nature cowardly. In this case, the people who need comfort are not just those feeling the blues. There were disciples who underwent daily pounding from their families, environment, and workplaces to give up on Christ. This section mirrors the teaching about being a "shepherd" in Ezek 34:4:

> You have not strengthened the weak or healed the sick or bound up the injured. You have not brought back the strays or searched for the lost. You have ruled them harshly and brutally.

Paul's words in this section show that he is a pastor of sensitivity. Pastors should know who is discouraged, who is disorderly, who is weak. Then they should attend to people according to their various needs.[14] For some this runs counter to intuition, since pastors often play to their personal strengths no matter the situation. One pastor is by nature encouraging and ends up encouraging the disruptive when what they really need is a reprimand. Another rebukes easily and so tells the weak and discouraged to "snap out of it." Paul is a superb model for pastors, since in his letters he runs the gamut from gentle encouragement to firm rebuke, depending on his audience.[15]

5:14d Stand by the weak (ἀντέχεσθε τῶν ἀσθενῶν). Another pastoral ministry is to help or stand by the "weak" (ἀσθενῶν, substantival use of the adjective). The adjective might refer to a variety of problems: physically weak (1 Pet 3:7), sick (Jas 5:14), or spiritually oversensitive (1 Cor 9:22). It may be that Paul is thinking of tending to the sick, but his directives in this context concern Christians of various psychological and spiritual states; hence, his theme here seems to be the "spiritually weakened" (cf. Isa 35:3: "Strengthen the feeble hands, steady the knees that give way"). This verse has no obvious connection with the strong and weak Christians in 1 Cor 8:7, where "weakness" denotes a person whose theological underpinnings are not firm and who thus has scruples about permitted practices.

5:14e Be patient toward everyone (μακροθυμεῖτε πρὸς πάντας). Now that he has mentioned various types of people, Paul gives the leaders a general charge: be patient with all people of the church.

13. So Malherbe, *Letters to the Thessalonians*, 308–9; Morris, *Thessalonians* (NICNT), 168–69, 252.

14. A similar passage is found in Jas 5:13–14, where James addresses various groups of people—the suffering, the cheerful, the sick—and gives them counsel appropriate to their situation.

15. The true pastor also knows the importance of discerning a person's true problems, which may be different from outward symptoms. For example, a person who complains of low self-esteem possibly has a deeper issue, such as a too-strong preoccupation with self.

Patience or long-suffering is often attributed to God in OT and intertestamental literature, as it is in Paul's letters (Rom 2:4; 9:22). It is a virtue that all Christians must practice (1 Cor 13:4; Gal 5:22). In his next letter, Paul will urge patient restraint even with those who have been flagrantly in disorder (2 Thess 3:14–15; cf. 2 Tim 2:24–26).

From the early second century comes a fine statement on how pastors should be patient with all. Ignatius warns Polycarp to "bear with all people, even as the Lord bears with you; endure all in love, just as you now do.... If you love [only the] good disciples, it is no credit to you" (Ign. *Pol.* 1.2; 2.1). It is no secret that in every church there are good or "easy" members, and there are those who drain more of the pastor's energy than is right. It doesn't matter — whether they need encouragement or rebuke, they should count on the pastor's patience.

5:15 See to it that no one returns evil for evil, but at all times [you are to] pursue good, both to one another and to all people (ὁρᾶτε μή τις κακὸν ἀντὶ κακοῦ τινι ἀποδῷ, ἀλλὰ πάντοτε τὸ ἀγαθὸν διώκετε [καὶ] εἰς ἀλλήλους καὶ εἰς πάντας). This verse implies three parties: those who have committed evil, those Christians tempted to reciprocate, and Christians who stand in the way of that retribution. We take this latter group as the church leaders who are responsible for leading their members away from sin. "See to it" (ὁρᾶτε) implies that they are keeping watch for when this occurs

"Return evil" (κακὸν ... ἀποδῷ) is typical language for revenge, whether that be done on a grand scale or on a petty level. This is one of a set of biblical sayings that forbids reciprocity in the face of wrongdoing against oneself.[16] What was taught in the OT is taken up and magnified in the example of Jesus, who suffered at the hands of his countrymen (2:15) and did not return insult for insult (1 Pet 2:23). As elsewhere, Paul's statement here is particularly suitable in a context where non-Christians may be actively trying to destroy the church. Yet even between believer and believer, vengeance must be left in God's hands (1 Thess 4:6).

This exhortation, which bans retaliation, calls the Synoptic tradition to mind. Jesus, too, taught his disciples to love both the neighbor and the enemy and not to resist evildoers or curse them in return (Matt 5:38–47; Luke 6:27–36). In 1 Thess 5:16, the command to "rejoice always," which Paul utters to Christians under persecution, reminds us of another aspect of the Beatitudes (see below). Since there is some evidence that Paul writes under the influence of Synoptic and especially Matthean tradition, it is possible that these two verses are based on the Jesus tradition.

Paul then contrasts the behavior to avoid with the correct model: "at all times ... pursue good." Contrary to expectation, he reverts to the second person plural imperative here: "*see* that others don't return evil for evil; *pursue* good (τὸ ἀγαθὸν διώκετε) at all times."

There is a textual tradition that eliminates the word "both" (καί); hence it appears in brackets in the NA[27] ("[both] to one another and to all people"). The textual evidence in favor of it includes a third-century papyrus 𝔓[30] plus א[2] B. It makes sense in context; not only to the church, the "one another," but also universally "to all people" (εἰς πάντας). Paul affirms a truth that the Thessalonians seem to have well in hand, that the Christian faith is not simply an intra-family matter, but a way of life played out before the whole world.

5:16 Rejoice always (Πάντοτε χαίρετε). These commands now are not specifically linked to the leadership; rather, the second person plural verbs

16. Prov 20:22; 24:29; Matt 5:44 and parallels; Rom 12:17–21; 1 Pet 2:23; 3:9.

are directed to the congregation. Rejoicing "always" stands in parallel with "pray without fail" and "in everything give thanks," denoting the constancy of the Christian's life. When Paul writes about how the Thessalonian Christians should pray, we hear echoes from the beginning of the letter, from the team's prayers to God. The Thessalonians are to imitate the model of Paul, and so they must be joyful always. In 3:9, "we [Paul and Silas] rejoice" (χαίρομεν) because the Thessalonians have survived Satan's attacks. Paul wrote to other churches too to tell them of the need to rejoice (Gal 5:22; Phil 3:1; 4:4, with "always," πάντοτε). But particularly apt for the Thessalonians was the teaching of Jesus that the disciples rejoice in tribulation (Matt 5:10–12).

What does it mean to "rejoice always," a command that runs counter to our contemporary philosophy of probing into and examining each negative feeling? One must take into account that Christians might properly feel anxious (3:1, 5), fearful (1 Cor 2:3), or angry (Gal 1:6; 5:12)—i.e., they are not called on to bury their feelings. Yet those same Christians must rejoice no matter the circumstances. Gordon Fee underscores the truth that Paul is not speaking about the feeling of joy but rather the deliberate choice to express joy before God. This is a truth Paul learned from a child as he read the psalms written by oppressed people. But Fee goes too far when he says that these commands have mostly to do with the gatherings of the church rather than to the individual's life before God.[17] It is not suggested by this context.

5:17 Pray without fail (ἀδιαλείπτως προσεύχεσθε). See comments on "without fail" (ἀδιαλείπτως) under 1:2–3a. To pray without fail means to invest oneself in regular extended and strenuous prayer. It is not limited to those who have given themselves over to a religious life, but a command for every disciple, as said the psalmist: "Look to the Lord and his strength; seek his face always" (Ps 105:4).

5:18a In everything give thanks (ἐν παντὶ εὐχαριστεῖτε). Once again the psalmists shed light on Paul's statement. For example, they command all nations to give him thanks (Ps 117:1). In Paul's ministry, the gospel was having concrete results in turning Gentiles to give thanks to the God of Israel (Rom 15:11). Paul lives a life of thankfulness; so must all followers of Christ. The phrase "in everything" does not yield to easy diluting. It does not ask for gratitude that is merely in proportion to the pleasantness of one's circumstances.

5:18b For this is the will of God in Christ for you (τοῦτο γὰρ θέλημα θεοῦ ἐν Χριστῷ Ἰησοῦ εἰς ὑμᾶς). With the use of "for" (γάρ) Paul explains the cause for the three preceding clauses (5:16–18a): God wills it. "This" (τοῦτο) refers to all three commands and not just 5:18a. (1) When one reads the section aloud in the original, it fits the rhythm of the section better to have it refer to all three. (2) Pronouns usually take the same case and gender as their antecedents; given that he speaks of three actions together, the neuter singular is appropriate.

5:19–20 Do not stifle the Spirit. Do not disdain prophetic messages (τὸ πνεῦμα μὴ σβέννυτε, προφητείας μὴ ἐξουθενεῖτε). Paul now turns from positive imperatives to negative ones, also known as "prohibitions." The interpretation of the passage is intertwined with the question of its structure. Does "stifling the Spirit" have something to do with prophetic messages? Does the command (lit.) to "discern all things" (v. 21) have something to do with the prophetic charism or is it a broader command, applicable to all areas of life?

Although this final section could be read as a

17. Fee, *Thessalonians*, 214.

list of unconnected imperatives, a careful reading shows that Paul has been grouping "like with like" as far back as 5:14. In vv. 14 – 15 is a set of exhortations, all of which have to do with relationships between people: how to help the weak, what to do when people harm you, and the like. Then, vv. 16 – 18 have to do, not with random points of the Christian life, but rather the "vertical" relationship between the believer and God, expressed principally in prayer: rejoicing, prayer, thanksgiving.

Paul now moves on to instructions regarding the moving of the Spirit in the congregation:

Do not stifle the Spirit.

Do not disdain prophetic messages.

He then speaks (v. 21a) of putting all things to the test. Paul is not thinking of "all things" generically, but all things that have to do with the Spirit's working. Verse 21 is connected syntactically with what goes before with "and" (δέ, or better, "but"). It is thus meant to explore further the meaning of v. 20. From there it is a logical step to attach the rest of the section (vv. 21b – 22) to the testing of prophetic messages (v. 21) — what is good must be honored and retained; what is not good should be rejected (v. 22). Verses 21b – 22 form a pair of imperatives that should be taken together as the two sides of the issue, not divided into two distinct ideas:

But rather put all things to the test:

hold on to what is proven good.

Keep away from every sort of evil.

We thus have to do with a four-part guide to the Spirit's activity, principally within the church meetings.

Paul begins by speaking about the "Spirit." Greek script in Paul's day did not provide for capitalizing divine names. Thus "Spirit" or "spirit" (πνεῦμα) is appropriate depending on the context. In contemporary English it is common to speak of spirituality or the human spirit. Nevertheless, in the Pauline idiom the predominant reference is to the "Spirit" of God. In this verse, he definitely speaks of the Holy Spirit, known in Rev 19:10 as the "Spirit of prophecy."[18]

Paul begins with a prohibition: "do not stifle [μὴ σβέννυτε] the Spirit." The verb could be used literally of quenching or extinguishing a fire (Eph 6:16; Heb 11:34). The sense here is the metaphorical "stifle." The passage is best read in conjunction with its more detailed parallel in 1 Cor 14. Those who speak in tongues or prophesy in the meeting live in the tension of speaking by and for the Spirit and at the same time being able to control their speech (1 Cor 14:27 – 33); that is, they are not to fall into ecstasy with an attendant loss of self-possession. The church is not to forbid tongues, if practiced in the apostolic fashion; yet prophecy has a higher value than does the gift of tongues (1 Cor 14:39).[19] While 1 Corinthians was written some years after 1 Thessalonians, it must be kept in mind that even as Paul was corresponding with the Thessalonians, he was giving oral instruction to the Corinthians, teaching that he would later reiterate in 1 Corinthians.

18. This observation helps greatly with Gal 5:16, "walk by the Spirit," or as the NLT helpfully suggests, "let the Holy Spirit guide your lives." This runs counter to the tendency of people to assert, "I'm not religious, but I'm a spiritual person." It then follows that when Paul speaks of the spiritual person in Gal 6:1 (lit., "let the one who is spiritual") is really the one who lives according to the Spirit's fruit in Gal 5:22 – 23; as the NRSV has it, "you who have received the Spirit…"

19. See the careful and detailed examination of Christian prophecy by G. Friedrich, "προφήτης," *TDNT*, 6:848 – 56. For the most part the Jews of the Second Temple took for granted that the gift of prophecy had been discontinued (1 Macc 4:46; 14:41). Nevertheless, this was not an absolute; Josephus attributed the prophetic gift to a number of Essenes: a certain Judas, Josephus, *Ant.* 13.11.2 (§311 – 13); Manahem and many other Essenes in *Ant.* 15.10.5 (§373 – 79); see also 17.13.3 (§345 – 48).

In the second century AD it was apparently the norm that messages were given within regular meetings of the church:

> ... when the man who has the divine Spirit comes into an assembly of righteous men who have faith in a divine Spirit, and intercession is made to God by the assembly of those men, then the angel of the prophetic spirit which is assigned to him fills the man, and being filled with the Holy Spirit the man speaks to the multitude, just as the Lord wills. (Herm. *Mand.* 11.9)

Thus 5:19 – 20 must be taken together: stifling the Spirit is done by devaluing prophetic words.[20]

A superb definition of NT prophecy was produced by the 1973 Seminar on Early Christian Prophecy of the Society of Biblical Literature:[21]

> The early Christian prophet was an immediately-inspired spokesperson for God, the risen Jesus, or the Spirit who received intelligible oracles that he or she felt impelled to deliver to the Christian community or, representing the community, to the general public.

The noun "prophecy" (προφητεία) may have two meanings: it could refer to the gift of prophecy,[22] or to a specific message given by prophecy.[23] This second meaning is the more common and is the sense here. Paul is "warning against a deliberate suppression of the extraordinary operations of the Spirit in the congregation."[24] Showing contempt (ἐξουθενεῖτε) toward prophecy was the very nature of Israel's transgression through the centuries (Neh 9:30; Matt 23:29 – 31; Acts 7:52). What the Thessalonians were doing or not doing in this regard, Paul does not say. He covers in 2 Thess 2:2 the possibility that the Thessalonians would be shaken and led astray by someone claiming a message from the Spirit. If Paul had written 1 Thess 5:19 – 20 *after* such a incident, he might have meant: *you've had a bad experience, but don't reject prophecy as such; rather, test it!* But Paul wrote this section without knowing what was about happen. In the end, we cannot be sure what prompted his words in 5:19 – 20.

5:21 But rather put all [of these] to the test. Hold on to what is proven good (πάντα δὲ δοκιμάζετε, τὸ καλὸν κατέχετε). This continues the instruction concerning charismatic activity. The initial "but rather" (our rendering of δέ) provides a contrast to what Paul has said in 5:20. "All things" (πάντα) in the context refers to utterances that claim to be from the Spirit; hence we render it "all *of these*." More than one person tests the prophecies, as shown by the plural of "test" (δοκιμάζετε); this finds its parallel in 1 Cor 14:29: "Two or three prophets should speak, and the others should weigh carefully what is said." The church must ensure that what passes for divine oracles are genuine and not from a lying spirit (see the important parallels in Matt 7:15 – 20; 24:11; 2 Thess 2:2; also Rev 2:20). The neuter substantival adjective "the good" (τὸ καλόν) seems to be "the good message" rather than "the good Spirit." The church should "hold on to" (κατέχετε) that spoken word, that is, value its content by letting the word shape its awareness of God and his will for them.

Paul does not here stipulate what sort of test is

20. "Prophecy" here can in no way be taken as the preaching of the Word; it is called "prophecy" because it is given in the authoritative style of the prophets. The "preaching" viewpoint is found in Calvin, *Thessalonians*, 299 – 300; likewise Ambrosiaster, *Commentary on Galatians – Philemon*, 111.

21. Found in M. E. Boring, "Prophecy: Early Christian," *ABD*, 5:496.

22. In the NT, only Paul uses "prophecy" (προφητεὶα) to mean the charism of prophecy, see Rom 12:6; 1 Cor 14:22. See C. H. Peisker, "Prophet," *NIDNTT*, 3:84.

23. Matt 13:14; 1 Cor 14:6; 1 Tim 1:18; 4:14; 2 Pet 1:20 – 21; throughout Revelation, with the possible exception of Rev 19:10.

24. F. Lang, "σβέννυμι," *TDNT*, 7:168.

appropriate for prophecy. Two clues are that he affirms the existence of another charism, the "distinguishing between spirits," in 1 Cor 12:10; yet even there it is not clear how the person puts that gift into operation. But a false spirit could give a message that is contrary to known apostolic teaching (2 Thess 2:2, 5; 1 John 4:1 – 3).[25] Paul seems to assume that the Thessalonians already know how to discern the right from the wrong; his only concern is that they make sure to do so and that these steps lead to the decisive embracing or rejection of the prophecy.

5:22 Keep away from every sort of evil (ἀπὸ παντὸς εἴδους πονηροῦ ἀπέχεσθε). Taken firmly in context, this imperative serves as the second half of 5:21 and concludes the theme of prophecy. Just as the church must hold firm to "good" or genuine prophecy, so it must reject and "keep away from" evil, false prophecy.

Paul says "every sort" because false revelation may come in many forms — for example, through a fake prophecy from some spirit or some sort of "message" (2 Thess 2:2). Beyond this call to discern prophecy, Paul seems to broaden the application: a Christian should avoid evil wherever it raises its head, whether it be false prophecy or some other evil. The KJV translation, "abstain from all appearance of evil" is unfortunate, although I am not certain whether the translators of the KJV or the users of that version are to blame for a longstanding misinterpretation. Its rendering of 5:22 has been the basis for what is virtually a special branch of ethics, that a believer should refrain from any practice which might *appear to be evil*, typically to another Christian, although in theory, to any person whatever.

This has led to the principle that one's behavior should be guided by the perception of others, even if no one has voiced an objection: "Well, you don't think it's wrong, and neither do I, and nobody has said anything about it, but to someone it might give an 'appearance of evil,' and therefore you must refrain from it." Usually this interpretation of 5:22 is linked with not being a stumbling block to other people (1 Cor 8:13). This is not at all the gist of Paul's command in 5:22. "All appearance of evil" must be laid aside in favor of "every sort" or "every kind" of evil, as the NIV and many other versions have.[26] Paul is not speaking of "what appears to be wrong" but "evil, which shows its face in many ways."

Thus we see how Paul, in 1 Thessalonians as in 1 Corinthians, speaks positively of the prophetic gift:

- prophecy is of great benefit to the church and may be a part of the meeting (1 Cor 14:3, 5, 26)
- it must not be stifled or despised (1 Thess 5:19 – 20)
- it must not be drowned out by the noise of others (1 Cor 14:30 – 31)
- its content must be discerned (1 Cor 14:29; 1 Thess 5:20 – 22)

25. So Malherbe, *Letters to the Thessalonians*, 333 – 34, concerning the false prophecy of 2 Thess 2.

26. There is a close parallel in Jos. *Ant.* 10.3.1 (§37): King Manasseh practiced *every sort of evil*; that is, in his apostasy he was a generalist.

Theology in Application

The converts in Thessalonica had joined a new spiritual family. This was not simply some useful sociological fiction, designed to achieve greater group coherence. Rather, this reality required specific attitudes and behaviors that expressed this gospel truth. For example, their membership in the family had implications for the way the meetings were run. This section of 1 Thessalonians gives us a glimpse of *life in the Christian community*.

The Church as Family

Although it may strike us as incredible, the Thessalonian believers, from the perspective of Greeks and Jews alike, could actually have been perceived as antifamily:

> [Those who] refused to participate in normal social and cultural activities could also have been accused of fracturing family relations and society as well. To cause divisions in the family unit was tantamount to helping bring about the disintegration of society and being regarded as a troublemaker.[27]

This is why the feeling of acceptance by the church was of such profound importance to the early disciples. For some it was the only family they had.

Paul's theology endorsed healthy family life as an expression of God's creation. Yet the church promotes the new, spiritual family as the higher reality. Membership in the church does not depend on the influence of powerful relations, nor did connection with the rich give anyone more status in the body of Christ. Within the Christian family, "intact" families were welcomed; so were single adults, older members, the divorced, and spouses of non-Christians. This should be a lesson to the contemporary church, which might give the impression that while everybody is acceptable, whole families, especially those with children, are the prize that the leadership would like to win.

Participation in the Church

The first-century synagogue included worship, teaching, and prayer. The teaching load of the synagogue was often shared; an out-of-town rabbi such as Paul would be allowed to give an extemporaneous word of exhortation if he chose (Acts 13:15). There was group participation, but it seems to have been only adult males who joined in the liturgy.

No synagogue would have countenanced the sort of "anarchy" that seemed to characterize a Pauline congregation. Women went so far as to pray and prophesy aloud (1 Cor 11:5), let alone the other activities they carried out within the congregation. In the house churches, in fact, it was expected that any member might bring

27. Burke, *Family Matters*, 173.

something to the meeting (14:26). This practice was more workable in these early congregations, where a few dozen members would be in attendance. Today it is one of the negative features of larger churches that meetings are carried out by relatively few leaders. In a church of ten thousand, perhaps 1 percent or fewer of the members actually bring something to the worship apart from singing. Sunday mornings would grind to a halt if multiple people arrived prepared to teach a lesson. Yet the church of today cannot simply bid farewell to the ancient practice of free participation. In some fashion it must seek to create an environment in which all members are able to express that which God has given them.

The Church as a House of Prayer

One term that Jews used for a synagogue was "a house of prayer." The church too is supposed to be the place where all participate in corporate prayer:

> The congregation is the place where prayer and praise are made to God. Although these activities are scarcely mentioned in Paul's descriptions of congregational practices, nevertheless, the calls to pray in his letters indicate that this was a significant aspect of the meeting.[28]

Throughout history some portion of the body of Christ or another has declared its intent to recover the apostolic pattern of "doing church." Nevertheless, most evangelicals focus on the element of teaching over other biblical activities. This has led to the growth of the sermon to at least one-half of the weekly meeting, with a single pastor teaching and conducting much of the other worship as well. The centrality of the pulpit in the sanctuary, while correctly emphasizing the ministry of the Word, has the unintended effect of deemphasizing the Lord's Supper, Scripture reading, and above all, prayer. As crucial as biblical teaching must always be, a church with good preaching and little prayer is not a church that Paul and Silas would have recognized.

The Church as the Temple of the Prophetic Spirit

Paul spoke often about spiritual gifts; in 1 Thess 5, he goes into some detail on the use of prophecy. It need hardly be mentioned how prickly is the issue of the prophetic gift today. The most prevalent danger is the practice of accepting prophetic words as a message that must not be questioned or in any way put to the test. The true biblical pattern is that the people of God must discern whatever purports to be a message from God.[29]

28. Marshall, *New Testament Theology*, 456.

29. Then there are those churches that reject all prophecy, arguing that the gift is moot now that the church has the completed canon and that prophecy by definition yields material of equal ranking as the NT books. It is helpful to examine how the postapostolic church handled prophecy; almost universally, the fathers did not rank prophecy at the level of apostolic writings. See Gary Steven Shogren, "Christian Prophecy and Canon in the Second Century: A Response to B. B. Warfield," *JETS* 40/4 (1997): 609–26.

Obedience to the Church's Leaders

The Christian who lives and breathes the values of Western democracy may feel tension when the Scriptures speak of obedience to leaders and maintaining unity. "Be at peace among yourselves" (v. 13), or as in 1 Cor 1:10, "be perfectly united in mind and thought," might sound like calls to rigid uniformity. We are raised to respond, *Don't I have the right to my opinion? Isn't it true that leaders make mistakes, and shouldn't we call attention to them?*

The NT implies that occasional dissent may in some cases be healthy. In Acts 6:1, the Hellenists' complaint that their widows were being neglected seems to have been justified. In another episode, Paul himself argued publicly with Cephas in Gal 2:11 – 14 when he perceived that the issue was fundamental to the gospel.[30] In both cases, good came out of a tense situation. But apart from unusual exceptions, disunity is typically caused by self-centered interests, the putting one's own desires ahead of another's (Rom 12:16; 1 Cor 1:10; 2 Cor 13:11; Phil 2:1 – 4). This means that to choose to break unity must be an extraordinary exception in God's family.

The Apostolic Vision for the Church

As with corporations, it is the vogue today to develop a mission and a vision for the church. This may be healthy, if the church can manage to capture the biblical vision and not import other values into the mix.

A church's "vision" should include at the least that every single member be growing in the true fundamentals of the faith, love, prayer, evangelism, holiness, and the other values that Paul deals with in these letters. As the apostles express it, "we give thanks to God all the time for every one of you" (1:2a-c). This was not an age when a Thessalonian could leave the Pauline church on one street and walk over to the Petrine church on the other. As good pastors, Paul and Silas worked with the assumption that everyone belongs. One doubts that Paul would have done as some pastors do today: tell a member of the Thessalonian church that if you don't agree with the direction we're headed, then you are "free" — that is, free to leave and find another church.

30. Calvin (*Thessalonians*, 293) recognizes this tension: "Unquestionably, in order that any one may be ranked among lawful pastors, it is necessary that he should shew that he *presides* in the Lord, and has nothing apart from him. And what else is this, but that by pure doctrine he puts Christ in his own seat, that he may be the only Lord and Master?"

CHAPTER 8

1 Thessalonians 5:23 – 28

Literary Context

Paul ends his letter, as was usually done in Greco-Roman correspondence, with a benediction and final greeting. But it does not follow that these are "mere" closing remarks. As with the introduction (1:1 – 2), he gears his conclusion to his particular audience. The prayer for their full sanctification, in light of Christ's parousia, is a reflection of his earlier petition that they be "blameless ... with regard to holiness, before our God and Father, in the coming of our Lord Jesus" (3:13). He reminds them of God's "call" (5:24) as he did in 2:12 and 4:7. He uses the language of "brothers and sisters" (5:25) and even asks them to give each other "a holy kiss" (5:26). He charges them to have this letter read aloud to all members of God's family (5:27). First Thessalonians thus concludes true to form, as the letter that most emphasizes Christian brother- and sisterhood.

It is worth comparing this letter with 1 Corinthians, in which Paul hints that he has not resolved every problem in Corinth (1 Cor 11:34), even after many labored chapters of instruction and correction. First Thessalonians, while touching on themes that would later become problematic (work, the time of the second coming), ends on a confident note.

VIII. Final Exhortations (5:12 – 22)

➡ **IX. Conclusion (5:23 – 28)**

- **A. The apostles pray for the Thessalonians' full sanctification at the return of Christ (5:23 – 24)**
- **B. The apostles ask the Thessalonians to pray for the apostles' work (5:25)**
- **C. The apostles direct the congregations to other actions (5:26 – 27)**
- **D. The apostles give a benediction to the Thessalonians (5:28)**

Main Idea

The goal of the Thessalonian church family is eschatologically oriented: to be holy, together, at Christ's appearing.

Translation

1 Thessalonians 5:23 – 28

23a	Entreaty	And now	**may God himself, the source of peace, make all of you perfectly holy;**
23b	Restatement	and	**may your spirit and soul and body be kept perfectly without blame**
23c	Time		at the coming of our Lord Jesus Christ.
24	Basis		**[The God] who calls you is faithful,** that is, **he who will do it.**
25	Exhortation		Brothers and sisters, **pray for us too.**
26	Exhortation		**Greet all the brothers and sisters** with a holy kiss.
27a	Exhortation		**I put you under oath**
27b	Agency		by the Lord [Jesus]
27c	Content		to have this letter read [aloud]
27d			to all the brothers and sisters.
28	Entreaty		**May the grace of our Lord Jesus Christ be with you.**

Structure

The closing of the letter contains, as does the introduction, typical elements from Greco-Roman rhetoric. Yet true to form, the apostle shapes convention to serve his own ends. He begins with a prayer in 5:23; as in 5:12 he marks it with "and now" (the preferred rendering of δέ in this context). His prayer uses two optatives: "may he make holy" and "may [your spirit] be kept" or "protected." He bases his prayer on the reality that God is faithful (5:24).

The remainder of the letter does not use discourse markers, and so it reads like a list of statements. Paul uses an imperative "pray," to ask the Thessalonians to intercede for his team's work (5:25). This is followed by an imperative, "greet all the brothers and sisters" (5:26). This sort of "family" emphasis leads naturally into 5:27, where he puts them under a formal oath that they read the letter to all brothers and sisters.

The final sentence (5:28) is a benediction, a prayer that the grace of the Lord Jesus Christ may be with them. It is identical to 2 Thess 3:18, except that the second letter reads "with you *all*." As throughout the two letters, prayer may be directed toward God the Father (5:23) or to the Lord Jesus (5:28).

Exegetical Outline

➡ **I. The Apostles Pray for the Thessalonians' Full Sanctification at the Return of Christ (5:23 – 24).**

II. The Apostles Ask the Thessalonians to Pray for the Apostles' Work (5:25).

III. The Apostles Direct the Congregations to Other Actions (5:26 – 27).

A. They should exchange the holy kiss (5:26).

B. They should carefully transmit this epistle (5:27).

IV. The Apostles Give a Benediction to the Thessalonians (5:28).

Explanation of the Text

5:23 – 24 And now may God himself, the source of peace, make all of you perfectly holy; and may your spirit and soul and body be kept perfectly without blame at the coming of our Lord Jesus Christ. [The God] who calls you is faithful, that is, he who will do it. (Αὐτὸς δὲ ὁ θεὸς τῆς εἰρήνης ἁγιάσαι ὑμᾶς ὁλοτελεῖς, καὶ ὁλόκληρον ὑμῶν τὸ πνεῦμα καὶ ἡ ψυχὴ καὶ τὸ σῶμα ἀμέμπτως ἐν τῇ παρουσίᾳ τοῦ κυρίου ἡμῶν Ἰησοῦ Χριστοῦ τηρηθείη. πιστὸς ὁ καλῶν ὑμᾶς, ὃς καὶ ποιήσει). Paul now prays directly for the Thessalonians. We translate δέ as "and now," since Paul is moving from exhortation to prayer. The long sentence is driven by two optatives, "may he sanctify" (ἁγιάσαι) and "may [your spirit] be kept" or "protected" (τηρηθείη); see comments on 3:12. He will invoke the "the Lord of peace" with an optative again in 2 Thess 3:16. He uses the descriptive genitive "of peace" (τῆς εἰρήνης) to show that peace comes from God (see also Gal 5:22). His reference to God is underscored with the intensive pronoun "himself" (αὐτός).

What is the content of this prayer? That God will wholly "sanctify" them or "make them consistently holy" (ἁγιάσαι). This is no casual blessing, since Paul has already prayed for their sanctification in 3:13 and apparently makes this a regular topic in his prayer for them. Paul also prays that the Thessalonians may be kept blameless. Earlier he prayed that the Thessalonians be kept entirely strong "in blamelessness" (3:13, using the adjective ἀμέμπτους), whereas here he prays that they may be kept "without blame" (using the adverb ἀμέμπτως); Paul's end goal for this prayer is the eschatological parousia of Jesus. While in 3:13 there is a past tense to Paul's theology of sanctification as well as a progressive work, here there is inherent a purposeful movement toward to the return of Christ, at which point the believer might be completely holy (cf. also 4:3 – 4; 1 Cor 1:8; 2 Cor 3:18).

Paul heaps up language and uses the triad "your spirit and soul and body." Some use this verse as a proof text for the tripartite view of human nature, that is, that an individual is composed of three sections.[1] While that is a possible reading, the context and other biblical passages must be brought to bear. First, the Scriptures in general, and Paul in particular, use strings of nouns to describe the entirety of the human person. For example, Deut 6:5 mentions heart, soul, and strength, yet few scholars argue that it teaches a three-part human nature; nor does Jesus' reference to that verse (Matt 22:37). Nor does the Lord Jesus in the Synoptic parallel (Mark 12:30) mean to say that heart, soul, mind, and strength point toward four-part human beings.

1. So Ambrose, *Cain* 2.6; Origen, *Comm. Matt* 14.3; both found in Gorday, *Colossians, 1 – 2 Thessalonians, 1 – 2 Timothy, Titus, Philemon* (ACCS), 100. For those who read French, see Rigaux, *Thessaloniciens*, 597 – 600, for a full analysis.

For his part, Paul casts the work of sanctification in terms of spirit and body in 2 Cor 7:1, again, with no sense that he is leaving out the soul.

Second, 5:23 is a Pauline triad (see comments on 1:3), that is, a point at which Paul uses effusive language of three terms to convey his idea. It is demonstrably fulsome already, with its dyad of "perfect" (ὁλοτελεῖς) and "complete" (ὁλόκληρον) and its long sentence structure. We take the spirit, soul, and body to be three aspects of human nature, not a statement of its tripartite nature.

It is theologically important to note that sanctification includes both the outer and inner person. As in 2 Cor 7:1, Paul asks for the sanctification of the physical person; sin may also infect the inner person, whether termed soul or (as in that verse) spirit. This truth overturns the misapplied Platonism that said that works of the body are not important to God and only the spiritual matters. It also short-circuits the notion (reflected in 1 John 1:8, 10) that the spirit is wholly sanctified in this life. No, teaches Paul, there are sins that touch the spirit and pollute it.

"The God who calls you" hearkens back to God's call of them in 1:4. Paul describes him with the relative clause "he who will do it" (ὃς καὶ ποιήσει). This future tense is oriented to the parousia of Christ; see below for the theological implications of 5:23–24.

5:25 Brothers and sisters, pray for us too (Ἀδελφοί, προσεύχεσθε καὶ περὶ ἡμῶν). Having just prayed for the Thessalonians, Paul asks that they in turn pray for the apostolic team. The "too" (καί) is missing from some ancient manuscripts, but was included with doubts by the NA^{27} committee.[2] Paul frequently asks his disciples to pray for him (e.g., Rom 15:30–32; 2 Cor 1:11; Col 4:3–4). As their model evangelist, Paul implies that when they go out with the gospel, the Thessalonians too need to recruit other Christians to pray for their work.

5:26 Greet all the brothers and sisters with a holy kiss (Ἀσπάσασθε τοὺς ἀδελφοὺς πάντας ἐν φιλήματι ἁγίῳ). Paul refers to the Christian kiss elsewhere, coincidentally, always in letters originating from Corinth or sent to Corinth (Rom 16:16; 1 Cor 16:20; 2 Cor 13:12; see too the use of a cognate verb in Acts 20:37; also 1 Pet 5:14). The word for "kiss" (φίλημα) is rooted in the love (φιλ-) word group. Here it consists of the kissing of people of both sexes.[3] Kissing was hardly normal within the Greco-Roman context. Kissing was a family matter, yet even between married couples, public displays of affection were considered *gauche*. Within Judaism, kissing was reserved for family members but was hardly common. In fact, "there is no basis in ancient texts, Jewish and Greco-Roman, outside the NT for the transformation of the kiss into a sign of religious community."[4]

For members of a congregation to kiss one other was not simply a show of affection; it was the affirmation that the church is the true family. The martyrs of Carthage went to their execution but "first kissed one another, that they might consummate their martyrdom with the kiss of peace."[5] The "holy kiss" became a part of the early liturgy; Justin Martyr places it just before the communion.[6] We are not certain of its role in the church in Paul's

2. See the note by Metzger, *Textual Commentary*, 565.

3. Fee, *Thessalonians*, 232 n. 91, states that this was a kiss on both cheeks, but this is hard to prove. The fact that Clement of Alexandria commanded that the kiss be close-mouthed is an indication that kissing on the mouth was the practice of the early church. See Clement of Alexandria, *Paed.* 3.11 (*ANF* 2:291) and the analysis of Clement's statement by G. Stählin, "φιλέω, etc.," *TDNT*, 9:142.

4. See the excellent analysis by William Klassen, "The Sacred Kiss in the New Testament: An Example of Social Boundary Lines," *NTS* 39 (1993): 122–35; esp. 128, 130. Also by Klassen, "Kiss," *ABD*, 4:89–92. See too "Kiss of Peace" in *Oxford Dictionary of the Christian Church*, 937.

5. *Perpetua and Felicitas* 6.4 (*ANF* 3:705).

6. Justin Martyr, *1 Apol.* 65.2 (*ANF* 1:185).

day, although its widespread reference suggests a regular practice. Nevertheless, Klassen goes too far when he claims that the Christians kissed each other whenever or wherever they met, whether in a meeting or in public.[7]

The kiss between sexes was bound to raise questions. Late in the second century, Athenagoras attributed to Jesus the chilling caveat: "The Logos again says to us, 'If any one kiss a second time because it has given him pleasure, [he sins];' adding, 'Therefore the kiss, or rather the salutation, should be given with the greatest care, since, if there be mixed with it the least defilement of thought, it excludes us from eternal life.' "[8] Around the same time, Clement of Alexandria wanted the emphasis to be shifted from the literal kiss to the inner feeling of love: "But love is not proved by a kiss, but by kindly feeling. But there are those, that do nothing but make the churches resound with a kiss, not having love itself within."[9] Somewhat later, Tertullian too was nervous about his wife meeting "any one of the brethren to exchange the kiss."[10] At least as early as the fourth century, by the time of the Apostolic Constitutions, it was taught, "then let the men give the men, and the women give the women, the Lord's kiss."[11] By the time of Augustine, not only was the kiss same-sex; the sexes were segregated in church.[12]

5:27 I put you under oath by the Lord [Jesus] to have this letter read [aloud] to all the brothers and sisters (Ἐνορκίζω ὑμᾶς τὸν κύριον ἀναγνωσθῆναι τὴν ἐπιστολὴν πᾶσιν τοῖς ἀδελφοῖς). Paul now solemnly charges the Thessalonians to ensure the spread and oral reading of 1 Thessalonians. The verb "adjure" is a *hapax legomenon* in the NT and is not easy to render in English. It means something like, "I hereby make you responsible before God, as if you yourself have taken an oath." The most memorable usage of a cognate is found in the mouth of the Jewish high priest when he tells Jesus, "I charge you under oath [ἐξορκίζω] by the living God" (Matt 26:63). The verb takes a double accusative, that is, the object of the adjuration "you" (ὑμᾶς) and "by whom or what" (τὸν κύριον, apparently the Lord Jesus, again assuming the attributes of divinity).

This oath obligates a course of action — in this case, that this letter "be read" (ἀναγνωσθῆναι) aloud. Paul makes plain that "all the brothers and sisters" should hear it. At the very least, this means all the Thessalonian Christians. Malherbe gives an excellent analysis of why Paul says this: the church was growing at such a rate that care must be taken that all hear the word. What is more, "this letter is ... part of an ongoing process of communication, and Paul wants to ensure it has wide a distribution as possible."[13] Yet Paul's words could be taken further, to apply to all Christians with whom they came into contact, beginning with all Macedonians (1 Thess 1:8; 4:10). In a similar vein, Paul would direct that the Laodiceans and the Colossians swap the letters they have received (Col 4:16).[14]

7. Klassen, "The Sacred Kiss," 130.

8. Athenagoras, *Leg.* 32 (*ANF* 2:146). The word from the "Logos" should be regarded as an *agraphon*, a saying attributed to Jesus that was not included in the canonical gospels or, by another definition, anywhere in the canon. Athenagoras goes on to state that sex within marriage must be strictly limited to procreation.

9. Clement of Alexandria, *Paed.* 3.11 (*ANF* 2:291).

10. Tertullian, *Ux.* 2.4 ("To his Wife"; *ANF* 4:46). On the other hand, Tertullian complains about those who refrain from kissing while they are on a fast in *Or.*18 (*ANF* 3:686 – 87).

11. *Apos. Con.* 2.57 (*ANF* 7:422); also 8.11 (*ANF* 7:486).

12. Augustine, *Civ.* 2.28.1 (*NPNF*[1] 2:41) — "a seemly separation of the sexes is observed."

13. Malherbe, *Letters to the Thessalonians*, 345.

14. See on this Raymond F. Collins, *Studies on the First Letter to the Thessalonians* (BETL 66; Leuven: Leuven Univ. Press, 1984), 370, on Col 4:16 — "not only does it attest to the reading of Christian texts in the context of a liturgical assembly, it also indicates that Christian 'letters' had a significance beyond that of an occasional letter." Collins affirms that this was so shortly after Paul's death; we would add that it was true even during Paul's life.

5:28 May the grace of our Lord Jesus Christ be with you (Ἡ χάρις τοῦ κυρίου ἡμῶν Ἰησοῦ Χριστοῦ μεθ' ὑμῶν). Paul concludes with a benediction, asking for the Lord's grace on them.[15] The wording is similar to that found in Rom 16:20 and 16:24 (Majority Text) and 2 Thess 3:18. Again, it is the Lord Jesus who gives divine grace, thus assuming the characteristics of the deity.

Theology in Application

Theology in Thessalonica

Just as an *exordium* signals the major themes of a letter (see 1:1 – 10, "Literary Context"), so the concluding words do the same. It comes, then, as no surprise that at the very end Paul returns to the sanctification of the Thessalonians. The letter, for all its brevity, has some of the strongest teaching on *Christian holiness.*

The Thessalonians know that their growth in sanctification lies at least in part in their own hands. Paul exhorts them "that you thrive even more" (4:1). Christians understand that God's principal goal is their holiness (4:3). They must accept, not reject, God's command (4:8). Believers who understand their own nature must live according to it (5:6 – 8).

The believer must also remain focused on the future. Paul's prayer in 3:11 – 13 includes apostolic intercession "that your entire person be made strong in blamelessness ... with regard to holiness, before our God and Father, in the coming of our Lord Jesus with all his holy angels." This eschatological center of attention is captured again near the conclusion of the letter, that God "make all of you perfectly holy; and may your spirit and soul and body be kept perfectly without blame at the coming of our Lord Jesus Christ." The reader will hear echoes in other verses, notably Phil 1:6: "being confident of this, that he who began a good work in you will carry it on to completion until the day of Christ Jesus." It is an important point, but little observed, that this too is a prayer: "I always pray with joy ... being confident of this ..." (Phil 1:4 – 6).

Biblical Theology

The doctrine of sanctification has long been a point of deep contention between Catholic, Reformed, Wesleyan, and other groups. The debate is an extraordinarily difficult to untangle, and it is impossible to do it justice here.[16] The special contribution of 1 Thessalonians is:

- complete holiness is eschatological; it is not said in this letter whether complete

15. Compare Num 6:25 and Deut 28:3 – 6 with Acts 14:26; Rom 15:15; 1 Cor 1:4; Titus 2:11; 1 Pet 5:12; see comment on 2 Thess 1:12.

16. See the full discussion of these perspectives in *Five Views on Sanctification* (ed. Stanley N. Gundry; Grand Rapids: Zondervan, 1987).

holiness may be found before the parousia or whether it is attained only at the parousia. Paul can pray for continual growth in holiness and for eschatological holiness in the same breath (5:23).

- holiness is based on the call of God, and the provision of God in already changing us to children of the day/the light.
- holiness is a walk, concerning which decisions and actions must be taken.
- holiness comes in part from the active participation of other believers in our lives. This work is most notable when we pray for other Christians, not just about their circumstances but about their growth in holiness.
- in the end, we may not congratulate ourselves on our level of holiness. Only God is able to provide the means for pleasing him, both by revealing his will to us and enabling us to fulfill it.

Message of This Passage for the Church Today

When it comes to sanctification, one might be tempted to reason: Why should I expend energy praying for my brother or sister to be holy at the return of Christ (3:13; 5:23), when we believe the resurrection will automatically consummate the work of sanctification? Truly, this is an area where we are to follow God's instructions, whether or not we fully grasp the mystery, and assume that our prayers are part of the recipe for our family's being made fully holy.

What one Christian prays for another, that prayer is being grounded in Scripture and also the direction of the Holy Spirit, who knows each person's heart. A prayer might be general or specific, as indicated by their need. For example, in 5:23, Paul prays that the Thessalonians be holy. In 3:12 he prays more specifically that their love might abound.

Evangelical Christians have begun to discover anew the worth of personal accountability between one believer and another. This is an excellent practice, and it should be widely applied. Nevertheless, no Christian will become sanctified simply by sharing with another his or her trials or victories. Only the Holy Spirit can effect real change within, and so it is to God in prayer that we must go.

CHAPTER 9

2 Thessalonians 1:1 – 12

Literary Context

Paul's dealings with the Thessalonians were not limited to these two short letters. Rather, the apostles received feedback from Thessalonica, consisting of greetings and perhaps letters from them. Most crucial would have been the observations of Timothy's trained eye.

In 2 Thess 1 Paul adds another segment to this dialogue. Again the apostle begins with a typical identification of sender and recipient, and a Christian greeting (1:1 – 2). As in 1 Thessalonians, he then moves into language of thanksgiving. In the *exordium* (see "Literary Context" of 1 Thess 1:1 – 10) he expresses his love but also recognizes and empathizes with their sufferings and then prays for them. As usual in the *exordium*, he leads his readers to think about what he will cover in the rest of the letter.

In the middle of his positive words about them, Paul suddenly invokes wrath from heaven (1:6 – 10), in a way that could have been expressed in the language of the psalms:

> O! the wickedness of those who are persecuting the righteous!
> O! the vengeful fire they will incur at the epiphany of Christ!

Paul is not principally concerned with the destiny of the wicked. Rather, he wishes to underscore that God is a God of justice. Before a holy God, only a portion of humanity will be accounted worthy of the future kingdom. This leads into the question about the day of the Lord in 2:1, whose underlying theme is similar: who is apostate and who is not; who is deceived by Satan and who is not; who has believed the gospel and who refuses it.

- **I. Introduction (1:1 – 2)**
- **II. Thanksgiving and Prayer for the Believers While in Tribulation (1:3 – 12)**
  - **A. The apostolic team gives thanks, since the Thessalonians' faith and love for one another are thriving (1:3)**
  - **B. The apostles have a positive opinion of how they have managed to live under persecution (1:4 – 10)**
  - **C. The apostles pray for the Thessalonians in accordance with their hard circumstances (1:11 – 12)**
- III. Instruction concerning the End Times (2:1 – 12)

Main Idea

God's judgment is righteous. Therefore, at the Lord's return, he will relieve the persecuted and take them into his kingdom. He will also bring about "eschatological reversal" — punishing the wicked persecutors of the church with eternal destruction.

Translation

(See next two pages.)

Structure

The first few verses of this chapter echo the language of 1 Thess 1, with the apostles' gratitude for the believers, their boasting of them, and a comment on church's sufferings. The letter begins with a typical Greco-Roman notation of the name of the sender, the name of the recipient, and a greeting (1:1 – 2). The difference between the two letters, according to the best witnesses, lies in the addition to the greeting: it is now "from God the Father and the Lord Jesus Christ."

Just as in the first letter, Paul advances in 1:3 to a report on their thanksgiving to God for the Thessalonians (see 1 Thess 1:1 – 10, "Structure"). The controlling theme for all that follows is "we are under obligation to give thanks to God" (1:3a). The following clauses rapidly develop that thought: when? — "all the time" (πάντοτε); for whom? — for "you, brothers and sisters"; a reference to the worthiness of the activity — "just as [καθώς] it is worthy;" and for what cause? — because of their faith and love.

Paul moves on to show a result (ὥστε) of their gratitude (1:4): the apostles boast to other churches about the way in which the Thessalonians are thriving amidst tribulation. Their endurance is proof (1:5) that they are bound for the kingdom. Paul uses highly compacted language to say that all of this shows that God judges fairly.

2 Thessalonians 1:1 – 12

1a	Sender	Paul, Silvanus and Timothy,
1b	Recipient	to the church of the Thessalonians,
1c	Identification	which is in God the Father and the Lord Jesus Christ:
2a	Greeting	Grace to you and peace
2b	Source	from God our Father and the Lord Jesus Christ.
3a	Thanksgiving	**We are under obligation to give thanks to God**
3b	Time	all the time
3c	Cause	because of you, brothers and sisters,
3d	Comparative	just as it is worthy [before God].
3e	List / Cause	That is because your faith has flourished, and
3f	List	your love has grown abundantly,
3g	List	[the love] that each one of you all has, one for the other.
4a	Result	As a result, we ourselves boast about you
4b	List	among the churches of God,
4c	List	about your endurance and
4d	List	faith
4e	Circumstance	during all your persecutions and
4f	Circumstance	all the tribulations that you are suffering.
5a	Inference	[All of this gives] evidence that God will pronounce a right verdict,
5b	Result	which will result in your being considered worthy of God's kingdom,
5c	Identification	for which you are also suffering.
6a	Inference	For it is indeed right for God to repay
6b		with tribulation those who cause you tribulation, and

7a	Contrast	you who are undergoing tribulation,
		relief,
7b	Association	along with us,
7c	Time	at the revealing of the Lord Jesus
7d	Source	from heaven
7e	Association	with his powerful angels,
8a	Manner	with blazing fire.
8b	Assertion	[The Lord Jesus] will dispense retaliation
8c	List	to those who do not know God and
8d	List	to those who do not obey the gospel of our Lord Jesus.
9a	Identification (of 8)	These are the very ones who will pay
		the penalty
9b	Description (of 9a)	of eternal destruction,
9c	Description (of 9a)	separated from the presence of the Lord and
9d	Description (of 9a)	his glorious might,
10a	Time	when he comes to be glorified among his saints and
10b	Time	to be worshiped among all who have believed,
10c	Cause	because our message to you was believed—
10d	Time	[he will be glorified and marveled at] on that Day.
11a	Cause	That is why **we pray**
		all the time for you,
11b	List / Content	that our God might consider you worthy of [his] calling and
11c	List	powerfully bring to completion his whole will,
11d	Purpose	to accomplish goodness [through you], and
11e	Purpose	[to complete] the work that comes from [your] believing.
12a	Purpose	[We keep praying]
		in order that the name of our Lord Jesus might be glorified among you, and
12b	Purpose	you [be glorified] in [him],
12c	Comparison	according
		to the grace
		of our God and
		of the Lord Jesus Christ.

When God judges thus, the result is that the Thessalonians will be deemed worthy to enter God's kingdom. "Consider worthy" (καταξιόω in 1:5b, likewise ἀξιόω in 1:11b) is eschatological; it is language of final judgment.

Verse 6 takes us into the subtheme of eschatological reversal. While what follows could possibly be seen as a new section, a glance at the larger context shows that Paul has not strayed away from the main theme of gratitude for the Thessalonians. In 1:7 and 10, he shows that his main interest lies still in God's vindication of his disciples, not the fate of the wicked as an interesting topic in itself. Our analysis is borne out in that he later returns to prayer for the disciples in 1:11 – 12, petitioning God that the Thessalonians be considered worthy. Thus, it is proper to view 1:6, 8 – 9 as parenthetical: the parousia of Jesus is also to bring retribution to unbelievers. God will do this, "for" (1:6a, εἴπερ used as a marker of accepted fact, not of conditionality) it is righteous.

The syntax of 1:6 – 10 is far from fluid. In part this is due to the parenthetical nature of some of the material; in part also because Paul inserts brief snatches here and there of tradition from the Olivet Discourse and from the OT (1:8a-b, 9c-d, 10a, 10d; also in 1:12a). There is an ellipsis in 1:10d, where "on that Day" does not follow what has gone before; we have supplied "he will be glorified and marveled at" in order to remind the reader where Paul is going.

The apostle returns to a prayer report (1:11 – 12), which he introduces with "that is why" (εἰς ὅ with a causal sense). As happens in 1 Thess 1:2 – 3 and 3:9 – 10, Paul has constructed an *inclusio* with 2 Thess 1:2; that is, two similar passages "bookend" the beginning and end of a section of text. How the apostles pray is explained first of all "that" God might consider them worthy, that God would accomplish his whole will in them. Paul unpacks their prayer further, this time using a word of purpose, that Jesus will be glorified and that the disciples too will be glorified when Jesus comes.

Exegetical Outline

➡ **I. Introduction (1:1 – 2)**

II. Thanksgiving and Prayer for the Believers in Tribulation (1:3 – 10)

A. The apostolic team gives thanks, since the Thessalonians' faith and love for one another are thriving (1:3).

B. The apostles have a positive opinion of how they have managed to live under persecution (1:4 – 10).

1. They boast to other churches about them, about their endurance and faith in tribulation (1:4).
2. God is using persecution to prepare them for the eschatological kingdom (1:5).
3. God will vindicate his people in Thessalonica at Christ's return (1:6 – 10).

a. Those who cause tribulation will receive tribulation (1:6).

b. Those who receive tribulation will be given relief (1:7).

c. The recipients of divine punishment are the unbelievers, who will be separated from the Lord and receive "eternal destruction" (1:8 – 9).

   d. Christ will give out punishment when he comes to be glorified in his saints, whose number includes the Thessalonians (1:10).

III. The Apostles Pray for the Thessalonians in Accordance with Their Hard Circumstances (1:11 – 12).

   A. That God will make them worthy of his calling (1:11a)
   B. That God will powerfully cause their works to flourish (1:11b-e)
   C. That Christ's name will be glorified among them and in them (1:12)

Explanation of the Text

1:1 Paul, Silvanus, and Timothy, to the church of the Thessalonians, which is in God the Father and the Lord Jesus Christ (Παῦλος καὶ Σιλουανὸς καὶ Τιμόθεος τῇ ἐκκλησίᾳ Θεσσαλονικέων ἐν θεῷ πατρὶ ἡμῶν καὶ κυρίῳ Ἰησοῦ Χριστῷ). Paul and Silas are still "orphaned" from the beloved church (1 Thess 2:17). Only Timothy is still able to travel back and forth from Thessalonica. The superscription (but not the greeting) is virtually identical to that of the earlier letter, naming the sender (nominative case), the recipient (dative case), and then a blessing or greeting. As in 1 Thess 1:1, he speaks to "the church of the Thessalonians" rather than, as he normally does, "the church in such-and-such a city."

Also as in 1 Thessalonians, while Paul was the author, Silas and to an extent Timothy are involved in the production of the letter. That is, the plural verbs and pronouns ("we," "us") are not "editorial" but truly reflect a plurality of people. Once again, Timothy's intimate involvement with the Thessalonians serves as a bridge between them and the apostles, Paul and Silas, making the naming of the three particularly apt; this same Timothy, who met with the Thessalonians, had been with the apostles as Paul wrote. As in the first letter, Paul slips in with "I" when he wishes to be emphatic (2:5). He also gives his personal greeting and signature (3:17) in order to lessen the possibility of forged letters (2:1 – 2).

1:2 Grace to you and peace from God our Father and the Lord Jesus Christ (χάρις ὑμῖν καὶ εἰρήνη ἀπὸ θεοῦ πατρὸς [ἡμῶν] καὶ κυρίου Ἰησοῦ Χριστοῦ). As in letters of that age, Paul greets his addressees. The better manuscripts add "our" (ἡμῶν) after "God the Father"; it is missing from the Textus Receptus and thus from the KJV. With "our" added, the greeting is identical to Rom 1:7; 1 Cor 1:3; 2 Cor 1:2; Gal 1:3; Eph 1:2; Phil 1:2; Phlm 3. It is longer than the greeting in 1 Thess 1:1, where the better manuscripts give the reading "grace to you and peace."

Grace and peace come from the Lord Jesus Christ: already here divine prerogatives are being assigned him. The language foreshadows the glorious coming of Jesus in 1:8 – 10 and the "epiphany" of 2:8, which texts draw from the language of Yahweh's coming in the OT.

1:3a-d We are under obligation to give thanks to God all the time because of you, brothers and sisters, just as it is worthy [before God] (Εὐχαριστεῖν ὀφείλομεν τῷ θεῷ πάντοτε περὶ ὑμῶν, ἀδελφοί, καθὼς ἄξιόν ἐστιν). Paul now begins a thanksgiving (1:3 – 10) and a report of their prayers (1:11 – 12). It becomes evident after the first few phrases that the language of Paul, while positive, is not as exuberant as that of his first letter (1 Thess 1:1 – 10). But there is no lack of joy on the part of the team, no disappointment, as if the church's confusion about the day of the Lord or the presence of disorderly believers has quenched the writers' enthusiasm. Rather, it is 1 Thessalonians that turns out to be exceptional, having been written after God gave them relief from the anxious waiting for word from the church. Second Thessalonians lies closer to the customary tone of a Pauline letter; it resembles Philippians, which likewise affirms a generally positive image of the church.

"To give thanks" (εὐχαριστεῖν) is prayer language, the infinitive echoing the finite verb (εὐχαριστοῦμεν) that Paul used in 1 Thess 1:2. The infinitive is complementary to the helping verb "we are under obligation" (ὀφείλομεν).[1] A translation such as "we ought ... to thank God" (NIV) is not the best, since in English it may come across as noncommittal: "we ought to, but we might not." Rather, the team feels that it is under a solemn obligation to thank God for what is taking place in the Thessalonian church; to fail to do so robs God of his due honor.

As in 1 Thess 1:2, Paul and his team are compelled to give thanks "all the time" (πάντοτε). To what is this adverb linked? Must they give thanks all the time or are they under obligation all the time? In favor of the former is that it is somewhat smoother to attach πάντοτε to the infinitive "give thanks"; on top of this, the decisive point is that in the parallel in 1 Thess 1:2 Paul states "we give thanks ... *all the time*." Paul also echoes his earlier words, saying that the team gives thanks "because of you"; 1 Thess 1:2 has "for *every one of* you."

Paul adds the comparative phrase "as is worthy [before God]" (καθὼς ἄξιόν ἐστιν), or as it might be literally rendered, "to give thanks is worthy"; "worthy" (ἄξιόν) is a neuter adjective, which is typical of a modifier of an infinitive. We have added "before God," since the implied standard of what is fitting behavior is God himself. The various English translations offer some version of "as is right" or "fitting." "Worthy" is less common English, yet it captures the parallel between 1:3 and 1:5, where the Thessalonians will be worthy of God's kingdom.

1:3e-g That is because your faith has flourished, and your love has grown abundantly, [the love] that each one of you all has, one for the other (ὅτι ὑπεραυξάνει ἡ πίστις ὑμῶν καὶ πλεονάζει ἡ ἀγάπη ἑνὸς ἑκάστου πάντων ὑμῶν εἰς ἀλλήλους). Timothy has now returned to Corinth to say that their faith and love have grown even more than the spiritual wealth that they had evidenced earlier. Now Paul explains their motive for thanksgiving: their faith and love are not some virtues of which the Thessalonians should be proud; rather, Paul regards these qualities as evidence that God is working in Thessalonica, and thus he should be thanked always. His statement is a partial parallel to 1 Thess 1:3, where their faith, love, and hope provide the basis for their Christian acts.

"Flourishing" (ὑπεραυξάνει) is a compound verb, the preposition transforming it from growth to wonderful growth. It is a *hapax legomenon* in the New Testament. Paul, like Jesus, favored agricultural metaphors when speaking of the success of the gospel (Matt 13:3 – 9; 1 Cor 3:6 – 9). The Thessalonians are a fine example of what an abundant, lasting harvest looks like, as in Matt 13:8 ("a hundred, sixty or thirty times what was sown"). Yes, faith was present from the first day they received the gospel; yet, in 1:3, the marvelous fact is that their faith has grown despite violent tribulation, which might have led them to stumble (Matt 13:21).

Their "love" (ἀγάπη) too has "grown abundantly" (πλεονάζει); this synonym too has the sense of profuse or even overabundant growth. Here is another striking parallel with the earlier letter, where Paul affirmed their family love (1 Thess

1. See Wallace, *Grammar*, 598 – 99.

4:9–10) while also praying, "may the Lord make you to increase [πλεονάσαι] and abound in love for one another and for all people" (3:12). Already the apostles and the Thessalonians witness how prayer may result in God's intervention.

The end of this verse runs smoothly in Greek. "The love of each one of you" (ἡ ἀγάπη ἑνὸς ἑκάστου) is a subjective genitive, meaning that "each one loves" (or more smoothly, "the love each one has"). "All of you" modifies "each one of you." "For the other" is a distinctively Christian use of the reciprocal adjective. In Thessalonica no one is merely a "taker"; all are givers. Chrysostom was impressed by the statement's implications and remarked:

> For what advantage is it, that you love such-and-such a person very much? That is a love that is wholly within the human faculty. But if it is not a merely human love, and you love for God's sake, then love all people. For so God has commanded, to love even our enemies. And if He has commanded to love our enemies, how much more must we love other Christians, who have never caused us any grief? *But*, you say, *I do love, but just not in that way*. The truth is, then, you don't really love at all.[2]

The fact that the love of the Thessalonians is increasing—no, going above all measure—is a sign that they are miraculously escaping one of the great snares that persecution brings: that many will hate and betray each other and the love of many will grow cold (Matt 24:10, 12).[3] Each believer faced his or her own unique burden from the loss of work, family unity, even physical safety. Yet they did not betray any of their group to the persecutors or let resentments grow up when one believer suffered more than another.

1:4 As a result, we ourselves boast about you among the churches of God, about your endurance and faith during all your persecutions and all the tribulations that you are suffering (ὥστε αὐτοὺς ἡμᾶς ἐν ὑμῖν ἐγκαυχᾶσθαι ἐν ταῖς ἐκκλησίαις τοῦ θεοῦ ὑπὲρ τῆς ὑπομονῆς ὑμῶν καὶ πίστεως ἐν πᾶσιν τοῖς διωγμοῖς ὑμῶν καὶ ταῖς θλίψεσιν αἷς ἀνέχεσθε). As in 1 Thessalonians, Paul does not simply remark on how pleased the apostolic team was; rather, he takes a step further and tells of how they speak of Thessalonica to other churches. This verse is in its entirety a result clause, begun with "so that" (ὥστε), which we have rendered "as a result." The intensive pronoun (αὐτοὺς ἡμᾶς) gives a rendering of "we ourselves"; that is, the team is not simply hearing good reports about the church (see 1 Thess 1:8), but are themselves speaking about them.

The rare verb "boast" (ἐγκαυχᾶσθαι) is used in the LXX to refer to prideful boasting,[4] but here it refers to glorying that is righteous, since it is done for God's honor. Five years later Paul would boast about the Macedonian Christians (including the Thessalonians, one feels certain) in 2 Cor 8:1–5, and lying behind that expression is his gratitude for "the grace that God has given the Macedonian churches" (2 Cor 8:1). Paul does not imply that the Thessalonians themselves needed convincing that they were doing well.[5] He is simply reminding them that they are on the right path, with the implicit message that they should continue on. There is no need to contrast "we ourselves boast about you" with the other letter's "so that we have no

2. We have paraphrased the translation of John Chrysostom, *Homilies on Second Thessalonians* 2 (*NPNF*[1] 13:381) to bring out his point more clearly.

3. Notable too is another statement given to believers in peril, 1 Pet 1:22: "love one deeply, from the heart."

4. "Why do you boast of evil, you mighty hero?" Ps 52:1 [see 51:3 LXX]; also Ps 74:4 [73:4 LXX]. See *1 Clem.* 21.5: "foolish and senseless men who exalt themselves and boast in the arrogance of their words, rather than God."

5. Malherbe, *Letters to the Thessalonians*, 389.

need to say anything" (1 Thess 1:8), as if the good reports about Thessalonica had now dried up and needed to be boosted by the apostles.

Their boasting takes place "among the churches of God." This designation for the churches appears elsewhere in Paul's letters, notably of the Judean congregations in 1 Thess 2:14. To which churches is Paul referring? Corinth and Athens naturally are candidates, but "the churches" seems to indicate more than just two. We are reminded yet again of the relative ease of communication in the first-century Roman Empire. Under normal circumstances, Christian churches could maintain regular communication with each other, particularly if they were in urban centers. The exception, of course, is when disruption was severe enough that only a single junior member of an apostolic team can slip in and out to meet with a church and take information back to the senior apostles. In the few months between the composition of 1 and 2 Thessalonians, the apostles might have heard a great deal about the church's patient endurance and then spread the good report about Thessalonica in their turn.

They are telling the churches "about your endurance" (ὑπὲρ τῆς ὑπομονῆς ὑμῶν). According to 1 Thess 1:3, they have endurance because they have hope. Throughout the NT, endurance is not simply holding on to one's faith, but holding fast despite tribulation. In the dominical tradition (Luke 21:36), the disciples must endure tribulation until the coming of Christ: "Be always on the watch, and pray that you may be able to escape all that is about to happen, and that you may be able to stand before the Son of Man" (cf. the strong parallel in Acts 14:22). No Christian should wish for hard times, but rather should pray for the government so that peace and tranquility will reign (1 Tim 2:1 – 2). Yet, when the quiet life is elusive, still the Christian may count on a benefit from tribulation, that it can lead to more endurance (see Rom 5:3; Jas 1:3). In this case, the Thessalonians have not simply gritted their teeth and hoped for better times. Rather, God has worked in them, allowing them to endure and to grow in steadfastness.

Paul does not minimize what the Thessalonians are going through. He is speaking realistically and pastorally. Their apostle recognizes in a letter, which they hear read aloud, that he understands the depth of their suffering. He tells other churches about how difficult it is to be a Thessalonian believer and for that reason emphasizes "your" and "you." Yet, they maintain their endurance and faith

> during all your *persecutions* (διωγμοῖς)
> [during] all the *tribulations* (θλίψεσιν)
> [persecutions and tribulations] that you are *suffering* (ἀνέχεσθε)

The fact that all three terms, with "endurance" (ὑπομονή), are so common in the NT stock of vocabulary reveals a great deal about the experience of the early church and also the church throughout the ages: "you will be handed over to be persecuted and put to death, and you will be hated by all nations because of me" (Matt 24:9). Yet, the Thessalonians are trusting God, and Paul is certain that relief is on the way (1:7) and prays that God will cause all things to end well for them (1:11).

1:5 [All of this gives] evidence that God will pronounce a right verdict, which will result in you being considered worthy of God's kingdom, for which you are also suffering (ἔνδειγμα τῆς δικαίας κρίσεως τοῦ θεοῦ, εἰς τὸ καταξιωθῆναι ὑμᾶς τῆς βασιλείας τοῦ θεοῦ, ὑπὲρ ἧς καὶ πάσχετε). Paul has used language of the church's suffering, which in the Olivet Discourse continues through this age and will escalate in the end times. He will now extrapolate from their sufferings to the end of the age, which is in God's hands.

This verse is relatively clear in the original, but as sometimes happens, the Greek sentence is cryptic when compared with common English usage and must be unpacked. What constitutes this "evidence" (ἔνδειγμα)? It is best to cast a glance backward to the whole content of the thanksgiving, beginning with 1:3. Then in 1:3 – 4, Paul shows why they know that it is a worthy work to give thanks to God — because of the evident faith and love of the Thessalonian disciples and because of their faith and endurance in tribulation.[6]

But evidence of what? There are two genitive nouns that show Paul's intention. First, "God's right judgment" (lit. trans. of τῆς δικαίας κρίσεως τοῦ θεοῦ) depends on taking "evidence" as an action noun, which means that it represents the action of someone "giving evidence."[7] The Thessalonians' behavior in tribulation "shows that God judges fairly."[8] Something similar happens with the expression "judgment of God" (κρίσεως τοῦ θεοῦ), a subjective genitive that means "God judges." In a passage so richly eschatological, a future reference is likely: in the end, "God will judge" or "pronounce a verdict."

The Gentile believers in Thessalonica share Abraham's faith, expressed in the rhetorical question: "Will not the Judge of all the earth do right?" (Gen 18:25). Still, they are being unfairly pounded with trials, while their persecutors live free of trouble. This tension has always caused the believer anguish, who looks on a world where might makes right. The psalmists of old faced the same problem. On the one hand they affirmed: "May the nations be glad and sing for joy, for you rule the peoples with equity and guide the nations of the earth" (Ps 67:4). But at the same time they pondered: "How long, LORD? Will you forget me forever? ... How long will my enemy triumph over me?" (Ps 13:1 – 2).

The Thessalonians too lived daily with the sharp "cognitive dissonance" of belief in a just God and seeing with their own eyes that the world is unfair. The apostle knows that good eschatology has a way of holding both those truths in proper alignment. Before God, there is a fundamental distinction between those moving toward the kingdom and those who will be taken by surprise by the final judgment. The Thessalonians need not avenge themselves but can do good to "all people" (1 Thess 5:15), nor need they ever doubt God's justice.

Verse 5b uses εἰς τό plus an infinitive to give the result of the foregoing: "you will be considered worthy." This is closely parallel to 1:11:

> 2 Thess 1:5: "which will result in you being considered worthy of God's kingdom"
>
> 2 Thess 1:11: we pray in order that "God might consider you worthy of his calling"

Given that God is the explicit subject of the verb in 1:11, we take "being considered worthy of God's kingdom" in 1:5 as a "divine passive": "God will consider you worthy of his kingdom." What leads Paul to this conclusion? It is not just that they have suffered tribulation; rather, it is the underlying certainty that *God's judgment is just*. With that truth, one may draw a straight line from the experience of persection to the certainty of their future entrance into the kingdom. See our comments concerning being "worthy of the kingdom" in 1 Thess 2:12.

Here in 2 Thess 1:5 the full form "kingdom of God" makes its first appearance in Paul's letters and hence in the NT. The ἄξιος word group often has to do with judgment (cf. Deut 25:2; Luke 12:48; 23:15).[9] Paul's two statements are similar to the Lukan form of Jesus' response to the Sadducees' question in Luke 20:35: "those who are considered

6. See Morris, *Thessalonians* (NICNT), 197.

7. On the "objective genitive," see Wallace, *Grammar*, 116 – 19.

8. As CEV; similarly GNB, NJB; Malherbe, *Letters to the Thessalonians*, 394.

9. The genitive follows either the adjective or verbs such as ἀξιόω and καταξιόω, in what Wallace calls "Genitive after certain adjectives (and adverbs)." Wallace, *Grammar*, 134 – 35.

worthy [καταξιωθέντες] of taking part in the age to come and in the resurrection from the dead will neither marry nor be given in marriage." It refers to the future age, when all believers will be together forever with the Lord, as the Thessalonians well know (1 Thess 4:17). As in 1 Thess 2:12, Paul speaks of a manner of life that conforms to God's future kingdom.

With only a slight amount of redundancy, noted by "also" (καί), Paul brings the verse around to connect sufferings with the kingdom: "for which you are also suffering" (ὑπὲρ ἧς καὶ πάσχετε); the preposition ὑπέρ has the sense of "for which" or "for the sake of which." Paul has already used the verb "to suffer" to describe the experience of the Thessalonian and the Judean Christians in 1 Thess 2:14.

There are two theological questions concerning "be considered worthy." First, given that God's true people will be persecuted, does the reverse follow, that people who are persecuted are proved to be God's people? Not at all, as even a cursory glance at history proves: people of every religion have suffered for their faith at some point. Two groups today speak often of their sufferings as an apologetic argument that their creed is the true one. The Jehovah's Witnesses argue that their sufferings of the past century and a half are a sign that they are the true remnant. The Baha'i use their suffering, particularly since the Iranian Revolution, as evidence for their correctness. This logic will not hold for Paul, who saw people suffering around him all the time. In the gospel, it is suffering in and for *Christ* that leads one along the kingdom path.

Second, is tribulation *salvific*; that is, does Paul teach that suffering tribulation is the path that leads to eschatological salvation? No, since his language in 1:5 speaks of *evidence* of how God will judge in the future. His language nicely matches other teachings of the NT, which makes persecution the concomitant of life en route to the kingdom, but not the ticket for entry. Tribulation and the inheritance of the kingdom go hand in hand in Paul's teaching, as they do in Jesus' (Matt 5:3 – 11; Rom 8:17; 2 Tim 2:11 – 12). Paul and Barnabas told the Galatian disciples that "we must go through many hardships to enter the kingdom of God" (Acts 14:22); they did *not* say that "*because* we suffer a lot, we will be permitted to enter into God's kingdom."[10] It is God's right judgment, not sufferings, that admits people to the future age. What defines the saved person is *belief in the gospel* (1:10); what often distinguishes the believer is *suffering*.

1:6 – 7b For it is indeed right with God to repay with tribulation those who cause you tribulation, and to you who are undergoing tribulation, relief, along with us (εἴπερ δίκαιον παρὰ θεῷ ἀνταποδοῦναι τοῖς θλίβουσιν ὑμᾶς θλῖψιν καὶ ὑμῖν τοῖς θλιβομένοις ἄνεσιν μεθ' ἡμῶν). If we speak of God's justice, we must also speak of his judgment. Thus throughout this chapter, the apostle carefully distinguishes two groups: those who will be accounted worthy of the kingdom and those who have rejected the gospel (1:8) and will face God's wrath. His anger falls most strongly on those who actively persecute his people (1:6), since the enemies of the church are by extension the enemies of God.[11] One may look at the trials that the church suffers during this age and take them as foreshadowings, because while "God thus spares the wicked for a time, and winks at the injuries inflicted upon his people, His judgment to come is shewn us as in a mirror."[12]

"Since" or "for" (εἴπερ) is not an easy particle to translate; here we are helped by an attentive study of the BDAG lexicon, which offers the translation

10. See S. J. Hafemann, "Suffering," *DPL*, 919 – 21.
11. So Rigaux, *Thessaloniciens*, 610 – 11.
12. Calvin, *Thessalonians*, 313.

"if indeed, if after all, since." In another context the very same word could express some conditionality; in a context such as this one, it refers to an accepted fact and means "since."[13] Several versions start a new sentence at this point, notably the CEV: "It is only right for God to punish everyone who is causing you trouble." The NRSV is better: "for it is indeed just of God" shows the connection with the previous verse.

In 1:5, because "God will pronounce a right verdict," the Thessalonian saints will be considered worthy of the end-time kingdom. In verse 6, that righteous verdict is paraphrased "it is indeed right with God"; if God's justice means that the Thessalonians will enter the kingdom, then that same divine justice means that he will "repay" (ἀνταποδοῦναι) their persecutors. In 1 Thess 3:9 Paul used the same verb to speak of repaying God with thanksgiving; now he speaks in terms of retribution. Both Paul (Rom 12:19) and Hebrews (Heb 10:30) quote Deut 32:35, that "it is mine to avenge; I will repay." From the Pentateuch also comes this promise to God's people: "If you listen carefully to what he says and do all that I say, I will be an enemy to your enemies and will oppose those who oppose you" (Exod 23:22).

The rest of verse 6 is replete with cognates of "tribulation." If reproduced in woodenly literal English it would sound something like: "He will repay the tribulators [participle of the verb θλίβω] with tribulation [accusative of θλῖψις], and to you who are tribulated (another participle), relief" (see the parallel in Rev 16:5 – 6). It was meant to comfort the Thessalonians that not only will the apostles be vindicated, but they too "along with us," that is, the apostolic team. There is no verb here; it is assumed from earlier in the verse ("repay," ἀνταποδοῦναι), but this time in the neutral sense of "recompense."

God will grant them eschatological "relief" (ἄνεσιν), a word that means "relief from a burden"; the burden is living as a Christian and having to face the world's persecution. In other Jewish and Christian literature, "rest" is a metaphor for the future kingdom or even for martyrdom: "they will rest from their labor, for their deeds will follow them" (Rev 14:13); by contrast, the followers of the beast will never have rest, day or night (14:11).

1:7c-e At the revealing of the Lord Jesus from heaven with his powerful angels (ἐν τῇ ἀποκαλύψει τοῦ κυρίου Ἰησοῦ ἀπ᾽ οὐρανοῦ μετ᾽ ἀγγέλων δυνάμεως αὐτοῦ). Paul now heightens the sense of what is evident through 1:7a, that we are dealing with the end-time coming of Christ to save and to judge. The use of "at" (ἐν) is a "marker of a period of time."[14] It is commonly used of the parousia (1 Cor 15:23; 1 Thess 2:19; 3:13) or other eschatological events. Here and in 1 Cor 1:7 Paul uses "revealing" (ἀποκάλυψις) to denote the coming of Christ; the cognate verb (ἀποκαλύπτω) will refer to the appearing of the Man of Lawlessness in 2 Thess 2:3, 6, 8 and the end-time wrath of God in Rom 1:18. The genitive "of the Lord Jesus" is likely an objective genitive — God is the implicit author of the action, so this means "[God] reveals the Lord Jesus."[15]

We have proposed (see the Introduction) that Paul and his team taught the Thessalonians something like Matt 24 when they originally evangelized them, although he switches out the term "Son of Man" for other titles of Christ. The Matthean tradition in turn rests upon Daniel 7:13:

> Dan 7:13: "In my vision at night I looked, and there before me was one like a son of man, coming with

13. For εἴπερ see under BDAG, εἰ 6. l.

14. BDAG, ἐν 10.

15. Wallace, *Grammar*, 116.

the clouds of heaven. He approached the Ancient of Days and was led into his presence."

Matt 24:30: "Then will appear the sign of the Son of Man in heaven. And then all the peoples of the earth will mourn when they see the Son of Man coming on the clouds of heaven, with power and great glory."

There has been a staggering amount of study as to whether "son of man" was a messianic title in Daniel, in books such as *1 Enoch* and *4 Ezra*, and in the canonical gospels and Revelation.[16] The best conclusion that can be made, with caution, is that "in Daniel 7 the phrase was used non-technically to refer to somebody 'like a man,' and hence the phrase came to be a means of reference to the person so described. Jesus took over this sense of the phrase, and thus identified his role with that of the figure in Daniel 7."[17]

In 1:7, Paul paints a picture of Jesus' glory, the clouds, the angels, and the judgment. He is particularly interested in the last point; the punishment of the wicked is a corollary of giving rest to the persecuted saints. Jesus is revealed "from heaven" (ἀπ' οὐρανοῦ) in what must be taken as a "descent," in the manner of Acts 1:11 and 1 Thess 4:16. He is accompanied by angels (see Matt 16:27; 25:31; 1 Thess 3:13).

The phrase that we have translated "with his powerful angels" (μετ' ἀγγέλων δυνάμεως αὐτοῦ) may be taken in one of two ways. First, "power" may be a descriptive genitive, making the phrase "the powerful angels of him" or "his powerful angels."[18] This makes sense within the context and has no good arguments against it. But it is also possible to take "power" as linked to "his," that is, that they are angels "of his power."[19] The first option is probable, since powerful angels are a key fixture in eschatological passages, not to mention noneschatological ones (note Ps 103:20: "Praise the Lord, you his angels, you mighty ones who do his bidding, who obey his word"; see also 2 Pet 2:11, "angels ... more powerful").

But whose angels are these? The syntax is not clear. It is possible that Paul means to say that "it is right with God to repay with tribulation ... at the revealing of the Lord Jesus ... with his [God's own] powerful angels." But this is more awkward, given that "God" lies farther back in the sentence; besides, there already existed Christian teaching that the angels were Jesus' angels (Matt 25:31). Since "Lord Jesus" lies closer to hand, it is best to take the angels as his. Once again, almost casually, an attribute of Yahweh is attributed to the Lord Jesus. The Lord of hosts, who comes with the armies of heaven, is now seen to be the Lord Jesus, who comes with his angelic army.

1:8 With blazing fire. [The Lord Jesus] will dispense retaliation to those who do not know God and to those who do not obey the gospel of our Lord Jesus (ἐν πυρὶ φλογός, διδόντος ἐκδίκησιν τοῖς μὴ εἰδόσιν θεὸν καὶ τοῖς μὴ ὑπακούουσιν τῷ εὐαγγελίῳ τοῦ κυρίου ἡμῶν Ἰησοῦ). Paul now brings the thought around to the fiery judgment that the persecutors will receive from God. The most natu-

16. *1 En.* 46:2 – 3 (Charles edition): "And I asked the angel who went with me and showed me all the hidden things, concerning that Son of Man, who he was, and whence he was, (and) why he went with the Head of Days? And he answered and said unto me: This is the Son of Man who hath righteousness, with whom dwelleth righteousness, and who revealeth all the treasures of that which is hidden, because the Lord of Spirits hath chosen him, and whose lot hath the pre-eminence before the Lord of Spirits in uprightness for ever." *4 Ezra* 13 refers indirectly to the Danielic Son of Man.

17. See the full review of the data and the scholarly discussion by I. H. Marshall, "Son of Man," in *Dictionary of Jesus and the Gospels* (ed. J. B. Green, S. McKnight, and I. H. Marshall; Downers Grove, IL: InterVarsity Press, 1992), 775 – 81.

18. Bruce, *1 & 2 Thessalonians*, 151.

19. Wanamaker, *Thessalonians*, 226; Malherbe, *Letters to the Thessalonians*, 399; Fee, *Thessalonians*, 256.

ral reading of 1:7 – 8 is that Christ will rescue the saints and inflict punishment on the wicked at one and the same coming.[20]

This commentary follows NA[27] and many versions in attaching "with blazing fire" to the previous sentence. Isaiah 66 seems to underlie Paul's language in these two letters, and that is clearly the case here, from Isa 66:14b – 15:

> The hand of the LORD will be made known to
> his servants,
> but his fury will be shown to his foes.
> See, the LORD is coming with fire,
> and his chariots are like a whirlwind;
> he will bring down his anger [ἀποδοῦναι
> ἐκδίκησιν] with fury,
> and his rebuke with flames of fire [ἐν φλογὶ
> πυρός].

The phrase "dispensing retaliation" (διδόντος ἐκδίκησιν) contains a genitive participle, to match the genitive "the Lord Jesus" (τοῦ κυρίου Ἰησοῦ) in 1:7. This yields the meaning "at the revealing of the Lord Jesus ... who will dispense...." Paul gives another nod to OT language, a further reference to Isa 66:15: as *Yahweh* comes with judgment in Isaiah, so the *Lord Jesus* comes to judge in 2 Thessalonians.[21]

Who will receive this fiery judgment? The first phrase is "those who do not know God." This is language similar to "the Gentiles, who do not know God" in 1 Thess 4:5, people who are said for that reason to lead sexually promiscuous lives (see also Eph 5:6). The second phrase is "those who do not obey the gospel of our Lord Jesus." While it is not common language today to speak of "obeying the gospel" — we prefer "receive" or "believe" — it is not an uncommon phrase in the NT. Paul speaks of rejecting the "truth" (Rom 2:8), of obeying a "pattern of teaching" (6:17), and of accepting "the good news" (10:16). In Galatians it is "obeying the truth" (Gal 5:7; outside the Pauline literature, see, e.g., Heb 5:9; 1 Pet 4:17). Obedience to the gospel means to believe it, but this is not mere assent; those who obey the gospel will turn from idols (1 Thess 1:9) and turn to a life of holiness (4:1 – 2).

Does Paul intend to delineate two groups here, as if Group A contains those who know not God (Gentiles?) and Group B those who hear and reject the gospel (Jews?).[22] We find it difficult to make a clear distinction, given the realities of the many human situations in which Paul preached. We might take into account that in biblical terms, "not knowing God" does not necessarily imply a lack of information. Some Bible characters, be they Jews or Gentiles, willingly refuse to "know" or acknowledge him, as in Jer 9:6: " 'They refuse to acknowledge me,' declares the LORD" (see Pharaoh in Exod 5:2). Besides this, we have to take into account a third description of the damned in 2 Thess 2:12, those "who do not believe the truth." All these terms are overlapping and to an extent, interchangeable.[23]

Some exegetes of 2 Thessalonians argue that, given the context of Thessalonica, Paul is only interested in the punishment of the small percentage of the population who were actively persecuting the church. In this way, it is thought to ameliorate the doctrine of hell by radically reducing the number of people who might face it. But this is not so; if Paul is focused on the persecutors in 1:6, he is

20. This juxtaposition of salvation and judgment causes great problems for a pretribulational view of the rapture; Paul D. Feinberg in Reiter, *Three Views on the Rapture*, 227, tries to make the difficult case that the pretribulation rapture is telescoped into the posttribulation punishment of the wicked seven years later: "The point being made is that in the whole eschatological complex of events, God is both going to bring rest for the Thessalonians and retribution on their persecutors."

21. Weima, "1 and 2 Thessalonians," 883 – 84.

22. So Marshall, *1 and 2 Thessalonians*, 177 – 78; contra Green, *Thessalonians*, 290; Wanamaker, *Thessalonians*, 227.

23. See Best, *Thessalonians*, 259 – 60.

entirely clear in 1:8 – 9 and 2:10 – 12 that all unbelievers are liable to the judgment Christ will bring.

1:9 These are the very ones who will pay the penalty of eternal destruction, separated from the presence of the Lord and his glorious might (οἵτινες δίκην τίσουσιν ὄλεθρον αἰώνιον ἀπὸ προσώπου τοῦ κυρίου καὶ ἀπὸ τῆς δόξης τῆς ἰσχύος αὐτοῦ). Paul moves on to describe the doom of the wicked. At last he anchors this in the eschaton, since "will pay" (τίσουσιν, from τίνω) is a future tense verb. "In its only appearance in the NT, 2 Thess 1:9, τίνω is used as in classical writers ... with δίκην = 'pay the penalty.' "[24] The verb occurs in biblical texts that speak of God's own retribution: "Do not say: 'I will repay my enemy' [τείσομαι, the middle voice of τίνω], but wait for the Lord that he may help you" (Prov 20:9c NETS = Prov 20:22 MT). The reader should make the connection with 1:6 – 7, where avenging the church rests with God, not with Christians.

We will deal with the theological issues surrounding "eternal destruction" (ὄλεθρον αἰώνιον) in the "Theology in Application" section. Here we raise the basic exegetical questions. The adjective we have translated "eternal" is based on the noun "age" or "eon" (αἰών). It is sometimes asserted that the Jews (and hence Jewish Christians) did not have a word for "eternal"; or alternatively, that αἰώνιος does not mean "everlasting" or "without end" but rather "for many ages," the implication being that it is punishment for a long time but not forever.

This argument contains two errors. First is the error that a people group does not grasp a concept such as "eternal" unless its language has some equivalent of the word "eternal" in another (Western!) language. One sometimes hears, for example, that "the x-y-z tribe doesn't have a word for jealousy," the implication being that they never experience jealousy and that they have not the language to describe it even if they saw it. The argument in the case of "everlasting" runs that the Greeks had precise words for "eternal," but the Jews could not describe anything longer than "a very long time." All of this is false reasoning.

The second error is the one about which all seminary students are warned: basing the meaning of the word on its etymology. In fact, the meaning of a word does not finally reveal itself in its etymology but rather in its actual usage. It is the use of the adjective that interests the exegete, and a study of the use of αἰώνιος in the NT shows that it patently takes the meaning of "eternal" (see 2 Thess 2:16; Heb 5:9; 1 Pet 5:10; 2 Pet 1:11); the only exception is when it is used of "before the beginning of time" (2 Tim 1:9). That it means everlasting is particularly apparent when used in the phrase "eternal life," which in Paul's letters signifies not "future life for a very long time" but "the unending resurrection life of the world to come."[25]

Christians and Jews of the first century AD did possess language that could denote "eternal"; the adjective αἰώνιος, though related to a cognate noun that could mean long but finite lengths of time (αἰών), in Christian texts refers to time unending. Then in the second century AD, Justin Martyr showed his awareness that "everlasting punishment" is not the same as "punishment for a long period of time." Rather, it is "upon the wicked in the same bodies united again to their souls which are now to undergo everlasting punishment [αἰωνίαν κόλασιν]; and not only, as Plato said, for a period of a thousand years."[26]

Paul speaks of the penalty of "eternal *destruc-*

24. MM, 636.

25. See, e.g., Morris, *Thessalonians* (NICNT), 204. Also G. S. Shogren, "Hell, Abyss, Eternal Punishment," *DLNT*, 459 – 62. See also H. Balz, "αἰώνιος," *EDNT*, 1:46 – 47: "Throughout the NT αἰώνιος can be rendered by *eternal*" as it is also used in the LXX.

26. Justin, *1 Apol.* 8 (*ANF* 1:165). We have altered the *ANF* translation from "spirits," since the original has "souls," ψυχῶν.

tion" (ὄλεθρον; a synonym of "destruction" is ἀπώλεια). His language here is similar to the Maccabean tradition of suffering and future vindication: those who torment the righteous "will deservedly undergo from the divine justice eternal torment by fire" (4 Macc 9:9).

It is at the parousia of Christ that the people of the world will experience "unexpected destruction" (αἰφνίδιος ... ὄλεθρος, 1 Thess 5:3). "Destruction" (ὄλεθρος) and its cognates are used of God's punishment in the LXX, for example, to speak of laying waste (e.g., "the land would be for annihilation," Ezek 14:16 NETS); that is, it is desolated rather than "annihilated" in any absolute sense. The same is true of the destruction of Egypt's firstborn in Heb 11:28 or Israel's being destroyed by serpents in 1 Cor 10:10 (see also Acts 3:23). The devil is a destroyer as well, as is seen by the appellation of his agent, the Man of Lawlessness, the "son of destruction" (2 Thess 2:3). Again, we will deal with the meaning of "destruction" in the "Theology in Application" section.

Paul has two prepositional phrases that help unpack the meaning of "eternal destruction," both with ἀπό. We take them to be based on the "ablative" use of the genitive, meaning separation.[27] The preposition "denotes alienation in some expressions, especially in Paul, which cannot be directly paralleled from the classical language."[28] "From the presence of the Lord and from his glorious might" is language of Isaiah, who describes the flight of the idolaters from the epiphany of Yahweh in Isaiah (Isa 2:10, 19, 21, "from before the fear of the Lord and from the glory of his strength," NETS); we have marked it as an OT allusion. Paul, in contrast with the LXX but like the Hebrew original, does not have the word "fear."[29] While the Hebrew text speaks of the presence of Yahweh, in Paul's hands it is separation from the Lord Jesus that is a portion of their punishment.

There are other parallels in the NT, notably, "Depart from me [ἀπ' ἐμοῦ; that is, from the presence of Son of Man] ... into the eternal fire" (Matt 25:41); likewise "cursed and cut off from [ἀπό] Christ" (Rom 9:3). Although it may imply that the wicked are absent at the parousia of Christ, the better interpretation, based on Jewish and Christian teaching, is that at his coming, the Lord Jesus will banish them from his presence.

The second prepositional phrase is "separated from ... his glorious might," a phrase parallel to the first "from" (ἀπό) phrase and is likely epexegetical, that is, stating the same truth in other phraseology: "separated from the Lord in his mighty glory."[30] It is paralleled by 1 Pet 4:13, "But rejoice, inasmuch as you participate in the sufferings of Christ, so that you may be overjoyed when his glory is revealed." The importance of this attribution of the Lord is that, during this age, he was killed in Judea (1 Thess 2:15; 4:14; 1 Cor 2:8 — they "crucified the Lord of glory"), and his followers are as a matter of course suffering persecution as well.

Now when the Lord comes, he comes in glory, but in the glory that is associated with the epiphany of Yahweh in the OT. For example, when Yahweh met with Moses on Sinai, "To the Israelites the glory of the LORD looked like a consuming fire on top of the mountain" (Exod 24:17). "The LORD came from Mount Sinai. From Edom, he gave light to his people, and his glory was shining from Mount Paran. Thousands of his warriors were with him, and fire was at his right hand" (Deut 33:2 CEV). Now it is the Lord Jesus who comes with that Shekinah glory that reveals his divine "might" (ἰσχύος, one of the attributes of God [see Eph 1:19; Rev 7:12] and of Christ [Rev 5:12]).

27. See BDF §180.

28. BDF §211.

29. Weima, "1 and 2 Thessalonians," 885.

30. See Malherbe, *Letters to the Thessalonians*, 403 – 4.

IN DEPTH: Did Jesus Teach That He Would Return at the End of the Age?

According to T. Francis Glasson, the notion that Christ will come in glory in the future was a theological innovation that did not come from Jesus' own teaching. Glasson opposed the so-called "consistent" eschatological approach to the gospel tradition as launched by Johannes Weiss and popularized by Albert Schweitzer. Glasson argued in various publications that Jesus did not teach an imminent coming of the Son of Man or an apocalyptic kingdom of God. Rather, his preaching had to do with a kingdom for the here and now and his predictions of glory had to do with his own resurrection. But afterward, the church distorted his statements into a gaudy package of end-time events, replete with a great tribulation and a Man of Lawlessness.

Where did these unnamed Christians come up with their ideas? According to Glasson, the eschatology in 1 – 2 Thessalonians "cannot be explained by anything in the teaching of Jesus but they are clearly from the OT." Thus, "the early church did not begin equipped with a fully formed theology and it was to the OT that they turned in order to explain and interpret their faith in Christ."[31] He pointed out, with some justification, that the picture of a Messiah descending from heaven in a parousia is not a feature of the intertestamental literature. He goes on, however, to claim that Jesus himself did not teach the idea, and that the eschatological passages in the gospels do not represent Jesus' own teaching or perhaps the proper understanding of that teaching. Therefore, the Thessalonian letters, as the earliest extant writings after Pentecost, are not a snapshot of a church that is carrying on the Jesus tradition, but a church that was just then creating the doctrine of the parousia. In turn, says Glasson, the church later imported that orientation back into the developing Jesus-tradition, the very oral teaching that would recrystallize into the Olivet Discourse and make it seem as if the Thessalonians had followed the Jesus tradition all along.

This clearly will not do. Yes, the earliest literary reference in the church to the return of Christ is found in 1 Thess 1:10, some two decades after Jesus. But when could the church have found the time to transform Jesus' teaching into something wholly new? Not at the writing of 1 Thessalonians, where Paul assumes it as settled that Christ will come in the eschaton. Not in the years prior, since 1 Thessalonians is based on previous oral teaching, which must have been a part of Paul's kerygma at least since the mid-40s. If 1 – 2 Thessalonians and the

31. T. Francis Glasson, "Theophany and Parousia," *NTS* 34 (1988): 261.

eschatological teaching of the Synoptic Gospels seem so cohesive (apart from their failure to grasp the resurrection doctrine, 1 Thess 4:13 – 18), it is because the earliest believers cherished and passed along Jesus' authentic teaching, particularly when they found themselves in the very type of tribulation that he himself had so recently predicted.

1:10 When he comes to be glorified among his saints and to be worshiped among all who have believed, because our message to you was believed — [he will be glorified and marveled at] on that Day (ὅταν ἔλθῃ ἐνδοξασθῆναι ἐν τοῖς ἁγίοις αὐτοῦ καὶ θαυμασθῆναι ἐν πᾶσιν τοῖς πιστεύσασιν, ὅτι ἐπιστεύθη τὸ μαρτύριον ἡμῶν ἐφ' ὑμᾶς, ἐν τῇ ἡμέρᾳ ἐκείνῃ). Every Thessalonian disciple knows that the return of Christ will be to rescue his people (see 1 Thess 1:10; 5:9). Paul now turns to them and shows the destiny of the rest of humankind when Jesus "comes" (the subjunctive ἔλθῃ). The exegete must be wary of a simplistic definition of the subjunctive mood, as if one were obliged to put a "should" or "might" before its every rendering in English. Here it is subjunctive because it follows the temporal particle "when" (ὅταν). When ὅταν + aorist subjunctive follows the main verb — the conditions that apply here — it means simply "then" or "when" and in fact is used in other eschatological passages (see, e.g., Matt 24:15 – 16, 33; 1 Cor 15:28, 54; Col 3:4).

Christ will come "to be glorified" (ἐνδοξασθῆναι). In extant literature this verb is found only in Jewish and Christian texts: eleven times in the LXX, but in the New Testament only in 2 Thess 1:10, 12. As noted in by G. Kittel, the present passage is yet another example of theophanic language (language of God appearing in glory) of Yahweh now applied to the coming of the κύριος Christ.[32] We note especially Ps 88:7 – 8 LXX (NETS; Ps 89:6 – 7 MT):

> Because who in the clouds shall be deemed equal to the Lord [κύριος in the LXX, Yahweh in the MT]? And who among the divine sons shall be compared with the Lord [again, κύριος/Yahweh]? God is glorified in [ἐνδοξαζόμενος ἐν] a council of holy ones [ἁγίων], great and awesome to all that are around him.

The parallels between Ps 88:7 – 8 LXX and 2 Thess 1 include the "incomparable" Lord, the heavenly beings, divine glory, and holy ones. The fact that the holy ones in the psalm are angelic beings leads some to interpret the "his holy ones" (τοῖς ἁγίοις αὐτοῦ) in 2 Thess 1:10 as angels,[33] the interpretation we gave "holy ones" in 1 Thess 3:13. But Paul does not always keep to the original referent when he uses Scripture in his arguments. Also, the eschatological "glory" seems to be associated with his holy *people* in this letter (2 Thess 2:14: "God called you unto this saving work through the gospel we preached, to obtain the glory of our Lord Jesus"). The near context of 1:12, "that the name of the Lord Jesus Christ might be glorified among you," is definitely related to God's people, not to his angels. Therefore, because of the poetic parallelism, the parallel terms do not denote two groups (angels, believers), but one:

> "when he comes to be glorified among his saints"
> and
> "to be worshiped among all who have believed"

The meaning of "glorified" lies parallel to the

32. G. Kittel, "ἔνδοξος, ἐνδοξάζομαι," *TDNT*, 2:254 – 55.

33. So BDAG, ἅγιος 2. d. α.

second infinitive (θαυμασθῆναι). Since Homer this infinitive (often meaning "to be marveled at") had another shade of meaning: "honour, admire, worship."[34] We may thus understand the two infinitives to be "glorified among the saints" and "worshiped among the believers," with the preposition (ἐν) speaking of a universal worship by the worldwide congregation (e.g., Rom 1:5; 15:6). Whereas the glorious coming of the Lord will be enjoyed and participated in by the believers, that same glory will mean destruction for the wicked. According to Rev 6:16 – 17, "They called to the mountains and the rocks, 'Fall on us and hide us from the face of him who sits on the throne and from the wrath of the Lamb! For the great day of their wrath has come, and who can withstand it?'"

"Among all who have believed" (ἐν πᾶσιν τοῖς πιστεύσασιν) is noteworthy first for its use of "all," a common theme in these two letters. Paul is not limiting himself to all the believers in Macedonia or even in Achaia (1 Thess 1:7). Rather, he is using universal language, as in 1 Cor 15:51: "We will not all sleep, but we will all be changed." It lies parallel to the universal condemnation of unbelievers that Paul preaches in 2 Thess 2:12: "in order that all might be judged, all who do not believe the truth but take pleasure in wickedness."

The phrase "those who believe" (τοῖς πιστεύσασιν) is capable of various translations; we must beware of an exegetical pitfall that awaits the reader who thinks that an aorist participle must of itself denote action in past time or a punctilear action.[35] Those who wish to translate the phrase as "those who believed" or "have believed" or "believed once and for all" or "believed once and for all, never to turn back" should not point to the aorist tense for proof. This is similar to the issue we encountered in 1 Thess 1:6 (see comments). We may translate the participle as "believers" or, as seems smoother *due to what comes next in the context*, "all who have believed."

Paul now turns back to anchor his eschatological teaching in the preaching of the gospel: "because our message to you was believed." There is an ellipsis here; that is, syntactically a clause is missing, but one that is easily supplied by common sense: "[The Lord will] be worshiped among all who have believed, *and you will be included in that number*, because our message to you was believed." "Was believed" (ἐπιστεύθη) is the aorist passive and stands for "you Thessalonians came to believe our testimony about the gospel," as opposed to those who disobeyed it (1:8). The subject of the verb is "our message" (τὸ μαρτύριον). Paul uses the cognate verbs "implored" (μαρτύρομαι) in 1 Thess 2:12 and "warned" (διαμαρτύρομαι) in 4:6, to speak of the teaching he had given the disciples. The noun form has the shade of meaning of a testimony of a witness (see Acts 4:33) and also of a solemn message in general (1 Cor 1:6; 2 Tim 1:8; Pol. *Phil.* 7.1). We have chosen the more general "message," since "testimony" implies another meaning in evangelical churches.

When Paul states "on that Day" (ἐν τῇ ἡμέρᾳ ἐκείνῃ), he is not, as could be misunderstood from the flow of the sentence, speaking of the day when the Thessalonians believed the gospel. Rather, he is using conventional scriptural language to refer to "the day of the Lord." This is the same "day" that comes like a thief in the night (1 Thess 5:2, 4; 2 Thess 2:2, 3; see comments on 1 Thess 5:2; 2 Thess 2:2). Our verse here probably has its roots in Isa 2:11 (also Isa 2:17): "The arrogance of man will be brought low and human pride humbled; the

34. See LSJ, θαυμάζω. It is worth looking at G. Bertram, "θαῦμα, θαυμάζω, θαυμάσιος, θαυμαστός," *TDNT*, 3:27 – 42, to get a sense of how (p. 37) "the Synoptists and Acts, the Johannine writings, Paul and Revelation reveal strong differences in the use of the word group."

35. See Wanamaker, *Thessalonians*, 231; Morris, *Thessalonians* (NICNT), 207.

Lord [κύριος in the LXX] alone will be exalted *in that day* [ἐν τῇ ἡμέρᾳ ἐκείνῃ, identical in 2 Thess 1:10]." In Isa 2, the day of the Lord is a day both of salvation for "many peoples" and destruction for the idolaters. "Whatever the nature of their present circumstances, with all the difficulties and suffering, Paul reassures them that they themselves will be among those who witness God's judgment on their enemies."[36]

1:11 That is why we pray all the time for you, that our God might consider you worthy of [his] calling and powerfully bring to completion his whole will, to accomplish goodness [through you], and [to complete] the work that comes from [your] believing (εἰς ὃ καὶ προσευχόμεθα πάντοτε περὶ ὑμῶν, ἵνα ὑμᾶς ἀξιώσῃ τῆς κλήσεως ὁ θεὸς ἡμῶν καὶ πληρώσῃ πᾶσαν εὐδοκίαν ἀγαθωσύνης καὶ ἔργον πίστεως ἐν δυνάμει). Paul now brings the section to a close with 1:11 – 12, a prayer report that forms an *inclusio* with 1:3, "We are under obligation to give thanks to God all the time because of you." Yet it is at this point that thanksgiving gives way to intercession. "For this reason" or "that is why" is formed from the preposition "because of, for" (εἰς) with its relative pronoun "which" (ὅ).[37] "We pray" (προσευχόμεθα) refers to the literal plural of Paul, Silas, and Timothy. As in 1 Thess 1:2, they pray "all the time" (πάντοτε) and "for you" (περὶ ὑμῶν), although 1 Thess 1:2 adds "everyone" of you.

"That" (ἵνα) is not used to show purpose but rather the content of the prayer: "We pray *that* this will happen."[38] Again, Paul assumes that their prayers actually influence the quality of life that the Thessalonian disciples will live out before God. That is to say, these prayers are not harmless, homogenized religious language or petitions limited to issues such as health or employment. In answer to their prayers, God himself might act to effect their sanctification; that is, the Thessalonians will become different people.

There are two petitions. The first is that "our God might consider you worthy" (ὑμᾶς ἀξιώσῃ … ὁ θεὸς ἡμῶν). "Consider worthy" (ἀξιόω) is, like "consider worthy" (καταξιόω) in 2 Thess 1:5, judicial language.[39] Worthy of what? Of the "call" (τῆς κλήσεως), with "of God" or "his" being implicit.[40] The fact of being "called" or "summoned" lies prior to their Christian experience. It comes through the preaching of the gospel (2 Thess 2:14). God calls Christians to his future kingdom (1 Thess 2:12), to live in moral purity (4:7) and to suffer (implicit in 2 Thess 1:5, among others). Paul speaks of living in a manner worthy of God's call, as he did in 1 Thess 2:12; Paul and his team taught the Thessalonians "to walk worthy of the God who called you." In the future, so we infer from 2 Thess 1:5, 11, God will determine whether they have walked worthily.

The second petition is that God might "powerfully bring to completion" (πληρώσῃ) that which was already begun.[41] The implied subject is again God, as befits a prayer request. This is patently an eschatological statement: while God will continue

36. Fee, *Thessalonians*, 262.

37. This is what Wallace calls an "Adverbial/Conjunctive Use" of the relative, used after a preposition. "In such instances, the [relative pronoun] either has no antecedent, or else its antecedent is conceptual, not grammatical." Wallace, *Grammar*, 342. He mentions this verse as an example.

38. See BDAG, ἵνα 2. a. γ. See also Matt 24:20; 26:41; Mark 14:35.

39. See BDAG, ἀξιόω; Green, *Thessalonians*, 296. LSJ too says that when the verb ἀξιόω is used with the accusative and the genitive, it means to "think *the accusative* worthy of *the genitive*." W. Foerster, however, says that solely "in view of the significance of κλῆσις," ἀξιόω does not mean to judge worthy but "1. 'To make worthy.' This meaning must be accepted in the case of 2 Th. 1:11." See "ἀξιόω, καταξιόω," *TDNT*, 1:380. Perhaps *TDNT* has had an affect on Bible translators, since "make worthy" is how the CEV, ESV, GNB, NJB, and NRSV take it.

40. It is in the genitive case for the same reason we noted under 2 Thess 1:5, that certain words such as "worthy" (ἄξιος) may be followed by the genitive case.

41. BDAG, πληρόω 3; also G. Delling, "πληρόω," *TDNT*, 6:297.

to work through the Thessalonians during this age, he will do so until the end (cf. Phil 1:6, where he uses the synonym, "accomplish, fulfill," ἐπιτελέω).

What comes next suffers badly if it is woodenly translated, as in the NASB, where the apostles pray that God would "fulfill every desire for goodness and the work of faith with power." But, whose desire? What goodness? Who does the "work"? How does power fit in?

First must come the lexical study. The first direct object of their prayer is "desire" or "will" (εὐδοκίαν), a word that causes difficulty. "It is almost completely restricted to Jewish and Christian literature," found typically in the Psalms and other wisdom books.[42] It may mean human "goodwill," as it does in Phil 1:15: "Some preach Christ out of envy and rivalry, but others out of *goodwill*." But this is not the common usage; G. Schrenk notes that "desire" (εὐδοκίαν), while at times applied to human intentions, is a near-technical term for the divine will or plan, synonymous with God's "counsel," "will," "purpose."[43]

This fits in well with other Pauline thought, for example, that living according to the "will of God" (lit. trans.) in 1 Thess 4:3 means living so as to be "pleasing to God" in 4:1. Here too one might assume that it speaks of the divine will since there is no indication to the contrary. If "will" (εὐδοκία) means "the divine goodwill," then "goodness" (ἀγαθωσύνης) must be an objective genitive, that is, the good works that God desires to accomplish in accordance with his purpose. There is yet another parallel to that other Macedonian letter: "for it is God who works in you to will and to act in order to fulfill his good purpose [εὐδοκίας]" (Phil 2:13; see Eph 1:5, 9; cf. 1:11).

Paul also asks that God will bring to completion the "work that comes from your believing" (ἔργον πίστεως). This language is reminiscent of 1 Thess 1:3, where faith produces the Thessalonians' good "works" (see comments on that verse). Here Paul prays that their works of faith will continue on and yield an appropriate harvest for God's judgment. Yet the good works that the disciples will produce are not in the end the fruit of their own dedicated labor, but ultimately a gift of God, for which Paul prays. Their entry into the kingdom is predicated on God's prior action. Decades later, Clement of Rome would agree: "All the generations from Adam to this day have passed away, but those who by God's grace were perfected in love have a place among the godly, who will be revealed when the kingdom of Christ visits us" (*1 Clem.* 50.3; see also 1 Cor 1:8).

The final part of the verse is the prepositional phrase "in power" (ἐν δυνάμει). While it could be attached grammatically to "work," that seems awkward; in these letters it is God who works with power (1 Thess 1:5; cf. 2 Thess 1:7). A better reading would be to attach it to the verb "bring to completion," so God, by his powerful action, makes himself known in believers' lives and takes them into the eschatological future.

1:12 [We keep praying] in order that the name of our Lord Jesus might be glorified among you, and you [be glorified] in [him], according to the grace of our God and of the Lord Jesus Christ (ὅπως ἐνδοξασθῇ τὸ ὄνομα τοῦ κυρίου ἡμῶν Ἰησοῦ ἐν ὑμῖν, καὶ ὑμεῖς ἐν αὐτῷ, κατὰ τὴν χάριν τοῦ θεοῦ ἡμῶν καὶ κυρίου Ἰησοῦ Χριστοῦ). Paul finishes this section of the letter, with its thanksgiving and prayer language, by bringing the apostolic prayer to a close. The verse starts with "in order that" or

42. G. Schrenk, "εὐδοκία," *TDNT*, 2:742–51. Meanwhile, its cognate "good pleasure" (εὐδόκησις) was the preferred form in Hellenistic Greek.

43. See Schrenk, "εὐδοκία," 2:747. "But the aim of this cumulative description [in Eph 1] demands that εὐδοκία should be seen as expressing a special side of this pre-temporal resolve of the divine will."

simply "that" (ὅπως). This word introduces us to the prayer's purpose.[44]

We take the reading that 1:12 is connected with the prayer report in 1:11a, "That is why we pray all the time for you," plus the content of that prayer. This allows this "purpose" verse (v. 12) the fullest possible antecedent as being the whole of 1:11. Thus we follow the NIV: "We pray this so that the name of our Lord Jesus ...," in contrast to most other English versions.

Paul extrapolates further, showing what results the apostles hope for: first, that Jesus' name be "glorified" (ἐνδοξασθῇ), the same verb he used in 1:10, when Jesus comes to be glorified among his holy ones. Here again we find ourselves in the language of Yahweh's epiphany as applied to Jesus: Isa 66:5 LXX (NETS) "that the name of the Lord may be glorified" (ἵνα ὄνομα κυρίου δοξασθῇ). It is seen most clearly when we note how "Jesus" is the added word in the clause: "in order that the name of our Lord *Jesus* might be glorified among you." The Isaiah passage is found in the context of the enemies of God, who hate those people who reverently "tremble at his word." We are also dealing with the language of parousia and may compare Paul with the Synoptic tradition: "Whoever acknowledges me before others, I will also acknowledge before my Father in heaven. But whoever disowns me before others, I will disown before my Father in heaven" (Matt 10:32 – 33); "if anyone is ashamed of me and my words in this adulterous and sinful generation, the Son of Man will be ashamed of them when he comes in his Father's glory with the holy angels" (Mark 8:38).

The second result is more complicated, since it is not clear what should be the antecedent of "in it" or "in him" (ἐν αὐτῷ). Grammatically it could refer either to the neuter noun "name" (τὸ ὄνομα) or to "our Lord Jesus." The first option would be unusual; the second option, chosen by most translations, lies in closer proximity to the pronoun and has the benefit of being more recognizably Pauline language. "Glory" is a resurrection term: Christ comes in glory, and those who are his add to and share in that same glory (see esp. Rom 2:7; 5:2; 8:17 – 21, 30; 9:23; also Titus 2:13). This is synonymous with the reception of eternal (resurrection) life. That "all have sinned and fall short of the glory of God" (Rom 3:23) is at least in part an eschatological statement, that apart from Christ there is no hope of being resurrected into God's glory. The apostles pray that the Thessalonians will experience that eschatological glory.

"According to the grace of our God and of the Lord Jesus Christ" uses typical Pauline names for God and Christ. If it sounds familiar, it is for good reason, for this is "the church of the Thessalonians, which is in God the Father and the Lord Jesus Christ" (1:1). Paul theologically roots the present and future tenses of salvation in the grace of God and Christ; he is also finishing a prayer report, in which the invocation of the divine names is fitting.

Theology in Application

It is to the nature of *eternal destruction* that we now turn. This section will be more extensive than others, given the questions that surround the topic today.

44. See BDAG, ὅπως 2.

Theology in Thessalonica

Before the gospel arrived in Thessalonica, most Jews held to a doctrine of resurrection and final judgment. A few Jews and a few Gentiles believed that the soul did not survive death. Nevertheless, most Thessalonians were sure that the dead were doomed to a dismal, shadowy afterlife as "poor feckless ghosts"; Odysseus reported that "many thousands of ghosts came round me and uttered such appalling cries."[45]

The Christians learned that the true God will punish the wicked and reward the righteous in the end time. Not only will God execute judgment on unbelievers (2:12); his work is properly understood as his "wrath" (1 Thess 1:10; 2:16; 5:9), "unexpected destruction" (5:3), "tribulation" (2 Thess 1:6), and "retaliation" (1:8). The wicked will experience separation from the Lord and "eternal destruction" (2 Thess 1:9).

God was taking special note of Christians and would not ignore their sufferings. While the church learned that their persecutors would suffer for their actions, they would be damned for reasons other than their opposition to believers. This is just as Chrysostom explained 1:8: "Paul does not say here 'on those who afflict you,' but 'on those who obey not.' So that not on the Thessalonians' account, but on His own account it is necessary to punish them."[46]

Biblical Theology

Given the deep emotional reactions that are associated with this doctrine, it is imperative to hold at bay as far as possible our prior assumptions and absorb the various texts.[47] It is also a matter of sound exegesis to give due consideration to the readings given these texts by other believers.[48]

The two most viable explanations of eternal punishment in 1:9 and in other passages are:

1. Eternal punishment means that the condemned are damned for eternity and *will experience conscious punishment forever.*[49]

45. Homer, *Odyssey* (trans. Butler), Book 9.

46. See John Chrysostom, *Homilies on Second Thessalonians* 2 (*NPNF*[1] 13:382), which I have paraphrased from the original. Paul's teaching in 2 Thess 1 gave the church a clear sociological identity, as Wanamaker (*Thessalonians*, 88) demonstrates.

47. It lies outside the scope of this commentary to discuss other important points such as the parable of the rich man and Lazarus, the meaning of Sheol and Hades, and the question of whether Christ "descended into hell" between his crucifixion and resurrection.

48. The book edited by W. Crockett, *Four Views on Hell* (Grand Rapids: Zondervan, 1992), does not live up to its full promise, precisely because the authors talk past each other and also focus on the texts that support their position.

49. Commentators on 2 Thessalonians, at least those who express one viewpoint or another, typically favor this interpretation: see Green, *Thessalonians*, 292; Beale, *Thessalonians*, 188–89; Witherington, *1 and 2 Thessalonians*, 196–97; Malherbe, *Letters to the Thessalonians*, 402. According to John Chrysostom, *Homilies on Second Thessalonians 3* (*NPNF*[1] 13:384) — "There are many men, who form good hopes not by abstaining from their sins, but by thinking that hell is not so terrible as it is said to be, but milder than what is threatened, and temporary, not eternal; and about this they philosophize much." He then quotes 1:9 and remarks, "How then is that temporary which is everlasting?"

2. Eternal punishment means that the condemned are damned for eternity, but that they *do not suffer consciously forever.*[50]

While the Bible student should study all relevant texts and consult with the early church fathers, the following are particularly important:

Matt 25:41: "Depart from me, you who are cursed, into the eternal fire prepared for the devil and his angels."

Rev 14:10b – 11a: "[The followers of the beast] will be tormented with burning sulfur in the presence of the holy angels and of the Lamb. And the smoke of their torment will rise for ever and ever."

Rev 20:10 (see also 19:20; 21:8): "And the devil, who deceived them, was thrown into the lake of burning sulfur, where the beast and the false prophet had been thrown. They will be tormented day and night for ever and ever."

Revelation 20:10 indicates that at least one being, if only the devil, will be consciously tormented in the lake of fire for eternity. If the beast and the false prophet are individual human beings as opposed to institutions or metaphors, then at least two human beings can and will be tormented forever. That is, we can treat "eternal conscious torment" as a viable category for human beings. The most crucial text of the lot is Rev 14:10 – 11, since it may possibly give a vital point of information that is not so explicit in the others:

"the smoke of their torment will rise for ever and ever"

This clause may mean:

the smoke from where they will have been tormented (tormented for a span of time, but not forever) *will continue to ascend for ever and ever*;

or,

they will be consciously tormented for ever and ever, and the smoke of that place of torment will therefore also ascend forever.

In comparing Rev 14:10 – 11 with 20:10, the reader should take "the smoke of their torment will rise for ever and ever" (14:11) to have the same time referent as "they will be tormented day and night for ever and ever" (20:10). Revelation 14:11

50. Commentaries on 2 Thessalonians that favor this viewpoint are scarce. Wanamaker, *Thessalonians*, 228, argues against "annihilation." Gaventa, *First and Second Thessalonians*, 105 – 07, does not deal directly with the issue, but she does offer an interesting essay on "Proclaiming Judgment" to a congregation that does not want to think about Christ's fiery condemnation. Within this second viewpoint, some distinguish between "annihilationism" and "conditional immortality." As John Stott writes, "According to [conditional immortality], nobody survives death except those to whom God gives life (they are therefore immortal by grace, not by nature), whereas according to [annihilationism], everybody survives death and will even be resurrected, but the impenitent will finally be destroyed." See David L. Edwards and John Stott, *Essentials: A Liberal-Evangelical Dialogue* (London: Hodder & Stoughton, 1988), 316. Stott's viewpoint must be distinguished from universalism, which holds that all or nearly all will be saved in the end. Interpretation 2 does not properly include Rob Bell's *Love Wins: A Book about Heaven, Hell, and the Fate of Every Person Who Ever Lived* (New York: HarperOne, 2011), which came out too late to be considered in this volume.

makes reference to the rising smoke as an image of the eternal burning, not in order to imply that the smoke keeps rising long after people are burnt up.

Is it fair to reference Revelation in order to explain a letter that was written decades earlier? In this instance, yes; although Paul is a writer of letters and thus works in a different genre, he moves within the thought world of the Apocalypse, and one can find many genuine conceptual parallels between the two. Both have roots in the Lord's teaching, such as Matt 25:41. In addition, for Paul (Acts 23:6; 24:15), as in Daniel (Dan 12:2), the Jesus tradition (Matt 10:28; John 5:25–29), and Revelation (Rev 20:11–13), the damned are resurrected in order to enter eternal punishment.[51] Therefore, the doctrine of eternal hell was not invented only in the second century, after the supposed introduction of the Greek idea that the human soul is immortal. The NT already affirms twin truths: that human beings are by nature mortal *and* that they are able to survive any time in hell because of the resurrection.[52]

With regard to 2 Thess 1:9 specifically, few understand Paul to be speaking of an instantaneous destruction; "destruction" seems to mean "in an ongoing state of being destroyed." Even a conditional immortality viewpoint typically allows that the damned enter into a *process* of perishing, even if their destruction plays out over a long time. This is the point that causes E. W. Fudge to contradict himself. First, says he, "nothing in Paul's language in 2 Thessalonians [1:9] requires or even hints at immortalized sinners or everlasting conscious torment.... They will perish, be destroyed, be burned up and be gone forever."[53] But second, he asserts that "there will be degrees of punishment, and the *destructive process* will allow plenty of opportunity for that ... [but] the unrighteous will all *finally* die."[54]

Here is the problem with that logic: if once it is allowed that the damned may perish over time, not at the instant of Christ's coming, then it must be assumed that they will be transformed in order to endure God's punishment. If, therefore, the resurrected may perish "over time," then logically they could perish forever. The sudden and eternal destruction of 2 Thess 1:9 (and 1 Thess 5:3) is not some instant annihilation of the wicked. Rather, it is the opening chapter of the decisive damnation of the unbelievers to everlasting punishment.[55]

51. So too Justin, *1 Apol.* 8 (*ANF* 1:165). In the second century, Justin Martyr was the most powerful proponent of everlasting torment, see Justin, *1 Apol.* 8, 12, 17, 20, 44.

52. The postapostolic teachers also taught that immortality was an eschatological endowment, not an inherent property of the human race (*Didache; 1 Clement;* Ignatius; *2 Clement;* Hermas; Polycarp; *Martyrdom of Polycarp;* Justin Martyr). See G. S. Shogren, "Mortality and Immortality," *DLNT*, 776–77. *Diogn.* 6.8 seems to be at variance from that consensus: "the soul, which is immortal, lives in a mortal dwelling." This change is probably due to a dependence on the Hellenized Wisdom of Solomon (see Wis 9:15; 16:14).

53. Edward William Fudge and Robert A. Peterson, *Two Views of Hell: A Biblical and Theological Dialogue* (Downers Grove, IL: InterVarsity Press, 2000), 60.

54. Ibid., 82, italics added. On p. 33 Fudge concedes that the wicked will be resurrected to enter punishment, that is, will be given bodies that are capable of enduring hell.

55. See esp. Green, *Thessalonians*, 292; Marshall, *1 and 2 Thessalonians*, 179. We may therefore identify 2 Thess 1:9 as a true parallel to the second-century *Barn.* 20.1, which speaks of "eternal death with punishment" as the destiny of those who follow the "black one"; that is, the concept of "eternal death" is completely in harmony with ongoing and everlasting punishment. Likewise, *Mart. Pol.* 2.3 warns against "eternal torment."

The doctrine of eternal conscious punishment has always been the majority viewpoint. In the last few decades, some prominent evangelicals have expressed their doubts about that traditional interpretation.[56] If such thinkers have not convinced me, it is not necessarily a reflection on their ability or a judgment that they are not good evangelicals; I simply do not find their arguments to be in the end convincing.

Message of This Passage for the Church Today

For the sake of simplicity, we will use the term "hell" to refer to the everlasting punishment by God at the return of Christ. By the same token, we will use "heaven" for everlasting bliss.

Pick up any book about hell; sit down for any sermon about eternal punishment; or even listen in on a dialogue between Christians or between Christians and unbelievers. Almost without fail the Christian will start in with qualifications, apologies, a distancing from medieval conceptions, and an affirmation that God is very loving. In fact, in the Western world the mention of hell seems to be the quickest way to silence a room.

For some, the doctrine of eternal security seems to mean that hell is not a relevant theme for an evangelical congregation; why threaten people with something they will never see? Others say that "people have heard about hell too much. Now they need to hear about grace." Others seem to imply that the sins that merit condemnation are those that are supposedly found outside the church (e.g., homosexuality, abortion) and not those inside. Above all, many pastors may sense that there is extreme resistance to the topic. Whether or not the parishioners pledge to an evangelical faith statement, they might in fact partake of the opinions voiced by typical North Americans that all good people go to heaven; that hell is for people like Hitler; and that, above all else, "I certainly won't go to hell."[57]

Beyond that, there are sociological factors that distinguish the North American church from the church in other times and places; the twenty-first-century Western message is at odds with most other expressions of Christianity.[58]

56. E.g., John Stott, whose evangelical credentials are not otherwise called into question. See Edwards and Stott, *Essentials*, 313 – 20. Likewise, Adventists and other groups have espoused conditional immortality for many years. Sometimes the line of evangelical orthodoxy is drawn at whether one holds to the "literal" fire of hell as opposed to "metaphorical" fire. This is unfortunate, since the Bible also uses other language to speak of the end of the wicked. Yes, hell is like being in fire; but it is also like being a worm-eaten corpse. At other times it is isolation from the Lord and others (2 Thess 1:9; Luke 16:23). In *Four Views of Hell* the editors chose to separate Literal from Metaphorical views of hell and to pit them against each other. In reality, the two views are expressions of the same position.

57. This is based on the research of the Barna Group, "Americans Describe Their Views about Life after Death," Oct 21, 2003, www.barna.org/barna-update/article/5-barna-update/128-americans-describe-their-views-about-life-after-death?q= @#!*%. Its findings: "Most Americans do not expect to experience Hell first-hand: just one-half of 1% expect to go to Hell upon their death. Nearly two-thirds of Americans (64%) believe they will go to Heaven. One in 20 adults (5%) claim they will come back as another life form, while the same proportion (5%) contend they will simply cease to exist."

58. The martyrs of Smyrna persevered in their suffering because of the doctrine of hell: "And turning their thoughts to the grace of Christ they despised the tortures of this world,

1. We live in a society where events that in other times and places might be interpreted as signs of God's wrath — plague, famine, storms, floods, drought — are (a) physically mitigated, so that even those who suffer directly can usually find food and shelter; (b) interpreted solely in scientific terms rather than theological; (c) attributed solely to human foolishness, such as ecological carelessness, as opposed to sin against God.
2. We live in a shrinking world, meaning that it is harder to relegate faceless masses on other continents to hell. In a global community, more and more of the lost have faces.
3. We also live in a world where the centuries-long battle between Islam and "Christendom" has resurfaced, meaning that a statement about the Muslim lost is naturally lent more geopolitical significance than we might wish.

How, then, might we reform our approach and preach about eternal condemnation as the apostles would have done, in the face of the belief system of North America?

1. We must take sin more seriously and preach about it more openly, showing why it merits God's eternal punishment.
2. We must preach against all sin, giving plenty of attention to those sins likely to have been committed within the congregation, not just those of people outside the church.
3. We must go to extraordinary lengths, given the difficulty of preaching about hell, to explain it clearly and appropriately. See "In Depth: How to Show Hell's Relevance."
4. We must emphasize that hell is by default the destiny for all, not simply for the extraordinarily wicked.
5. We must take away from church attendees the notion that their decision to raise their hand to receive Jesus and attend church is a guarantee against hell.
6. We must emphasize that works condemn, but that salvation is in Christ alone. This runs contrary to the shared opinion of many North Americans, including many evangelicals, who view heaven as the destiny for good or sincere people.

purchasing at the cost of one hour an exemption from eternal punishment. And the fire of their inhuman torturers felt cold to them, for they set before their eyes the escape from that eternal fire which is never extinguished" (*Mart. Pol.* 2.3). See other early patristic references to get an idea of how the doctrine of eternal punishment was applied in different situations: *1 Clem.* 11.1 – 2; Herm. *Sim.* 9.18.2; Justin, *1 Apol.* 17.

IN DEPTH: How to Show Hell's Relevance

One time I wanted to get the threat of hell across to people in their late teens and early twenties, people who I suspected might be immune to a "hell-fire" sermon. I wanted to catch them off-balance, and so as I prepared, I put some questions to some people from that age. They emphasized how young people are driven to be connected with others. They mentioned the communication media in particular.

I decided to preach on how hell means being isolated in the "outer darkness."[59] I pointed out that "hell as fire" is important, but that Jesus, Paul, Peter, and Jude also spoke of the fate of the damned as being "cut off from the presence of the Lord" or as "outer" or "eternal darkness":

> Some people think that death is nothing, that you just click off and you're done. No — for a person without Christ, it's being in darkness, but you're still conscious forever. Imagine going down to a dark basement with a flashlight and then there is no flashlight, and your eyes never get adjusted ... but you're still there. There are worse things than ceasing to exist. And living in the outer darkness is not in a nice sense of "I'd like some down time by myself." Rather it's "I'll never be in touch with anyone again." Whatever our dead heroes are doing now [I had spoken about a rock singer who had died of a drug overdose], they're not keeping in touch with their friends. You think our church is picky about turning off your cell phones? Well, in hell they make you check your devices at the door: no texting, no cell phone, no Facebooking, not even email, no face-to-face, no sharing a cappuccino and comparing notes on the afterlife! "See you in hell"? No, you won't....

I joked that my subtitle was "Will There Be Texting in Hell?" It might be hard for some of us older folk to imagine, but for some people being disconnected and forgotten is infinitely more horrifying than the lake of fire ... and it is equally biblical.

59. This is the polar opposite of Sartre's "hell is other people." See Jean-Paul Sartre's famous play *No Exit* (1944).

CHAPTER 10

2 Thessonians 2:1 – 12

Literary Context

In 2 Thess 1, Paul has spoken about Christ's return to punish the wicked, using vivid language of judgment. But he cannot end his letter there, since Timothy brought back a question regarding the time of the end. Paul ties together language of the return of Christ from his own oral teaching, the Matthean tradition, Daniel, and 1 Thessalonians. Yet the modern reader must interpret the passage with only an incomplete knowledge of Paul's earlier teaching. We are confronted with a puzzle with pieces missing, but we are not sure how many there are or what they contain. Nevertheless, Paul's main interest is clear: Christ will come to judge the wicked, avenging his people. If people follow the devil's lies, it is the sure sign that they are outside the people of God.

The description of the Man of Lawlessness might seem disproportionate to the problem. After all, Paul could have simply stated that the Apostasy and the Man of Lawlessness must precede the day of the Lord; therefore, the Day has not come. Yet he continues in 2:4 – 12 with a recital of the "restrainer" doctrine, a declaration of how the Man of Lawlessness will be destroyed, and an assertion of how this evil has its source in Satan. In so doing, he demonstrates that the whole section plays an important role in the greater message of the letter: there is righteousness, and there is evil. God is just and true and the devil is a deceiver. Some follow Christ, but most remain under satanic deception. Above all, the gospel is the message that rescues people such as the Thessalonians (2:13 – 17) and might have success in the apostles' Corinthian mission (3:1 – 2).

II. Thanksgiving and Prayer for the Believers in Tribulation (1:3 – 12)

➡ **III. Instruction concerning the End Times (2:1 – 12)**

A. The Thessalonians must not become confused about the end of the age (2:1 – 3a)

B. The apostles remind them that they already possess the information they need to stay on course (2:3b – 12)

IV. A Second Thanksgiving, an Exhortation, and a Prayer for the Thessalonians (2:13 – 17)

Main Idea

The Thessalonians should not be shaken by a rumor that the day of the Lord is upon them. That event will not arrive before the coming of the Apostasy and the Man of Lawlessness. They should remember that lies, deceit, and confusion about the Lord's return are always a possibility and that they are due to satanic machinations.

Translation

(See next two pages.)

Structure

With "and now" (δέ) Paul moves from presenting eschatological justice to handle the central doctrinal issue of the letter: confusion about the coming of the day of the Lord. Paul seizes the attention of his readers with "we appeal to you, brothers and sisters." Rather than go immediately to the specific point — *has the day of the Lord come?* (2:2e) — Paul makes the listeners wait through several further clauses, with each one making them pay closer and closer attention. This issue has to do with (ὑπέρ) the parousia, which is also the "gathering" of the saints; for the latter Paul harks back to language of the previous letter (1 Thess 4:14) and probably also the Olivet tradition (Matt 24:31).

Paul urges the believers (2:2) not to fall for misleading information, which might come through different media: perhaps a prophecy or a letter. He also summarizes the point in 2:3a: "let no one deceive you in any way." While the immediate problem for the Thessalonians was whether the end was nigh, the overarching theme of 2:1 – 12 is "every kind of unrighteous deception" (2:10a), which is fostered by Satan. Paul's audience for their part must realize that confusion about the day of the Lord is not simply a minor misunderstanding; it is part of a larger satanic scheme to spread lies and to lead people away from God, right up until the moment of Christ's coming.

Thus "Satan's deception" is the real problem in Thessalonica. On that basis the reader may see more readily that the chapter is not principally about the Man of Lawlessness or the restrainer. Rather, Paul's point in giving out all this detail is summed up in his abrupt statement in 2:3a: "let no one deceive you in any way." He will also remind them that he had already forewarned the Thessalonians about the end times (2:5, 6a). If the seed of deceit has been planted in the church, a good apostle knows he must sweep it away before it does more harm.

Paul uses an ellipsis in 2:3b, that is, an incomplete sentence: "because if there has not first come the Apostasy and the Man of Lawlessness is revealed. . . ." While this is technically incorrect syntax, Paul was not averse to using ellipsis when his thoughts

2 Thessalonians 2:1 – 12

1a	Entreaty	And now **we appeal to you**, brothers and sisters,
1b	Reference	with respect to the coming of our Lord Jesus Christ,
1c	Reference	when [God] gathers us together to [Christ],
2a	Entreaty	**that you not be quickly shaken or disturbed,**
2b	Means / List	whether "through the Spirit" or
2c	List	through a message or
2d	List	through a letter coming, supposedly, from us,
2e	Content of 2b, c, d	[through anything that says] that the day of the Lord has come.
3a	Entreaty	**Let no one deceive you** in any way,
3b	Cause	because [it will not come]
3c	List / Condition	if there has not first come the Apostasy and
3d	List	the Man of Lawlessnesss is revealed,
3e	Identification	the son of destruction.
4a	List/ Identification	He is the one who opposes and
4b	List	exalts himself over any so-called god or religious object,
4c	Result	so that he installs himself in the sanctuary of God,
4d	Result	proclaiming himself to be a god.
5	Reminder language	**Do you not remember that when I was with you I told you these things?**
6a	Reminder language	And as it is, **you know what it is that restrains [him],**
6b	Purpose	in order that he be revealed
6c	Time	in his right time.

7a	Cause	For **the hidden force of lawlessness is already at work**;
7b	Condition	only **the one who now restrains it [will do so]**
7c	Time	until he is taken away.
8a	Sequence	And then **the Man of Lawlessness will be revealed**,
8b	Identification	whom the Lord [Jesus] will kill
8c	Means	by the breath of his mouth and
8d	Identification	destroy
8e	Means	by the glorious appearance of his coming.
9a	Assertion	The coming [of the Man of Lawlessness] is
9b	List / Means	by the powerful influence of Satan,
9c	List	with all power and signs and wonders that mislead and
10a	List	in every [kind of] unrighteous deception
10b	Disadvantage	for those who are perishing.
10c	Cause	[This is] because they did not receive the love for the truth
10d	Result	so that they might be saved.
11a	Result (of 10c)	And so **God will send them a powerful influence of deception**
11b	Result (11a)	so that they believe a lie
12a	Result or Purpose	in order that all might be judged,
12b	Identification	[all who] do not believe the truth but
12c	Identification	take pleasure in wickedness.

ran ahead of his grammar: *The final Apostasy and the ultimate sacrilege of the Man of Lawlessness must precede the day of the Lord (2:3 – 4); thus, the day of the Lord could not have come already.* Paul does not give further details about a final Apostasy, but he does go on to describe this man, using language from Daniel and the Synoptic tradition.

He continues to describe the flow of events. The restrainer is active now (2:6); he will work until the removal of the restraint (2:7). The key phrase is coming next, to contrast with present time in 2:6: "and then" (καὶ τότε) — then and only then! — the Man of Lawlessness will be revealed (2:8). Paul then returns (2:8) to the rough style he displayed in 1:6 – 10, and for the same reasons: he is speaking parenthetically and also touching on snippets of biblical language. The Man of Lawlessness will be killed by the Lord Jesus at the parousia.

This man is an important character in this chapter, because the apostle needs to play off his absence in order to prove that the restrainer is still in place and that the day of the Lord cannot have arrived. These are not piquant topics for a conference on eschatology; rather, people are heading toward eternal destruction (1:8) because they do not believe the true gospel and us are not saved (2:10). What the Thessalonians have just experienced in 2:1 – 2, what could be shrugged off ("How silly of me! I thought the world was coming to an end!"), was, when writ large, the same dynamic by which their pagan neighbors would face God's fiery wrath.

Verse 11 describes further this theme, but, perhaps shockingly, it includes deception sent by God. God will influence them to believe lies, "with the result that" or "in order that" (the use of ἵνα in 2:12a is not clear) they all might be judged by him. The perishing of the lost is the mirror image of the gospel: the wicked have faith, but the object of their belief is a lie (2:10 – 11a). They follow not Christ but Satan, although most of them unwittingly; they will not be saved but will perish (2:10, 12). Thus Paul concludes by distinguishing as strongly as he can between two groups: those who receive the truth, and those who believe the lie. The apostles thank God at the start of the next section (2:13) for the salvation of the Thessalonians through belief in the truth. But may no Thessalonian Christian believe even a "little white lie" of Satan when he makes a misleading suggestion about the timing of the end!

Exegetical Outline

➡ **I. The Thessalonians Must Not Become Confused about the End of the Age (2:1 – 3a).**

A. Their focus is the parousia of Christ and the gathering of the church (2:1).

B. It is possible that false information has distressed the church, namely, that *the Day of the Lord is at hand* (2:2).

C. They must guard against being deceived (2:3a).

II. The Apostles Remind Them That They Already Possess the Information They Need to Stay on Course (2:3b – 12).

A. The end-time Apostasy and the revelation of the Man of Lawlessness will precede the day of the Lord (2:3b-e).

B. The Man of Lawlessness will commit the ultimate sacrilege of setting himself up as god over all other religion (2:4).

C. The Thessalonians already know all this from Paul's oral teaching (2:5).

D. The "restrainer" will hold the Man of Lawlessness back until the proper time (2:6 – 8a).

E. The Lord Jesus will destroy the Man of Lawlessness at his parousia (2:8b-e).

F. The Man of Lawlessness will come with satanic power — signs, wonders, deception of unbelievers (2:9 – 10a).

G. If unbelievers are deceived, it is because they reject the gospel (2:10b-d).

H. In addition to satanic deception, God himself will confirm unbelievers in their deception (2:11 – 12).

Explanation of the Text

2:1 And now we appeal to you, brothers and sisters, with respect to the coming of our Lord Jesus Christ, when [God] gathers us together to [Christ] (Ἐρωτῶμεν δὲ ὑμᾶς, ἀδελφοί, ὑπὲρ τῆς παρουσίας τοῦ κυρίου ἡμῶν Ἰησοῦ Χριστοῦ καὶ ἡμῶν ἐπισυναγωγῆς ἐπ᾽ αὐτόν). Here is the principal doctrinal teaching of the letter. Unlike 1 Thess 4:13 – 18, Paul indicates that the content is no surprise to the Thessalonians; he is reminding them of what should already have been understood. The theme once again is the parousia (1 Thess 4:15; 2 Thess 2:8), one aspect of which is the gathering of believers to Christ (1 Thess 4:14, 17; 2 Thess 2:1). The apostles (plural) "appeal" (ἐρωτῶμεν) that the Thessalonians be calm and not fall into ungodly panic. We need not imagine that Timothy had kept silent about this theme when he was with the Thessalonian disciples. Nevertheless, Paul also put the truth in writing, so that Timothy might return with a signed letter that would quell any competing opinions.

"Our" (ἡμῶν) is an objective genitive, giving the sense that he "gathers us [ἐπισυναγωγῆς] together to Christ." "God" is the implied subject; it is he who performs this gathering in 1 Thess 4:14. The LXX had used "gather" in a similar way, to refer to the regathering of Israel to their land:[1] "When Jeremiah learned of it, he rebuked them and declared: "The place shall remain unknown until God gathers [συναγάγῃ] his people together again and shows his mercy" (2 Macc 2:7; cf. Isa 27:13).

The gathering of the elect is carried out by the angels in Matt 24:31, using the cognate verb "to gather together" (ἐπισυνάγω). It is the Lord Jesus who gathers the saints: "Jesus Christ might also gather me together with his elect into his heavenly kingdom" (*Mart. Pol.* 22.3b; see also *Did.* 9.4). The two primary nouns (τῆς παρουσίας ... καὶ ... ἐπισυναγωγῆς), in a woodenly literal translation would be, "the coming and gathering together" or "the coming, that is, the gathering together." But the Greek syntax of "the coming and gathering" follows the familiar pattern of the Granville Sharp Rule: *article-noun-καί-noun*. This rule indicates that the parousia and the "gathering" should be understood as the same event or as events that

1. As points out Best, *Thessalonians*, 274.

are closely identified. Paul means to say that Christ gathers the church at his parousia, when he also destroys the Man of Lawlessness (see παρουσία in 2:8).[2]

2:2a That you not be quickly shaken or disturbed (εἰς τὸ μὴ ταχέως σαλευθῆναι ὑμᾶς ἀπὸ τοῦ νοὸς μηδὲ θροεῖσθαι). One bad reaction in the face of the coming day of the Lord would be a dangerous sense of "Peace and security!" (1 Thess 5:3). Here is what another false teaching might look like: *the day of the Lord has come … we should panic!* The Thessalonians must be self-possessed. Paul uses litotes (the negation of a negative) in order to make a positive statement (see comments on 1 Thess 1:2): "not quickly shaken" is an indirect wording of a positive, "be steadfast."[3] Grammatically, it is unclear whether they are already experiencing a case of bad nerves or whether Paul is trying to prevent a possibility; the former is more likely to be true and thus "quickly" (the adverb ταχέως) may contain a subtle rebuke. These Christians were well-versed in doctrine, and so they should be slow to embrace false teaching.

Paul is not concerned about two types of anxiety, being "shaken in mind" (σαλευθῆναι … ἀπὸ τοῦ νοὸς) and also "disturbed" (θροεῖσθαι).[4] Rather, this is another example of the hendiadys so common in these letters, where two words refer to the same thing. The verbs "shaken" and "disturbed" in other contexts could refer to physical movement; here they refer to a psychological state. Few commentaries appreciate that Paul is echoing the eschatological vocabulary of Jesus. "Shaken" (σαλεύω) is a sign of the impending appearance of the Son of Man in Matt 24:29, that the powers of heaven (in context, the sun, moon, stars) will be "shaken" in the physical sense. Jesus in turn is alluding to Joel 2:10 LXX (see similar language in 4:16 LXX = 3:16 MT), which uses a synonymous verb for "shaken."

"Disturbed" (θροέω) too is known language from the Matthean eschatological discourse, where Jesus warns the disciples, in the face of some initial signs of trouble, "not to be alarmed" (Matt 24:6). It is a scriptural truth that when Satan is unable to harm the saints by persecution (1 Thess 3:3), he tries to neutralize them by confusion. Paul is foreshadowing that which is implicit in 2:3 and explicit in 2:5, that they have already received the appropriate apostolic teaching and possess a solution to any anxiety that the devil might send along.

2:2b-d Whether "through the Spirit" or through a message or through a letter coming, supposedly, from us (μήτε διὰ πνεύματος μήτε διὰ λόγου μήτε δι' ἐπιστολῆς ὡς δι' ἡμῶν). Paul mentions three media by which the Thessalonians might be led astray. The first two are worded vaguely — perhaps because they are Pauline idioms that are already known, perhaps because Paul wants to cover all possible contingencies. The Pauline use of "spirit/Spirit" (πνεῦμα) refers to the Holy Spirit unless there is evidence to the contrary.[5] The language is parallel to 1 Thess 5:19 – 20 (see comments there), making this phrase "through the Spirit by a word of prophecy" (thus the REB's "prophetic utterance"). The congregation should in theory have been able to identify and reject false prophecy all on its own without additional apostolic help (1 Thess 5:21 – 22; cf. 1 Cor 14:29).

2. Wallace expresses some doubts about applying the Granville Sharp Rule to this verse, since the two nouns in question refer to impersonal events rather than to a person; see *Grammar*, 290. He concludes "This is not to say that one could not see a post-tribulational rapture in the text, for even if the words do not have an identical referent, they could have simultaneous ones."

3. The English versions interpret the infinitive clause as indirect discourse, that is, a command that is embedded in the sentence beginning with "we appeal" (ἐρωτῶμεν) in 2:1.

4. As suggests Fee, *Thessalonians*, 273.

5. The translation "a spirit" of the NASB does not reflect the Pauline idiom.

The second clause is harder, given the broad meaning that "word" (λόγος) could have. When this verse is compared with 1 Thess 1:5 and 2 Thess 2:15, it suggests an oral communication. "A message" (διὰ λόγου) could be a message allegedly from the apostles; or, again, a supposed "revelation" (as the NLT); or any other type of communication, even "preaching" (GNB).

The third point, "through a letter" (δι' ἐπιστολῆς) is clearer language. "As if" (ὡς) denotes that which is "objectively false or erroneous,"[6] in this case, erroneously said to have come from the apostolic team. A letter's authenticity could not be confirmed by a quick phone call. It would be simple enough for a rival or opponent of Paul to string together language with enough of a Pauline feel to fabricate a convincing letter — or at least one that was not readily *dis*provable.[7] In 3:17 we will see how Paul in part resolves this problem, by signing his own name. In 2:15 Paul affirms that the Thessalonians should heed the authentic apostolic teaching given by word of mouth or by (authentic) letter; he is not willing to give up on the epistolary medium, which in the early 50s was just beginning to mature into a major teaching tool.

Why does Paul give this warning about false teaching? Why does he find it necessary to remind the disciples about the end-time chronology? These questions are more difficult than might appear on the surface, especially when one must mentally juggle the chronology of the two letters and the visits of Timothy. It is possible that Timothy had originally (see 1 Thess 3:6) brought back information to Paul concerning their vulnerability to panic. If this is so, the Thessalonians would have fallen into the trap during the period of time *after* Timothy had left them to visit Paul and *before* he returned with 1 Thessalonians. *That is, the church would have had to have fallen into some fresh anxiety even before they had received the first letter.* Part of the difficulty with long-distance conversation by letter was that by the time the church received the answer to one question, new ones had arisen.

Nevertheless, we must not lightly set aside the possibility that nothing of this sort had happened in Thessalonica: that is, that there was never any false prophecy, no "word," and no faked letter, and that Paul was simply guarding against a potential danger.[8] He would know from the Synoptic eschatology that followers of Jesus might interpret fierce but "normal" persecution as a reason for alarm (Matt 24:6a). Hadn't Jesus warned the original disciples not to panic, that despite what looked like eschatological signs, "the end is still to come" (24:6b)? After all, Paul does not single out any actual letter or prophecy; and if Timothy had brought news of one, it might have been mentioned and refuted more specifically.[9] We do not know what caused Paul to write this verse, but whatever was the case, in 2 Thess 2 the apostle is painting with a

6. BDAG, ὡς 3. c.

7. The fourth-century AD "Epistle to the Laodiceans," a complete fabrication, shows the possibilities of what form a forged Pauline letter might take. For example, verses 3 – 4: "I give thanks unto Christ in all my prayers, that you continue in him and persevere in his works, looking for the promise at the day of judgement. Neither do the vain talkings of some overset you, which creep in, that they may turn you away from the truth of the Gospel which is preached by me."

8. Contra Fee, *Thessalonians*, 273; Green, *Thessalonians*, 302 – 3, who believe that there was definitely a rumor going around.

9. The church father Hippolytus tells in his *Commentary on Daniel* 4.19 (AD 235) the story of a man of Pontus who had dreams and announced to his church, "Recognize it, brothers and sisters, that the Judgment will happen in one more year." There was a panic and many left off their work, sold their possessions, and canceled their wedding plans. See Boring, Berger, and Colpe, eds., *Hellenistic Commentary*, 496 – 97. The parallel between Pontus and Thessalonica is striking; nevertheless, Hippolytus's story does not prove that people who were not working in 2 Thess 3 did so because of eschatological speculation.

broad brush because he may not have known from which quarter misinformation had come.

This chapter is one of those passages that prove that a knowledge of Greek does not immediately lay bare the author's intention. In this case, Paul is speaking in a kind of shorthand, in part because the Thessalonians had previously received his oral teaching (2:5, etc.), in part because they have interacted with Timothy already, in part because Timothy can answer any further questions that they have, and in part even because Paul might be reticent about putting in writing what could be seen as anti-Roman sentiment.

2:2e [Through anything that says] that the day of the Lord has come (ὡς ὅτι ἐνέστηκεν ἡ ἡμέρα τοῦ κυρίου). The Thessalonians believed that the day of the Lord and Christ's coming were imminent, as will be demonstrated below. At this spot, many manuscripts (D^2, the Majority Text, and the Textus Receptus), the KJV, and the NKJV read "the day of Christ" instead of the "day of the Lord" (see comments on 1 Thess 5:2 for an analysis of "day" expressions). In favor of "day of the Lord" are all the important older manuscripts. In some dispensationalist circles, this textual variant "the day of Christ" has been used to mean "as if *the rapture* had already come." But that makes little sense, given that Paul's proofs have to do with the Man of Lawlessness and the great Apostasy, signs that in a dispensationalist scheme should not have preceded the rapture. As acknowledged by many dispensationalists, their problem in part is solved by following the better reading, "day of the Lord." See "In Depth: The Critical Text and the Textus Receptus in 2 Thessalonians."

IN DEPTH: The Critical Text and the Textus Receptus in 2 Thessalonians

Since the name of "Christ" is an important textual factor in 2 Thess 2:2, it is worth mentioning here a common attack from the Textus Receptus Only or King James Only factions against critical Greek editions of the New Testament and the translations that rest on them. It is said, for example, that the NIV strikes out the name of the Lord Jesus 178 times, and that this is an attack against his person or authority.

There are several camps that prefer the TR or the Majority (Byzantine) Text. Some do so because of a belief that it better represents the original text than does the critical text. Others go further and create a conspiracy theory, according to which the editors of the critical text have plotted to remove Christ's lordship from the NT.

As a test case, let us examine 2 Thessalonians. Jesus, by whatever combination of names, is referenced some twenty-two times.[10] Of these, eighteen times show no difference whatever between the 1550 Elzevir version of the TR and the latest critical edition, NA^{27}.

10. These references are: 2 Thess 1:1, 2, 7, 8, 9, 12 (2x); 2:1, 2, 8, 14, 16; 3:1, 3, 4, 5 (2x), 6, 12, 16 (2x), 18.

There are four verses that do show a change between the editions:

- "our Lord Jesus Christ" in the TR is "our Lord Jesus" in the critical text (1:8)
- "our Lord Jesus Christ" is "the Lord Jesus" (first reference in 1:12)
- "day of Christ" is "day of the Lord" in 2:2
- "the Lord" is "the Lord Jesus" in 2:8 (i.e., the critical text has the additional name "Jesus")

These differences are not due to some whim of the editors but are based on what are considered to be the better manuscripts of the NT. In addition to that principle, one might add the demonstrable fact that over the centuries, pious scribes tended to expand the divine names as they copied manuscripts, for example, augmenting "Jesus Christ" into "the Lord Jesus Christ." A good example of this is found in 1 Cor 5:4, where "our Lord Jesus Christ" (first reference) is "our Lord Jesus" in earlier manuscripts. Of the twenty-two examples in 2 Thessalonians, the main significant difference between the TR and the NA^{27} is from "day of Christ" to "day of the Lord." Twice "Lord Jesus Christ" becomes "Lord Jesus," but the critical text leaves in "Christ" the other nine times! The other change in 2:8 actually *expands* the divine name from "the Lord" to "the Lord Jesus." In addition, it should be noted that the critical text contains a reference to "the Lord Jesus Christ" in 1 Thess 1:1, a reference that is missing from the TR. These sorts of data stretch the imagination of conspiracy theorists, who must explain why those in the plot to diminish the person of Christ did such slipshod work.

The Day will come "like a thief in the night" in 1 Thess 5:2 (see comments). It comes as a destroying thief to those unprepared for Jesus' coming. The believer for his or her part *may be startled by the event*, but must focus on staying alert to face the Lord on his Day. For the believer, the day of the Lord will primarily be salvation; for the unbeliever, it is judgment.

The rumor that is (or might be) circulating was a distortion of Paul's own eschatology. The principal interpretations of 2:2 are:

1. *The day of the Lord has arrived already.*[11] Most English versions have one form or another of "has come" or "is here."
2. *The day of the Lord has drawn near.* A few translations follow this viewpoint (e.g., the KJV has "is at hand").[12]

The rendering of the NLT, "has already begun," perhaps represents a hybrid of the two interpretations — *it has started, it is in the process of being fulfilled, and will arrive fully in the future.*

Much hangs on the translation of the principal verb. "Has come" (ἐνέστηκεν) is the perfect tense of ἐνίστημι, a verb sometimes used for the arrival

11. Best, *Thessalonians*, 276, translates "is present." Malherbe, *Letters to the Thessalonians*, 417, "has come." Fee, *Thessalonians*, 273, goes with the translation "has come," but admits that we cannot know what the errorists meant by it.

12. So A. Oepke, "ἐνίστημι," *TDNT*, 2:544; Green, *Thessalonians*, 305.

of an event. The future tense is used of an eschatological event in 2 Tim 3:1 (KJV): "in the last days perilous times *shall come*." This is clearly a case where fuller lexical study is needed. To begin with, BDAG suggests the possibility of "to be about to occur, w[ith the] connotation of threatening, *be imminent, be impending*." The problem is that the examples given are ambiguous at best and could just as easily be rendered "to be present."

Pressing further, however, one discovers that the LSJ lexicon has firmer evidence for the definition "to begin" or "to be at hand."[13] For example, Polybius, *Hist.* 1.71.4 (trans. Shuckburgh), says: "They were *confronted by* [lit., "it was impending," imperfect tense of ἐνίστημι] an outbreak of war still more difficult and formidable" (see also *Hist.* 3.97.1). That is, while the verb typically means *to come*, in a few cases it means *to be impending*.

In addition to the lexical evidence, the early versions reveal that the church understood the verb as "is imminent." For example, the Latin Vulgate has "*instet*" (from *insto*) = "is at hand." Augustine, using the Old Latin (also "*instet*"), unpacked the clause to mean "the coming of the Lord was already at hand" and "the imminent approach of the last day."[14] Chrysostom, preaching to a *koinē*-speaking audience, said: "Here he seems to me to intimate that certain persons went about having forged an Epistle, as if from Paul, and showing this, said that the Day of the Lord is at hand, that thence they might lead many into error."[15] When he paraphrases Paul, Chrysostom uses a verb that clearly means "to be at hand" (ἐφίστημι) rather than Paul's "has come" (ἐνίστημι). In other words, Chrysostom equated the two compound verbs, interpreting the false teaching as *the day of the Lord is near, but not now present.*

A final lexical datum comes from the rumor mentioned above, from the second century AD. Hippolytus tells the story of a man of Pontus who had dreams and announced to his church, "Recognize it, brothers and sisters, that the Judgment will happen in one more year." Hippolytus summed up the man's teaching with "they heard him as he said that the Day of the Lord is near."[16] The Greek text is identical to that of 2 Thess 2:2e. It is likely that the letter's text had shaped the language of the false prophet or Hippolytus or both. Of great importance is the fact that it was possible to use the language of 2:2, including the use of the verb in question (ἐνέστηκεν), to say that the Day had not arrived but that it was imminent.

What would Paul have been talking about if it meant (1) "the day of the Lord has come already"? It is unlikely that he could have meant that "the final tribulation period has arrived." In the prophets, the Synoptic tradition, and Pauline vocabulary, the day of the Lord does not include the signs that lead up to that final event. In Matt 24 the Day itself is equated with the coming of the Son of Man or the parousia.

Therefore, some see a connection between this rumor and the doctrine that "the resurrection has already taken place" (2 Tim 2:18, using the adverb "already," ἤδη). That is to say, the Thessalonians have come across a "spiritualizing" interpretation of the day of the Lord. For example, Jewett observes that "the most likely implication of 2 Thess 2:2 is that Christ has already returned, in one form or another, and thus that for the prophetic circle

13. There was a legal meaning of the verb to mean "pending" in the sense of an *ongoing* lawsuit in the present time, not pending in the sense of an imminent event. This technical legal sense does not apply in 2 Thess 2:2.

14. Augustine, Letter 199.1.2, found in Gorday, *Colossians, 1–2 Thessalonians, 1–2 Timothy, Titus, Philemon* (ACCS), 108. So too Ambrosiaster, *Commentaries on Galatians-Philemon*, 114.

15. John Chrysostom, *Homilies on Second Thessalonians* 3 (*NPNF*[1] 13:386).

16. Boring, Berger, and Colpe, *Hellenistic Commentary*, 497. Greek text from *Commentarium in Danielem* 4.19.4 (SC).

that issues the oracle, there would be no further need to remain in preparedness for the Parousia."[17] The weakness of this viewpoint is that nothing in the text speaks of radically realized eschatology.

Viewpoint 2, that "the day of the Lord has drawn near," has some lexical data to back it and a great deal of evidence from the context 2:1 – 12. Paul's refutation has to do, not with a spiritualized resurrection of day of the Lord, but with the Thessalonians' inability to correctly apply the chronology of that Day's arrival as given by Jesus and then by Paul.[18] Jesus had warned that "the day" or the "end" (Matt 24:14) would come, but not before other signs took place. He also warned that the disciples might misinterpret the signs of the times as harbingers of the imminent end of the world. As for the Thessalonians, they already know that certain events must take place first. Despite the terror of what is going on around them, they can easily observe that the final Apostasy and the Man of Lawlessness have not yet appeared.

If some sort of radically realized eschatology were the problem in Thessalonica, Paul's response would have been beside the point. As Bruce points out, "it would not have helped the situation for them to be given further futurist eschatology such as is presented in vv 3 – 8."[19] If one objects that perhaps Paul did not understand the false teaching, we must point to 1 Cor 15, where he is entirely adept at parsing the Corinthians' rejection of the bodily resurrection with an appeal to the Scripture, apostolic tradition, logic, and philosophical reasoning. In the case of Thessalonica, the possibility for confusion was reduced almost to nil: Timothy was now on his third trip to them, moving back and forth between the church and Paul and Silas with eyewitness and verbatim descriptions of what he had seen and heard.

Therefore, as nearly as we can tell, rumor had it that *the signs of the end are upon us already! They fulfill the predictions made by the prophets and the Lord Jesus. Therefore the day of the Lord and return of Christ are imminent.* Paul refutes this by showing that, based on what they already know, the day of the Lord and thus the parousia cannot be imminent. If the Man of Lawlessness has not appeared, the "restrainer" is still in place. *Ipso facto*, the day of the Lord has not come, nor is it even necessarily close; thus, they should not be in distress.

2:3a Let no one deceive you in any way (μή τις ὑμᾶς ἐξαπατήσῃ κατὰ μηδένα τρόπον). Paul's language is emphatic, yet not strong enough to be called a rebuke to his readers. Deceit is a tool of the devil, and he will use it up to the very end; this is nowhere more apparent than in 2:9 – 11. Paul once again has strong gospel tradition to stand on: when asked about the end of the age, Jesus' initial response was, "Watch out that no one deceives you" (Matt 24:4); false prophets will lead many astray (24:11). There will come fake parousias, pseudomessiahs, and deceptive signs (Matt 24:23 – 24).

It is fitting that Paul uses the verb "deceive" (ἐξαπατήσῃ), a common verb to describe Satan's tricks. Genesis 3:13 uses the simple form (ἀπατάω) of Eve's accusation of the serpent; Paul uses the compound form here "to deceive" (ἐξαπατάω) and in 2 Cor 11:3, and he uses both verbs in 1 Tim 2:14 to speak of the serpent's deception of Eve. This deception is no mere alternate interpretation that originates from some human teacher; it is a part of the devil's ploy to throw the church into

17. Jewett, *Thessalonian Correspondence*, 100; also; Malherbe, *Letters to the Thessalonians*, 428 – 29. Schmithals, *Paul & the Gnostics*, 203 – 5, roots the error in the Gnostic doctrine of spiritual resurrection.

18. So Best, *Thessalonians*, 276 – 77.

19. Bruce, *1 & 2 Thessalonians*, 166. Also Green, *Thessalonians*, 305, who concludes that "the concern was not about whether the day had already come but its imminence."

bewilderment (see also Rom 16:18) and thus leave it vulnerable.[20]

2:3b-e Because [it will not come] if there has not first come the Apostasy and the Man of Lawlessness is revealed, the son of destruction (ὅτι ἐὰν μὴ ἔλθῃ ἡ ἀποστασία πρῶτον καὶ ἀποκαλυφθῇ ὁ ἄνθρωπος τῆς ἀνομίας, ὁ υἱὸς τῆς ἀπωλείας). Paul gives the information that will help them to calm down: the day of the Lord will come only after two other events.

He uses a causal (ὅτι, "because"), which leads into an ellipsis, an incomplete sentence, literally: "because if there has not first come the Apostasy ..."; there is no "then" clause to follow. The NAB translates it literally, making it an incomplete sentence that concludes with the "reminder language" of 2:5 — " For unless the apostasy comes first and the lawless one is revealed ... — do you not recall that while I was still with you I told you these things?" The protasis or "if" (ἐάν) clause in this context is not some hypothetical possibility, but what Paul states confidently will occur.

The future event is called an "apostasy" or a "falling away" (ἡ ἀποστασία). The word could denote a political rebellion. Josephus used the cognate verb (ἀφίστημι) of Judas of Galilee's "rebellion" against Rome (Josephus, *Ant.* 13.7.1 [§219]). In the LXX, the "fall away" (ἀφίστημι) word group is found everywhere; but the noun form "rebellion" (ἀποστασία) occurs only in Josh 21:22; 2 Chr 29:19; and Jer 2:19 in the canonical books. In the Apocrypha Jews apostatized under Antiochus IV in 1 Macc 2:15 (NRSV): "The king's officers who were enforcing the *apostasy* came to the town of Modein to make them offer sacrifice" to Greek gods. Paul himself was accused of the sacrilege of teaching Diaspora Jews (lit.) "*apostasy* from Moses" (Acts 21:21). The verb form also appears in a warning against apostasy in Heb 3:12 and in the Lukan version of the parable of the sower to speak of those who fall away because of persecution (Luke 8:13). Paul uses ἀφίστημι of the end-time falling away once in 1 Tim 4:1; he uses the noun form (ἀποστασία) only here in 2 Thess 2:3.[21]

Such an end-time falling away was a running theme in the Jewish eschatology. The majority will abandon God's law, while a small remnant will keep itself righteous:

> After that in the seventh week an apostate
> generation shall arise;
> its deeds shall be many, and all of them criminal.
> (*1 En.* 93.9, ed. Charlesworth)

Jesus predicted a final end-time apostasy (Matt 24:10, which uses a synonym for "fall away," σκανδαλίζω). Implicit in 2 Thess 2:5 is that Paul had taught them about the final apostasy while present in Thessalonica: "Do you not remember that when I was with you I told you these things?"[22] The Pastoral Letters have a pair of predictions that may have in part had reference to the immediate future, but which are also expressed in apocalyptic language:

1 Tim 4:1: "The Spirit clearly says that in later

20. Once that is granted that false teaching is not random but part of a conscious deception, one may find a parallel in the world of intelligence-gathering. Espionage is the acquisition of knowledge that the enemy wishes to keep secret. Counterespionage is the attempt to feed the enemy a lie. The clever operative assembles a set of information, most of which is verifiably true, in order to include in those data a falsified datum that will appear by its context to be the truth. So it may have been in Thessalonica. Perhaps the false teaching was in the main true (Christ is coming; the day of the Lord is a day of judgment; Christ will vindicate the righteous and punish the wicked) and in one small part false (the Day is upon us, so panic!).

21. See the overview of this word group by W. Bauder, "Fall, Fall Away," *NIDNTT*, 1:606 – 11. Lampe's *A Patristic Greek Lexicon* shows that in the Greek church ἀποστασία meant "revolt, defection," usually religious.

22. As notes Malherbe, *Letters to the Thessalonians*, 418.

times some will abandon the faith and follow deceiving spirits and things taught by demons."

2 Tim 3:1: "But mark this: There will be terrible times in the last days."

A few dispensationalists have suggested that 2:3 should be translated not as "the Apostasy" but as a "removal" or "departure."[23] To be sure, the cognate verb (ἀφίστημι) has "to depart" as one of its meanings (Luke 2:37; Acts 15:38). But one cannot simply import that meaning into its cognate noun. The noun form (ἀποστασία) is a Jewish and Christian technical term for religious apostasy, being used to describe Judas Iscariot, the Antichrist, and the end time religious rebellion; that is its meaning here.

We have found that Paul's eschatological teaching, while not quoting Matthean tradition directly, seems to track parallel with it in point after point (see the Introduction):

the disciples should not be alarmed
there will come deception and false prophets
many will go apostate
the antichrist figure will appear

Since it refers to a specific eschatological event, we will capitalize the word "Apostasy."[24] Who will apostatize in the end times? The major options are: (1) the world in general;[25] (2) the Jews as a nation;[26] (3) the church.[27]

The difficulty with (1) and (2) seems insurmountable. By definition apostasy is possible only when one has already confessed the faith. This would seem to rule out those who do not affirm Christ. Also, in Matt 24 the recipients of the eschatological teaching are the disciples of Jesus.[28] Due to persecutions and satanic deceptions, they themselves face the danger of falling away from *faith in the gospel*: "many" will fall away, and the one who endures to the end will be saved (24:10, 13). Jesus is describing a heightened danger of "falling away" that he warned about in Matt 13:21.[29] Even within the first years of the church there were people falling into apostasy. A member of Paul's team, Demas, had apparently left the faith (2 Tim 4:10). In Johannine theology, the "antichrist" is eschatological, but his "spirit" is at work among the believers leading them to error and falling away from the community (1 John 2:18 – 19; also 2:22; 4:3; 2 John 7). Around the time of John's letters, some Christians in Pontus (N. Turkey) denied the faith when they encountered persecution. Governor Pliny the Younger recorded:

> Others named by the informer declared that they were Christians, but then denied it, asserting that they had been but had ceased to be, some three years before, others many years, some as much as twenty-five years. They all worshipped your image and the statues of the gods, and cursed Christ.[30]

But there is a positive side taught in Matthew and the Thessalonian letters: Jesus emphasizes that

23. Consult Reiter, *Three Views on the Rapture*, 32. Years ago, dispensationalists Kenneth Wuest and Schuyler English said this was a "departure," i.e., the rapture; see also H. W. House "Apostasia in 2 Thessalonians 2:3: Apostasy or Rapture?" in *The Return: Understanding Christ's Second Coming and the End Time* (ed. Thomas Ice and Timothy J. Demy; Grand Rapids: Kregel, 1999); John Walvoord and most other dispensationalists have rejected the "rapture" interpretation.

24. That this is "the" Apostasy is not due to ἀποστασία having the definite article. Rather, it is the context that shows that it is the final eschatological Apostasy.

25. Bruce, *1 & 2 Thessalonians*, 166.

26. So Best, *Thessalonians*, 282 – 83; Wanamaker, *Thessalonians*, 244.

27. Malherbe, *Letters to the Thessalonians*, 431. Contra Fee, *Thessalonians*, 281 – 82, who rejects the "church" interpretation, not giving due weight to the warnings about apostate disciples in the Synoptic tradition and in 1 – 2 Timothy.

28. It is special pleading to reason, as some dispensationalists do, that the Twelve who listened to the Olivet Discourse should be interpreted as representatives of Israel during the tribulation, as opposed to representative followers of Jesus.

29. See Green, *Thessalonians*, 307.

30. "Medieval Sourcebook: Pliny on the Christians, Letters 10.96 – 97"; see www.fordham.edu/halsall/source/pliny1.html.

"the elect" will not be deceived or fall away. For their sake the days will be cut short (Matt 24:22); the elect cannot be deceived (24:24); they will be gathered up (24:31). Yet the hearers and followers of Jesus must stay firm until the end if they wish to retain the hope of entering the kingdom (24:13; 2 Thess 1:5). Apparently, many Christians will imagine themselves as having a guaranteed place in the kingdom only to find themselves abandoning Christ as the tribulation worsens. Yet again we run into the same tension that one encounters in Matt 13:24 – 25 and the Thessalonian letters: "see that you endure to the end" and "the elect will endure" do not form a contradiction but parallel truths.

The other indispensable sign of the end is the revelation of the "Man of Lawlessness." "Revealed" (ἀποκαλυφθῇ) hints that we are entering into eschatology, as do "in his right time" in 2 Thess 2:6 and "hidden force" in 2:7. The verb is an example of the so-called "divine passive" (he is revealed = God reveals him; cf. also Rom 1:18). God is sovereign over history, and in the end time events his sovereignty grows ever more visible.

The terminology used of this figure (ὁ ἄνθρωπος and ὁ υἱὸς) should be interpreted as references to a *male human being*: first because of these masculine terms, and second because "he" (αὐτόν) in v. 6 is masculine, not a generic "some person." Paul identifies him with the so-called descriptive genitive: the man will be *characterized by* lawlessness. "Man of Lawlessness" is "Man of Sin" (ὁ ἄνθρωπος τῆς ἁμαρτίας) in a number of manuscripts and in the Majority Text; Sinaiticus and Vaticanus support the reading of "lawlessness" (ἀνομίας). The editorial committee of the critical text chose "lawlessness" because of the relative rareness of the word in Paul and because it seems to be presupposed in the "mystery of lawlessness" in 2:7.[31] That lawlessness will increase is another aspect of the Matthean apocalypse (24:12; cf. 13:41).[32] We need not restrict "lawlessness" (ἀνομία) to a meaning such as "without the *Mosaic* law." Rather, it refers more broadly to "the refusal to submit to the authority of God as creator, the refusal to acknowledge God as God."[33] Paul gives a second description: as the "son of destruction" (τῆς ἀπωλείας) he will live under the threat of God's coming judgment. See 1 Thess 5:4 – 5 for the meaning of "child of" in theological language.

Bruce offers the unlikely idea that Paul "does not say from whom or when his readers had heard of the coming of Antichrist; it was part of the common stock of early Christian eschatology."[34] This interpretation might work if the Thessalonian disciples had for some time been plugged into the network of Christian congregations around the eastern empire, absorbing various circulating traditions. But surely at this early chapter in their story, most of what they knew about Christianity had come from the Pauline team. He simply reminds them of what the apostles have already taught them.

2:4 He is the one who opposes and exalts himself over any so-called god or religious object, so that he installs himself in the sanctuary of God, proclaiming himself to be a god (ὁ ἀντικείμενος καὶ ὑπεραιρόμενος ἐπὶ πάντα λεγόμενον θεὸν ἢ σέβασμα, ὥστε αὐτὸν εἰς τὸν ναὸν τοῦ θεοῦ καθίσαι, ἀποδεικνύντα ἑαυτὸν ὅτι ἔστιν θεός). The apostle continues the thought of 2:3, giving greater detail about the identity of this Man of Lawlessness in terms that the Thessalonians know. Paul describes this man with substantival participles: "the one who opposes and exalts himself over." That there

31. Metzger, *Textual Commentary*, 567.

32. As an interesting side note Justin Martyr refers to him as the "man of *apostasy*," thus uniting the two signs of the end found in this verse. See Justin, *Dial.* 110 (*ANF* 1:253).

33. Gaventa, *First and Second Thessalonians*, 111. See also W. Gutbrod, "ἀνομία," *TDNT*, 4:1085 – 86; Malherbe, *Letters to the Thessalonians*, 419.

34. Bruce, *1 & 2 Thessalonians*, 179.

is a tight connection between these two actions is shown by their connection with "and" (καί) and by the omission of the article before the second participle, making this another example of the Granville Sharp Rule.[35] "Opposes" (ἀντικείμενος) carries the sense of antagonism: "he is the enemy of."[36] "Exalts himself" (ὑπεραιρόμενος) refers to an arrogant lifting up of oneself.

The blasphemy of the man is far-ranging, not only against God but against every "so-called god or a religious object."[37] The latter term is broad: "the adversary exalts himself above everything that can be an object of reverent awe. Paul makes his statement as general and comprehensive as possible."[38]

The enemy of God seats himself "in the sanctuary of God." "To sit" (καθίσαι) in this context is cultic; that is, he "installs himself as an object of worship." This interpretation is reinforced by what follows, that he claims that he is a god. The referent of the "temple of God" can only with great difficulty be made to speak of a pagan temple of a god, as if it were some cultic center in Thessalonica. Unless Paul in his oral teaching had indicated otherwise, the hearer would naturally think of the Jerusalem temple, which would stand for two decades more. "Temple" or "sanctuary" (ναός) may refer to the Holy Place plus the inner temple,[39] or it may be restricted to the Holy Place.[40] In the Matthean parallel of the abomination (Matt 24:15), he stands (not "sits") in the "holy place"; Mark 13:14 says it is "standing where it does not belong." Matthew is echoing the language of Daniel, which has as its referent the abomination of Jerusalem by Antiochus IV Epiphanes in 167 BC (Dan 9:27; 11:31; 12:11). Antiochus's sacrilege took place on the main altar, not in the innermost sanctuary (see 1 Macc 1:54 (NRSV): "they erected a desolating sacrilege on the altar of burnt-offering."

The verb "proclaiming himself" sometimes indicates that someone has declared something out loud; here it refers to a demonstration through action (1 Cor 4:9). In some fashion, the Man of Lawlessness communicates his blasphemy "that he is god/God" (ὅτι ἔστιν θεός). This is one of those times when it is problematic in English to refer to the true God with a capital letter and pagan gods in lowercase, for it is not certain what is the point of θεός at the end of this verse. It lacks the article. The Man might be making himself a god or God, and the Greek would be the same in both cases. The NAB renders this "a god," whereas most other English versions have "God."

Making oneself either "a god" or "God" would be apostasy from the truth, so either one could make sense in context. The Man of Lawlessness has already spoken against every sort of deity with the "so-called god," not only against the true God but every other god that he or anyone might imagine, whether as reality or as myth. Other evidence suggests that the NAB is correct and that "a god" is Paul's meaning. This is the meaning of the Seleucid king's name Antiochus II Theos in the third century BC — that he was divine but not *the* God. It was also the significance of the crowd's acclamation of Agrippa I as "a god" in Acts 12:22.[41]

A few short years before the evangelization of Macedonia, the emperor Gaius (Caligula) became

35. See Wallace, *Grammar*, 270 – 73.

36. BDAG, ἀντίκειμαι. See *1 Clem.* 51.1, "the tricks of the adversary."

37. σέβασμα refers to the varied cult objects of the Athenians in Acts 17:23.

38. W. Foerster, "σέβασμα," *TDNT*, 7:173.

39. So Jos., *Ant.* 15.11.3 (§391).

40. So Bruce, *1 & 2 Thessalonians*, 168 (see 1 Kgs 6:5).

41. The Acts account is paralleled, with some differences in detail, in Josephus, *Ant.* 19.8.2 (§343 – 352). Josephus too states that he was acclaimed a god (θεός), a boast that Agrippa did not reject. See too the king of Tyre in Ezek 28:2; most versions have him saying "I am a god," not "God."

mentally imbalanced and made himself a god, taking literally the emperor worship that was growing in vogue in the eastern empire. Because Gaius wished to insult the Jews, he ordered his general Petronius to put his statues in the Jerusalem temple. Thousands of Jews volunteered to lay down their lives in the temple's defense, whereupon Petronius risked his own life and defied his emperor. The noble Petronius was spared by the arrival of news of Caligula's assassination in AD 41.

The NT presupposes that the sin of Antiochus IV Epiphanes is a harbinger of the ultimate, eschatological blasphemy. That connection gives further weight to the interpretation "a god" in 2 Thessalonians: Antiochus did not set himself up in the Jerusalem temple as Yahweh, but he committed sacrilege in the same way that the Man of Lawlessness does. Daniel comments: "The king ... will exalt himself and magnify himself above every god [πάντα θεόν] and will say unheard-of things against the God of gods" (Dan 11:36).

Only within that context of Daniel, the history of the Second Temple, and the Olivet tradition may the reader hope to find the meaning of the Man's blasphemous action. Three notable blasphemers provide us with good parallels: Antiochus IV Epiphanes, the emperor Gaius Caligula, and the Judean king Herod Agrippa I:

- Like Antiochus IV Epiphanes, Gaius, and Agrippa I, the Man of Lawlessness *receives adoration.*
- Like Antiochus and Gaius, he *compels worship.* A parallel in Rev 13:15 states that the "second beast" punishes those who refuse to worship the first beast.
- Like all three of these, the Man of Lawlessness is characterized by unbridled sacrilegious arrogance (see also Rev 13:4 – 6).
- Antiochus and Gaius were set on desecrating the Jerusalem temple; Antiochus succeeded, but Gaius did not. Agrippa was two days journey from Jerusalem when he committed his sin and had no designs of desecrating the temple.

Jesus predicts "the abomination that causes desolation" in Matt 24:15 and Mark 13:14. In Luke 21:20, "the desolation" seems to have become transformed into the destruction of Jerusalem by the Roman army. It seems likely that all three gospels derive from the same teaching of Jesus, with Matthew and Mark retaining more of the Danielic language. We will adopt as a working hypothesis that the text as it stands refers both to the Roman action in AD 70 *and* to an eschatological event; the language, after all, was already fulfilled in Antiochus, and if it is to take place yet again, it might just as well be capable of two future fulfillments — by Rome and by the Man of Lawlessness.[42]

Paul was aware of the incident with Gaius in AD 40 – 41. The Second Temple period had seen a smattering of blasphemers, yet Paul was certain that the worst was still to come. The eschatological Man of Lawlessness, like those monsters before him, will make himself "a god." He will proclaim himself as a supernatural power to be reckoned with, not because of some fresh take on monotheism but because his supreme arrogance leads them into the ultimate blasphemy.

We return to Paul's reference to "the sanctuary of God," which presents the interpreter with number of possibilities.[43]

1. The Second Temple. The language in Daniel undoubtedly refers to the Jerusalem temple. Gaius

42. The fact that Paul seems influenced by Daniel's "abomination that causes desolation" is evidence that Jesus himself made a prediction concerning it in Danielic language, and that the Synoptic passages are not simply prophecies placed in Jesus' mouth by the oral tradition after the actual events of AD 70 — a so-called *vaticinium ex eventu*, or prediction that follows after the fact.

43. See esp. Green, *Thessalonians*, 310 – 13, for the options.

promoted emperor worship around the empire, but the Jews were primarily shaken by its incursion into the temple precinct.[44] An alternative interpretation is that the destruction of the Jerusalem temple is the sign that the Son of Man is glorified, which event takes place in AD 70 (this is a version of the "preterist" position).

2. A third temple, which will be desecrated in the eschaton.[45] This is a highly popular interpretation around the world today, since masses of Christians are convinced that the Bible predicts a rebuilding of the Jerusalem temple as a sign of the end times. A ruler will halt sacrifices in that future temple and then commit sacrilege in it (Dan 9:27).
3. The temple as metaphor. While the "temple" is taken from traditions that deal with the literal temple in Jerusalem, in this prophecy and in Matt 24:15 and parallels we are not speaking of a particular building, either present or future; it is a metaphor of claiming to be god in a broad sense.[46]
4. The temple as heaven. The Man of Lawlessness will try to seize hold of God's temple in heaven, as foretold in Rev 12:7.[47]
5. The true temple, that is, the Christian church (1 Cor 3:16 – 17; 2 Cor 6:16; Eph 2:21 – 22).[48]

Which of these is most likely? Paul does use "temple" to refer to the Christian individual or the Christian church. What is more, #5 might yield a parallel to the final apostasy in 2 Thess 2:3 — Apostasy will take place as the Man of Lawlessness takes over God's place in the church. Nevertheless, there is no evidence that Paul used that metaphor as early as 2 Thessalonians. Neither Daniel, Jesus, nor Revelation indisputably use "temple" as a cipher for "God's people." The case for these two interpretations is not convincing.

According to #4, Rev 12:7 records an attempted coup to take over the heavenly temple. This was apparently the view of Victorinus in his commentary on Revelation from the late second century AD: the fall of Satan "is the beginning of antichrist" and (perhaps also according to Victorinus) the "falling away."[49] This seems an unlikely key to 2 Thess 2:4; the antichrist figure (our Man of Lawlessness) does not show up until Rev 13, not in 12:7. That is, the order of events in Revelation is reversed.

With regard #1, Jesus predicted the coming of false religion both before and after the desolating sacrilege; what interests Paul here is the *final* Apostasy and the Man of Lawlessness, future signs that are unique and unmistakable. He refers to the day of the Lord, the referent of which is none other than the unexpected Day in 1 Thess 5:1 – 2, that is, the time of Christ's parousia and the bodily resurrection of the dead. In addition to this eschatological

44. Wanamaker, *Thessalonians*, 248; Witherington, *1 and 2 Thessalonians*, 211 – 12.

45. This may be the intended meaning of *Barn.* 16.4, which condemns the Jews for trusting in their temple and (apparently) for their plans to shortly rebuild it: "For because they went to war, it was torn down by their enemies, and now the very servants of their enemies will re-build it." The prediction of a third temple is a staple of much popular evangelicalism. The so-called Temple Institute in Jerusalem (see www.templeinstitute.org/) has attracted the attention of those who foresee a third temple. Some Christians who support their goals seem to follow the logic: rebuild the temple, and then the Man of Lawlessness will have something to desecrate; then the tribulation may begin and Christ will shortly come. It is this sort of apocalyptic calculus that the NT discourages and certainly has no place in this or other Pauline letters.

46. Bruce, *1 & 2 Thessalonians*, 169; Best, *Thessalonians*, 286 – 87, since the other positions strike him as too difficult. Contra Wanamaker, *Thessalonians*, 247. The Adventist position may be included as one expression of this "metaphorical" view, see below.

47. James E. Frame, *A Critical and Exegetical Commentary on the Epistles of St. Paul to the Thessalonians* (ICC; Edinburgh: T&T Clark, 1912), 256 – 57.

48. See Beale, *Thessalonians*, 220: "The prophesied latter-day temple has also started to appear in the form of the church community (see on 2:4), into which 2:7 says the antichrist has already begun to enter and defile."

49. Victorinus, *Commentary on the Apocalypse*, on Rev 12:7 – 9 (*ANF* 7:356).

tie-in of the Man of Lawlessness, the church in the second century still regarded the desolation of the temple as future-eschatological.[50]

With regard to #2, the case is built on implication: if there is a desecration of the temple in the tribulation, and if there hasn't been a Jerusalem temple since AD 70, then in the interim it must have to be rebuilt. But nowhere is it predicted in Scripture that someone will rebuild the temple only to see it desecrated in the end. This is one way to read Dan 9:24, but it is only one interpretation.[51] Some try to refute #2 by noting that in the new covenant there is no need for the temple, as in Heb 10:9: "He sets aside the first to establish the second." This is true from the Christians' vantage point, but it does not mean that a temple cannot stand in Jerusalem during the time of the church, as it did for four decades in the first century.

The Adventist position is a version of the metaphorical viewpoint #3: the Man of Lawlessness is the Roman Catholic Church, which was foretold in the "little horn" prediction of Dan 7:25 (KJV) — he "shall wear out the saints of the Most High, and think to change times and laws." This is taken to mean that Rome, so the theory goes, by changing the day of worship from Saturday to Sunday, has committed sacrilege against the law of God, as if it were in the place of God.[52] This interpretation stresses that no one individual can fulfill the prediction of the Man, since its work takes place over centuries, until the coming of Christ. "Claiming to be God," in that case, is not really literal, but rather the claiming of some of God's prerogatives: the right to forgive sins, to be the sole means to salvation, and to demand the total obedience of Christians. The difficulties with this view are: (a) "thinking to change times and laws" is a general statement and could be applied to any number of actions; (b) there is not the least evidence that Constantine changed the Christian day of worship; he merely affirmed the long-standing practice of the church;[53] (c) neither Jesus, Paul, or Revelation link the sacrilege with the abrogation of the Sabbath.

To conclude: the metaphorical view #3 makes good sense of this passage, and it passes the test of Occam's razor, since it must make fewer assumptions than other interpretations.[54] If the metaphorical interpretation is true, then the participle "proclaiming" might be taken as an adverbial participle of means: "he installs himself in the sanctuary of God, *by* proclaiming himself to be a god."[55] Yes, this spiritual crime could be fulfilled within a

50. Irenaeus, *Haer.* 3.6.5 (*ANF* 1:420), "and Antichrist shall be lifted up"; Tertullian, *Res.* 24 (*ANF* 3:563), the Man of Lawlessness will be revealed after the fall of the Roman Empire; Lactantius, *Inst.* 7.17 (*ANF* 7:214 – 15). This puts a large question mark on the preterist interpretation, which implies that no one would think to look for eschatological signs after the day of the Lord had come in AD 70. Yet the earliest of the church fathers continued to regard 2 Thess 2:4 as wholly future. Beyond that, preterists have found a great deal of difficulty in satisfactorily identifying any one historical person as the Man of Lawlessness. Wanamaker, *Thessalonians*, 248, states that "the passage can no longer be understood as valid" after AD 70.

51. J. E. Goldingay, for example, believes that it refers to the consecration of a new holy place under the Hasmoneans. See *Daniel* (WBC 30; Nashville: Nelson, 1989), 260.

52. This traditional Adventist approach is taken by the popular TV program *Amazing Facts*, see www.amazingfacts.org/FreeStuff/OnlineLibrary/tabid/106/ctl/ViewMedia/mid/447/IID/8/LNG/en/7/The-Beast-The-Dragon-and-The-Woman/SC/R/Default.aspx#!; also by The Sabbath Truth Research Institute at SabbathTruth.com. The official Seventh-day Adventist website SeventhDayAventist.org is more politic and does not criticize the Catholic Church as such.

53. Acts 20:7; also Ign. *Magn.* 9.1: Christians are "no longer keeping the Sabbath but living in accordance with the Lord's day, on which our life also arose through him"; also *Diogn.* 4; Justin, *Dial.* 10. See the excellent treatment in *From Sabbath to Lord's Day: A Biblical, Historical, and Theological Investigation* (ed. D. A. Carson; Grand Rapids: Zondervan, 1982).

54. So Bruce, *1 & 2 Thessalonians*, 169; Malherbe, *Letters to the Thessalonians*, 421.

55. Wallace, *Grammar*, 628 – 30. A participle of *cause* might work equally well, see ibid., 631 – 32.

specific temple precinct in Jerusalem, and therefore we need not rule out #2. Nevertheless, the important point of 2:4 is what takes place and when it happens, but not where the blasphemy takes place. Before the day of the Lord, a mere man, energized by Satan, will exalt himself as a god, opposed to and exalted over any other god — including the true God — or any religious object. This interpretation does not make the statement a "mere" metaphor, nor does it in any way lessen the enormity of the deed.

2:5 Do you not remember that when I was with you I told you these things? (Οὐ μνημονεύετε ὅτι ἔτι ὢν πρὸς ὑμᾶς ταῦτα ἔλεγον ὑμῖν;). Reminder language (see comments on 1 Thess 1:5) helps the disciples recall that they already have the answer; it helps to forestall panic in the face of what might have looked like new and puzzling information. As is common in reminder language, Paul uses a rhetorical question: "Do you not remember?" The particle οὐ indicates that Paul is expecting a positive answer ("You remember, don't you?"; μή is its opposite). This teaching device has the effect of giving comfort: *your apostles have already foreseen and provided for your need.*

Paul did not expect the Thessalonians to piece together their eschatology based solely on the data from the two Thessalonian letters. Rather, he draws on his own broader theology, as expressed in his oral teaching. The points that they already possessed were:

- The Apostasy will come before the day of the Lord.
- The Man of Lawlessness will be revealed before the day of the Lord.
- The Man of Lawlessness will set himself up as a god.
- There is a restrainer that keeps the Man of Lawlessness from appearing.
- The Thessalonians know who/what the restrainer is.
- They know that the restrainer is presently doing the work of restraining.

2:6 And as it is, you know what it is that restrains [him], in order that he be revealed in his right time (καὶ νῦν τὸ κατέχον οἴδατε, εἰς τὸ ἀποκαλυφθῆναι αὐτὸν ἐν τῷ ἑαυτοῦ καιρῷ). Paul reiterates the reminder language he has used in 2:5 ("you know," οἴδατε) and returns to the description of the Man of Lawlessness given in 2:3 – 4. But now he adds a new element. The "now" could go with "you know"[56] or the "restraining" (τὸ κατέχον).[57] The syntax of the former is more graceful, and we choose to render it "as it is, you know."

The compound verb "to restrain" (κατέχω = κατά + ἔχω) is critically important in this passage. It appears commonly in the LXX and seventeen times in the Greek NT. Apart from 2:6 and 7, its other appearance in the Thessalonian letters occurs in 1 Thess 5:21, where the church is told to "hold on" to the good that comes through charismatic revelation. This is not its sense in 2 Thess 2, where the meaning is "hold back" or "check."[58] In this verse Paul uses a neuter participle, "that which restrains" (τὸ κατέχον). In 2:7 it changes from a neuter to a masculine.

The restraint is put on the Man of Lawlessness for a purpose, "in order that" only at the due time he should be revealed. "In his own time" (ἐν τῷ ἑαυτοῦ καιρῷ) could be paraphrased as: "in the time that is right for his revealing."[59] As we have

56. So CEV, KJV, NIV, NKJV, NJB.

57. ESV, NASB, NRSV, GNB, HSCB. It is unlikely that Paul is referring to some recent event that had happened "just now," as suggested by H. Hanse, "κατέχω," *TDNT*, 2:829 – 30.

58. So BDAG, κατέχω 1. See, e.g., Luke 4:42; Phlm 13: "I would have liked to *keep* [Onesimus] with me."

59. See BDAG, καιρός 1. a.

noted before, this is the language of apocalyptic; "in order that he might be revealed" means "in order that God will reveal him only when God says that it is his time to be revealed."

2:7a For the hidden force of lawlessness is already at work (τὸ γὰρ μυστήριον ἤδη ἐνεργεῖται τῆς ἀνομίας). Paul explores further the relationship between the delay of the revelation of the Man of Lawlessness and the work of this restrainer. There is a mystery surrounding the revelation of the Man of Lawlessness. In this sort of context, a mystery is a chain of cause and effect that is known to God and made known to humans only through revelation. This too is apocalyptic language; for example, Daniel uses μυστήριον "in a very definite theological sense, that of 'eschatological secret,' the vision of what God has decreed shall take place in the future."[60] Daniel proclaims that "there is a God in heaven who reveals mysteries [μυστήρια]. He has shown King Nebuchadnezzar what will happen in days to come" (Dan 2:28). Satan is propagating lawlessness; nevertheless, that work is appropriated by God to fit into his own program. We might paraphrase Paul: *lawlessness is already at work, but forced to operate in part as a mystery or as it were "underground" until God takes the restraint out of its way.*

The mystery "is at work" or "in operation" (ἐνεργεῖται). The Thessalonian believers were blessed to have God's Word "active" in them (1 Thess 2:13). But Satan too is active. The statement anticipates 2 Thess 2:9, where the coming of the Man of Lawlessness will be according to the working of Satan (the cognate noun "working, operation, action," ἐνέργεια; see also 2:11). We are not told directly how lawlessness is already at work. From these two letters one may learn that Satan works against the apostles (1 Thess 2:18); he tries to deceive Christians (2 Thess 2:1 – 3); and he is confirming unbelievers in their rejection of the gospel (2:10). Beyond that, of course, he sponsors a select group of men who in their arrogance proclaim themselves to be gods: Antiochus IV Epiphanes, Gaius, Herod Agrippa I. In the Johannine language one finds a similar pattern of present activity reaching a future climax. The "antichrist" is at work in the present and in the eschatological time: "This is the spirit of the antichrist, which you have heard is coming and even now is already in the world" (1 John 4:3).

2:7b-c Only the one who now restrains it [will do so] until he is taken away (μόνον ὁ κατέχων ἄρτι ἕως ἐκ μέσου γένηται). Paul completes his thought by reworking what he said in 2:6, harking back to it with "only." It is God's plan that the one that hinders will do so until a point of time; at that moment, the restrainer will be taken aside, and then the Man of Lawlessness will be revealed to do his blasphemous deeds.

"Now" (ἄρτι) belongs to "he who restrains"; it is yet one more "time" word to delineate between *then* and *now*. "Until" (ἕως) goes with the verb "is" (γένηται). The prepositional phrase "from among" (ἐκ μέσου) gives it the idea of moving from the midst or being removed. The reader must be able to think beyond merely human movement in three dimensions; spiritual forces can "restrain" or "be removed" on an invisible plane.

Paul transforms the neuter substantival adjective "what ... restrains" (2:6) to the masculine "the one who restrains" (ὁ κατέχων). Paul may appear to be posing a riddle: "what is it that restrains, is this an 'it' or a 'he'?" This has led many readers to conclude that "he is the Spirit," since Spirit is a "he" but is also represented by a neuter noun "Spirit" (πνεῦμα). Some have taken a different path, that

60. G. Finkenrath, "μυστήριον," *NIDNTT*, 3:502.

Paul is the man, and the "gospel" (εὐαγγέλιον) is the neuter noun. But, without the missing data, this is speculation, and it is next to impossible to interpret the referent of the word based merely on its gender.[61]

As is well known, there are many interpretations of the restrainer: the preaching of the gospel;[62] God himself;[63] more specifically the Holy Spirit residing in the church on earth (with or without the removal of the restrainer as a rapture of the church);[64] civil authority, perhaps the Roman empire;[65] an angelic force or even the devil himself, who holds back the Man of Lawlessness until a time that suits him.[66] The Thessalonians apparently know the answer to this riddle, or at least know more about it than we do. All of our theories must be inferential and based on a humble acknowledgment of our lack of evidence.[67]

One promising direction is to take Paul's thought world as a starting point. He has an apocalyptic worldview, within which God and Satan are at war over the spread of the gospel, particularly because of its spread among the Gentiles and their abandonment of idols. Paul has not "demythologized" the spirit world. In fact, the other example of "restrain" in these letters occurs in 1 Thess 2:18: Satan has hindered Paul and Silas from returning to Thessalonica, using a synonym for "hinder" (ἐνκόπτω instead of κατέχω). The Danielic tradition includes both restraining angels and a blasphemous king, making that book the most attractive candidate as a source for the "restrainer" motif.

In fact, Dan 10 records a battle involving four major angelic figures. Two are from God and two are evil and oppose the others. The first good angel (unnamed) appears and tells Daniel that he was held up for twenty-one days by the "prince of Persia." The powerful angel prince Michael came to help him by holding off the prince of Persia while the first angel went on to Daniel. Then he would return and Michael would fight the prince of Persia as well as the prince of Greece. That is to say, Daniel has a long section that involves angels fighting and blocking one another. Later on, Michael stands up for the people of Israel in Dan 12:1.

This sort of angelic combat occurs also in the NT. In Jude 9 Michael contends with the devil himself for the body of Moses. Michael with his angels expels the dragon and his angels from heaven in Rev 12:7 – 9. There are also four angels who hold back the four winds in Rev 7:1, using yet another synonym for "hold back" (κρατέω). Likewise, an angel is told to let go the four angels bound at the river Euphrates (9:13 – 15). They are released in order to kill a third of humankind. They had been

61. See 1 Cor 13:10 for a parallel exegetical problem: "but when the perfect [τὸ τέλειον] comes." Some readers assume that "the perfect" must be a *thing*; others conclude that if "the perfect" is grammatically neuter, then its referent must be a neuter noun. Neither inference is true of necessity.

62. Oscar Cullmann, *Christ and Time: The Primitive Christian Conception of Time and History* (Philadelphia: Westminster, 1950), 164 – 66; Cullmann appeals to Matt 24:14 and parallels and also understands "he who restrains" as the apostle himself.

63. See R. D. Aus, "God's Plan and God's Power: Isaiah 66 and the Restraining Factors of 2 Thess 2:6 – 7," *JBL* 96/4 (1977): 537 – 53.

64. So House, "Apostasia in 2 Thessalonians 2:3," 162 – 63; Hiebert, *Thessalonians*, 313 – 14. Along with Ryrie, Hiebert makes a razor-fine distinction between the Spirit's "residence" on earth prior to the rapture and his "presence" in every place.

65. A popular view since Tertullian, see *Res.* 24 (*ANF* 3:563): " 'And now ye know what detaineth, that he might be revealed in his time. For the mystery of iniquity doth already work; only he who now hinders must hinder, until he be taken out of the way.' What obstacle is there but the Roman state, the falling away of which, by being scattered into ten kingdoms, shall introduce Antichrist upon (its own ruins)?"

66. Frame, *Thessalonians*, 265; Paul S. Dixon, "The Evil Restraint in 2 Thess 2:6," *JETS* 33/4 (1990): 445 – 49.

67. See the summary by Best, *Thessalonians*, 295 – 301; also Malherbe, *Letters to the Thessalonians*, 432 – 34; Green, *Thessalonians*, 314 – 16. Fee, *Thessalonians*, 286 – 88, shows admirable restraint in identifying the restrainer.

"kept ready for this very hour and day and month and year"; that is, much like the Man of Lawlessness, they were bound by God precisely until his plan was ready, then loosed by him to do their work of destruction. Another passage that yields some light is 9:1 (and probably 20:1 – 3), where an angel holds the keys to the abyss and can lock up or let loose the devil and other demonic beings.[68]

There is thus a substantial amount of background that suggests that in 2 Thess 2 a restraining angel is the agent whom God sends to hold back the work of Satan's man until God's own time.[69] This chapter fits neatly within the image of the jousting and battling between angels that is a part of the apocalyptic backdrop to the Thessalonian letters. It is probable that the Thessalonians had heard from Paul: *A great angel is now restraining the Man of Lawlessness, in order that he be revealed in his right time. Satan is working behind the scenes, pushing for lawlessness; yet the angel will hinder that force until God takes him away.*

2:8 And then the Man of Lawlessness will be revealed, whom the Lord [Jesus] will kill by the breath of his mouth and destroy by the glorious appearance of his coming (καὶ τότε ἀποκαλυφθήσεται ὁ ἄνομος, ὃν ὁ κύριος ['Ιησοῦς] ἀνελεῖ τῷ πνεύματι τοῦ στόματος αὐτοῦ καὶ καταργήσει τῇ ἐπιφανείᾳ τῆς παρουσίας αὐτοῦ). After the removal of the restraint on the Man of Lawlessness, "then" he will be revealed according to God's plan, not just the scheme of Satan. Paul uses the future passive verb "will be revealed" (ἀποκαλυφθήσεται), which in this context functions as the technical language of eschatological unveiling by God.

It is the final end of the Man of Lawlessness that really interests Paul; it will be as sudden as it is certain. Jesus kills him "by the spirit" or better "by the breath" (τῷ πνεύματι) of his mouth.[70] Paul speaks in parallelism, using two future verbs, followed by dative clauses of means or instrument:

> whom the Lord Jesus will kill by the breath of his mouth
> and
> [whom he will] destroy by the glorious appearance [ἐπιφανεία] of his coming [παρουσία].

This is the only NT verse that describes the coming of Jesus using two of the principal eschatological terms, epiphany and parousia. "Appearance" (ἐπιφανεία) was used in the LXX and in particular 2 Maccabees to speak of divine intervention to rescue the saints and to crush their opponents.[71] In broader usage, it was used "to denote any conspicuous intervention on the part of higher powers."[72] More importantly for our purposes, it was used to speak of the glory of God (cf. Acts 2:20) or gods.

Things took a sinister turn in Hellenism when the word group came to be appropriated by arrogant human rulers who were making claims to divinity. One prime example among others is Antiochus IV Epiphanes (lit., Antiochus the Divinely Glorious). The "accession" of Gaius was labeled as

68. There are other references to angels binding someone, such as Tob 8:3, where Raphael binds a demon hand and foot; *Acts Pil.* 22 (*Desc.* 6) (*ANF* 8:437) says of the "harrowing of hell": "Then the King of glory seized the chief satrap Satan by the head, and delivered him to His angels, and said: With iron chains bind his hands and his feet, and his neck, and his mouth. Then He delivered him to Hades, and said: Take him, and keep him secure till my second appearing."

69. This is well argued by Colin Nicholl, *From Hope to Despair in Thessalonica*; see my review in *JETS* 48/2 (2005): 396 – 97. He understands Dan 12:1 to mean that Michael will "step aside" (not, as most understand it, "arise"); that is, he will stop restraining Satan, at which point the church will enter the tribulation. He is followed, cautiously, by Witherington, *1 and 2 Thessalonians*, 208 – 12.

70. For "breath of his wrath" see Exod 15:8; 2 Sam 22:16; Job 4:9; Ps 18:15. All major English versions of 2 Thess 2:8, except for the KJV, have "breath."

71. See Spicq, "ἐπιφαίνω, ἐπιφανεία, ἐπιφανής," *TLNT*, 2:67.

72. MM, 250.

a divine epiphany.[73] The idea that Jesus' coming is an epiphany may in part be an intentional foil of the divine glory being usurped by the Roman emperors: Jesus, not Caesar, is the true manifestation of God's glory. "His visible presence or second coming will be victorious, like that of an emperor who is visiting or making a joyous entry into a city, granting favors (*philanthrōpa*) to his subjects but also punishing his adversaries."[74]

But while it is true that the political background of the day provided Paul with relevant material, it must not be forgotten that within the LXX, as well as in Philo and other Second Temple sources, the word group had deep Jewish roots. Jesus' coming, as seen in 2 Thess 1, was the fulfillment of the prophecies of the glorious coming of Yahweh to judge, to destroy his enemies, and to save. On top of that, Jesus' appearance at the parousia is the coming of Yahweh the true God, the mortal adversary of the eschatological satanic pretender. In addition to 2:8, "glory" is especially characteristic of the gospel and of the coming of Jesus in this letter (see 1:9 – 10, 12; 2:14; 3:1).

Apart from here, "appearance" is found in Paul's letters only in the Pastoral Letters (1 Tim 6:14; 2 Tim 1:10; 4:1; 4:8; Titus 2:13). In 2 Tim 1:10 it refers to the coming of Jesus to earth in the incarnation. Otherwise it has the meaning of a glorious second coming, as in Titus 2:13, "the appearing [ἐπιφανεία] of [his] glory." Some have buttressed their arguments against the authenticity of 2 Thessalonians by pointing out its use of ἐπιφανεία. Just as the Pauline authorship of the Pastorals is attacked because of its use of this supposedly post-Pauline term, so 2 Thessalonians is also put into doubt and dated in the post-Pauline period following the Jewish War. This is hardly a necessary inference. Although Paul typically uses παρουσία, he is hardly wed to that term (see, e.g., "revelation," ἀποκάλυψις, in 1 Cor 1:7, also 2 Thess 1:7). "Appearance" (ἐπιφανεία) could be found throughout Paul's Greek Bible, in other Jewish writings, and in the political language of his day. An apostle writing in the 50s would have had the language of appearing within easy reach as a well-known symbol.

We are not told why God would wish to hold back the coming of the Man of Lawlessness or why at some future point he will allow him to be unfettered. A parallel may shed light; 2 Pet 3:9 – 10 promises that the delay of the end has benefits for humankind: "The Lord is not slow in keeping his promise, as some understand slowness. Instead he is patient with you, not wanting anyone to perish, but everyone to come to repentance. But the day of the Lord will come like a thief." Paul himself will later give details of his theology of "the full number of the Gentiles," a time when the number of non-Jewish believers will reach completion (Rom 11:25). If that is the case in 2 Thess 2, the apostle does not say.

2:9 – 10b The coming [of the Man of Lawlessness] is by the powerful influence of Satan, with all power and signs and wonders that mislead and in every [kind of] unrighteous deception for those who are perishing (οὗ ἐστιν ἡ παρουσία κατ' ἐνέργειαν τοῦ Σατανᾶ ἐν πάσῃ δυνάμει καὶ σημείοις καὶ τέρασιν ψεύδους καὶ ἐν πάσῃ ἀπάτῃ ἀδικίας τοῖς ἀπολλυμένοις). Paul describes the arrival of the Man of Lawlessness as a "coming" (παρουσία), a word that may be used technically of the second coming of Christ or depending upon context, of Paul or of any other person. Nevertheless, the counterbalance between the parousia of the Man of Lawlessness and that of the Lord Jesus indicates that Paul has chosen the word deliberately for contrast.

Not only does the Man of Lawlessness proclaim himself to be a god, he is able to deceive people

73. See ἐπιφανεία in BDAG; LSJ; MM.

74. Spicq, "ἐπιφαίνω, ἐπιφανεία, ἐπιφανής," *TLNT*, 2:67.

through Satan's remarkable working through him. His coming is "in accordance with" or "by" (κατ' from κατά) the powerful influence of Satan.[75] The noun translated here as "powerful influence" (ἐνέργεια) in this sort of context means "working" or "operation," and takes us back to the working of Satan (the cognate verb ἐνεργέω) already during this age (2:7).[76] In the LXX (as in the NT), the noun is used "almost exclusively for the work of divine or demonic powers."[77]

Finally, we are told what has been lurking in the background since 2:3, that it is Satan himself who is the patron of this Man of Lawlessness. The devil is apparently now able to produce more false miracles than he could before the restrainer was removed. Paul's prediction is in full accordance with the Olivet Discourse: there will be *many* false prophets (Matt 24:11; Mark 13:22). According to Mark, the "false messiahs and false prophets will appear and perform signs and wonders to deceive, if possible, even the elect." Luke focuses on those who come in Jesus' name (Luke 21:8): "Watch out that you are not deceived. For many will come in my name, claiming, 'I am he,' and, 'The time is near.' Do not follow them."

In fact, just a few years prior to the evangelization of Thessalonica, one Theudas led a rebellion of Jews against Rome, claiming that he would divide the waters of the river Jordan. Josephus remarks that "many were deluded by his words," but then the Roman army made fast work of him.[78] We assume that Paul knew of the incident, but he does not mark it as an end-time sign or link it to the Man of Lawlessness. For more on the identity of the end-time figure, see "In Depth: Who Is the Man of Lawlessness?"

IN DEPTH: Who Is the Man of Lawlessness?

Paul was but one of the canonical teachers to expound on the ultimate apostate, known originally from the pages of Daniel. The Jewish members of the Thessalonian church may have believed in some sort of eschatological tribulation and antichrist figure before they had even heard of Paul. Recent detailed research shows that a wide spectrum of opinions was circulating during the Second Temple period. The fact that this enemy of God predates Paul is proof against the idea that 2 Thessalonians could only have been written after the fall of Jerusalem or the death of Nero.[79]

75. BDAG, κατά 5. a.

76. It can be attributed to God (1 Cor 12:10 [some mss]; Eph 1:19; 3:7; Col 1:29; 2:12; 2 Thess 2:11) or to Satan, but always used "of transcendent beings" (BDAG, ἐνέργεια).

77. G. Bertram, ἐνέργεια, *TDNT*, 2:652.

78. Josephus, *Ant.* 20.5.1 (§97 – 99).

79. Brant Pitre, *Jesus, the Tribulation and the End of the Exile: Restoration Eschatology and the Origin of the Atonement* (WUNT 2/204; Tübingen: Mohr Siebeck, 2005), 41. The classic work on the subject is by Wilhelm Bousset, *The Antichrist Legend: A Chapter in Christian and Jewish Folklore* (trans. A. H. Keane; 1896; reprint, Atlanta: Scholars, 1999). Today Bousset must be read with caution, since he attempts to create a unified model out of elements from various strata of Judaism, data that must be manipulated in order to make them add up to one coherent picture. Better and more up-to-date works are in G. W. Lorein, *The Antichrist Theme in the Intertestamental Period* (JSPSup; Sheffield: Sheffield Academic, 2004), and L. J. Lietaert Peerbolte, *The Antecedents of Antichrist: A Traditio-Historical Study of the Earliest Christian Views on Eschatological Opponents* (JSJSup 49; New York: Brill, 1996). See also Gregory C. Jenks, *The Origins and Early Development of the Antichrist Myth* (New York: de Gruyter, 1991). On p. 361 he counters Bousset, stating that a fully-developed antichrist teaching *can-*

This eschatological blasphemer appears throughout the NT. Three times the Johannine letters give evidence (1 John 2:18, 22; 4:3; 2 John 7) that "antichrist" was a known term among Christians for the eschatological man of evil. Although it is not explicit within the canon, it is certainly implicit that the "one abomination that causes desloation," the "Man of Lawlessness," the "antichrist," and one "beast" or the other from Rev 13 are intended as the same eschatological figure. It was also typical in the church of the next century to understand the Man of Lawlessness and the antichrist as one and the same person. To give but one example, Irenaeus taught that the "antichrist" would sit for three and one-half years in Jerusalem.[80]

The NT does not identify the Man of Lawlessness. In Revelation, the mark of the beast (666; Rev 13:18) has been interpreted in myriad ways. The idea that it stands for some permutation of the name "Nero Caesar" has won the greatest support, but it has not commanded a majority. Other candidates have been Mohammed, the Roman Catholic Church (by Protestants, see the Westminster Confession), and the Protestant movement (by Catholics).

Bruce tries to narrow down the search by focusing on the context of Thessalonica in AD 50:

> No identification of the mystery of lawlessness can be acceptable if it would not have been intelligible to the Christians to whom 2 Thessalonians was first addressed. Individuals or systems figuring in the subsequent course of Christian history cannot be considered when the primary application of the apostolic words is being decided.[81]

This observation must be heavily qualified. Those who believe in supernatural prophecy must allow that Paul was in fact predicting the future and that the fulfillment might be something well beyond the capacity of first-century Christians to understand. In addition, if Paul does not write down who the Man of Lawlessness is, it is entirely plausible that he himself has no idea of his identity. The question of his identity is left wide open.

A syntactical issue appears with the use of ψεύδους (trans. "that mislead"; lit., "of a lie"). We take it as a "descriptive genitive," that is, that it functions something like an attribution of the previous noun or nouns. The question is, how far back in the

not be reconstructed from Judaism alone. In fact it only makes sense in the christocentric gospel, making the Antichrist a foil for the true Christ. A more accessible essay is found in F. F. Bruce, *1 & 2 Thessalonians*, "Excursus on Antichrist," 179–88.

80. Irenaeus, *Haer.* 5.30.4 (*ANF* 1:560). He speaks several times of antichrist being the fulfillment of 2 Thess 2. For example, in *Haer.* 3.6.5 (*ANF* 1:420) he quotes 2 Thess 2:4. *Barn.* 4.4–5 identifies the antichrist with the "little horn" from Dan 7.

81. Bruce, *1 & 2 Thessalonians*, 187.

list "power and signs and wonders" (δυνάμει καὶ σημείοις καὶ τέρασιν) does this attribution function? Some English versions take it to refer to the last term (τέρασιν; "power, signs, lying wonders," NRSV), some to the last two terms (σημείοις καὶ τέρασιν; "signs and wonders that serve the lie," NIV), and some to all three words ("counterfeit power and signs and miracles," NLT; GNB is similar). Since the three words greatly overlap in meaning, the view of the NLT and GNB is best.

This leads to a theological problem, both for Paul's contemporaries and later readers of the Scriptures: Paul's miracles were the evidence of true apostleship. In 2 Cor 12:12 Paul said, "I persevered in demonstrating among you the marks of a true apostle, including signs, wonders and miracles." This is a pattern reminiscent of Moses before the magi of Egypt (see the progressive stages in Exod 7:10 – 13; 7:22; 8:7; 8:18 – 19; 9:11); Paul did signs while the super-apostles could not. So then, how do we reconcile this principle with what happens when "the restrainer" is removed and Satan enters to work signs?

View 1: Satan can in fact perform supernatural actions; yet during the time of the restrainer, while the gospel is going forth to the nations, satanic miracles are so limited that *as a rule* false prophets and apostles do not perform apostolic signs. Then, when the restrainer is removed, his power will manifest itself and cause confusion. These "power and signs and wonders that mislead" mean "genuinely supernatural acts that lead people to believe a lie."[82] This reading seems to have the backing of Deut 13:1 – 3: false prophets might arrive with "a sign or wonder," which might lead gullible Israelites into apostasy.

View 2: During the eschatological time, what is let loose is not Satan's power to do miracles, but his power to deceive. Here, "lie" (ψεύδους) is used as follows: "power and signs and wonders that mislead" means "counterfeit miracles"; that is, people become more gullible and fall for fakes and tricks that are not supernatural.[83] The CEV, with most English versions, represents this viewpoint: "Satan will pretend to work all kinds of miracles, wonders, and signs." Similar language is used of deceitful magical arts in the Exodus account in Jos. *Ant.* 2.13.3 (§284); Pharaoh accused Moses of practicing "deceitful tricks, and wonders and magical arts, to astonish him." Further parallels are found in Acts 13:6 – 12 (Bar-Jesus is a false prophet and sorcerer, but Paul blinds him) and 2 Cor 11:13 – 15, 12:12 (the super-apostles are boastful, but do not perform apostolic miracles).

The best resolution might not lie in the context of 2 Thessalonians, but rather in other passages. For Paul is not writing this statement upon a *tabula rasa*. He is recalling material that he has already taught them, including the apocalyptic worldview that underlies the Matthean apocalypse. Jesus taught that "false messiahs and false prophets will appear and perform great signs and wonders to deceive" (Matt 24:24; cf. Mark 13:22). There is no indication that Jesus is speaking of sleights of hand; everything indicates a supernatural show of power. Therefore we choose as a translation for 2:9, "power and signs and wonders that mislead."[84]

If the Thessalonians must take care now that no one deceives them in any way (2:3), and if Satan successfully ran the blockade and confused them with a false prophecy (2:2), they must extrapolate what might happen when the day of the Lord is truly drawing near. Yes, during the period of the "restrainer," Satan already deceives those who re-

82. So Best, *Thessalonians*, 306; Morris, *Thessalonians* (NICNT), 232; Malherbe, *Letters to the Thessalonians*, 425; especially Fee, *Thessalonians*, 293 – 94.

83. Green, *Thessalonians*, 321 – 22.

84. See the same solution in Witherington, *1 and 2 Thessalonians*, 223 – 26.

ject the gospel truth (2:10, 12; contrast 2:13; cf. Rev 20:7 – 8). But in the future the world will face the onslaught of Satan unleashed; he will attack with "every kind of ... deception." Satan's deceit is of course "unrighteous" (ἀδικίας), a genitive of description. His target is "those who are perishing." We may compare this with 1 Cor 1:18, where "those who perish" is contrasted with those "who are being saved." For those who are perishing, the gospel message is foolishness.

2:10c-d [This is] because they did not receive the love for the truth, so that they might be saved (ἀνθ' ὧν τὴν ἀγάπην τῆς ἀληθείας οὐκ ἐδέξαντο εἰς τὸ σωθῆναι αὐτούς). Now we have come full circle and returned to the message of salvation: anyone may receive the gospel in faith, escape God's wrath, and enter into the kingdom (1:3 – 10). But the world does not wish to turn to God. Why?[85] Because the unbelievers did not "receive the love for the truth." In "love for the truth" (τὴν ἀγάπην τῆς ἀληθείας), "love" is an action noun, to which is attached the objective genitive = "they [do not] love the truth." Paul implies that if someone receives the gospel, their favorable response was an endowment of God.

"So that they might be saved" can be understood as purpose or result; the difference is negligible. The use of an aorist infinitive "be saved" does not prove that salvation is in the *past*; nor that it is of necessity *once and for all*, as if it demonstrated the doctrine of eternal security. An aorist infinitive simply describes the fact of the action, without regard to time and without giving information concerning the nature of the action. Paul usually speaks of salvation as an eschatological action (see 1 Thess 1:10; 2 Thess 1:7) and that seems theologically likely here: *so that they, with us, might be rescued from God's wrath at Jesus coming.*

2:11 And so God will send them a powerful influence of deception so that they believe a lie (καὶ διὰ τοῦτο πέμπει αὐτοῖς ὁ θεὸς ἐνέργειαν πλάνης εἰς τὸ πιστεῦσαι αὐτοὺς τῷ ψεύδει). God now makes his reappearance in the narrative. Unbelievers have rejected the truth, refusing to be enabled to love it; now God will act to confirm their stubbornness. Paul uses the present tense of "send" (πέμπει), but in the context this is a future event, coming as it does after people have followed the deception of Satan and his Man of Lawlessness.

Paul surprisingly uses the noun attributed to Satan in 2:9. "Working of deception" (ἐνέργειαν πλάνης) is an action noun with an objective genitive ("he works deception"). The thought is indirectly expressed, and it looks as if Paul wishes to avoid a straight declaration that God is capable of deceit. A paraphrase is indicated, given that it is difficult to make both 2:9 and 11 have a similar English rendering and still make good sense. The NIV has "how Satan works [ἐνέργειαν]" and then "God sends them a powerful [ἐνέργειαν] delusion." The ASV is accurate, but ungraceful: "the working of Satan" and "the working of error" (similarly the GNB). We choose "powerful influence," which lies within the semantic range of the noun "working" (ἐνέργεια) and also plays up what is important in both verses, that God or Satan powerfully apply themselves to the influencing of human opinion.

As in Rom 1:24, 26, 28, those who rebel are punished by God with further degradation and rebellion. One truth that made itself felt in the ministry of Isaiah as well as that of Jesus and the apostles is that God sometimes sends his messengers out *in order to* make their hearts hard (Isa 6:9 – 10). In the case of Ahab and Jehoshaphat, twice it is recorded that God sent a spirit to energize false prophets in order to bring down their unholy alliance (see 1 Kgs 22:19 – 23; 2 Chr 18:18 – 22). Finally, Rev 17:17

85. See the analysis of "because" (ἀνθ' ὧν) in BDF §208(1).

shows that God compels the kings of the earth to give their authority over to the beast. Paul teaches that the Spirit influences people to receive the gospel; at the same time God confirms people in their rejection of it.

The world loves a lie, and in the end time it will fall more deeply into deception. Some have wished to load too much meaning to the Greek article with "the lie." They link it with Rom 1:25, where "lie" with the Greek article refers to worshiping the created rather than the Creator. Therefore, some propose that it must refer to *the lie*, the Big Lie. But this is not so; the Greek article does not function as does the English, and it may be rendered in English as *the* lie or *a* lie. The lie is whatever Satan happens to be offering a human being as an alternative to the truth of the gospel.

2:12 In order that all might be judged, [all who] do not believe the truth but take pleasure in wickedness (ἵνα κριθῶσιν πάντες οἱ μὴ πιστεύσαντες τῇ ἀληθείᾳ ἀλλὰ εὐδοκήσαντες τῇ ἀδικίᾳ). "That all might be judged" could syntactically denote purpose or result. A purpose clause is the most common usage, though result is not impossible. In this use of the conjunction (ἵνα), it seems unlikely that a differentiation can be made:

> In many cases purpose and result cannot be clearly differentiated, and hence ἵνα is used for the result that follows according to the purpose of the sub[ject] or of God. As in Semitic and Greco-Roman thought, purpose and result are identical in declarations of the divine will.[86]

For those who are put off by the idea of God deceiving unbelievers, neither the "result" nor the "purpose" interpretation will relieve them from offense. God is sending the deceiving power toward those who "delight in" their wicked lifestyles and who stand firm in their rejection of the gospel, that "all might be judged/condemned."

The subject of the verb "judged" is "all who do not believe the truth but take pleasure in wickedness." These are not two distinct groups, but one, as our translation shows. The objects of eschatological justice are "all" who do not believe. They not only practice wickedness; they "take pleasure" in it. Unlike believers, who are fulfilling God's good pleasure in good works (2 Thess 1:11), these people actively pursue wickedness. Implicit in Paul's condemnation is that their state is in part a result of Satan's work in 2:10. Satan leads them into unrighteousness, but his dupes would not have it any other way. "Wickedness" (ἀδικία) may relate back to the "unrighteous deception" of 2:10, a sign that before the end time is being felt in the experience of the Macedonian church.

As in 1 Thess 1:10, 5:9 and particularly in 2 Thess 1:8, Paul here does not allow for a third category, that of "righteous pagans" who follow the light of their conscience and de facto live more righteously than patrons of the synagogue (see Rom 2:14 – 16 and the standard commentaries). Rather, his eschatology is similar to what is found in Rom 2:12a: "All who sin apart from the law will also perish apart from the law." Outside the pale of the small church of Thessalonica are the masses who live in lies and wickedness. While Paul has focused in ch. 1 on the condemnation of the church's persecutors, he also predicts Christ's judgment of those who "do not believe" (here and in 1:8).

86. BDAG, ἵνα 3.

Theology in Application

A first-time reader might be surprised at how this chapter unfolds. After all, the central pastoral problem lay in whether the day of the Lord was at hand. Could not Paul have simply said it was not, since the Apostasy and the Man of Lawlessness were not present, and then moved on? Instead, he goes on for many verses to give details about that man, including the only canonical information about the so-called "restrainer." The reason for this apparent detour is that deeper within the story, it is not the Man of Lawlessness who is the chief protagonist, but Satan with his lies. The reader might take a blank copy of 2:1 – 12 and, highlighting anything having to do with lies, deception, or truth, will discover that little remains unmarked. Therefore, our main theological application will be an imperative: watch out for deception!

Theology in Thessalonica

In 2:2 Paul gives the Thessalonians a gentle scolding; whether or not they have already succumbed to anxiety, they should never "be quickly shaken or disturbed." To do so, we read in the Olivet tradition, would mean that they have fallen into the very temptation Jesus had warned about, that of pouncing on frightening events as a reason to panic (Matt 24:4 – 8). The power of Satan and of his Man of Lawlessness lies precisely in the fact that he can terrorize Christians. His puppet, the antichrist, "fights with two weapons, and they are power and lies."[87] There will be a future mass delusion among the unbelievers, fueled by Satan on the one hand and reinforced by God (2:11 – 12) on the other. This deception is eschatological, but it resonates with the present experience of the Thessalonians — their pagan and also Jewish neighbors are in lock-step with the devil in rejecting God and persecuting his chosen ones. How much more, then, will this clash of truth systems reveal itself in the end times, when all restraints are released and Satan and God are fighting the final battle for human beings?

Biblical Theology

Before the day of the Lord, a mere man will set himself up as a god. He will be backed by the power of the devil, fully unleashed because of the removal of the "restrainer." This means that while in Paul's day signs and wonders were proof of God's activity through the true gospel, in the end times they may come from the devil and be "signs that lie" (2:9).

Three events in redemptive history are parallels to this eschatological deception:

1. In Eden, the serpent deceived the woman by telling her that God was jealously

87. Stauffer, *New Testament Theology*, 213.

keeping the knowledge of good and evil from human beings (Gen 3:4 – 5). Eve and then Adam took the fruit, signaling that they had accepted Satan's lie. Their apostasy is the prototype of all rebellion against God.

2. During the exodus, the children of Israel rejected Moses, and by extension, Yahweh (Exod 32; Acts 7:35).
3. Jesus was invited to follow Satan as his god in Matt 4:8 – 10 (Luke 4:5 – 8) in return for all the kingdoms of the earth.

We might mention a fourth biblical figure, Simon of Samaria, the so-called "Magus" (Acts 8:9 – 11, 13, 18 – 24). He started off as a self-proclaimed manifestation of divine power and supposedly did miracles. He then seems to have been converted, but the author leaves open the question of whether he was an apostate. While Simon makes only a brief appearance in Acts, he looms large in the church fathers of the second century. It was supposedly Simon "from whom all sorts of [Gnostic] heresies derive their origin."[88] Irenaeus was not shy about calling such false teachers precursors of the antichrist, following the lead of 1 John 4:3.[89]

The Bible states that there is God's truth and Satan's deception. It also challenges today's readers to evaluate their assumptions concerning truth:

1. *Rationalism.* Here we speak of a rationalist approach to finding truth and discerning what is false. But finding God's truth cannot be a pure science as long as the seeker for truth is vulnerable to compromise from spiritual forces.
2. *The construction of the self.* In our Western culture, people are fanatically devoted to the creed "I am free to choose" and "I am the sum of my choices." People in our culture must grapple with the reality that they are not free as they think; in fact, they are not even able to say what blocks or compels their choices. In that case, Paul's theology should remind them to place less confidence in the power of their own choices and more trust in the God who answers prayer.
3. *Postmodernism.* Paul writes this chapter assuming that there exists the truth of God and that deviations from God's truth are false. The Christian who lives in an postmodernism environment must declare that if there is a God, and if God has said that truth matters, then Christianity cannot concede that one version of the truth is as valid as another.

In all three cases, it is God's truth in Christ that gives us a framework to say this or that is true; and it is the humility, peace, and patience that arise from confidence in God that best captures the Christian's deportment in the world.

88. Irenaeus, *Haer.* 1.23.1 – 2 (*ANF* 1:347 – 48).

89. Ibid.. 1.13.1 (*ANF* 1:334).

Message of This Passage for the Church Today

Since neither the Son of Man nor the angels know when the parousia will come, neither does Satan know the "times and seasons." It follows that he does not know when the Man of Lawlessness is scheduled to appear. He might be setting forth "*Men* of Lawlessness" — the Napoleons, the Stalins, the Hitlers — banking against that day when the end does begin to draw near and some candidate or another is able to step forward without hindrance as *the* Man.[90]

Read the history of the church, and you might draw the conclusion that Satan loves to mock Christians with "red herrings." That is, just as he wants to deceive the world with "false messiahs," he might also enjoy confusing the church by making them chase after one supposed antichrist after another, and all the while the restrainer is still in place. Then, when the Man of Lawlessness finally appears, all the forces of hell will be unleashed to convince Christian and non-Christian that he is not what he seems to be. Guile is the heart of hell's game plan.

Who is qualified to break the seals and interpret biblical prophecy? Within evangelical circles there is no lack of end-time calculators and speculators who hope to brag of their new information about the eschaton. Serious Bible students might be tempted to laugh these people off, but in that direction there lies danger. We need to protect the church from this sort of peril. Whenever believers wander off after some new eschatological fad, somebody will sustain permanent spiritual damage when those predictions fail to come to pass. We are not limiting ourselves to groups such as the Jehovah's Witnesses, but also speaking about evangelical teachers who can now count exbelievers among their former followers. This is no more than what we should have expected from reading 2 Thessalonians or Revelation: Satan does not simply amuse himself with fallible human beings; he is a destroyer.

If the devil exploited first-century media such as a charismatic utterance or a letter, he knows how to manipulate modern media as well. Hardly a day goes by in which I do not receive an electronic message about the identity of the antichrist or some other theory about globalism or the mark of the beast. It is said by some that the end must be nigh because the Middle East peace process is faltering; and at another time *by those same people* that the end must be nigh because the peace process seems to be succeeding. I have seen people argue that Prince Charles of England must be the Man of Lawlessness; I have heard equally earnest Spanish-speakers prove that King Juan Carlos of Spain is the *anticristo*.

The healthy Christian must develop an aversion to the "X-Files" type of logic. He

90. I am indebted to Dr. Robert C. Newman for this very useful idea. See www.ibri.org for a number of his essays and presentations.

or she should also know how to spot an urban legend, such as the tale of the "vanishing hitchhiker," where a stranger relates that Jesus' coming is right around the corner, just before disappearing from the backseat.[91] Christ taught that "many false prophets will appear and deceive many people" (Matt 24:11; see also 24:23 – 24). It does not matter whether "inside information" comes through some charismatic utterance or through some private decoding of the Bible. Such people are alive today and are by definition "false prophets."

91. See Jan Harold Brunvand, *The Vanishing Hitchhiker: Urban Legends and Their Meanings* (New York: Norton, 1989), 24 – 46. The story has been circulating in one form or another for centuries. I first heard it in the 1960s, and it is still circulating today.

CHAPTER 11

2 Thessalonians 2:13 – 17

Literary Context

In language reminiscent of 1:3, Paul turns from the condemnation of the wicked (2:1 – 12) to offer thanks to God for the believers. It is obvious that the Thessalonian disciples are beloved and chosen of God, in contrast with the lost in 2:1 – 12, who walk in Satan's lies. In the following section (3:1 – 5) Paul enlists the Thessalonians to pray that others might hear the powerful gospel.

III. Instruction concerning the End Times (2:1 – 12)

➡ **IV. A Second Thanksgiving, an Exhortation, and a Prayer for the Thessalonians (2:13 – 17)**

- **A. The apostles give thanks because of God's election and call (2:13 – 14)**
- **B. They remind the Thessalonians that they are responsible to hold fast to apostolic doctrine (2:15)**
- **C. They pray that the God of salvation will encourage and strengthen the Thessalonians (2:16 – 17)**

V. A Request for the Thessalonians' Prayer (3:1 – 5)

Main Idea

Paul draws together three genres to make three theological statements; *thanksgiving* to God for the Thessalonians' election and call; *reminder language* that they are responsible to follow what they have been taught; *prayer* that God will strengthen and encourage them in their walk.

Translation

2 Thessalonians 2:13 – 17

13a	Assertion	But for our part, **we are under obligation to give thanks to God**
13b	Time	all the time
13c	Advantage	for you,
13d	Description	brothers and sisters, whom the Lord loves,
13e	Cause	because God has chosen you
13f	Purpose/Result	to be the firstfruits of people
	Description	who would receive salvation
13g	Means	by means of the sanctifying work of the Spirit and
13h	Means	faith in the truth.
14a	Assertion	God called you unto [this saving work]
14b	Means	through the gospel we preached,
14c	Result	to obtain the glory of our Lord Jesus Christ.
15a	Exhortation	Consequently, brothers and sisters, **be firmly committed** and
15b	Exhortation	**hold tight to the traditions that you were taught**,
15c	Means	whether through a message or letter from us.
16a	Prayer	Now **may our Lord Jesus Christ himself and God our Father,**
16b	Description / List	who loved us and
16c	List	gave us eternal encouragement and
16d	List	good hope
16e	Means	by [his] grace,
17a	Prayer	**. . . encourage your whole person and**
17b	Prayer	**strengthen you**
17c	Respect	with respect to every good work and word.

Structure

This section is the perfect foil to the preceding section. The Thessalonians are saved through "faith in the truth" (2:13h); the pagans for their part believe a lie (2:10 – 11). God elected and called his people to salvation and righteousness (2:13); God is reinforcing the delusions of those who love unrighteousness (2:11 – 12). Most of all, the saints will obtain the glory of the Lord Jesus Christ (2:14c); the wicked will be condemned (2:12). The last point has deep roots in 1:5 – 11.

We may neatly divide these verses into three parts. It is entirely appropriate for Paul to state these thoughts in terms of *thanks to God* (2:13 – 14), an *exhortation* (2:15), and a report on their *ongoing prayers* (2:16 – 17).

The *thanksgiving* is marked by "but for our part, we" (expanded translation of δέ, which connects with ἡμεῖς). Their gratitude (2:13a) is an obligation (ὀφείλομεν), as seen already in 1:3; once again, Paul uses language of "all the time" and "for you" (2:13b-c). The cause (ὅτι) for their thanksgiving is God's election (2:13) and his call (2:14).

In the *exhortation* section (2:15), God has worked in the Thessalonians from the start, and "consequently," those disciples are obligated to hold firmly to the apostolic teaching. Here too Paul refers back to the previous section: let no Thessalonian decide that, if it is possible to forge a letter or fake a Pauline teaching (2:2), those media may be set aside when properly used.

Third (2:16 – 17), Paul offers a *benediction/prayer*, that the Thessalonians might live in the manner that the gospel demands. This is marked by "now" (δέ), which, as we have noted before, might introduce a prayer (1 Thess 3:11; 5:23). The petition focuses primarily on the Thessalonians, who being encouraged and strengthened will grow in good works.

Exegetical Outline

➡ **I. The Apostles Give Thanks because of God's Election and Call (2:13 – 14).**

II. They Remind the Thessalonians That They Are Still Responsible to Hold Fast to Apostolic Doctrine (2:15).

III. They Pray That the God of Salvation Will Encourage and Strengthen the Thessalonians (2:16 – 17).

Explanation of the Text

2:13a-d But for our part, we are under obligation to give thanks to God all the time for you, brothers and sisters, whom the Lord loves (Ἡμεῖς δὲ ὀφείλομεν εὐχαριστεῖν τῷ θεῷ πάντοτε περὶ ὑμῶν, ἀδελφοὶ ἠγαπημένοι ὑπὸ κυρίου). Paul captures again the thankfulness of the team as they stand in awe of God's work in Thessalonica. He uses what is technically known as *inclusio*: employing similar language at the beginning and ending of a section of text in order to come full circle to his original thought. In 1:3 he said, "We are under obligation to give thanks to God all the time because of you, brothers and sisters"; he then goes into a detailed discussion of how those outside the faith will face God's wrath. He now returns to thank God for the Thessalonians: *you* are not part of *they*, "the outsiders"; *you* are distinct as God's people, and it is all due to God's intervention (see comments on 1:3 and 1 Thess 1:2–4). The perfect participle "beloved" (ἠγαπημένοι) echoes 1 Thess 1:4 and anticipates the love of God the Father for them in 2 Thess 2:16. Here it is "the Lord" who loves the Thessalonians, and if this reference follows Paul's normal pattern, it is the Lord *Jesus*.

2:13e-h Because God has chosen you to be the firstfruits of people who would receive salvation by means of the sanctifying work of the Spirit and faith in the truth (ὅτι εἵλατο ὑμᾶς ὁ θεὸς ἀπαρχὴν εἰς σωτηρίαν ἐν ἁγιασμῷ πνεύματος καὶ πίστει ἀληθείας). Paul is grateful, not just because there *are* converts but because these individuals in particular belong to God.

There is a textual variant, with one letter making a substantial difference in meaning:

- God chose them "from the beginning" (ἀπ' ἀρχῆς), that is, from the primeval beginning (KJV, HCSB, NASB, NJB, NKJV, REB)
- God chose them as the "firstfruits" (ἀπαρχήν) (CEV, ESV, GNB, NIV, NLT, NRSV)

Both readings have solid manuscript support and both make sense; the UBS committee chose ἀπαρχήν because it is a Pauline expression whereas the former is not. God chose "you" (accusative ὑμᾶς) to be the "firstfruits" (a second accusative, ἀπαρχήν) — a double accusative that is not grammatically objectionable, but might have tempted some scribe to smooth it into a simpler "from the beginning."

In Judaism as in paganism, people would present "firstfruits" at the temple, a token of the first of the season's agricultural produce. It was a foreshadowing of a future, greater harvest (Exod 23:16). Paul at times used the term of a harvest of *people*. In 1 Cor 15:20, Christ is the "firstfruits" of the resurrection (the full eschatological harvest). "Firstfruits" can also serve as a metaphor of "first converts": Epaenetus was the "first convert ... of Asia" (Rom 16:5), and the household of Stephanus of Achaia (1 Cor 16:15). Paul never specifies of what the people are the firstfruits. Is the household of Stephanus, for example, part of the firstfruits that anticipates a larger harvest in Achaia during this age? At the resurrection? In the case of the Thessalonians, Paul does not mention their geographical location, so we cannot determine if he wishes to say that they are the initial converts of Thessalonica/Macedonia, or that they are among the earliest converts to the gospel in the Gentile world.

"God has chosen you ... [to] receive salvation." In this manner, Paul drew a firm contrast between the disciples and the world in 2:10–12; the wicked refuse to believe in the truth, and God has further confirmed them in their love for a lie. In the case of the Thessalonians, however, God has chosen them to be the firstfruits of those who would receive the gospel and enter salvation. Salvation is to be understood, as it is in these two letters, as eschatological — the disciples are saved from God's wrath at Christ's return; for this God has chosen them. The doctrine of election is key to understanding the Thessalonian letters; we will treat it in the "Theology in Application" section.

The "sanctifying work of the Spirit" (ἁγιασμῷ πνεύματος) is the means through which God will save believers. Normally Paul uses "spirit/Spirit" to refer to the Holy Spirit rather than the human spirit. This in itself makes a translation of "Spirit" as the natural one. Nevertheless, Paul has shown himself capable of speaking of God's sanctifying work in the human spirit in 1 Thess 5:23 ("may God himself ... make all of you perfectly holy; and may your spirit and soul and body be kept perfectly without blame at the coming of our Lord Jesus Christ"). If that were the case, "sanctification of [your] spirit" (objective genitive) is a possible alternative to "sanctification done by the Spirit" (subjective genitive). While this possibility exists, it is a remote one, and it is telling that the English versions do not mention it.

The general tenor of Paul's language in these letters is that the *Spirit makes people holy*. Because of "the Spirit," we may identify this verse as one of those passages that contain an implicit reference to what eventually came to be called the Trinity: the Lord (Jesus) loves them, God chooses them, the Spirit sanctifies them (see likewise 1 Pet 1:2).[1]

There are other passages that speak of sanctification as a past event in which God has set men and women apart to be his holy people (1 Cor 6:11: "But you were washed, you were sanctified, you were justified in the name of the Lord Jesus Christ and by the Spirit of our God"). But that is not Paul's emphasis in the Thessalonian letters, where holiness is always a goal and sanctification is the ongoing divine work in which people cooperate and by which Christians will attain that end.[2]

Their "faith in the truth" (πίστει ἀληθείας) is an objective genitive: "they believed the truth." Paul moves back and forth in this part of the letter, distinguishing those who follow the truth with the followers of Satan, who believe a "lie" (2:9, 11) and hate the truth (2:10). By contrast, the Christians received the gospel as God's own Word (1:10; also 1 Thess 2:13).

2:14 God called you unto [this saving work] through the gospel we preached, to obtain the glory of our Lord Jesus Christ (εἰς ὃ ἐκάλεσεν ὑμᾶς διὰ τοῦ εὐαγγελίου ἡμῶν, εἰς περιποίησιν δόξης τοῦ κυρίου ἡμῶν Ἰησοῦ Χριστοῦ). Not only has God chosen the Thessalonians; he also called them to salvation through the preaching of the gospel and sets them on the path to being glorified in the future.

"Unto which" (εἰς ὅ) with its neuter pronoun would normally direct the reader back to find a neuter antecedent. But there is no neuter singular noun. This is a known usage and is similar to what Wallace calls the "Conceptual Antecedent" use of the neuter of the pronoun "this" (τοῦτο), which refers backward to a general concept rather than a particular word.[3] This is most famously used in Eph 2:8: "For it is by grace you have been saved, through faith — and *this* (τοῦτο) is not from yourselves" (i.e., "this whole process"). "This saving work" is a fitting summary of 2:13.

God is the implied subject of "he called you" (ἐκάλεσεν ὑμᾶς) and is parallel to other references to God's call (1 Thess 2:12; 4:7; 5:24; 2 Thess 1:11).

1. See the comments by Fee, *Thessalonians*, 300, who states that there are nearly forty such passages in the Pauline corpus.

2. See 1 Thess 3:13; 4:1, 3, 7, 10; 5:23 – 24; 2 Thess 1:11; 2:14, 17; 3:5.

3. See Wallace, *Grammar*, 333 – 35.

As always, God's call is not considered apart from the preaching of the gospel (see the various levels of "call" in the "Theology in Application" section). Another parallel lies between this verse and 1 Thess 5:9, where Paul spoke of obtaining eschatological salvation. "To obtain the [end-time] glory" (εἰς περιποίησιν δόξης) is again a phrase with an objective genitive.[4]

"Glory" is a Pauline symbol of the final resurrection. Believers will enter glory in the kingdom (1 Thess 2:12); in the end they will glorify Christ but also be glorified by him (2 Thess 1:12; cf. Rom 8:30); glory is sought by the righteous (Rom 2:7); the saints hope for it (Rom 5:2; 8:17–23; 2 Cor 4:17; 2 Tim 2:10). As in 2 Thess 2, it is the goal of God's election and call (Rom 8:30). The resurrection body is a body of "glory" (1 Cor 15:40, 41, 43).

The genitive "of our Lord Jesus Christ" has two possibilities: source (Jesus will give you glory) or descriptive (glory like that which Jesus has). The parallel in that other Macedonian letter (Phil 3:21) suggests the second option: Christians will receive a body like his "glorious body" (see also Col 3:4).

2:15 Consequently, brothers and sisters, be firmly committed and hold tight to the traditions that you were taught, whether through a message or letter from us (ἄρα οὖν, ἀδελφοί, στήκετε, καὶ κρατεῖτε τὰς παραδόσεις ἃς ἐδιδάχθητε εἴτε διὰ λόγου εἴτε δι' ἐπιστολῆς ἡμῶν). Paul gives the first word of exhortation in this letter. "Consequently" (ἄρα οὖν) points back to what has been said, leading to an overarching exhortation, as in 1 Thess 5:6. His word is that they conserve what they have gained or will have learned of the apostolic teaching. Paul further catches their attention with "brothers and sisters" (ἀδελφοί)—he means to be listened to and taken seriously.

The two imperatives in this verse do not have physical meanings ("grab hold of something") but metaphorical. "Hold fast to" (κρατεῖτε) implies a firm commitment; apart from here, this verb is found only in Col 2:19 in Paul's letters, where the errorists were (lit.) "*not* holding fast to the Head." "Be firmly committed" (στήκετε) shows up in 1 Thess 3:8 and elsewhere in Paul's letters.

The Thessalonians must continue firm in "the traditions [παραδόσεις] that you were taught." Paul uses the verb form "pass on tradition" (παραδίδωμι) when he refers to creedal language in 1 Cor 11:2, 23 and 15:3, the latter being "what I received I passed on [παρέδωκα] to you."[5] Yet we need not limit Paul's thought in 2 Thess 2:15 to creeds—the language is broad enough to include all teaching, oral or written ("through a message or letter from us"), including the full content of the two letters at hand (so 2 Thess 3:14).

Paul has to maintain a careful balance here, reinforcing the importance of tradition while also warning about the pitfalls of the various media of the early church (see 2:2 and comments). The disciples at Thessalonica must be fully attentive to genuine apostolic teaching, that is, what they have already received along with further instruction in the future. After all, there will probably be more visits, and there have been at least two letters. Despite the dangers inherent in the sending of letters, which he will try to mitigate in 3:17, Paul is clearly unwilling to give up on written communication.

4. Wallace, *Grammar*, 116–19.

5. See the analysis of tradition language in Paul in Caroline Vander Stichele, "The Concept of Tradition in 1 and 2 Thessalonians," in *The Thessalonian Correspondence* (ed. Raymond F. Collins; BETL 87; Leuven: Leuven Univ. Press, 1990), 499–504.

IN DEPTH: "Tradition" in 2 Thessalonians

The word "tradition" strikes our ears in different ways, depending in part on one's religious background. For the Eastern Orthodox Church and Roman Catholicism, tradition is an authentically apostolic deposit of truth that is broader than the written canon. The Roman expression is:

> In keeping with the Lord's command, the Gospel was handed on in two ways: *orally* "by the apostles who handed on, by the spoken word of their preaching, by the example they gave, by the institutions they established, what they themselves had received—whether from the lips of Christ, from his way of life and his works, or whether they had learned it at the prompting of the Holy Spirit"; *in writing* "by those apostles and other men associated with the apostles who, under the inspiration of the same Holy Spirit, committed the message of salvation to writing."[6]

That is to say, the apostles' teaching, the writings of the church fathers, and the living apostolic authority of Rome are all sources of tradition, which work together with the NT to inform the church of God's will. In popular Catholicism this unfortunately gets boiled down to "the priest tells us what the Bible means."

The Westminster Confession expresses a Reformed viewpoint, that the

> whole counsel of God ... is either expressly set down in Scripture, or by good and necessary consequence may be deduced from Scripture: unto which nothing at any time is to be added, whether by new revelations of the Spirit, or traditions of men.[7]

Some, but by no means all, of the NT references to tradition reinforce this negative sense of tradition.[8]

With regard to Paul's statement here, a Catholic might underscore that Paul is referring to tradition that was not coterminous with the written letters; that before the penning of 1 Thessalonians there *was* no NT, whereas true apostolic doctrine did already exist. A Protestant might respond that from the standpoint of today, apart from the NT text the church does not possess any *certain* apostolic tradition,[9] that many of Rome's "apostolic traditions" may be demonstrated

6. See Catechism of the Catholic Church (www.vatican.va/archive/catechism/p1s1c2a2.htm#I).

7. Westminster Confession of Faith 1.6.

8. Consistently in Matthew and Mark; Gal 1:14; Col 2:8. See also 2 Tim 2:2: "the things you have heard me say in the presence of many witnesses entrust to reliable people who will also qualified to teach others." It is from liberal Protestants that the interpretation arose that the Pastoral Letters are postapostolic, that the church had grown beyond the dynamic theology and preaching of the founders and clung to the passing along of "sound teaching." The Pastoral Letters are, supposedly, an example of that so-called "Early Catholicism."

9. Even the useful *Teaching of the Twelve Apostles*, the *Didache*, while old and with some roots in the first century, cannot be dependably shown to be from the Twelve.

to be historically postapostolic and theologically not in line with the Bible, and that God has ordained that only the canonical books constitute the church's instruction.[10]

The question of knowability is an epistemological and a historical one, namely, how we gain access to all of God's truth. The Roman Church claims for its traditions a historical pedigree that cannot be fully verified in canonical texts. The Reformed faith focuses on data that can be verified by those same texts. It is that position that underscores the exegete's true task: there are the texts, and there are inferences that may be drawn from the texts. With regard to "what did the Thessalonians know, and when did they know it," we cannot go behind the text of the correspondence (or inferences from Acts or other books) to hear Paul's voice, and so as far as authoritative teaching is concerned, the text is "it."

By the same token, those who desire to know what the Thessalonians knew, no more and no less, must reckon with the loss of data. In one tantalizing case, within a window of time in the mid-first century, the Thessalonians knew more than we do concerning what or who restrains the Man of Lawlessness during this age (2:6 – 7). In a parallel instance, Irenaeus (*Haer.* 5.30.3) states that neither he nor any Christian knows the meaning of 666 from Rev 13, but believes that John may have known it but did not write it down. These examples should serve as warnings that the exegete should remain humble.

2:16 Now may our Lord Jesus Christ himself and God our Father, who loved us and gave us eternal encouragement and good hope by [his] grace (Αὐτὸς δὲ ὁ κύριος ἡμῶν Ἰησοῦς Χριστὸς καὶ [ὁ] θεὸς ὁ πατὴρ ἡμῶν, ὁ ἀγαπήσας ἡμᾶς καὶ δοὺς παράκλησιν αἰωνίαν καὶ ἐλπίδα ἀγαθὴν ἐν χάριτι). Paul moves to a prayer/benediction, which reflects the elements of the first two chapters with their emphasis on hope and good works. The sentence continues in 2:17, where the main verb appears, which can be attached either to the Lord or to God the Father. This has a strong parallel in 1 Thess 3:11 – 13, and one comparison in particular is instructive: in 3:11 the divine names are reversed: "our God and Father" comes first, followed by "our Lord Jesus Christ." In addition, the optative verbs that follow are in singular, even though the subject is plural. In the next sentence (3:12), the results for which Paul prays there are to be carried out by "the Lord" Jesus.

Here in the second letter, by contrast, the "Lord Jesus Christ" is followed by "God our Father," and it is the *Father* who is the active person, as shown by two attribute participles "who loved us and gave

10. We do not even begin to explore the role of tradition in hermeneutics. One does not have to be a postmodernist to appreciate the gravitational pull of the sum of one's religious culture and experiences. This truism must be countered with the apostles' own implication that their written word is capable of being heard, understood, and obeyed; and that the Holy Spirit is God's agent to redirect the hearer of inspired text away from assumptions and toward truth.

us" (ὁ ἀγαπήσας ἡμᾶς καὶ δοὺς) and then by the optative verb in 2:17. This means that by comparing two similar Pauline prayers, the reader arrives at a subtle but undeniable attestation of the divinity of Christ. In both cases, God the Father and the Lord Jesus are petitioned in prayer, and one or the other who might answer that prayer. What Paul explored a few times in explicit propositions (Rom 9:5; Phil 2:6; Titus 2:13) becomes clear when he turns to God and the Lord Jesus in prayer; it is in prayer that he shows who he really thinks the Lord Jesus is.

Greek participles do not communicate the time of an action, and so it is doubtful that the Greek implies past time with the two aorist participles, "who loved us and gave us." The only help we are given here is the context, which most likely points to God's elective love in the past, God who then gave the Christian hope through the reception of the gospel message.

God has given the Thessalonians "eternal encouragement and good hope by his grace" (παράκλησιν αἰωνίαν καὶ ἐλπίδα ἀγαθὴν ἐν χάριτι). We take "by his grace" to be connected to both of these phrases. The two direct objects are uncommon. "Eternal encouragement" anticipates Paul's prayer in the optative of "encourage you" in 2:17. The encouragement is not merely of some eternal quality; Paul means to say that it chronologically extends into the age to come. The same is true of "good hope"; the Thessalonians can look forward to the welcome they will receive into the kingdom (1:5).

2:17 Encourage your whole person and strengthen you with respect to every good work and word (παρακαλέσαι ὑμῶν τὰς καρδίας καὶ στηρίξαι ἐν παντὶ ἔργῳ καὶ λόγῳ ἀγαθῷ). Paul speaks in language reminiscent of 1 Thess 3:11 – 13. The main verb of this prayer/benediction is the aorist optative, "encourage" (παρακαλέσαι; see 1 Thess 3:11 for comments on the optative). Since it is prayer language, we translate it "may he encourage."

Once again, we avoid translating the object of the verb (ὑμῶν τὰς καρδίας) as "your hearts," since that implies something different in English than it does in Greek (see comments on 1 Thess 3:13; see there also for comments on the translation of "strengthen you"). Paul does not ask simply that they be blessed or confirmed; he wants God and the Lord to empower them to lead a life of "goodness" (ἀγαθῷ, cf. 1 Thess 4:3). This adjective modifies both nouns. The Christian life expresses itself holistically, from the innermost person, outwardly into the interaction of the individual with others in word and deed.

Theology in Application

One cannot study the Thessalonian letters without being impressed with the central importance of *divine election*.

Theology in Thessalonica

The majority of Paul's audiences (i.e., the relatively few who even bothered to listen to him in the first place) rejected and even lampooned the gospel. Even as he was dictating this letter, the Corinthian multitude was labeling his word "foolishness" (1 Cor 1:18). But during his three stops in Macedonia and two in Achaia, some few had a radically distinct reaction: they "received the word." To Paul's delight, the Thessalonians not only acted on the gospel, but they held on to it despite fierce trials and even actively promoted its spread. It was within this matrix that Paul thinks about cause and effect in God's kingdom.

Perhaps we have debated the issues of election and human will in classrooms and coffee shops. But when Paul broaches the topic of God's election, he cannot do so in a sterile environment. He speaks as evangelist and pastor of real men and women. He claims to know that the Thessalonians are chosen and shows them how their behavior patterns strike an apostle as the fruit of divine election. He reminds them that, as Calvin put it, "it was not a bare preaching that had been brought to them."[11] There were miracles and the presence of the Spirit and a gripping sense of the truth of the gospel in the minds of its envoys (1 Thess 1:5). A Thessalonian in the middle of confusion, hardship, and death is, therefore, hearing from leading experts in the gospel: "Believe us, you have had the real experience; we'd recognize it anywhere." The joy of the apostolic team "God has chosen you" in turn bolsters the believers' confidence and urges them further in godliness.

Yet if the Thessalonians showed every indication of being among God's elect and thus on their way to the kingdom (1 Thess 2:12; 2 Thess 1:5), election is not the only relevant doctrine to consider. These very people, who have demonstrable signs of having been elected and called, must endure to the end if they are to receive salvation. Salvation is principally an eschatological goal (1 Thess 1:10; 5:9; 2 Thess 1:10 – 12; 2:14, 16), and along the pathway lies the real possibility of disaster (1 Thess 3:5). As in Jesus' teaching and that of the other letters and Revelation, the apparently elect might apostatize and fail to receive that for which they started.

Biblical Theology

How might we handle the prickly doctrines of election and perseverance? If we would follow Paul, we will not start a debate over free will versus predestination. Instead, we will acknowledge these realities from the Thessalonian texts.

1. *There exists a spectrum of data.* One must agree to take all biblical evidence with seriousness. "God chose you" (cf. 1 Thess 1:4; 2 Thess 2:13) and "you received/believed the message" (cf. 1 Thess 1:6; 2 Thess 2:13) will be paid equal attention. Paul's anxiety about whether their evangelistic work had been "in vain" (1 Thess 3:5) should also be included in the data pool. We must show ourselves capable of allowing seemingly contradictory data to exist side-by-side, even as we try to synthesize them.[12]

2. *The "call" to salvation seems to take two meanings, depending on the context.*

11. Calvin, *Thessalonians*, 240.

12. The very variety of data should lead us to listen with care to other ways of interpreting them. Although J. Matthew Pinson, ed., *Four Views on Eternal Security* (Grand Rapids: Zondervan, 2002) should be a useful resource, the book is somewhat disappointing — the authors here address different issues; they talk past one another.

First Thessalonians 2:12 speaks of God's calling or summoning the Thessalonians into his eschatological kingdom; 4:7 speaks of God's call to purity; 5:24 speaks of God's call without further detail. Similarly, 2 Thess 1:5 speaks of being worthy of his calling; 2:14 of calling them by means of the gospel presentation.

On the one hand, God uses preachers to call everyone to believe (Rom 1:5). On the other, there is a "call" to become a Christian that was experienced only by those who believed. This is why Paul can say in Rom 1:6 that "you also are among those Gentiles who are called to belong to Jesus Christ"; in the context only the predestined receive that call (see Rom 8:28: 8:30; 11:29) while, logically, other people have not been so called. See also Rev 17:14: those "with [the Lamb] will be his called, chosen and faithful followers."

One of the points of contention between Arminians and Calvinists has been precisely the nature of that second kind of call. The former hold that God's call was given within a context of "prevenient grace"; that is, after the fall of Adam, God gave all people a measure of grace sufficient to overcome their hardness and to receive the gospel. The other view is that God's grace is effective in carrying out God's elective will. Hence the Westminster Confession 10.1: "All those whom God hath predestinated unto life, and those only, He is pleased, in his appointed and accepted time, effectually to call ... effectually drawing them to Jesus Christ." Critical to this definition, yet at times overlooked, is the qualifier, "they come most freely, being made willing by his grace."[13]

3. *God is the subject, not the object, of "election."* "Were chosen" in 1 Thess 1:4 and "has chosen" in 2 Thess 2:13 and other verbs or action nouns in the New Testament predicate a free choice on God's part. This is why John Calvin (like Augustine before him) was infuriated when one of his detractors accused him of teaching "predestination *and* fate." The confusing of the two concepts, said he, was "outraging all decency ... to confound things the most opposite":

> Fate, according to the Stoics, is a necessity springing out of a changeable and complicated labyrinth, and binding in some measure God himself. Instructed by the Scriptures, I define predestination as the free counsel of God, by which he regulates the human race, and all the individual parts of the universe, according to his own immense wisdom, and incomprehensible justice.[14]

The personal, living God is the All-Free One, who chooses to initiate a relationship with yet unborn persons; Paul states in Eph 1:4 that it took place prior to the creation itself.

4. *The apostles spoke of election within different contexts.* Noteworthy passages

13. Highly recommended is a Calvinist presentation for the nonspecialist by Robert A. Peterson, *Election and Free Will: God's Gracious Choice and Our Responsibility* (Phillipsburg, NJ: Presbyterian and Reformed, 2007); he displays a most irenic spirit in an effort to engage his opponents and win a hearing.

14. John Calvin, *On Secret Providence* (trans. John Lillie; New York: Robert Carter, 1840), xi – xii.

about divine election are Rom 8:28 – 30; 1 Thess 1:4; and 1 Pet 1:2; it is striking that all do so in the context of persecution. That is, the authors affirm God's election and love in situations where doubt might have crept in. In other situations, the authors seem to use the doctrine to warn their audiences about apostasy (all throughout Hebrews) or to exhort them (2 Pet 1:10) to "make very effort to confirm your calling and election." That is, the doctrine of election is no hope for those who drift away from the faith.

5. *Both the church and the individual may be said to be "elect."* According to 1 Pet 2:9 God's people as a corporate whole are a "chosen people." In 1 Thess 1:4, however, it would be awkward to regard election as "corporate." It would involve Paul in a tautology (a statement that is true by necessity and thus not worth saying): that he was certain that God had chosen the Thessalonian church because that group received the gospel. It makes better sense if Paul is thinking of the faith that he detects in the believers as individuals.

6. *Election is demonstrable only by its effects on human behavior.* The so-called "free grace theology" maintains that good works are not a necessary proof of faith in Christ. In fact, this viewpoint goes on to say that those who insist on visible works do not truly believe in justification by faith. With regard to perseverance, one popular preacher writes that

> God's love for His people is of such magnitude that even those who walk away from the faith have not the slightest chance of slipping from His hand.... [We] are not saved because we have an enduring faith. We are saved because at a moment in time we expressed faith in our enduring Lord.[15]

This notion would never have passed muster with Paul. He satisfied himself that the Thessalonians were God's people by examining how they conducted their lives, not by the fact that they professed faith at some point in time. He follows the teaching of Jesus (Matt 7:16 – 20; John 3:8) that the relationship of a person to the Father is detectable to other human beings by the evidence of a changed life, visible only after the conversion of that individual.[16]

7. *The doctrine of election, far from making prayer moot, makes it a vital component in the saints' perseverance.* Success in the Christian life consists in the work of

15. Charles Stanley, from the chapter "For Those Who Stop Believing," in *Eternal Security: Can You Be Sure?* (Nashville: Nelson, 1991), 74, 80. These are not isolated statements: "Even if a believer for all practical purposes becomes an unbeliever, his salvation is not in jeopardy" (93); "believers who lose or abandon their faith will retain their salvation, for God remains faithful" (94).

16. See I. H. Marshall, "Election and Calling to Salvation in First and Second Thessalonians," in *The Thessalonian Correspondence* (ed. Raymond F. Collins; BETL 87; Leuven: Leuven Univ. Press, 1990), 265: "Paul's claim to knowledge of their election is related to his knowledge of their conversion." Grudem, a Calvinist, says "as soon as they came to faith Paul concluded that long ago God had chosen them, and therefore they had believed when he preached" (Wayne Grudem, *Systematic Theology: an Introduction to Biblical Doctrine* [Grand Rapids: Zondervan, 1995], 672). While both statements are essentially correct, it should be added that it was not simply the initial moment of conversion that led the apostles to believe they were among the elect, but also their perseverance in the faith up until the moment of Timothy's departure from Thessalonica for Corinth. Witherington, *1 and 2 Thessalonians*, 67,

God, and God works mightily through the prayers of a pastoral figure (1 Thess 3:12; 5:23; 2 Thess 2:17). Of course, theologians may argue over what is the exact relation between prayer, perseverance, and election. Do believers persevere because they are elect? Or do they remain elect because they continue in the faith? It is clear that God works to have them persevere (1 Thess 5:23; 2 Thess 3:3; cf. Phil 1:6). It is also clear that Paul prays that they will do so, and by implication, believes that pastoral prayer and effort are ingredients in their persistence (see 2 Tim 2:10).

8. *The doctrine of election is not a deterrent but a spur to seeking the lost.* Paul is yet again a model for his disciples, showing how prayer and thanksgiving are a vital part of the gospel work (2 Thess 3:1; see too Col 4:2–3a). When we pray that the gospel will be received, it happens that it meets with success. God works so that people turn to Christ in faith.

Summary. God chose both a people, which included the church of the Thessalonians and its members, bestowing on them his covenant love. His intervention and the coming promised Spirit of the new covenant bring about what Israel of old did not consistently do: the Gentiles put away idols; serve God; experience the eschatological love, joy, and hope while living in an age of tribulation; and await future salvation. Being part of God's people demands a life of service to God; that is, Spirit-bred works are a necessary adjunct to election. That is why when the devil tried to "shake" the Thessalonians, Paul felt genuine fear and was not certain apart from Timothy's testimony that they had endured Satan's pounding.[17] He viewed prayer as a factor in people's reception of the gospel and their endurance.

Message of This Passage for the Church Today

If election is a biblical doctrine, it is also clear that the Christian is an active agent in the proclamation, reception, and incarnation of the gospel. I speak here, being persuaded of the Reformed doctrine of election, but I think brothers and sisters from across the spectrum will benefit by these comments.[18]

puts it: "Paul says that not only he but also the Thessalonians can 'know' that the Thessalonians are God's chosen.... This 'knowing' comes from recognition of the positive response to the gospel received with joy and of changed lives, turning from idols to the living God. Indeed the chosen are all too visible and are enduring persecution because of it."

17. See I. H. Marshall, "Election and Calling," 261—"[Paul's] was a real fear; we do not find Paul saying, 'but of course this fear which I had for you was totally unjustified because I know that God will keep you regardless of whatever may happen'; instead he says they *continued* to show faith and love, and he prays to God to keep them." We recommend two volumes that provide careful exegesis of the texts that deal with endurance and falling away. First, I. Howard Marshall's *Kept By the Power of God: A Study of Perseverance and Falling Away* (reprint, Minneapolis: Bethany Fellowship, 1974); second is the more recent offering by Thomas R. Schreiner and Ardel B. Caneday, *The Race Set Before Us: A Biblical Theology of Perseverance and Assurance* (Downers Grove, IL: InterVarsity Press, 2001); on 158–60 they offer a discussion of the Olivet Discourse's "those who endure to the end will be saved." Marshall comes from a Wesleyan perspective, Schreiner and Caneday from a Calvinist. Both volumes are praiseworthy because of the care that the authors take to try not to import a theological system into the texts, but to let them speak for themselves.

18. All readers should profit by the minor classic by J. I. Packer, *Evangelism and the Sovereignty of God* (Downers Grove, IL: InterVarsity Press, 2009; orig. 1961). In the first chapter he shows that it is mandatory that people pray for others to be saved.

Evangelistic methodology. Paul himself was a brilliant strategist who planted a string of self-replicating congregations in key cities. We know from Acts that he knew how to contextualize his message. He strikes us as a man who would have had no tolerance for unclear preaching or sloppy organization.

Nevertheless, some people put so much emphasis on strategizing that it leads to the idolization of method. That is, we implicitly decide that God cannot or will not work outside of our set of assumptions — be they traditional, Pentecostal, or emergent. The election doctrine for its part "reminds the contemporary church that to be a church is to participate in an activity *initiated by God*."[19] We exist because God chose a new people and intervened in power at this time and not another; our own conversions were a late chapter in this story and our personal actions long postdate the Spirit's work. This is hard to swallow when we are daily told that we create our own reality by our own choices.

Paul, Silas, and Timothy become our "models" in these letters. They do not simply give a treatise about God's work or even a treatise about prayer. Rather, they report how they always speak to God and thus enter into what he is doing, and they invite the Thessalonians and us to join in. Calvinists and Arminians — all Christians must agree on the efficacy of intercession for drawing people into the flock and keeping them there.[20] We are never more in line with the reality of God's doings than when we are praying and giving thanks for his work in people.

Overthinking the doctrine of election. Most Christians do not give the doctrine of election sufficient thought. Yet there are also those who brood over the mysteries of God's sovereignty and risk falling into paralysis. Looked at this way, some say: perhaps Abraham defied God when he interceded for the cities of the plain, who were already under God's judgment. In that case, who is to know whether we should pray for Bill or for Mary, when for all we know they are already under God's condemnation?

Now and again I have been struck with a sudden realization that God wanted me to pray for or share my faith with a specific individual. But I can hardly exegete my experience to mean that I should pray for a person *only if and when* the Holy Spirit tips me off that they are fair game for evangelism. This perspective is out of harmony with the apostolic pattern. Paul prayed for groups and for individuals to come to Christ, and he did not seem to worry that he would offend God's sovereignty. Do we imagine that we are so spiritually sharp that we won't misidentify our run-of-the-mill coldness of heart as the Holy Spirit's saying "don't bother to pray"? By all means let us pray for discernment, but within a vital active lifestyle of prayer and evangelism.

19. Donfried and Marshall, *Shorter Pauline Epistles*, 74, italics in the original. See too John Chrysostom, *Homilies on First Thessalonians* 1 (*NPNF*[1] 13:324): "For to give thanks to God for them is the act of one testifying to their great advancement, when they are not only praised themselves, but God also is thanked for them, as Himself having done it all. He teaches them also to be moderate, all but saying, that it is all of the power of God."

20. Calvin, for example, so prayed; cf. his strong words in his commentary on 1 Tim 2:1.

CHAPTER 12

2 Thessalonians 3:1 – 5

Literary Context

Paul introduces a new theme, that his converts should pray for the apostles. It is a context ripe for this request. After all, his formal prayer language in 2:13 – 17 reveals many of the areas concerning which an apostle might pray — notably, the conversion of the lost. He now enlists their help to pray for the current stage of the gospel work. We will suggest with regard to 3:6 – 15 that evangelism continues to be the topic throughout 2 Thess 3.

IV. A Second Thanksgiving, an Exhortation, and a Prayer for the Thessalonians (2:13 – 17)

➡ **V. A Request for the Thessalonians' Prayer (3:1 – 5)**

- **A. The apostles ask the Thessalonians to pray that Paul's team will have success in their current evangelistic work (3:1)**
- **B. They ask for prayer that the team be delivered from evil people (3:2)**
- **C. They affirm that the Lord is faithful and will protect the Thessalonians (3:3)**
- **D. They are convinced that through the Lord's faithfulness, the Thessalonians will carry out the apostolic commands (3:4)**
- **E. They pray that the Thessalonians will grow, particularly with regard to love and endurance (3:5)**

VI. *Paraenesis:* The Problem of Disorderly Thessalonian Disciples (3:6 – 15)

Main Idea

Paul recruits his recent converts in Thessalonica to support the apostles in prayer — in this context, as they labor in Achaean Corinth. This reference to prayer leads Paul to affirm that the Thessalonians themselves will continue to grow, especially in love and obedience.

Translation

2 Thessalonians 3:1 – 5

1a	Entreaty	Beyond that, **pray for us**, brothers and sisters,
1b	Content	that the word of the Lord might run [well] and
1c	Content	be glorified [by its hearers],
1d	Comparison	just as it was with you, and
2a	Content	that we might be delivered from wicked and evil people;
2b	Cause	for **not everyone possesses faith.**
3a	Contrast	But **the Lord is faithful,**
3b	Description	who will strengthen you and guard you from evil.
4a	Assertion	And **we are persuaded** in the Lord concerning you,
4b	Content	that whatever we command,
4c	Content	you are already doing and
4d	Content	will continue to do.
5a	Prayer	Now **may the Lord direct your entire person**
5b	Direction	unto [living] in the love that comes from God and
5c	Direction	the endurance that comes from Christ.

Structure

Paul changes direction in this short section with "beyond that" (τὸ λοιπόν). This phrase does not mean "finally," as if to mark the conclusion; rather, it indicates a new direction that lies after the principal teaching of a letter (see esp. Phil 3:1). The underlying assumption that Paul here explores is the difference between the believers and the world.

The Thessalonians should pray for the evangelistic work of the Pauline team (3:1 – 2). Paul delineates what their prayers should accomplish: that God's word might run well, that the hearers might receive it with approval, and that the team will be protected from God's enemies. The comparative "just as" (καθώς) reinforces the apostles' joy over the Thessalonians: they truly received the word. Paul develops the distance between "you" and "them" further: there are evil and wicked people out there, and the reason is that (γάρ) "not everyone possesses faith."

In v. 3 Paul turns from the world's wickedness to speak to the spiritual life of the Thessalonians. First, one must think theocentrically: God is at work in them; he will strengthen and guard them (3:3). Second, the apostles have confidence in them, but only because "we are persuaded in the Lord concerning you" that they will obey their apostolic teaching (3:4).

The section ends with yet another prayer, marked by "now" (δέ, see also 1 Thess 3:11; 5:23; 2 Thess 2:16). The apostles pray that the Thessalonians will live lives full of love and endurance (3:5).

Exegetical Outline

➡ **I. The Apostles Ask the Thessalonians to Pray That Paul's Team Will Have Success in Their Current Evangelistic Work (3:1).**

II. They Also Ask for Prayer That the Team Be Delivered from Evil People (3:2).

III. They Affirm That the Lord Is Faithful and Will Protect the Thessalonians (3:3).

IV. They Are Convinced That through the Lord's Faithfulness, the Thessalonians Will Carry Out the Apostolic Commands (3:4).

V. They Pray That the Thessalonians Will Grow in Love and Endurance (3:5).

Explanation of the Text

3:1 Beyond that, pray for us, brothers and sisters, that the word of the Lord might run [well] and be glorified [by its hearers], just as it was with you (Τὸ λοιπὸν προσεύχεσθε, ἀδελφοί, περὶ ἡμῶν, ἵνα ὁ λόγος τοῦ κυρίου τρέχῃ καὶ δοξάζηται καθὼς καὶ πρὸς ὑμᾶς). Beyond that" (τὸ λοιπόν) does not mean "finally" here, but rather "now, on another theme."[1] Paul charges them to "pray." The ministry of prayer has shown up with particular clarity in the Thessalonian letters, as the Pauline team conformed to the practice of the earliest church: "[we] will give our attention to prayer and the ministry of the word" (Acts 6:4).

Paul has just offered thanks for them and prayed for them (2:13, 16 – 17). Now he asks them for a mutual blessing: "pray for us" (see 1 Thess 5:25). To Paul, one of the obligations that his disciples bore, having received the message of salvation from him, was that they pray for the gospel's advance into other areas (2 Cor 1:11; Eph 6:19 – 20; Col 4:3). People might also pray for other aspects of the apostles' work; for example, Paul asks the Romans to pray that he will be able to deliver the Jerusalem offering and then visit Rome (Rom 15:30 – 32); the author of Hebrews asks for prayers to be released from prison (Heb 13:18 – 19).

The specific object of prayer in this verse is that "the word of the Lord might run well and be glorified." Paul is perhaps thinking of Psalm 147:

> He who sends out his saying to the earth;
> his word will run swiftly. (Ps 147:15 LXX [NETS]; Ps 147:15 MT)

Likewise, Acts and other letters speak of the word growing and advancing (see, e.g., Acts 12:24; 13:49). "Be glorified" (δοξάζηται) could have the eschatological sense that it takes throughout these two letters; that is, that those who receive the word will participate in Christ's glory when he returns (1 Thess 2:12; 2 Thess 1:10 – 12; esp. 2:14). Nevertheless, since Paul says "as it was with you," this verse almost certainly has the sense of "glorified by being received with approval." There are parallel references to the glorifying of God's word;

1. BDAG, λοιπός 3. b.; MM, 380. Cf. 1 Thess 4:1; 2 Thess 3:1; Phil 3:1.

for example, "When the Gentiles heard this, they began rejoicing and glorifying the word of the Lord" (Acts 13:48 ESV; cf. Ps 138:2).

The sense of the comparative phrase "just as it was with you" (καθὼς καὶ πρὸς ὑμᾶς) is clear enough, the preposition (πρός) meaning "with" in this context.[2] The Thessalonians were remarkable examples of the success of the gospel; why not enlist them to pray that the same work of the Spirit be reproduced in Corinth and elsewhere?

3:2 And that we might be delivered from wicked and evil people; for not everyone possesses faith (καὶ ἵνα ῥυσθῶμεν ἀπὸ τῶν ἀτόπων καὶ πονηρῶν ἀνθρώπων· οὐ γὰρ πάντων ἡ πίστις). Paul delineates what he wishes their prayers to accomplish. He wants to "be delivered" (ῥυσθῶμεν). The verb is a divine passive; that is, "that we might be delivered" means "that God [or the Lord Jesus?] might deliver us."

Who are the sources of the team's troubles? Certain "people" who are "wicked and evil" (ἀτόπων καὶ πονηρῶν). The first adjective (ἄτοπος) is relatively uncommon. The KJV's "unreasonable" does not capture the sense; "bigoted" (NJB) reads more into the text than is there. The "wicked" of most English versions is adequate.

Paul observes, in an elliptical phrase, that "not everyone possesses faith." In this context Paul is referring to faith in the gospel. Whereas the faith of the Thessalonians has gained notoriety, the lack of Christian faith on the part of others has produced noxious fruit. Paul engages in serious understatement when he asserts that not everyone believes.

3:3 But the Lord is faithful, who will strengthen you and guard you from evil (πιστὸς δέ ἐστιν ὁ κύριος, ὃς στηρίξει ὑμᾶς καὶ φυλάξει ἀπὸ τοῦ πονηροῦ). Far more interesting to Paul is what the Lord can do with a hard situation, and so he changes his focus with "but" (δέ). At this point the apostle turns from "we" in the previous verse and begins to speak again of "you," the Thessalonians; he is moving toward giving them an exhortation and a prayer in 3:4–5.

There is a play on "faith" (πίστις, v. 2) and "faithful" (πιστός): not everyone has *faith*, but God is *faithful* (see a parallel in 2 Tim 2:13). That the Lord is faithful (1 Cor 1:9; 10:13; 1 Thess 5:24) is not an unusual theme in Paul and has its roots in the OT covenant: "Know therefore that the Lord your God is God; he is the faithful God, keeping his covenant of love to a thousand generations of those who love him and keep his commands" (Deut 7:9). Again, in Paul's mouth "the Lord" is Jesus, who is the Yahweh of the covenantal faithfulness (*ḥesed*). In 1 Thess 5:24 he states that *God* is faithful in carrying through their sanctification (cf. Phil 1:6).

The relative clause "who" (ὅς) expands on the person of the Lord Jesus. There are two future tense verbs: he will "strengthen you" (στηρίξει; see comments on 1 Thess 3:13; 2 Thess 2:17) and "guard" (φυλάξει) you. What follows is almost certainly taken from some version of the Lord's Prayer. "Deliver" in 3:2 is followed up with "from evil" (ἀπὸ τοῦ πονηροῦ) in 3:3 (see Matt 6:13). As in the Lord's Prayer, it is possible to take the substantival adjective as "the evil one," though it is difficult to prove which one is intended.

3:4 And we are persuaded in the Lord concerning you, that whatever we command, you are already doing and will continue to do (πεποίθαμεν δὲ ἐν κυρίῳ ἐφ' ὑμᾶς, ὅτι ἃ παραγγέλλομεν [καὶ] ποιεῖτε καὶ ποιήσετε). Paul's affirmation of the Thessalonians' obedience is heartening, and it is also the key to understanding the general tone of the letter. Paul is not speaking to a rogue congregation, even though he will go on in 3:6–15 to correct a few of the members about their work ethic.

2. BDAG, πρός 3. g.

With "we are persuaded" (πεποίθαμεν) Paul expresses the opinion of the apostolic team with regard to the church. Although it is a perfect tense, it has a present meaning, "to be so convinced that one puts confidence in something."[3] Paul also uses this verb to speak of the confidence he has in the Corinthians (2 Cor 2:3). This confidence now is not principally grounded in the behavior of the Thessalonians but "in the Lord"; that is, he has just spoken of the Lord's ongoing work in them, and within that sphere he can rest more easily about them.

The apostles are convinced that the Thessalonians will obey "whatever we command" (ἃ παραγγέλλομεν), with the relative clause referring generally to their instructions. This harks back to 2 Thess 2:15, where Paul tells them to hold fast to the traditions he has taught them. It also anticipates what he is about to say in 3:6 – 15: those who do not wish to work will obey the apostles and change their course; the rest of the church will obey the apostles and take the appropriate stance toward the disobedient. Paul emphasizes his confidence by using two tenses of the verb "to do" (ποιέω) — present and then future: "already doing and will continue to do" capture the contrast.

3:5 Now may the Lord direct your entire person unto [living] in the love that comes from God and the endurance that comes from Christ (Ὁ δὲ κύριος κατευθύναι ὑμῶν τὰς καρδίας εἰς τὴν ἀγάπην τοῦ θεοῦ καὶ εἰς τὴν ὑπομονὴν τοῦ Χριστοῦ). It is not unusual for Paul to insert a blessing or prayer before the closing verses of a letter. Here we already see in this small letter the second of four prayers.

Paul uses the optative "may [he] direct" (κατευθύναι), as he had in 1 Thess 3:11. There he meant it quite literally, that God and Christ would "guide their steps" to travel to see the Thessalonians again. Here he uses the same form to speak of the Lord Jesus' direction of the Thessalonians' spiritual walk toward a goal. "Your entire person" translates a word often rendered "heart" (καρδία), but here the term speaks not as the seat of the emotions but of the whole person (see comments on 1 Thess 2:4; 3:13). In the same way he prayed for their whole "spirit and soul and body" in 1 Thess 5:23.

The two virtues Paul mentions underlie much of the two letters, *love* and *endurance*:

> "the love that comes from God" (εἰς τὴν ἀγάπην τοῦ θεοῦ)
>
> "the endurance that comes from Christ" (εἰς τὴν ὑπομονὴν τοῦ Χριστοῦ)

The phrase "endurance of Christ" (lit. trans.) is the easier of the two, probably a genitive of source.[4] That is, Paul prays that the Thessalonians may receive the endowment of endurance in tribulation from Christ himself. The genitive "love of God" is more difficult. As with "labor of love" in 1 Thess 1:3, this phrase might mean *love for God* or *love for others*. In 1 Thess 1:3, the second choice was preferable, given that the theme of mutual love runs throughout these letters. We will therefore choose "love that comes from God" for this text as well, translating both as genitives of source. The fact that both love for other believers and endurance are mentioned in 2 Thess 1:3f – 4 means that 3:5 closes off a so-called *inclusio*:

> 2 Thess 1:3f – 4f: "Your love has grown abundantly, [the love] that each one of you all has, one for the other … your endurance and faith during all your persecutions and all the tribulations that you are suffering."
>
> 2 Thess 3:5: "Now may the Lord direct your entire person unto living in the love that comes from God and the endurance that comes from Christ."

3. BDAG, πείθω 2. a.

4. Wallace, *Grammar*, 109 – 10.

Theology in Application

Theology in Thessalonica

Paul asks the Thessalonians to pray for his work in Corinth, just as months earlier unnamed others might have been interceding for his work in Macedonia. By this point they would have been no strangers to the task of praying for lay evangelists. Besides Paul's team, the disciples might also be praying for missionaries who had gone out from their own church.

The Thessalonians learned about prayer, not just as an abstract doctrine but by actually praying with Paul's team. They came to realize during the first few months of their church's existence that Satan could block even the great missionary to the Gentiles (1 Thess 2:18), and that it was their duty to invoke God's powerful intervention against the forces of evil (2:17 – 19; 2 Thess 3:2).

Biblical Theology

Prayer for missionaries has elements both defensive and offensive. The defensive side is emphasized in the Thessalonian letters. Paul is going to face evil people (see the parallel in Rom 15:30 – 32) and invisible spiritual forces. Some Christians find a demon under every stone, while others cannot imagine that they've ever run across the devil. Both of these extremes are approved by hell itself, since either one ties up the Christian from meaningful prayer. Satan endeavors to ruin the harvest of new believers by any means possible, be it killing or shaming the messenger, or using the tools of superficiality, distraction, or persecution of new disciples (see Matt 13:3 – 9, 18 – 23). He might use the foolishness of other Christians to try to discourage those who are walking the right path. Paul tries to counter this effect here; believers must pray against these attacks.

The offensive side of prayer, found in other texts, is just as imperative. Jesus spoke in Matt 9:38 of praying to the Lord of the harvest for "reapers" to enter the field. There is a sense of urgency, to bring in the harvest when it is ready but before it spoils, is burnt by the sun, or is destroyed by rain. In another parable, workers are brought in without thought to how much it might cost (see Matt 20:1 – 16). If Christians follow Jesus' teaching, they not only labor in the harvest but they also pray for God to recruit workers.

In Eph 6:10 – 20, believers put on God's armor to battle against angelic forces. Even there we find offensive weapons — the sword of the Spirit is the Word of God, that is, Christ's gospel (6:17). The Ephesians must pray so that Paul might declare the gospel boldly (6:19 – 20), just as he did in Thessalonica (1 Thess 1:5). This is the church's counterattack against Satan; it is not simply prayer for the defense of the missionaries, but prayer that they inflict damage against Satan's strongholds.

Message of This Passage for the Church Today

Each missionary associated with your church must be able to depend on prayer, both from the congregation as a whole and even more importantly from a smaller, more deeply committed group, perhaps composed of members of various churches.

We can assume that the prayer time of Paul's congregations included local needs of health, employment, and so on. Yet, given what we may infer from the letters, it seems that they would have prayed more for missionaries than for, to name one example, the sick; also they would have prayed for the mission in an informed manner. Believers of an earlier age with their intelligent prayer might put us to shame, despite our rapid advances in communication technology.

Of course, missionaries themselves must be careful to communicate to churches "back home." Some post information as much as daily; others communicate rarely, starting with, "We're so sorry it's taken so long, we've been so busy. . . ." A missionary of the Pauline mold knows how important it is to teach the church that prayer changes things. If the missionary is incommunicado, it transmits the message that prayer is less than efficacious.

Missionaries distribute cards with options that may be checked off: financial support and/or prayer support. Perhaps the recipient is thinking, "I'll check off prayer support, it's the easier of the two." In fact, prayer support is not the easier path. When our family goes out to raise missionary funds, we suggest the figure of fifty dollars per month from a family or individual. We also ask people to commit themselves to pray for us. I am sure when someone truly carries through on a commitment to be prayer partners with us (daily, with focus, in a substantial fashion), it demands far greater time and effort than a pledge of money.

CHAPTER 13

2 Thessalonians 3:6 – 15

Literary Context

On the whole, the church in Thessalonica was obeying the apostles' commands (3:4), but there were a few troublemakers. The question of context is complicated by the enigma of who these disruptive people were and what precisely they were doing. The approach of this commentary is that Paul is not dealing with people who are, as one commentator puts it, simply "loafing." Rather, a small number of Thessalonians have arrogated for themselves the apostolic right to financial support for their ministry. Paul goes back to his apostolic work ethic in order to warn certain Thessalonians not to expect a living from the church.

The section fits nicely within the flow of the letter. First, it is an ethical exhortation, and it is typical of Paul that he places such *paraenesis* close to the end of a letter. Second, the section suits what he has just said 3:1 – 5, where Paul is thinking both of his own ongoing mission and of the steady obedience of the Thessalonian church.

V. A Request for the Thessalonians' Prayer (3:1 – 5)

➦ **VI. *Paraenesis:* The Problem of Disorderly Thessalonian Disciples (3:6 – 15)**

- **A. The church should stay away from members who are living disruptively (3:6)**
- **B. The church knows full well that Christians should work to support themselves (3:7 – 10)**
- **C. Some Thessalonians are living disruptively, not working but "meddling" (3:11)**
- **D. The apostles command these disorderly persons to work for their living and to cease their troublesome behavior (3:12)**
- **E. The church must not allow these new distractions to discourage them from doing the right thing (3:13)**
- **F. The church must stay aloof from disorderly members but not cut them out from the fellowship of the church (3:14 – 15)**

VII. Conclusion (3:16 – 18)

Main Idea

Paul addresses the problem of certain "disorderly" members of the church. They cause disruption by not supporting themselves through their own employment and by seeking their livelihood from other Christians. He gives the church instructions about how to manage the situation, telling them to withdraw from the disruptive and to not give them provisions.

Translation

(See next two pages.)

Structure

Paul steers the letter in a new direction, a final ethical exhortation marked with "and now" (δέ). Whereas in 1 Thessalonians the *paraenesis* section was introduced with "we appeal to you" (1 Thess 5:12), in 2 Thess 3:6 Paul uses a stronger verb ("we command you") and even invokes the name of our Lord Jesus Christ as his authority. In 1 Thess 5:12 – 22 the teaching was generalized; in 2 Thess 3 it is laser-sharp and focused on one issue: How should the church handle a "brother or sister who lives in a disorderly fashion"? Throughout the passage Paul addresses the church as a whole; only in 3:12 does he give a brief command to the disorderly people themselves.

Paul's exhortation in 3:6 is that the church should "keep aloof" from the disorderly (3:6c). What it means to keep aloof is developed at the end (3:14 – 15). In between these two commands, he gives readers some hints as to what was going on. Apparently some members were out of line with the apostolic teaching (3:6e, 7b, 11a). The translation of the ἀτάκτος word group as "disorderly" and not "lazy" lies at the heart of my understanding of the text (see comments on 3:6). Paul has also heard that these people were "meddling" (3:11c; again, see below for the possible interpretations of this activity). Finally, it is probable they were asking other Christians for daily food (3:10, 12).

Paul uses the causal marker "because" (γάρ) in 3:7a, which takes in all the material from 3:6e – 10. The apostles had taught them and provided a pattern for their disciples to imitate. Paul uses antithesis throughout this section, a favorite technique in the two letters: "not this, but [ἀλλά] that." Thus, the whole issue is one that the apostles have already handled in their first visit and need never have been a problem.

Paul again uses the causal "because" (γάρ) in 3:11 to indicate why he feels compelled to revisit the command now: the apostles have heard it is being disobeyed in Thessalonica. He uses antithesis here as well: they are "not working, but rather [ἀλλά] meddling." Paul addresses these disruptive people directly with "so" (δέ in

2 Thessalonians 3:6 – 15

6a	Exhortation	And now **we command you**, brothers and sisters,
6b	Invocation	in the name of our Lord Jesus Christ,
6c	Content #1	that you keep aloof from every brother or sister
6d	Description	who lives
		in a disorderly fashion, rather than
6e	Description	according to the tradition that they received from us.
7a	Cause	For **you yourselves know**
		how [you] must imitate
		our ways,
7b	Description	in that we did not act in a disorderly manner among you.
8a	Description	Nor did we eat food [taken] from anyone [without payment], but rather
		in labor and toil, night and day,
		we worked
8c	Purpose	in order not to be a burden to any one of you.
9a	Contra-expectation	Not that we lacked the authority to do so; but
9b	Contrast	[we lived this way] in order that we might provide you a model
9c	Purpose	so that you might imitate us.

10a	Time	And when we were with you, even then
10b	Exhortation	**we commanded you**
10c	Content	that, if someone does not wish to work,
		he or she shouldn't be given leave to eat.
11a	Cause	[We say this now] because **we hear that some among you are living in a disorderly manner,**
11b	Manner	not working, but rather
11c	Contrast	meddling in matters where they should not.
12a	Exhortation	So, **such people we command and exhort**
		in the Lord Jesus Christ
12b	Content	that they work quietly and eat their own food.
13	Exhortation	And **as for you**, brothers and sisters, **do not lose enthusiasm for doing good.**
14a	Condition	Now, if people do not obey the message we give through this letter,
14b	Content	**take note [of them] to not associate with them**,
14c	Purpose	in order that they might be shamed.
15a	Content	But **do not treat them as enemies**;
15b	Contrast	rather, **admonish them as a brother or sister.**

3:12), telling them to find gainful employment and support themselves. Since the exhortation in 3:13 seems to be the twin of the one in 3:12, I have translated it "and as for you" (ὑμεῖς δέ): Thessalonians who had been behaving rightly all along should not lose heart, that is, not let their disorderly companions make them grow cynical or discouraged.

The section ends as it began, with "now" (δέ) to mark the conclusion (3:14). Paul charges the church as a whole what to do if some continue to be disruptive: not to feed them and not to associate with them (3:14). With another antithesis (3:15) Paul states that the church should not treat them as enemies but as members of the Christian family. They should maintain enough contact with the disorderly so that they can try to dissuade them from their actions.

We do not follow the verse division of NA^{27}, which puts 3:16 as the conclusion to this section; rather, it is the beginning of the letter's closing in 3:16 – 18.

Exegetical Outline

➡ **I. The Church Should Stay Away from Members Living Disruptively (3:6).**

II. The Church Knows Full Well That Christians Should Work to Support Themselves (3:7 – 10).

A. Paul and the team gave them an example by their own behavior (3:7 – 9).

B. Paul and the team also gave them oral instruction that covered this very situation (3:10).

III. Some Thessalonians Are Living Disruptively, Not Working but "Meddling" (3:11).

IV. The Apostles Command These Disorderly Persons to Work for Their Living and to Cease Their Troublesome Behavior (3:12).

V. The Church Must Not Allow These New Distractions to Discourage Them from Doing the Right Thing (3:13).

VI. The Church Must Stay Aloof from Disorderly Members but Not Cut Them Out from the Fellowship of the Church (3:14 – 15).

Explanation of the Text

3:6 And now we command you, brothers and sisters, in the name of our Lord Jesus Christ, that you keep aloof from every brother or sister who lives in a disorderly fashion, rather than according to the tradition that they received from us (Παραγγέλλομεν δὲ ὑμῖν, ἀδελφοί, ἐν ὀνόματι τοῦ κυρίου ἡμῶν Ἰησοῦ Χριστοῦ, στέλλεσθαι ὑμᾶς ἀπὸ παντὸς ἀδελφοῦ ἀτάκτως περιπατοῦντος καὶ μὴ κατὰ τὴν παράδοσιν ἣν παρελάβοσαν παρ' ἡμῶν). Paul turns to the major ethical exhortation in this pair of letters. He grabs their attention by using the serious language of "we command" (παραγγέλλομεν), alerting the listeners by calling their attention with "brothers and sisters" (ἀδελφοί). As in 1 Thess 4:1 he invokes the Lord's authority.

The verb "keep aloof" (στέλλεσθαι) needs to be compared with the specific directions found in 3:14 – 15 concerning how they interact with those who live outside of the boundaries of behavior set by the apostles. "Who lives" means a way of life (lit., "walks," περιπατέω, see comments on 1 Thess 2:12). They are walking "in a disorderly fashion" (ἀτάκτως in 3:6, 11); Paul is using the adverb form of the adjective used in 1 Thess 5:14 for "the disorderly" (see comments there). He uses the cognate verb (ἀτακτέω) in 2 Thess 3:7 to state that the apostolic team "did not act in a disorderly manner."

The lexicons agree about the meaning of the "disorderly" (ἀτάκτ-) word group, giving definitions along the lines of "disorderly" or "disruptive" (see BDAG; LSJ; LEH; MM; *TDNT*; *TLNT*). The single use of the word group in the LXX clearly reveals that meaning for the adjective (ἄτακτος): "Others who had just now dressed for their wedding abandoned the chambers appointed for the occasion, as well as the appropriate modesty, and made a mad [i.e., disorderly] dash through the city" (3 Macc 1:19 NETS). Some English versions render the adjective properly, while others have "lazy" (GNB), "idle" (NIV, NLT, NRSV) or, to stretch it to the limit, "loaf around" (3:11, CEV).[1] These translators are making the text say more than it really does, apparently basing their renderings upon this reasoning:

> Some Thessalonians do not wish to work, but want to receive a handout.
>
> Paul uses the Greek word (ἀτάκτως) to describe their action.
>
> Therefore, the Greek word (ἀτάκτως) must mean a person who is idle or lazy.

This is loose logic. Spicq is wholly justified when he complains:

> It would not be necessary to insist on the meaning of *ataktos* — "not remaining in his/her/its place, out of order, undisciplined" — if a certain number of exegetes did not suggest translating it "idle, lazy." But the usage of the verb, the adjective, and the adverb in the Koine, notably in the first century AD, confirms that the word covers any breach of obligation or convention, disorders of life in general; and the usage is decisive.[2]

The disruptive disciples, of course, should be engaging in gainful employment, in accordance with the apostolic "tradition" (παράδοσιν), just as they were obligated to obey all of the apostles' oral teaching (2:15).[3] In fact, it may be this reference to tradition that will help us unlock the specific nature of these persons' disorderliness.

3:7 For you yourselves know how [you] must imitate our ways, in that we did not act in a disorderly manner among you (αὐτοὶ γὰρ οἴδατε πῶς δεῖ μιμεῖσθαι ἡμᾶς, ὅτι οὐκ ἠτακτήσαμεν ἐν ὑμῖν). Paul again points to himself, Silas, and Timothy as models. The Thessalonians do not simply need to follow oral tradition; they must also imitate behaviors they saw in their leaders. He uses reminder language for the second time in 2 Thessalonians, this time to make them recall with the eyes of their memory the way in which the apostles maintained themselves in good order. Paul had spoken

1. The English words "idle" and "lazy/indolent" are not precisely synonymous; people can be idle for reasons other than laziness. The Lord Jesus happens to illustrate this point when he speaks of field hands who were *idle* because they couldn't find work. Nevertheless they were not *lazy* for they leaped immediately to work when they could get it (parable of the vineyard, Matt 20:1–16).

2. Spicq, "ἀτακτέω, ἄτακτος, ἀτάκτως," *TLNT*, 1:223; esp. C. Spicq, "Les Thessaloniciens 'inquiets' étaient-ils des paresseux?" *Studia Teologica* 10 (1956): 1–13. Pointed too is the observation by G. Delling in "ἄτακτος (ἀτάκτως), ἀτακτέω," *TDNT*, 8:48: "Outside Christianity the verb, when applied to work, does not in the first instance lay emphasis on sloth but rather on an irresponsible attitude to the obligation to work." Rigaux, *Thessaloniciens*, 704–5, notes that these people are not passive (lazy) but active (busybodies).

3. This is one of those passages that should be read aloud, in order to hear it as the Thessalonians did, with its staccato use of the letter π.

generally of their good imitation in 1 Thess 1:6, but now some have failed to conform to the apostolic model.

The next clause is not tightly joined syntactically to what precedes it; we have translated the conjunction (ὅτι) as "*in* that" in order to smooth the English. Here Paul turns to the cognate verb "to be disorderly" (ἀτακτέω). As we saw in 3:6, the text does not say "we were not idle" but rather "we did not act in a disorderly manner."

3:8 Nor did we eat food [taken] from anyone [without payment], but rather in labor and toil, night and day, we worked in order not to be a burden to any one of you (οὐδὲ δωρεὰν ἄρτον ἐφάγομεν παρά τινος, ἀλλ' ἐν κόπῳ καὶ μόχθῳ νυκτὸς καὶ ἡμέρας ἐργαζόμενοι πρὸς τὸ μὴ ἐπιβαρῆσαί τινα ὑμῶν). Paul gives more details about the apostles' behavior in Thessalonica, advancing further with "nor" (οὐδέ). "Without payment" (the accusative form δωρεάν used as an adverb) is the same form he used in 2 Cor 11:7, to say that he preached the gospel to the Corinthians *gratis*. As he asserts in Acts 20:33 – 35 and in the tradition of Samuel (1 Sam 12:3 – 5), Paul could not be accused of taking anything from anyone — not even his "food" (ἄρτον, lit., "bread" as a metonymy of daily food). In an economy where daily bread was never certain, a request for food might be a warning sign: false apostles might reveal their true motives when they asked for rations (see *Did.* 11.6, 9).

Paul then uses language that is almost identical to 1 Thess 2:9: "labor and … hardship" (see comments on this verse).

3:9 Not that we lacked the authority to do so; but [we lived this way] in order that we might provide you a model so that you might imitate us (οὐχ ὅτι οὐκ ἔχομεν ἐξουσίαν, ἀλλ' ἵνα ἑαυτοὺς τύπον δῶμεν ὑμῖν εἰς τὸ μιμεῖσθαι ἡμᾶς). Paul adds, as he so typically does, that while he does not exercise his right, still the right is his to use or to set aside as he wishes. This verse, as 3:7, does not flow smoothly in the original, and so we have paraphrased slightly.

In 1 Thess 2:7 Paul had expressed the thought as "even though we could have insisted on acting all important and being a burden to you" as apostles. Here, Paul and his team have the "authority" (ἐξουσίαν) to require financial support of the Thessalonians while ministering to them. Yet they worked, first, in order to propel the gospel along without unnecessary hindrance, and second, to provide a "model" (τύπον) of a Christian work ethic.

3:10 And when we were with you, even then we commanded you that, if someone does not wish to work, he or she shouldn't be given leave to eat (καὶ γὰρ ὅτε ἦμεν πρὸς ὑμᾶς, τοῦτο παρηγγέλλομεν ὑμῖν, ὅτι εἴ τις οὐ θέλει ἐργάζεσθαι μηδὲ ἐσθιέτω). Paul and his companions gave the Thessalonians specific teaching "when we were with you." The verb "we commanded" (παρηγγέλλομεν) is a form of the verb Paul uses to begin this section (3:6).

Paul uses a simple conditional sentence. The protasis or "if" clause anticipates the situation they are facing now. What happens when a person "does not wish" (οὐ θέλει) to work? The verb (θέλω) could refer to one's personal taste ("does not like to work"); more likely in this context Paul is describing a volitional act (as we might say today, "does not choose to work") without revealing what drove that decision. Paul was not compelled to work, but he "voluntarily" made the decision to do so (1 Cor 9:17). The disorderly made the opposite decision. Apparently it was not the case that the Thessalonians could not find suitable employment.

Few commentators remark on the significance of the infinitive "to work" (ἐργάζεσθαι). The verb has a variety of applications in Classical and *koinē*

Greek. When it was used intransitively — that is, without a direct object — it often had the significance of "labor" or "work with one's hands."[4] Paul uses it in connection with manual labor in some passages (e.g., 1 Cor 4:12; Eph 4:28; 1 Thess 4:11; probably 1 Thess 2:9). This evidence probably indicates that Paul is referring to manual labor in 2 Thess 3:10: "if someone does not wish to work [with their hands]." Such an interpretation suits well the context of the two letters. The apostles had worked with their hands; so too must all Christians (1 Thess 4:11 – 12), and so should these disorderly people in 2 Thess 3.

The apodosis, or "then" clause, shows the church how to manage such a situation: "he or she shouldn't be given leave to eat" (μηδὲ ἐσθιέτω). Perhaps church authorities stand behind the action, as in NJB (see also ESV) — "not to let anyone eat who refused to work." It means that those who won't follow Paul's example of industry should not be allowed to eat *gratis*, whether at the invitation of the individual believer or the assembly or its leaders.

It is worth pointing out that Paul does *not* say that the church is already giving food to the disorderly. That may be the implication of 3:10, but it is not explicit. Paul could merely be warning them not to do so in the future.

3:11 [We say this now] because we hear that some among you are living in a disorderly manner, not working, but rather meddling in matters where they should not (ἀκούομεν γάρ τινας περιπατοῦντας ἐν ὑμῖν ἀτάκτως, μηδὲν ἐργαζομένους ἀλλὰ περιεργαζομένους). Finally, for the first time in two letters, Paul puts his finger on a known sin in the Thessalonian church! "We say this now" is an expansion of the causative conjunction "because" (γάρ). "We hear" (ἀκούομεν) is probably due to the report from Timothy, although perhaps some third party has passed on the information (see 1 Thess 1:8 – 9).

Paul makes a play on words that works well in the Greek but not in English: *they do not work, but "meddle"* (μηδὲν ἐργαζομένους ἀλλὰ περιεργαζομένους), the second term being the compound of the first. The NIV (similarly the ESV) makes a good attempt with "not busy; they are busybodies."

Once again, it must be insisted that the Greek text still says nothing of "loafing around," "lazy," "idling their time away" (REB), or "do nothing except"; this is all eisegesis, a reading *into* the text. What Paul actually says is that rather than "working," they are engaging in "meddling" (περιεργαζομένους).

IN DEPTH: Lexical Note on "Meddle" (περιεργάζομαι)

This verb may be taken in two directions. The more common usage is certainly suited to this context. It is *socially imposing upon other people*, wasting other people's time and distracting them from their daily responsibilities. Here the "meddlesome" would be neglecting their own work as well as annoying their fellows; they "do nothing except meddle in other people's business" (GNB). In a parallel, younger widows (1 Tim 5:13) are likely to become "busybodies" (the cognate noun περίεργοι), gadding about and gossiping instead of focusing on

4. See LSJ. So Homer, *Od.* 2.272 (captive soldiers used as forced labor); Herodotus, *Hist.* 2.124.3 (work in the quarries); Demosthenes, *Orat.* 42.31 (work in the mines); Thucydides, *Hist.* 2.72.3 (cultivate the ground).

their own domestic work. There is a useful parallel in the scorn that was sometimes directed toward Greco-Roman philosophers: they were regularly called "busybodies," while they replied that they were busy with important matters. "Thus Paul uses a well-known term of opprobrium that was applied by his contemporaries to people who thought of themselves as representing higher values."[5]

Second is a sense that is scarcely mentioned in the commentaries but shows up with surprising regularity in Hellenistic, Jewish, and Christian Greek: *prying inappropriately into divine matters.*[6] Such presumptuous trespassing into the divine realm is no mere wasting of your neighbor's time; it is an offense to God/the gods. This significance of the word group could fit in with 2 Thess 3:11. Paul does not indicate the nature of their meddling, but they could be interloping in the sphere of the Lord's work, crossing the line into areas where they should not presume to go. Like Uzzah touching the ark (2 Sam 6:6 – 7), like Uzziah intruding into the temple (2 Chron 26:16 – 21), they have trespassed into the holy.

The difficulty with choosing between either significance is that in practice they tend to overlap. People who meddle in God's business tend also to make pests of themselves on a horizontal level (see Col 2:18; 1 Tim 1:3 – 7; and the full host of sectarian movements since time immemorial). See further "In Depth: Summary and Conclusion: Who Were These Disruptive People?" for a summary analysis of their wrongdoing.

3:12 So, such people we command and exhort in the Lord Jesus Christ that they work quietly and eat their own food (τοῖς δὲ τοιούτοις παραγγέλλομεν καὶ παρακαλοῦμεν ἐν κυρίῳ Ἰησοῦ Χριστῷ ἵνα μετὰ ἡσυχίας ἐργαζόμενοι τὸν ἑαυτῶν ἄρτον ἐσθίωσιν). Paul finally moves with a δέ to a command concerning "such people." His words mirror the charge to the church in general that they distance themselves from disorderly people (3:6). Again he invokes the name of the Lord Jesus Christ to give the command a most solemn air.

Believers are to work hard (see definition of ἐργάζομαι above). They should live "quietly" (μετὰ ἡσυχίας), an ideal that Paul had already taught them (1 Thess 4:11 – 12). As in 3:8, "eating their own bread" (τὸν ἑαυτῶν ἄρτον ἐσθίωσιν) is metonymy,

5. Malherbe, *Letters to the Thessalonians*, 453.

6. Among other references are *Let. Aris.* 315 (ed. Charlesworth): "it was revealed to him in a dream that it was due to his meddlesome desire to disclose the things of God to common man"; Philo, *Names* 72, criticizes those who would trespass in God's cosmic secrets: "On what account dost thou investigate the motions and periods of the stars...? Is it merely that you may indulge your curiosity [from περιεργάζομαι] with respect to those matters? And what advantage could accrue to you from all this curiosity [from περίεργος]?"; Acts 19:19: there are those in Ephesus who "meddle" in magic; Josephus, *Ant.* 12.2.14 (§112), refers to the third-century BC Ptolemy II Philadelphus of Egypt: "his distemper befell him while he *indulged too great a curiosity* about divine matters [i.e., the Jewish Law]"; Herm. *Sim.* 9.2.7: "Let what you cannot see alone, and do not *trouble* yourself about it [or *meddle in it*]"; Plato, *Apol.* 19b, used the verb in this sense when he reported the charge that Socrates meddled in things heavenly and earthly.

representing a lifestyle in which they earn their own keep and cause no trouble to the church family. Paul does not develop in this passage another purpose of work—that one is then able to help the less fortunate (see Acts 20:35; Eph 4:28).

3:13 And as for you, brothers and sisters, do not lose enthusiasm for doing good (ὑμεῖς δέ, ἀδελφοί, μὴ ἐγκακήσητε καλοποιοῦντες). Paul turns from the "disruptive" Thessalonians to the larger group, calling their attention with "and as for you, brothers and sisters." "Doing good" (καλοποιοῦντες) is a *hapax legomenon* in the New Testament and is unusual outside the canon. Paul later says the same thing with slightly different language in Gal 6:9 (τὸ καλὸν ποιοῦντες), which also emphasizes service to the Christian community. Paul's statement is especially appropriate in a context where people of good conscience might grow disgusted at those who presumed upon them and become cynical about being generous.

3:14 Now, if people do not obey the message we give through this letter, take note [of them] to not associate with them, in order that they might be shamed (εἰ δέ τις οὐχ ὑπακούει τῷ λόγῳ ἡμῶν διὰ τῆς ἐπιστολῆς, τοῦτον σημειοῦσθε, μὴ συναναμίγνυσθαι αὐτῷ, ἵνα ἐντραπῇ). Paul moves on to instructions about what to do with the disruptive numbers, addressed to the church as a whole. He harks back to 3:6, but rather than reminding them of "tradition," he speaks of the message he has just given "through this letter." The church should not ignore what is going on or tolerate it, but act. "Take note" (σημειοῦσθε) in the middle voice means "to take note of, to mark," occasionally with the sense of take note of with disapproval.[7] The believers, no matter their eagerness for being kind people (3:13), should not "associate" or "intermingle" (συναναμίγνυσθαι) with the troublemakers. This verb may be compared with "keep aloof from" (στέλλεσθαι) in 3:6.

Paul would later write in 1 Cor 5:9, 11 that the church should not "associate with" (συναναμίγνυσθαι) Christians who did wicked deeds. But despite the use of the same verb, the sin in the Corinthian case was much more grave. A man had committed incest; he should be turned over to Satan (5:5) and thrust from the church: "Expel the wicked person from among you" (1 Cor 5:13). This is the sort of language that, in the context of Deuteronomy, might have been followed by a call for the death penalty.

The appropriate discipline in Thessalonica is less strict than in 1 Cor 5. One is reminded that religious communities usually have grades of punishment; the Rule of the Community (1QS) of Qumran, for example, allowed for full expulsion (as in Corinth) but also for temporary disciplines. A minor offense—interrupting another member while he is speaking—incurred a penalty of ten days.[8]

Paul's orders to the Thessalonian church are meant to correct wrong behavior by social disapproval: "that they might be shamed" (ἵνα ἐντραπῇ). English versions tend to translate the verb as if it were a description of the sinner's feelings: "until he is ashamed of himself" (REB) or "that they may feel ashamed" (NIV). Nevertheless, "that they might *be shamed*" is more accurate, since it takes into account the system of shame and honor that underlay social interaction in Paul's day. In modern times, self-esteem or its absence is thought to be an individual matter. In the first century, shame was pressed on the individual from without. In Thessalonica, the erring believers would be "shamed" by those refusing to intermingle with them. Paul

7. MM, 573; see Polybius, *Hist*. 5.78.2, where an eclipse was "noted" as a bad omen.

8. 1QS VII, 9–10 (Martínez and Tigchelaar, 1:87).

does not say whether he wanted them put out of the church.

3:15 But do not treat them as enemies; rather, admonish them as a brother or sister (καὶ μὴ ὡς ἐχθρὸν ἡγεῖσθε, ἀλλὰ νουθετεῖτε ὡς ἀδελφόν). Here the conjunction (καί) must have its sense of "but," providing a contrast: Paul does not counsel harshness, since this level of sin does not constitute a rupture of the family relation that is so fundamental to these letters.

"Regard" or "treat" gives us information on how Paul categorizes such people. "Not as enemies" (μὴ ὡς ἐχθρόν) indicates that the discipline of the church is not a matter of animosity by people who have been dunned for support. These offenders are still part of the family of God; brothers and sisters are inside the circle, enemies outside (see Rom 5:10). In this particular case they were apparently not to be "shunned,"[9] that is, denied all contact, as with the incestuous man of Corinth. The church is to continue speaking with disorderly Christians, in order to confront them with "admonition" (νουθετεῖτε), that is, reproving and instructing them regarding God's way.

Paul has sketched out for us the broad strokes of discipline in this particular instance: don't treat them as unbelievers on the one hand; keep away from them on the other. This doesn't seem to be sufficiently clear direction for the church to know what to do, and that is why Malherbe's observation rescues the exegete: "It is most likely that he expected the person who carried this letter to its recipients to supply the details or that he left matters of procedure to the church, so long as his commands were carried out."[10]

In the second century, Polycarp would quote 2 Thess 3:15 (Pol. *Phil.* 11.4) in the context of a presbyter and his wife who "loved money."

> Therefore, brothers, I am deeply grieved for him and for his wife; may the Lord grant them true repentance. You, therefore, for your part must be reasonable in this matter, "and do not regard" such people "as enemies," but, as sick and straying members, restore them, in order that you may save your body in its entirety. For by doing this you build up one another.

We are not told how the Philippian church handled the situation either — most likely the facts were already well-known to both Polycarp and the recipients of his letter.

Paul's letter to the Philippians yields yet another dimension. He identifies certain teachers as "enemies" of the cross of Christ (Phil 3:18), that is, beyond the pale of God's family. We see nothing in 2 Thessalonians that indicates that there was any offense so unspeakable in Thessalonica. But Paul deals with another group in Phil 1:15 – 17, evangelists preaching the true gospel with low motives, a spiteful rivalry against Paul. They are members of God's family, no matter how irritating they could be. Perhaps the sin of the disorderly people was closer in rank to that of Phil 1.

9. Witherington, *1 and 2 Thessalonians*, 256, says that "withdrawal cannot mean absolute avoidance in all aspects." See contra, Wanamaker, *Thessalonians*, 289 – 90, who thinks that Paul is counseling their excommunication and that members of the church "reprove" the excommunicated outside of the meetings. The comments by Green, *Thessalonians*, 354 – 55, show the difficulty of determining what precisely Paul wanted to happen; they are not excommunicated, says Green, but also not "in communion."

10. Malherbe, *Letters to the Thessalonians*, 460.

IN DEPTH: Summary and Conclusion: Who Were These Disruptive People?

We possess only partial data, a fact that should lead the interpreter to be cautious.

I. *At what point in time did these people stop working?* As it turns out, the question of "when" is an important clue. One can narrow down the possibilities by taking into account other data in the two letters:

- During their first visit, the apostles had taught about the Christian's work habits.
- Paul later praised their willingness to work hard (1 Thess 1:3). He told them to keep going on in this direction and to not neglect their labor (4:11).
- He told them to reprove any "disorderly" people (the ἄτακτ- word group) in the church (5:14). As demonstrated above, the word group does not mean "lazy."
- Later, some did indeed become "disorderly" (3:10 – 11); they did not wish to work and were "busybodies" (3:6 – 15).
- Possibly the "disorderly" asked for support, whether from individuals or from the congregation (3:8); or it is conceivable that Paul is merely anticipating the possibility.
- Someone — probably Timothy — reported them to Paul (3:11).

It seems best to infer that after Timothy's initial reconnoitering of Thessalonica, Paul assessed that the matter was not (yet) serious, and so he fired a "warning shot" in his first letter (4:11 – 12; 5:14). The situation grew worse during the time between Timothy's two trips and drew forth Paul's detailed comments in 2 Thess 3.

II. *What was the motivation for their disorderliness?* Paul simply does not give an explanation for their rejection of the apostolic model.[11] The principal hypotheses are:

1. They decided that if the eschatological day was at hand, there was no need for them to keep working.[12]
2. They were some variety of charismatic "enthusiasts," Christians who were so caught up in the Spirit that they neglected normal earthly concerns.[13]
3. They did not wish to work because of their own character flaws.[14]

11. It is apparently for this reason that Fee, *Thessalonians*, 332, does not explain the cause for this disruptive behavior.

12. Best, *Thessalonians*, 334. Also Morris, *Thessalonians* (NICNT), 253.

13. So says Mearns, "Early Eschatological Development in Paul: The Evidence of 1 Corinthians," 23: "we may presume that the giving up of regular work in the case of many Thessalonians probably stemmed from the enthusiastic motive of living in 'heaven now' and enjoying a proleptic paradise."

14. Malherbe, *Letters to the Thessalonians*, 457, seems to fall into this category: some Thessalonians made a "perverse decision *not* to work." Malherbe (ibid., 454 – 57) gives a careful analysis to the passage, but in the end does not offer a solution as to why people would not work.

4. They followed the culture of "patronage"; that is, they were people who sought to ally themselves with a powerful patron or "godfather" figure, who in return offered his "clients" enough for their basic living expenses.[15]
5. They emulated Paul and Silas by doing evangelistic work, but unlike them they asserted that they deserved support from the churches.[16]

Many commentators regard #1 as the natural result of reading the passage in its literary context. In a time of eschatological panic, some quit their jobs and lived off the common fund of the church. Paul, having dismissed the mistaken theology in 2 Thess 2:1 – 12, goes on to handle its behavioral fruit in 3:6 – 15. Hence Best makes a leap from one point to the other: "We are not told why the minority does not work, and as at 1 Th. 4.11 *we can only surmise* from the completely eschatological atmosphere that they reasoned within themselves, 'The End is near, work is a waste of time.'"[17]

But this exegesis of 2 Thessalonians could be based on the fallacy of *post hoc, ergo propter hoc*: that is, if A happens and afterward B, then A must have caused B. It is possible, of course, that faulty eschatology may have been the cause of a mistaken work ethic. But the data we possess do not yield that as a necessary conclusion. For example, we are not even sure of the historical sequence: Did the work issue in fact arise *after* the eschatological panic (if there even was "panic")? With regard to the literary sequence, yes, in 2 Thessalonians Paul deals with theological problems first, and ethical problems second. But this is his normal style, since he follows the Greco-Roman rhetoric of dealing with ethical issues toward the end of his letters. That does not mean they occurred in that order; people might have refrained from working in Thessalonica *before there was any sign of eschatological confusion.*

In fact, Paul already sensed the need to reinforce the Christian work ethic in 1 Thess 2:9; 4:11 – 12, before Timothy had returned to him from Thessalonica, and only then prompting Paul to write 2 Thess 2:1 – 12. Witherington is surely correct to underscore the absence of any connection between the ethical ex-

15. The "patronage" viewpoint has recently grown in popularity. See Green, *Thessalonians*, 341 – 42; Witherington, *1 and 2 Thessalonians*, 247 – 49; Wanamaker, *Thessalonians*, 286; Andrew D. Clarke, *Serve the Community of the Church: Christians as Leaders and Ministers* (Grand Rapids: Eerdmans, 2000), 200 – 201; R. Russell, "The Idle in 2 Thess 3.6 – 12: An Eschatological or a Social Problem?" *NTS* 34 (1988): 105 – 19; Bruce W. Winter, "'If a Man Does Not Wish to Work ...' A Cultural and Historical Setting for 2 Thessalonians 3:6 – 16," *TynBul* 40 (1989): 303 – 15.

16. See Jewett, *Thessalonian Correspondence*, 105.

17. Best, *Thessalonians*, 334, emphasis added. Some people naturally look at a letter and try to explain all the data by one grand unified theory (Gnosticism, for example, or eschatological fervor). On the other hand, a pastor who reads 2 Thessalonians might have a different method, knowing that a single congregation may experience a range of problems — this group is fanatical about eschatology; this person seems unable to hold a job; this one has strong temptations toward sexual sin — and that their various problems might have absolutely no connection with each other!

hortation in 3:6–15 and the Thessalonians' eschatology: "Attempts to connect the problem of idleness with the problem of eschatology fail to recognize that Paul deliberately separates these two issues by three segments of prayer."[18]

With regard to the "sociological" interpretation (#4), nowhere does Paul mention in 1 Thess 4:11–12 or 2 Thess 3:6–15 *why* anyone would not wish to work; that is, he does not state that their motive is personal laziness or based in eschatology or anything else, such as a reliance on "patronage." Those who argue for this latter viewpoint state that patronage was so ingrained in the culture that Paul did not have to mention it. This only serves to indicate that #4, like #1, is an argument from silence.

Neither does the "enthusiasm" viewpoint (#2) find support from the text. The "laziness" interpretation (#3) does have some evidence, albeit slight: Paul might be saying in 3:10 that these people simply don't "feel like" working (one possible rendering of θέλω). Nevertheless, he never says that laziness is the problem. Lazy people might cause disruption, but the disorderly are not necessarily lazy.

It is #5 that best explains the situation in Thessalonica.

a. When Paul speaks of a work ethic, it is always in connection with his ministry and the model he gave them. In other words, he is not simply a pattern for *Christian behavior*, but more specifically for the *behavior of Christians who evangelize.*
b. Paul held to a specific ideal of self-support, which he applied to himself, Silas, and Barnabas. Although an apostle has the right to food and drink from his churches (1 Cor 9:4, 6, 14), it is better for pioneering evangelists to pay their own way through manual labor.
c. The Thessalonians were noteworthy for being evangelistic, as demonstrated in 1 Thess 1–2. We have argued that the reason for Paul's description of the apostles' work in 2:1–12 was not self-defense, but rather to provide a model for the Thessalonians, including in particular any Thessalonian evangelists.
d. In later Christian texts, one encounters a strong indication that the church had regular trouble with parasitical teachers who looked to the church for goods or money. For example:
   - teachers of false doctrines who infiltrated house churches with their teaching: "they are disrupting whole households by teaching things they ought not to teach—and that for the sake of dishonest gain" (Titus 1:11; likewise 1 Tim 3:3, 8; 6:5; 2 Tim 3:2; Titus 1:7, 11; 2 Pet 2:3).
   - "apostles" who are condemned not for their doctrine but because of economic impropriety: "Let every apostle who comes to you be welcomed as if

18. Witherington, *1 and 2 Thessalonians*, 245.

he were the Lord. But he is not to stay for more than one day, unless there is need, in which case he may stay another. But if he stays three days, he is a false prophet. And when the apostle leaves, he is to take nothing except bread until he finds his next night's lodging. But if he asks for money, he is a false prophet" (*Did.* 11.4 – 6). If teachers come to a town and wish to receive money from the church, then they are "trading on Christ" (*Did.* 12.5). The *Didache* uses language similar to 2 Thess 3; it is better that they should work with their hands and not be "unemployed" (12.4).[19] The *Didache* tradition could well have roots in the first century and may be a response to a problem that began as early as the 50s.

Some have argued that this viewpoint would only be convincing if 2 Thessalonians were written significantly later than Paul — such as the late first or early second century.[20] But this is hardly necessary, given that already in the mid-40s through the mid-50s Paul had a fine sensibility of how financial questions could inhibit the work of the gospel and knew of people who were wrongfully taking money from others (cf., e.g., 2 Cor 11:5 – 9).

What then is Paul saying? First, *as apostles, we worked for our own living, even though we were doing the Lord's work; that is because all Christians should support themselves.* The apostolic team was not "disorderly" (3:7); neither should the Thessalonians be (see 1 Thess 5:14). But there may be a more specific application here: *as apostles we worked for our own living, even while doing the Lord's work;*[21] *people who go out from our churches to evangelize should follow our pattern.*

III. *To what sort of behavior does "busybody" refer (2 Thess 3:11)?* The language of 2 Thess 3:11 indicates that the disorderly Christians are guilty of "meddling" (περιεργάζομαι, see comments on 3:11). There is a special meaning of the verb that happens to work neatly here: they are trespassing in divine matters that are not their business, by usurping the privilege of financial support for their ministry; they are interlopers. They might even have been willing to justify themselves, that they are doing good work and should be recompensed for it.

19. "Unemployed" in this text is not ἀτακτός but the synonym ἀργός. The Holmes version of *Didache* translated it as "idle," but "unemployed" or "not gainfully employed" is a better rendering of ἀργός. It is the nonpejorative meaning that the adjective has in the parable of the unemployed field workers (Matt 20:3, 6). In all other uses of ἀργός in the NT, it has a negative meaning (Matt 12:36; 1 Tim 5:13; Titus 1:12; Jas 2:20; 2 Pet 1:8).

20. See the overview in Marshall, *1 and 2 Thessalonians*, 219.

21. Paul's rule was not absolute: in fact, he himself had around the time he wrote 1 – 2 Thessalonians devoted himself to full-time ministry in Corinth (the probable meaning of Acts 18:5). In addition, he affirms the right of any apostle to receive financial support in 1 Cor 9:4, 6 – 7. In different circumstances, the pastor Chrysostom allows that people in ministry should be supported by the church if they "teach, and are wholly occupied in the business of teaching." See John Chrysostom, *Homilies on Second Thessalonians* 5 (*NPNF*[1] 13:394).

Our viewpoint, like all the others, contains an element of guesswork. Yet it takes all the data into account and rests on the fewest number of assumptions. Because of this link between evangelism and work in these letters, the best reading of this passage is this: *some Thessalonians are availing themselves of an apostolic right that Paul and his team have not taken for themselves, requesting support from Thessalonica or from the new churches they are planting. They are not lazy and perhaps are very busy; but they do not have gainful employment, and they are proving to be disruptive.*

Theology in Application

Paul is dealing with a Christian *work ethic* in this section, one that applies to ministers of the Word and to believers in general. We have sought to demonstrate that the problem in Thessalonica was not the common fund for the poor, but certain Christians who believed that their gospel ministry deserved financial maintenance.

Theology in Thessalonica

The Thessalonian church received the gospel from a team that performed manual labor to support itself. The new disciples quickly turned from being learners to being evangelists and teachers of others (1 Thess 1:6 – 8). Paul in 2:1 – 12 explained to them in detail the sort of lifestyle they must follow if they wanted to carry on the sort of work that Paul's team did. Included in 2:9 is the fact that they worked hard with their own hands, because that was the way they showed love to their disciples. Paul contrasts their decision to not avail themselves of their apostolic rights, while other, less deserving, people presume to use them.

Today's young person is faced with thousands of career options, and it is no surprise that professional vocational help is needed. Until just a few decades ago, people did what they were told to do — boys followed in their father's footsteps or were ordered by their fathers what to do; girls married or worked as secretaries or teachers or domestics. For his part, Paul lived in a world where the vocational options for most people were more limited still. For the majority, working with one's own hands was the sole alternative to thievery, slavery, or charity. Paul in 1 Thess 4:10b – 12 reiterates the need for all Christians to be orderly, quiet, and good workers. He does not connect this doctrine with their possible confusion with the resurrection of the dead in 4:13 – 18 or with the rest of the eschatological teaching in 1 Thess 5:1 – 11 or 2 Thess 1 – 2.

Then in 2 Thess 3:6 – 15 the issue of work resurfaces. Paul labels as "disruptive" certain people who did not wish to work. These evangelists/teachers went from house to house in Thessalonica or even throughout Macedonia, asking for support and heedlessly causing harm with their inflated self-perception. After all, they reasoned, had not Jesus taught them that "the worker is worth his keep" (Matt 10:10; see also Gal 6:6; 1 Tim 5:17 – 18)? Paul does not charge them with being false teachers.[22] Still, he tells them, as the saying goes, "not to quit their day jobs."

The Thessalonians were likewise known for their love toward others (1 Thess 4:9 – 10a). These kindhearted people might have allowed themselves to be taken advantage of by Christians who seemed to have a solid claim on their largesse. The best solution for everyone, says Paul, is that the church should maintain family relations with them and kindly yet firmly refuse to give them support.

Biblical Theology[23]

God created humanity to work in paradise, but the fall twisted that gift into dehumanizing drudgery. Now that Christ has come, God has begun to redeem work. Even in the future kingdom, God's people will work together as co-heirs with Christ (2 Tim 2:12). Christians manifest love when they engage in meaningful employment and find a life of "quiet." This is not the inner freedom from a troubled heart, as was the ideal in Stoicism, nor the serenity that the Epicurean sought when he withdrew from society. Rather, it is the undisturbed tranquility that comes from communion with God and with the church in the supernatural power of the Spirit.

The Protestant Reformation sought to recapture the biblical doctrine of "vocation." While God may call some to special service, the distinction between clergy and layperson is functionally reduced. Since every believer is a priest, every good work that is done by any believer is a sacred offering to God. Therefore our work must be done with cheerfulness, honesty, integrity, and excellence. As Calvin put it, "no task will be so sordid and base, provided you obey your calling in it, that it will not shine and be reckoned very precious in God's sight."[24] One area where the Reformers are not entirely relevant today is that they argued against changing professions, since in that culture it was a sign of rootlessness. Today, with the shifting patterns caused by industrialization and technologies, people often find themselves called to change their work in order to make a worthwhile contribution.

While I was researching this topic, I discovered that not every Christian comes

22. Schmithals, *Paul & the Gnostics*, 198, makes the useful observation: "Most suggestive is the reference to the example Paul gave during his stay in Thessalonica, which calls to order members of the community with a missionary activity similar to Paul's." Nevertheless, Schmithals attempts to link these Thessalonian preachers with, and it comes as no surprise, Gnosticism. They were supposedly otherworldly because their theology encouraged it: "the disorderliness of their activity consists in the fact that in their missionary busyness they neglect their existence in this world." Once again, Schmithals detects an elaborate theological structure behind what was more likely a simpler issue.

23. We heartily recommend Craig L. Blomberg, *Neither Poverty Nor Riches: A Biblical Theology of Material Possessions* (New Studies in Biblical Theology; Grand Rapids: Eerdmans, 1999), for a holistic treatment of all the Bible's teaching on economics.

24. Calvin, *Institutes* 3.10.6 (trans. Battles, 725).

from a background similar to mine. I will focus my comments on the message I've often heard:

- Industriousness will lead to prosperity (Prov 6:6 – 11).
- People should not be allowed to live on welfare (based on 2 Thess 3:11 – 12).
- People should be content with what they have; that is, they should not desire or seek higher pay (1 Tim 6:6).
- Workers should obey their bosses in everything and not talk back (Col 3:22; Eph 6:5 – 6; 1 Tim 6:1; Titus 2:9; also 1 Pet 2:18). If they are asked to do something that is patently wrong, they should tell their bosses respectfully that they cannot act in that manner and, if necessary, leave and find another job.[25]

What is wrong with this message? It errs by omission of some key doctrines that the Bible repeats over and again:

1. *While the Bible affirms cheerful industry, it also recognizes that it will not always lead to prosperity or even to subsistence level.* We might mention the parable of the prodigal son (Luke 15:15 – 17) and that of the workers in the vineyard (Matt 20:1 – 16); while fictitious, they are true to life and indicate an environment in which people might labor and yet not earn enough for daily food. "Working poor" was a category of high relevance for the early church. In much of the Two-Thirds World and even in the West, many people cannot find work that will support them, even if they were to labor around the clock.
2. *In 2 Thess 3, Paul is not dealing with those who want to draw from the church's charity for the poor.* From its earliest days, the church followed the synagogue's example (Tob 1:8) and made a daily distribution of a food allowance, for example, to the widows in Jerusalem (Acts 6:1). Although there is little reference to a daily distribution in the rest of the NT, it was probably a common practice not worth mentioning unless some problem arose (see, e.g., 1 Tim 5:3 – 16, esp. Paul's sharp word in 5:8). In the mid-second century Justin Martyr spoke in praise of the church that "the wealthy among us help the needy."[26] That is, the early church always recognized that some people could not support themselves and made allowance for them. Taken in that light, 2 Thess 3 does not contain a well-rounded ethic of work or of economics.
3. *When Paul comments about being content with what one has (1 Tim 6:8), he is speaking to people who presumably have adequate food and clothing but beyond*

25. Typical of this viewpoint is John MacArthur, Submission in the Workplace, Part 1. Online: www.biblebb.com/files/mac/sg60 – 26.htm. "Because God has sovereignly established the social order, we are to serve our employer as though we are serving the Lord (cf. Col. 3:17, 22 – 25). If employers are unfair, God will deal with them. The mandate is to submit, not strike or demonstrate." If readers will search the internet for passages about slavery and masters in the New Testament, they will find that plenty of North American churches are preaching that same message.

26. Justin, *1 Apol.* 67 (*ANF* 1:185).

that want to get rich. It is this desire that causes people to be drawn away from the true path and fall into all sorts of problems. Paul is not addressing a situation in which a free worker or a union of workers negotiates with management for a higher wage; it is an unwarranted leap of exegesis to brand salary negotiations as unchristian based on that text.

4. *When Paul speaks of obedience, he is speaking in the context of slavery.* He knows very well the difference between slavery and free labor (1 Cor 7:21 – 24). There is no hermeneutical justification for taking Eph 6:5 – 8 and other passages and casually transmuting the concept of "slave" to "employee" and "master" to "employer." Of course, the principles of working to please God, not stealing, showing respect, and the like are appropriate in every circumstance.
5. *Nowhere in his letters does Paul address employers of free workers*. But Paul is not the only biblical author. The OT law speaks more often to employers or slave-owners than it does to workers and slaves. When the prophets preach, it is rarely to scold laborers for not putting in a fair day's work, but the masters and employers for exploiting their workers (Jer 22:3; Ezek 22:29). In the NT, James directs his preaching to those who neglect the needy (Jas 1:27; 2:14 – 17), look down on the working poor (2:1 – 7), exploit workers (5:1 – 6), or hanker for high profits (4:13 – 17). Pastors should ask themselves when was the last time they preached against unfair management practices.

Message of This Passage for the Church Today

For some years I have guided seminary students through their academic programs. One of the areas we look into is their undergraduate training. How dismaying to hear, over and over, things like: "Well, I studied accounting (or business management or chemistry) but I'm through with that secular work. Now I want to prepare to serve the Lord!"[27] Part of my direction to them is that God in Christ redeems whatever field they studied and that they need to learn how to serve him in and through it.

Here are two further issues that have to do with so-called vocational Christian ministry. First, what might Paul say to a modern Western pastor, who is often paid full-time and is dedicated wholly to the work of the church? The pastorate, contrary to popular belief, is not the highest rung of the vocational ladder. Evangelicals tend to elevate the role of pastor, and in much of evangelical culture that means a single person and not the group of elders (as was the apostolic custom). Some pastors magnify their own role in the church rather than hammer on the doctrine of the priesthood and giftedness of all believers. When they speak of ministry, they speak of what God

27. This attitude is exacerbated, I've concluded, by the fact that I work in Latin America. The culture is steeped in the Catholic doctrine of clergy and laity, and its influence will be felt for generations more, even among evangelicals.

is doing through the pastor, not through others. The extreme form of this misshapen doctrine is the notion that "God has a man" (and it usually is a *man*, not a woman), an idea that finds some justification in the old covenant but not much in the new.

The NT does not teach a polity of one full-time pastor receiving a full-time salary. It does imply that a group of elders might receive financial compensation for their work in the church (1 Tim 5:17). Nevertheless, it is not the intent of the NT to offer a general plan that is applicable in every situation. Here is an example of how one might apply biblical principles. Years ago, a pastor of mine spent his life ministering in small churches while at the same time working full-time in industry (in Human Resources). While this double load was a drain on him, his work experience added a dimension that made him an excellent counselor to the men of the church; they felt that he was "one of them."

How does Paul's teaching inform the missionary? One way in which the church shows its interest in God's values is by underwriting missions. That is, it demonstrates that the planting of a church in another culture, the drilling of a well, or the training of Christian workers in the Two-Thirds World is of greater worth than expanding and improving its own physical plant or adding to its staff.

For their part, missionaries should critically evaluate how to apply Paul's approach to finances to their own situation. Paul was utterly against self-enrichment (1 Thess 2:5; see too 2 Cor 11:20). To a lesser degree he was disapproving of pioneering evangelists who took pay for their work. His "tent-making" was a legitimate alternative model for ministry. Yet Paul with equal intensity declared that, so long as apostles are authentically from God, they have the "right" to receive pay for their pioneering efforts (1 Cor 9:1 – 18).

One group whose literature I have read asserts that tent-making is *the* biblical pattern. It is not. Paul's tent-making method is *an* apostolic model, and one that has produced good fruit over the centuries; but it is not the only possibility that the Bible offers. For Paul it was a decision he took for pragmatic reasons. He worked only so far as he had need, to support himself as a single adult. Because he worked in an *agora*, he had a natural space for human interaction. Paul could work and still talk to seekers or to people off the street — now discussing the gospel, now turning his attention to a customer. Paul was his own boss and his work hardly interfered with being a full-time missionary. Try doing this with an office job today and in a country where you do not know the language!

"Tent-making" today is a necessary means for gaining creative access to closed countries. It is also an important option for missionaries who are going out from poorer nations and who cannot count on support from home. In every case, the missionary must be a hard-nosed realist, recognizing that in many cases, tent-making raises as many problems as it solves.

CHAPTER 14

2 Thessalonians 3:16 – 18

Literary Context

This brief section of blessing wraps up the letter. If this conclusion seems abrupt, it is because there was only one issue that needed addressing in the final *paraenesis* (ethical teaching) section of the letter. The reference to Paul's signature refers back to the possibility of a forged letter in 2 Thess 2:2.

VI. *Paraenesis:* The Problem of Disorderly Thessalonian Disciples (3:6 – 15)

➦ **VII. Conclusion (3:16 – 18)**

- **A. The apostles give the Thessalonians a blessing of peace (3:16)**
- **B. Paul signs the letter with his own handwritten greeting, in order to authenticate it (3:17)**
- **C. The apostles give a benediction to the Thessalonians (3:18)**

Main Idea

Paul concludes the letter with two blessings. He also pens a greeting, demonstrating how he signs his name, in order to reduce the chances of forged letters.

Translation

2 Thessalonians 3:16 – 18

16a	Benediction	Now **may the Lord himself,**
16b	Description	**the Lord of peace,**
16c	Benediction	**bestow on you peace**
16d	Time	at all times and
16e	Manner	in every way.
16f	Benediction	**May the Lord be with you all.**
17a	Greeting	The greeting by my own hand, PAUL,
17b	Description	which is the sign in every letter of mine:
17c	Explanation	**this is how I write [it].**
18	Benediction	**The grace of our Lord Jesus Christ be with you all.**

Structure

We do not follow the versification of NA[27], which makes 3:16 the conclusion of the previous section. It is more natural to take the benediction as the start of the letter's conclusion, as it is in 1 Thess 5:23.

The structure is simple and characteristically Pauline. He begins in 3:16 with a double benediction, marked with "now" (δέ, as in 2:16); that the Lord of peace will give them peace is perhaps the foil to 3:6 – 15, where the disruptive people are enemies to the church's peace. Then Paul prays that the Lord will be with the Thessalonians. As is typical in his epistolary conclusions, there is no connective that marks this blessing, nor for the next two parts, the greeting and the final benediction.

The second element is that Paul gives a greeting in his own hand (3:17). Given the customs of ancient letter writers, it is likely that the whole verse and perhaps all of 3:16 – 18 were originally penned in his own handwriting. His signature was apparently written in some distinctive fashion. When he says "this is how [οὕτως] I write it," he may be implying earlier letters, now lost.

Third is the final benediction (3:18). As in 1 Thess 5:28, it is a prayer that the grace of the Lord Jesus Christ be with you; the only difference is that Paul states "you all" in this letter. It is altogether fitting that both letters, which are richly christocentric, should conclude with the divine grace of the Lord Jesus.

Exegetical Outline

- **I. The Apostles Give the Thessalonians a Blessing of Peace (3:16).**
- **II. Paul Signs the Letter with His Own Handwritten Greeting, in Order to Authenticate It (3:17).**
- **III. The Apostles Give a Benediction to the Thessalonians (3:18).**

Explanation of the Text

3:16 Now may the Lord himself, the Lord of peace, bestow on you peace at all times and in every way. May the Lord be with you all (Αὐτὸς δὲ ὁ κύριος τῆς εἰρήνης δῴη ὑμῖν τὴν εἰρήνην διὰ παντὸς ἐν παντὶ τρόπῳ. ὁ κύριος μετὰ πάντων ὑμῶν). Paul gives the Thessalonians another benediction (see 2:16 – 17) as he closes the letter. Again, it is the "Lord himself" who gives peace, the phrase similar to the prayer language of 1 Thess 3:11. As in 2 Thess 3:6, 12, and then in 3:18, this is the Lord Jesus Christ. The main verb is the optative mood "give" (δῴη), which we have chosen to translate with the archaic-sounding "bestow." Paul uses old-fashioned language in his prayers, and so we reproduce it here. For other uses of the optative in prayer language, see 1 Thess 3:11 – 12 and 5:23 and comments.

In Rom 15:33 Paul invokes a blessing from the "God of peace." Especially striking is the parallel with the Aaronic benediction of Num 6:26: "the LORD ... give you peace" (κύριος ... δῴη σοι εἰρήνην). In the Hebrew, Yahweh stands behind the "Lord" (κύριος) of the LXX. In clear, if implicit, terms, Jesus assumes the role of Yahweh, as he does in his parousia (1 Thess 4:13 – 18) and in the epiphany of his coming to judge the wicked (2 Thess 1:7 – 10).

Isaiah had prophesied that those who brought the gospel of God's kingdom would be bringing a message of peace (Isa 52:7), which stands in contrast with the false security of the wicked (Jer 6:14, et al.; cf. 1 Thess 5:3). The peace of the Lord is qualified in two ways: first "at all times." The second extends the benediction through all circumstances ("in every way").

Not content with this, Paul also invokes the Lord Jesus' *presence* with every Thessalonian Christian: "the Lord be with you all" (ὁ κύριος μετὰ πάντων ὑμῶν). This is similar to the greeting "Yahweh be with you" (or as the LXX has it, κύριος μεθ' ὑμῶν), as Boaz greeted his reapers (Ruth 2:4; see also 2 Tim 4:22).

3:17 The greeting by my own hand, PAUL, which is the sign in every letter of mine: this is how I write [it] (Ὁ ἀσπασμὸς τῇ ἐμῇ χειρὶ Παύλου, ὅ ἐστιν σημεῖον ἐν πάσῃ ἐπιστολῇ· οὕτως γράφω). "By my own hand" is the signature that marks the letter's authenticity. This action, summarized by the neuter relative pronoun (ὅ), is in every letter of Paul a "sign" (σημεῖον).[1]

Papyrus letters from the period show it was common for a sender to dictate the message, then sign the letter and give a personal greeting at the end. In Paul's case, it seems he also signed his name in some unique and recognizable fashion. Similarly, in my adopted country of Costa Rica, people

1. LSJ, σημεῖον 1. b. cites examples of this term as "proof of the genuineness of a communication" and gives some *koinē* examples.

design for themselves elaborate signatures, partly for flair and partly to make them difficult to falsify. Although Paul does not mention a "signature" in 1 Thessalonians, it is probable that he wrote some or all of 1 Thess 5:23–28; otherwise the Thessalonians would not have a handwriting sample with which to compare 2 Thessalonians.

Paul gives an explicit reference to giving a greeting in his own hand in 1 Cor 16:21; Gal 6:11; Col 4:18; Phlm 19; he allows his scribe Tertius to sign his own greetings in Rom 16:22. If one day we were to find a first-century manuscript of a Pauline letter, we might count it a candidate for the original autograph if it ended with a sentence or two in a second handwriting.

Easy to miss is the note at the end of the verse: "in every letter of mine: this is how I write it." "Every letter" can hardly mean only 1 and 2 Thessalonians, although conceivably Paul is saying "this is how I'll do it in every letter from now on." No, it is more likely that Paul is already a letter-writer. We certainly are missing some of Paul's letters, most notably letters to the Corinthians (1 Cor 5:9; probably another in 2 Cor 7:8). Had he also written to disciples in Arabia, Damascus, Syria, Cilicia, or Cyprus? We may only speculate, but given the fact that letter-writing was such a universal medium in his day, it seems more than possible.

3:18 The grace of our Lord Jesus Christ be with you all (ἡ χάρις τοῦ κυρίου ἡμῶν Ἰησοῦ Χριστοῦ μετὰ πάντων ὑμῶν). Finally, Paul invokes the grace of the Lord Jesus for them. The verb is not written; it would have been a form of "to be" (εἰμί). Again, what is noteworthy is the christocentricity of his letter. To get the gauge of a man's theology, one might observe who it is he turns to in his devotions and the manner in which he prays. For Paul there is no experience of God apart from the Lord Jesus Christ and his grace. This grace, Paul desires, will be upon "you all," repeating once again a motif of these two letters: "may every single Thessalonian believer experience God in Christ to the fullest!"

Theology in Application

It is stunning to imagine that the Thessalonians — in tribulation, perhaps losing members to death, subject to deception, and in every way beaten about by their Hellenistic environment — can be told to have "peace" from the God of peace. This divine peace is not the gift of occasional spaces of tranquility, but it is for "all times"; it is not felt in some special circumstance but "in every way." Jesus Christ, the scriptural Yahweh and the Lord of peace, will ensure their well-being through his presence, since he is with them always. These two letters could hardly conclude with a more fitting tribute to the existence that the new disciples enjoy in Christ.

Theology of 1 and 2 Thessalonians

The two Thessalonian letters are sometimes identified as the "eschatological epistles." This reputation is partly deserved, given that the parousia is developed in every chapter. Paul's thought world includes spirit beings, fiery judgment, the Man of Lawlessness, and other points apocalyptic. Yet to limit the two letters to eschatology is reductionist. The two letters are above all *pastoral*. His "children" are under the barrage of the deceiver and need apostolic reminders of the truth. His teaching is aimed to help the disciples thrive in a Christian outpost deep within the pagan world.

Almost all of the material found in these letters is teaching that the disciples had already heard from Paul and Silas. Yet he weaves together what is known (labeled with "reminder language") with a small amount of new material in order to give the Thessalonians what they need to remain steadfast and to thrive in their faith. The reader should consult the relevant sections of this commentary for details about these topics.

God the Creator

Most Thessalonian Christians came from a background of popular paganism and had no previous acquaintance with the synagogue. Their divinities did not include a Creator. Their gods were not the source of the material universe; they did not create humanity, nor would they hold the human race accountable at a future judgment. Heaven was the battleground for civil war; the gods fought constantly and formed alliances to gain the upper hand. Beyond this system of checks and balances, the gods were subject to the Fates, just as were human beings.

The apostles had passed on a new paradigm. That is why these letters do not introduce God in a systematic way. The apostles can assume a Christian (and scriptural) conception of God on the part of their hearers. They know, for example, that God is a God of justice, who will rescue his people when that Jesus comes to judge the wicked (1 Thess 5:10; 2 Thess 1:6–9).

The Thessalonians now affirm that the Deity's interests extend to every part of one's life, not simply the spheres of civic and domestic religion. That is to say, it was within the character of God that one find a true ethic of holiness (1 Thess 4:3), not through tradition or custom or philosophical reasoning. This too constitutes a paradigm shift that stretches the imagination of the ex-pagans, since now all issues — including sexual ethics, the redefining of friendship and *philadelphia*, the dignity of manual labor, and all other questions of human existence that might be imagined — have become "religious" topics. And the true God cannot be duped, since he is able to test everyone's "heart," that is, inner motives (2:4).

As Paul preached shortly before writing 1 Thessalonians, God "is not far from any one of us" (Acts 17:27). The "living and true" God (1 Thess 1:9) is not bound by Fate, nor is he frustrated by his own failures or by competing gods. He may "choose" (1:4) to establish a relationship with people through his own free will. We can barely imagine the shift that this has caused in the lives of converts from Hellenism. They came to realize that they could have a personal and communal relationship with the Creator of the universe, and that nothing stood in his way when he came to save them. This seeking God is revealed in Christ.

Christology

Paul knows well the power of myth to shape the self-understanding of both the individual and the community. In preaching Jesus, however, he does not simply ask people to replace old myths with new ones. Rather, he calls them to discard myth as a category of knowledge in favor of following one who died in a certain way at a recent time in Judea (1 Thess 2:15; 4:14) and was then resurrected (1:10; 4:14). In Paul's theology, one cannot accept the ethical and existential features of the gospel without accepting its historical matrix.

For Paul, Jesus is "Lord," the one to whom all the world is held accountable. Christians must follow his authority (1 Thess 4:1 – 2; 2 Thess 3:6, 12); his word is a divine oracle (1 Thess 4:15). But "Lord" does not simply mean someone with some sort of authority. Paul regularly mines motifs from the Scriptures, verses that spoke in the Hebrew of Yahweh, rendered in LXX as references to "the Lord"/κύριος. In his hands, these verses can be applied to the Lord *Jesus*. For example, when Jesus comes, people will be separated "from the presence of the Lord [Jesus] and his glorious might" (2 Thess 1:9). Paul's language is taken from Isa 2:10, where *Yahweh* is the judge who inspires terror in the wicked.

In verse after verse Jesus and the Father interchange roles and actions. Although we modern Christians might not be fazed by this fact, its import would not have escaped Paul. The former Pharisee prayed to a crucified and resurrected man; he offered praise and thanks to the Son as he did to God the Father; he expected Christ to answer prayers as would the Father (cf. 1 Thess 3:11 – 13; 2 Thess 2:16 – 17). Paul, who had probably heard the Aaronic blessing of Num 6:24 – 26 every week of his life — "The Lord bless you and keep you; the Lord make his face shine on you and be gracious to you; the LORD turn his face toward you and give you peace" — now blesses the chosen people in the name of the Lord *Jesus*: "Now may the Lord himself, the Lord of peace, bestow on you peace at all times and in every way. . . . The grace of our Lord Jesus Christ be with you all" (2 Thess 3:16, 18). Jesus is Yahweh Sabaoth, Lord of the heavenly armies (2 Thess 1:7). He is the divine Avenger (1 Thess 4:6), the divine Savior (1:10).

In 1 – 2 Thessalonians, eschatology is key, and it is christocentric. This too might seem unremarkable for us who were raised to equate the end of the age with the second coming of Christ. Yet in Second Temple Judaism, the Messiah typically played a subordinate role in the final judgment. Eschatology consisted in the coming of God himself, who might also use a human Davidic king, or angels, or a heavenly Son of Man. But the focus was always on God, and the glorious epiphany was the coming of God. I have had cause to remark throughout this commentary that Paul may have taught the Thessalonians something like the Matthean Olivet Discourse. There too, Jesus' teaching was focused on his own coming as the Son of Man. The kingdom of God comes, Jesus taught, but where is God himself when the age draws to a close? Paul follows neatly this line of thought, that God's kingdom comes in and through Jesus.

Nowhere is this more apparent than in 1 Thess 3:13, which we have interpreted as "the coming of our Lord Jesus with all his holy angels." Here Paul gives a clear nod to Zech 14:5 — and perhaps Matt 24:31 — as he applies a passage about Yahweh's coming to Jesus: "Then the LORD my God will come, and all the holy ones with him." The parousia of Jesus *is* the divine epiphany, at which he will kill the Man of Lawlessness (2 Thess 2:8). It is Jesus' name that is glorified at his coming (1:12). The day of Yahweh from the OT prophets has been transformed into the day of the Lord Jesus Christ (see comments on 1 Thess 5:2). For the saints, eternity is defined as being forever with the Lord Jesus (4:17; see also 5:10; 2 Thess 2:1).

Holy Spirit

There is a handful of specific references to the Spirit; Paul seems to assume his operation even when it goes unmentioned. The Holy Spirit performed miracles when the apostles evangelized the city (1 Thess 1:5 – 6). It is he who inspired some believers to utter prophecies (5:19 – 20). He empowered Christians — even those from a Gentile background — to live in holiness (4:8; 2 Thess 2:13). Paul anticipates his teaching on the "fruit of the Spirit" in Gal 5:22 – 23 when he traces the Thessalonians' joy to the Spirit (1 Thess 1:6).

Second Temple Judaism thought of the Spirit of Yahweh as the power behind the prophets of old. The Spirit would also come in the last days, as part of the new covenant (e.g., Ezek 36:22 – 32). This Jewish theology contrasts sharply with the new understanding that the church is a people of the Spirit. In these early letters, Paul does not develop the doctrine of the Spirit as he does in Galatians, 1 Corinthians, and Romans. Yet he strongly underscores the truth that the eschatological gift of the Spirit had come during this present age (1 Thess 4:8).

Satan

Although Satan appears in the OT, it is in Second Temple Judaism and in the NT that he begins to figure prominently as the chief enemy of God. In 1 – 2 Thessalonians, Satan appears in many of the roles for which he is well-known. He lurks behind false gods (2 Thess 2:4, 9 – 10; cf. also 1 Thess 1:9), deceives human beings, and leads them away from the living and true God.

It is small wonder then, that once men and women join themselves to God's camp, Satan exerts himself to harm them. He puts believers to the test, pushing them to give up on the gospel (1 Thess 3:5; Satan seems to be the persecutor in 2 Thess 1:4 as well). As a deceiver he circulates the rumor that the current persecution is the day of the Lord and tries to fill the Christians with fear. Perhaps most cruelly of all, he tries to keep new disciples apart from their apostles, depriving them of the spiritual nourishment they need (1 Thess 2:18).

Paul does not state so explicitly in these letters, but it is implicit that when Jesus comes to destroy Satan's proxy, the Man of Lawlessness, he comes for Satan as well. Paul is in line with the Olivet Discourse, which foresees eternal fire for the devil and his angels (Matt 25:41).

The New Covenant

God was bringing to pass in pagan Macedonia a set of prophecies that he originally offered to Israel. Centuries earlier, the new covenant had promised a rewriting of the inner heart so that the Israelites could and would obey the Torah (Ezek 36:27).

The Jewish nation of AD 50 should have been enjoying life within this new covenant. Yet only a minority received Christ. The Judean establishment had even participated in killing Jesus and hindered the spread of his message to the nations (1 Thess 2:14 – 16). The Thessalonian synagogue was particularly vociferous in rejecting the gospel (Acts 17:5 – 7, 13).

Nevertheless, the new covenant was making astounding headway among some Jews and a greater number of Gentiles. One cannot begin to understand the Thessalonians' experience without first appreciating how in the new covenant, the Spirit had transformed them into "children of light and children of the day" (1 Thess 5:5).

The Apostles as Pastors

It is by historical accident that 1 and 2 Thessalonians have 1 Timothy as their neighbor in the canon. Yet if one compares the three letters, the Thessalonian letters come off looking as "pastoral" as that which follows in our NT. The apostolic work is summed up in 1 Thess 2:7 – 12: they worked "night and day"; they nurtured their disciples as "a wet-nurse might cherish her very own little ones"; "as a father with his own sons and daughters; that's how we entreated you, that's how we comforted you, that's how we implored you to walk worthy of the God who called you." Their occupation was no mere job, no list of goals to be set and fulfilled. They sacrificed their very selves in order to seek the good of others. John Chrysostom said it well: "For merely to preach is not the same thing as to give the soul."[1]

As makers of disciples, the team made broad use of *mimēsis*, that is, providing in their persons a pattern for the disciples to follow. This model was often enough visual; for example, Paul branded on their sense memory the image of him and Silas working with their hands. At the same time they had also verbally "instructed" them how to live (with regard to the work ethic, see 1 Thess 4:11; see 2 Thess 3:6, 10, 12).

The Work of Prayer

Looked at from a certain angle, 1 Thessalonians may be viewed as a prayer report, which also happens to include an itinerary and apostolic instruction. The apostles' prayers include both intercession and thanksgiving. Christian prayer is not a manipulation of the cosmic laws, as in magic. Rather, it is an appearing before the presence of the almighty God to ask for his intervention. They pray against the work of Satan, but also and principally that their disciples might flourish in the faith. Here too, Paul and the team serve as patterns for the new converts, so that they too might learn how to enter God's presence in prayer.

Evangelism and Discipleship

In his letters, Paul rarely instructs his disciples to become evangelists. The best explanation of this is that "basic evangelism" was a theme covered in the early days of discipleship and thus did not need to be brought up in the letters.[2] In the case of Thessalonica, the gospel broke forth from a small church to a larger region. Paul simply reminds them how to be people worthy of sharing the gospel. He cannot bear

1. John Chrysostom, *Homilies on First Thessalonians* 2 (NPNF[1] 13:330).

2. First Timothy is a probable exception to that rule: the Ephesian church had fallen into an inward-looking mysticism (1 Tim 1:3 – 4) that cut off concern for the outer world (indicated by 2:1 – 2). Timothy should reinstruct them to be evangelists by being a pattern for them (2 Tim 4:5).

to have the gospel spread by anyone who would soil its reputation and — through displeasing God — short-circuit its transforming power. Therefore when he says "we were this, we were not that" (1 Thess 2:1 – 12), he is speaking not exclusively of himself, Silas, and Timothy, but of a pattern that they set for all makers of disciples. An evangelist should give of him- or herself (2:8) and should be prepared for hard work, even manual labor (2:9). An evangelist should be prepared for a negative reaction, including persecution (2:2, 15).

According to Acts, the Lord commissioned Paul "to open [the Gentiles'] eyes and turn them from darkness to light, and from the power of Satan to God" (Acts 26:18), and sent him "far away to the Gentiles" (Acts 22:21). Some years later and many hundreds of kilometers away from the Damascus Road, Paul and his team found themselves carrying a word from God, the "gospel."[3]

The saving message is centered in the work of Christ: that he died and rose again to save his people (1 Thess 4:14; 5:9 – 10). Yet one cannot separate the basic gospel from what we sometimes call "follow-up" or discipleship. For the apostles there is no break in continuity from the moment of belief to following Jesus as Lord and growing in holiness.

We need not limit "evangelism" to one method or another or imagine that Paul was always speaking to a gathering from a pulpit. The ministry of the word might take place in a large meeting, a small group, or an intimate conversation. A "successful" proclamation of the message takes place when people accept it and repent, recognizing that it is a message from God and not of mere human origin (1 Thess 2:13). The apostles believe that for the gospel to be successful, it is necessary to invoke divine intervention (2 Thess 3:1). It is a dreadful sin to oppose its spread (1 Thess 2:16), and those who do so are taking part in the devil's schemes. The hellish parallel to receiving the gospel is to believe and follow "the lie" (2 Thess 2:10 – 12).

Work Ethic

For the apostles, manual labor was concrete proof of their love for the church. Paul thus has no hesitation in reproaching a group within the Thessalonian church that falls short of the "tradition" of the apostolic work ethic (2 Thess 3:6 – 15). Apparently some were depending on the church for their daily needs rather than working to support themselves. We have interpreted these people as would-be evangelists

3. The "word" (always λόγος, never ῥῆμα) in the sense of the Christian message is called "the word of God" (1 Thess 2:13), "of the Lord" (1:8; 2 Thess 3:1) or simply "the word/message" (1 Thess 1:6; 2:13 in the Greek). In these cases "word" refers to the oral proclamation, not the written canon. It is also used more generally to mean a "message" (2 Thess 3:14). The "gospel" is "of Christ" (1 Thess 3:2), "of our Lord Jesus" (2 Thess 1:8), "of God (1 Thess 2:2, 8, 9), or simply "the [or 'our'] gospel" (1 Thess 1:5; 2:4; 2 Thess 2:14). Its cognate verb "to announce good news" (εὐαγγελίζομαι) appears once (1 Thess 3:6), but not in the sense of "evangelize." Paul also uses the term "tradition" (παράδοσις) to refer to the content of the apostolic message (2 Thess 2:15; 3:6).

and teachers who were claiming the right to take support, as Jesus had permitted (Matt 10:11).

The Family That Is the Church

The church cannot easily be made to fit into the sociological category of "fictive family," that is, an organization where people "act as if" their fellow members are a family. The church truly is family, the Spirit making each one a child of the Father and brother or sister to one another. Within the new covenant, "family values" have their primary reference to what goes on between members of the church. Each person, male or female, young or old, of whatever social stratum, belongs to the other. The members go so far as to give their fellows the holy family kiss (1 Thess 5:26).

Within the meetings of the church (1 Thess 5:12 – 22), there was a group dynamic of mutual support, prayer, prophecy, and its companion, "discernment." While Paul implies the existence of church leaders (5:12 – 13), they are by no means the primary focus of the church's ministry, which is carried out by the congregation. As responsible partakers of that group, each member must be made aware of the content of Paul's teaching (5:27).

Sexual Ethic

Sanctification is no mere human struggle; rather, it is a realization that in the new covenant, Christians are "of the day" and "of the light" already (1 Thess 5:4 – 8). Yet the Thessalonians also must make holiness their business; as Paul wrote them, "thrive even more" (4:1). First Thessalonians contains some of the strongest apostolic teaching on Christian sexuality, instruction made necessary by the environment of pagan Macedonia. Paul speaks about both men and women possessing their own bodies in holiness and honor (4:4).

This divine interest in human holiness is in part a result of the resurrection doctrine, that God has an interest in what is done in the physical body, as well as in the mind or spirit. That is what makes it so relevant that Paul speaks of sex in the section prior to the resurrection teaching of 1 Thess 4:13 – 17. He concludes the letter with a prayer that they may be holy in all aspects, including the physical (5:23). As Irenaeus would say in the next century: "For it is manifest that those acts which are deemed righteous are performed in bodies."[4]

4. Irenaeus, *Haer.* 2.29.2 (*ANF* 1:403).

Eschatology

The Gentile Christians learned a new way of understanding history. They came to see that it was not aimless or cyclical but "telic," that is, moving toward an end that is under the control of almighty God. Only at that future point will God fully demonstrate his wrath and his salvation — not capriciously, but in accordance with his character.

Paul's teaching about the light and the day are predicated on the salvation of God that will appear in the parousia (1 Thess 1:10), and also on the operation of the Holy Spirit during this age. Whether time is long or short before the return of Christ, believers have what they need to serve God.

These two letters are like the rest of the NT, which gives little eschatological detail for its own sake and discourages calculations of times and seasons. Instead, each reference to the end times exists in order to direct the listener to God, which in turn results in changes in their behavior. First Thessalonians 5:6 is an excellent example of the NT pattern: "So then, let us not let ourselves fall asleep, as do other people, but let us keep alert and exercise self-control."

Paul addresses a number of eschatological issues.

Persecution

The majority of Paul's audiences — i.e., the relatively few who even bothered to listen to him in the first place — rejected and even burlesqued the gospel. Even as he was dictating these letters, the Corinthian multitude was labeling his message as "foolishness" (1 Cor 1:18). But during his three stops in Macedonia and two in Achaia, some few had a radically distinct reaction: they "received the word." They, like the apostles, experienced tribulation, which Paul describes in terms reminiscent of Jesus' own warnings. To Paul's deep pleasure, the Thessalonians not only acted on the gospel, but they held on to it despite fierce trials.

Deception

Before the day of the Lord, a mere man will set himself up as a god. He will do so by the unleashed power of the devil, fully manifested because of the removal of the "restrainer." In Paul's day, signs and wonders were strong proof of God's presence; in the end times, however, they might also come from the devil and be "signs ... that mislead" (2 Thess 2:9). Whether the Lord's return is near or distant, believers should always be on guard against misdirection (2:1 – 3a).

Apostasy

The Thessalonian Christians were standing firm against apostasy — so far. But Paul knew that the end times will bring about a horrific falling away from the truth (2 Thess 2:3). It will be pushed by Satan and engineered through the deceptive Man of Lawlessness.

This final Apostasy was a staple of Jewish eschatology. While the OT prophets usually focused on the ongoing apostasy of the nation, Second Temple Judaism laid greater emphasis on an eschatological "apostate generation" (so *1 En.* 93.9; see also *Jub.* 23.14 – 23; 1QM XIII, 7 – 9). Eschatological apostasy also features in the teaching of Jesus: "Many will turn away from the truth and will betray and hate each other" (Matt 24:10). While the world will be led away by Satan, Christians need to keep on the alert: the one who endures faithful to the end will be saved (24:13). During the apostolic age, the church received prophetic oracles about apostasy either in the short term (Acts 20:29 – 30) or in the undefined "later times" (1 Tim 4:1).

The Apostasy in 2 Thess 2 refers to the falling away of Christians, as do the predictions in 1 Tim 4:1 and 2 Tim 3:1 (see also in 2 Peter and Jude; 1 John 2:18 – 19; Revelation). Paul encountered examples of apostasy during his own lifetime: some Galatians began to fall from the gospel (Gal 1:6); Demas wandered off (2 Tim 4:10). Although the Thessalonian Christians are God's elect (2 Thess 2:13), still, they must take care to stand firm (2:15). After all, people who look just like them will in the end times be casualties to Satan's lies.

Watchfulness

Salvation is principally a future, eschatological goal (1 Thess 1:10; 5:9; 2 Thess 1:10 – 12; 2:14, 16). Along the pathway lies the real possibility of disaster (1 Thess 3:5). That is why all believers must be constantly on their guard (5:1 – 11).

Order of the End

Paul states that the day of the Lord could not be immediately at hand in AD 50, given the current circumstances. Neither the final Apostasy nor the appearance of the Man of Lawlessness is present, and both are expected before the Lord's coming (2 Thess 2:1 – 12). Some agent of God, perhaps as we have suggested one of the principal angels, is "hindering" the appearing of the Man of Lawlessness until such time as God decides to remove him (2:6 – 8).

Destruction of Unbelievers

The disciples hear that God is just; that is, he will reward the righteous in the end time and punish the wicked in his "coming wrath" (1 Thess 1:10; 2:16; 5:9). This will be manifested in the parousia of Jesus, who brings with him "unexpected destruction" (5:3), "tribulation" (2 Thess 1:6; cf. 2:12), and "retaliation" (1:8). The unbelievers will experience separation from the Lord and "eternal destruction" (1:9). God's judgment is proof that he does not stand aloof from his creation, nor, as in other systems, is he himself unjust or capricious.

Second Thessalonians 1:5 – 10 may properly be correlated with Rev 14:10 – 11 as predictions of the eternal conscious torment for the wicked. They will not be annihilated, whether instantly or after a period of suffering.

Resurrection

Although it would probably be some years before the gospel of Matthew is published, Paul knows and teaches something that resembles the Olivet Discourse in its Matthean form. It is thus noteworthy that Matt 24 – 25, while speaking of the "gathering" of the saints (24:31), does not speak of their resurrection as such.

Yet in Thessalonica, some members of the church had died within the short space of time between Paul's hasty departure and the writing of 1 Thessalonians (1 Thess 4:13). We cannot now determine how they died; we need not think in terms of large numbers or of death by martyrdom — even one or two deaths would have shaken up the small "family." Thus, Paul gives them a doctrine that, in the most reasonable interpretation, they had heard but forgotten or, better, forgotten how to apply: the resurrection of the saints. He puts the data together for the Thessalonians: Jesus has risen from the dead; Jesus is our eschatological Savior; therefore, Jesus will save us by raising us from the dead at the parousia (1 Thess 4:13 – 18). The manner in which Paul links their resurrection anticipates the fuller expression in a later letter (1 Cor 15).

Final Note

In the decades after the apostles, Christians concluded the Lord's Supper with this prayer:

> Remember your church, Lord,
> to deliver it from all evil
> and to make it perfect in your love;
> and gather it, the one that has been sanctified,
> from the four winds into your kingdom,
> which you have prepared for it;
> for yours is the power and the glory forever.[5]

5. *Did.* 10.5.

This encapsulates as well as any commentary the heart of 1 and 2 Thessalonians: not a fascination with the end time as such, but pastoral help for a church as it grows in holiness and looks toward the coming of Christ.

As their pastor, then, and not as an armchair theologian, Paul shows the Thessalonians the meaning of their election by God and their entry into a new (and truer) family, the manner in which they must teach and model the gospel in the world, the fact that the persecution they feel will not last forever, and the ramifications of Christ's second coming for the unbeliever.

Above all else, Paul sketches out a cosmovision at the center of which is Christ. In these earliest extant Christian texts, in passage after passage, the Lord Jesus fulfills the OT passages concerning the intervention of Yahweh to save and to judge. In the earliest written testimony about Easter, a message from the AD 40s, but having its roots in the earliest Christian proclamation, it is written: "he whom God raised from the dead, Jesus our Savior from God's coming wrath" (1 Thess 1:10).

This is why even dying in Jesus is no tragedy. Mortality is grievous, but its powers are temporary for the follower of the resurrected Lord. And it is Jesus himself who is the focus of true life:

No Loss at All

"This way, please," the angel urges,
shaking your all-too-tangible elbow,
an arm now filled with incomparable vigor,
fine hairs alit from finer glory within,
senses that bear the brilliance and the trumpet.

Ascending, the way grows steadily busier,
ancients mingling together with moderns,
myriads in togas and loincloths and business suits,
shouting and marveling, each tongue a known one,
every word and tonal and click with ease deciphered.

Church members, martyrs, children, great-great-greats,
better known than during life, call greetings.
Yet the fascination is ever with the center,
the focus is personal, the one like a Son of Man.
You lost nothing by dying in Him.

GARY S. SHOGREN

Scripture Index

Luke

John

Acts

Romans

1 Corinthians

2 Corinthians

Galatians

Ephesians

Philippians

Colossians

1 Thessalonians

2 Thessalonians

Other Ancient References

Greek and Roman Literature

Jewish Literature

Christian Literature

Subject Index

Author Index

ZONDERVAN EXEGETICAL COMMENTARY ON THE NEW TESTAMENT

Luke

David E. Garland

Luke sought to assure believers about the truth of the gospel (1:4) and to advance their understanding of God's ways in the world as revealed in Christ's ministry, death, and resurrection. Luke wrote as a historian, theologian, and pastor, and Garland's commentary strives to follow suit in assisting those who will preach and teach the text and those who seek to understand it better. The commentary presents a translation through a diagram that helps visualize the flow of thought, provides a summary of the central message of the passages, reveals how they function within the gospel, and offers an exegetical outline and verse-by-verse commentary that takes notice of Jewish and Greco-Roman background evidence that sheds light on the text. Christians interpret the Bible to make sense of their lived experience, and the commentary highlights theological emphases of each passage and applies them to the everyday struggles of faith and practice.

Available in stores and online!